HEATH ENGLISH

An Integrated Approach to Writing

J. A. Senn
Carol Ann Skinner

HEATH

D.C. Heath and Company
Lexington, Massachusetts • Toronto, Ontario

Editorial	Barbara Brennan, Christopher Johnson, Kathleen Kennedy Kelley, Peg McNary
Series Design	Robin Herr
Book Design	Joan Paley, Caroline Bowden
Cover Design	Len Massiglia
Production	Donna Lee Porter

Acknowledgments start on page 857.

Published simultaneously in Canada

Printed in the United States of America

International Standard Book Number: 0-669-37741-4

1 2 3 4 5 6 7 8 9 10-KP-98 97 96 95 94

Consultants and Reviewers

Program Consultant

Henry I. Christ
Former Chairman of the English Department
Andrew Jackson High School
St. Albans, New York

Program Reviewers

Arizona
Patricia Nash
North High School
Chandler Unified School District
Chandler, Arizona

Florida
Carol Alves
Apopka High School
Apopka, Florida

Ohio
Linda Fulton
Lincoln High School
Gahanna, Ohio

Oklahoma
Sandra L. Benson
Edison High School
Tulsa, Oklahoma

Pennsylvania
Bernadette Fenning
Cardinal O'Hara High School
Springfield, Pennsylvania

Tennessee
Alan F. Kaplan
Hume-Fogg Academic High School
Nashville, Tennessee

Texas
Victor Valenzuela
South Grand Prairie High School
Grand Prairie, Texas

Jan W. Blount
Berkner High School
Richardson, Texas

Contents

Unit 1
Exploring the Writer's Craft

Chapter **2**   **Developing Your Writing Style**   **50**

Unit 2
Achieving the Writer's Purpose

Editing and Publishing:

Chapter **8**   **Writing Summaries**   **290**

Chapter **10**   **Creative Writing**   **372**

Editing and Publishing:

Unit 3
Applying Communication
and Study Skills

Chapter **12**   **Speaking and Listening**   **430**

Unit 4
Language Skills Resource

Grammar

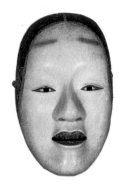

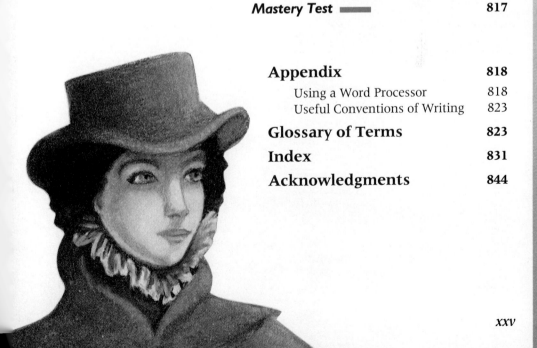

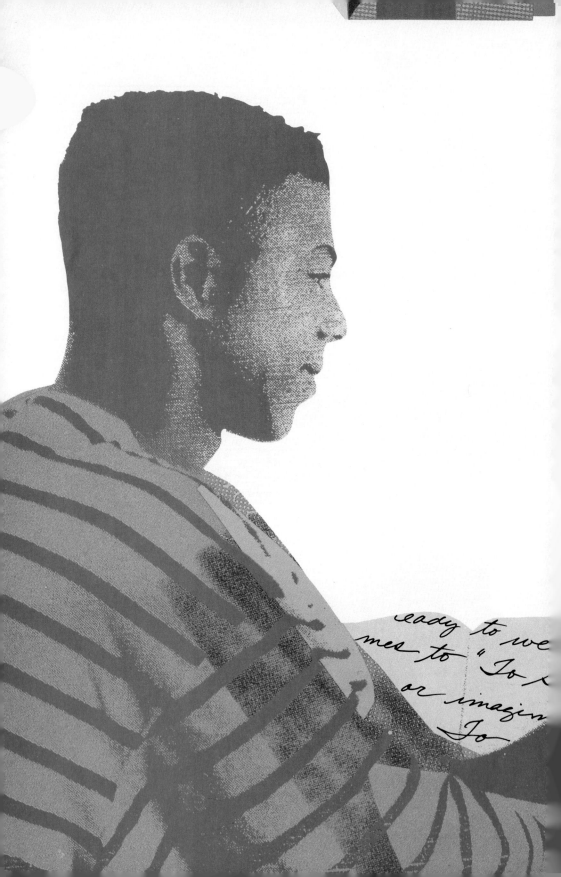

eady to we
mes to "Jo &
or imagin
Jo

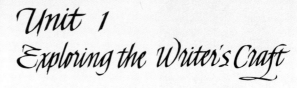

Unit 1
Exploring the Writer's Craft

WRITING

C h a p t e r

1 The Writing Process

Part 1   *Reading to Write*

THEME: *Communication*

People affect one another through the variety of ways they communicate with each other. A comedian can make an entire room—or nation—laugh just by telling a few well-timed jokes. A coach can have a dramatic effect on an athlete's performance by giving a few well-timed words of praise and encouragement.

You too can have an effect on people—not only in your daily interaction with them but through your writing. With a well-written poem about a football game on a clear autumn afternoon, you can make your readers call to mind a similar experience. By writing an effective essay on a controversial issue, such as acid rain or global warming, you can persuade people that they should care about those issues.

As you learn about the writing process in this chapter, you will be thinking and writing about how people communicate with each other and how communication affects people. Katherine Mansfield, an English author, was herself interested in this theme, and she explored it in the following story, "The Singing Lesson." As you read the story, think about how communication is central to the story's development. For example, how does the main character's personal life affect her communication with others?

The Singing Lesson

K a t h e r i n e   M a n s f i e l d

With despair—cold, sharp despair—buried deep in her heart like a wicked knife, Miss Meadows, in cap and gown and carrying a little baton, trod the cold corridors that led to the music hall. Girls of all ages, rosy from the air, and bubbling over with that gleeful excitement that comes from running to school on a fine autumn morning, hurried, skipped, fluttered by; from the hollow classrooms came a quick drumming of voices; a bell rang; a voice like a bird cried, "Muriel." And then there came from the staircase a tremendous knock-knock-knocking. Someone had dropped her dumbbells.

The Science Mistress stopped Miss Meadows.

"Good mor-ning," she cried, in her sweet, affected drawl. "Isn't it cold? It might be winter."

Miss Meadows, hugging the knife, stared in hatred at the Science Mistress. Everything about her was sweet, pale, like honey. You would not have been surprised to see a bee caught in the tangles of that yellow hair.

"It is rather sharp," said Miss Meadows, grimly.

The other smiled her sugary smile.

"You look fro-zen," said she. Her blue eyes opened wide; there came a mocking light in them. (Had she noticed anything?)

"Oh, not quite as bad as that," said Miss Meadows, and she gave the Science Mistress, in exchange for her smile, a quick grimace and passed on. . . .

Forms[1] Four, Five, and Six were assembled in the music hall. The noise was deafening. On the platform, by the piano, stood Mary Beazley, Miss Meadows' favorite, who played accompaniments. She was

---

1. **Forms:** Grade levels in British secondary schools.

3

turning the music stool. When she saw Miss Meadows she gave a loud, warning "Sh-sh! girls!"and Miss Meadows, her hands thrust in her sleeves, the baton under her arm, strode down the center aisle, mounted the steps, turned sharply, seized the brass music stand, planted it in front of her, and gave two sharp taps with her baton for silence.

"Silence, please! Immediately!" and, looking at nobody, her glance swept over that sea of colored flannel blouses, with bobbing pink faces and hands, quivering butterfly hair blows, and music books out-spread. She knew perfectly well what they were thinking. "Meady is in a wax."[2] Well, let them think it! Her eyelids quivered; she tossed her head, defying them. What could the thoughts of those creatures matter to someone who stood there bleeding to death, pierced to the heart, to the heart, by such a letter—

. . . "I feel more and more strongly that our marriage would be a mistake. Not that I do not love you. I love you as much as it is possible for me to love any woman, but, truth to tell, I have come to the conclusion that I am not a marrying man, and the idea of settling down fills me with nothing but—" and the word "disgust" was scratched out lightly and "regret" written over the top.

Basil! Miss Meadows stalked over to the piano. And Mary Beazley, who was waiting for this moment, bent forward; her curls fell over her cheeks while she breathed, "Good morning, Miss Meadows," and she motioned toward rather than handed to her mistress a beautiful yellow chrysanthemum. This little ritual of the flower had been gone through for ages and ages, quite a term and a half. It was as much part of the lesson as opening the piano. But this morning, instead of taking it up, instead of tucking it into her belt while she leaned over Mary and said, "Thank you, Mary. How very nice! Turn to page thirty-two," what was Mary's horror when Miss Meadows totally ignored the chrysanthemum, made no reply to her greeting, but said in a voice of ice, "Page fourteen, please, and mark the accents well."

Staggering moment! Mary blushed until the tears stood in her eyes, but Miss Meadows was gone back to the music stand; her voice rang through the music hall.

"Page fourteen. We will begin with page fourteen. 'A Lament.'[3] Now, girls, you ought to know it by this time. We shall take it all together; not in parts, all together. And without expression. Sing it, though, quite simply, beating time with the left hand."

2. **in a wax:** Being angry.
3. **'A Lament':** A sorrowful song.

She raised the baton; she tapped the music stand twice. Down came Mary on the opening chord; down came all those left hands, beating the air, and in chimed those young, mournful voices:—

Fast! Ah, too Fast Fade the Ro-o-ses of Pleasure;
Soon Autumn yields unto Wi-i-nter Drear.
Fleetly! Ah, Fleetly Mu-u-sic's Gay Measure
Passes away from the Listening Ear.

Good Heavens, what could be more tragic than that lament! Every note was a sigh, a sob, a groan of awful mournfulness. Miss Meadows lifted her arms in the wide gown and began conducting with both hands. ". . . I feel more and more strongly that our marriage would be a mistake. . . ." she beat. And the voices cried: *Fleetly! Ah, Fleetly.* What could have possessed him to write such a letter! What could have led up to it! It came out of nothing. His last letter had been all

about a fumed-oak bookcase he had bought for "our" books, and a "natty little hall stand" he had seen, "a very neat affair with a carved owl on a bracket, holding three hat brushes in its claws." How she had smiled at that! So like a man to think one needed three hat brushes! *From the Listening Ear,* sang the voices.

"Once again," said Miss Meadows. "But this time in parts. Still without expression." *Fast! Ah, too Fast.* With the gloom of the contraltos[4] added, one could scarcely help shuddering. *Fade the Roses of Pleasure.* Last time he had come to see her, Basil had worn a rose in his buttonhole. How handsome he had looked in that bright blue suit, with that dark red rose! And he knew it, too. He couldn't help knowing it. First he stroked his hair, then his moustache; his teeth gleamed when he smiled.

"The headmaster's wife keeps on asking me to dinner. It's a perfect nuisance. I never get an evening to myself in that place."

"But can't you refuse?"

"Oh, well, it doesn't do for a man in my position to be unpopular."

Music's Gay Measure, wailed the voices. The willow trees, outside the high, narrow windows, waved in the wind. They had lost half their leaves. The tiny ones that clung wriggled like fishes caught on a line. ". . . I am not a marrying man. . . ." The voices were silent; the piano waited.

"Quite good," said Miss Meadows, but still in such a strange, stony tone that the younger girls began to feel positively frightened. "But now that we know it, we shall take it with expression. As much expression as you can put into it. Think of the words, girls. Use your imaginations. *Fast! Ah, too Fast,*" cried Miss Meadows. "That ought to break out—a loud, strong *forte*[5]—a lament. And then in the second line, *Winter Drear,* make that *Drear* sound as if a cold wind were blowing through it. *Drear!*" said she so awfully that Mary Beazley, on the music stool, wriggled her spine. "The third line should be one crescendo.[6] *Fleetly! Ah, Fleetly Music's Gay Measure.* Breaking on the first word of the last line, *Passes.* And then on the word, *Away,* you must begin to die . . . to fade . . . until *The Listening Ear* is nothing more than a faint whisper. . . . You can slow down as much as you like almost on the last line. Now, please."

---

4. **contraltos** [kən tral′tōz]: Female singers having the lowest voices.
5. *forte* [fôr′tā]: Loud and forceful, as in music.
6. **crescendo** [krə shen′dō]: A gradual increase in musical sound.

Again the two light taps; she lifted her arms again. *Fast! Ah, too Fast.* ". . . and the idea of settling down fills me with nothing but disgust—" Disgust was what he had written. That was as good as to say their engagement was definitely broken off. Broken off! Their engagement! People had been surprised enough that she had got engaged. The Science Mistress would not believe it at first. But nobody had been as surprised as she. She was thirty. Basil was twenty-five. It had been a miracle, simply a miracle, to hear him say, as they walked home from church that very dark night, "You know, somehow or other, I've got fond of you." And he had taken hold of the end of her ostrich feather boa, *Passes away from the Listening Ear.*

"Repeat! Repeat!" said Miss Meadows. "More expression, girls! Once more!"

Fast! Ah, too Fast. The older girls were crimson; some of the younger ones began to cry. Big spots of rain blew against the windows, and one could hear the willows whispering, ". . . not that I do not love you. . . ."

"But, my darling, if you love me," thought Miss Meadows, "I don't mind how much it is. Love me as little as you like." But she knew he didn't love her. Not to have cared enough to scratch out that word "disgust," so that she couldn't read it! *Soon Autumn yields unto Winter Drear.* She would have to leave the school, too. She could never face the Science Mistress or the girls after it got known. She would have to disappear somewhere. *Passes away.* The voices began to die, to fade, to whisper . . . to vanish. . . .

Suddenly the door opened. A little girl in blue walked fussily up the aisle, hanging her head, biting her lips, and twisting the silver bangle on her red little wrist. She came up the steps and stood before Miss Meadows.

"Well, Monica, what is it?"

"Oh, if you please, Miss Meadows," said the little girl, gasping, "Miss Wyatt wants to see you in the mistress's room."

"Very well," said Miss Meadows. And she called to the girls, "I shall put you on your honor to talk quietly while I am away." But they were too subdued to do anything else. Most of them were blowing their noses.

The corridors were silent and cold; they echoed to Miss Meadows' steps. The head mistress sat at her desk. For a moment she did not look up. She was as usual disentangling her eyeglasses, which had got caught in her lace tie. "Sit down, Miss Meadows," she said very kindly. And then she picked up a pink envelope from the blotting pad. "I sent for you just now because this telegram has come for you."

"A telegram for me, Miss Wyatt?"

Basil! He had committed suicide, decided Miss Meadows. Her hand flew out, but Miss Wyatt held the telegram back a moment. "I hope it's not bad news," she said, so more than kindly. And Miss Meadows tore it open.

"Pay no attention to letter, must have been mad, bought hat stand today—Basil," she read. She couldn't take her eyes off the telegram.

"I do hope it's nothing very serious," said Miss Wyatt, leaning forward.

"Oh, no, thank you, Miss Wyatt," blushed Miss Meadows. "It's nothing bad at all. It's"—and she gave an apologetic little laugh—"it's from my *fiancé* saying that . . . saying that—" There was a pause. "I *see*," said Miss Wyatt. And another pause. Then—"You've fifteen minutes more of your class, Miss Meadows, haven't you?"

"Yes, Miss Wyatt." She got up. She half ran toward the door.

"Oh, just one minute, Miss Meadows," said Miss Wyatt. "I must say I don't approve of my teachers having telegrams sent to them in school hours, unless in case of very bad news, such as death," explained Miss Wyatt, "or a very serious accident, or something to that effect. Good news, Miss Meadows, will always keep, you know."

On the wings of hope, of love, of joy, Miss Meadows sped back to the music hall, up the aisle, up the steps, over to the piano.

"Page thirty-two, Mary," she said, "page thirty-two," and, picking up the yellow chrysanthemum, she held it to her lips to hide her smile. Then she turned to the girls, rapped with her baton: "Page thirty-two, girls. Page thirty-two."

We come here To-day with Flowers o'erladen,
With Baskets of Fruit and Ribbons to boot,
To-oo Congratulate. . . .

"Stop! Stop!" cried Miss Meadows. "This is awful. This is dreadful." And she beamed at her girls. "What's the matter with you all? Think, girls, think of what you're singing. Use your imaginations. *With Flowers o'erladen. Baskets of Fruit and Ribbons to boot.* And *Congratulate.*" Miss Meadows broke off. "Don't look so doleful, girls. It ought to sound warm, joyful, eager. *Congratulate.* Once more. Quickly. All together. Now then!"

And this time Miss Meadows' voice sounded over all the other voices—full, deep, glowing with expression. ◆

Responding to the Theme

Communication

Responding in Your Journal   Throughout the composition units of this textbook, you will find ideas and suggestions for writing in a journal. For your journal select a loose-leaf notebook so that you can remove personal entries, if necessary, before sharing your journal with your teacher. *(See page 15 for more about journal writing.)*

In "The Singing Lesson," Basil profoundly affects Miss Meadows by writing ". . . our marriage would be a mistake." She, in turn, has a great effect on her students. In your journal for the next few days, write about specific incidents in which someone's words affected, or changed, someone else's life. For example, relate a time when a teacher or an adviser boosted your confidence or a time when you cheered up a friend. Start today by writing about one such incident. Then, in the next several days, write about other incidents.

Speaking and Listening   Plan with your teacher to watch a particular movie or television show and observe closely how the characters communicate with one another. Does one character try to persuade another to do something? How does he or she use language? Gestures? Tone of voice? Facial expressions? Then, with your teacher's permission, form a small group with three or four other students and discuss your impressions of the characters you have studied. From your discussion draw conclusions about how characters affect one another through their means of communication.

Critical Thinking: Contrasting   Contrast Miss Meadows's behavior *before* and *after* she receives the telegram from Basil, telling her to ignore his earlier note. How does she behave differently toward the students? What are the clues to her change in behavior? Write a paragraph describing the differences in her behavior.

Extending Your Vocabulary   In the story "The Singing Lesson," the author uses a few terms and expressions not common to everyday vocabulary. For example, *forms* in the sentence "Forms Four, Five, and Six were assembled in the music hall" is the term used for *grades* in British secondary schools. Using a dictionary, look up the meaning of the following British words: *lorry, roundabout, zebra crossing, tube, bobby.* Then use them in a paragraph.

The Artist's Sister, Mme. Pontillon, Seated on the Grass, Berthe Morisot (French 1841–1895), 1873, Oil on Canvas, 17¾ × 28½"

Part 2 / *Writing*

In "The Singing Lesson," Katherine Mansfield effectively communicates Miss Meadows's despair when she receives the first note from her fiancé and her happiness when she receives the second note. How effectively do you communicate with others? This chapter will help you sharpen your communication skills by providing you with a process for writing—stages to go through in developing an excellent and effective composition.

As a writer you will plan, draft, revise, and polish your writing. These stages of the writing process remain the same no matter what the writing task. Your passage through these stages, however, will vary. Sometimes you will move slowly at the beginning as you search for and explore a topic. At other times you will start out with a clear topic and barely pause at the early stages. Later, however, in the revising stage, you may go back and explore the topic further. The passage from idea to finished piece of writing is rarely a direct, straightforward journey. You will take detours, travel back and forth, and linger on certain steps.

In this chapter you will learn a number of strategies that are helpful at different stages of the writing process. Keep these strategies in your repertoire so that you can call on them when you need them.

The Writing Process

The following diagram illustrates the different stages of the writing process. Notice that the diagram loops back and forth. This looping shows how writers often move back and forth between various stages instead of going step-by-step from beginning to end. They can go back to any stage until they are satisfied with the quality of their writing.

Prewriting includes all the planning steps that you can take before you write the first draft. During prewriting you find a subject, develop it, and organize the details.

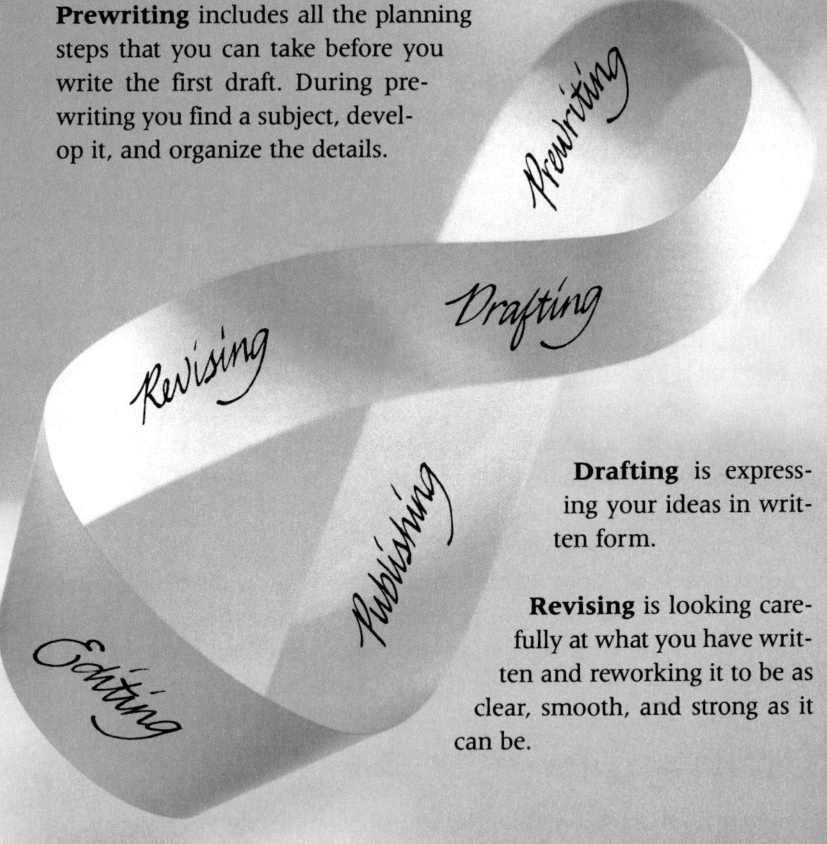

Prewriting

Drafting

Revising

Publishing

Editing

Drafting is expressing your ideas in written form.

Revising is looking carefully at what you have written and reworking it to be as clear, smooth, and strong as it can be.

Editing means checking your final draft for mistakes in grammar, usage, spelling, and mechanics and correcting any errors you may find.

Publishing means presenting your finished work to others in an appropriate way.

Prewriting

The process of putting words on paper begins long before those words are actually written. By the time you take pen in hand for your first draft, you should know what you want to say and how you want to say it. *Prewriting* includes all of the planning that precedes the writing of the first draft. In this first, critically important stage, you plan the substance and structure of your composition. Take your time, because careful planning will simplify your writing task and help you write effectively.

Keep a writing folder as you work through the following prewriting strategies. It is quite possible that you will be able to use at some later time many of the ideas you will discover.

Strategies for Finding a Subject

Writing ideas lurk everywhere—in a memory, a friendship, a conversation, an ocean wave. The world within your mind and the world around you are teeming with ideas, but you need to bring them within reach—to make yourself aware of them. Following are strategies that will help you tap this vast store of writing subjects. As you become acquainted with the many different techniques, you will be able to determine which will work best for you.

Taking Stock of Your Interests You write more effectively when you write about a subject you personally find interesting. As a result, you should begin your search for ideas with your own interests. The following activity will help you explore those interests.

WRITING ACTIVITY *Exploring Your Interests*

Complete each statement thoughtfully and completely. Then save your notes in your writing folder.

1. To communicate effectively with others, one should _____.
2. If I were producing a TV program called *Admirable People,* some of the people I would include would be _____.
3. The most interesting projects I have completed are _____.
4. In the next five years of my life, I would like to _____.
5. Courses that I would like to take are _____.

6. As President the issues that I would deal with are _____.

7. I disagree with my friends about _____.

8. My favorite places are _____.

9. I worry about _____.

10. I would like to know more about _____.

Freewriting   The search for subjects involves uncovering some of the countless ideas that lie buried in your mind. Freewriting is one way to dig deeply into your mind. *Freewriting* means writing down anything and everything without pausing to reflect. You can begin writing about anything, or you can do *focused freewriting,* in which you use a word, a topic, or a question to start your mind moving. Write sentences, fragments, unconnected words—whatever encourages your thoughts. Following is an example of how freewriting led one student writer to the subject of performing before audiences.

Student Model: *Freewriting*

Here I go again – writing, writing to find something to write about. My cat? The importance of recycling? What I'd do if I were president? I've written about that stuff a million times – lots of other stuff too. Any topics left? Sure doesn't feel like it. Think I'm all written out by now. But – got to come up with something. My teacher says any word, any object, any anything can make you think of a subject. All right. Try some words... plant – light bulb – glue – enemy – stormy – crowd – audience. Audience. Well, there are all the plays I've been in. But I've written about those many times. Audience. Audiences still make me nervous. Stage fright is a horror. But I've learned to deal with it. How?

WRITING ACTIVITY *Freewriting*

Timing yourself, write freely for five full minutes. Let your thoughts pour out onto the page. Do not even lift your pen or pencil from the paper. If you find your thoughts drying up, then just note that fact. Write anything, as long as you keep writing. When your time is up, place your notes in your writing folder for later use.

WRITING ACTIVITY *Focused Freewriting*

Freewrite for five minutes on one of the following subjects about the future. Focus on that subject in the beginning, but let your thoughts take you in whatever direction they want to go. When you finish, be sure to place your notes in your writing folder for possible later use.

1. transportation
2. different means of communication
3. fashions and hairstyles
4. scientific discoveries
5. occupations

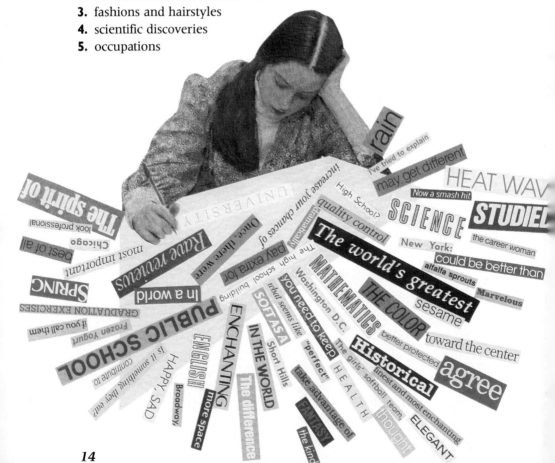

Keeping a Journal   A journal is a notebook in which you make daily entries about your experiences, observations, and reflections. When you write in your journal, you should date each entry. In doing so, you will be chronicling certain stages of your life. You will find this record of your personal feelings and observations to be a rich source for writing ideas.

In addition to using your journal for personal entries, you will find journal-related activities to do in this textbook. These activities will add to your source for writing ideas and will help you perfect your writing style. The additional uses for your journal are as follows.

Additional Uses of the Journal

RESPONDING TO LITERATURE   A journal is a good place to record your responses and reactions to books, stories, poems, and other literature. After reading each literature selection in this book, you will have the opportunity to use your journal for this purpose, as you did on page 9. Be sure to start each entry with the author's name and the title of the selection.

LEARNING LOG   The Learning Log is a special section of your journal where you can write down ideas and information about math, science, history, health, or any other subject that you find particularly interesting.

PERSONALIZED EDITING CHECKLIST   The Personalized Editing Checklist is a section of your journal where you can keep a list of errors that recur in your writing. You might include words you frequently misspell, usage mistakes, and mechanical errors. When you edit a composition, refer to this checklist. *(See page 38 for more information about the Personalized Editing Checklist.)*

WRITING ACTIVITY *Writing in Your Journal*

Every day of your life you are bombarded with other people's words. You hear and read comments from teachers, friends, family, people standing next to you on the bus, books and magazines, radio and TV, and even popular songs. Of the countless statements that come your way, some undoubtedly will start you thinking. They may excite you or puzzle you, move you or irritate you. Beginning today write in your journal whatever you heard or read that made an impression. Then write your thoughts about it.

15

Exploring Literature for Writing Ideas   So far in this chapter, you have learned to explore your personal experience and interests for writing ideas. However, you can also find interesting ideas for writing subjects in your reading. For example, after reading the short story "The Singing Lesson," you could explore the subject of teaching or music.

The following box lists strategies for getting writing ideas from fiction and nonfiction. Even though stories, plays, and poems are imaginative, they often deal with issues and events that can serve as good subjects for nonfiction writing.

Exploring Literature for Writing Ideas

FICTION, POETRY, AND DRAMA

1. Write about the piece of literature itself, exploring plot, character, setting, author's style, or some other aspect of literature. *(See "Writing Essays about Literature," on pages 246–289.)*
2. Write about the theme, or central message, of a story, poem, or play. For example, if a story deals with preserving the environment, you may choose to address this issue in your writing.
3. After reading a story or play, write about some aspect of one of the characters, such as the character's personality. For instance, if you read about a character in a story who is frequently jealous of other people, you may decide to write about the issue of jealousy between people.

NONFICTION

1. Decide whether you agree or disagree with an editorial in a newspaper.
2. Look through newpapers and magazines to find issues or subjects that you could explore and write about.
3. Think about biographies and autobiographies that you have read. Write about the subject of any of them.

WRITING ACTIVITY   *Exploring Literature for Writing Ideas*

Scan the front page of a newspaper. Then list five subjects you could write about. Save your work in your writing folder.

Choosing and Limiting a Subject

Writing gives you the valuable opportunity to know yourself better and to present your ideas and interests to others. You should make the most of this opportunity by writing about subjects you personally find stimulating and challenging. The following guidelines will help you choose such subjects.

Guidelines for Choosing a Subject

1. Choose a subject that genuinely interests you.
2. Choose a subject that will interest your readers.
3. Choose a subject you can cover thoroughly through your own knowledge or a reasonable amount of research.

WRITING ACTIVITY **6** *Writing on Your Own*

WRITING
ABOUT THE
THEME

 Look over your prewriting notes in your writing folder and journal. Jot down five to ten writing ideas that have to do with how people communicate with one another and what the effects of that communication are. For instance, you might write about a teacher whose encouraging words gave you the confidence to enter a writing contest. Once you have listed your ideas, mark each one *strong, average,* or *weak* in terms of how it fulfills the guidelines above. Finally, consider carefully the subjects you have labeled *strong* and circle the one you would most like to write about. Save your work in your writing folder.

Limiting a Subject   Once you have chosen a subject, you may have to limit it, or narrow it. Very broad subjects, such as *Europe* or *education,* could not be covered in a single composition. To limit a broad subject, use the following strategies.

Strategies for Limiting a Subject

1. Limit your subject to one example that represents the subject.
2. Limit your subject to a specific time or place.
3. Limit your subject to a specific event.
4. Limit your subject to a specific condition, purpose, or procedure.

17

For example, if you were given the broad subject *automobiles,* you could limit it in several ways.

GENERAL SUBJECT   automobiles
LIMITED SUBJECTS   the first horseless carriage [example]
      transportation in the early 1900's [time]
      assembly-line production [event]
      the effects on the environment [condition]

The student writer who, through freewriting, came up with the broad subject *performing before audiences* was able to narrow that subject in the following way.

GENERAL SUBJECT   performing before audiences
LIMITED SUBJECT   developing stage presence

WRITING ACTIVITY *Limiting a Subject*

Following the example above for limiting a subject, choose three of the following subjects and limit them.

1. football   **5.** contemporary music
2. college   **6.** immigration
3. environment   **7.** Japan
4. London   **8.** islands

WRITING ACTIVITY *Writing on Your Own*

Return to the subject on the theme of communication that you chose to write about in Writing Activity 6. Then, using the Strategies for Limiting a Subject, narrow your subject. Save your work in your writing folder for later use.

Considering Your Purpose and Audience

Often your writing has a very particular goal, such as completing a school assignment or sending a letter to a friend. At the same time, every piece of writing also has a more general purpose. For example, the purpose of the school assignment may be to explain something, or the purpose of your letter may be to express your feelings. The following chart lists the most common purposes for writing and gives examples of each one.

Writing Purposes

- to **explain** or **inform** (scientific essay, research paper)
- to **create** (a poem or short story)
- to **persuade** (editorial)
- to **express** your thoughts and feelings (a diary or journal)
- to **describe** (descriptive paragraph)

Writing purposes, of course, may overlap. You can write an essay to explain a new product and at the same time persuade people to try it. You can write a poem that describes your neighborhood and that also expresses your feelings about it. Whatever your purpose, always keep it in mind as you write.

Your writing purpose is also related to the audience that you are addressing. You write to convey a certain kind of message to certain people. Who are they? How interested will they be? You must consider the answers to such questions if you are to get your message across.

Audience Profile Questions

1. Who will be reading my work?
2. How old are they? Are they adults, teenagers, or children?
3. What background do they have in the subject?
4. What interests and opinions are they likely to have?
5. Are there any words or terms I should define for them?

WRITING ACTIVITY *Writing for Different Audiences*

Write two paragraphs that explain the telephone. Address the first paragraph to a child. Address the second to an adult contemporary of George Washington.

WRITING ACTIVITY *Writing on Your Own*

In Writing Activity 8, you limited your subject on the theme of communication. Return to it now and decide your writing purpose and audience. Refer for guidance to the list of Writing Purposes and the Audience Profile Chart. Save your notes.

19

Strategies for Developing Your Subject

Once you have chosen a subject, limited it, and determined the purpose and audience, you can move on to fleshing out your ideas with *supporting details*. Supporting details are the facts, examples, incidents, reasons, procedures, or other specific points that back up your main idea. A composition with adequately developed supporting details will enable you to achieve your writing purpose effectively.

Observing   Your best source of supporting details is often your own senses, especially if you are writing a description. When you observe, you open all your senses, focusing on one sense at a time and on one detail at a time. Following are some techniques that will help you use your powers of observation to gather details for your writing.

Techniques for Observing

1. Be aware of the reason why you are observing. Keep your purpose in mind as you decide what and how to observe.
2. Be aware of and use all your senses. Look, listen, smell, touch, taste.
3. Use your mind. Think about what your observations mean or what the details have in common.
4. Observe from different viewpoints. Examine the subject from all angles: near and far, above and below, inside and out, and even upside down.
5. Sketch your subject. Make a drawing of the person or scene you observe.
6. Take notes. Keep a record of your observations.

WRITING ACTIVITY *Observing*

Review your journal entries and writing folder for subjects that you can observe in person for the purpose of gathering descriptive details. You may want to do some additional focused freewriting, starting with *When I think about sitting and observing, I think about . . .* Then observe that subject for at least a half an hour, making notes as you observe. Try to write down at least 25 details. Finally, place your notes in your writing folder for possible later use.

Brainstorming for Details   Brainstorming, like freewriting, is a way of digging into your mind for ideas. However, brainstorming always begins with a chosen subject. Furthermore, when you brainstorm, you write a list of words and phrases rather than a continuous stream of words. In addition, you may take time to pause and think as you brainstorm. When you brainstorm, let the ideas flow freely. Write them all down as they occur to you. Encourage one notion to lead to another. Each idea—even one that may seem silly or useless— unlocks a new one. You will not use all the items, but the longer the chain, the more likely you are to find the ideas you are seeking. Below is a part of the brainstorming notes made by one student on the subject of performing.

Student Model: *Brainstorming List*
          Subject: *developing stage presence*

- thrill of being in front of an audience
- awful stage fright sometimes
- need to turn nervous energy into performing energy
- excercise can help
- some actors have more energy than others
- stage presence
- audience's eyes always on actors
- project confidence
- rehearse, rehearse, rehearse
- knows lines perfectly
- always need to be "on" when onstage

Group Brainstorming   When the entire class is writing on the same subject, you can brainstorm in a group to generate supporting details. With your teacher's permission, start by forming a small group of three to five other students. The following guidelines will help you. *(See page 444 for information about cooperative learning.)*

Guidelines for Group Brainstorming

1. Set a time limit on the brainstorming session.
2. Write the subject on a piece of paper and assign one group member to be the recorder. If your group meets frequently, take turns recording ideas.
3. Start brainstorming for supporting details, such as facts, reasons, and examples. Since you can eliminate irrelevant ideas later, contribute any and all ideas.
4. Build on the ideas of other group members. Add to those ideas or modify them to improve them.
5. Avoid criticizing the ideas of other group members.

When you finish brainstorming, you should get a copy of all the material from the group recorder and then choose those details that are most appropriate for your composition.

WRITING ACTIVITY *Group Brainstorming*

TV and movie writers often develop their ideas in group brainstorming sessions. Get together with one or more classmates to brainstorm ideas for a new TV game show. For example, the purpose of the game show could be one in which contestants have to write song lyrics on the spot. Following the Guidelines for Group Brainstorming, come up with the details of how the show will work and then brainstorm to find a catchy title. Save your notes in your writing folder because you may want to develop them later.

Clustering *Clustering* is a visual form of brainstorming that is a good technique to use for developing supporting details. Instead of just listing ideas, however, you connect them. You begin with a single word or phrase and then arrange associated ideas around that nucleus, linking the ideas back to the original word or phrase. You continue this process by linking each of the surrounding words, in turn, to other words as they occur to you. In the end you have a diagram that provides you not only with details but also with the paths that connect them. As a result, you can see groups, or clusters, of related details.

The following is a portion of the cluster developed by the student planning a composition about developing stage presence. Notice how various ideas are clustered together.

Student Model: *Cluster*

WRITING ACTIVITY 13 *Clustering*

Create a cluster about what you will be doing a year from now. Save
your cluster in your writing folder for possible later use.

Inquiring To explore a writing topic, you can also use the technique of inquiring—a method that journalists use to gather information. Ask questions that begin with *who, what, where, when, why,* and *how.* For certain kinds of writing, such as narratives and expository pieces, finding the answers to such questions can provide many of your supporting details.

The model below shows some questions one writer used to guide her in finding details about early musical instruments. Notice that the writer developed more than one question using *what* and *how.*

Student Model: *Inquiring to Develop Supporting Details*

Early Musical Instruments

Who played musical instruments in ancient times?
What are the oldest instruments known?
What sounds did the instruments make?
What did they look like?
Where have ancient instruments been discovered?
When were they discovered?
Why did different instruments develop in different places?
How were the instruments made?
How were they played?

WRITING ACTIVITY   *Inquiring*

Write a series of questions that would help you develop supporting details on the subject of how viewers can influence TV programming. Write at least one question beginning with each of the six question words: *who, what, where, when, why,* and *how.* Save your questions in your writing folder for possible use later on.

WRITING ACTIVITY   *Writing on Your Own*

WRITING
ABOUT THE
THEME

Return to your notes from Writing Activity 10. Try observing, brainstorming, clustering, or asking *Who?, What?, Where?, When?, Why?, How?*—or a combination of these strategies—to develop supporting details for your composition on communication. Use whichever strategies seem appropriate for your subject and whichever work well for you. Continue until you have more than enough supporting details to cover your subject. Save your work in your writing folder.

Recalling

Your own experiences often furnish you with some of the most interesting subjects to write about. As you explore such subjects, you will use the skill of *recalling*. You probably will be surprised to find out how many past experiences, events, and reactions have left lasting impressions in your mind.

Suppose that one of your most vivid memories is your first trip to New York City and that you now want to develop the subject for a class assignment. Focus your thoughts on the subject and think about who was with you. When did you go there? What happened? What sensory details do you recall? Sketch a chart like the following one to help you focus and recall the details.

Memory: First Trip to New York City	
Who? When? Where?	parents, sister, and I; visited cousins one week last July, hottest days of summer New York City
Events	toured city; saw Statue of Liberty, Empire State Building, Central Park, Metropolitan Museum, Chinatown
Sights Sounds Smells	tall buildings, crowded streets, theater marquees car horns, street vendors, sirens pretzels, ethnic foods, raindrops on hot pavement
Reactions	amazement, curiosity, excitement, sore feet

Thinking Practice   Choose one of the following topics or a subject of your own. Then make a chart like the one above to help you recall your memories.

1. learning how to dance
2. the art of paddling a canoe or making popcorn
3. the first part-time job after school

Strategies for Organizing Details

When you are searching for and exploring subjects, you unlock your thoughts and set them free. After you have collected your ideas, however, it is time to give your thoughts focus and structure. Instead of relaxed, creative thought, you need concentration. Instead of opening your mind, you need to focus it—to examine the details you have gathered in an organized, logical way so that you can make sense of them. The strategies that follow will help you to organize your details in preparation for writing.

Focusing Your Subject   To determine how best to organize your details, you first need to determine your focus. Exactly what do you want to say about your subject? Your answer to this question will become your focus, or main idea. To help you decide on a main idea, use the following guidelines.

Guidelines for Deciding on a Focus

1. Look over your supporting details. Think of meaningful generalizations, or general statements, that you can draw from some or all of the details.
2. Choose a main idea that holds great interest for you.
3. Choose a main idea that suits your purpose and audience.

Recall the student who wants to write on the subject of performing. After reviewing his prewriting notes, he has decided to focus on the best ways to develop stage presence. As a performer in school plays, he is interested in the subject and can say something meaningful about it. His purpose is to write a composition that informs his classmates about something. His main idea suits this purpose, and since all students have participated in performances in some way, his audience is likely to find the subject appealing.

WRITING ACTIVITY   **16**    *Writing on Your Own*

WRITING
ABOUT THE
THEME

Look over your details from Writing Activity 15. Choose a focus for your composition on communication by using the guidelines above. Then write down your main idea and put it in your writing folder.

Classifying Your Details   Many of the supporting details you collect for a composition, especially a long composition, are likely to fall into certain groups, or categories. As you study your details, some of these categories will become obvious. If you are explaining weather forecasting, for example, some of the details may deal with kinds of weather, some with forecasting methods, and some with forecasting successes and failures. If you are comparing and contrasting the United States Congress and the British Parliament, your details will fall into the categories of similarities and differences.

When you classify, be sure to use categories that fit your purpose and main idea. If some of your details do not fit into any category, discard them. The following sample shows how the student writing about developing stage presence classified some of the supporting details he had gathered into two groups. He labeled the first group *During rehearsals,* and the second group he labeled *Before performance.*

Student Model: *Classifying Details*

During rehearsals
— practice movements, gestures as well as script
— study your character
— practice staying in character
— develop confidence
— know your part perfectly
— practice reacting to what's happening onstage

Before performance
— exercise; stretch, shake
— get into character
— do *not* practice lines
— rechannel nervous energy

WRITING ACTIVITY   *Writing on Your Own*

WRITING
ABOUT THE
THEME

Look back at your details from Writing Activity 15. Keeping your purpose and main idea in mind, choose some suitable categories and classify as many of the details as you can. You may find that you need to do additional observing, brainstorming, clustering, or questioning to generate more details.

Ordering Your Details Your next step is to order your details so that they progress logically from one to the other. A clear method of organization helps your reader follow and understand the details you present. Below is a summary of the most common types of organization.

Types of Order	Arrangement of Details
CHRONOLOGICAL	According to the order in which events occurred
SPATIAL	According to the location of details (right to left, etc.)
ORDER OF IMPORTANCE	According to degrees of importance, size, or interest
DEVELOPMENTAL ORDER	According to a logical progression, with one detail growing out of another
COMPARISON/CONTRAST	According to similarities or differences

Zero Mostel, Actor, on stage in *Fiddler on the Roof*

The order you choose will depend on your writing purpose and your details. For example, for a narrative you would probably choose chronological order, while for a description you might choose spatial order. The student writer of the composition on stage presence, whose purpose was to inform, chose a combination of chronological order and order of importance, going from most to least important. The following is the list he made.

Student Model: *Ordering Details*

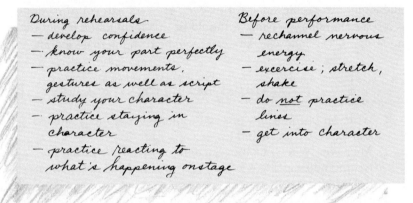

During rehearsals
— develop confidence
— know your part perfectly
— practice movements,
  gestures as well as script
— study your character
— practice staying in
  character
— practice reacting to
  what's happening onstage

Before performance
— rechannel nervous
  energy
— excercise ; stretch,
  shake
— do *not* practice
  lines
— get into character

WRITING ACTIVITY   18 *Organizing Details*

Decide which organizing method would be most suitable for each of the writing subjects listed below. Then write *chronological, spatial, order of importance or degree, developmental order,* or *comparison/contrast* after the proper number.

1. differences between European and American schools
2. description of night sky on a particular date
3. accomplishments of your current United States senator
4. the history of the bicycle
5. thoughts on academic freedom

WRITING ACTIVITY   19 *Writing on Your Own*

WRITING
ABOUT THE
THEME
Review your groups of details from Writing Activity 17. Do you need more details? If so, repeat some of the strategies for developing your subject and then classify the new details. Decide which ordering would be best, given your purpose and your subject, and arrange all your details in that order.

Drafting

Writing Process

The word *draft* is related to *draw,* in the sense of drawing a net from the sea or drawing votes in an election. When you write a draft, you draw together your ideas on paper. Just as a fisher pulls in the net repeatedly to assure a worthwhile catch, you write more than one draft to assure a worthwhile composition. In your additional drafts, you will be able to look for more ideas, rethink your ideas, or even find a more workable subject. However, even though your first draft is just a preliminary version, it should be in a form that a reader can understand. The following strategies will help you prepare a draft.

Strategies for Drafting

1. Write an introduction that will capture the reader's interest and express your main idea.
2. After you write your introduction, use your organized pre-writing notes as a guide but depart from those notes when a good idea occurs to you.
3. Write fairly quickly. Do not worry about spelling or phrasing. You will have the opportunity to go back and fix such problems when you revise.
4. Stop frequently and read what you have written. This practice will help you move logically from one thought to the next.
5. Do not be afraid to return to the prewriting stage if you find that you need some more ideas or need to clarify your thinking.
6. Write a conclusion that drives home your main idea.

The following model shows the first draft of the student's composition about stage presence.

Student Model: *First Draft*

~~There are certain perfo~~

~~Do you~~ Have you ever felt yourself watching a minor character in a play instead of the star? Some actors always ~~hold~~ catch and hold the audience's eye, ~~even if they have~~ no matter how small a part they play. These performers have stage presence. This is a certain something that is

transmitted and sent to the audience. Stage presence is not
magic. You too can have it. Just work on your technique
during rehearsals. Also learn to ~~control~~ channel your
emotions at performance time.

~~Be conf~~ Stage presence is based on confidence. Your
first and most important step then is to lern your part.
Know it as if it was really part of you. Try different
deliveries, moves, and gestures until you find just the
right ones. Then rehearse them until they come naturally.
Another important thing is to ~~work on your movements~~ develop
your character ~~you are playing~~ as you rehearse. Think about
what the person is like. Practice staying in character
every moment. Listen and react to everything that happens
onstage. Do that even when you have no lines. Finally,
consentrate onthe way you move. Avoid halfway movements.
If you grin grin from ear to ear. if you do turn your head,
really turn it. Transform yourself into the character so
that you behave like the character. When performance time
arrives you ~~will~~ can expect to be nervous. Expereinced
actors do not try to calm themselves. They draw on their
nervous energy instead. That way they can increase their
energy level. By the way, avoid the temtation to practice
you're lines, especially trouble some ones. Misteaks only
will end up making you nervouser. The best way to rechanel
your nervus energy is to get into character. Chat with
others as your character would walk around as your character
would. Another importent strategy is Exercise. Even just a
healthy stretch and shake of your limbs, head and body will
help.

~~What is Achieving stage presence~~ Stagepresence depends
on ~~wor~~ concsciousness--of your character, of your emotions,
and of your audience above all. According to Ms Keller
Drama Teacher "There are no small parts, only small actors.
When you use the techniques above, you can always be a big
actor.

WRITING ACTIVITY *Studying a Draft*

Write answers to these questions about the student's first draft.

1. Which part did the writer seem to have the most trouble with? Why do you think that was so?

2. Where did the writer change the order of the details in his prewriting notes? Why, do you think, did he make the change?

Drafting a Title   The final step in writing the first draft is to think of a suitable title for your composition. A good title will express the main idea of the composition and at the same time catch the reader's attention. Many times words or phrases found within the composition are used as titles.

WRITING ACTIVITY *Drafting a Title*

Review the first draft of the student's composition about stage presence. Then brainstorm a list of five possible titles for the composition.

WRITING ACTIVITY *Writing on Your Own*

WRITING
ABOUT THE
THEME

Review all your prewriting notes and, using the plan you developed in Writing Activity 19, write your first draft. Follow the strategies outlined on page 30. Then brainstorm a list of five possible titles for your composition and choose the one you think is most suitable.

32

Revising

Writing Process

Although you can and should be making revisions at every stage of the writing process, your major revising job comes after your first draft. In the revising stage, your purpose is to evaluate and improve your first draft. A helpful technique when revising is to put yourself in your reader's place and ask yourself, "Will my reader understand exactly what I mean?" For most writers this is very helpful.

Keep in mind that revising is not a one-time procedure—you may feel a need to write a second, third, or even a fourth draft. Of course, if you are able to use a word processor, you will find the task of revising easier and more efficient.

Revising on Your Own

Your first approach to revising your draft will be self-evaluation. Think about the overall organization and effect and zero in on the smallest details. Put your draft away for a time and then review it once more. Next look at it objectively, as if you were seeing it for the first time. Do you need to refine your subject? Generate more details? After you have evaluated your draft, make whatever changes are needed. The following strategies will help you revise your draft.

Adding Ideas Look over your composition. Have you covered every aspect of the subject? Do your ideas seem lively? Are they ideas that will spark people's interest? Are the ideas sound—or do you need to explore the subject in greater depth? If so, you may need to think of new ideas. Try freewriting about the subject or talking it over with someone more knowledgeable than you.

Adding Details and Information Do you have enough details to support your main idea? Do you have enough details to make your ideas clear and interesting? Look for places where additional details and information would be helpful.

Rearranging Consider carefully the organization of your ideas and facts. Are any ideas out of place? Does one idea lead logically to another so that the reader can easily follow your train of thought? Would a different order be more effective? If so, rearrange your ideas so that one flows smoothly and logically into another.

Deleting Unnecessary Words or Ideas   Unnecessary repetition clouds your ideas. Are there words that are not needed? Have you repeated yourself unnecessarily? Are there ideas that stray from the main point? Delete what you do not need.

Substituting Words and Sentences   Once again read over your draft. Will any parts of it confuse the reader? If so, think of a clearer way to express the same idea. If any words or phrases sound dull, think of more original ways to say the same thing. If your sentences sound monotonous, revise them so that they are of varying lengths.

Using a Revision Checklist   Revising is a challenging process that requires you to look at your writing many times and in many ways. To help you keep track of what you have done and what you still need to do, use a revision checklist. The general checklist below is a good place to start. As you become more familiar with the checklist, you may want to tailor it to suit your particular writing style. Other checklists will appear in the composition chapters to come.

Revision Checklist

1. Did you clearly state your main idea?
2. Does your composition have a strong introduction, body, and conclusion?
3. Did you include enough interesting details?
4. Did you present your ideas in a logical order?
5. Do any of your sentences stray from the main idea?
6. Are your ideas clearly explained?
7. Are your words specific?
8. Are any words or ideas repeated unnecessarily?
9. Are your sentences varied and smoothly connected?
10. Is the purpose of your composition clear?
11. Is your writing suited to your audience?
12. Is your title effective?

WRITING ACTIVITY   *Studying a Revision*

On the next page is the revision of the first part of the composition on stage presence. (Remaining errors in spelling, capitalization, and usage will be corrected later.) After you read it carefully, answer the questions that follow.

Stage Presence

Have you ever felt yourself watching a minor character

in a play instead of the star? Some actors always catch and

hold the audience's eye, no matter how small a part they

play. These performers have stage presence. ~~This is~~ a

certain ~~something~~ *poise and energy* that is transmitted ~~and sent~~ to the

audience. Stage presence is not magic. ~~You too can have~~

~~it. Just work~~ *By working* on your technique during rehearsals. ~~Also~~ *and*

~~learn to~~ channel *ing* your emotions at performance time. *you*
too can project that special quality when you step onstage.

Stage presence is based on confidence. Your first and

most important step then is to lern your part. Know it as

if it was really part of you. ~~Try~~ *Practice* different deliveries,

moves, and gestures until you find just the right ones.

Then rehearse them until they come naturally. Another

important ~~thing~~ *tactic* is to develop your character as you

rehearse. Think about what the person is like. *- how he or*
she talks, feels, thinks, moves, eats, and sleeps. Practice
staying in character every moment. Listen *ing* and react *ing*
appropriately
to everything that happens onstage. ~~Do that~~ even when you

have ~~no lines~~ *nothing to say*. Finally, consentrate onthe way you move.

Avoid halfway movements. If you grin grin from ear to ear.

if you do turn your head, really turn it. *Learn to* Transform
automatically walk as the character
yourself into the character so that you ~~behave like the~~
walks, cough as the character coughs, even fidget as
~~character.~~ *the character fidgets.*

1. For what reason were the words *and sent* in the first paragraph deleted?
2. Where were details added? Why?
3. Which idea was shifted? Why?
4. Why was *thing* replaced with *tactic* in the second paragraph? Where was another change like that made?
5. Where were groups of sentences replaced with a single sentence? Why?

WRITING ACTIVITY *Revising a Draft*

The following paragraphs are from the student's model of a first draft on pages 30–31. Rewrite the paragraphs, using the Revision Checklist as a guide to make improvements. Ignore any spelling, punctuation, and usage errors for now.

> When performance time arrives you can expect to be nervous. Expereinced actors do not try to calm themselves. They draw on their nervous energy instead. That way they can increase their energy level. By the way, avoid the temtation to practice you're lines, especially trouble some ones. Misteaks only will end up making you nervouser. The best way to rechanel your nervus energy is to get into character. Chat with others as your character would walk around like your character would. Another importent strategy is Exercise. Even just a healthy stretch and shake of your limbs, head and body will help.
>
> Stagepresence depends on concsciousness—of your character, of your emotions, and of your audience above all. According to Ms Keller Drama Teacher "There are no small parts, only small actors." When you use the techniques above, you can always be a big actor.

Revising through Conferencing

No matter how hard you try to distance yourself from your writing, the words and thoughts remain your own. Therefore, as you revise, you may find it helpful to get an objective reaction from someone else. With your teacher's permission, ask a classmate, friend, or relative to read your draft and comment on what works well and what needs improvement. Do not try to defend your work; just listen. Then think about which comments you want to act on.

Peer Conferencing When you use peer conferencing, you form a small group with three or four other students and read one another's compositions. You then take turns discussing each person's composition, offering praise for what each writer has done well and providing suggestions to make the composition better.

No matter which form of conferencing you choose—one-on-one or small-group—the following guidelines will help you get the most out of this revising technique.

Guidelines for Conferencing

1. Read your partner's work carefully.
2. Start your comments by saying something positive like, "Your opening really captured my interest."
3. Be specific. Refer to a specific word, sentence, or section of the composition when you comment.
4. Phrase criticisms as questions. For example, "Do you think your details might be stronger if you . . . ?"

WRITING ACTIVITY ◆25 *Writing on Your Own*

WRITING
ABOUT THE
THEME
 If your teacher agrees, exchange your first draft from Writing Activity 22 with a classmate and follow the guidelines above to comment on your partner's paper. Then listen to your partner's comments on your paper and revise your work as you see fit. Also use the revision strategies and the checklist on pages 33–34.

Editing and Publishing

Writing Process

Throughout the first three stages of the writing process, you have been concentrating on the form and substance of your work. While you may have noticed—and sometimes corrected—slips in spelling, usage, punctuation, and capitalization, your focus has been on more substantive concerns. Editing is the stage in which you locate and correct such errors.

Strategies for Editing

Although editing is a less complicated process than revising, it still demands that you read your manuscript several times. Review your manuscript for one type of error at a time. This approach you will find more effective than looking for many types of errors at once. As you edit your work, use the following checklist as a guide for locating common errors in mechanics.

Editing Checklist

1. Are the sentences free of errors in grammar and usage?
2. Did you spell each word correctly?
3. Did you use capital letters where needed?
4. Did you punctuate each sentence correctly?
5. Did you indent paragraphs as needed and leave proper margins on each side of the paper? (*See page 43.*)

Creating a Personalized Editing Checklist You also should reserve an eight-page section at the end of your journal as a personalized editing checklist. Write one of these headings on every other page: *Grammar Problems, Usage Problems, Spelling Problems, Mechanics Problems.* Then use these pages to record any mistakes that you commonly make in your writing.

Using Proofreading Symbols *Proofreading* means "reading and marking corrections." To make the process of proofreading efficient, most writers use shorthand notations, called *proofreading symbols.* The most common symbols are listed below. Use them, for they will save you time when you edit your work.

Proofreading Symbols

∧ insert	Ms. Tey spoke ^*about* graduation.
⋏ insert comma	We ate corn, hamburgers ⋏ and salad.
⊙ insert period	The party ended at eleven ⊙
⌿ delete	The fair was a great ~~enormous~~ success.
....let it stand	Pago Pago is in ~~American~~ Samoa.
⊂ close up	Each set of finger‿prints is different.
∩∪ transpose	They ⌒only⌒arrived⌒yesterday.
¶ new paragraph	¶ Dunn Field resounded with cheers.
≡ capital letter	Is Ohio in the southwest or Midwest?
/ lowercase	To the /southwest lay barren desert.

The following model shows how the student edited a section of his composition on developing stage presence.

Student Model: *Edited Draft*

¶ When performance time arrives ⋏ you can expect to be nervous.

Exper⌒ienced actors, rather than trying to calm themselves ⋏

draw on *their* nervousness to increase their energy level. The

best way to rechan^n^el your nerv^o^us energy is to get into

character. Chat with others as your character would ⊙ walk

around as your character would. Another import^a^ant

strategy is /exercise. Even just a ~~healthy~~ stretch and

shake of your limbs, head and body will help. ⋏

Editing

Grammar in the Writing Process

The letter from Miss Meadows's fiancé in "The Singing Lesson" is just one example of how powerful words can be. However, some of that power can be lost if the words are not written correctly, following the rules of standard English. For this reason, editing is an important part of the writing process.

When you edit, you pull together, or integrate, what you know about usage and mechanics skills. As you review the different language skills in each composition chapter, write them in your personalized editing checklist. Then, at the end of the composition section, you will have covered every major language skill in this book.

Sentence Fragments   A subject and a verb are the foundation of each sentence you write. In fact, without these two main sentence parts, you have no sentence at all. You have only a *sentence fragment*, a group of words that does not express a complete thought. As a result, when you read through a piece of writing, you should look for any missing subjects and verbs. *(For information about sentence fragments and practice in correcting them, see pages 631–639.)*

SENTENCE FRAGMENT   The first and most important step in building stage presence. [This fragment is missing a verb.]

SENTENCE   The first and most important step in building stage presence **is learning your part.**

Subject and Verb Agreement   After correcting any sentence fragments, you should read through your composition again, making sure that the subject and the verb in each sentence agree in number. *Number* refers to whether a subject and verb are singular or plural. Therefore, if a subject is singular, its verb must also be singular, or if a subject is plural, its verb must also be plural. *(For more information about subject-verb-agreement problems and practice in correcting them, see pages 695–713.)*

In the following examples, the subject is underlined once, and the verb is underlined twice.

SINGULAR SUBJECT AND VERB   That <u>actor</u> with only a few lines <u>has</u> stage presence.

PLURAL SUBJECT AND VERB   The <u>actors</u> wearing masks <u>have</u> stage presence.

Run-on Sentences   Before you write a final copy of your composition, check to see if you have included an end mark—a period, a question mark, or an exclamation point—at the end of each sentence. Forgetting to put an end mark will result in a *run-on sentence*—two sentences mistakenly written as one. One way to correct a run-on sentence during editing, therefore, is to separate the sentences with an end mark and a capital letter. *(For information about run-on sentences and practice in correcting them, see pages 634–639.)*

RUN-ON SENTENCE   Stage presence is not magic you can have it just like famous actors have it.

CORRECT SENTENCE   Stage presence is not magic. You can have it just like famous actors have it.

Although editing takes time, think of that time as an investment. When you have edited well, you have unleashed the maximum power of your words, and those words will produce the maximum effect on your readers.

Editing Checklist

1. Are there any sentence fragments? *(See pages 631–633.)*
2. Do the subject and verb in each sentence agree? *(See pages 695–709.)*
3. Does each sentence begin with a capital letter and end with an end mark? *(See pages 753–770.)*
4. Are there any run-on sentences? *(See pages 634–635.)*

WRITING ACTIVITY   **26**    *Writing on Your Own*

WRITING ABOUT THE THEME   As you edit your work from Writing Activity 25, make sure you cover the problems in the checklist above. Also review the Editing Checklist on page 38 and your own Personalized Editing Checklist. To make your editing as easy as possible, remember to use the proofreading symbols on page 39. Then save your work in your writing folder for later use.

41

Ways to Publish

Although some of what you write is for your eyes alone—such as your journal or diary—most of what you write is for others to read. The final stage of the writing process, then, involves putting your writing in an appropriate form for an audience. That form may be as simple as a letter to a friend or as formal as a business letter. This stage is called *publishing*.

Your first step after the editing stage is to copy your work over neatly, incorporating your revisions and corrections. Follow your teacher's guidelines for headings and margins. Then, if you have not done so already, select an appropriate way to publish the piece, taking into account your purpose and audience. Following are some possible choices.

Ways to Publish Your Writing

1. Display your final draft on a bulletin board and include illustrations.
2. Give an oral presentation to your class or to another audience, using audiovisual aids such as charts, graphs, maps, and so forth.
3. Create a class library to which you submit your work. The library would be a collection of folders devoted to different types of student writing.
4. Submit your work to a local or national newspaper or to a student magazine.
5. Enter your work in a writing contest. For information on writing contests, write to National Council of Teachers of English, 1111 Kenyon Road, Urbana, IL 61801.
6. Create a class anthology to which every student contributes a piece of his or her writing.
7. Share your work with the school by creating a literary magazine or booklet. Display the magazine or booklet in the school library.
8. Publish your work in your school newspaper, yearbook, or literary magazine.
9. Form a writing group with classmates. Share your compositions by reading them aloud and comment on one another's writing.
10. Create a video based on your writing and present it to your class.

Using Standard Manuscript Form The appearance of your composition may be almost as important as its content. A paper with jagged margins and words crossed out or crowded together is difficult to read. A neat, legible paper, however, makes a positive impression on your reader. Use the following guidelines for standard manuscript form to help you prepare the final copy of a composition or report.

Standard Manuscript Form

1. Use standard-sized, 8 1/2- by 11-inch, white paper. Use one side of the paper only.

2. If handwriting, use black or blue ink. If typing, use a black typewriter ribbon and double-space the lines.

3. Leave a 1 1/4-inch margin at the left and a 1-inch margin at the right. The left margin must be even. The right margin should be as even as possible, without too many hyphenated words.

4. Put your name, the course title, the name of your teacher, and the date in the upper right-hand corner of the first page.

5. Center the title about 2 inches from the top of the first page. Do not underline or put quotation marks around your title.

6. If handwriting, skip 2 lines between the title and the first paragraph. If typing, skip 4 lines.

7. If handwriting, indent the first line of each paragraph 1 inch. If typing, indent 5 spaces.

8. Leave a 1-inch margin at the bottom of all pages.

9. Starting on page 2, number each page in the upper right-hand corner. Begin the first line 1 inch from the top.

The final copy of the model student composition on the next page shows how to use standard manuscript form. Notice the placement of the name, class, teacher, date, and composition title. Notice, in addition, that the margins are a consistent width. When writing your composition, be sure it is clear and easy to read. When typing or using a word processor, be sure that your paper is double-spaced.

WRITING ACTIVITY **27** *Writing on Your Own*

WRITING
ABOUT THE
THEME

Following standard manuscript form, make a neat final copy of your edited composition from Writing Activity 26. Then select an appropriate way to publish it.

Student Model: *Final Composition*

½ inch

Andrew Dunn

English: Ms. Jones

2 inches

February 14, 1992

Stage Presence

4 lines

5 spaces

Have you ever felt yourself watching a
minor character in a play instead of the star?
Some actors always catch and hold the audience's
eye, no matter how small a part they play.
These performers have stage presence--a certain
poise and energy that is transmitted to the
audience. Stage presence is not magic. By
working on your technique during rehearsals and
channeling your emotions at performance time,
you too can project that special quality when
you step onstage.

1¼ inches   1 inch

        Stage presence is based on confidence.
Your first and most important step, then, is to
learn your part. Know it as if it was really
part of you. Practice different deliveries,
moves, and gestures until you find just the
right ones. Then rehearse them until they come
naturally. Another important tactic is to
develop your character as you rehearse. Think
about what the person is like--how he or she
talks, feels, thinks, moves, eats, and sleeps.
Learn to transform yourself into the character

1 inch

1 inch

so that you automatically walk as the character
walks, cough as the character coughs, even
fidget as the character fidgets. Practice
staying in character every moment, listening and
reacting appropriately to everything that
happens onstage--even when you have nothing to
say. Finally, concentrate on the way you move.
Avoid halfway movements. If you grin, grin from
ear to ear. If you do turn your head, really
turn it.

When performance time arrives, you can
expect to be nervous. Experienced actors,
rather than trying to calm themselves, draw on
their nervousness to increase their energy
level. The best way to rechannel your nervous
energy is to get into character. Chat with
others as your character would. Walk around as
your character would. Another important
strategy is exercise. Even just a healthy
stretch and shake of your limbs, head, and body
will help. Finally, avoid the temptation to
practice your lines, especially troublesome
lines. Mistakes will only end up making you
more nervous.

Stage presence depends on consciousness--of
your character, of your emotions, and of your
audience above all. According to Ms. Keller,
drama teacher, "There are no small parts, only
small actors." Using the techniques sketched
above, you can always be a big actor.

1¼ inches

1 inch

1 inch

A Writer Writes

  ## An Informational Booklet for Freshmen

PURPOSE: to inform incoming students about your high school
AUDIENCE: freshmen and other entering students

Prewriting   Students advising other students are often more effective than adult advisors. In some high schools around the country, seniors have prepared information booklets to aid incoming students. How would you describe your school to new students—for example, the location, the physical layout, the faculty, and the student body? What information would they need to know? Are there selected activities, classes, or special events that they should know about? What information would you like to have had communicated to you when you entered the school? What recommendations would you now make to benefit incoming students? With teacher approval you might want to prepare the booklet as a class project.

STEP 1: To help you decide on a subject, recall your first weeks at school—the way you felt and the questions you had. Use brainstorming or freewriting to think of and explore ideas.

STEP 2: Choose an idea that interests you and that will be of value to your readers.

STEP 3: Use a variety of techniques, observing, brainstorming, clustering, and questioning, to recall as much as possible, including appropriate details.

STEP 4: Review your notes. Decide on a focus for your subject and then group and order your details.

Drafting Use your prewriting notes to help you write a first draft of a composition that informs new students about your high school. As you write, always keep in mind that you want to supply information that will be helpful. Use the Strategies for Drafting on page 30. As you draft, stop occasionally to read over what you have written.

Revising *Peer Conferencing:* If possible, and if your teacher agrees, exchange papers with a partner. Refer to the Guidelines for Conferencing on page 37 and answer the following questions about each other's work.

1. Which part of the composition did you find most informative? Why?
2. Which sections need more work? Why?
3. Are the ideas logically connected?
4. Are there enough specific details and information to support your main idea?
5. Is the purpose of the composition clearly expressed?

Act on those readers' comments that you think will improve your composition. Then use those comments, the revision strategies on pages 33–34, and the Revision Checklist on page 34 to revise your writing. Remember that, if necessary, you should repeat any of the prewriting strategies for finding a subject, developing the subject, or organizing your ideas.

Editing and Publishing When you are satisfied with the form and content of your draft, edit it, using proofreading symbols and the Editing Checklists on pages 38 and 41. Then prepare a neat final copy of your composition and include it with your classmates' compositions to form a booklet.

Independent Writing

The advance of technology in the latter half of this century has brought about many new forms of communication. Today people are well-informed about current events, whether it is the launching of a space shuttle in Florida or a cultural celebration in China. Think about what communication methods, both old and new, exist today and brainstorm a list. What form of communication do you think has had the most powerful and influential effect on the world today? Express your thoughts in the form of a composition.

Creative Writing

Return again to the statements you have recorded in your journal for Writing Activity 4. Choose two or three that are especially entertaining and create a character who might have made the statements. What would the character look like? Act like? Do? Under what conditions might he or she have made the statements? Use the character, situation, and statements as the basis for a one-act play.

Writing about Literature

The perspective from which a story is told is called *point of view.* In "The Singing Lesson," Katherine Mansfield uses the third person point of view. Through the thoughts and actions of Miss Meadows, the reader becomes acquainted with other characters, particularly Basil. Suppose the story were told from Basil's point of view. How might the narration of the events in the story have changed? How might the reader's reactions to Basil and Miss Meadows be different? In a composition, explain how this different point of view would change the story.

Writing in Other Subject Areas

Physics   Space flight is one of science's most rapidly developing fields of study. One goal of scientists today is the establishment of space stations—manned satellites orbiting Earth. What exactly are space stations? What effects will they have on people's lives? Write a composition on a subject related to space stations.

Foreign Language   Write about the capital city of a country whose language you have studied. Explain why you would like to visit this city. Include informaton about its historical landmarks and features.

1

Checklist

The Writing Process

Prewriting

✔ Remember that writing is a back-and-forth process. *(See pages 10–11.)*

✔ Find a subject to write about by taking stock of your interests, freewriting, keeping a journal, and exploring literature. *(See pages 12–16.)*

✔ Choose and limit a subject. *(See pages 17–18.)*

✔ Consider your purpose and audience. *(See pages 18–19.)*

✔ Develop your subject by observing, brainstorming, clustering, and inquiring *(See pages 20–24.)*

✔ Organize your material by focusing your subject, classifying your details, and ordering your details. *(See pages 26–29.)*

Drafting

✔ Write a first draft and choose a title, using the strategies on page 30. *(See pages 30–32.)*

Revising

✔ Revise your draft by adding ideas, adding details and information, rearranging, deleting unnecessary words and ideas, and substituting words and sentences. *(See pages 33–34.)*

✔ Use a revision checklist as a reminder and guide. *(See page 34.)*

✔ Use conferencing to help you revise your draft. *(See pages 36–37.)*

✔ Revise your draft as often as needed. Repeat some of the prewriting and drafting strategies if necessary.

Editing and Publishing

✔ Use the Editing Checklists to find errors in grammar, usage, capitalization, and punctuation. *(See pages 38 and 41.)*

✔ Use proofreading symbols to correct errors. *(See pages 38–39.)*

✔ Follow standard manuscript form and make a neat final copy of your work. Then publish it, using any of the ways listed on page 42.

C
h
a
p
t
e
r

2 Developing Your Writing Style

Part 1 Reading to Write

THEME: *Passage of Time*

Suppose that you are having a great time with some friends at the beach. At one point you glance at your watch and see that it is noon. After what seems like a short time, you look again at your watch, and you are surprised to see that it is already 4:00 P.M. "Where did the time go?" you ask yourself.

With that question you have raised a subject that writers have explored many times—the passage of time. According to some writers, the best way to deal with the passage of time is to live each day to the fullest. Other writers offer the message that although time may seem to pass quickly, people can stay in touch with the past through their memories.

In expressing their thoughts about this subject—or any subject—writers use unique styles. That is, they choose words and shape sentences to make their writing powerful and concise. In this chapter you will learn ways of developing your own writing style. You will also have the opportunity to apply what you learn by writing about the passage of time, as well as other subjects. To start thinking about the theme of time, read the following two poems by William Shakespeare and Percy Bysshe Shelley.

50

Reading Woman with a Parasol, Henri Matisse, 1921, Oil on Canvas

Sonnet 73

W i l l i a m   S h a k e s p e a r e

That time of year thou mayst in me behold
When yellow leaves, or none, or few, do hang
Upon those boughs which shake against the cold,
Bare ruined choirs where late the sweet birds sang.
5   In me thou see'st the twilight of such day
As after sunset fadeth in the west,
Which by and by black night doth take away,
Death's second self that seals up all in rest.
In me thou see'st the glowing of such fire,
10   That on the ashes of his youth doth lie,
As the deathbed whereon it must expire,
Consumed with that which it was nourished by.[1]
   This thou perceivest, which makes thy love more strong,
   To love that well which thou must leave ere long.

1. **Consumed . . . by:** Smothered by the very ashes that had once fueled its flame.

Ozymandias[1]

P e r c y   B y s s h e   S h e l l e y

I met a traveler from an antique land
Who said: Two vast and trunkless legs of stone
Stand in the desert. Near them, on the sand,
Half sunk, a shattered visage lies, whose frown,
5   And wrinkled lip, and sneer of cold command,
Tell that its sculptor well those passions read
Which yet survive, stamped on these lifeless things,
The hand that mocked them and the heart that fed:
And on the pedestal these words appear:
10   "My name is Ozymandias, king of kings:
Look on my works, ye Mighty, and despair!"
Nothing beside remains. Round the decay
Of that colossal wreck, boundless and bare,
The lone and level sands stretch far away.

1. **Ozymandias** [oz'i man'de əs]: Greek name for the Egyptian pharaoh Rameses II
(thirteenth century B.C.). During his reign he had temples and palaces built, as
well as many statues of himself.

Responding to the Theme
Passage of Time

Responding in Your Journal Both Shakespeare and Shelley show that time waits for no one—not even the greatest of kings. Although you cannot slow down time, you can learn to appreciate each day fully by focusing on what is going on around you. In this chapter use your journal to recall and write about recent days that may have slipped by you. Perhaps, for instance, you will recall yesterday's basketball game. At the time you did not think much about the game, but now you recall and can write about the skill and the intensity of the players. Start today by writing about one such experience in your journal.

Speaking and Listening "Ozymandias" is about an artifact—a statue that is representative of the once-powerful King Ozymandias. What artifact from your own time would be representative of your society if an archaeologist found it 1,000 years from now? Would it be an automobile? A television set? A special toy? Some other item? In a group with three or four other students, and with your teacher's permission, discuss what the most representative artifact would be and why it is representative. After your discussion, write a summary of the conclusions of your group. Be prepared to present your conclusions to the rest of the class.

Critical Thinking: Inferring An *inference* is a conclusion that you draw based on a set of clues or details. Make inferences about the poem "Ozymandias" and write answers to the two following questions. In your answers include the details on which you based your inferences.

1. How did Ozymandias view his power?
2. What point does the poet make about Ozymandias's power?

Extending Your Vocabulary The Shakespearean poem that you have just read was written in the form of a *sonnet*. Using a dictionary or a glossary of literary terms, define what an English, or Shakespearean, sonnet is. Then read "Sonnet 73" once more and write an explanation of how it fulfills the criteria of what an English sonnet should be. Be sure to use specific quotations from the poem as examples of the characteristics of a sonnet.

Secret of the Sphinx (Homage to Elihu Vedder), Mark Tansey, 1984, Oil on Canvas

Part 2   *Writing*

"How do I know what I think until I see what I say?" pondered E. M. Forster. As a writer Forster realized that putting words on paper is a way of exploring ideas as well as expressing them. Writers who start out with a general notion of what they want to say often find their own words and sentences leading them to better-formulated and sometimes-unexpected ideas.

Whether you are writing a letter, a research report, a poem, or a story, a well-chosen word can reveal new avenues of thought. A singular detail like the description of Ozymandias—". . . sneer of cold command"—can open the eye of the imagination. A creative simile or metaphor can help you see things in new ways—as does the metaphor Shakespeare uses to describe the leafless boughs of a tree: "Bare ruined choirs where late the sweet birds sang."

In this chapter you will discover ways to select that well-chosen word, be more expressive, and write more concisely. In the process you will develop an effective writing style of your own.

Choosing Vivid Words

Words with rich, precise meanings give life to your thoughts and your writing. Look for vivid words in this scene, which describes a famous moment in horror-story history.

Model: *Vivid Words*

It was on a dreary night of November that I beheld the accomplishment of my toils. With an anxiety that almost amounted to agony, I collected the instruments of life around me, that I might infuse a spark of being into the lifeless thing that lay at my feet. It was already one in the morning. The rain pattered dismally against the panes, and my candle was nearly burnt out. Then, by the glimmer of the half-extinguished light, I saw the dull yellow eye of the creature open. It breathed hard, and convulsive motion agitated its limbs.   MARY SHELLEY, *Frankenstein*

Just as Dr. Frankenstein sparks life into his creature, Shelley sparks life into her writing with carefully chosen words. Indeed, her own words may have helped her to visualize the scene as she wrote—just as they have helped readers ever since.

When you write, search for words that paint vivid mental pictures. The selection of such words will help you develop an effective writing style.

Scene from the Movie, *Son of Frankenstein*

Specific Words

Use specific words to convey clear messages and create clear images. In each example below, a general word is replaced by one of the specific words Mary Shelley used in the preceding passage. The specific word may be a more precise synonym or a word with a different, richer sense.

GENERAL VERB   The rain **fell** against the window.
SPECIFIC VERB   The rain **pattered** against the window.
GENERAL ADJECTIVE   The **big** blast shook the house.
SPECIFIC ADJECTIVE   The **convulsive** blast shook the house.

Writing Tip   Choose **specific words** over general words.

WRITING ACTIVITY   *Choosing Specific Words*

Write two specific words for each of the following underlined general words.

1. Nothing ever stopped Lou and Henry from <u>talking</u>.
2. The <u>book</u> kept Andrew reading late into the night.
3. As the rocket blasted off, the earth <u>moved</u>.
4. It was an <u>awful</u> defeat, but the season had just begun.
5. Whenever Anna <u>came</u> into a room, everyone knew it.
6. The new state champions marched <u>happily</u> around the field.
7. That summer was a <u>great</u> time for the entire Diaz family.
8. Prince never behaved like an ordinary <u>dog</u>.
9. Surprisingly, all three beginners skated <u>well</u>.
10. The <u>nice</u> breeze carried the scent of lilacs.

Denotation and Connotation   Every word has a literal meaning, or *denotation*. Sometimes a word also has a *connotation*—a meaning that comes from attitudes attached to the word. Often the connotation of a word will be either positive or negative. Specific words tend to be richer in connotation than general words.

GENERAL WORD   work—little or no connotation
SPECIFIC WORDS   vocation, profession—positive connotation
               drudgery, toil—negative connotation

Writing Tip   Choose words with **connotations** that suit your meaning.

WRITING ACTIVITY *Different Connotations*

Write two specific words that could replace each underlined word. One word should have a positive connotation; the other, a negative connotation. You may consult a thesaurus for help.

EXAMPLE   Dramatically he pointed to his new <u>car</u>.
POSSIBLE ANSWER   sedan [positive]   jalopy [negative]

1. The meeting room at the school had not been designed for such a <u>throng</u>.
2. She <u>smiled</u> at the mention of his name.
3. Tall <u>plants</u> almost hid the front steps from view.
4. Thomas Rutherford lived on a nearby <u>roadway</u>.
5. Jennifer was a young woman with <u>great</u> ambition.
6. Every morning at 6:22, Arnold Ling <u>walks</u> out of his house and picks up the morning paper from his front lawn.
7. The wallpaper he chose for his bedroom had an <u>unusual</u> pattern.
8. On that late November day, the weather turned <u>cold</u>.
9. The halls were <u>crowded</u> with students hurrying to class.
10. Once inside the cabin, he closed his eyes and listened to the <u>sound</u> of the raging storm.
11. The locomotive <u>pulled</u> out of the station.
12. Although I was nervous, Megan was <u>calm</u>.
13. The room was filled with <u>interesting</u> furnishings.
14. Wait until you hear *this* <u>information</u>!
15. The <u>leader</u> of the newly formed government told his people that there were to be many new reforms.

Jargon   *Jargon* refers to the specialized, often wordy language used in a certain field—such as government, psychology, or computer technology. Jargon often interferes with clear thinking and writing. First of all, readers unfamiliar with the field may not understand its jargon. Furthermore, jargon may be used to create the impression that something is more precise or scientific than it really is.

Compare the following two sentences. Notice how much clearer the simple statement is than the one that contains jargon.

JARGON   The determination was made that employees conducted themselves in ways consistent with the achievement of optimum goals.

SIMPLE LANGUAGE   The employees were working efficiently.

WRITING ACTIVITY *Translating Jargon*

Translate each jargon-filled sentence below into simple, direct language. If any of the words are unfamiliar to you, look them up in a dictionary.

1. The maternal instinct in dolphins is developed to such a degree that a female dolphin is believed to experience emotional trauma upon the death of her young.
2. Negotiations to terminate the military conflict fell short of achieving an agreement that effectively specified the terms of the demilitarization of the area.
3. One of the curriculum objectives is to enhance students' skills in written and oral communication.
4. The chief-attending physician convened with the patient's nearest of kin to review the prognosis.
5. Mr. Robertson repeatedly exhibits an element of instability with regard to employment relationships.

Figurative Language

A good writer knows how to use language figuratively as well as literally—to stretch the literal meaning of words so that they appeal to the imaginations of readers. Figurative language is usually composed of *figures of speech*—expressions that use words in inventive ways. Compared to literal language, figurative language is a more powerful tool for creating strong images, as shown in the following example.

LITERAL LANGUAGE   The moon appeared in the cloudy sky.

FIGURATIVE LANGUAGE   The moon was a ghostly galleon tossed upon cloudy seas.

ALFRED NOYES, "The Highwayman"

Here the poet appeals to the reader's imagination with his choice of imagery. Rather than simply stating that the night sky was cloudy, the poet compares the moon to a galleon, or ship, being tossed upon a sea of clouds.

Writing Tip   Use **figurative language** to appeal to your reader's imagination.

Similes and Metaphors   Similes and metaphors fire the imagination by making unusual comparisons. Similes use *like* or *as* to show a comparison. Whereas metaphors, on the other hand, imply a comparison without using *like* or *as,* or they simply state that one thing *is* another. Such figures of speech can enrich your writing and help your reader view ideas or things in new ways.

SIMILE   Here he stopped again, and glanced suspiciously to right and left, **like a rabbit that is going to bolt into its hole.**   E. M. FORSTER

METAPHOR   The days ahead **unroll in the mind, a scroll** of blessed events in the garden and the barn.

E. B. WHITE

Forster uses *like* to compare the suspicious man to a rabbit. White implies a comparison between the days ahead and a scroll.

When you use figurative language, beware of two hazards—the mixed metaphor and the cliché. In a *mixed metaphor,* two different comparisons are illogically combined.

MIXED METAPHOR   His car was a spoiled child, drowning him in the waves of its demands.

IMPROVED   His car was a spoiled child, eternally whining for his attention.

A spoiled child cannot drown someone in its waves, but a spoiled child can certainly whine for attention.

A *cliché* is an overused comparison that has lost its power to evoke a strong mental image. If you find clichés in your writing, replace them with new similes. The following are some examples of clichés.

happy as a lark   stubborn as a mule   good as gold

| Critical |
| Thinking |

Writing Is Thinking

Comparing

When you *compare,* you think of similarities or differences between people, places, things, or even ideas. One effective way to compare is to create a simile or metaphor in which you show how two essentially dissimilar things are similar. For example, if you compared the human brain to a computer, you would find several similarities. Both a brain and a computer process large amounts of information quickly. They both have extensive memories, and they both can classify related pieces of information into groups.

Effective similes and metaphors are based on creative comparisons that make people look at things in new and different ways. The simile below compares an angry crowd of people to a swarm of bees.

> Angered by events, the crowd of people flew down the street like a swarm of bees.

Making a chart like the following one will help you write your own powerful comparisons.

Comparison Chart		
PERSON, PLACE, THING, OR IDEA	**SIMILAR QUALITIES**	**COMPARISON**
SUBJECT 1 CROWD OF PEOPLE	angry, threatening	CROWD OF PEOPLE = SWARM OF BEES
SUBJECT 2 SWARM OF BEES	angry, threatening	

Thinking Practice   Create your own powerful comparisons by making a chart like the one above for one of the following phrases. Then write a resulting simile.

1. The truck was like . . .
2. A friendship is like . . .
3. The bridge spanned the bay like . . .

60

Personification   When you attribute human qualities to objects or ideas, you are using *personification.* Here are examples.

PERSONIFICATION   The book **beckoned** to me from the shelf.
The trees **danced** to the rhythm of the wind.
Darkness **crept** silently into the house.
The mountain **dared** me to try its slopes.

Of course, books cannot beckon, trees cannot dance, darkness cannot creep, and mountains cannot dare. Yet the meaning of each sentence is clear, since the actions described are understandable human actions. Through personification, objects and ideas take on fresh, new identities.

Sound Effects   Some figures of speech rely on the sounds of words to create vivid impressions. *Onomatopoeia,* for example, is a figure of speech in which the word's sound matches its meaning. The following are examples of onomatopoeia.

crash	slither	ooze
thump	hiss	quiver
boom	whistle	jangle

Another figure of speech that relies on sound effects is called alliteration. *Alliteration* is a sequence of words that begin with the same consonant sound. Often the sound enhances the meaning of the words, as in the following line from a poem. In that line the *b* sounds imitate the beating of the drum.

ALLITERATION   **B**ooth led **b**oldly with his **b**ig **b**ass drum . . .
VACHEL LINDSAY

Both onomatopoeia and alliteration are figures of speech that are more widely used in poetry than in prose. Used sparingly, however, they can enrich prose writing by calling on the reader's sense of hearing to bring a passage to life.

WRITING ACTIVITY *Experimenting with Sound Effects*

Write one sentence about each subject. Use onomatopoeia and/or alliteration to add sound effects appropriate to the subject.

1. doorbell   **2.** surf   **3.** busy office   **4.** traffic   **5.** cat

WRITING ACTIVITY *Identifying Figures of Speech*

The following sentences are from a novel by Stephen Crane. Identify the underlined figure of speech in each case by writing *personification, simile, metaphor,* or *onomatopoeia.*

The Red Badge of Courage

1. The trees began softly to <u>sing a hymn of twilight</u>.
2. The regiment was <u>like a firework</u> . . .
3. There was <u>a little flower of confidence</u> growing within him.
4. The red sun was pasted in the sky <u>like a wafer</u>.
5. The <u>regiment was a machine</u> run down.
6. War, <u>the red animal</u>, war, <u>the blood-swollen god</u> . . .
7. The <u>voices of the cannon</u> were clamoring in interminable chorus.
8. The guns <u>belched</u> and <u>howled</u> . . .
9. . . . <u>the black weight of his woe</u> returned to him.
10. Thus, many men of courage, he considered, would be obligated to desert the colors and <u>scurry like chickens</u>.

WRITING ACTIVITY *Using Figurative Language*

Write a paragraph about something that moves, such as the ocean, clouds, or a car. Include literal language, a simile or a metaphor, and personification.

WRITING ACTIVITY *Writing on Your Own*

WRITING ABOUT THE THEME

Prewriting With the passage of time, people change—not only in appearance, but in attitude and emotions. Think about how you have changed in the past ten years. What object would symbolize the "you" of ten years ago—a game, your diary, or a favorite place? What object makes a statement about who you are now? Choose the two objects and explore why you associate yourself with them by asking the questions *Who? What? Where? When? Why?* and *How?*

Drafting Use your prewriting notes to draft a composition—serious or humorous—in which you describe the two objects and why they are representative of you.

Revising Look for opportunities to use more specific words or figurative language; however, eliminate any clichés. Save your draft for later use.

Writing Concise Sentences

Just as a hiker carries only the essentials in order to move easily, a writer should use only the words needed to communicate clearly. Lighten your reader's load by avoiding needless words.

Writing Tip Keep your sentences concise by eliminating needless words and phrases.

Redundancy and Empty Expressions

Redundancy means unnecessary repetition of words or phrases. Find the redundancy in the first sentence of each pair below. Then notice how it is eliminated without any loss of meaning.

REDUNDANT Our memorable trip to London was unforgettable.
CONCISE Our trip to London was unforgettable.

REDUNDANT Animals who are members of the mammal family are warm-blooded.
CONCISE Mammals are warm-blooded.

Empty expressions are mere fillers—words that contribute no meaning to a sentence. Reduce empty expressions to a single meaningful word or eliminate them entirely, as shown below.

EMPTY The thing of it is that I cannot turn in my paper due to the fact that I forgot it.
CONCISE I cannot turn in my paper because I forgot it.

EMPTY It seems there were 20 people at the party.
CONCISE Twenty people attended the party.

Some Empty Expressions

on account of	so, as you can see
what I want/believe/think is	the reason that
it seems as if	the thing of it is that
due to the fact that	there is/are/was/were
in my opinion	I believe/feel/think that

Arena, Salome, 1982, 200 × 240 cm

WRITING ACTIVITY *Eliminating Redundancy and Empty Expressions*

Revise the following sentences to eliminate redundancies and empty expressions. A sentence may need more than one revision.

Sports in Japan

1. Many of the popular sports that many people enjoy in Japan are contests of strength and power.
2. There is *sumo* wrestling, for example, which pits two huge, giant men against each other.
3. The first wrestler to touch the floor before the other with anything but his feet loses the match.
4. Preceding the match the contestants enact a traditional ritual that they perform before the wrestling begins.
5. After clapping their hands, they extend their arms out with open hands to show the fact that they carry no weapons.
6. Finally they stamp their feet on the ground at the end to symbolize driving away evil.
7. It seems that *kyudo,* a centuries-old form of archery, dates back hundreds of years.
8. Also, fencing with swords, or *kendo,* is centuries old too.

9. *Kendo* is well-known due to the fact that it is taught in Japan's schools, where students can learn it.

10. The thing of it is that Japanese police and law enforcement officers are experts in *kendo* and *judo,* and they carry no firearms.

Wordiness

The expression "less is more" may sound illogical, but it makes good sense for writing. In general your writing style will be sharper if you use as few words as possible to express your point.

Reduce *wordy* constructions—constructions that use more words than necessary—to shorter phrases or words. The following are examples of various ways to reduce wordiness.

Phrase to Word

WORDY   Winds on Greenland's ice cap howl **in a fierce way.** [prepositional phrase]

CONCISE   Winds on Greenland's ice cap howl **fiercely.** [adverb]

WORDY   Dry snow, **having the quality of sand,** covers the ice. [participial phrase]

CONCISE   Dry, **sandlike** snow covers the ice. [adjective]

Clause to Phrase

WORDY   Because of the winds, scientists **who work in Greenland** do not venture far from their stations. [adjective clause]

CONCISE   Because of the winds, scientists **working in Greenland** do not venture far from their stations. [participial phrase]

or

Because of the winds, scientists **in Greenland** do not venture far from their stations. [prepositional phrase]

WORDY   The ice cap, **which is a perilous wilderness,** appears serene from the air. [adjective clause]

CONCISE   The ice cap, **a perilous wilderness,** appears serene from the air. [appositive phrase]

Clause to Word

WORDY   A glare **that is blinding** rises from the ice cap on a sunny day. [adjective clause]

CONCISE   A **blinding** glare rises from the ice cap on a sunny day. [adjective]

Archaeological dig
at Kampsville, Illinois

WRITING ACTIVITY *Reducing Wordy Sentences*

Revise the sentences below by reducing wordy phrases and clauses.

Going on a
Dig

1. Kampsville, which is a center for archaeological research and training, is located in west central Illinois.
2. Every year young students who are interested in archaeology go to Kampsville in order to dig up the past.
3. The remains of 2,000 communities of prehistoric times are being uncovered.
4. Students are taught to dig in a very careful way.
5. The site is divided into areas measuring six feet square.
6. Items that are excavated are identified by the number of the square in which they are found.
7. On unearthed bones and shells, students look for points, notches, and grooves, which are signs of human handiwork.
8. A student who is at Kampsville learns much about the life that ancient people led every day.
9. Bones that come from animals can be revealing.
10. Zooarchaeologists, who are experts in animal bones, surmise that early American Indians kept dogs as pets.

WRITING ACTIVITY *Writing on Your Own*

WRITING
ABOUT THE
THEME

Return to the essay about the passage of time that you drafted for Writing Activity 7. If your teacher agrees, exchange papers with another student. Look for any redundancies, empty expressions, and wordy constructions in your partner's paper. Then return to your own paper and make changes that will enable you to express your ideas more concisely.

Creating Sentence Variety

Clothing with an appealing style flatters the human form. Similarly an appealing writing style shows ideas to their best advantage. One important feature of writing style is sentence construction. An interesting pattern of sentences appeals to the reader's ear and gives a graceful shape to ideas.

Writing Tip Vary the length and structure of your sentences.

Sentence-Combining Strategies

Short, choppy sentences suffer from two important weaknesses. First, their rhythm soon becomes tiresome to the reader. Second, they obscure the relationships between ideas.

Compare the following two examples. The first presents a series of short, choppy sentences, while the second combines the short sentences into one. Notice how the relationships among the ideas become clearer when the sentences are combined.

SHORT SENTENCES Alfonso beat John in the mile race. John was Alfonso's best friend. John was also Alfonso's chief rival in track. Alfonso felt proud of his victory. He also felt sorry about John's defeat.

COMBINED After Alfonso beat John in the mile race, he felt proud of his victory but sorry about the defeat of his best friend and chief rival in track.

The following techniques of sentence combining will help you link related ideas and vary the lengths of your sentences.

Combining Sentences with Phrases Two sentences can be combined by turning one sentence into a phrase that modifies the main idea expressed in the other sentence.

A. Police departments today use computers. **Computers store important information about suspects.**
Police departments today use computers **to store important information about suspects.** [infinitive phrase]

67

B. In 1967, the first computer system used to fight crime was developed. **The FBI developed it.**

In 1967, the first computer system used to fight crime was developed **by the FBI.** [prepositional phrase]

C. The National Crime Information Center provides information by computer. **It aids police nationally.**

The National Crime Information Center provides information by computer, **aiding police nationally.** [participial phrase] *(See pages 591–593 and 782–783 for comma use.)*

D. CATCH can call up a picture of a suspect on a computer screen. **It is a highly advanced system.**

CATCH, **a highly advanced system,** can call up a picture of a suspect on a computer screen. [appositive phrase] *(See pages 589 and 781 for comma use.)*

WRITING ACTIVITY *Combining Sentences with Phrases*

Combine each of the following sets of sentences, using one or more of the preceding techniques. Add commas where needed.

A Long Flight
1. Birds navigate the long distances of their migration routes. They use innate compasses and clocks.
2. The arctic tern holds the distance record. It is an amazing bird. It flies a round-trip distance of 23,000 miles. It goes from the Arctic to the Antarctic every year.
3. Many birds use the sun. It helps them navigate.
4. Tens of millions of shearwaters land on islands off Australia. The time they all arrive is one November day.
5. The shearwaters land within a 20-minute period. They have come from many different places. These include Japan and Canada.

Combining Sentences by Coordinating   Ideas of equal importance can be joined with a coordinating conjunction *(and, but, or, for, nor, yet,* and *so)*. Following are some examples of sentences that were combined by coordination.

A. In many science-fiction novels, robots grow too powerful. They try to take over the world.

In many science-fiction novels, robots **grow** too powerful **and try** to take over the world. [compound verb]

B. Robots in most early works were dangerous. In *Star Wars*, C3PO and R2D2 are friendly.

Robots in most early works were dangerous, **but** in *Star Wars*, C3PO and R2D2 are friendly. [compound sentence] *(See page 774 for comma use.)*

C. One famous movie robot is Gort in *The Day the Earth Stood Still*. Another is Robbie the Robot in *Forbidden Planet*.

Two famous movie robots are **Gort** in *The Day the Earth Stood Still* and **Robbie the Robot** in *Forbidden Planet*. [compound predicate nominative]

WRITING ACTIVITY *Combining Sentences by Coordinating*

Combine each of the following pairs of sentences, using the conjunction shown.

Last but Not Least
1. Animals' tails are used for communication. They are also used for locomotion. [and]
2. The position in which an animal holds its tail may indicate aggression. The position may also be an indicator of the animal's social rank. [or]
3. Running cheetahs bend their tails in the direction they want to turn. Running wolves bend their tails in the direction they want to turn. [and]
4. Australian rat kangaroos sweat through their tails. They are kept cool by the evaporation. [and]
5. For many animals, tails are rudders. For many animals, tails are balances. [both/and]

Combining Sentences by Subordinating Ideas of unequal importance can be combined by *subordination*—by turning the less important idea into a subordinate clause. Following are some words that introduce subordinate clauses. *(For a longer list, see page 613.)*

Relative Pronouns		Subordinating Conjunctions	
who	that	after	because
whom	which	until	whenever
whose	whoever	unless	although

A. Capitol pages have a chance to see government in action. **They are aides to lawmakers.**

Capitol pages, **who are aides to lawmakers,** have a chance to see government in action. [adjective clause] *(See pages 616–617 for comma use.)*

B. **The Supreme Court uses only three students as pages.** The chances of becoming a Supreme Court page are slim.

Because the Supreme Court uses only three students as pages, the chances of becoming a Supreme Court page are slim. [adverb clause] *(See pages 612–613 for comma use.)*

C. **A person may want to become a Capitol page.** That person should write to his or her senator and representative for information.

Whoever wants to become a Capitol page should write to his or her senator and representative for information. [noun clause]

WRITING ACTIVITY *Combining Sentences by Subordinating*

Combine each of the following sentences, using the joining word given in brackets. Add commas where needed.

A Capitol Page

1. Senate pages may be between fourteen and seventeen years old. Pages in the House must be high school juniors or seniors. [while]
2. The *Capitol Page School Handbook* tells pages about their jobs. It is issued by the House of Representatives. [which]
3. The tasks of Capitol pages are varied. They include running errands and handling phone calls. [which]
4. Parliamentary rules must be followed strictly. Pages sound bells to call House members to a vote. [because]
5. Capitol pages serve out the terms to which they are appointed. They must still attend school. [while]
6. The school is part of the Washington, D.C., public school system. The schedule is adjusted for the pages. [although]
7. Regular classes begin in the morning. Capitol pages have already finished their special early classes. [when]
8. Pages attend school. They rush to Capitol Hill for a day's work. [after]
9. Someone may come from outside Washington, D.C., to be a page. He or she must arrange for room and board. [whoever]
10. Pages are well paid. Living expenses are high. [although]

Varying Sentence Structure

By combining sentences, you can create sentences that have different lengths and different structures. Using a mix of the four basic sentence types will improve your writing style. *(See pages 622–623.)*

SIMPLE	Rita read the letter.
COMPOUND	Rita read the letter, and Sam waited.
COMPLEX	While Rita read the letter, Sam waited.
COMPOUND-COMPLEX	While Rita read the letter, Sam waited, but she never uttered a word.

Varying Sentence Beginnings   Beginning every sentence with a subject can become monotonous. Use the following sentence starters for a change of pace.

ADVERB	**Probably** the largest meteor to fall within recorded history landed in Siberia in 1947.
ADJECTIVE	**Brittle** as glass, the meteor broke into thousands of pieces on its way to Earth.
PREPOSITIONAL PHRASE	**In its original form,** it probably weighed 200 tons.
INFINITIVE PHRASE	**To trace the source of the meteor,** scientists studied the debris at the site.
PARTICIPIAL PHRASE	**Landing with great destructive force,** the meteor felled all trees within 40 miles.
ADVERB CLAUSE	**If the meteor had fallen two hours later,** it would have hit Leningrad.

WRITING ACTIVITY *Varying Sentence Beginnings*

Write a sentence for each type of sentence starter listed above. Then challenge yourself by selecting a topic and writing a paragraph in which you use several different types of sentence beginnings.

WRITING ACTIVITY *Writing on Your Own*

WRITING
ABOUT THE
THEME
Return to your composition about the passage of time from Writing Activity 10. If your teacher agrees, exchange papers with another student. As you review your partner's draft, ask the following questions: Is there variety? Can related sentences be combined? Then review your own paper and make appropriate changes.

71

Correcting Faulty Sentences

Most writers, when writing their first draft, concentrate on just the content and organization. Only later do they go back to polish their sentences and correct any errors. In this section, you will find ways to revise your sentences to eliminate some common sentence faults.

Writing Tip Revise your sentences to eliminate faulty coordination and faulty subordination, rambling sentences, and overuse of the passive voice.

Faulty Coordination

You can prevent problems in faulty coordination in three ways. First, avoid using the wrong coordinator, which will blur the meaning of your sentence. Notice in the following example how the writer sharpens the meaning by supplying the appropriate coordinator.

FAULTY COORDINATION   It began to rain, **so** the ball game continued.

CORRECT   It began to rain, **but** the ball game continued.

The following lists some common coordinators according to their use.

Some Common Coordinators			
TO SHOW SIMILARITY	**TO SHOW CONTRAST**	**TO SHOW ALTERNATIVE**	**TO SHOW RESULT**
and	but	either/or	so
both/and	still	neither/nor	therefore
furthermore	nevertheless	or, nor	as a result

Second, coordinate only those ideas that are related to each other. If the ideas are not related, express them in separate sentences.

FAULTY COORDINATION   Planes fly over our house every hour, and flying is really a safe way to travel.

CORRECT   Planes fly over our house every hour. Flying is really a safe way to travel.

Finally, coordinate only those ideas that are equally important. If the ideas are not equal, subordinate one of them by putting it in a phrase or a subordinate clause.

FAULTY COORDINATION	Inez forgot our phone number, and she did not call us.
CORRECT	**Forgetting our phone number,** Inez did not call us. [phrase]
CORRECT	**Since Inez forgot our phone number,** she did not call us. [subordinate clause]

Faulty Subordination

Subordination can also lead to two types of problems: (1) using the wrong subordinator, and (2) subordinating the wrong idea. To avoid the first problem of faulty subordination, be sure to use the connecting word that shows exactly how the ideas are related.

FAULTY COORDINATION	Yuki trained for months **even though** he would be ready for the Olympic trials.
CORRECT	Yuki trained for months **so that** he would be ready for the Olympic trials.

Following are common subordinators, listed according to their use.

Some Common Subordinators			
TO SHOW TIME	**TO SHOW CAUSE**	**TO SHOW PURPOSE**	**TO SHOW CONDITION**
after	because	that	if
before	since	so that	even though
whenever	as	in order that	unless

To avoid the second problem, use a subordinator and turn the less important idea into a subordinate clause. Then express the more important idea as an independent clause. *(See pages 611–623.)*

FAULTY COORDINATION	Although they took a walk, it was snowing.
CORRECT	Although it was snowing, they took a walk.

73

Use the following guidelines as you revise. They will help you examine your sentences for the faults discussed in this section.

Correcting Faulty Coordination and Subordination

1. Use the connecting word that best expresses how the ideas are related.
2. Express unrelated ideas in separate sentences.
3. If related ideas are equally important, use a coordinating word to combine them.
4. If related ideas are not equally important, turn the less important idea into a phrase or a subordinate clause.

WRITING ACTIVITY *Correcting Faulty Coordination and Subordination*

Use the guidelines in the box above to revise each of the following sentences.

Early Cowhands

1. Tales of western cowhands depict adventurous heroes, and actually their lives were exhausting and dangerous.
2. On the range water was scarce and raiders were common; furthermore, cowhands on the open range endured many hardships.
3. The cowhands' most precious possessions were their horses; also, horses were their only means of transportation.
4. A cowhand might give the last drop of water in his canteen to his horse, since he himself was thirsty.
5. A western saddle was designed for support because a cowhand could even nap in the saddle without falling off.
6. A cowhand had to be skilled with a rope, and it was his most important tool.
7. Cowhands in different regions had different names for the rope, for in the Southwest it was a lariat, while along the Pacific coast it was a lasso.
8. The cattle roundup was an important part of the cowhand's work, so it was also a type of social gathering.
9. They finished their work, and they competed in contests of skill called rodeos.
10. Because rodeos are still popular today, they have become more commercialized.

Rambling Sentences

Sentences that ramble on and on are usually the result of excessive coordination. To break up rambling sentences, separate ideas into concise sentences of their own.

RAMBLING   Some lions live in groups, which are called prides, and the lions who live this way can be said to be more fortunate than solitary lions, because the members of a pride of lions share all of the important tasks—for example, tasks such as hunting and protecting their turf—while solitary lions must feed themselves and must protect themselves on their own.

IMPROVED   Lions who live in groups, called prides, are more fortunate than solitary lions. Members of a pride share important tasks such as hunting and protecting their turf, while solitary lions must feed and protect themselves.

WRITING ACTIVITY *Correcting Rambling Sentences*

Revise the following rambling sentences. Capitalize and punctuate the new sentences correctly.

1. The Beatles were an immensely popular singing group in the years during the 1960's and 1970's, and they expressed in their words and in their music the feelings of the young people of those times, but even though they were controversial and their records and appearances were banned in some places, still their popularity held steady for many years, and at least one university now offers a college course on the music and impact of the Beatles.

2. People who are interested in a research career in the field of chemistry must choose between basic research and applied research, and the choice is an important one because there are significant differences between the two types of research, since in basic research the main goal of chemists is to expand knowledge about nature, while in applied research, chemists strive to make improvements in or develop particular products and services, and there are generally more jobs available in applied research.

3. Denim is a durable fabric used for making jeans, and the name *denim* evolved from the French, who called the fabric *serge de Nimes*, because it was originally woven in Nimes, France, but Levi Strauss was the first to popularize denim, and he used it to make pants for gold miners in the San Francisco area in the mid-1800's.

4. "What's in a name?" asked Shakespeare 400 years ago. and some psychologists are still asking the very same question today, for they maintain that people's names can have an effect that is profound on their attitudes and behavior, and so these psychologists make a plea for parents' devoting considerably more thought to what they name their children than to what they name their pets.

5. The sign language that is used by many deaf people can be very descriptive, and the signs for animals are especially so, since *elephant*, for example, is signed with the hand extending from the nose, like an elephant's trunk, and the sign for *monkey* is the famous chest-scratching motion.

Alligator

Elephant

Rabbit

Faulty Parallelism

A parallel structure is one in which two or more ideas linked with coordinate or correlative conjunctions are expressed in the same grammatical form. Ideas being contrasted should also be parallel. Parallelism helps readers understand related ideas. *Faulty parallelism*, on the other hand, adds a jarring effect to a sentence.

FAULTY   The committee members were **enthusiastic, energetic,** and **of great diplomacy.** [two adjectives and one prepositional phrase]

PARALLEL   The committee members were **enthusiastic, energetic,** and **diplomatic.** [three adjectives]

FAULTY   Neither soft **words** nor **offering treats** could coax the kitten down from the tree. [noun, gerund]

PARALLEL   Neither soft **words** nor **treats** could coax the kitten down from the tree. [both nouns]

FAULTY   **Doing** your best is more important than **to win.** [gerund, infinitive]

PARALLEL   **Doing** your best is more important than **winning.** [both gerunds]

PARALLEL   **To do** your best is more important than **to win.** [both infinitives]

WRITING ACTIVITY *Correcting Faulty Parallelism*

Revise the faulty parallelism in the following sentences.

1. Vernetta's goals are to study law and saving money for the future.
2. Some toys are neither of any educational value nor safe.
3. After the audition, Tom felt both disappointed and relief.
4. Roberto proved himself trustworthy and a hardworking person.
5. The sense of smell is more powerful in evoking memories than how things sound.
6. Police dogs must be both good retrievers and good at barking.
7. Neither raking nor to sweep can remove all the fallen leaves.
8. The club members discussed how to recruit new members, where to go for the club outing, and the pros and cons of raising dues.
9. The acting in the movie was better than the people who wrote the script.
10. As we watched the sailboat race from the shore, we saw billowing sails, rippling waves, and that the gulls swept by.

77

Active Voice and Passive Voice

Writers always have a choice between the active and passive voice. The active voice stresses the doer of an action. The passive voice stresses the receiver of an action; in fact, the doer is sometimes left out of a sentence written in the passive voice. *(See pages 662–663.)*

ACTIVE   The plumber just fixed the kitchen sink.

PASSIVE   The kitchen sink was just fixed by the plumber.

PASSIVE   The kitchen sink was just fixed.

The passive voice not only requires more words, but it can also rob a sentence of its feeling of action. In general choose the active voice over the passive except when the doer of the action is either obvious or unimportant, as in these examples.

PASSIVE   Jimmy Carter was elected President in 1976.

PASSIVE   The old library has been completely remodeled.

WRITING ACTIVITY   *Changing Passive Voice to Active Voice*

Rewrite each of the following sentences in the active voice instead of the passive voice.

EXAMPLE   The car was driven by me while my sister followed the map.

ANSWER   I drove the car while my sister followed the map.

I. A yard full of holes was dug by the persistent husky.
2. A decision was made by the company president to present employees with year-end bonuses.
3. A foul ball was called by the first-base umpire.
4. The plan for a new shopping mall was vetoed by the mayor.
5. The World's Fair was attended by thousands of people.
6. The telephone bill was handed to me by my mother with a stern look in her eyes.
7. A donation was made by our graduating class to the school library.
8. Survival techniques were learned from the Indians by the Pilgrims.
9. A cool midsummer's evening was ushered in by the passing thundershower.
I0. An enormous amount of money was being spent by executives on business travel and entertainment.

WRITING ACTIVITY *Writing Effective Sentences*

Rewrite each of the following sentences to correct the problem indicated in brackets.

1. Stan repeated the phrase in his mind over and over again. [redundancy]
2. The book that is sitting on my desk is about people who work as archaeologists. [wordiness]
3. Becky wanted the job more than anything else in her life, but she knew she could do it well. [faulty coordination]
4. Rhoda has always had an easy time making conversation with strangers and to bring out the best in people. [faulty parallelism]
5. The gymnasium was emptied by the spectators after the disappointing defeat. [misuse of the passive voice]

WRITING ACTIVITY *Correcting Faulty Sentences*

Revise the paragraph below to correct faulty coordination and subordination, rambling sentences, and overuse of the passive.

Patterns in the way in which we use our language have been traced by language researchers who work in the field called statistical linguistics, and interesting statistical regularities have been found by them. For example, the 50 most common words in the language account for almost half of what is written by us. Furthermore, about 60 percent of what we say is composed of consonants, so the other 40 percent is composed of vowels, in addition to which certain letters occur more frequently than others. You may know that the most commonly occurring letter in English is *e,* and do you know the letters that come next? You guessed correctly unless you chose *t* and *a,* which are second and third in frequency.

WRITING ACTIVITY *Writing on Your Own*

WRITING
ABOUT THE
THEME

Return to the composition about the passage of time, which you last worked on in Writing Activity 15. Are any of your sentences unclear because of faulty coordination or faulty subordination? Do any sentences ramble and need to be broken up? Can you rewrite any passive-voice sentences to be in the active voice? Make any necesssary revisions. Then save your work in your writing folder.

79

Language Integrating Skills

Editing and Publishing

| **Grammar in the Writing Process**

With the passage of time, memories fade and things change. Yet some of these memories can be preserved through written accounts, such as those in a journal, a diary, or a letter. Written words, of course, last longer than spoken words. In this chapter you have read that the most memorable words are ones that are specific. They make a greater impact on readers than general words because they create clear images in the minds of readers. However, to ensure the clarity of your words, you need to edit your composition for correct capitalization, punctuation, and spelling.

Capitalization of Proper Nouns   One way to make some nouns more specific is to substitute proper nouns for common nouns. A *common noun* is any person, place, or thing; but a *proper noun* is a particular person, place, or thing. All proper nouns, of course, begin with a capital letter. *(For examples of words that should be capitalized and for practice in capitalizing proper nouns, see pages 753–767.)*

COMMON NOUNS   The **poet** wrote a sonnet about a **pharaoh** who once ruled that **country.**

PROPER NOUNS   **Shelley** wrote a sonnet about **Rameses II** who once ruled **Egypt.**

Punctuation with Possessive Nouns   To form the possessive of a singular noun, simply add *'s*. However, to form the possessive of a plural noun, you need to do one of two things: Add only an apostrophe to a plural noun that ends in *s* or add *'s* to a plural noun that does not end in *s*. *(For examples and rules concerning possessive nouns and for practice in writing possessive nouns correctly, see pages 789–790.)*

SINGULAR POSSESSIVE   This is the **traveler's** report about his trip to Egypt.

PLURAL POSSESSIVE   These are the **travelers'** reports about their trip to Egypt.

Punctuation with a Series   A *series* is three or more similar items listed in consecutive order. A series of nouns—or any other series of words, phrases, or clauses—would be confusing to read if the words in the series were not separated by commas. *(For examples of commas separating words in a series and for practice in writing words in a series correctly, see pages 772–774.)*

INCORRECT   Lying in the desert were trunkless legs a shattered face and a broken pedestal.

CORRECT   Lying in the desert were trunkless legs, a shattered face, and a broken pedestal.

Spelling the Plurals of Nouns   Simply add *s* to form the plural of most nouns. The endings of a few nouns must be changed, however, before you add *s*. For instance, if a word ends in a consonant and *y*, you must change the *y* to *i* and add *es. Jury,* for example, becomes *juries. (For other spelling rules that affect plural nouns and for practice in spelling plural nouns correctly, see pages 473–476.)*

SINGULAR NOUNS   My **memory** of the **statue** is vague.

PLURAL NOUNS   **Memories** of the **statues** are vague.

Editing Checklist

1. Are all proper nouns capitalized? *(See pages 753–763.)*
2. Is an apostrophe used correctly with possessive nouns? *(See pages 789–790.)*
3. Do commas separate any series of words? *(See pages 772–773.)*
4. Are plural nouns spelled correctly? *(See pages 473–476.)*

WRITING ACTIVITY   23   *Writing on Your Own*

WRITING ABOUT THE THEME

Editing   Give a final reading to your composition about time in Writing Activity 22. Look specifically for the items about nouns listed in the checklist above. Use the Editing Checklist on page 38 and your own Personal Editing Checklist to find other errors.

Publishing   After making a final copy, read your composition to a family member and compare that person's recollections with yours.

A Writer Writes

A TV News Feature

PURPOSE: to inform viewers about the life of a person who has just turned one hundred—namely, you

AUDIENCE: viewers of a TV news show

Prewriting   What kind of life would you like to look back on when you turn one hundred? For what would you like to be remembered? Use clustering, brainstorming, freewriting, or questioning to think of what you might have done, where you might have gone, whom you might have met, how you might have felt during your long life. Then choose your favorite details, making sure that they fit together to create a finished portrait of yourself. After you arrange the details in time order, from youth to old age, write a lead sentence that will engage your audience.

Drafting   Write a draft of a TV news feature covering your 100th birthday. Include details that not only tell the events of your century-long life but also reveal what kind of person you are—your interests, your attitudes, your personality. You do not have to be totally likable, but you should be interesting.

Revising   Read your feature aloud and, if possible, tape it. Listen to yourself carefully. Do your words paint a clear picture? Where can you add specific words or figurative language? Are there any redundancies, empty expressions, or wordy structures? Does your writing have a smooth flow, or do you need to combine some sentences? Are there any faulty sentences that need to be corrected?

   Peer Conferencing: After you have made some revisions, read the feature to a sample audience—a student, friend, or relative. Ask your listener if the hundred-year-old you comes alive in your newscast. Is the listener able to suggest any ways to improve the feature? Incorporate those suggestions that you think are appropriate.

Editing and Publishing   Refer to the Editing Checklists on pages 38 and 81 to edit your TV news feature. Then copy your story neatly. If your teacher agrees, read the story to the class as if you were the newscaster and the students were the audience.

WRITING
ABOUT THE
THEME

Independent Writing

If you could put time in a bottle, what memorable time would you save? What would you do with the bottle? How would you use the time stored in it? Would you tell others about your method for storing time? Plan and write a composition expressing your thoughts about this memorable experience. Be sure to include vivid words and figurative language in your description and make your sentences concise and varied.

Creative Writing

During an ordinary day, you come upon countless scenes and events. Choose a place that you observed in detail and picture it in your mind. What might happen there? Who might turn up? What if something about that scene or event suddenly changed? Use the scene as the setting for a short story. *(For information about writing a short story, see Chapter 10, "Creative Writing.")*

Writing about Literature

As in "Sonnet 73," Shakespeare would often compare nature with the stages of one's life. In order to do this, he would use a figure of speech called a metaphor. A *metaphor* is an implied comparison between two things that are usually perceived as being different. In "Sonnet 73" to which stage of life is Shakespeare comparing nature? What three metaphors does he use to make this comparison? In the form of a composition, cite the metaphors he uses and explain what they mean.

Writing in Other Subject Areas

Economics   A popular form of enterprise today is the *franchise*. As a *franchisee* a person or a group buys the legal right to market the goods and services of a company and uses its trade name. For example, a franchise could be a restaurant that is duplicated in neighboring towns or throughout the country. Imagine that you have decided to invest in a franchise. What type would you buy? Would you simply like to sell the product and use the trade name, as a car dealership does, or would you buy the entire management package as offered by the fast-food chains? Write a brochure describing your franchise. Keep your words specific and use figures of speech to highlight your description.

Biology   Write a description of a trip through the human body from the point of view of a molecule of oxygen, a white blood cell, a grain of sugar, or anything else that travels through the body. Explain the sights, sounds, feelings, smells, and tastes, as well as the events that you encounter. You might want to write about the journey as if you were preparing an article for a travel magazine.

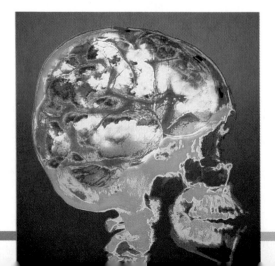

2

Checklist

Developing Your Writing Style

Choosing Vivid Words

✔ Choose specific words over general words. *(See page 56.)*
✔ Choose words with appropriate connotations. *(See page 56.)*
✔ Avoid using jargon. *(See page 57.)*
✔ Use figurative language—personification, similes and metaphors, sound effects—to appeal to your reader's imagination. *(See pages 58–61.)*

Writing Concise Sentences

✔ Keep your sentences concise by eliminating redundancies and empty expressions. *(See page 63.)*
✔ Eliminate unnecessary words by reducing clauses to phrases and phrases to words where possible. *(See page 65.)*

Creating Sentence Variety

✔ Vary the length and structure of your sentences by combining short sentences into longer ones by means of phrases, coordination, or subordination. *(See pages 67–70.)*
✔ Vary the structure of your sentences by expanding them with details and by shifting different elements to the beginning. *(See page 71.)*

Correcting Faulty Sentences

✔ Revise your sentences to correct faulty coordination and subordination. *(See pages 72–74.)*
✔ Break up rambling sentences by expressing separate ideas in separate sentences. *(See page 75.)*
✔ Avoid using the passive voice except when the performer of the action is obvious or unimportant. *(See page 78.)*

3 Writing Different Kinds of Paragraphs

Part 1 | *Reading to Write*

THEME: *Traditions*

The dictionary defines *tradition* as "a mode of thought or behavior followed by people continuously from generation to generation and passed down by oral communication." In these modern days of instant replay, electronic marvels, and space shuttles, traditions do not seem very important anymore. Still, a few traditions have remained. Do you celebrate birthdays with a cake with candles on it? That is one tradition. Do you watch fireworks on the Fourth of July? That is another tradition.

In the story you are about to read, called "Dead Men's Path," an old African priest tells a modern schoolmaster to let "the hawk perch and let the eagle perch." In this colorful analogy, the priest is saying that new ideas ought to be able to coexist with old ideas—with traditions—because he believes that both have value. The schoolmaster, on the other hand, sees no value in traditions at all. How do you feel about traditions? Do they have any value or purpose in this last decade of the twentieth century? Consider your answer as you read the story.

Dead Men's Path

C h i n u a   A c h e b e

Michael Obi's hopes were fulfilled much earlier than he had expected. He was appointed headmaster of Ndume Central School in January 1949. It had always been an unprogressive school, so the Mission authorities decided to send a young and energetic man to run it. Obi accepted this responsibility with enthusiasm. He had many wonderful ideas and this was an opportunity to put them into practice. He had had sound secondary school education which designated him a "pivotal teacher" in the official records and set him apart from the other headmasters in the mission field. He was outspoken in his condemnation of the narrow views of these older and often less-educated ones.

"We shall make a good job of it, shan't we?" he asked his young wife when they first heard the joyful news of his promotion.

"We shall do our best," she replied. "We shall have such beautiful gardens and everything will be just *modern* and delightful . . ." In their two years of married life she had become completely infected by his passion for "modern methods" and his denigration of "these old and superannuated people in the teaching field who would be better employed as traders in the Onitsha[1] market." She began to see herself already as the admired wife of the young headmaster, the queen of the school.

The wives of the other teachers would envy her position. She would set the fashion in everything . . . Then, suddenly, it occurred to her that there might not be other wives. Wavering between hope and fear, she asked her husband, looking anxiously at him.

"All our colleagues are young and unmarried," he said with enthusiasm which for once she did not share. "Which is a good thing," he continued.

1. **Onitsha** [o nich'ə]: Business district in Nigeria.

"Why?"

"Why? They will give all their time and energy to the school."

Nancy was downcast. For a few minutes she became skeptical about the new school; but it was only for a few minutes. Her little personal misfortune could not blind her to her husband's happy prospects. She looked at him as he sat folded up in a chair. He was stoop-shouldered and looked frail. But he sometimes surprised people with sudden bursts of physical energy. In his present posture, however, all his bodily strength seemed to have retired behind his deep-set eyes, giving them an extraordinary power of penetration. He was only twenty-six, but looked thirty or more. On the whole, he was not unhandsome.

"A penny for your thoughts, Mike," said Nancy after a while, imitating the woman's magazine she read.

"I was thinking what a grand opportunity we've got at last to show these people how a school should be run."

Ndume School was backward in every sense of the word. Mr. Obi put his whole life into the work, and his wife hers too. He had two aims. A high standard of teaching was insisted upon, and the school compound was to be turned into a place of beauty. Nancy's dream-gardens came to life with the coming of the rains, and blossomed. Beautiful hibiscus and allamanda hedges in brilliant red and yellow marked out the carefully tended school compound from the rank neighborhood bushes.

One evening as Obi was admiring his work he was scandalized to see an old woman from the village hobble right across the compound, through a marigold flower bed and the hedges. On going up there he found faint signs of an almost disused path from the village across the school compound to the bush on the other side.

"It amazes me," said Obi to one of his teachers who had been three years in the school, "that you people allowed the villagers to make use of this footpath. It is simply incredible." He shook his head.

"The path," said the teacher apologetically, "appears to be very important to them. Although it is hardly used, it connects the village shrine with their place of burial."

"And what has that got to do with the school?" asked the headmaster.

"Well, I don't know," replied the other with a shrug of the shoulders. "But I remember there was a big row some time ago when we attempted to close it."

"That was some time ago. But it will not be used now," said Obi as he walked away. "What will the Government Education Officer think of this when he comes to inspect the school next week? The villagers might, for all I know, decide to use the schoolroom for a pagan ritual during the inspection."

Heavy sticks were planted closely across the path at the two places where it entered and left the school premises. These were further strengthened with barbed wire.

Three days later the village priest of *Ani* called on the headmaster. He was an old man and walked with a slight stoop. He carried a stout walking stick which he usually tapped on the floor, by way of emphasis, each time he made a new point in his argument.

"I have heard," he said after the usual exchange of cordialities, "that our ancestral footpath has recently been closed . . ."

"Yes," replied Mr. Obi. "We cannot allow people to make a highway of our school compound."

"Look here, my son," said the priest bringing down his walking stick, "this path was here before you were born and before your father was born. The whole life of this village depends on it. Our dead relatives depart by it and our ancestors visit us by it. But most important, it is the path of children coming in to be born . . ."

Mr. Obi listened with a satisfied smile on his face.

"The whole purpose of our school," he said finally, "is to eradicate just such beliefs as that. Dead men do not require footpaths. The whole idea is just fantastic. Our duty is to teach your children to laugh at such ideas."

"What you say may be true," replied the priest, "but we follow the practices of our fathers. If you reopen the path we shall have nothing to quarrel about. What I always say is: let the hawk perch and let the eagle perch." He rose to go.

"I am sorry," said the young headmaster. "But the school compound cannot be a thoroughfare. It is against our regulations. I would suggest your constructing another path, skirting our premises. We can even get our boys to help in building it. I don't suppose the ancestors will find the little detour too burdensome."

"I have no more words to say," said the old priest, already outside.

Two days later a young woman in the village died in childbed. A diviner was immediately consulted and he prescribed heavy sacrifices to propitiate ancestors insulted by the fence.

Obi woke up the next morning among the ruins of his work. The beautiful hedges were torn up not just near the path but right round the school, the flowers trampled to death and one of the school buildings pulled down . . . That day, the white Supervisor came to inspect the school and wrote a nasty report on the state of the premises but more seriously about the "tribal-war situation developing between the school and the village, arising in part from the misguided zeal of the new headmaster." ◆

Responding to the Theme

Traditions

Responding in Your Journal   Whether you are a villager in Ndume or a resident of New York City, you will encounter—if not practice—traditions; for all cultures have traditions. Think about the traditions that are part of your society. Do you follow any of them? In your journal this week, write about traditions—what they are and why they are important to you. Begin today by writing about any family traditions, such as special birthday privileges. On another day write about school traditions—for example, graduation ceremonies and the senior prom. Also consider any local, state, or national traditions. You probably will discover most of your traditions, however, when you write about national traditions, such as Thanksgiving.

Speaking and Listening   The dictionary definition of *tradition* emphasizes that traditions are usually passed down by word of mouth to younger generations. If possible, get a tape recorder and record a family tradition. Describe what happens and why that tradition is important to you. Then, after you play your recording for various family members, ask them to record other family traditions. When you have recorded as many traditions as possible, give the tape to the youngest member of your family—either then or on his or her next birthday. If you do not have a tape recorder, then interview family members and write their responses on paper.

Critical Thinking: Evaluating   In "Dead Men's Path," the supervisor who inspects the village school reports that the problem between the school and villagers results "in part from the misguided zeal of the new headmaster." Focusing on this statement by the supervisor, review the story and evaluate the actions of the headmaster. Then, using specific examples, explain whether or not the headmaster's zeal was misguided.

Extending Your Vocabulary   The following ten words are from the story "Dead Men's Path." Using a dictionary, define each one and list its part of speech. Then develop a paragraph using five or more of the vocabulary words.

ancestral	colleagues	condemnation	cordialities	diviner
eradicate	propitiate	superannuated	denigration	pivotal

Rocky Mountains and Tired Indians, © David Hockney, 1965, Acrylic on Canvas,
67 × 99½"

Part 2   *Writing*

Traditions, passed down to younger generations by word of mouth, become lost when they are no longer practiced. However, if you write down traditions and other important thoughts and ideas, you prevent them from becoming lost. As you write, remember that in a longer piece of writing, paragraphs provide a way to break up ideas so that a reader can easily follow them. When a paragraph stands alone, it is a short composition, complete with an introductory sentence, a body of supporting sentences, and a concluding sentence. Many essay tests call for answers in the form of a paragraph composition.

Although you may come across a variety of types of paragraphs in your reading, most good paragraphs have certain features in common that ensure clarity. As in all writing, the main purpose of a paragraph is to help readers understand your message, clearly and simply.

Writing Term   A **paragraph** is a group of related sentences that present and develop one main idea.

Analyzing Paragraphs

Whenever and whatever you write, your purpose is to convey a message to your reader. As a writer you must bear the responsibility for providing a message with substance and an easy-to-follow structure. Notice how much you can understand and learn in the following paragraph.

Model: *Paragraph*

Stellar Compromises

TOPIC SENTENCE: STATES MAIN IDEA

Director George Lucas considers *Star Wars* a "real low-budget movie." He had to pare down his original budget estimate of $18 million, and, as a result, the film is full of compromises.

BODY OF SUPPORTING SENTENCES: DEVELOPS MAIN IDEA WITH SPECIFICS

He cut out over a hundred special effects shots. New sets were made from old sets. Space weapons were made out of cut-down machine guns. On such a low budget, the robots didn't work right at first. The original R2-D2 couldn't go more than three feet without running into something. (Extra footage had to be shot later for some scenes in the beginning.) Even the cantina scene, in which Luke and Ben Kenobi hire Han Solo and Chewbacca from among a roomful of bizarre, other worldly creatures, is only a shadow of what was in Lucas's imagination. The designer fell sick, and the studio wouldn't give Lucas enough money to have someone fully complete it.

CONCLUDING SENTENCE: REINFORCES MAIN IDEA

"The film is about 25 percent of what I wanted it to be," he has said.

DIAN G. SMITH
American Filmmakers Today (Adapted)

For a number of reasons, this paragraph succeeds in delivering its message. Its clear structure is relatively easy to follow. The main idea of the paragraph is stated plainly in the topic sentence and is amply supported with specific details. The sentences in the body of the paragraph all relate to the main idea and are presented in a smooth, logical order. In short, this model includes the basic features needed for an effective paragraph.

Paragraph Structure

A paragraph that stands alone should include the three main parts noted in the previous example: (1) a topic sentence, (2) a body of supporting sentences, and (3) a concluding sentence. The following chart summarizes the function of each of these elements.

Elements of a Paragraph

1. The **topic sentence**
- states the main idea.
- limits the main idea to one aspect of the subject that can be covered in one paragraph.
- controls all the other sentences in the paragraph.
- is more general than the sentences that develop it.

2. The **supporting sentences**
- explain, develop, or prove the topic sentence.
- provide details, events, facts, examples, or reasons.

3. The **concluding sentence,** or clincher,
- provides a strong ending.
- restates, summarizes, evaluates, or adds an insight to the main idea.

The topic sentence can appear at the beginning, in the middle, or at the end of a paragraph. The main idea may also be stated in two sentences or not stated at all, but merely implied. All these alternatives are available to help you, the writer, express your main idea clearly, as in the examples that follow.

Model: *Topic Sentence in the Middle*

Japan is a collection of large islands, strung along the eastern shore of the mainland of Asia. The islands are very rugged and very mountainous. High over all the other peaks rises the one supreme peak—the perfect cone of snowclad Fuji. Like most of the high mountains of Japan, Fuji is a volcano, sleeping, but far from dead. Compared to the Alps and the Himalayas, Fuji is not especially high. It seems high, however, because it rises in one superb sweeping curve right from the shore to the sky, a curve that can be seen for a hundred miles on every side.

RICHARD HALLIBURTON, *Complete Book of Marvels*

Model: *Implied Main Idea*

When the newborn seal pup slips from the warmth of his mother's body onto the ice, crystals form on his wet little body and his skin temperature falls to 70°F. He shivers so vigorously that in about 45 minutes he has produced enough heat to bring his skin temperature to 93.4°F. Only a light coat of baby fur, the lanugo, protects him from the zero temperatures of the Antarctic spring. His metabolism, however, is exceedingly high during his early life, and he can take in great quantities of milk. Seal mothers' milk is richer than heavy cream; it is half butterfat. On this creamy diet the pup gains about 250 pounds in six weeks and has a good coating of fat.   LUCY KAVALER

Life Battles Cold (Adapted)

Implied main idea: Seal pups have natural mechanisms to help them survive frigid temperatures.

WRITING ACTIVITY *Identifying the Main Idea*

Find and write the topic sentence of each paragraph. If the main idea is implied, write a sentence expressing that idea.

1. Forest Rangers

Park rangers' work includes planning and carrying out conservation efforts to protect plant and animal life in the parks from fire, disease, and heavy visitor traffic. Rangers plan and conduct programs of public safety, including law enforcement and rescue work. They set up and direct interpretive programs such as slide shows, guided tours, displays, and occasionally even dramatic presentations. These programs are designed to help visitors become aware of the natural and historic significance of the areas they visit.   WALTER OLEKSY

Careers in the Animal Kingdom

2. Starry Neighbors

Easter Island is the loneliest inhabited place in the world. The nearest solid land the islanders can see is above in the firmament, the moon and the planets. They have to travel farther than any other people to see that there really is land closer. Therefore, living nearest the stars, they know more names of stars than of towns and countries in our own world.

THOR HEYERDAHL, *Aku-Aku*

Critical Thinking

Writing Is Thinking

Generalizing

Generalizing is the process of developing a general principle based on specific facts or experiences. Many topic sentences are generalizations that are supported by ideas, facts, examples, and details in the body of the paragraph. To be valid, however, generalizations must avoid exaggeration. Therefore, when you write generalizations, avoid using words like *all, always,* or *never.*

All teenagers like loud music. [broad generalization]

This generalization is not valid because no amount of facts could ever prove that *all* teenagers like loud music. The generalization should be rewritten by replacing *all* with *some, many, most,* or *few.*

Some teenagers like loud music. [valid generalization]

To evaluate and revise generalizations, make a chart like the one written below, which is based on *All students litter the school campus.*

Generalization Chart	
SUPPORTING FACTS	**NONSUPPORTING FACTS**
1. The campus has accumulated litter. **2.** You saw some students throwing empty bottles on the lawn. **3.** You noticed that some cans were knocked over.	**1.** The wind blows some papers onto the campus. **2.** Many students, however, throw trash away in trash receptacles. **3.** Some animals knock over trash cans.
Revised: Some students litter the school campus.	

Thinking Practice   Test one of the following topic sentences or your own generalization by making a chart like the one above.

1. Students turn to cheating because of a variety of pressures.
2. All teenagers are influenced by what they see on televison.

Features of a Good Paragraph

Not every paragraph with a topic sentence, supporting sentences, and a concluding sentence is an effective paragraph. What the sentences actually say and how they say it are as important as the way in which they are put together. Important features of a good paragraph are (1) adequate development, (2) unity, and (3) coherence.

Adequate Development   The supporting sentences in a paragraph have the job of developing the main idea with specific details. These details explain, illustrate, describe, or argue for the main idea. They may take one or more of the forms listed below, depending upon what kind of idea is being developed.

Types of Supporting Details		
facts	reasons	descriptive details
examples	events	comparisons and contrasts

Whatever their form, supporting details must be numerous enough and specific enough to do their job—that is, to develop the main idea. If the main idea is not strongly supported, the reader may not understand it or believe it.

Compare the following two paragraphs. Both open with the same topic sentence. In the first paragraph, however, the main idea is weakened because the supporting details are so sparse and general. On the other hand, in the second paragraph there are enough specific details to support the full weight of the main idea. In that paragraph the details take the form of facts and examples.

Sample: *Inadequately Developed*

Around the turn of the last century, child-labor practices led to a grueling life for many American children. Many children worked instead of going to school. They had hard jobs and worked long hours for little pay. Since their families often needed the money, these children had little choice but to work hard. Eventually, though, earlier in this century some laws were passed that put an end to some of these practices. Yet, it was not until the 1930's that a law was passed about the hiring age for children.

97

Model: *Adequately Developed*

Around the turn of the last century child-labor practices led to a grueling life for many American children. In 1900, at least 1.7 million children under the age of sixteen worked for wages. Children working at night were kept awake by having cold water splashed in their faces. Some girls under sixteen worked sixteen hours a day in canning factories, capping forty cans per minute. Ten-year-old boys crouched over dusty coal chutes for ten hours a day to pick slate out of the coal sliding past. In city tenements many children seven years and younger made artificial flowers at night to be sold the next day at street stands. Some states began passing laws protecting child laborers after 1905. Not until 1938 was a federal law passed that prevented employers in most industries from hiring children under the age of sixteen.

CLARENCE L. VER STEEG, *American Spirit* (Adapted)

Writing Tip   Use sufficient **specific details** to develop your main idea adequately.

WRITING ACTIVITY *Improving Development*

Using the facts in the following table, revise the paragraph below so that the main idea is adequately developed. Retain the first sentence and the last sentence, which is the topic sentence.

Cities Take Over

Between the years 1860 and 1910, the nation's population increased enormously. Many people came from Europe. The new population moved to both rural and urban areas, but more people moved to cities. The number of cities increased dramatically. Ever since the early 1900's, the United States has been a nation of cities.

Facts	1860	1910	Percent of Growth
overall population	31 million	92 million	200
rural population	25 million	50 million	100
urban population	6 million	42 million	600
number of cities	400	2200	450

number of immigrants from Europe (1865–1910): 19 million

Unity In a paragraph that has *unity*, all the sentences support and develop the main idea. A unified paragraph is easy to follow, for the reader is not distracted by ideas or details that stray from the primary thought.

Writing Tip Achieve **unity** in a paragraph by making sure that all the supporting sentences relate directly to the main idea.

In the following paragraph, the crossed-out sentences stray from the main idea. If you read the paragraph without those sentences, you will notice how much easier it is to follow.

Model: *Paragraph Unity*

Sammy Lee

Sammy Lee, a second-generation Korean American, has devoted his life to athletic excellence and physical fitness. In 1948, he won the Olympic medal for high diving. When he repeated his feat at the Olympics four years later, he became the first male diver to win two consecutive times. ~~Another Korean American, Richard You, was an Olympic weight-lifting coach.~~ Lee also won the James E. Sullivan award for outstanding sports achievement in 1958. He now practices medicine and has served on the President's Council on Physical Fitness. ~~Richard You is also a doctor at present.~~

At first the crossed-out sentences may seem related—such as the sentence "Like Lee, You is a Korean doctor and a famed athlete." The topic sentence, however, limits the main idea of the paragraph to Sammy Lee. When you write and revise, ask yourself whether each sentence in a paragraph really is related to the main idea.

WRITING ACTIVITY *Revising for Unity*

Each of the following paragraphs contains sentences that stray from the main idea and weaken the paragraph's unity. Find and write the sentences in each paragraph that do not belong.

1. Science or Magic?

Although the alchemists of long ago are often regarded as superstitious magicians, they did help pave the way for some important discoveries. In their vain search for an elixir of life and a way to turn metals into gold, they discovered chemicals that are now common in such products as dye, varnish, medicine, glass, and steel. Alchemists also developed waterproofing, smelling salts, and some painkillers. Some alchemists, nonetheless, were undoubtedly frauds. One early alchemist developed a theory of gas, and others led the way to an understanding of blood circulation and enzymes and hormones. One famous alchemist, Merlin, may have existed only in legend. Although their work was limited by a lack of scientific knowledge, many alchemists were serious scientists whose discoveries opened new doors.

2. Director of Volunteer Services

Because volunteers are so important in the smooth running of a hospital, the director of volunteer services is usually a well-paid professional. The requirements for this position often include a college education, normally in sociology, psychology, or management. In fact, many of the jobs available in a hospital require advanced training of some kind. The salary of the director of volunteers varies according to the person's previous experience and the size and resources of the hospital. Most doctors, of course, earn more money than the volunteer director. Still the job is so important that most directors do earn a good wage.

Coherence   The details in a paragraph must relate not only to the main idea but also to one another. A *coherent* paragraph is one in which the ideas are smoothly and logically related. The keys to a coherent paragraph are (1) logical organization and (2) appropriate connecting devices.

Writing Tip   Achieve **coherence** in a paragraph by ordering the ideas logically and using suitable connectives.

The following chart shows the most common ways to organize paragraphs and longer pieces of writing as well.

Ways to Organize Ideas	
CHRONOLOGICAL ORDER	Arrange details in the order in which they occurred (time order).
SPATIAL ORDER	Arrange details according to their location—near to far, top to bottom.
ORDER OF IMPORTANCE	Arrange details from most to least or from least to most important.
DEVELOPMENTAL ORDER	Arrange details in a logical progression, in which one idea grows out of another.
COMPARISON/CONTRAST	Arrange details to show how two items are similar or different. Describe one item and then the other or compare and contrast feature by feature.

A writer can use various devices, as shown below, to help the reader understand how the ideas in a paragraph are related.

Ways to Connect Ideas

1. Repeat key words occasionally to link ideas.
   Ten years ago the tree was a sapling, barely able to stand alone. **Ten years ago** I was a child, leaning on my parents.

2. Use synonyms to connect back to key words.
   My **parents** guided me through that long period of growth. **Mother and father** sustained me with their love.

3. Use pronouns to relate back to key nouns.
   My **father** believed in being strict with his only **child,** and **his** training served **me** well in later years.

4. Use *transitions*—words and phrases that show how ideas are related to one another.
   Finally I felt ready to set out on my own.
   The tree, **furthermore,** had grown tall and sturdy.

The following box lists some common transitions and the types of order with which they are most often used. Most transitions may actually be used with more than one kind of organization.

Common Transitions	
CHRONOLOGICAL ORDER	first, second, then, by evening, in the beginning, soon, immediately, finally
SPATIAL ORDER	above, below, right, next to, beyond, inside, behind
ORDER OF IMPORTANCE	first, second, more, most important, the largest, above all, furthermore, also, another
DEVELOPMENTAL ORDER	furthermore, besides, however, despite, another, as a result, therefore
COMPARISON/CONTRAST	similarly, like, just, as, but, on the other hand, in contrast to, however

WRITING ACTIVITY **4** *Recognizing Paragraph Organization*

Write *chronological, spatial, order of importance, developmental,* or *comparison/contrast* to describe the organization of each paragraph.

I. Zookeepers Then and Now

The job of animal keeper in a zoo once required no advanced education. The primary responsibilities of the keeper were to feed the animals and keep their cages clean, and working with wild animals was not considered a particularly desirable activity. Recently, however, more and more zoos have begun to hire college graduates to fill the role of keeper. In contrast to earlier times, the job of animal keeper has expanded to include more challenging activities, such as presenting educational programs to the public and studying the animals' habitats. Furthermore, unlike years ago, zoos are deluged with applications from college graduates interested in working with animals. The educated and concerned zookeeper of today is quite different from the simple caretaker of the past.

2. Tail Snaring

"Catch and release" has become a popular slogan for those who fish for sport rather than for food. As a result the search is on for ways to land fish without harming them. One such device is the tail snare, which catches fish by lassoing their tails. Besides being useful to people who fish, tail snares help conservationists in tagging fish. Furthermore, they can prevent damage to the meat of big game fish. In short, tail snares hold advantages for people who enjoy fishing.

3. The Distant Past

Throughout most of the Mesozoic era, sometimes called the Age of Reptiles, primitive mammals scurried about, lost in the shadows of the mighty dinosaurs who lumbered through the gloomy swamps and giant softwood forests. In the beginning of the Cretaceous, the period which marks the last chapter in the reign of the giant reptiles, the earth cooled. Inland seas receded, marshes dried up, and the monster dinosaurs clambered out onto the trembling uplands and began to live on open ground. Great hardwood forests of oak, walnut, beech, and laurel bloomed and soon covered the land. Life for the small, ancestral mammals was perilous, and while the terrible dinosaurs ruled, the little animals hurried about in the deep green shade of the forests or took refuge in the branches of bushes and trees, often venturing forth only at night. They waited, unaware of the kingdom they were soon to inherit, and used their wits and mammalian advantages to survive.   JUDITH GROSCH, *You and Your Brain*

Gary Larson, The Far Side

The picture's pretty bleak, gentlemen. . . . The world's climates are changing, the mammals are taking over, and we all have a brain about the size of a walnut.

103

4. A Man of Many Talents

Benjamin Franklin accomplished many things in his eighty-four years. He was a recognized inventor. Franklin gave to the world the stove, bifocals, and the lightning rod. He invented a draft for fireplaces and a combination chair and stepladder for the kitchen. He was also a city planner. Franklin reorganized the British Post Office, established a city police system in Philadelphia, and an efficient fire-control organization. He was instrumental in providing his city with a public hospital and a subscription library. Furthermore, Franklin was a military strategist. He organized a successful defense of his colony when it was threatened by attack by the French. He led a force of men into the wilderness near Bethlehem and supervised the building of three important forts in that area. Finally Franklin was an active statesman. He was a member of the committee which drew up the Declaration of Independence, a delegate to the Constitutional Convention, and a very popular and valuable ambassador to England and France for over twenty-five years.   P. JOSEPH CANAVAN

5. Whose Desk Is It?

There was no name on the office door, but I recognized the desk immediately. Its surface was hidden beneath tall, precarious mounds of paper. Just visible behind a pile of folders stood a framed photo of my parents and me, smiling out over the rubble. On the wall above hung a painting I had done in second grade. "For Dad!" it proclaimed in shaky but bold green letters. Undoubtedly this was my father's desk.

WRITING ACTIVITY *Recognizing Transitions*

Find and write the transitional words and phrases used in each of the paragraphs in Writing Activity 4.

WRITING ACTIVITY *Writing on Your Own*

WRITING
ABOUT THE
THEME

Find an interesting paragraph about a school tradition like graduation in a magazine or newspaper. Then analyze the paragraph in a paragraph of your own. What are its parts? How are the details ordered? What gives it unity and coherence? Revise and edit your paragraph, following the steps on pages 34 and 38.

The Process of Writing Paragraphs

You use different types of writing for a variety of purposes, particularly in longer compositions. Most paragraphs serve one of four main
functions: (1) to tell a story, (2) to describe, (3) to explain, or (4) to
persuade. Therefore, paragraphs can be classified into one of four basic
types: (1) narrative, (2) descriptive, (3) expository, or (4) persuasive.
Although each of these four types of writing calls for special techniques, the main stages in the writing process remain the same. These
stages, which you worked through in detail in Chapter 1, are summarized below.

The Process of Writing Paragraphs

PREWRITING
  1. Tap your interests, knowledge, and experience for ideas.
  2. Make a list of subjects.
  3. Determine the purpose and audience of your paragraph.
  4. Choose a subject and limit it.
  5. Brainstorm a list of supporting details.
  6. Arrange your details in a logical order.

DRAFTING
  7. Write a topic sentence that states the main idea.
  8. Use your prewriting notes to write supporting sentences.
  9. Add a concluding sentence.

REVISING
  10. Check your paragraph structure. Is your topic sentence strong?
      Are your supporting sentences appropriate and adequate?
      Is your concluding sentence strong?
  11. Check your paragraph for unity and for coherence.
  12. Check your sentences. Are they varied? Have you combined
      sentences that go together? Are they concise? Have you
      avoided faulty parallelism and overuse of the passive?
  13. Check your words. Did you use specific words with appro-
      priate connotations? Did you use figurative language?

EDITING AND PUBLISHING
  14. Use the Editing Checklist on page 38 to check your gram-
      mar, usage, spelling, and mechanics.
  15. Find an appropriate way to publish your paragraph.

Writing Narrative Paragraphs

When you want to tell a story or relate an incident, you are writing *narration*. Narration is used in short stories, news stories, novels, histories, biographies, and letters.

Writing Term   A **narrative paragraph** tells a real or imaginary story with a clear beginning, middle, and end.

Most narratives involve a *conflict,* or problem, at their core. In the following narrative paragraph, the conflict is between a polar bear and the crew of a coast-guard vessel. As you read the paragraph, be aware of its main elements and transitional words and phrases.

Model: *Narrative Paragraph*

A Curious Clown

TOPIC SENTENCE: MAKES A GENERAL STATEMENT

The polar bear has an insatiable curiosity, and sometimes he can be quite a clown. **In 1969,** a coast-guard vessel in the Canadian Arctic received a visit from an adult male polar bear traveling atop a drifting ice-floe. The animal was obviously bent on a shopping expedition, and the crew obliged

SUPPORTING SENTENCES: TELL STORY EVENT BY EVENT

by throwing it a carton full of black molasses which the bear **soon** spread all over itself and the ice. This was **followed by** some jam, salt pork, two salami sausages, an apple which it spat out in disgust, and a jar of peanut butter which disappeared in about two seconds flat. It refused to touch bread or potatoes but loved chocolate bars. **Eventually** the food supply ran out, but the 363 kg (800 lb.) bear, its appetite now thoroughly whetted, decided to investigate further. It stuck its head through one of the port-holes in search of further nourishment. **When** nothing turned up, it decided to climb aboard, much to the alarm of the crew, who decided to open up the hoses on it. This was a big mistake, however, because the bear absolutely loved the drenching and raised its paws in the air to get the

CONCLUDING SENTENCE: GIVES THE OUTCOME

jet of water under its armpits. **In the end** the coastguards were forced to fire a distress rocket rather close to the interloper **before** it reluctantly moved away.

GERALD L. WOOD
Animal Facts and Feats

The writer of the preceding paragraph used the following guidelines. Apply them to your own narrative paragraphs.

Guidelines for Writing a Narrative Paragraph

1. Write a topic sentence that captures attention, sets the scene, or makes a general statement about the events.
2. Write supporting sentences that relate the events of the story.
3. Organize the supporting sentences in chronological order and use transitions that show when the events occurred.
4. Write a concluding sentence that resolves the conflict or makes a general statement about the meaning of the story.

Point of View   The person who tells the story is called the *narrator.* Who the narrator is determines the *point of view* of the story. With a first person point of view, the narrator is involved and uses first person pronouns. With a third person point of view, the narrator tells what happens to others, using third person pronouns. When you write a narrative, choose a point of view and use it consistently.

FIRST PERSON   In **my** disappointment, **I** wanted only to sleep, but **my** mind kept wandering back to the rally.

RALPH ELLISON, *Invisible Man*

THIRD PERSON   In **his** disappointment, **he** wanted only to sleep, but **his** mind kept wandering back to the rally.

Writing Tip   Use **first person point of view** if you are a character in the story. Use **third person point of view** if you relate what happens to others.

WRITING ACTIVITY *Writing a First Person Narrative*

Prewriting   As a senior you will soon be closing many chapters in your life. "Last times" are not new to you, however. Over the years you have said good-bye to friends, to places, to activities, and even to some hopes and dreams. Think back to moments when you experienced something or saw someone for the last time.

- Use freewriting, brainstorming, and/or clustering to recall as many "last times" as you can.
- Choose the experience that would make the best narrative paragraph.
- Relive the experience in your mind. How did the "last time" start? If there was a conflict, what was it? What was the outcome?
- Develop a list of details and events by brainstorming answers to the questions *Who? What? Where? Why? When?* and *How?*
- Arrange the events in chronological order.
- With the agreement of your teacher, tell your story to a small group or to a partner without using notes. Pay careful attention to your listeners' reactions and incorporate suggestions that seem sound.

Drafting   Making use of your oral story and the listeners' comments, draft your paragraph. Follow the guidelines on page 103.

Revising   Review your draft carefully. Then use the revising guidelines on page 103 to revise your paragraph.

Editing and Publishing   Refer to the checklist on page 38 to edit your draft. Then copy it neatly to share with your classmates.

WRITING ACTIVITY *Writing a Third Person Narrative*

Often an embarrassing moment becomes a humorous story. Write a third person narrative based on such an incident. Follow the steps on page 105 and the guidelines on page 107.

WRITING ACTIVITY *Writing on Your Own*

WRITING ABOUT THE THEME   A school tradition like a graduation ceremony is a special time. Write a narrative paragraph telling about a special moment during a senior's graduation. If you need ideas, refer to your journal. Then follow the steps on page 105 and the guidelines on page 107.

Writing Descriptive Paragraphs

Descriptive writing uses sensory details to bring a subject to life. It re-creates for the reader the sights, sounds, and other sensory impressions of people, places, and objects.

Writing Term  A **descriptive paragraph** paints a vivid picture of a person, scene, or object by appealing to the reader's senses.

When you write a description, you cannot record everything around you. Instead, you need to focus on the aspects of your subject that convey one strong overall impression. In describing a city street, for example, you might choose features that convey an exciting hustle and bustle, or you might focus on different features to convey a tense, chaotic scene. Once you have your focus, state the overall impression in a topic sentence, as in the following examples.

> The aged tree brooded over the pond like a father over an ill child. [overall impression: concern, gloom]

> From his twinkling green eyes to his ever-present smile, he was a picture of good cheer. [overall impression: cheerfulness]

Then, in your supporting sentences, you should supply specific and sensory details that bear out the overall impression. For example, the man described above might have a lilting voice, a roaring laugh, and high, round eyebrows. Rather than telling what the impression is, *show* your reader through sensory details, specific words, and figurative language. *(See pages 55–61.)*

Writing Tip Use **sensory details, specific words,** and **figurative language** to paint a vivid picture.

Spatial order is the most common method of organizing descriptive details. You may, for example, present the details from top to bottom, right to left, outside to inside, or near to far. Alternatively, you may record the details in the order in which they strike you. Such ordering is especially useful for descriptions that involve several senses. Then use appropriate transitions to help the reader piece the details together.

Notice the abundance of specific, sensory details in the example on the following page. The transitions appear in heavy type.

Model: *Details Ordered as Observed by the Writer*

The memories of Beach Haven run all to smells and sounds and sights; they are physical, of the blood and appetite, as is natural to summertime. **At the west end** of Coral Street the marshes began, turning soft with color at sunset, pink and lilac and golden green. The ocean beach at low tide lay hard **underfoot,** wet sand dark **below the waterline. On the dunes—** we called them sandhills—we played King of the Castle or slid down on our bloomer seats, yelling with triumph and pure joy. The floors of Curlew Cottage, the chairs, even the beds were sandy. Always a lone sneaker sat **beneath the hall sofa;** by August our city shoes were mildewed in the closets, and towels were forever damp. CATHERINE DRINKER BOWEN

"Beach Haven"

Guidelines for Writing a Descriptive Paragraph

1. Suggest an overall impression in the topic sentence.
2. Write supporting sentences that include specific and sensory details that communicate the overall impression.
3. Organize the supporting details in spatial order, adding transitions to guide the reader through the description.
4. Write a concluding sentence that reinforces the overall impression conveyed in the paragraph.

© Joel Meyerowitz

WRITING ACTIVITY *Describing a Scene*

Prewriting   Ordinary settings can take on extraordinary qualities when conditions change. A normally crowded playground or theater can turn tranquil or eerie, inspiring or haunting, when it is deserted. Prepare to describe a place under unusual conditions—a beach in the rain, a rural area teeming with people, a house before or after you move in, a street decked out for a festival, or your high school during summer vacation.

- Begin by listing places familiar to you—classrooms, outdoor sites, homes, rooms, stores. For each one, jot down an unusual condition—one you have seen or imagined.
- Choose a scene that is particularly vivid to you, one that conveys a strong overall impression.
- Brainstorm or use a cluster to compile sensory details about the scene that also support the overall impression.
- Decide which type of spatial order suits your details best.

Drafting   Use the guidelines on page 105 and your notes to write a draft of your paragraph. Picture the scene as you write.

Revising   If your teacher agrees, share papers and reactions with a classmate. Then use your partner's comments and the guidelines on page 105 to revise your draft. Be sure to save your work in your writing folder for later use.

WRITING ACTIVITY *Describing a Person*

Put a person in the scene you described in Writing Activity 10. Give the person a personality and a reason for being there and write a descriptive paragraph that conveys a strong overall impression. Use the guidelines on page 110 and the chart on page 105. Revise your work and save it for later use.

WRITING ACTIVITY *Writing on Your Own*

WRITING
ABOUT THE
THEME   A traditional place to hold a graduation ceremony is the school auditorium. Write a paragraph that describes the school auditorium—or some other place where graduation could be held—an hour after graduation is over. Follow the steps on page 105 and the guidelines on page 110.

111

Editing and Publishing

In the story "Dead Men's Path," Chinua Achebe lets you see the schoolmaster through the eyes of his wife.

> He was <u>stoop-shouldered</u> and looked <u>frail.</u> But he sometimes surprised people with <u>sudden</u> bursts of <u>physical</u> energy.

The underlined words in the description are adjectives, words that describe nouns and pronouns. Without the adjectives you would have no mental picture at all of the schoolmaster.

Regular Comparison of Adjectives   All one-syllable adjectives and most two-syllable adjectives add *-er* to form the comparative degree. All adjectives with three or more syllables, use *more.*

ONE OR TWO SYLLABLES	Mr. Obi was **younger** than the previous headmaster of Ndume Central School.
THREE OR MORE SYLLABLES	Mrs. Obi was **more enthusiastic** about the appointment than her husband was.

When you use adjectives to compare three or more people or things, you use the superlative degree. To form the superlative degree, you add *-est* to all adjectives with one syllable and to most adjectives with two syllables. Adjectives with three or more syllables use *most.*

ONE OR TWO SYLLABLES	Mr. Obi was the **youngest** headmaster to be appointed at Ndume Central School.
THREE OR MORE SYLLABLES	Mrs. Obi was the **most enthusiastic** wife of all of the headmasters.

Irregular Comparison of Adjectives   The following adjectives change form completely when used to make comparisons. *(For additional information and practice on the comparisons of adjectives and problems with modifiers, see pages 715–727.)*

ADJECTIVE	bad	good	little	many
COMPARING TWO	worse	better	less	more
COMPARING THREE OR MORE	worst	best	least	most

Capitalization of Proper Adjectives Proper adjectives, formed from proper nouns, begin with a capital letter. For example, *Columbian* coffee is more specific than simply *coffee*. *(For examples of proper adjectives and for practice in writing them correctly, see pages 760–761.)*

Punctuation of Adjectives When a conjunction does not connect two adjectives before a noun, a comma is sometimes used. To decide if you should use a comma, read the sentence with *and* between the adjectives. If the sentence sounds natural, a comma is needed. *(For information about the punctuation of adjectives and for practice in using punctuation correctly, see pages 773–774.)*

COMMA NEEDED   The next day the small**,** bushy hedges were torn up. [*Small* and *bushy* sounds natural.]

COMMA NOT NEEDED   The next day the small green hedges were torn up. [*Small* and *green* does not sound natural.]

Editing Checklist

I. Have you used the correct form when writing the regular and irregular comparison of adjectives? *(See pages 715–716.)*

2. Are proper adjectives capitalized? *(See pages 760–761.)*

3. Have you correctly punctuated adjectives? *(See page 773.)*

WRITING ACTIVITY *Editing Descriptive Paragraphs*

Using the checklist above and the Editing Checklist on page 38, edit the paragraphs from Writing Activities 10 and 11. Then make final copies of both paragraphs.

WRITING ACTIVITY *Writing on Your Own*

WRITING ABOUT THE THEME   **Editing** Edit your paragraph about an empty graduation hall from Writing Activity 12. Refer to the Editing Checklist above and the one on page 38.

Publishing After you have written a final copy, read it to a recent graduate and ask that person if your description is accurate.

Writing Expository Paragraphs

Expository, or explanatory, writing is the most common and practical of the four types of writing. Expository writing usually involves the classification of information. Whenever the purpose of your writing is to explain, you will be writing exposition.

Writing Term   An **expository paragraph** explains or informs.

Methods of Development   In an expository paragraph, you can explain a subject in a variety of different ways. Often the main idea expressed in your topic sentence will suggest the most suitable way to explain the subject.

Methods of Developing Exposition	
facts and examples	comparison and contrast
steps in a process	analogy
set of directions	analysis of parts
incident	cause and effect
definition	grouping into types

Classifying Supporting Details   In order to select the best method for developing your subject, *classify* or group your details into categories. Notice how the ideas expressed in the following topic sentences lead to the most appropriate way to classify supporting details.

1. MAIN IDEA   Many areas of the country have their own colorful traditions for celebrating the Fourth of July.

DETAILS   **Classify** information according to facts about Fourth of July traditions and examples of cities or areas that follow such traditions.

METHOD OF DEVELOPMENT   Facts and examples

2. MAIN IDEA   The process by which the Declaration of Independence was prepared and approved demonstrated democracy in action.

DETAILS   **Classify** information according to the steps followed in the preparation and approval of the Declaration of Independence.

METHOD OF DEVELOPMENT   Steps in a process

3. MAIN IDEA   After the flag is lowered, it must be folded properly.

DETAILS   **Classify** information about folding the flag in a set of directions.

METHOD OF DEVELOPMENT   Set of directions

4. MAIN IDEA   I did not realize the depth of my patriotism until I visited a foreign country for the first time.

DETAILS   **Classify** information about what patriotism means to you in relation to your first visit to a foreign country.

METHOD OF DEVELOPMENT   Incident

5. MAIN IDEA   Patriotism involves both emotions and actions.

DETAILS   **Classify** information according to the characteristics of patriotism.

METHOD OF DEVELOPMENT   Definition

6. MAIN IDEA   The British government of today, while deeply rooted in tradition, differs significantly from the British government of colonial times.

DETAILS   **Classify** information according to similarities and differences.

METHOD OF DEVELOPMENT   Comparison and contrast

7. MAIN IDEA   Britain treated its colonies as a parent treats a child.

DETAILS   **Classify** information according to similar characteristics.

METHOD OF DEVELOPMENT   Analogy

8. MAIN IDEA   The Constitution of the United States created a government with three distinct branches.

DETAILS   **Classify** information according to the three distinct branches.

METHOD OF DEVELOPMENT   Analysis of parts

9. MAIN IDEA   A long series of grievances against the British Crown led to the final break and the creation of a new nation.

DETAILS   **Classify** information into cause (grievances) and effect (creation of new nation).

METHOD OF DEVELOPMENT   Cause and effect

10. MAIN IDEA   The grievances against the British Crown can be classified as economic, political, and idealistic concerns.

DETAILS   **Classify** grievances according to three concerns.

METHOD OF DEVELOPMENT   Grouping into types

Two techniques you can use to classify information are charting and outlining. The following model shows how one student used the technique of charting to classify information from example 8 on page 115. *(For more information about outlining, see pages 148–152.)*

Student Model: *Charting to Classify Details*

> **MAIN IDEA:** The Constitution of the United States created a government with three distinct branches.

BRANCHES	**Legislative**	**Executive**	**Judicial**
MEMBERS	Congress	President and the Cabinet Members	Supreme Court and other Federal Courts
FUNCTIONS	Makes laws	Approves or disapproves of laws	Decides whether laws are constitutional
	Approves or disapproves of Presidential appointments	Appoints Supreme Court Justices	The President appoints Supreme Court Justices

Notice how the student writer developed the following expository paragraph based on the preceding chart.

Student Model: *Expository Paragraphs (Analysis of parts)*

Three Branches of Government

TOPIC SENTENCE: STATES MAIN IDEA

   The Constitution of the United States created a national government with three distinct branches. They are the legislative branch (Congress), the executive branch (the President/Cabinet), and the judicial branch (the federal court system). No one

SUPPORTING SENTENCES: EXPLAIN THE THREE BRANCHES OF GOVERNMENT

branch has absolute power; each one has its own duties and limitations. For example, the President is the one to appoint Supreme Court justices, but those appointees must be approved by Congress. When Congress, on the other hand, makes a law, the president has the right to veto it, and the Supreme Court may determine whether it is con-

CONCLUDING SENTENCE: ADDS A STRONG ENDING

stitutional or not. This separation of powers prevents any one branch or person from becoming too powerful.

WRITING ACTIVITY *Analyzing Expository Paragraphs*

Identify the method of development used in each of the following paragraphs. Refer to page 114 for a list of the methods.

1. Police Officer with the K-9 Unit

Dogs and the officers who handle them are carefully trained from the start. Dogs are obtained from the public, preferably between the ages of 6 months and 16 months. They are, in the first instance, kept at the Dog Training Establishment for a period varying from one week to three weeks in order to assess their health, physique, and working abilities. On completion of this period, if found satisfactory, they are given to a handler, who takes a five days' course of instruction. The dog is then taken to the home of the handler to begin a period of familiarization, which is very important, as it is essential to build trust and understanding between dog and handler before serious training is undertaken.

SCOTLAND YARD OF LONDON, "Metropolitan Police Dogs"
(Adapted)

2. Qualities of a Good Broadcaster

To help broadcasters decide which candidates to hire for a position in radio or television, the National Association of Broadcasters drew up a list of qualities to look for in job applicants. The most successful broadcasters have most, if not all, of these qualities. One important trait is enthusiasm. Another is a sense of public relations, since broadcasters must anticipate the needs and interests of viewers and listeners. Creativity is also a desired trait; developing entertaining programming amidst fierce competition requires a lively imagination. A balanced temperament and reliability are two other important qualities that go hand in hand. The pressures in the field of broadcasting can be very strong, and a person who can get the job done and work well with others is very valuable. While cooperation is important, so is initiative, since employees in responsible positions are expected to monitor their own work schedules and progress. Finally, a good broadcaster has a good business sense. Without the ability to manage budgets and handle other financial matters, a broadcaster is not likely to rise very high in the professional ranks.

Organization and Transitions   The way you order details in an expository paragraph is determined in large part by your method of explanation. If the supporting details are steps in a process or a set of directions, chronological order is usually the most appropriate. In some paragraphs of analysis, in which the parts of an object are explained in relation to the whole, spatial order may be the most useful. Most expository paragraphs, however, use order of importance or developmental order, with transitions clearly showing the relationship of ideas. Notice how the details are ordered in the following models. The transitions are shown in heavy type. *(See page 102 for a listing of common transitions.)*

Model: *Facts and examples—Order of importance*

The Tennessee Valley Authority (TVA), a federal agency set up in 1935, brought significant progress to the people of its region. **First,** before 1935, flood damage in the area averaged two million dollars a year. The TVA dams were successful in controlling floodwaters and putting them to good use. **Another** accomplishment was educating the region's farmers in methods of soil conservation. Through techniques **such as** contour plowing, strip-cropping, and tree planting, the region's soil was restored. **Probably the most important** benefit of the TVA, **however,** was the generating of electric power. Without electricity the once-depressed region could not have kept pace with the rest of the country. **Now** people from all over the world visit the region to learn how to improve river valleys in their own countries.

Model: *Definition—Developmental order*

Artificial Intelligence is the study of ideas that enable computers to be intelligent. Note that wanting to make computers *be* intelligent is not the same as wanting to make computers *simulate* intelligence. Artificial Intelligence seeks to uncover principles that all intelligent information processors use, not just those made of wet neural tissue (human brains) instead of dry electronics (computers). **Consequently** there is neither an obsession with mimicking human intelligence nor a prejudice against using methods that seem involved in human intelligence. **Instead,** there is a new point of view that brings along a new methodology and leads to new theories.   PATRICK HENRY WINSTON
Artificial Intelligence

Guidelines for Writing Expository Paragraphs

1. The topic sentence states a main idea, making clear your purpose.

2. To explain the main idea, the supporting sentences can use facts, examples, steps in a process, set of directions, incident, definition, comparison and contrast, analogy, analysis of parts, cause and effect, or grouping into types.

3. The paragraph may be organized according to order of importance, developmental order, chronological order, or spatial order, depending on the type of details. Use transitions to show how the details are related.

4. The concluding sentence summarizes the main idea, adds an insight, or evaluates the details in the paragraph.

WRITING ACTIVITY *Writing to Explain a Process*

Prewriting   Recent years have witnessed a surge of interest in physical fitness and health. Suppose you are working on a newsletter for and by students on fitness and health. It offers the reader explanations of processes, not how-to directions. Subjects range from the process of tooth decay and how exercise builds muscles to how the heart works. What health-related process could you write about? What process would you like to learn more about?

- Use brainstorming or clustering to think of subjects.
- Choose a process that will interest you and your audience. It can be one that you know or one that requires research.
- Do any need research? Then list the steps in the process in chronological order.
- Read the steps aloud to a partner. Do they make sense? Then listen carefully to your partner's steps and share comments.

Drafting   Use your notes and the guidelines on page 105 to write a paragraph that explains the process.

Revising   Review your paper carefully. Is each step in the process clear? Does each lead logically to the next? Are the steps in order? Revise your draft, using the guidelines on page 105.

Editing and Publishing   Refer to the checklist on page 38 to edit your draft. Then copy it neatly for inclusion in the newsletter.

WRITING ACTIVITY *Writing a Paragraph of Definition*

"Graduation is the intermission between school and real life." What are the various meanings of the word *graduation?* What does graduation mean to you? In a paragraph of definition, explore the meaning of *graduation* or a related word, such as *diploma* or *commencement.* Use the chart on page 105 and the guidelines on page 119.

WRITING ACTIVITY *Writing on Your Own*

WRITING
ABOUT THE
THEME

Write an expository paragraph that explains the value or importance of school traditions like graduation ceremonies. Use the steps on page 105 and the guidelines on page 119.

Writing Persuasive Paragraphs

When you write persuasion, you try to convince others that they should share your opinion or take a certain course of action. Advertisers use persuasion to sell products, and book reviewers use persuasion to defend their opinions. Whenever your purpose for writing is to state and support an opinion, you are writing persuasion.

Writing Term

A **persuasive paragraph** states an opinion and uses facts, examples, reasons, and the testimony of experts to convince readers.

In contrast to an expository paragraph, the topic sentence of a persuasive paragraph states an opinion, not a fact. Propositions that can be argued make good subjects for persuasive paragraphs; simple preferences do not. The test of an appropriate opinion for a persuasive topic sentence is the availability of reliable facts, examples, and expert judgments to back it up.

Order of importance is probably the most effective way to organize your arguments. Usually you will build from least to most important, although sometimes the reverse order is more effective. Then make sure you use transitions to show how the ideas are related.

The persuasiveness of your writing will depend in large part on how well you use the tools of persuasion summarized in the following chart.

Tools of Persuasion

1. Use logical arguments that are free of fallacies. *(See pages 206–208.)*
2. Use reliable facts, examples, and statistics that support instead of using more opinions.
3. Use the testimony of experts in the field.
4. Use polite and reasonable language. Avoid charged, emotional words.
5. Anticipate arguments on the other side of the issue. Concede the opposition's valid points but show why they do not change your position.

Conceding a Point   As you write, always keep in mind the fifth tool of persuasion. If you ignore opposing viewpoints, you will weaken your appeal. By admitting that your opponent has a good point, you help to establish your credibility and forestall objections. Of course, you must then go on to show why that good point is not convincing enough to tip the argument in your opponent's favor. Following are some transitions to use when conceding a point.

Transitions for Conceding a Point

while it is true that	nevertheless	however	despite
notwithstanding	granted that	although	

The following paragraph demonstrates the use of the tools of persuasion. The transitions are shown in heavy type.

Model: *Persuasive Paragraph*

The Fall of Rome

Historians have long been fascinated by the fall of the Roman Empire and the causes of that fall. **Although** at one time most historians blamed Rome's collapse on the invasion of barbarians, a more careful study shows that Rome contained the seeds of its own destruction. **For one thing,** the economy of Rome was in serious disorder. The historian Max Weber argues that the decline of

TOPIC
SENTENCE:
STATES AN
OPINION

121

SUPPORTING SENTENCES: FACTS, EXAMPLES, TESTIMONY OF EXPERTS

slavery and cities, coupled with the development of self-sufficient manors, left the city-based governments in poverty. **At the same time,** wealthy Romans indulged in lavish luxuries, widening the gap between the social classes. **Another** historian, Mikail Rostovtzeff, adds an intellectual crisis to the causes of Rome's collapse. He claims that the influx of conquered nationalities "barbarized" Rome, sapping it of its intellectual vigor. **Perhaps most important,** Rome's political structure was in disarray. Uncertainty over who held the ruling power, the people or the Senate nobles, led to rev-

CONCEDING A POINT

olutions and massacres. **Although** no single one of these forces would have been sufficient to topple the great empire, the combination of internal

CONCLUDING SENTENCE

weaknesses ultimately left it unable to defend itself against the barbarian invaders.

Guidelines for Writing a Persuasive Paragraph

1. The topic sentence states an opinion.
2. The supporting sentences use facts, examples, reasons, and the tools of persuasion to convince readers.
3. The ideas in the supporting sentences are usually organized in order of importance, from least to most important. Transitions show how the ideas are related.
4. The concluding sentence reinforces the main idea or summarizes your arguments.

WRITING ACTIVITY *Writing a Persuasive Paragraph*

Prewriting Seniors are being polled for their opinions on the recruitment of athletes by colleges. Should athletes be recruited? Should they be held to the same standards as other students?

- Explore your ideas by brainstorming or freewriting.
- Choose one opinion that you feel strongly about, one that you think you can defend.
- Gather whatever information you need to defend your opinion. You may want to speak to college students, coaches, and athletes. Listen carefully to opposing as well as supporting arguments.
- Arrange your arguments from least to most important. Discard any that are mere opinions.

Drafting Use your notes to write a first draft of your persuasive paragraph, beginning with a topic sentence that states your opinion.

Revising Read your draft. Are your arguments persuasive? Why or why not? Use your partner's comments and the relevant steps on page 105 to revise your draft.

Editing and Publishing Refer to the checklist on page 38 to edit your draft. Then copy your paragraph neatly. If your teacher permits, share your ideas with your class.

WRITING ACTIVITY *Writing an Advertisement*

A current trend in radio and TV advertising involves dealers "selling" their own products. Car dealers announce the virtues of their own dealerships, and furniture dealers declare their prices to be the best. Prepare to "sell" something of yours on TV. Write a paragraph that will persuade the audience to buy something you own or have made. If you add emotional appeals to your arguments, be sure the arguments are good ones. Use the charts on pages 121 and 122.

WRITING ACTIVITY *Writing on Your Own*

WRITING ABOUT THE THEME
Write a persuasive paragraph that argues for or against school traditions like graduation ceremonies. Follow the process outlined on pages 121 and 122.

A Writer Writes

WRITING
ABOUT THE
THEME

A Letter about a Family Tradition

PURPOSE: to inform, describe, narrate, and persuade
AUDIENCE: your children

Prewriting   Because traditions should be passed on to younger generations, write a letter to your children. (Since they will probably not be born for many years, keep your letter in a safe place for them.)

Prepare to write each of the following paragraphs—one after another in your letter. (1) The first paragraph, a narrative paragraph, should reenact a family tradition. For example, tell what happens—as if it were happening. (2) The second paragraph should describe where the tradition takes place and any objects used to perform the tradition.

Dear Amy

Your letter arrived yesterday and I was very glad to hear from you. I hope you can visit me when you come home again.

The courses you are taking sound interesting. Please tell me more about them. When does the semester end? Will you find time to tour the other provinces?

I am still effort to go for a walk morning. park

(3) The next paragraph should be expository, explaining the reasons why this tradition means so much to you. (4) The last paragraph should persuade your children to continue that tradition.

Use brainstorming or freewriting to think of and explore ideas for all of your paragraphs. Choose the most interesting and the most important ideas to include. Then, after developing a list of appropriate details for each one, arrange the details in a logical order.

Drafting   Write a topic sentence that captures the main idea of each of your paragraphs. Then write your letter, including your lists of details with each paragraph. Finally, add a concluding sentence to each one to sum up what you have said in that paragraph.

Revising   Before revising your letter, take it home and read it to a member of your family. Ask that person if each paragraph was clear, interesting, and helpful. Why or why not? Then review the letter yourself. Are there enough supporting details in each paragraph? Are the details covered by each main idea? Have you used connecting devices to lead your readers from one idea to another? Does each paragraph fulfill its purpose? Keeping in mind the comments of your family member, revise your letter.

Editing and Publishing   Use the Editing Checklists on pages 38 and 113 as guides to correcting any mistakes in usage and mechanics. As you write your final letter, follow the form of a friendly letter. Before putting your letter away for safekeeping for your children, read it to another member of your family—a younger brother or sister if possible. Afterward ask that family member if the tradition is more meaningful to him or her now that you have written about it.

Independent Writing

Write a narrative, descriptive, expository, or persuasive paragraph, following the steps on pages 107, 110, 119, or 122. To find a subject, look at the pictures in a magazine. For example, if you see a picture about baseball, you could write a narrative paragraph about a particular play your favorite team recently made. If you see an ad for a new car, you could describe the car of the future. However, if you see an article for protecting the environment, you could write a persuasive paragraph about how a person could participate in this effort on a local level. After you have revised and edited your paragraph, prepare a neat final copy. Then read your paragraph to your classmates and ask them to identify what type of paragraph it is.

Creative Writing

Myths are traditional stories that often answer questions about the phenomena of nature. They were written, especially in ancient times, to provide answers to questions such as *Why is the sky blue?* and *What makes the thunder roar?* For example, Greek mythology explains that a rainbow was made from the trail left by the multicolored gown of Iris, Hera's messenger, every time she raced between Earth and Mount Olympus. Imagine that you are an ancient Greek who is baffled by the wonders of nature. First write a list of questions about the universe. What causes rain? Why are there tornadoes? What mysteries lie beneath the ocean? After you decide on one question, write a myth that uses the actions of gods and goddesses to explain the answer. Keep in mind that you can use either the traditional Greek or Roman gods and goddesses, or you can make up a whole new set of your own.

 ## Writing about Literature

A *symbol* is any object, person, place, or event that represents an abstract idea or concept. For example, in the poem "Ozymandias" by Percy Bysshe Shelley the statue of the pharaoh symbolizes power, vanity, and the hope for immortality. What, do you think, does the path symbolize in the story "Dead Men's Path"? What, do you think, does the village priest mean by saying, "The whole life of this village depends on it"? Write a composition that explains the symbolism of the path. As you write, consider how the symbol of the path contributes to the meaning of the story.

Writing in Other Subject Areas

Astronomy   Write a descriptive paragraph, including many vivid details, about a celestial body or a phenomenon such as a planet, a comet, or a black hole. Remember to organize your details logically and to use clear connecting devices.

Government   What do you think are the limits to the freedom of speech guaranteed by the First Amendment to the Constitution? For example, should someone whose opinions are highly inflammatory or unpopular with the majority be permitted to speak to a school club or other school group? Take a stand and write a persuasive paragraph on this issue.

3

Checklist

Writing Different Kinds of Paragraphs

Narrative Paragraphs *(See pages 106–107.)*

✔ Write a topic sentence that sets the scene or gets the story moving.
✔ Develop supporting sentences that tell the story event by event.
✔ Order the events chronologically and use transitions.
✔ End with a concluding sentence that tells the outcome of the story or makes a point about its meaning.

Descriptive Paragraphs *(See pages 109–110.)*

✔ Develop a topic sentence that suggests an overall impression of the subject.
✔ Include specific sensory details in your supporting sentences.
✔ Use figurative language.
✔ Use spatial order and appropriate transitions.
✔ Write a concluding sentence that reinforces the overall impression.

Expository Paragraphs *(See pages 114–119.)*

✔ Write a topic sentence that states a factual main idea and makes your purpose clear.
✔ Select the method of development that is most appropriate for your subject. Make sure it follows naturally from your topic sentence.
✔ Use an appropriate method of organization, along with clear transitions.
✔ Check that your concluding sentence summarizes, adds insight, or evaluates the supporting details.

Persuasive Paragraphs *(See pages 120–123.)*

✔ Write a topic sentence that states an opinion.
✔ Develop supporting sentences that use the tools of persuasion.
✔ Use a logical order with appropriate transitions.
✔ Check that your concluding sentence either reinforces the main idea or summarizes the argument.

Unit 2
Achieving the Writer's Purpose

4 Writing Essays to Inform

Part 1 *Reading to Write*

THEME: *Opportunities*

Because an *opportunity* is "a favorable or advantageous combination of circumstances," people often use this word synonymously with *chance*. Are all opportunities, however, the result of luck, or do you think you have some control over the creation or the shaping of the opportunities that come your way?

Consider the teenager who wants a part-time job. After overhearing two people talking about a job, she introduces herself, asks for more information, and applies. If she gets the job, her friends probably will think she was lucky to have had the opportunity. However, she went out of her way to make the opportunity hers. Also consider the teenager who wants very much to learn to play the guitar. After earning money to buy a guitar, he persuades his uncle to teach him to play. Did he have an opportunity that his friends did not have? Yes, but he helped to create that opportunity.

In the following selection, "Shakespeare's Sister" by Virginia Woolf, you will read about the lack of opportunity accorded women in sixteenth-century England. As you read the selection, think about how much life and its opportunities have changed, especially in this past century.

Shakespeare's Sister

V i r g i n i a   W o o l f

*In 1928, Virginia Woolf addressed the women students of
Cambridge University, England. There she gave two lectures focusing
on the position of women in society. Later on, these lectures were
published as one work entitled* A Room of One's Own.

In the following excerpt from A Room of One's Own, *Virginia
Woolf narrowed her focus to the role of women in Elizabethan society.
Her search for information about the Elizabethan woman, however,
produced very little. She did, though, find that a contradiction existed
between the woman portrayed in the literature of that day and the
woman in real life. In developing her essay, she imagined what would
have happened if Shakespeare had had a sister who was as gifted as
he. Would his sister have had the same opportunities?*

Here am I asking why women did not write poetry in the
Elizabethan age, and I am not sure how they were educated; whether
they were taught to write; whether they had sitting-rooms to themselves; how many women had children before they were twenty-one;
what, in short, they did from eight in the morning till eight at night.
They had no money evidently; according to Professor Trevelyan they
were married whether they liked it or not before they were out of the
nursery, at fifteen or sixteen very likely. It would have been extremely
odd, even upon this showing, had one of them suddenly written the
plays of Shakespeare, I concluded, and I thought of that old gentleman, who is dead now, but was a bishop, I think, who declared that
it was impossible for any woman, past, present, or to come, to have
the genius of Shakespeare. He wrote to the papers about it. He also
told a lady who applied to him for information that cats do not as a
matter of fact go to heaven, though they have, he added, souls of a
sort. How much thinking those old gentlemen used to save one! How
the borders of ignorance shrank back at their approach! Cats do not
go to heaven. Women cannot write the plays of Shakespeare.

Be that as it may, I could not help thinking, as I looked at the works of Shakespeare on the shelf, that the bishop was right at least in this; it would have been impossible, completely and entirely, for any woman to have written the plays of Shakespeare in the age of Shakespeare. Let me imagine, since facts are so hard to come by, what would have happened had Shakespeare had a wonderfully gifted sister, called Judith, let us say. Shakespeare himself went, very probably—his mother was an heiress—to the grammar school, where he may have learnt Latin—Ovid, Virgil and Horace—and the elements of grammar and logic. He was, it is well known, a wild boy who poached rabbits, perhaps shot a deer, and had, rather sooner than he should have done, to marry a woman in the neighborhood, who bore him a child rather quicker than was right. That escapade sent him to seek his fortune in London. He had, it seemed, a taste for the theatre; he began by holding horses at the stage door. Very soon he got work in the theatre, became a successful actor, and lived at the hub of the universe, meeting everybody, knowing everybody, practicing his art on the boards, exercising his wits in the streets, and even getting access to the palace of the queen.

Meanwhile his extraordinarily gifted sister, let us suppose, remained at home. She was as adventurous, as imaginative, as agog to see the world as he was. But she was not sent to school. She had no chance of learning grammar and logic, let alone of reading Horace and Virgil. She picked up a book now and then, one of her brother's perhaps, and read a few pages. But then her parents came in and told her to mend the stockings or mind the stew and not moon about with books

and papers. They would have spoken sharply but kindly, for they were substantial people who knew the conditions of life for a woman and loved their daughter—indeed, more likely than not she was the apple of her father's eye. Perhaps she scribbled some pages up in an apple loft on the sly, but was careful to hide them or set fire to them. Soon, however, before she was out of her teens, she was to be betrothed to the son of a neighboring wool-stapler. She cried out that marriage was hateful to her, and for that she was severely beaten by her father. Then he ceased to scold her. He begged her instead not to hurt him, not to shame him in this matter of her marriage. He would give her a chain of beads or a fine petticoat, he said; and there were tears in his eyes. How could she disobey him? How could she break his heart?

The force of her own gift alone drove her to it. She made up a small parcel of her belongings, let herself down by a rope one summer's night and took the road to London. She was not seventeen. The birds that sang in the hedge were not more musical than she was. She had the quickest fancy, a gift like her brother's, for the tune of words. Like him, she had a taste for the theatre. She stood at the stage door; she wanted to act, she said. Men laughed in her face. The manager—a fat, loose-lipped man—guffawed. He bellowed something about poodles dancing and women acting—no woman, he said, could possibly be an actress. He hinted—you can imagine what. She could get no training in her craft. Could she even seek her dinner in a tavern or roam the streets at midnight?

Yet her genius was for fiction and lusted to feed abundantly upon the lives of men and women and the study of their ways. At last—

for she was very young, oddly like Shakespeare the poet in her face, with the same grey eyes and rounded brows—at last Nick Greene the actor-manager took pity on her; she found herself with child by that gentleman and so—who shall measure the heat and violence of the poet's heart when caught and tangled in a woman's body?—killed herself one winter's night and lies buried at some crossroads where the omnibuses[1] now stop outside the Elephant and Castle.[2]

That, more or less, is how the story would run, I think, if a woman in Shakespeare's day had had Shakespeare's genius. But for my part, I agree with the deceased bishop, if such he was—it is unthinkable that any woman in Shakespeare's day should have had Shakespeare's genius. For genius like Shakespeare's is not born among laboring, uneducated, servile people. It was not born in England among the Saxons and the Britons. It is not born today among the working classes. How, then, could it have been born among women whose work began, according to Professor Trevelyan, almost before they were out of the nursery, who were forced to it by their parents and held to it by all the power of law and custom? Yet genius of a sort must have existed among women as it must have existed among the working classes. Now and again an Emily Brontë or a Robert Burns blazes out and proves its presence. But certainly it never got itself on to paper.

When, however, one reads of a witch being ducked, of a woman possessed by devils, of a wise woman selling herbs, or even of a very remarkable man who had a mother, then I think we are on the track of a lost novelist, a suppressed poet, of some mute and inglorious Jane Austen, some Emily Brontë who dashed her brains out on the moor or mopped and mowed about the highways crazed with the torture that her gift had put her to. Indeed, I would venture to guess that Anon, who wrote so many poems without signing them, was often a woman. It was a woman Edward Fitzgerald, I think, suggested who made the ballads and the folksongs, crooning them to her children, beguiling her spinning with them, or the length of the winter's night. ◆

1. **omnibuses:** Buses.
2. **Elephant and Castle:** A British inn.

Responding to the Theme

Opportunities

Responding in Your Journal   This week in your journal, explore the theme of opportunities. Think about what opportunities you have had in your life. Have they all just presented themselves to you or do you think you have played a part in shaping or creating some of them? Also think about any missed opportunities. Analyze why you allowed an opportunity to pass by. Did you fail to recognize it until it was too late or was there some other reason?

Later in the week, write freely about various opportunities you have that teenagers did not have as recently as 50 years ago. Were there some opportunities that you have today that simply did not even exist back then? Consider areas such as education, home life, recreation, job possibilities, and health.

Speaking and Listening   Talking to a person who lived centuries ago could be a fascinating experience. Suppose, for instance, that you had the opportunity to talk to Shakespeare's fictitious sister, Judith. Write an imaginary dialogue between you and her, using the information in the selection as the basis for her words. When you have finished, ask a classmate to practice reading Judith's portion of the dialogue. Then, if time permits, your teacher may have you and the other student read your dialogue to a small group.

Critical Thinking: Applying   In the selection "Shakespeare's Sister," what do you think was Virginia Woolf's purpose for creating the character Judith Shakespeare? What was the author's message? How does her message *apply* to today's society? Express your thoughts in the form of a paragraph.

Extending Your Vocabulary   In the essay that you have just read, Virginia Woolf places her fictional character, Judith Shakespeare, in the historic time period called the *Elizabethan Age*. Using a dictionary, an anthology of English literature, or other reference materials, explore the origin of this term. When was the Elizabethan Age? What is the meaning of the term *Elizabethan*? Who were the prominent writers of this time period? Once you have gathered sufficient information about the Elizabethan Age, organize and write your findings in the form of a paragraph.

Virginia Woolf, (1882–1941)

Part 2 / *Writing*

When you write an *essay*—a composition of three or more paragraphs—you have the opportunity to explore and develop your ideas in depth. In the selection you have just read, for instance, Virginia Woolf uses the essay form to explore thoroughly an aspect of women's rights.

The expository essay is probably the most common type of essay. It can be used to explain factual subjects, such as how to land the space shuttle or what causes acid rain. It can also be used to explain ideas and insights, such as why people laugh or what freedom means. In all cases, the success of the essay depends on how clearly the writer explains and communicates.

Writing Term   An **expository essay** informs or explains.

As a writer of exposition, you will often use *narration* and *description* to assist you in your explanations. *(See pages 106–111.)* In addition, you will often be able to use *classification. (See pages 114–116).* Finally, you may be able to use the skill of *evaluating. (See Writing Is Thinking on page 202.)*

Essay Structure

Virtually all forms of communication can be divided into the same basic parts—a beginning, a middle, and an ending. Just as a phone call begins with a hello and ends with a good-bye, a complete piece of writing is framed by an introduction and a conclusion. As the following chart illustrates, the same basic structure applies to a single paragraph as well as an essay.

Paragraph Structure	Essay Structure
1. Topic sentence expressing the main idea of the paragraph	1. Introductory paragraph(s) including a thesis statement expressing the main idea of the essay
2. Body of supporting sentences	2. Body of supporting paragraph(s)
3. Concluding sentence	3. Concluding paragraph(s)

In the following essay, the three basic parts and the thesis statement are labeled at the left.

Model: *Expository Essay*

But Did They Floss?

INTRODUCTION
As anthropologists imagine it, early humans sat by the fire after a hard day at the hunt, chewing on roasted mammoth and picking their teeth with sticks cut to sharp points. At other times, they just picked their teeth idly, while contemplating what a daub of paint might do for drab cave walls. The

THESIS
STATEMENT
simple toothpick, recent discoveries reveal, may have been one of the first "tools" of human design.

BODY
Evidence of Stone-Age toothpicks is indirect but compelling, anthropologists say. Fossil teeth, the most durable relics of early life, seem to tell the tale. Analysis of grooves on ancient teeth has led to a consensus that these are the marks of heavy toothpick use by early humans. The journal *Nature*

137

has reported that the earliest known example of the grooved-teeth phenomena was found in 1.8-million-year-old fossils. The grooves were especially common in the teeth of Neanderthals and other archaic Homo sapiens of Europe and Asia between 130,000 and 35,000 years ago. Researchers considered whether the grooves could have been the result of tooth decay, dietary grit or stripping and processing fibers in making domestic goods. "None of these, however, really fits the evidence," *Nature* reported. The similarity of the prehistoric grooves to toothpick-caused abrasions in historical and modern populations of American Indians and Australian Aborigines argued for the toothpick interpretation of the data.

CONCLUSION   In a recent article in *Current Anthropology,* Christy G. Turner 2d, professor of anthropology at Arizona State University, concluded, "As far as can be empirically documented, the oldest human habit is picking one's teeth."

JOHN NOBLE WILFORD, *The New York Times*

The *introduction* of an essay does just what its name implies: it introduces the subject. Depending on the length of the essay, the introduction may be one or two paragraphs long. Included within the introduction is the *thesis,* a statement that expresses the main idea of the essay. While the thesis statement is frequently the last sentence in the introduction, as it is in the model, it may occur anywhere within the introduction.

In addition to containing the thesis statement, the introduction sets the tone of the essay. *Tone* is the writer's attitude toward his or her subject and audience. The tone may be straightforward, reflective, casual, bitter, comic, joyous, or any other human attitude. For example, the introduction of the essay "But Did They Floss?" sets the tone as comic.

Writing Term   The **thesis statement** states the main idea of the essay and makes clear the writer's purpose.

Writing Term   The **tone** of an essay is the writer's attitude toward his or her subject and audience.

138

The middle section, or *body,* of the essay contains the supporting paragraphs. Like the supporting sentences in a paragraph, the supporting paragraphs of an essay back up the main idea with specifics. These specifics may take the form of facts, examples, or any of a variety of other details. Usually each paragraph in the body of an essay develops one main supporting point. For example, the following are the supporting points in the model essay on pages 137–138.

SUPPORTING PARAGRAPH 1   the fossil evidence
SUPPORTING PARAGRAPH 2   interpreting the fossil evidence

Writing Term   The **supporting paragraphs** in the body of an essay develop the main idea with specific and numerous details.

If you do not provide a definite ending for your writing, you will leave your reader dangling. Your essay needs a *conclusion,* a paragraph that reinforces the main idea and ends the essay in a satisfying way.

Writing Term   The **conclusion** of an essay completes the essay and drives home the main idea.

WRITING ACTIVITY *Analyzing an Expository Essay*

Identify the tone and the three main parts of the following expository essay. Then write the thesis statement and the main point developed in each supporting paragraph.

The Fosbury Flop

In Mexico's Estadio Olimpico, a crowd of 80,000 gasped as high jumper Dick Fosbury flew over the bar at seven feet, four and a half inches to win a gold medal in the 1968 Olympics and set an Olympic record. It was not only the height that astounded them but also Fosbury's novel approach: head first and flat on his back.

Before jumping, Fosbury would stand at the start of the runway, sometimes for several minutes, meditating, worrying, visualizing himself clearing the bar. "I have to psych myself up," said the nervous jumper. "It's positive thinking, convincing myself that I'll make it." Then he would bolt down the runway, just left of center, plant his right (outside) foot firmly parallel to the bar and spring up, pivoting quickly so his back was to the bar, which

139

he glimpsed behind, then beneath him from the corner of one eye. With his back parallel to the ground and crosswise to the bar, his legs dangled on the starting side, till he jackknifed them up to clear the bar and land—appallingly enough—on his back or the nape of his neck. The usual pile of sawdust did not make for a welcoming base, so Fosbury finished his backward flight on three feet of foam.

Fosbury did not deliberately set about to revolutionize the world of high jumping, nor even to invent a sensational method for himself. The Fosbury Flop, as the jump is commonly called, evolved over time. "I didn't change my style," Fosbury told Roy Blount of *Sports Illustrated*. "It changed inside me." Fosbury started jumping in fifth grade and was still using the scissors method in high school to clear five-four. (This is a sideways jump in which the athlete kicks up the leg nearer the bar, crosses in a sitting position, and then brings the trailing leg up and over as the other leg comes down.) He tried the conventional straddle (crossing the bar on one's stomach, with one's body parallel to the bar), but it just didn't feel right, so he went back to the scissors. "As the bar's height increased," Fosbury recollects, "I started lying out more, and pretty soon I was flat on my back." He cleared five-ten at the time and the seed was planted for the Fosbury Flop.

Fosbury met with a lot of resistance from skeptical coaches along the way. It took a flying flop of about seven feet over a six-six bar to convince Fosbury's college coach Berny Wagner that the flop was more than a funny spectacle. "The physics of his jump are good," Wagner told *The New York Times*. "Dick exposes less of himself to the bar than any other high jumper."

Not only did Fosbury go on to glory with his backward, potentially hazardous leap, but the technique also became widely used among high jumpers. However, the innovator himself said in 1968, "Sometimes I see movies, and I really wonder how I do it."   CAROLINE SUTTON, *How Did They Do That?* (Adapted)

WRITING ACTIVITY *Studying an Essay*

Find an interesting short essay in a newspaper or magazine and write a paragraph that analyzes it. In your paragraph identify the parts of the essay: the introduction, the thesis statement, the main point of each supporting paragraph, and the conclusion.

Prewriting

Writing Process

As you know by now, you do not begin a composition by simply composing an opening sentence. Instead, careful thinking and planning need to take place before you ever write that first sentence. All of this thinking and planning come during the first stage in the writing process—the prewriting stage. You begin this stage with the search for an idea and end it with the shaping of that idea into an organized plan for a composition. Your initial step in writing an expository essay, therefore, is to discover possible subjects by using prewriting strategies.

Discovering Subjects

How can the seniors raise money to defray the cost of the senior class trip? What do birds do when it rains? What strategy do you use to get a good seat at a baseball game? Why was George Washington an effective President? How has popular music changed in the last five years? Possible subjects for an expository essay, such as these, are limited only by your own interests and knowledge. Once you begin to tap the vast store of information you carry around, your challenge will not be to find a subject to write about but to choose one from the great number available to you.

Countless ideas for subjects are inside your head right now. The task is to bring them to the surface by letting your mind relax or by asking yourself some probing questions. Start by using the strategies discussed in Chapter 1 on pages 12–16: taking stock of your interests, freewriting, and using your journal. You can also skim books and magazines and afterward ask yourself questions about what you saw or read. Another idea is to look over your textbooks and class notes for possible topics.

Drawing by C. Barsotti; © 1977
The New Yorker Magazine, Inc.

WRITING ACTIVITY *Discovering Ideas through Questions*

Answer each of the following questions as thoroughly as you can. Then put your answers in your writing folder for later use.

1. What subjects do I enjoy talking about at school? At home? With friends?
2. What faraway places have I had the opportunity to visit? What nearby places?
3. What sports, musical, dramatic, or other activities do I enjoy?
4. What kind of advice do my friends ask me for? What do they consider me knowledgeable about?
5. What subjects outside myself do I think about when I am alone? What kinds of problems have I solved?

WRITING ACTIVITY *Discovering Ideas through Other Sources*

Answer each question thoroughly. Then put your answers in your writing folder.

1. What topics in history class have I found interesting?
2. What have I been reading about in other classes that interests me?
3. What magazine articles or television shows have caught my attention recently?
4. What people has the media been covering lately?
5. What lessons have I had the opportunity to take outside of school?

Choosing and Limiting a Subject

The following guidelines will help you choose a subject from the many ideas you gather.

Guidelines for Choosing a Subject

1. Choose a subject that you would enjoy writing about.
2. Choose a subject that you know enough about to develop adequately in a short essay.
3. Choose a subject that your readers want to know about.

Your next step is to make sure that your subject is narrow enough to be covered adequately in a short essay. The following questions will help you limit your subject.

Questions for Limiting a Subject

1. What aspect of my subject do I want to explain?
2. How can I narrow it even further?
3. Who are my readers? What do they need to know to understand my subject?
4. What insight can I draw from my subject?
5. How might I express my main idea in one sentence?

Suppose you chose a subject you had read about in psychology class and had found fascinating: a boy who was discovered living in the wild in Aveyron, France, in the early 1800's. The answers to the five questions for limiting a subject might look like the following.

Answers to Questions

1. I want to explain what happened to the wild boy after he was discovered.
2. I can explain how the wild boy was educated.
3. Because my readers probably have not heard of the wild boy, they will need some background information.
4. Finding the wild boy gave scientists a chance to study how heredity and environment influence human development.
5. Work with the wild boy has led to new ideas in education and psychology.

WRITING ACTIVITY *Limiting a Subject*

Use the questions on page 143 to help you limit each subject below to one that is appropriate for a short expository essay.

1. summer	**3.** household chores	**5.** the American
2. baseball	**4.** earning money	Revolution

WRITING ACTIVITY *Writing on Your Own*

WRITING
ABOUT THE
THEME

Use the answers you wrote to Writing Activities 3 and 4 and your journal notes to list ten possible subjects for an expository essay about opportunities. You could write about opportunities you have had or ones you have lost. You also could write about any ideas you have about opportunities. Then choose a subject and limit it. Save your work for later use.

Gathering Information

Once you have limited your subject, you can begin to gather information that will help you explain it. Make use of the techniques discussed in Chapter 1: observing, brainstorming a list, clustering, and questioning. Choose whichever techniques seem to work best for your approach and subject. Use one or two or try them all. Go back and forth among them as different ideas occur to you. If you need more information, research your subject—use the reference materials in your library, magazines, newspapers, and other sources. Remember that your goal is to accumulate enough details to cover your subject most effectively. The specific types of details you select will usually indicate the method of development you should use. *(For more information about Methods of Development in expository writing, see pages 114–115.)* Your list may include any of the following types of details.

Types of Details Used in Expository Essays		
facts	steps in a process	similarities/differences
examples	incidents	analogies
reasons	definitions	causes/effects

The following notes are on the subject of the wild boy of Aveyron. They are not, however, arranged in any logical order.

Model: *List of Details*

LIMITED SUBJECT: education of the wild boy of Aveyron

- doctor's name was Jean-Marc-Gaspard Itard
- François Truffaut made a movie about the boy
- Itard named the boy Victor
- Victor was found in France in 1800, age twelve
- had 23 scars on him
- couldn't talk
- trotted instead of walked
- learned how to fetch water
- learned how to say *milk*
- had a nice smile
- expressed only joy and sorrow at first
- Itard made sure the boy's needs were met before educating him
- Tarzan and Mowgli are fictional wild children
- insensitive to heat and cold and some sounds
- responded only to sounds related to foods
- hard to imagine how boy survived by himself
- Itard played games with him to develop thinking powers; games Victor was most interested in involved food
- could reach into boiling water and not express pain
- work with Victor helped Itard develop ideas about how to teach deaf people and also mentally retarded people
- educator Maria Montessori was influenced by Itard's work

WRITING ACTIVITY *Listing Supporting Details*

Use observing, brainstorming, clustering, and/or questioning to develop at least five details for each of these subjects.

1. the importance of teamwork in school sports
2. reasons for getting a high school diploma
3. why endangered species are protected
4. the qualities of a good television show

WRITING ACTIVITY *Writing on Your Own*

WRITING
ABOUT THE
THEME
Using your limited subject from Writing Activity 6, observe, brainstorm, cluster, question, and/or do research to develop supporting details about opportunities. Save your list of details.

Writing Is Thinking

Developing Analogies

An effective device for explaining unfamiliar ideas or processes in an expository essay is an analogy. An *analogy* is an extended comparison that uses a familiar object to explain something abstract or unfamiliar by pointing out a number of similarities between the two things. For example, suppose you want to explain your ideas about the process of interviewing for a job by comparing interviewing for a job to advertising a new car. To think through the analogy, make a chart like the following. Begin by writing your idea for the analogy (interviewing for a job *is like* advertising a new car) at the top of the chart. Then list parallel processes on both sides of your chart.

Analogy Chart

INTERVIEWING FOR A JOB	ADVERTISING A NEW CAR
• Make experience and qualifications clear	• Make features of car (comfort, reliability) apparent
• Make best appearance by dressing neatly, combing hair, polishing shoes	• Present product attractively by using good photography in beautiful surroundings
• Emphasize what you can do for employer: do quality work, solve problems	• Emphasize what new car can do for consumer: provide comfortable transportation, communicate an image

Thinking Practice   Choose one of the following analogies or make up your own. Then make a chart like the one above to help you draw parallels between the abstract concept and the familiar concept.

1. success is like mountain climbing
2. fear is like a virus
3. friendship is like a mirror

Developing a Working Thesis

No matter what information-gathering technique you use, the process of generating details will uncover a variety of information and ideas. At this point you need to pull together all the information you have gathered and identify a main idea that grows out of connections and patterns you see in the information. This main idea around which you will select and organize your details is called the *working thesis*. Later, as you develop your expository essay, you will refine your working thesis into a polished thesis statement.

Steps for Developing a Working Thesis

1. Review your prewriting notes and the questions you answered to limit your subject. *(See page 143.)*
2. Express your main idea.
3. Look closely at your notes to see that your working thesis covers all of your information and ideas.

Using the steps above, you might develop the following working thesis about the wild boy of Aveyron.

WORKING THESIS   The methods Dr. Itard used to help the wild boy had an influence on education and psychology.

Selecting Details   The methods you use to develop details are aimed at opening your mind. Not all the details that spill out, of course, will be usable. Once you have chosen a working thesis, go over your list of details and check off only those that directly fit within the thesis. These are the details that you will use in your essay. Given the working thesis above, you would *not* use the following details about the wild boy of Aveyron.

- François Truffaut made a movie about the boy
- Tarzan and Mowgli are fictional wild children
- hard to imagine how boy survived by himself

Irrelevant details such as these, no matter how interesting, can detract from the unity of your essay if you include them in the body of your essay. Hold them in reserve, however, for you may be able to use them to enliven your introduction or conclusion.

147

WRITING ACTIVITY *Writing on Your Own*

WRITING
ABOUT THE
THEME

After you review the list of supporting details you produced for Writing Activity 8, develop a working thesis for your essay about opportunities. Then select the details in your list that fit within your thesis. Save your work in your writing folder.

Organizing and Outlining

The final step in prewriting involves the arranging of your ideas in a logical order. The thoughts that occurred to you as you generated details now need to be grouped into categories and arranged in an order that the reader can easily follow. Many writers use a two-step process to create an outline for their essay: (1) grouping supporting details into categories and (2) arranging those categories in a logical order with letters and numbers.

Writing Tip   Organize your notes in an **outline** that shows how you will cover the **main topics, subtopics,** and **supporting details** of your subject.

Grouping Supporting Details into Categories   Scan your list of supporting details, asking yourself what each detail might have in common with the other details. Try to create three to five main categories into which most of your details will fit. Details that do not easily fit into one of your main categories may be usable in the introduction or conclusion of your essay. The following categories have been created from the notes about the wild boy of Aveyron.

Model: *Grouping Details*

Itard's methods and successes in helping Victor

- Itard made sure boy's needs were met before educating him
- Itard played games with him to develop thinking powers; games Victor most interested in involved food
- learned how to fetch water
- learned how to say *milk*

How Itard's work influenced later educational practices

- work with Victor helped Itard develop ideas about how to teach deaf people and also mentally retarded people
- educator Maria Montessori was influenced by Itard's work

Boy's state when found

- had 23 scars on him
- trotted instead of walked
- had a nice smile
- expressed only joy and sorrow at first
- couldn't talk
- insensitive to heat and cold and some sounds
- could reach into boiling water and not express pain
- responded only to sounds related to foods

Arranging Categories in Logical Order The categories you create when you group your supporting details are the main topics that you will use to support your thesis statement. Your next step is to arrange these topics in a logical order. If your essay presents steps in a process or uses an incident to explain something, *chronological order* is probably best. If your essay analyzes an object, *spatial order* might be the most logical. If your essay focuses on the similarities and differences between two items, the method of *comparison and contrast* would be the best. Otherwise you will probably want to use either *order of importance* or *developmental order,* the most common arrangements for expository essays. *(See page 101.)*

Tetrahedral Planetoid, Maurits Cornelis Escher (Dutch, 1898–1972), 1954, Woodcut printed from two blocks, National Gallery of Art, Washington

The most logical organization for the main topics about the wild boy is developmental order. If a Roman numeral is assigned to each category, a simple outline for the body of this essay would appear as follows.

Model: *Simple Outline*

I.   Boy's state when found
II. Itard's methods and successes in helping Victor
III. Itard's influence on later educational practices

Notice that the wording of the third main topic is different from the wording on page 148. The change was made so that the three main topics would be expressed in *parallel form*. The main topics and each group of subtopics in an outline should always be parallel expressions. *(See page 77.)*

After your simple outline is complete, you continue the outlining process by arranging the items within each category in a logical order. These items, called *subtopics,* are assigned capital letters. As you build your outline, you may add new ideas as you think of them, provided there is a logical place for them in your outline.

The following is an appropriate outline for an essay about the wild boy of Aveyron. Notice the indentation of the topics.

Model: *Outline*

MAIN TOPIC   I.   Boy's state when found
SUBTOPICS   A. Physical appearance
                   B. Emotions
                   C. Insensitivities
MAIN TOPIC   II. Itard's methods and successes in helping Victor
SUBTOPICS   A. First step: meeting boy's needs
                   B. Second step: developing boy's sensitivities
                   C. Third step: playing thinking games
                   D. Fourth step: teaching language and chores
MAIN TOPIC   III. Itard's influence on later educational practices
SUBTOPICS   A. Idea of good learning environment
                   B. Education for deaf and mentally retarded
                   C. Influence on Montessori

Your final step in outlining is to add any necessary supporting points under the subtopics. These supporting points are assigned Arabic numerals. If your supporting points can be broken down even further, use lowercase letters to show the divisions.

The following pattern indicates the correct form for an outline, adding supporting points and details.

Model: *Outline Form*

I. (Main topic)
   A. (Subtopic)
      1. (Supporting point)
      2. (Supporting point)
         a. (Detail)
         b. (Detail)
   B. (Subtopic)
      1. (Supporting point)
        (etc.)

The following is the final outline for the essay on the wild boy of Aveyron.

Model: *Final Outline*

I. Boy's state when found
   A. Physical appearance
      1. Scars
      2. Method of walking
   B. Emotions
      1. Smile
      2. Expression of only joy or sorrow
   C. Insensitivities
      1. Heat and cold
      2. Certain sounds
         a. Failure to take notice of speech
         b. Ready notice of sounds relating to food
II. Itard's methods and successes in helping Victor
   A. First step: meeting boy's needs
   B. Second step: developing boy's sensitivities
   C. Third step: playing thinking games
   D. Fourth step: teaching civilized ways
      1. Language
      2. Chores
III. Itard's influence on later educational practices
   A. Idea of good learning environment
   B. Education for deaf and mentally retarded
   C. Influence on Montessori

After you have finished a draft of your outline, use the following checklist to verify its form.

Questions for Checking an Outline

1. Did you use Roman numerals for main topics?
2. Did you use capital letters for subtopics?
3. Did you use Arabic numerals for supporting points?
4. If your supporting points are broken down, did you use lowercase letters?
5. If you put subtopics under topics, do you have at least two?
6. If you included supporting points under subtopics, do you have at least two?
7. If you broke down your supporting points, do you have at least two items in the breakdown?
8. Does your indentation follow the model of the final outline on page 151?
9. Did you capitalize the first word of each entry?
10. Are your main topics and each group of subtopics expressed in parallel forms?

WRITING ACTIVITY *Grouping Ideas into Categories*

The following prewriting notes are on the subject of machines that play a role in classical music. Find three categories into which you can group all of the ideas—except one. Then list the ideas under the appropriate category. Save your work for later use.

- spinning-wheel sound imitated in Richard Wagner's opera *The Flying Dutchman* (1843)
- George Antheil composed *Airplane Sonata* for piano in 1922
- Arthur Honegger portrayed sound of express train in *Pacific 231* (1923)
- Richard Strauss imitated sound of telephone ring in his opera *Intermezzo* (1924)
- Mikhail Glinka wrote "Song of the Railways" (1846)
- Alban Berg imitated telephone sound in his opera *Lulu* (1936)
- George Antheil used two aircraft propellers as instruments in his *Ballet Mècanique* (1924)
- Gian-Carlo Menotti wrote opera called *The Telephone* (1947)

WRITING ACTIVITY *Outlining*

Use the categories you created in Writing Activity 10 to prepare an outline. The outline should include three main topics, with at least two subtopics under each one. Organize the main topics and subtopics in a logical way. Save your work for later use.

Organizing Comparison and Contrast A common type of expository essay is the comparison and contrast essay. In a *comparison* you explain how two subjects are similar. For example, you might give an idea about how a computer works by comparing it to an airport terminal. A *contrast*, on the other hand, emphasizes the differences rather than the similarities. For instance, you might explain how made-for-television movies are different from movies made for the theater. In a comparison and contrast essay, you will examine both the similarities and the differences between two subjects.

If the comparison and contrast method of development is appropriate for your essay, you can choose one of two patterns for organizing your information. In one pattern, called the *AABB* pattern, you include all that you have to say about subject *A* before you discuss subject *B*. You can discuss subject *A* in one paragraph and subject *B* in another paragraph, or you can explain both in the two halves of the same paragraph. In one section of an essay about Robert E. Lee and Ulysses S. Grant, the historian Bruce Catton uses this *AABB* pattern.

Ulysses S. Grant Robert E. Lee

Model: *AABB Pattern of Organization*

(A)Lee was tidewater Virginia, and in his background were family, culture, and tradition . . . the age of chivalry transplanted to a New World which was making its own legends and its own myths. **(A)He** embodied a way of life that had come down through the age of knighthood and the English country squire. . . **(A)Lee** stood for the feeling that it was somehow of advantage to human society to have a pronounced inequality in the social structure. There should be a leisure class, backed by ownership of land; in turn, society itself should be keyed to the land as the chief source of wealth and influence. It would bring forth (according to this ideal) a class of men with a strong sense of obligation to the community; men who lived not to gain advantage for themselves, but to meet the solemn obligations which had been laid on them by the very fact that they were privileged.

(B)Grant, the son of a tanner on the Western frontier, was everything Lee was not. **(B)He** had come up the hard way and embodied nothing in particular except the eternal toughness and sinewy fiber of the men who grew up beyond the mountains. **(B)He** was one of a body of men who owed reverence and obeisance to no one, who were self-reliant to a fault, who cared hardly anything for the past but who had a sharp eye for the future. These frontier men . . . stood for democracy, not from any reasoned conclusion about the proper ordering of human society, but simply because they had grown up in the middle of democracy and knew how it worked. . . No man was born to anything, except perhaps to a chance to show how far he could rise. Life was competition. Bruce Catton

"Grant and Lee: A Study in Contrasts" (Adapted)

The second way to organize a comparison and contrast essay is to use the *ABAB* pattern. In this pattern you point out one similarity or one difference between subject *A* and subject *B* and then go on to another similarity or difference. For instance, if you are contrasting travel by airplane and travel by car, you might start with one difference: the amount of time it takes to travel the long distances. In a sentence or two, you would state that for long distances, travel by airplane is faster. Then you would go on to another difference: the expense. Later, in his essay on Grant and Lee, Bruce Catton shifts to this *ABAB* pattern of organization.

154

Model: *ABAB Pattern of Organization*

Yet it was not all contrast, after all. Different as they were—in background, in personality, in underlying aspiration—these two great soldiers had much in common. . . Each man had, to begin with, the great virtue of utter tenacity and fidelity. **(A)Lee** hung on in the trenches at Petersburg after hope itself had died. **(B)Grant** fought his way down the Mississippi Valley in spite of acute personal discouragement and profound military handicaps. In each man there was an indomitable quality . . . the born fighter's refusal to give up as long as he can still remain on his feet and lift his two fists. Daring and resourcefulness they had, too; the ability to think faster and move faster than the enemy. These were the qualities which gave **(A)Lee** the dazzling campaigns of Second Manassas and Chancellorsville and won Vicksburg for **(B)Grant.**   BRUCE CATTON

"Grant and Lee: A Study in Contrasts" (Adapted)

WRITING ACTIVITY *Writing a Comparison and Contrast Essay*

Choose one of the following pairs of items and make a list of their similarities and differences. If you need additional information, use encyclopedias and other reference materials in your library. Then organize your information according to either the *ABAB* pattern or the *AABB* pattern.

1. an office building and a beehive
2. movies made for television and movies made for the theater
3. the telephone and the mail
4. the offices of the President of the United States and the prime minister of Great Britain
5. a mountain and a goal in life

WRITING ACTIVITY *Writing on Your Own*

WRITING
ABOUT THE
THEME

Following the model of an outline on page 151, use your list of supporting details from Writing Activity 9 to prepare an outline for your essay about opportunities. When you have completed your outline, review the Questions for Checking an Outline on page 152. Then save your outline in your writing folder for later use.

Drafting

Writing Process

With the use of your outline and other prewriting notes, you are ready to write your essay. During this drafting stage, you will transform the bits and pieces you have accumulated into complete sentences and paragraphs.

As you go about writing your first draft, you are likely to think of new ideas. You may incorporate them into your draft, as long as they relate to your main idea and help to clarify and develop it. Although this first draft does not have to be polished or neat, it should include all the parts of an essay: an introduction with a thesis statement, a body of supporting paragraphs, and a conclusion.

Drafting the Thesis Statement

Even if your essay does not begin with your thesis, you should first refine your working thesis to keep your main idea in focus. The steps shown in the following chart will help you draft your thesis statement.

Steps for Drafting Your Thesis

1. Review your outline and revise your working thesis so that it covers all of your main topics.
2. Avoid expressions that weaken your thesis, such as "In this paper I will . . . " or "This essay will be about . . . "

Review the prewriting notes and the outline on the wild boy of Aveyron on pages 144–145 and 148–152. Then study the problems in the following thesis statements.

WEAK THESIS STATEMENT   When he was first captured in 1800, the wild boy of Aveyron was very different from a normal child. [too narrow: does not cover boy's education and the influence of Itard's work]

WEAK THESIS STATEMENT   Wild children exist in both fiction and fact. [too general: does not even mention the wild boy of Aveyron]

WEAK THESIS STATEMENT   This essay will be about the wild boy of Aveyron. [focuses reader's attention on the essay instead of on the wild boy]

In contrast the thesis statement below is appropriately specific and covers all the supporting details.

STRONG THESIS STATEMENT   Dr. Itard's methods in attempting to civilize the wild boy from Aveyron led to new developments in education and psychology that people take for granted today.

WRITING ACTIVITY *Refining Thesis Statements*

Review your notes from Writing Activities 10 and 11 on machines in music. Write the following thesis statements on your paper, leaving a blank line after each one. Then, in each blank space, explain in one sentence what is wrong with the thesis statement. Use the models on pages 156–157 as a guide.

1. Airplanes and telephones have been celebrated in classical music.
2. In this essay I will show how composers have paid tribute to machines.
3. Composers often try to reflect in their music the social changes of the day.
4. This paper will be about music and machines.
5. George Antheil's *Airplane Sonata* is a good example of how composers celebrate machines.

WRITING ACTIVITY *Writing a Thesis Statement*

Following the steps on page 156, write a thesis statement for an essay about machines and music. Be sure your thesis statement is appropriately specific and covers all of the main topics in the outline you wrote for Writing Activity 11.

WRITING ACTIVITY *Writing on Your Own*

WRITING
ABOUT THE
THEME
After reviewing your outline from Writing Activity 13, refine the working thesis for your essay about opportunities so that it takes into account the ideas and details in your outline.

Drafting the Introduction

The introduction is the place to state your subject and thesis and to set the tone for the entire essay. Following are suggestions for some effective ways to open your essay.

Strategies for Drafting an Introduction

1. Begin with an incident that shows how you became interested in your subject.
2. Begin by giving some background information.
3. Begin with an example or an incident that catches the reader's attention.

When you write your introduction, you may need to revise your thesis statement to make it work with the other sentences. Notice in the following introduction about the wild boy that the thesis statement has been reworked to fit smoothly into the introduction. Notice also that some of the original ideas that could not fit under any of the outline headings have been included in the introduction as part of the background information.

Model: *Introduction of an Expository Essay*

The idea of a child's growing up away from all other humans and being raised by animals has turned up again and again in popular tales. *Tarzan of the Apes,* a creation of Edgar Rice Burroughs, and Rudyard Kipling's Mowgli the wolf boy are two famous examples. Wild children turn up in fact as well as in fiction, although there is no evidence that any were raised by animals. One of the most interesting and famous factual cases is that of Victor, the wild boy of Aveyron, France. The doctor who worked with the boy after he was captured in the wild in 1800 was Jean-Marc-Gaspard

REFINED THESIS
STATEMENT

Itard. The young doctor's methods in trying to civilize the boy, whom he named Victor, led to new ideas in education and psychology—ideas that people take for granted today.

WRITING ACTIVITY *Identifying Introductions*

Write *personal incident, background information,* or *attention-getting example* to indicate how each essay introduction begins.

1.

I remember, to start with, that day in Sacramento, in a California now nearly thirty years past, when I first entered a classroom—able to understand about fifty stray English words. The third of four children, I had been preceded by my older brother and sister to a neighborhood school. Neither of them, however, had revealed very much about their classroom experiences. They left each morning and returned each afternoon, always together, speaking Spanish as they climbed the five steps to the porch.

Their mysterious books, wrapped in brown shopping-bag paper, remained on the table next to the door, closed firmly behind them.   RICHARD RODRIGUEZ
"Aria: A Memoir of a Bilingual Childhood"

2.

With his 47-pound bow drawn taut, a carbon graphite arrow held close to his cheek and EEG wires flowing from his scalp to monitor his brain, Rick McKinney seemed to be gazing absently at the majesty of Pikes Peak towering above the U.S. Olympic Training Center in Colorado Springs. Suddenly, he released the arrow and hit a perfect bull's eye that stood 98.6 yards downrange. Dr. Daniel Landers, an exercise scientist from Arizona State University, looked up from his EEG monitor, smiled and nodded with approval. McKinney had really not been thinking during the shot; the left side of his brain had shown diminished electrical activity.   LEE TORREY
"How Science Creates Winners"

3.

For almost three-quarters of a century, James Van DerZee has with rare artistry compiled a sweeping photographic survey of a way of life among black people of eastern America, particularly Harlem, that is unique and irreplaceable. It is both an historical record of value and an achievement of disciplined and feeling art. Van DerZee is only now beginning to be recognized as one of the notable photographers of middle-class people of the country.
CLARISSA K. WITTENBERG, *Smithsonian*

WRITING ACTIVITY   *Drafting Essay Introductions*

Write two different introductory paragraphs that include the following thesis. In the first introduction, provide background information; in the second, use a personal incident or an attention-getting example. You should revise the thesis statement as needed to fit each introduction.

THESIS STATEMENT   Parks come in a variety of sizes and offer a variety of attractions, from the neighborhood park to the sprawling national park.

WRITING ACTIVITY   *Writing on Your Own*

WRITING ABOUT THE THEME   Based on your work from Writing Activity 16, draft an introduction for your essay about opportunities. Use the Strategies for Drafting an Introduction on page 158 as your guide.

Drafting the Body

Use your outline to draft the body of your essay, moving from point to point in the same order as the outline. You may add new ideas that would improve your essay. Check, however, to make sure each new idea relates to the main idea expressed in your thesis statement.

As you write the body of your essay, you will also need to supply transitions to connect your thoughts within and between paragraphs. In each case select the transition that will best direct your reader from thought to thought. *(See page 102 for transitions.)* Using transitions will help give your essay *coherence*, the quality that makes each sentence seem related to the one before. *(See pages 100–102.)* Following are some other ways you can achieve coherence.

Strategies for Achieving Coherence

1. Repeat a key word from an earlier sentence.
2. Repeat an idea from an earlier sentence using new words.
3. Use a pronoun in place of a word used earlier.

In the following draft, the outline on the wild boy of Aveyron on page 151 has been fleshed out into complete sentences and paragraphs. The transitions, which have been added, are in heavy type. Keep in mind that this first draft must still undergo revising and editing.

Model: *Body of an Expository Essay*

FROM I
IN OUTLINE

Itard and other scientists were interested in finding out how much of a human's development is inborn and how much is learned through civilization. Victor provided an opportunity to study this question, for when he was captured at the age of twelve, he was in an extremely uncivilized state. Twenty-three scars from burns, bites, and scratches covered his dirty body, and he trotted instead of walking. He had a pleasing smile, but he expressed only extremes of emotion: joy, especially when he was fed or taken on walks, and sorrow about not being free. He could not speak, and he appeared insensitive to heat and cold. He could reach into a pot of boiling water and pull out a potato. The only sounds of interest to him related to food. For Itard, working with Victor was a rare chance to study a human raised in isolation and to examine the influence of environment on human behavior.

FROM II
IN OUTLINE

Itard's first step in educating Victor was attending to his needs and desires. He gave Victor the foods he liked (mainly vegetables), plenty of rest, privacy, and exercise. **Then** he began developing the boy's sensitivities, such as those of sight and hearing, for Itard believed that no attempt to teach him to talk would succeed unless he was first sensitive to sound. **Next** he tried to play games with Victor to stretch the boy's mental powers. He **soon** learned that only when food was involved did Victor pay any attention. To motivate Victor, Itard devised a game in which Victor would find a chestnut under one of three inverted cups. When he **finally** began teaching Victor to speak and read, **however,** Itard met with very little success. **After** years the only words Victor learned were *milk* and *Oh God,* the latter expression having been picked up by imitating his caretaker, Madame Guérin. Victor never learned to read. He did, **however,** learn some simple chores, including fetching water and sawing wood. He never became what most

161

FROM III
IN OUTLINE

people would consider a normal person, although he did respond to the affectionate concern of those around him.

Itard's methods, whatever their failings with Victor, opened new doors in education. **First,** the idea that a child can learn only after his or her needs are met showed the importance of a good learning environment. **In addition,** working with Victor enabled Itard to make discoveries about teaching deaf children to speak, and it helped him create a whole new field of study: teaching the mentally retarded. **Finally,** Maria Montessori, a pioneer in educating very young children, was influenced by Itard's work with Victor.

A Scene from Truffaut's Movie, *The Wild Child*

WRITING ACTIVITY *Analyzing the Body of an Essay*

Refer to the draft of the essay about Victor, the wild boy of Aveyron, on pages 161–162 to answer the following questions.

1. In the first supporting paragraph, the last sentence refers to an earlier idea. Where is that earlier idea expressed?
2. What transitions are used in the second supporting paragraph?
3. Find the sentence that begins *After years the only words* near the end of the second supporting paragraph. What key word appears in that sentence that is repeated in the next two sentences? What pronoun is repeated in the last two sentences of the paragraph?
4. In the third supporting paragraph, the words *whatever their failings with Victor* appear. To what earlier idea does the phrase refer?
5. What transitions are used in the third supporting paragraph?

WRITING ACTIVITY

WRITING
ABOUT THE
THEME

Using your outline, thesis, and introduction from Writing Activities 13, 16, and 19, draft the body of your essay about opportunities. As you write, use transitions to achieve coherence.

Drafting the Conclusion

Like the introduction the conclusion of an essay is usually more general than the supporting paragraphs in the body. In fact, the conclusion provides a good opportunity to express whatever insight your subject has inspired. One or a combination of the following may be an effective way to end an expository essay.

Strategies for Concluding an Essay

1. Summarize the essay or restate the thesis in new words.
2. Refer to ideas in the introduction to bring the essay full circle.
3. State your personal reaction to the subject.
4. Draw a conclusion from the details in the essay body.
5. Relate an incident supporting your thesis or conclusion.
6. Ask a question that leaves the reader thinking.
7. Appeal to the reader's emotions.

The following closing to the essay about Victor draws a conclusion based on the supporting details in the essay body. The last sentence, often called a *clincher* because it fixes the message firmly in the reader's mind, provides a strong ending.

Model: *Conclusion of an Expository Essay*

After Itard stopped working with Victor, the French government paid for Victor's care for the rest of his life. He never fit into normal society. Itard concluded that the early years of human life are precious periods of learning; and if a child is deprived of a human environment during those years, full learning can never take place. Although scientists and psychologists are still debating the influences of heredity and environment, Itard drew

CLINCHER

his own conclusion. It is human society—civilization—that makes us what we are, and no amount of inborn humanity could make up for the loss of companionship that Victor endured in the wild.

A Scene from Truffaut's Movie, *The Wild Child*

Drafting a Title   To complete your first draft, you need to think of an appropriate title. You may take your title from words and phrases within the essay, or you may compose a headline-type phrase.

Writing Tip   A good **title** suggests the main idea and makes your reader want to read on.

WRITING ACTIVITY *Analyzing a Concluding Paragraph*

Use the entire draft of the essay about Victor on pages 158, 161–162, and 164 to write answers to the following questions.

1. Where in the essay besides the concluding paragraph is some form of the word *civilized* used?
2. To which sentence in the first supporting paragraph do the last two sentences of the conclusion refer?
3. Which names in the last sentence of the body are repeated in the first sentence of the conclusion?
4. What other key word in the last sentence of the body is repeated in the first sentence of the conclusion?
5. What information is offered in the concluding paragraph to reinforce the conclusion drawn?

WRITING ACTIVITY *Writing a Concluding Paragraph*

Reread the introduction and body of the essay about Victor on pages 158 and 161–162. Then write an alternative concluding paragraph. Make your paragraph appeal to the reader's emotions.

WRITING ACTIVITY *Drafting Titles*

Draft five possible titles for the essay about Victor. Use words or phrases from the essay for two of the titles and a headline style for the others.

WRITING ACTIVITY *Writing on Your Own*

WRITING
ABOUT THE
THEME

Draft a paragraph to conclude the essay about opportunities in Writing Activity 21. Then experiment with possible titles. Save your conclusion and titles in your writing folder.

Revising

Writing Process

In the revising stage, your aim is to improve your first draft—to make it clearer, smoother, livelier, and more readable. Always leave yourself time to put your composition away for a while before revising it. Distancing yourself from your work can clear your mind and help you think of new and better ways to express your meaning.

Sometimes you may need to write a second or third draft before you are satisfied with the effectiveness of your essay. Your main concern in the revising stage, of course, is your audience. Ask yourself over and over again, "Will my readers understand exactly what I mean?"

Checking for Unity, Coherence, and Emphasis

In an expository essay having unity, the paragraphs work together to develop a single thesis. The topic sentence of each supporting paragraph relates directly to the thesis, and each sentence within a paragraph relates directly to the topic sentence. As you revise, watch for and delete ideas that stray from the main point.

Also be on the alert for transitions that are needed to keep your essay coherent. *(See pages 100–102 and page 160.)* Look for ways to improve the organization and flow of ideas. Your writing should guide your reader along a logical path of thought.

As you revise, check for appropriate emphasis. *Emphasis* is the quality in essays that makes the most important points stand out clearly in the reader's mind. You can achieve the proper emphasis by devoting more space to the most important ideas, by using transitional words and phrases to indicate relative importance, and by repeating the most important points.

Writing Tip   A good essay has **unity, coherence,** and **emphasis.**

Using a Revision Checklist

Because of the number and variety of points to be checked in the revision stage, you should read through your essay several times. A revision checklist—like the one on the next page—can help you keep track of what you are looking for and what you have completed.

166

Revision Checklist

CHECKING YOUR ESSAY

1. Does the introduction set the tone and capture attention?
2. Does the thesis statement make your main idea clear?
3. Does your essay have unity? Does the topic sentence of each paragraph relate directly to the thesis statement?
4. Does your essay have coherence?
    a. Are the paragraphs arranged in a logical order? *(See page 101.)*
    b. Do transitions smoothly connect the paragraphs? *(See pages 100–102.)*
    c. Did you use the techniques for achieving coherence between paragraphs? *(See page 160.)*
5. Does your essay have the proper emphasis?
    a. Did you use transitions to show the importance of your ideas?
    b. Did you devote the most space to the most important ideas?
    c. Did you repeat key ideas to show their importance?
6. Do you have a strong concluding paragraph?
7. Did you add a title?

CHECKING YOUR PARAGRAPHS

8. Does each paragraph have a topic sentence? *(See pages 94–95.)*
9. Is each paragraph unified and coherent? *(See pages 99–102.)*

CHECKING YOUR SENTENCES AND WORDS

10. Are your sentences varied? *(See pages 67–71.)*
11. Are your sentences clear and concise? *(See pages 63–65.)*
12. Did you avoid faulty sentences? *(See pages 72–78.)*
13. Did you use specific words with correct connotations? *(See pages 56–57.)*
14. Did you include figurative language? *(See pages 58–59.)*

WRITING ACTIVITY 26  *Writing on Your Own*

WRITING
ABOUT THE
THEME

Use the Revision Checklist to revise the essay about opportunities that you finished drafting in Writing Activity 25. Save your revision.

Editing and Publishing

Grammar in the Writing Process

In her description of what would have happened to Judith Shakespeare in London, Virginia Woolf wrote the following sentences.

> The manager—a fat, loose-lipped man—guffawed. He bellowed something about poodles dancing and women acting—no woman, he said, could possibly be an actress.

Partly because of her choice of the verbs *guffawed* and *bellowed*, this scene is particularly easy for readers to picture in their minds. The following lines, however, would have produced a fuzzy image.

> The manager—a fat, loose-lipped man—laughed. He shouted something about poodles . . .

This is just one example of how important verbs are not only to nonfiction essays but to every other kind of writing as well. *(For more information about verbs and for practice in using colorful verbs, see pages 542–546 and 641–663.)*

Tenses of Verbs   After you revise your writing, you should edit your work to make sure that all verbs are written in the correct tense. *Tense* expresses a particular time and makes the order of events clear to your readers. Following are examples of the six main tenses.

PRESENT	Judith **lives** in London.
PAST	Judith **lived** in London last year.
FUTURE	Judith **will live** in London next year.
PRESENT PERFECT	Judith **has lived** in London most of her life.
PAST PERFECT	Judith **had** never **lived** in London.
FUTURE PERFECT	By June she **will** already **have lived** in London for two years.

Shifts in Tense   As you edit, you also need to correct any shifts in tense. If you began to write in the past tense, for example, watch for any accidental shift to the present tense. *(For more information about tenses and practice in using tenses correctly, see pages 658–660.)*

168

SHIFT IN TENSE   She **stood** at the stage door and **asks** the manager for a job. [Tense shift from the past to the present.]

CORRECT TENSE   She **stood** at the stage door and **asked** the manager for a job. [Now both verbs are in the past tense.]

Principal Parts of Verbs   The six tenses are formed from the principal parts of a verb. The *principal parts* are the *present,* the *present participle,* the *past,* and the *past participle.* Most verbs, called *regular verbs,* form their past and past participle by adding *-ed* or *-d* to the present. A few verbs, called *irregular verbs,* form their past and past participle in other ways. Following are examples of the principal parts of a few irregular verbs. *(For lists of the principal parts of irregular verbs and practice in using the verbs correctly, see pages 641–649.)*

Irregular Verbs

PRESENT	PRESENT PARTICIPLE	PAST	PAST PARTICIPLE
hurt	hurting	hurt	(have) hurt
leave	leaving	left	(have) left
speak	speaking	spoke	(have) spoken
know	knowing	knew	(have) known
begin	beginning	began	(have) begun
fall	falling	fell	(have) fallen

Editing Checklist

1. Have you used the correct tense? *(See pages 650–656.)*
2. Are there any shifts in tense? *(See pages 658–661.)*
3. Have the correct principal parts of verbs been used in forming the tenses? *(See pages 641–647.)*

WRITING ACTIVITY  *Writing on Your Own*

WRITING ABOUT THE THEME **Editing**   Use the checklist above and the one on page 38 to edit your essay about opportunities from Writing Activity 26.

Publishing   After you write a final copy, ask an adult to read it and discuss with you your ideas about opportunities.

A Writer Writes

A Comparison and Contrast Essay about Opportunities

PURPOSE: to explain the similarities and/or differences between
             opportunities teenagers have now and those they had
             50 years ago

AUDIENCE: teenagers

Prewriting   How have opportunities for teenagers changed over
the past 50 years? Have they changed very much since the 1940's,
when the world was still caught up in World War II? To begin to
explore this subject, read over the ideas you wrote in your journal
and then talk to people who were teenagers during the 1940's or who
knew teenagers during the 1940's. Ask questions about different areas
such as schooling, work, recreation, and health. Then choose the one
area that interests you the most or zero in on one significant difference
or similarity in opportunities from then to now. If necessary, limit
your subject so that you can handle it effectively in a short essay.

Then, in addition to brainstorming for all the information you know, follow up on any helpful interviews you had and also look for additional details in reference books in the library. To develop a working thesis, concentrate on the main similarities and/or differences you discovered. Then group relevant details into categories and choose a pattern—either *AABB* or *ABAB*—for your comparison and contrast essay. Finally, use your categories as the basis of an outline.

Drafting   After you refine your thesis statement to cover all of your ideas and details, draft your essay. Make sure that your introduction includes your thesis statement, captures your reader's interest, and sets the tone. For the body of your essay, draft a supporting paragraph for each main category of details. Then, after you draft a concluding paragraph, think of an interesting title for your essay.

Revising   If you can put your draft away for a time, you will be able to revise it with fresh eyes. During your revision read through your essay several times, each time looking for a different item on the Revision Checklist on page 167. *Peer Conferencing:* If possible, also get a friend's or classmate's comments. Then make whatever changes or adjustments you think will make your essay more effective.

Editing and Publishing   When you are pleased with your revised essay, edit it, using the checklists on pages 38 and 169. Then give your essay to your teacher, who will publish it in a classroom book called "Then and Now." You also may want to share a copy of your essay with anyone you interviewed during prewriting.

Independent Writing

Write an expository essay about one of the following subjects or about one of your own choosing.

1. how working at a part-time job affects academic performance
2. how the nature of friendship changes as a person grows older
3. how inexpensive steps can be taken to cut pollution.

Creative Writing

Like essays poems can be written about differences. In fact, Richard Wilbur developed a special kind of poetry called *Opposites*. In rhymed verse he humorously pairs opposite things. Read the example on the following page and then write an "opposite" of your own.

Not To Be Reproduced, René Magritte,
1937, Oil on Canvas, 81.3 × 65 cm

38

What is the opposite of *mirror?*
The answer hardly could be clearer:
It's *anything which, on inspection,*
Is not all full of your reflection.

For instance, it would be no use
To brush your hair before a moose,
Or try a raincoat on for size
While looking at a swarm of flies.

RICHARD WILBUR, *Opposites*

WRITING
ABOUT THE
THEME

Writing about Literature

The *tone* of an essay is the writer's attitude toward his or her subject
and audience. What is the tone of Virginia Woolf's essay "Shakespeare's Sister?" Do you think it is bitter? Angry? Sarcastic? Resigned?
Write a paragraph that states the tone and then explain how you think
the tone contributes to the meaning of the essay.

Writing in Other Subject Areas

Government   Although you live under a system of government
in which the people rule, it is rare when all the people agree on any
one issue. What part is played by those who disagree? Have you ever
been in the minority on an important issue? Write an essay about the
role of the minority in a democracy.

Foreign Language   While Shakespeare is generally considered
to be the greatest writer of the English language, other languages have
their great writers too. Who is the "Shakespeare" of the language you
are studying? Write an essay that explains why that author is so
important.

4 Checklist

Writing Essays to Inform

Prewriting

✔ Find ideas by asking yourself questions and by reading. *(See pages 141–142.)*

✔ Choose a subject to develop into an essay from a list of possible subjects. *(See page 142.)*

✔ Limit your subject by asking questions about your subject and your audience. *(See page 143.)*

✔ Develop a list of supporting details. *(See page 144.)*

✔ Develop a working thesis based on the supporting details. *(See page 147.)*

✔ Organize your details into an outline. *(See pages 148–152.)*

Drafting

✔ Refine your thesis. *(See pages 156–157.)*

✔ Draft an introduction that includes your thesis. *(See page 158.)*

✔ Use your outline to write a first draft of the body of the essay. *(See pages 160–162.)*

✔ Use connecting devices to link your thoughts. *(See page 160.)*

✔ Draft a concluding paragraph. *(See pages 163–164.)*

✔ Draft a title. *(See page 165.)*

Revising

✔ Use the Revision Checklist to revise your essay for structure, well-developed paragraphs, unity, coherence, emphasis, and varied and lively sentences and words. *(See page 167.)*

Editing and Publishing

✔ Use the Editing Checklists to check your essay for errors in grammar, spelling, and mechanics. *(See pages 38 and 169.)*

✔ Follow standard manuscript form and make a final copy of your work. Then publish it, using any of the ways listed on page 42.

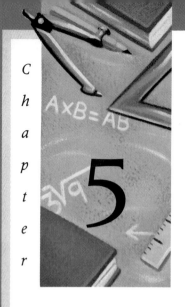

C
h
a
p
t
e
r

5 Writing Essays to Persuade

Part 1 *Reading to Write*

THEME: *Education*

This year, your senior year, is an excellent time to look back and take stock of the education you have received for the past 12 years. What do you think have been the most valuable experiences you have had? Did they involve good courses or teachers that you had? Were they activities, such as sports or the band, that helped you develop a special talent? Then think about how education has changed in the years since you started first grade. For instance, are there more computers in school now? Finally, how do you think your education could have been improved? What would your answer be, for example, if you were asked this question: *What aspects of your education would you change to guarantee that a younger brother or sister would have a better education than you had?*

In the following selection, you will read an excerpt from Charles Dickens's novel *Hard Times*. In this novel, published in 1854, Dickens portrays a very different kind of educational system than what you are used to. In the scene that you will read, Thomas Gradgrind, an illustrious citizen and educator, visits a school to persuade students to deal only with "Fact, fact, fact!" As you read the excerpt, think about Gradgrind's beliefs about education and about your own.

from

Hard Times

C h a r l e s   D i c k e n s

Thomas Gradgrind, sir. A man of realities. A man of facts and calculations. A man who proceeds upon the principle that two and two
are four, and nothing over, and who is not to be talked into allowing
for anything over. Thomas Gradgrind, sir—peremptorily Thomas—
Thomas Gradgrind. With a rule and a pair of scales, and the multiplication table always in his pocket, sir, ready to weigh and measure
any parcel of human nature, and tell you exactly what it comes to. It
is a mere question of figures, a case of simple arithmetic. You might
hope to get some other nonsensical belief into the head of George
Gradgrind, or Augustus Gradgrind, or John Gradgrind, or Joseph
Gradgrind (all supposititious,[1] non-existent persons), but into the head
of Thomas Gradgrind—no sir!

In such terms Mr. Gradgrind always mentally introduced himself,
whether to his private circle of acquaintance, or to the public in general. In such terms, no doubt, substituting the words "boys and girls"
for "sir," Thomas Gradgrind now presented Thomas
Gradgrind to the little pitchers before him,
who were to be filled so full of facts.

1. **supposititious** [sə poz'ə tish' əs]:
   Supposed, hypothetical.

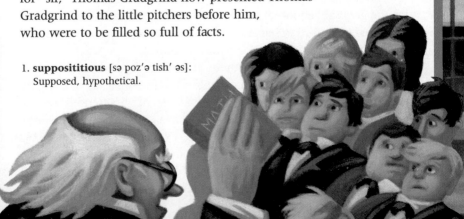

Indeed, as he eagerly sparkled at them from the cellarage before mentioned, he seemed a kind of cannon loaded to the muzzle with facts, and prepared to blow them clean out of the regions of childhood at one discharge. He seemed a galvanizing apparatus, too, charged with a grim mechanical substitute for the tender young imaginations that were to be stormed away.

"Girl number twenty," said Mr. Gradgrind, squarely pointing with his square forefinger, "I don't know that girl. Who is that girl?"

"Sissy Jupe, sir," explained number twenty, blushing, standing up, and curtsying.

"Sissy is not a name," said Mr. Gradgrind. "Don't call yourself Sissy. Call yourself Cecilia."

"It's father as calls me Sissy, sir," returned the young girl in a trembling voice, and with another curtsy.

"Then he has no business to do it," said Mr. Gradgrind. "Tell him he mustn't. Cecilia Jupe. Let me see. What is your father?"

"He belongs to the horse-riding, if you please, sir."

Mr. Gradgrind frowned, and waved off the objectionable calling with his hand.

"We don't want to know anything about that here. You mustn't tell us about that here. Your father breaks horses, don't he?"

"If you please, sir, when they can get any to break, they do break horses in the ring, sir."

"You mustn't tell us about the ring here. Very well, then, describe your father as a horse-breaker. He doctors sick horses, I dare say?"

"Oh yes, sir."

"Very well, then. He is a veterinary surgeon, a farrier, and horse-breaker. Give me your definition of a horse."

(Sissy Jupe thrown into the greatest alarm by this demand.)

"Girl number twenty unable to define a horse!" said Mr. Gradgrind, for the general behoof of all the little pitchers. "Girl number twenty possessed of no facts in reference to one of the commonest of animals! Some boy's definition of a horse. Bitzer, yours."

The square finger, moving here and there, lighted suddenly on Bitzer, perhaps, because he chanced to sit in the same ray of sunlight which, darting in at one of the bare windows of the intensely white-washed room, irradiated Sissy. For, the boys and girls sat on the face of the inclined plane in two compact bodies, divided up the centre by a narrow interval; and Sissy, being at the corner of a row on the sunny side, came in for the beginning of a sunbeam, of which Bitzer, being at the corner of a row on the other side, a few rows in advance, caught the end. But, whereas the girl was so dark-eyed and dark-haired that she seemed to receive a deeper and more lustrous color from the sun when it shone upon her, the boy was so light-eyed and light-haired that the selfsame rays appeared to draw out of him what little color he ever possessed. His cold eyes would hardly have been eyes, but for the short ends of lashes which, by bringing them into immediate contrast with something paler than themselves, expressed their form. His short-cropped hair might have been a mere continuation of the sandy freckles on his forehead and face. His skin was so unwholesomely deficient in the natural tinge, that he looked as though, if he were cut, he would bleed white.

"Bitzer," said Thomas Gradgrind, "your definition of a horse."

"Quadruped. Graminivorous. Forty teeth, namely, twenty-four grinders, four eye-teeth, and twelve incisive. Sheds coat in the spring; in marshy countries, sheds hoofs too. Hoofs hard, but requiring to be shod with iron. Age known by marks in mouth." Thus (and much more) Bitzer.

"Now, girl number twenty," said Mr. Gradgrind, "you know what a horse is."

She curtsied again, and would have blushed deeper, if she could have blushed deeper than she had blushed all this time. Bitzer, after rapidly blinking at Thomas Gradgrind with both eyes at once, and so catching the light upon his quivering ends of lashes that they looked like the antennae of busy insects, put his knuckles to his freckled forehead, and sat down again.

The third gentleman now stepped forth. A mighty man at cutting and drying he was; a government officer; in his way (and in most other people's too) a professed pugilist; always in training, always with a system to force down the general throat like a bolus,[2] always to be heard of at the bar of his little Public Office, ready to fight all England. To continue in fistic phraseology, he had a genius for coming up to the scratch, wherever and whatever it was, and proving himself an ugly customer. He would go in and damage any subject whatever with his right, follow up with his left, stop, exchange, counter, bore his opponent (he always fought All England) to the ropes, and fall upon him neatly. He was certain to knock the wind out of common sense, and render that unlucky adversary deaf to the call of time. And he had it in charge from high authority to bring about the great Public Office Millennium,[3] when Commissioners should reign upon earth.

2. **bolus** [bō′ ləs]: A large, round pill.
3. **Millennium** [mə len′ē əm]: A period of peace, joy, and prosperity.

"Very well," said this gentleman, briskly smiling, and folding his arms. "That's a horse. Now, let me ask you girls and boys, Would you paper a room with representations of horses?"

After a pause, one-half of the children cried in chorus, "Yes, sir!" Upon which the other half, seeing in the gentleman's face that Yes was wrong, cried out in chorus, "No, sir!"—as the custom is in these examinations.

"Of course, No. Why wouldn't you?"

A pause. One corpulent slow boy, with a wheezy manner of breathing, ventured the answer, Because he wouldn't paper a room at all, but would paint it.

"You *must* paper it," said the gentleman, rather warmly.

"You must paper it," said Thomas Gradgrind, "whether you like it or not. Don't tell *us* you wouldn't paper it. What do you mean, boy?"

"I'll explain to you, then," said the gentleman, after another and a dismal pause, "why you wouldn't paper a room with representations of horses. Do you ever see horses walking up and down the sides of room in reality—in fact? Do you?"

"Yes, sir!" from one-half. "No, sir!" from the other.

"Of course, no," said the gentleman, with an indignant look at the wrong half. "Why, then, you are not to see anywhere what you don't see in fact; you are not to have anywhere what you don't have in fact. What is called Taste is only another name for Fact."

Thomas Gradgrind nodded his approbation.

"This is a new principle, a discovery, a great discovery," said the gentleman. "Now, I'll try you again. Suppose you were going to carpet a room. Would you use a carpet having a representation of flowers upon it?"

There being a general conviction by this time that "No, sir!" was always the right answer to this gentleman, the chorus of No was very strong. Only a few feeble stragglers said Yes; among them Sissy Jupe.

"Girl number twenty," said the gentleman, smiling in the calm of strength of knowledge.

Sissy blushed and stood up.

"So you would carpet your room—or your husband's room, if you were a grown woman, and had a husband—with representations of flowers, would you?" said the gentleman. "Why would you?"

"If you please, sir, I am very fond of flowers," returned the girl.

"And is that why you would put tables and chairs upon them, and have people walking over them with heavy boots?"

"It wouldn't hurt them, sir. They wouldn't crush and wither if you please, sir. They would be the pictures of what was very pretty and pleasant, and I would fancy—"

"Ay, ay, ay! But you mustn't fancy," cried the gentleman, quite elated by coming so happily to his point. "That's it! You are never to fancy."

"You are not, Cecilia Jupe," Thomas Gradgrind solemnly repeated, "to do anything of that kind."

"Fact, fact, fact!" said the gentleman. And "Fact, fact, fact!" repeated Thomas Gradgrind.

"You are to be in all things regulated and governed," said the gentleman, "by fact. We hope to have, before long, a board of fact, composed of commissioners of facts, who will force the people to be a people of fact, and of nothing but fact. You must discard the word Fancy altogether. You have nothing to do with it. You are not to have, in any object of use or ornament, what would be a contradiction in fact. You don't walk upon flowers in fact; you cannot be allowed to walk upon flowers in carpets. You don't find that foreign birds and butterflies come and perch upon your crockery; you cannot be permitted to paint foreign birds and butterflies upon your crockery; you never meet with quadrupeds going up and down walls; you must not have quadrupeds represented upon walls. You must use," said the gentleman, "for all these purposes, combinations and modifications (in primary colors) of mathematical figures which are susceptible of proof and demonstration. This is the new discovery. This is fact. This is taste."

The girl curtsied, and sat down. She was very young, and she looked as if she were frightened by the matter-of-fact prospect the world afforded.

"Now, if Mr. M'Choakumchild," said the gentleman, "will proceed to give his first lesson here, Mr. Gradgrind, I shall be happy, at your request, to observe his mode of procedure."

Mr. Gradgrind was much obliged. "Mr. M'Choakumchild, we only wait for you."

So, Mr. M'Choakumchild began in his best manner. He, and some one hundred and forty other schoolmasters, had been lately turned at the same time, in the same factory, on the same principles, like so many pianoforte legs. He had been put through an immense variety of paces, and had answered volumes of head-breaking questions. Orthography, etymology, syntax, and prosody, biography, astronomy, geography, and general cosmography, the sciences of compound

The Lambeth "Ragged School" for Girls—a school for poor students in London. This picture first appeared in the *Illustrated London News* on April 11, 1846.

proportion, algebra, land surveying and levelling, vocal music, and drawing from models, were all at the ends of his ten chilled fingers. He had worked his stony way into her Majesty's most Honorable Privy Council's Schedule B, and had taken the bloom off the higher branches of mathematics and physical science, French, German, Latin, and Greek. He knew all about all the Water Sheds of all the world (whatever they are), and all the histories of all the peoples, and all the names of all the rivers and mountains, and all the productions, manners, and customs of all the countries, and all their boundaries and bearings on the two and thirty points of the compass. Ah, rather overdone, M'Choakumchild! If he had only learnt a little less, how infinitely better he might have taught much more!

He went to work, in this preparatory lesson, not unlike Morgiana in the Forty Thieves: looking into all the vessels ranged before him, one after another, to see what they contained. Say, good M'Choakumchild. When, from thy boiling store, thou shalt fill each jar brimful by and by, dost thou think that thou wilt always kill outright the robber Fancy lurking within—or sometimes only maim him and distort him? ◆

Responding to the Theme

Education

■ ***Responding in Your Journal***   As a senior in high school, you can now look back and reflect on many years of close participation in and observation of the educational system. In fact, you now could be considered an education expert. As an expert what are your views about education? What is good about education? What ideas do you have for improving the educational system? Express your ideas and opinions about all of these and any related subjects in your journal this week. First, however, think and write about your education. What value does an education have? Does your education end when you receive your diploma or is there some lifelong learning that goes on after your formal education ends?

■ ***Speaking and Listening***   In the scene you just read, Dickens presents an exaggerated but pointed picture of a particular approach to education. With your classmates discuss the characters and the way Dickens presents them. Then, after your discussion, your teacher will assign the parts of Mr. Gradgrind, Sissy Jupe, Bitzer, the third gentleman, and a narrator. Those students assigned speaking parts should be sure to use a lot of expression. When they finish, others should volunteer to take the speaking parts and improvise a continuation of the scene.

■ ***Critical Thinking: Analyzing***   Near the end of the scene, the third gentleman makes a passionate speech about the importance of "fact." Reread the speech, concentrating on the part that begins, "You don't walk upon flowers in fact ... " Which of the statements are actually facts? Which are opinions? Do they make sense? Why or why not? Explain your answers in a paragraph.

■ ***Extending Your Vocabulary***   Knowledgeable young Bitzer used the word *graminivorous* in his definition of a horse. *Gramin* refers to "grass" and *vorous* to "eating." There are other *vorous* words that relate to the eating habits of human beings; some words also refer to lizards, cows, and cats. Using a dictionary, make a list of at least five *-vorous* words with their meanings and then create some of your own. For example, what word might describe the eating habits of an earthworm, a python, or your car?

Part 2   *Writing*

Mark Twain once wrote, "It were not best that we should all think alike; it is difference of opinion that makes horse-races." Twain can rest assured that modern society will never lack for "horse-races," for there is probably no question on which everyone thinks alike. As a result, to obtain agreement on a certain issue, you sometimes must try to convince people to accept the position you feel is best. One way to do so is to write a persuasive essay, in which your purpose is to win readers over to your side of an issue or to motivate them to take a certain action.

Writing Term   A **persuasive essay** states an opinion and uses facts, examples, and reasons to convince readers to accept that opinion and/or take a specific action.

When you write essays for the purpose of persuading, you can draw on several types of writing, including *narrative writing* and *descriptive writing. (See pages 106–111.)* You will also be able to use different methods of *classification* to organize information you are using to support your opinions. *(See pages 114–116.)* Finally, you will find the skill of *evaluating* helpful in writing persuasion. *(See Writing Is Thinking on page 202.)*

Analyzing Persuasive Essays

A persuasive essay is like other essays in its structure but not its substance. The core of a persuasive essay lies in its arguments—the logical presentation of facts designed to move the reader to believe or act in a certain way. To analyze a persuasive essay, then, it is necessary to analyze its arguments. This section will examine not only the structure of persuasive essays but also the specifics of their substance.

Structure

Like other kinds of essays, a persuasive essay is composed of three basic parts—an introduction, a body of paragraphs, and a conclusion. The following chart shows the function of each of these three parts.

Structure of a Persuasive Essay
1. The **introduction** presents the issue and the writer's opinion on the issue, which is expressed in the thesis statement.
2. The **body** of supporting paragraphs presents facts, reasons, statistics, incidents, examples, the testimony of experts, and other kinds of evidence to support the writer's opinion.
3. The **conclusion** provides a strong summary or closing that drives home the writer's opinion.

Read the following persuasive essay, in which the main parts are labeled. Notice how the writer presents the issue and his opinion in the introduction, supports his opinion in the body, and reinforces his main idea in the conclusion.

Model: *Persuasive Essays*

Controlling Alaska's Wolves

INTRODUCTION:
PRESENTS THESIS
STATEMENT; LAYS
OUT ISSUE

The plan to eliminate humanely some of Alaska's soaring number of wolves makes good sense. Those who would deny Alaska's right to control its bourgeoning wolf population have failed to realize the ability of the wolf population to bounce back.

183

FIRST BODY PARAGRAPH: GIVES EXAMPLES AND FACTS

At one time, up to six federal varmint hunters ranged the Territory, poisoning, trapping, and shooting wolves from the air. As a result, at statehood few wolves remained. Since then, Alaska has worked hard to bring its wolves back. It added the wolf to its big game trophy and fur animal lists, which brought it under protection of bag limits and other regulations. It has shown flexibility in adjusting these regulations in response to wolf population changes. It has banned hunting wolves from an airplane as a sport. Finally, it has supported wolf research to learn how the animal lives.

SECOND BODY PARAGRAPH: GIVES STATISTICS

The wolf, with its remarkable resilience, has responded dramatically. In fact, there are so many wolves in some areas they are destroying their own food supply. In Alaska, the wolf's diet varies regionally but is mainly moose, deer, and caribou. Such prey is scarce in parts of the state now. The Arctic caribou herd crashed from 240,000 in 1970 to 60,000 in 1976; wolves may be killing up to 12,000 annually. The Tanana Flats near Fairbanks once supported 6,000 to 12,000 moose; now, the region contains only 3,000. In southeastern Alaska, deer herds thinned by severe winters have been kept at dangerously low levels by wolves. The wolves also starved, as deer became depleted.

THIRD BODY PARAGRAPH: CONCEDES THAT WOLVES ALONE ARE NOT TO BLAME

Besides severe winters, there are a number of other reasons behind these alarming trends, including hunting by humans. Game is the main food for many wilderness residents. Nevertheless, in specific areas, there is little doubt that wolves have decimated moose, caribou, and deer.

CONCLUSION: REINFORCES MAIN IDEA

For many years, Alaska's game managers have demonstrated good wolf management. Now, unless the state can control soaring wolf numbers in specific areas, by humane and strictly controlled means, Alaska stands to lose many more caribou, moose, and deer—and, ultimately, its wolves.

JIM REARDEN
National Wildlife

WRITING ACTIVITY ◀ I ▶ *Analyzing Persuasive Essays*

The following essay takes a different view of the plan to eliminate some of Alaska's wolves. Read it carefully and answer the questions that follow it. The paragraphs are numbered for easy reference.

Wolves as Scapegoats

(1) The Alaska fish and game department has chosen the wolf as a scapegoat for its own disastrous mistakes in game management. In 1970, the Nelchina caribou herd numbered only 10,000 animals. Five years before, there had been 80,000. The same trend has been true of the Tanana moose herd. The great western Arctic caribou herd, which in 1972 contained 240,000 animals, numbered only 60,000 in 1977.

(2) Is this decimation of the western Arctic herd the wolf's doing? State game officials have declared that it is. However, they have no research to support that view. They do not even have a scientific count of how many wolves there are. Undaunted by what they do not know, they are determined to use aerial gunner teams to kill eight out of every ten western Arctic wolves. The caribou they want to defend, however, are the same ones they allowed hunters to kill without limits or closed seasons from 1959 until April of 1976. In 1976 alone, native hunters killed over 30,000 western Arctic caribou.

(3) In January of 1977, the fish and game department was caught trying to hush up the results of its own research on the Nelchina moose herd—research designed to demonstrate scientifically, once and for all, what effect wolves have on calf survival. The research showed no significant wolf impact. So, instead, the department released to the press totally unscientific data.

(4) One department official in Anchorage said in April of 1977 that if every wolf in Alaska were killed, the western Arctic caribou herd would still not be helped. He added that, because the natives in the area were paying so little attention to the new seasons and limits set by the state, nothing could save the herd.

(5) In the spring of 1977, one house of the Alaska legislature passed a bill to ban all cow and calf moose hunting. We can hope that the blame for wildlife crises will now be placed where it belongs—on the shoulders of the Alaska fish and game department.   James L. Pitts, *National Wildlife*

1. What is the thesis statement of this essay?
2. What statistic in the introduction is also used in the opposing essay by Jim Rearden in his essay on pages 183–184?
3. Which is a better statement of the main idea of paragraph 2?
   a. Wolves are not responsible for the decimation of the western Arctic herd.
   b. Game officials have insufficient evidence to blame wolves for the decimation of the western Arctic herd.
4. What statistic in paragraph 2 is omitted from Jim Rearden's opposing essay? What persuasive purpose does it serve here, in the essay by James L. Pitts?
5. One of Rearden's arguments is that the Alaska fish and game department has been doing a good job. What information in paragraph 3 of Pitts's essay counters that argument?
6. To what authority does Pitts refer in paragraph 4?
7. Which is a better statement of the main idea of paragraph 4?
   a. Immoderate hunting threatens caribou more than wolves do.
   b. Even a department official believes that immoderate hunting threatens caribou more than wolves do.
8. Which word in the last sentence of paragraph 3 is repeated in the first sentence of paragraph 4 as a transition?
9. The last sentence of the essay restates an idea and adds a new emphasis. Write the earlier sentence to which it refers.
10. Explain in a paragraph which essay you found more persuasive.

Facts and Opinions

Every persuasive essay is composed of two types of statements: facts and opinions. The soundness of the essay hangs on the writer's awareness of the difference between the two; facts can be proven true while opinions cannot.

Writing Terms A **fact** is a statement that can be proved. An **opinion** is a judgment that cannot be proved.

One plus one equals two. That is a fact, for it can be demonstrated within your own experience. If you add one pencil or orange or shoe to another, you will always end up with two. Some facts, however, cannot be verified by you directly, as shown in the following example.

FACT During a solar eclipse, the moon's shadow covers the sun.

Even if you have witnessed a solar eclipse, you cannot state from your own experience that the moon's shadow was the cause. Astronomers, however, can establish the cause by using sophisticated observations and calculations. Therefore, statements by experts can be used to verify facts that lie outside your experience.

Writing Tip Use your own experience and reliable authorities to verify facts.

Opinions can vary from person to person, and they can take the form of judgments, interpretations, predictions, or preferences. The following are some examples of opinions.

OPINIONS *Dick Tracy* was a better movie than *Batman*.

To protect riders in accidents, car manufacturers should be required to install air bags in cars.

Alfred, Lord Tennyson is the most highly respected English poet.

Broccoli tastes better than spinach.

By the early twenty-first century, robots will be part of every household.

Opinions, by definition, cannot be proved. Some, however, can at least be supported with convincing evidence. Opinions that can be backed up with facts are called *arguable propositions*.

187

Writing Term An **arguable proposition** is an opinion that can be supported by factual evidence.

Arguable propositions, as their name implies, can be argued. Opinions that express only personal preferences, on the other hand, are not worth arguing, for there are no facts to support them.

ARGUABLE PROPOSITION The performers' waiting room should be painted green. [Experiments have provided evidence that green has a calming effect.]

PREFERENCE Green is a prettier color than blue. [No facts are available to back up this statement.]

Always remain alert to the distinction between fact and opinion and remember that opinions need to be supported by facts, not by other opinions. As a writer be sure to back up every opinion with facts. As a reader be on your guard for unsupported opinions and for opinions offered up as facts. Remember that only arguable propositions form a solid basis for a persuasive essay.

WRITING ACTIVITY *Identifying Arguable Propositions*

Identify each statement as *an arguable proposition* or a *preference*.

Taking Off

1. Airplane rides are more exciting than train rides.
2. There should be more rigorous training for flight mechanics in order to improve airline safety.
3. Aircraft of the future will be controlled almost entirely by computers.
4. An airplane takeoff is the most thrilling sight there is.
5. Air-traffic controllers should have more frequent rest periods in order to perform more effectively.
6. Takeoff is the most exciting part of a flight.
7. Takeoff is one of the riskiest parts of a flight.
8. Passengers should pay careful attention to the safety instructions at the beginning of each flight.
9. Flying remains a relatively safe way to travel.
10. After a number of flights, flying loses its excitement and becomes monotonous.

The Sorrows of the King, Henri Matisse, 1952, Paper Cutout

WRITING ACTIVITY *Supporting Opinions with Facts*

Write one fact that, if verified, you would accept as evidence to back up each of the following arguable propositions.

EXAMPLE   The guitar is one of the most versatile of musical instruments.

POSSIBLE ANSWER   The guitar is used in playing folk, classical, and rock music.

1. Too much television watching can have a harmful effect on performance in school.
2. Raising fines can help to keep people from double-parking.
3. Americans should consume more fruits and vegetables.
4. Electrical appliances should not be used near water.
5. New sources of energy should be developed.
6. On hot days joggers should run only in the morning or evening.
7. Using a computer will make writing easier and more fun.
8. Police work has become increasingly dangerous.
9. Eva Ramirez is a better candidate for mayor than Nelson Gooden.
10. The minimum age for a driver's license should be eighteen.

189

WRITING ACTIVITY *Analyzing Persuasive Writing*

In a newspaper or other publication, choose an editorial or some other piece of persuasive writing. List the opinions and facts that are found in the text. Then identify each opinion as either a preference or an arguable proposition. Finally, write a paragraph using the arguable propositions to support your analysis. Save your work for later use.

WRITING ACTIVITY *Writing on Your Own*

WRITING
ABOUT THE
THEME
  Write an arguable proposition of one sentence arising from your own experience in school. Then list three facts you could use to back up your proposition. Finally, with your teacher's permission, exchange papers with a classmate and check the following points.

1. Is the proposition arguable?

2. Is it supported by facts and not more opinions?

3. Are the facts verifiable?

Reasoning

As you have seen, personal experience and the statements of experts can provide evidence for an opinion. However, facts by themselves do not form a solid argument. What do the facts mean? Why are they relevant? How do they fit together? Interpreting facts in these ways to construct an argument requires reasoning power, or logic.

Logic is clear, organized thinking that leads to a reasonable conclusion. To understand how logical thinking applies to persuasive writing, you must understand inductive reasoning and deductive reasoning.

Inductive Reasoning and Generalizations *Inductive reasoning* is a formal term for something that you do quite naturally, that is, use known facts to make a generalization. A *generalization* is a statement about a group of things based on observations about a few items in that group. If one or two encounters with roses have left you sneezing, you may conclude that roses make you sneeze. You draw a general conclusion from specific facts, or evidence.

Writing Tip Use **inductive reasoning** to form a qualified general conclusion based on known facts about particulars.

The following chain of thoughts about naval officers is another example of inductive reasoning.

SPECIFIC FACT	A fleet admiral is the highest officer in the navy.
SPECIFIC FACT	A fleet admiral wears one large gold stripe and four smaller gold stripes.
SPECIFIC FACT	An admiral is lower in rank than a fleet admiral.
SPECIFIC FACT	An admiral wears one large gold stripe and three smaller gold stripes.
GENERAL CONCLUSION	The rank of navy officers can probably be detected by the number of gold stripes on their uniforms.

Notice the word *probably* in the general conclusion. Unless the stripes of every naval officer are examined, the conclusion cannot be stated with absolute certainty. The conclusions reached by the inductive method should always be qualified or limited in some way. A conclusion may be reasonable and sound, but it is not a fact. It is always open to new evidence. Suppose, for example, you learned these new facts about the stripes on Navy uniforms.

NEW FACT	A commodore wears one two-inch gold stripe.
NEW FACT	An ensign wears one half-inch gold stripe.
NEW FACT	A commodore has a much higher rank than an ensign.

The first conclusion equated rank with the number of gold stripes. However, if both a commodore and an ensign wear just one stripe, that conclusion cannot hold. The conclusion, however, can be expanded to accommodate the new facts as follows.

NEW CONCLUSION	The rank of navy officers can probably be detected by the number and size of the gold stripes on their uniforms.

Hasty Generalizations   Beware of *hasty generalizations*—generalizations that are too broad. If a poodle growls at you, you cannot conclude that all poodles are unfriendly. If your family does not like anchovies, you cannot conclude that no one likes anchovies.

HASTY GENERALIZATION	No one ever likes anchovies.
SOUND GENERALIZATION	Some people do not like anchovies.

Boston Common at Twilight,
Frederick Childe Hassam,
1885–6, Oil on Canvas,
42 x 60", Gift of
Miss Maud E. Appleton

The writer of the following paragraph attempts to use inductive reasoning but arrives at a conclusion too hastily.

Model: *Hasty Generalization*

SPECIFIC FACTS

If you dislike hot weather, you need to avoid not only the obvious places in the South and Southwest, but also a more surprising "hot spot" in the Northeast. I have visited Boston three times, and every time I have been there the temperature has been 90 degrees or above. My first visit took place in May of 1987. On the day I arrived, the mercury reached 95 degrees. I was there again in the summer of 1989, when the temperature hit 98 degrees. In late September of 1991, I passed through Boston again, and even at that time of year, the temperature reached 91 degrees. Heat haters, beware!

HASTY
GENERALIZATION

Boston is one of the hottest cities in the nation.

The writer bases the generalization on only three days over a four-year period. In addition, the writer fails to compare Boston's temperatures with those of other cities. The hasty generalization could have been avoided if the writer had followed these guidelines.

Avoiding Hasty Generalizations

1. Examine a sufficient number of facts and examples.
2. Be sure your examples are representative of the whole group.
3. Check reliable authorities to confirm the generalization.
4. Be able to explain any exceptions.
5. Limit the generalization by using words like *some, many, most.*
6. Avoid words like *all, complete, always, never, none.*

WRITING ACTIVITY *Using Inductive Reasoning*

Read each set of facts below. Then write a generalization based on the facts. Be sure to limit your generalization appropriately.

EXAMPLE   FACTS   Two weeks ago my new computer jammed. On the day it jammed, the weather was very hot and humid. Yesterday, on a hot and humid day, my computer jammed again.

    GENERALIZATION   High temperature and high humidity sometimes cause a computer to jam.

1. FACTS   At my brother's college, my cousin's college, and my friend's college, more students major in business than in liberal arts.

2. FACTS   *The Day the Earth Stood Still, E.T.,* and *Close Encounters of the Third Kind* are all science-fiction movies about visitors from outer space. All have remained popular.

3. FACTS   When the Chicago White Sox meet the Toronto Blue Jays in Chicago, "The Star-Spangled Banner" is played before "O Canada." When the Chicago White Sox meet the Toronto Blue Jays in Toronto, "O Canada" is played before "The Star-Spangled Banner."

4. FACTS   In winter, goats, sheep, and antelope leave the alpine zone of mountains for lower snow-free slopes. In winter squirrels and marmots in the alpine zone hibernate.

5. FACTS   Two friends who moved to the country are bored and unhappy. They put their house up for sale.

Deductive Reasoning   While induction moves from the particular to the general, deduction moves from the general to the particular. In *deductive reasoning,* you begin with a general statement and then apply it to a particular case. The following chain of thoughts illustrates the deductive process.

GENERALIZATION   No mail is delivered on legal holidays.

PARTICULAR   Today is a legal holiday.

CONCLUSION   Therefore, no mail will be delivered today.

Writing Tip   Use **deductive reasoning** to prove that what is true about a group (generalization) will be true about an individual member of that group (particular).

The steps in the deductive process can be expressed in a three-part statement called a *syllogism*. Each part of the syllogism has a name.

MAJOR PREMISE   All members of the jazz band are seniors.
MINOR PREMISE   Kristin is a member of the jazz band.
CONCLUSION   Therefore, Kristin is a senior.

The following diagram illustrates how the conclusion must follow from the premises.

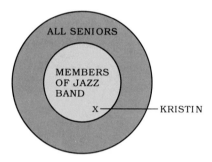

Since the smaller group is part of the larger group, and Kristin is in the smaller group, then she must also be in the larger group. As long as the premises are true, then the conclusion, like the one about Kristin, is also true, or *sound*. However, if either or both of the premises are false, then the conclusion is also false, or *unsound*.

In the following example, on the other hand, the conclusion is not logical even if both of the premises are true.

MAJOR PREMISE   All members of the jazz band are seniors.
MINOR PREMISE   Kristin is a senior.
CONCLUSION   Therefore, Kristin is a member of the jazz band.

The following diagram shows why the reasoning here is not logical.

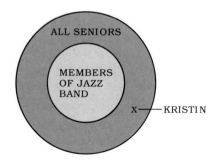

The fact that Kristin belongs to the larger group, seniors, does not guarantee that she belongs to the smaller group, the jazz band. The conclusion is illogical, or *invalid*.

Writing Term A syllogism is **sound** if the premises are true. A syllogism is **valid** if the reasoning is logical.

WRITING ACTIVITY *Recognizing Flaws in Deductive Reasoning*

Each syllogism below is unsound or invalid. Write *unsound* if the premises are not true. Write *invalid* if the reasoning is illogical.

1. All late papers will be given failing grades.
   Bill's paper was given a failing grade.
   Therefore, Bill's paper was late.
2. All seniors are honor students.
   Sondra is a senior.
   Therefore, Sondra is an honor student.
3. All southern states begin with the letter *M*.
   Florida is a southern state.
   Therefore, Florida begins with the letter *M*.
4. All four-legged animals are cows.
   My cat is a four-legged animal.
   Therefore, my cat is a cow.
5. All cats are four-legged animals.
   My cow is a four-legged animal.
   Therefore, my cow is a cat.

WRITING ACTIVITY *Using Deductive Reasoning*

Study the following example of deductive reasoning. Then supply the logical conclusion for each of the following sets of premises.

EXAMPLE All city officials live within the city boundaries. Sal Savetti is a city official.

ANSWER Therefore, Sal Savetti lives within the city boundaries.

I. All Triple Crown winners have won the Kentucky Derby. Seattle Slew was a Triple Crown winner.
2. All bowling team members must have a minimum average of 175. Carl is a bowling team member.
3. All of the fruit in this basket is either apples or oranges. This piece of fruit from the basket is not an apple.
4. All Marx brothers movies are comedies. *A Day at the Races* is a Marx Brothers movie.
5. The seniors do not have to come to school this Thursday and Friday. Jonathan is a senior.

Combining Inductive and Deductive Reasoning The arguments in a persuasive essay are not neatly arranged in three-part syllogisms. Actual reasoning normally involves a back-and-forth process of induction and deduction. For example, a writer may gather evidence in order to draw a general conclusion (induction) and then use that conclusion as the premise of a syllogism (deduction).

EVIDENCE Scientific studies have shown that walking, running, and swimming benefit the heart and lungs.
CONCLUSION Aerobic exercises benefit the body.

MAJOR PREMISE Aerobic exercises benefit the body.
MINOR PREMISE Dancing is an aerobic exercise.
CONCLUSION Therefore, dancing benefits the body.

One famous example of combining inductive and deductive reasoning is the Declaration of Independence. This document can be viewed as a persuasive essay that sought to persuade Great Britain and the rest of the world that the American colonies were justified in severing their ties with the British Crown. As you read the following excerpt from the Declaration of Independence, use the side labels to help you follow the reasoning.

Model: *Combining Inductive and Deductive Reasoning*

Declaration of Independence

MAJOR PREMISE
OF SYLLOGISM

MINOR PREMISE
OF SYLLOGISM

FACTS SUPPORTING
MINOR PREMISE

We hold these truths to be self-evident, that all men are created equal, that they are endowed by their Creator with certain unalienable Rights, that among these are Life, Liberty and the pursuit of Happiness. That to secure these rights, Governments are instituted among Men, deriving their just powers from the consent of the governed. That whenever any form of Government becomes destructive of these ends, it is the Right of the People to alter or to abolish it, and to institute new Government . . . Such has been the patient sufferance of these Colonies; and such is now the necessity which constrains them to alter their former Systems of Government. The history of the present King of Great Britain is a history of repeated injuries and usurpations, all having in direct object the establishment of an absolute Tyranny over these States. To prove this, let Facts be submitted to a candid world.

He has refused his Assent to Laws, the most wholesome and necessary for the public good.

He has combined with others to subject us to jurisdictions foreign to our constitution, and unacknowledged by our laws; giving his Assent to their Acts of pretended Legislation:

For quartering large bodies of armed troops among us:

For protecting them, by a mock Trial, from punishment for any Murders which they should commit on the Inhabitants of these States:

For cutting off our Trade with all parts of the world:

For imposing Taxes on us without our Consent:

For depriving us in many cases, of the benefits of Trial by Jury . . .

In every stage of these Oppressions We Have Petitioned for Redress in the most humble terms:

197

Our repeated Petitions have been answered only by repeated injury. A Prince, whose character is thus marked by every act which may define a Tyrant, is unfit to be the ruler of a free people . . .

We, therefore, the Representatives of the United States of America, in General Congress, Assembled, appealing to the Supreme Judge of the world for the rectitude of our intentions, do, in the Name, and by Authority of the good People of these Colonies, solemnly publish and declare, That these United Colonies are, and of Right ought to be Free and Independent States . . .

CONCLUSION OF
SYLLOGISM

The Declaration of Independence is based on a deduction that can be expressed in the following syllogism.

MAJOR PREMISE   When a government violates natural rights, the people have a right and duty to abolish it.

MINOR PREMISE   The British Crown violated the natural rights of the colonists.

CONCLUSION   Therefore, the colonists have a right and duty to break their ties with Great Britain.

Inductive reasoning also plays its part. The minor premise—that Great Britain violated the colonists' rights—is a generalization based on specific facts presented about the behavior of the king.

WRITING ACTIVITY 9 *Analyzing Persuasive Writing*

Continue your analysis of the selection that you chose for Writing Activity 4 or find some other piece of persuasive writing on the subject of education. Then write a paragraph of analysis, answering questions like these.

1. What inductive reasoning is involved? That is, what facts are presented to support each general conclusion?
2. Is the conclusion sound or is it hasty?
3. What deductive reasoning is involved? That is, what general statement is applied to a particular case?
4. Is the reasoning valid? Is it sound?
5. Where and how are inductive and deductive reasoning used together?

Writing a Persuasive Essay

As you prepare to write a persuasive essay of your own, always keep your purpose in sight. Your efforts at every stage are directed at finding a means of convincing the reader to think a certain way or to act a certain way. Clear, logical arguments and a strong, consistent approach to your position are your most effective tools.

Prewriting

The prewriting stage is the most critical in the development of a persuasive essay. Take time to prepare and organize your arguments thoroughly before you write. The more carefully you think through your position, the more forcefully you will be able to present it. In the prewriting stage, you will choose your subject, develop your thesis, and gather and organize your evidence.

Choosing a Subject   The world is full of opinions, but not every opinion makes a good subject for a persuasive essay. Only certain issues will stir your thoughts and your emotions. Furthermore, of the many opinions you hold, only some will be arguable propositions. Others, such as a liking for apples over pears, would be difficult to defend. Only an issue that you care about and that you can support makes an appropriate subject for a persuasive essay.

Try to be more aware of the controversial issues all around you—in the newspapers, on TV, in your school, and in your home. Notice matters about which you can say, "I think" or "I believe." Brainstorm or freewrite answers to questions such as "What do I care about?" When you have accumulated a list of possible subjects, use the following guidelines to help you choose among them.

Guidelines for Choosing a Subject

1. Choose an issue that has at least two sides.
2. Choose an issue that you feel strongly about.
3. Choose an issue for which there is an audience whose belief or behavior you would like to influence.
4. Choose an issue that has a position you can support with facts, examples, and reasons.

WRITING ACTIVITY *Brainstorming Subjects*

Brainstorm or freewrite completions to each of the following statements. Keep your answers for later use.

1. The things I care about at school are . . .
2. The things I worry about at school are . . .
3. The things that seem to concern other people at school are . . .
4. Some things I would like to change at school are . . .
5. If I had a million dollars to give to the school system, I would want it used for . . .

WRITING ACTIVITY *Writing on Your Own*

WRITING
ABOUT THE
THEME
     Use your notes from Writing Activity 10, your journal, school publications, and other sources to list possible subjects about an educational issue for a persuasive essay. Your audience will be the local school board. Then, with the help of the guidelines on page 199, select an appropriate subject. Save your work.

Developing a Thesis Statement   Once you have selected a subject, you should develop a thesis statement. Often the statement will be a recommendation that includes a word such as *should, ought,* or *must.* Stay away from statements of fact or preference, for they do not make suitable thesis statements for a persuasive essay.

        FACT   In some areas wolves are near extinction.
   PREFERENCE   I am horrified by the killing of wolves.
      THESIS   Laws protecting wolves must be strengthened.

     After you write your thesis, ask yourself the following questions. If your thesis does not meet all of these guidelines, you should rethink your position or look for a more appropriate issue.

Guidelines for Developing a Thesis Statement

1. Can you state the thesis simply in one sentence?
2. Is the statement either a judgment or a recommendation rather than a fact or a preference?
3. Is the point of view debatable as you have expressed it? Can you think of any opposing arguments?

WRITING ACTIVITY *Choosing a Suitable Thesis*

Write *suitable* or *unsuitable* to tell whether each statement would make a suitable thesis for a persuasive essay. If the statement is unsuitable, write the number of the guideline it violates.

I. Despite its great potential for education and communication, TV has developed into a negative influence in our society, and we must somehow find a way to reverse that trend without violating the principles of free speech on which our nation was founded.

2. Our society is becoming increasingly dependent on computers.

3. We must learn to make better use of the sun for energy if we are to conquer the problems of pollution.

4. The incidence of violent crime in our nation is horrifying.

5. We must all learn to respect one another more.

WRITING ACTIVITY *Writing on Your Own*

WRITING
ABOUT THE
THEME

Write a one-sentence thesis statement on your subject from Writing Activity 11. Remember that your purpose is to persuade your school board about an educational issue. Does the thesis meet the guidelines on page 200? If not, revise the thesis or start over with a new subject from your list.

Writing Is Thinking

Evaluating Evidence

When you write to persuade, you make your argument convincing by presenting evidence that strongly supports your opinions. When you choose facts, examples, incidents, statistics, and expert opinions, you should use the skill of *evaluating* to judge each piece of evidence critically as to its strength in support of your position. To evaluate a piece of evidence, use the following criteria.

- Is evidence clearly related to the thesis and up-to-date?
- Is the source of the evidence reliable?
- Is the evidence unbiased and objective?

Suppose, for example, that you are arguing in favor of allowing seventeen-year-olds in your state to vote in primary elections. The following chart shows how you could evaluate evidence on this issue.

Evidence	Evaluation
• Polls show that seventeen-year-olds are as knowledgeable as eighteen-year-olds.	• Supports thesis— explains logical reason to extend vote to seventeen-year-olds.
• A low percentage of eighteen-year-olds turn out to vote.	• Does not support thesis—evidence focuses on eighteen-year-olds.
• Seventeen-year-olds claim that such a law will encourage civic awareness.	• Does not support thesis—source of evidence may be biased and not objective.

Thinking Practice   Choose one of the arguable propositions below or one based on an issue that is important to you. Make a chart like the one above to evaluate the evidence for your position.

1. Leash laws should be strictly enforced in public parks.
2. Public libraries should be open longer hours.
3. Good personal grooming is essential to obtaining a job.

Developing an Argument   Once you are satisfied with your thesis statement, you should gather and evaluate evidence to support it. First think about your audience. List arguments they might find convincing and then search for the appropriate evidence. You will want to find not only material that supports your position but also material that refutes it so that you can offer counterarguments. Your evidence will normally take the form of facts, examples, incidents, reasoning, and expert opinions. This needed information can be found in library reference material, books, magazines, newspapers, personal interviews, and your own experience. Once you have collected evidence and evaluated it, use the following guidelines to help you build an argument.

Guidelines for Developing an Argument

1. List pros and cons (and positions in between) in your prewriting notes and be prepared to address the opposing views point by point.
2. To support your opinion, use facts—not more opinions—and refer to well-respected experts and authorities who support your opinion.
3. If the opposing view has a good point, admit it. *Conceding a point* in this way will strengthen your credibility.
4. Use logical reasoning, both deductive and inductive, to pull your evidence together and draw conclusions from it.
5. Express your arguments in polite and reasonable language.

WRITING ACTIVITY   *Listing Pros and Cons*

For each of the following thesis statements, list three facts, examples, incidents, or personal experiences that support the statement and three that oppose it. Save your notes for later use.

1. A greater percentage of our tax money should go to improving the quality of education.
2. We should make our holidays less commercial.
3. We should live for the moment and not worry about the future.
4. The 55-mile-per-hour speed limit should be raised throughout the country.
5. For many people a college education is the most important investment for the future.

Organizing an Argument After you have gathered the information you need to build your argument, you should organize your ideas in a logical way. Many persuasive essays use order of importance or developmental order. Spatial order and chronological order, however, do not usually serve the persuasive purpose as well. Whatever organization you choose, however, you will need to use transitions like the following to guide the reader through your arguments. *(See pages 99–102.)*

Transitions Showing Concession or Contrast		
while it is true that	nonetheless	despite
although	however	even though
admittedly	still	nevertheless

WRITING ACTIVITY *Organizing Persuasive Ideas*

Choose one thesis from Writing Activity 14 and decide which side you want to support. Then follow the instructions below.

1. Amend the thesis statement as necessary to express your view.
2. List the three supporting points from least to most important.
3. Assign each point a Roman numeral as in an outline.
4. Add at least two supporting points under each Roman numeral. Your outline should look like this.

    I. (Least important point)
        A. (Supporting point)
        B. (Supporting point)
    II. (More important point)
        A. (Supporting point)
        B. (Supporting point)
   III. (Most important point)
        A. (Supporting point)
        B. (Supporting point)

WRITING ACTIVITY *Writing on Your Own*

WRITING
ABOUT THE
THEME
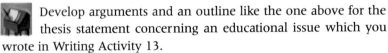
Develop arguments and an outline like the one above for the thesis statement concerning an educational issue which you wrote in Writing Activity 13.

Drafting

If you have been thorough in working through the steps of the prewriting stage, then the drafting stage should essentially be a matter of putting your prewriting notes together. Nevertheless, you may find as you write that some of your ideas need to be modified or that new ideas occur to you. Always remember that because you are beginning with a first draft, you will be able to review and rewrite.

Begin by writing your thesis, which you may want to refine. Then write an introduction that includes the thesis. Because your introduction will explain your subject and state your position, you must capture the reader's attention. Make the reader both aware of the importance of the subject and interested in what you have to say.

Next draft the body of the essay, devoting one or more paragraphs to each main topic in your outline. In addition to presenting your own supporting evidence, include counterarguments and concede points where appropriate. Also remember to add transitions to guide the reader. Finally, write a concluding paragraph that summarizes your argument and, if appropriate, urges the reader to take action.

Persuasive Language   In general you will be more persuasive if the tone of your essay is calm and reasonable. Inflamed, emotional language, on the other hand, may only convince your reader not to support your proposition.

INFLAMED   Nasty, unruly dogs are terrorizing decent citizens.

REASONABLE   We need a leash law to discourage pet owners from allowing their animals to run free.

If you choose your words carefully, however, you can make effective use of *persuasive language*—language with strong positive or negative connotations that appeals to the reader's emotions. When you use persuasive language, be sure to support statements with facts.

PERSUASIVE   Tens of thousands of our precious young people are
LANGUAGE   massacred and maimed each year by drunk drivers.

WRITING ACTIVITY   17

WRITING
ABOUT THE
THEME

Using the outline you prepared in Writing Activity 16, as well as any other prewriting notes, write a draft of your persuasive essay about education.

Revising

No matter how carefully you have prepared and drafted your essay, it can still benefit from revising. You may need to bolster your opening, strengthen your arguments, refine your language, or add evidence or counterarguments. Review your essay several times, focusing on a different aspect each time. However, reserve at least one reading to check your logic, looking especially for the fallacies discussed below. *(For information about recognizing different forms of propaganda, see pages 439–441.)*

Eliminating Logical Fallacies   A *fallacy* is a flaw in reasoning like the hasty generalization and the faulty syllogism. *(See pages 191–195.)* The following six fallacies also merit special attention, since they often surface in a poorly reasoned argument.

Attacking the Person instead of the Issue   This fallacy is often called *argumentum ad hominem,* which is Latin for "argument against the man." Writers who commit this fallacy target the character of their opponent instead of the real issue.

AD HOMINEM FALLACY	Senator Moreland has missed every important vote this year. How could his new bill have any merit?
AD HOMINEM FALLACY	Sally Jones has never been late to work. She should be mayor of our city.

Although Moreland's voting record may be irresponsible, his new bill may have merit. Promptness is not a mayor's most important quality.

Either-Or/If-Then Fallacies   Writers guilty of these fallacies assume that there are only two sides to an issue; they ignore other viewpoints. Notice how the following issues are limited to two choices.

EITHER-OR FALLACY	Either we stop using nuclear power for energy or we face certain disaster.
IF-THEN FALLACY	If you are against the new social center, then you are against the young people of our town.

In the first example, "certain disaster" might be averted by better nuclear waste management. In the second example, the plans for the social center might be faulty. Between the two extreme positions on most issues lie a number of valid viewpoints.

The Fallacy of *Non Sequitur* In Latin, the words *non sequitur* mean "it does not follow." You have already seen some examples of conclusions that do not necessarily follow from the evidence. Most *non sequiturs* are the result of illogical deductive thinking.

NON SEQUITURS   My sister liked this book; therefore, it must be good.

John's car was more expensive than mine; he must be richer than I am.

Like the fallacy of *either-or,* the *non sequitur* can neglect possible alternatives. Judgments about the quality of books vary greatly, and your sister's taste may not match your own. John may have gone into serious debt to buy an expensive car.

Confusing Chronology with Cause and Effect This fallacy assumes that whatever happens after an event was caused by that event.

CAUSE-EFFECT   On my birthday I wished that I would win something. That week I won two concert tickets in a raffle. Wishing really works!

The roof collapsed today because of yesterday's snowfall.

In the first example, only coincidence relates the two events. In the second example, the snowfall may, indeed, have contributed to the collapse of the roof. The fallacy lies in assuming that the snow was the only cause, for if the roof had been sound, it probably could have withstood the snowfall. Such errors in reasoning often result from failing to consider more than one cause.

False Analogies An *analogy* is a comparison between two things that are alike in some significant ways. A *false analogy* attempts to compare two things that are not enough alike to be logically compared.

FALSE ANALOGY   The phone company's discontinuation of my service was unfair, since even a criminal gets one phone call.

There are no logical grounds for comparing the situation of a free citizen who has not paid his or her telephone bill and that of a person arrested for a crime.

207

Begging the Question   A writer who "begs the question" builds an argument on an unproved assumption.

BEGGING THE QUESTION   That unethical doctor should not be allowed to practice medicine.

George Bernard Shaw was a great playwright because he wrote a number of superb plays.

In the first example, the writer bases the conclusion—that the doctor should not be allowed to practice medicine—on the unproved assumption that the doctor is unethical. The second sentence provides an example of circular reasoning, which affords no proof. All the sentence says is that Shaw was a great playwright because he was a great playwright.

WRITING ACTIVITY *Recognizing Fallacies*

Write the name of the fallacy committed in each statement.

attacking the person instead of the issue	confusing chronology with cause and effect
either-or/if-then	false analogy
non sequitur	begging the question

  1. Either you allow the hunting of wolves or you end up with slaughtered farm animals.
  2. The dog is barking; someone must have rung the doorbell.
  3. The sun reappeared after the cave dwellers chanted a hymn during the eclipse. The chanting must have caused the sun to reappear.
  4. I didn't hear Jennifer's speech, but I know I disagree with it. She's always so disorganized!
  5. These unnecessary taxes are a burden on taxpayers.
  6. Just as a car needs gasoline to keep running, a hospital needs volunteers.
  7. If you don't clean your room, then you obviously do not care what people think about you.
  8. The show was a flop; the actors must not have rehearsed enough.
  9. Since I have been running regularly, my grades have improved. Running must make me smarter.
  10. The shortsighted plan to cut the trees down will have unpleasant future consequences.

Using a Revision Checklist   Use the following checklist to help you revise your persuasive essay.

Revision Checklist

CHECKING YOUR INTRODUCTION

1. Does your thesis statement express your opinion clearly?
2. Does the introduction capture attention?
3. Are your emotional appeals, if any, sincere and restrained?

CHECKING YOUR BODY PARAGRAPHS

4. Does each paragraph have a topic sentence? *(See page 94.)*
5. Is each paragraph unified and coherent? *(See pages 99–102.)*
6. Have you chosen an appropriate order for your arguments and followed that ordering consistently? *(See page 204.)*
7. Have you supported your main points? *(See page 187.)*
8. Have you evaluated your evidence? *(See page 202.)*
9. Have you considered counterarguments? *(See page 203.)*
10. Did you concede a point if appropriate? *(See page 203.)*
11. Did you avoid logical fallacies? *(See pages 206–208.)*

CHECKING YOUR CONCLUSION

12. Does your conclusion summarize the main points?
13. Do you restate your thesis forcefully?
14. Have you asked your reader to take some action, if that was your purpose?
15. Are your emotional appeals, if any, sincere and restrained?

CHECKING YOUR WORDS AND SENTENCES

16. Are your sentences varied and concise? *(See pages 63–71.)*
17. Did you avoid faulty sentences? *(See pages 72–79.)*
18. Did you use specific words with correct connotations? *(See pages 56–57.)*

WRITING ACTIVITY ⟨19⟩  *Writing on Your Own*

WRITING
ABOUT THE
THEME
If your teacher permits, choose a partner and exchange essays from Writing Activity 17. Then use the above checklist to suggest revisions in your partner's work. Refer to the checklist again as you go over your partner's suggestions and review your own persuasive essay about education.

Editing and Publishing

Grammar in the Writing Process

In the excerpt from *Hard Times* that you read, Dickens describes Thomas Gradgrind as "A man of realities. A man of facts and calculations. A man who proceeds upon the principle that two and two are four, and nothing over. . . . " In other words Thomas Gradgrind was a man of precision and exactness. Often your writing needs to be like Thomas Gradgrind—precise and exact.

The chapter called "A Writer's Glossary of Usage" can help you make your writing precise and exact. In that chapter you will find an alphabetical list of commonly made writing errors. A good habit to form would be to turn to this chapter each time you edit a piece of writing, skim over the list, and check those items you have used. Following are a few examples of the items you will find in the Glossary. As you look at them, you will occasionally see the words *standard* and *nonstandard. Standard English* is the form you should use when you write; *nonstandard English* should be avoided in writing. *(For more information about standard and nonstandard English, see pages 729–730.)*

advice, advise   *Advice* is a noun that means "a recommendation." *Advise* is a verb that means "to recommend."

ADVICE   Thomas Gradgrind gave the children good **advice.**

ADVISE   He **advised** them to think "Fact, fact, fact!"

among, between   *Among* is used when referring to three or more people or things. *Between* is used when referring to two people or things.

AMONG   Gradgrind stood **among** the children.

BETWEEN   The conversation **between** Gradgrind and Sissy Jupe was quite short.

bad, badly   *Bad* is an adjective and often follows a linking verb. *Badly* is used as an adverb and often follows an action verb. In the first two examples on the next page, *felt* is used as a linking verb. *(For more information about adverbs and comparison of adverbs, see pages 715–718.)*

210

NONSTANDARD Sissy Jupe felt **badly** when she could not answer.

STANDARD Sissy Jupe felt **bad** when she could not answer.

STANDARD Mr. Gradgrind thought she had performed **badly.**

double negative Words such as *hardly, never, no, not,* and *nobody* are considered negatives. Do not use two negatives to express one negative meaning. *(See page 721 for a complete list of negative words.)*

NONSTANDARD Sissy Jupe had**n't never** heard of a farrier.

STANDARD Sissy Jupe had**n't** heard of a farrier.

STANDARD Sissy Jupe had **never** heard of a farrier.

principal, principle As an adjective *principal* means "main" or "chief." As a noun *principal* means "the head of a school" or "leader." *Principle* is a noun that is synonymous with *law, truth,* or *doctrine.*

PRINCIPAL The **principal** for the day was Mr. Gradgrind.

PRINCIPLE He tried to teach the children an important **principle.**

than, then *Than* is usually a subordinating conjunction and is used for comparisons. *Then* is an adverb that means "at that time" or "next." *(For other Glossary entries and practice in writing all of the Glosssary items correctly, see pages 728-751.)*

THAN Bitzer seemed smarter **than** Sissy.

THEN Mr. Gradgrind first talked to Sissy and **then** to Bitzer.

Editing Checklist

1. Is your essay written in standard English? *(See pages 729–730.)*
2. Have you checked your writing with "A Writer's Glossary of Usage"? *(See pages 728–750.)*

WRITING ACTIVITY 20 *Writing on Your Own*

WRITING ABOUT THE THEME   **Editing** Use the checklist above and the Editing checklist on page 38 to guide you through the editing of your essay about education from Writing Activity 19. Then write a final copy.

Publishing Ask your guidance counselor or one of your teachers to read your essay.

A Writer Writes

  A Proposal for a New School Course

PURPOSE: to persuade your school administration to offer a
specific new course

AUDIENCE: your school community

Prewriting   What subjects do you wish were offered at your school?
Why? For example, would you like to learn how to be a wise shopper?
Influence TV programming? Buy stock? Help the environment? Choose
a career? Fix a car? Identify the stars? Speak Japanese? Prepare to
write a letter to be printed in the school newspaper in which you
present a favorable evaluation of a course of interest to you. Your letter
will also be sent to the principal and other school officials. Your purpose will be to persuade school officials to offer the course.

STEP 1: To help you explore some subjects, brainstorm or freewrite completions to the following sentences. Use your imagination to include subjects that are challenging and original.

1. If I could study anything I like, I would study . . .
2. It is important for young people today to understand . . .
3. After I graduate, I will need to know how to . . .

STEP 2: Speak to students at other schools and find out what different or unusual courses are offered in your area. Then explore in a library what courses are taught in other states and in other countries. After you review all your notes, list the subjects that interest you most. For each subject jot down facts, examples, and reasons to support its being taught. For example, is it practical? Will it motivate students to do more? Will it help students cope in today's world? Is it something from which students can derive benefit throughout their lives?

STEP 3: Choose a subject that you can support effectively and write about enthusiastically.

STEP 4: Write a one-sentence thesis in the form of a recommendation that a certain subject should be offered at your school.

STEP 5: Speak to teachers and other students to find out their reactions to your recommendation. Then build an argument to support it, using the guidelines on page 203.

STEP 6: Organize your ideas in outline form based on order of importance or developmental order.

Drafting   Draft your letter, keeping your audience and purpose in mind. Remember that you are addressing adults in a position of authority and choose your language, tone, and content accordingly. Feel free to make use of humor, persuasive language, and emotional appeals but suit all of these to your audience and back them with facts.

Revising   Try to read your letter to one or more adult listeners and ask for suggestions. Do your listeners find the letter persuasive? Can they spot any logical fallacies? Then use the Revision Checklist on page 209 to go over your work.

Editing and Publishing   Go over your letter for grammatical and mechanical errors, using the Editing Checklists on pages 38 and 211 as a reminder. Then copy it neatly in appropriate letter form and submit it to your school newspaper.

WRITING
ABOUT THE
THEME ## Independent Writing

In your journal you have been writing about issues that have come up at your school. Some of these probably relate to critical questions in education today—such as effective courses of study, student motivation, budget restrictions, and parental participation. While such matters seem overwhelming, they—like all big issues—are made up of many little situations that can be dealt with by individuals. What small action could you take to advance a bigger cause? For example, could you organize a tutoring service? Help out with day care for young children? Form a cleanup squad? Paint a mural? Write a proposal for a student-faculty disciplinary committee? Help form some new school clubs or other groups? Think of a constructive activity you could participate in. Then propose it in an essay and submit it to the editor of your school or local newspaper.

Creative Writing

The selection from *Hard Times* at the beginning of this chapter included some interesting ideas for designs on carpets, wallpaper, and crockery. Imagine that the gentlemen who put forth these ideas have become interior decorators and have hired you to create their advertising. Write a magazine advertisement or a TV commercial to advertise their unique decorating services.

WRITING
ABOUT THE
THEME ## Writing about Literature

Satire is a work of literature that often uses exaggeration to ridicule something that is wrong with some aspect of human behavior or with society in general. Write a paragraph that explains what Dickens was satirizing in the excerpt from *Hard Times*. Include specific examples from the literature to support your explanation.

Writing in Other Subject Areas

Biology/Chemistry   Using your knowledge of the makeup, or chemistry, of the human body, write a persuasive essay convincing people to avoid—or consume—certain foods.

Government   Read some political columns and editorials in the newspaper to find examples of logical fallacies. Then write a letter to the editor pointing out the fallacy or fallacies.

Checklist

Writing Essays to Persuade

Prewriting

✔ Use brainstorming, freewriting, or clustering to identify subjects about which you have strong opinions. *(See pages 199–200.)*

✔ Develop a thesis statement that states your opinion. Then collect the evidence needed to support it. *(See pages 200–201.)*

✔ Use your own experiences and reliable authorities to verify facts. *(See page 203.)*

✔ Develop an argument by listing pros and cons, facts and examples, and counterarguments. *(See pages 203–204.)*

✔ Construct an argument by using logical reasoning: inductive and/or deductive. *(See pages 190–198.)*

✔ Avoid hasty generalizations, unsound syllogisms, and invalid syllogisms. *(See pages 191–195.)*

Drafting

✔ Draft an introduction that presents the issue and states your opinion in the thesis statement. *(See page 205.)*

✔ Draft the body of the essay, presenting facts, reasons, statistics, incidents, examples, the testimony of experts, and other kinds of evidence to support your opinion. *(See page 205.)*

✔ Draft a conclusion that provides a summary and a strong closing that drives home your opinion. *(See page 205.)*

Revising

✔ Revise to eliminate logical fallacies—including false analogies and non sequiturs. *(See pages 206–208.)*

✔ Use the Revision Checklist. *(See page 209.)*

Editing and Publishing

✔ Use the Editing Checklists to correct errors in grammar, spelling, and mechanics. *(See pages 38 and 211.)*

✔ Follow standard manuscript form and make a neat final copy of your work. Then publish your essay in an appropriate form.

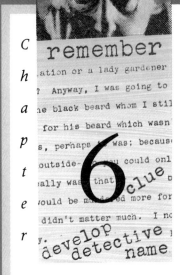

C
h
a
p
t
e
r

6 Writing Personal Essays

Part 1 Reading to Write

THEME: *Memories*

How good is your memory? Do you remember what you ate for dinner a week ago? Can you recall what you wore on this day a month ago? Some people who cannot answer questions like these may still be able to tell you with great precision and accuracy what they did on a certain day six years ago! How the memory works—selecting only some items and events to remember and forgetting the others—is one of the most fascinating mysteries of the human mind.

Although how the memory works may not be clear, the importance of memories to people is very clear. Your memories account for much of what you are today. They are your past, your history, and therefore the foundation on which you build your life. If you are able to remember a time, for example, when you handled a difficult situation, you will have more confidence in your ability to handle the next difficult situation you face.

In the following excerpt from her autobiography, the mystery writer Agatha Christie recounts a memory that was critical in her development as a writer. As you read this excerpt, think about why you remember some experiences more vividly than others. Why do you think, for instance, that people tend to remember positive experiences more than they remember negative experiences?

216

from

Agatha Christie:
An Autobiography

A g a t h a   C h r i s t i e

It was while I was working in the dispensary that I first conceived the idea of writing a detective story. . . . My present work seemed to offer a favorable opportunity. Unlike nursing, where there always was something to do, dispensing consisted of slack or busy periods. Sometimes I would be on duty alone in the afternoon with hardly anything to do but sit about. Having seen that the stock bottles were full and attended to, one was at liberty to do anything one pleased except leave the dispensary. I began considering what kind of a detective story I could write. Since I was surrounded by poisons, perhaps it was natural that death by poisoning should be the method I selected. I settled on one fact which seemed to me to have possibilities. I toyed with the idea, liked it, and finally accepted it. Then I went on to the *dramatis personae.*[1] Who should be poisoned? Who would poison him or her? When? Where? How? Why? And all the rest of it. It would have to be very much of an *intime*[2] murder, owing to the particular way it was done; it would have to be all in the family, so to speak. There would naturally have to be a detective. At that date I was well steeped in the Sherlock Holmes tradition. So I considered detectives. Not like Sherlock Holmes, of course: I must invent one of my own, and he would also have a friend as a kind of butt or stooge—that would not be too difficult. I returned to thoughts of my other characters. Who was to be murdered? A husband could murder his wife—that seemed to be the most usual kind of murder. I could, of course,

1. **dramatis personae** [dram′ə tis pər sō′nē]: The actors or characters in a play or story (Latin).
2. **intime** [ăn′tēm′]: Intimate (French).

have a very *unusual* kind of murder for a very *unusual* motive, but that did not appeal to me artistically. The whole point of a *good* detective story was that it must be somebody obvious but at the same time, for some reason, you would then find that it was *not* obvious, that he could not possibly have done it. Though really, of course, he *had* done it. At that point I got confused, and went away and made up a couple of bottles of extra hypochlorous lotion so that I should be fairly free of work the next day.

I went on playing with my idea for some time. Bits of it began to grow. I saw the murderer now. He would have to be rather sinister-looking. He would have a black beard—that appeared to me at that time very sinister. There were some acquaintances who had recently come to live near us—the husband had a black beard, and he had a wife who was older than himself and who was very rich. Yes, I thought, that might do as a basis. I considered it at some length. It might do, but it was not entirely satisfactory. The man in question would, I was sure, never murder anybody. I took my mind away from them and decided once and for all that it is not good thinking about real people—you must create your characters for yourself. Someone you see in a tram or a train or a restaurant is a possible starting point, because you can make up something for yourself about them.

Sure enough, next day, when I was sitting in a tram, I saw just what I wanted: *a man with a black beard, sitting next to an elderly lady who was chatting like a magpie.* I didn't think I'd have *her,* but I thought *he* would do admirably. Sitting a little way beyond them was a large, hearty woman, talking loudly about spring bulbs. I liked the look of her too. Perhaps I could incorporate her? I took them all three off the tram with me to work upon—and walked up Barton Road muttering to myself.
Very soon I had a sketchy picture of some of my people. There was the hearty woman—I even knew her name: Evelyn. She could be a poor relation or a lady gardener or a companion—

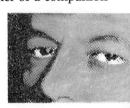

perhaps a lady housekeeper? Anyway, I was going to have her. Then there was the man with the black beard whom I still felt I didn't know much about, except for his beard, which wasn't really enough—or *was* it enough? Yes, perhaps it was; because you would be seeing this man from the *outside*—so you could only see what he liked to show— not as he really was: that ought to be a clue in itself. The elderly wife would be murdered more for her money than her character, so she didn't matter much. I now began adding more characters rapidly. A son? A daughter? Possibly a nephew? You had to have a good many suspects. The family was coming along nicely.

I left it to develop, and turned my attention to the detective. Who could I have as a detective? I reviewed such detectives as I had met and admired in books. There was Sherlock Holmes, the one and only— I should never be able to emulate *him*. There was Arsene Lupin—was he a criminal or a detective? Anyway, not my kind. There was the young journalist Rouletabille in *The Mystery of the Yellow Room*—that was the *sort* of person whom I would like to invent: someone who hadn't been used before. Who could I have? A schoolboy? Rather difficult. A scientist? What did I know of scientists? Then I remembered our Belgian refugees. We had quite a colony of Belgian refugees living in the parish of Tor. Everyone had been bursting with loving kindness and sympathy when they arrived. People had stocked houses with furniture for them to live in, had done everything they could to make them comfortable. There had been the usual reaction later, when the refugees had not seemed to be sufficiently grateful for what had been done for them, and complained of this and that. The fact that the poor things were bewildered and in a strange country was not sufficiently appreciated. A good many of them were suspicious peasants, and the last thing they wanted was to be asked out to tea or have people drop in upon them; they wanted to be left alone, to be able to keep to themselves;

they wanted to save money, to dig their garden and to manure it in their own particular and intimate way.

Why not make my detective a Belgian? I thought. There were all types of refugees. How about a refugee police officer? A retired police officer. Not too young a one. What a mistake I made there. The result is that my fictional detective must really be well over a hundred by now.

Anyway, I settled on a Belgian detective. I allowed him slowly to grow into his part. He should have been an inspector, so that he would have a certain knowledge of crime. He would be meticulous, very tidy, I thought to myself, as I cleared away a good many untidy odds and ends in my own bedroom. A tidy little man. I could see him as a tidy little man, always arranging things, liking things in pairs, liking things square instead of round. And he should be very brainy—he should have little grey cells of the mind—that was a good phrase: I must remember that—yes, he would have little grey cells. He would have rather a grand name—one of those names that Sherlock Holmes and his family had. Who was it his brother had been? Mycroft Holmes.

How about calling my little man Hercules? He would be a small man—Hercules: a good name. His last name was more difficult. I don't know why I settled on the name Poirot; whether it just came into my head or whether I saw it in some newspaper or written on something—anyway it came. It went well not with Hercules but Hercule—Hercule Poirot. That was all right—settled, thank goodness.

Now I must get names for the others—but that was less important. Alfred Inglethorpe—that might

Drawing of Hercule Poirot was done by W. Smithson Broadhead to accompany Agatha Christie's series of Poirot stories published in *The Sketch*, March 21, 1923.

do; it would go well with the black beard. I added some more characters. A husband and wife—attractive—estranged from each other. Now for all the ramifications—the false clues. Like all young writers, I was trying to put far too much plot into one book. I had too many false clues—so many things to unravel that it might make the whole thing not only more difficult to solve, but more difficult to read.

In leisure moments, bits of my detective story rattled about in my head. I had the beginning all settled, and the end arranged, but there were difficult gaps in between. I had Hercule Poirot involved in a natural and plausible way. But there had to be more reasons why other people were involved. It was still all in a tangle.

It made me absent-minded at home. My mother was continually asking why I didn't answer questions or didn't answer them properly. I knitted Grannie's pattern wrong more than once; I forgot to do a lot of things that I was supposed to do; and I sent several letters to the wrong addresses. However, the time came when I felt I could at last begin to write. I told Mother what I was going to do. Mother had the usual complete faith that her daughters could do anything.

"Oh?" she said. "A detective story? That will be a nice change for you, won't it? You'd better start."

It wasn't easy to snatch much time, but I managed. I had the old typewriter still and I battered away on that, after I had written a first draft in longhand. I typed out each chapter as I finished it. My handwriting was better in those days and my longhand was readable. I was excited by my new effort. Up to a point I enjoyed it. But I got very tired, and I also got cross. Writing has that effect, I find. Also, as I began to be enmeshed in the middle part of the book, the complications got the better of me instead of my being the master of them. It was then that my mother made a good suggestion.

"How far have you got?" she asked.

"Oh, I think about halfway through."

"Well, I think if you really want to finish it, you'll have to do so when you take your holidays."

"Well, I did mean to go on with it then."

"Yes, but I think you should go away from home for your holiday, and write with nothing to disturb you."

I thought about it. A fortnight[3] quite undisturbed. It *would* be rather wonderful.

---

3. **fortnight** [fôrt′ nīt]: Two weeks.

"Where would you like to go?" asked my mother. "Dartmoor?"

"Yes," I said, entranced. "Dartmoor—that is exactly it."

So to Dartmoor I went. I booked myself a room in the Moorland Hotel at Hay Tor. It was a large, dreary hotel with plenty of rooms. There were few people staying there. I don't think I spoke to any of them—it would have taken my mind away from what I was doing. I used to write laboriously all morning till my hand ached. Then I would have lunch, reading a book. Afterwards I would go out for a good walk on the moor, perhaps for a couple of hours. I think I learned to love the moor in those days. I loved the tors and the heather and all the wild part of it away from the roads. Everybody who went there—and of course there were not many in wartime—would be clustering round Hay Tor itself, but I left Hay Tor severely alone and struck out on my own across country. As I walked I muttered to myself, enacting the chapter that I was next going to write; speaking as John to Mary, and as Mary to John; as Evelyn to her employer, and so on. I became quite excited by this. I would come home, have dinner, fall into bed and sleep for about twelve hours. Then I would get up and write passionately again all morning.

I finished the last half of the book, or as near as not, during my fortnight's holiday. Of course that was not the end. I then had to rewrite a great part of it—mostly the overcomplicated middle. But in the end it was finished and I was reasonably satisfied with it. That is to say it was roughly as I had intended it to be. It could be much better, I saw that, but I didn't see just how *I* could make it better, so I had to leave it as it was. I rewrote some very stilted chapters between Mary and her husband John, who were estranged for some foolish reason, but whom I was determined to force together again at the end so as to make a kind of love interest. I myself always found the love interest a terrible bore in detective stories. Love, I felt, belonged to romantic stories. To force a love motif into what should be a scientific process went much against the grain. However, at that period detective stories always had to have a love interest—so there it was. I did my best with John and Mary, but they were poor creatures. Then I got it properly typed by somebody, and having finally decided I could do no more to it, I sent if off to a publisher—Hodder and Stoughton—who returned it. It was a plain refusal, with no frills on it. I was not surprised—I hadn't expected success—but I bundled it off to another publisher. ◆

Responding to the Theme
Memories

■ **Responding in Your Journal**   How do you think memories are formed? Are they based entirely on what you have actually seen or experienced, or could they be composed of several factors? For example, could what you actually remember about a certain event be influenced over the years by what you have heard others recall about that event or by what you have seen repeatedly in old photographs of that event? Today in your journal, write an answer to this question—as well as any other thoughts and ideas you have about the theme of memories. Then, during the rest of the week, write about some of your own memories. For example, what one event or occasion do you remember more completely and more accurately than any other? Why, do you think, this one memory is so clear? Also write about other memories of yours—such as your funniest memory, your happiest memory, and maybe even your scariest memory.

■ **Speaking and Listening**   To learn about how others feel about memories, take an opinion poll. First write some questions to ask friends and family members. For example, you could ask why they think memories are or are not important or how accurately they think they remember things. As various people answer your questions, take notes or tape their responses so that you can develop a consensus at the end. Be prepared to share and compare your results with others in your class. For instance, were your classmates' results similar to yours? Were there any unusual responses?

■ **Critical Thinking: Organizing**   As you review the selection from Agatha Christie's autobiography, make a list of the steps she followed when writing her first detective story. For example, did she create the crime or the detective first? How did she choose the characters for her story?

■ **Extending Your Vocabulary**   The first footnote in the literary selection defines *dramatis personae* as "the actors or characters in a play or story." In a dictionary look up this term and the following terms: *deus ex machina, exeunt,* and *in medias res.* For each one write the language from which it comes and a short explanation of its meaning in relation to its origin.

Agatha Christie at home, 1946

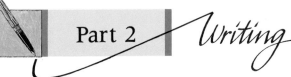

Part 2 *Writing*

In the excerpt from her autobiography, Agatha Christie has recalled one of the most important experiences of her life—her creation of the famous fictional detective, Hercule Poirot. While memories of your personal experiences may not have results as world-famous as Agatha Christie's are, they are still important and can serve as the inspiration for a type of composition called a personal essay.

Writing Term  A **personal essay** expresses the writer's personal point of view on a subject drawn from the writer's own experience.

Personal essays have the flavor of conversations, for in them you can directly express your thoughts, feelings, observations, and insights. For instance, you may write about your first week on a new job or the experiences of an athletic team on which you played. Because you are expressing personal thoughts and reflections, you should use the pronouns *I* and *me* as well as a conversational style of writing when you write a personal essay.

Prewriting

A personal essay may grow out of one of life's big events, such as a graduation, or it may grow out of a seemingly minor event, such as a camping trip or a rock concert. In the following excerpt from a personal essay, the writer Hal Borland wrote about a simple, common experience—yet one that had significance for him.

Model: *Personal Essay*

I suspect that a midsummer dawn is so special because so few people are up and trying to manage or improve it. It is a tremendous happening in which man has no part except as an occasional fortunate witness. And it happens with neither haste nor confusion. The stars aren't hooked to a switch that turns them all off at once. The birds don't bounce out of bed and immediately start singing in unison. Darkness doesn't rise like a theatrical curtain and reveal the sun crouched like a sprinter ready to race across the sky.

I was up at four o'clock the other morning to go fishing before breakfast. First streaks of light were in the sky and the lesser stars had begun to dim when I got up, but I brewed a pot of coffee, had a first cup, filled a vacuum bottle, gathered bait and gear, and still had only half-light when I cast off my boat. By then the first birds were wakening and uttering first sleepy calls. But I went almost half a mile up the river before they really began to sing.

I had boated three fish before the full light of dawn, and even then the sun hadn't risen. Time was so deliberate that when I looked at my watch I thought it had stopped. I had been caught up in a different rhythm, one that seemed to have no relation to clocks. So I sat and watched and listened, and it was like seeing the earth emerge from the ancient mists. I was alone with creation; I and the birds who were in full voice now, a vast chorus of sheer celebration.
HAL BORLAND
"Summer and Belief"

The preceding excerpt has three important characteristics of a personal essay. First, the writer draws on a personal experience—watching a midsummer dawn. Second, he uses the pronoun *I*. Finally, he uses a conversational style, as if he were talking personally to you.

Drawing on Personal Experience

Hal Borland's essay may have grown out of random observations that he had made in his journal. Like many writers of personal essays, you will find your journal to be a rich source of possible subjects. Look for a subject by going through your journal and circling any experiences you have written about repeatedly, as well as the feelings that you expressed about those experiences. Also circle your observations of people, accounts of places, or reflections about objects that are promising subjects. In addition to using your journal, try clustering and freewriting. Then, explore the following sources.

Sources of Subjects for Personal Essays	
photograph albums	school newspapers
letters from friends	newspapers and magazines
family stories	souvenirs from vacations
friends' stories	school yearbooks
scrapbooks	items in your desk

WRITING ACTIVITY   *Writing on Your Own*

WRITING
ABOUT THE
THEME

After you look through your journal and the sources suggested in the box above, list five possible subjects for a personal essay on the theme of memories. Then examine your list and select the one subject that you remember vividly or that is most significant to you. Write this subject on a piece of paper and save it for later use.

Determining the Meaning of an Experience

A personal essay should express a main idea to readers. Sometimes you will state this main idea directly, but other times you may simply imply that idea, giving clues to it in your descriptions and the incidents you narrate. Either way, the main idea of the essay will evolve from the meaning, or significance, that the experience had for you.

Suppose, for example, that you have decided to write a personal essay about a time you helped to renovate a state park in your region. That experience probably would have been important to you for several reasons, any one of which could become the main idea of a personal essay.

- The experience taught you about the ecology of your region.
- Because the experience deepened your interest in the outdoors, you may seek a career in a related field.
- Because you worked with 15 other students, you learned the value of cooperation in accomplishing a goal.

In the following continuation of Hal Borland's essay about a summer dawn, notice how he explores the meaning of his experience.

Model: *Personal Essay*

And at last came the silence, the hush—not a birdsong, not a rustled leaf. It was a kind of reverence, as though everything was awaiting the daily miracle. It lasted until the first ray of sunlight lit the treetops. Then the silence ended. The birds began to sing again, a vast jubilation. The sun had risen. A new day had begun. But it would be still another hour or two, until diurnal human beings were up and stirring, before the . . . haste would start all over again. Meanwhile, I had witnessed the deliberation of the dawn.

That is what I mean by perfection. Everything is right, at dawn. Nothing is hurried. Everything necessary to the day's beginning is in order and happening on its own schedule. Time is reduced to its true, eternal dimensions.   HAL BORLAND

"Summer and Belief"

Impression, Sunrise, Claude Monet, 1872, Oil on Canvas

As Borland makes clear, dawn is significant to him because it reveals the perfection that he sees in the natural world. He expresses this meaning directly in sentences like "That is what I mean by perfection. Everything is right, at dawn." However, he also expresses the meaning indirectly through details such as "The birds began to sing again . . . The sun had risen."

WRITING ACTIVITY ②

WRITING
ABOUT THE
THEME

Think about the experience related to memories that you selected as your subject in Writing Activity 1. Then in a sentence or two, express the main idea you wish to convey about the experience. *(See Writing Is Thinking on page 229.)* Save your work for later use.

Determining Purpose and Audience

After you have thought through the significance of an experience, you need to decide on an appropriate purpose and audience for your essay. Usually your overall purpose in a personal essay is to express your thoughts and feelings in a way that entertains readers. To achieve this purpose, you may use narration, description, or exposition. *(See pages 106–119.)* For example, if you were writing a personal essay about helping to renovate a state park, you might use paragraphs having the specific purposes shown in the following box.

Purpose in Personal Essays

General Purpose: to express how the experience of renovating a state park teaches the value of teamwork

SPECIFIC PURPOSES	KINDS OF PARAGRAPHS
• to describe the conditions of the park before work was started	descriptive
• to explain the process of renovating a campsite and the reasons why this effort requires cooperation	expository
• to tell an anecdote about how teamwork achieved a goal	narrative

---

Writing Is Thinking *Writing Is Thinking*

Critical Thinking

Interpreting Experience

When you select an experience for a personal essay, you may know intuitively that the experience was important, but you may not know why. To figure out why, you need to interpret that experience. *Interpreting* first involves recalling your feelings and impressions at the time of the experience. Then you must examine your thoughts and feelings by asking questions like those in the following chart. The questions have been answered by a student planning an essay about being reprimanded by his new boss at Sampson's Market.

Questions for Interpreting an Experience

QUESTIONS	ANSWERS
What do you remember most about the experience?	Mrs. Jones was more strict and critical than my first boss.
How did the experience affect you at the time?	It made me angry.
How have your feelings about the experience changed?	I'm not angry anymore. Mrs. Jones is still strict, but she also helps me become a better salesperson.
If those feelings have changed, explain why.	Mrs. Jones is a good teacher, and I respect her.

INTERPRETATION: This experience helped me learn to delay judgments about people until I have learned more about them.

Thinking Practice Select one of the following experiences or one of your own choice and interpret that experience by answering the questions above. Then write a statement that interprets the experience.

1. an incident in which your opinion of a person changed
2. an incident that revealed a facet of human nature to you
3. an incident that taught you about leadership

229

Considering Your Audience   Give special consideration to your audience when writing a personal essay. Because you are writing from your personal experience, you need to relate your subject to your readers' experiences. For instance, suppose that you have planned to write about several funny and interesting individuals whom you observed at your family reunion. However, introducing the members of your family to your readers and establishing the relationships among them could be a problem.

To overcome this problem, you might develop the essay by using anecdotes. For instance, do not simply tell readers that Uncle Bob is hilarious. Instead, include a story or two that show his sense of humor and tell readers some of the funny things he has said. In using this strategy, you will have considered your audience and shaped your writing to suit that audience.

WRITING ACTIVITY *Determining Purpose and Audience*

Select four of the following eight subjects for personal essays and write an appropriate purpose and audience for each one.

1. learning to drive a car
2. participating in an activity in which you made a difference or had an effect on other people
3. achieving an important personal goal
4. participating in an activity with friends
5. going on a trip or a vacation
6. creating something new, such as a drawing, an invention, or a computer program
7. learning something new about a place or person you thought you knew very well
8. going to a concert or other live performance that impressed you

WRITING ACTIVITY *Writing on Your Own*

WRITING
ABOUT THE
THEME

Review the main idea of the subject related to memories that you wrote in Writing Activity 2. Evaluate your statement of that main idea to see whether it still accurately summarizes the meaning of the experience for you. If not, revise the statement. Then make notes on the purpose of your essay and its audience and put those notes into your writing folder for later use.

Developing and Selecting Details

Details are the lifeblood of a personal essay because they make the experience you are writing about seem real and compelling. After settling on a purpose and audience, therefore, you should brainstorm for vivid details. The following strategies will help you.

Strategies for Developing Details

EVENTS Close your eyes and slowly visualize the experience that you are writing about. Then write down the details as you "see" them.

PEOPLE Visualize each person that you are writing about. Start by visualizing the head of each person and slowly move down to the feet.

PLACES Visualize the places you are describing. Start at the left side of the setting and visualize slowly to the right.

FEELINGS Imagine yourself once again undergoing the experience that you are writing about. Focus on your feelings and thoughts as you move through the experience.

After making your list of details, choose those that you will include when you write the first draft of your essay. The following guidelines will help you decide which details to include.

Guidelines for Selecting Details

1. Choose details appropriate for your purpose and audience.
2. Use factual details to provide background information.
3. Use vivid descriptive and sensory details to bring your experience to life.

In the following excerpt from a personal essay, writer Annie Dillard describes a creek that has overflowed because of a hurricane. She has carefully selected details to develop her main idea—that the flood has completely transformed what was once a peaceful and quiet setting.

Model: *Details in a Personal Essay*

That morning I'm standing at my kitchen window. Tinker Creek is out of its four-foot banks, way out, and it's still coming. The high creek doesn't look like our creek. Our creek splashes transparently over a jumble of rocks; the high creek obliterates everything in flat opacity. It looks like somebody else's creek that has usurped or eaten our creek and is roving frantically to escape, big and ugly, like a blacksnake caught in a kitchen drawer. The color is foul, a rusty cream. Water that has picked up clay soil looks worse than other muddy waters, because the particles of clay are so fine; they spread out and cloud the water so that you can't see light through even an inch of it in a drinking glass.

ANNIE DILLARD, *Pilgrim at Tinker Creek*

WRITING ACTIVITY *Writing on Your Own*

WRITING
ABOUT THE
THEME

Refer to the Strategies for Developing Details on page 231 to brainstorm for details for your personal essay on the theme of memories. In addition, try other strategies such as clustering and freewriting, which you learned about in Chapter 1, "The Writing Process." After making a complete list of all your details, evaluate them and cross out any that are not related to your purpose or main idea. Then save your details in your writing folder.

Organizing Your Essay

Like any essay a personal essay should be well-organized to be logical and easy to follow. The overall organization of personal essays is often developmental order. In this type of order, one idea grows out of the previous idea and leads into the next idea. However, as was indicated earlier in the section on "purpose," within this overall pattern of organization you will often use narrative writing, descriptive writing, or expository writing. To organize the details when using these different kinds of writing, use the following methods of organization.

Organizing Details		
KIND OF WRITING	**KIND OF DETAILS**	**TYPE OF ORDER**
narrative	events in a story, narrated from the beginning to the end	chronological order
descriptive	details to help readers visualize a person, object, or scene	spatial order (left to right, top to bottom, far to near, etc.)
expository	background details and details explaining the meaning of a particular experience	order of importance (most to least important or least to most important)

WRITING ACTIVITY *Writing on Your Own*

WRITING
ABOUT THE
THEME

Take out the brainstorming notes you compiled in Writing Activity 5 for your personal essay about memories. Arrange your details in major groups, or categories, which will become the paragraphs of your personal essay. Then organize in logical order the details within each group or category, using chronological order, spatial order, or order of importance. To help you order your details, write an outline and save it for later use. *(See pages 148–152 for more information about outlining.)*

233

Drafting

Writing Process

Personal essays are more informal in structure than expository or persuasive essays. Nevertheless, a personal essay should have the three parts of an essay: an attention-getting introduction, a body that develops the subject in an interesting way, and a striking conclusion.

Drafting the Introduction

In a personal essay, you will be writing about a subject that may not be important or relevant to readers at first glance. Therefore, your goal in the introduction is to make an immediate impact on your readers. Following are some strategies for beginning a personal essay.

Ways to Begin a Personal Essay

1. Begin with a startling statement that catches readers by surprise, as Eudora Welty begins her essay "A Sweet Devouring."

> When I used to ask my mother which we were, rich or poor, she refused to tell me. I was nine years old and of course what I was dying to hear was that we were poor.

2. Begin with a statement that promises interesting things to follow, as John Updike introduces his essay "Central Park."

> On the afternoon of the first day of spring, when the gutters were still heaped high with Monday's snow but the sky itself was swept clean, we put on our galoshes and walked up the sunny side of Fifth Avenue to Central Park.

3. Begin with an interesting detail related to the setting of your essay, as N. Scott Momaday does in "A Kiowa Grandmother."

> A single knoll rises out of the plain in Oklahoma, north and west of the Wichita Range.

Tone in Personal Essays   In addition to building interest, your introduction should establish the *tone,* which is your attitude toward the subject. To choose an appropriate tone, think about the effect the subject had on you. If it made you laugh, for example, you would use a humorous tone. Personal essays have a variety of tones, as the following excerpts show.

Model: *Tone of Alarm*

There is something uneasy in the Los Angeles air this after-noon, some unnatural stillness, some tension. What it means is that tonight a Santa Ana will begin to blow, a hot wind from the northeast whining down through the Cajon and San Gorgonio Passes, blowing up sandstorms out along Route 66, drying the hills and the nerves to the flash point. For a few days now we will see smoke back in the canyons, and hear sirens in the night. I have neither heard nor read that a Santa Ana is due, but I know it, and almost everyone I have seen today knows it too. We know it because we feel it. The baby frets. The maid sulks. I rekindle a waning argument with the telephone company, then cut my losses and lie down, given over to whatever it is in the air.   Joan Didion, "Los Angeles Notebook"

Joan Didion creates a tone of alarm through phrases like "something uneasy," "hot wind," and "drying hills and nerves to the flash point." Now notice how another writer creates a different tone.

Model: *Reflective Tone*

The sound of the sea is the most time-effacing sound there is. The centuries reroll in a cloud and the earth becomes green again when you listen, with eyes shut, to the sea—a young green time when the water and the land were just getting acquainted and had known each other for only a few billion years and the mollusks were just beginning to dip and creep in the shallows; and now man the invertebrate, under his ribbed umbrella . . . pulls on his Polaroid glasses to stop and glare and stretches out his long brown body at ease upon a towel on the warm sand and listens.   E. B. White, "On a Florida Key"

E. B. White's details like "the earth becomes green again when you listen, with eyes shut, to the sea" create a reflective tone. Like E. B. White and Joan Didion, choose words carefully to create the tone.

WRITING ACTIVITY *Analyzing for Tone*

Review the selection from Agatha Christie's autobiography on pages 217–222, considering what the tone is. Then write a paragraph explaining what you think the tone is. Be sure to support your opinion by including examples and specific quotations from the essay.

WRITING ACTIVITY *Writing on Your Own*

WRITING
ABOUT THE
THEME Write two first drafts of an introduction for your essay on the theme of memories, for which you organized details in Writing Activity 6. Each introduction should establish a different tone. Then save your work in your writing folder.

Drafting the Body

Once you have written an introduction that piques the interest of your readers, move on to draft the body of your essay. While writing the body, include the details that you selected earlier in your planning. The following guidelines will help you draft the body of your essay.

Guidelines for Drafting the Body

I. Make sure that each supporting paragraph has a topic sentence that supports the main idea.

2. Follow a logical order of ideas and details.

3. Use transitions between sentences and paragraphs to give your essay coherence.

4. If you discover new ideas and details as you write, go back and make changes in those sections of the essay that are affected by the new insights or details.

As you draft the body, use narrative writing, descriptive writing, and expository writing as appropriate. In her autobiographical essay at the beginning of this chapter, Agatha Christie effectively uses different types of writing. For example, early in the essay, she describes how she first visualized the appearance of Hercule Poirot.

Model: *Descriptive Writing in a Personal Essay*

Sure enough, next day, when I was sitting in a tram, I saw just what I wanted: *a man with a black beard, sitting next to an elderly lady who was chatting like a magpie.* I didn't think I'd have *her,* but I thought *he* would do admirably. Sitting a little way beyond them was a large, hearty woman, talking loudly about spring bulbs. I liked the look of her too. Perhaps I could incorporate her? I took them all three off the tram with me to work upon—and walked up Barton Road muttering to myself.

Later in the essay, she uses expository writing to explain the thought process by which she arrived at the name *Hercule Poirot*.

Model: *Expository Writing in a Personal Essay*

How about calling my little man Hercules? He would be a small man—Hercules: a good name. His last name was more difficult. I don't know why I settled on the name Poirot; whether it just came into my head or whether I saw it in some newspaper or written on something—anyway it came. It went well not with Hercules but Hercule—Hercule Poirot. That was all right—settled, thank goodness.   AGATHA CHRISTIE
Agatha Christie: An Autobiography

WRITING ACTIVITY ◆ 9 *Writing on Your Own*

WRITING
ABOUT THE
THEME

From the two introductions that you wrote for your essay in Writing Activity 8, choose the one that establishes the appropriate tone and will better capture your readers' attention. Then draft the body of your personal essay on the theme of memories. Be sure to include the details you developed in Writing Activity 5 and to use narrative, descriptive, and expository writing as appropriate. Save your work for later use.

Drafting the Conclusion

The conclusion of your personal essay should leave the readers with a memorable impression of the personal experience or insight that serves as your subject. The following strategies will help you write a striking conclusion.

Ways to End a Personal Essay

1. Summarize the body of the essay or restate the main idea in new words.
2. Add an insight that shows a new or deeper understanding of the experience.
3. Add a striking new detail or memorable image.
4. Refer to ideas in the introduction.
5. Appeal to your readers' emotions.

The following paragraph concludes the E. B. White essay from which you read a paragraph on page 235. The conclusion adds a new insight that reveals a further understanding of his subject.

Model: *Conclusion of a Personal Essay*

The sea answers all questions, and always in the same way; for when you read in the papers the interminable discussions and the bickering and the prognostications and the turmoil, the disagreements and the fateful decisions and agreements and the plans and the programs and the threats and the counter threats, then you close your eyes and the sea dispatches one more big roller in the unbroken line since the beginning of the world and it combs and breaks and returns foaming and saying: "So soon?"

E. B. WHITE, "On a Florida Key"

WRITING ACTIVITY ◆10◆ *Writing on Your Own*

WRITING ABOUT THE THEME

Review the introduction and body of your essay about memories, which you drafted in Writing Activities 8 and 9. Think about the type of conclusion that would be most appropriate for your essay and then draft two different conclusions. After a day or two, review your two conclusions and choose the one that seems more effective to you. Give your personal essay an interesting title and set aside your completed first draft in your writing folder.

The South Ledges, Appledore, Frederick Childe Hassam, 1913, Oil on Canvas

Revising

After you have drafted your personal essay, put it aside for a few days so that you will be able to reread it with a fresh perspective. When you review it, read it aloud to yourself and ask yourself whether the essay sounds lively. Do you hear the voice of your personality in it? Do your feelings about the subject come through?

Once you have evaluated your draft in this way, revise it with the goal of making it as fresh and natural sounding as possible. The following box shows some common problems with first drafts of personal essays and ways to fix them.

Strategies for Revising Personal Essays

PROBLEM	STRATEGY
1. The essay is too short, general, or vague.	Find more details. Visualize again the people, places, things, or experiences you are writing about. *(See page 231.)*
2. The tone is inconsistent.	Revise parts of the essay that stray from the tone set in the introduction. For example, if you start the essay in a serious tone, keep it serious.
3. The essay sounds too stiff and formal.	Replace any formal or technical words with words that are in most people's everyday vocabulary. Such words sound more natural and are, therefore, more suitable for a personal essay.

WRITING ACTIVITY *Writing on Your Own*

WRITING ABOUT THE THEME

Evaluate your personal essay on the theme of memories by asking yourself whether it is adequately developed and natural sounding. Pay attention to whether your impressions or feelings about the experience will come across to the readers. Then revise the essay, using the strategies above and the Revision Checklist on page 34 as a guide. Save your essay in your writing folder.

	Grammar in the
Editing and Publishing	Writing Process

Referring to the completion of her first book, Agatha Christie wrote, "Of course that was not the end. I then had to rewrite a great part of it—mostly the overcomplicated middle." Revising and editing a story or an essay are a natural part of every writer's efforts. These steps allow you, for example, to streamline your writing so that it flows smoothly. One tool in this streamlining process is the skillful use of phrases—groups of words that do not have a subject and verb.

Prepositional Phrases   A *prepositional phrase* begins with a preposition and ends with a noun or pronoun and modifies, or describes, another word in a sentence. You can use prepositional phrases to add information to a sentence. The prepositional phrases in heavy type in the following example, for instance, provide the reader with necessary, specific details. *(For information about the different kinds of prepositional phrases, see pages 585–588.)*

PREPOSITIONAL PHRASES   I settled **on a Belgian detective . . .** I could see him **as a tidy little man,** always arranging things **in pairs.**

Punctuation with Prepositional Phrases   When a prepositional phrase four words or longer comes at the beginning of a sentence, place a comma after it. Using prepositional phrases at the beginnings of some sentences will help you create sentence variety. *(For other examples and for practice in punctuating prepositional phrases correctly, see pages 775–776.)*

PREPOSITIONAL PHRASE   **On the following morning,** I saw two interesting characters sitting opposite me on the tram.

Appositive Phrases   An *appositive phrase* is a phrase that identifies or explains a noun or a pronoun in a sentence. *(For other examples and for practice in writing appositive phrases correctly, see pages 589–590.)*

APPOSITIVE PHRASE   I could use Rouletabille, **a journalist in** *The Mystery of the Yellow Room,* as a model.

Punctuation with Appositive Phrases   If an appositive phrase is not essential in identifying a noun, that phrase should be set off with commas from the rest of the sentence. In the preceding example, the appositive phrase, "a journalist in *The Mystery of the Yellow Room*," is not essential in identifying the noun "Rouletabille." *(For practice in writing appositive phrases correctly, see pages 781–782.)*

Combining Sentences by Using Phrases   You can use prepositional phrases and appositive phrases to combine short, choppy sentences into fluid, mature ones. *(For practice in combining sentences, see pages 67–68 and 602–603.)*

TWO SENTENCES	There were difficult gaps. They were between the beginning and the end of my story.
ONE SENTENCE	There were difficult gaps **between the beginning and the end of my story.**
TWO SENTENCES	I sent my story off to Hodder and Stoughton. That is a publishing company in London.
ONE SENTENCE	I sent my story off to Hodder and Stoughton, **a publishing company in London.**

Editing Checklist

1. Have phrases been used to add information and variety? *(See page 71.)*
2. Are all phrases punctuated correctly? *(See pages 775–776 and 781–783.)*
3. Could phrases be used to combine any sentences? *(See pages 67–68.)*

WRITING ACTIVITY   *Writing on Your Own*

WRITING
ABOUT THE
THEME

Editing   Use the checklist above and the Editing Checklist on page 38 to check your revised personal essay from Writing Activity 11 for any errors in usage, mechanics, and spelling. Also check for any fragments or run-on sentences. *(See pages 631–635.)*

Publishing   Read, give, or send your personal essay to someone who was involved in the memory you recounted in it. Then, if possible, discuss that person's recollections of the same event.

A Writer Writes

WRITING
ABOUT THE
THEME

A Personal Essay about a Memory

PURPOSE: to inform and entertain by sharing a memory of a
           teenage experience

AUDIENCE: parents and readers of *Today's Parent* magazine

Prewriting   Imagine that *Today's Parent* magazine is sponsoring a
writing contest. In the interest of providing parents with insights into
the world of teenagers, the magazine has invited high school students
to submit a personal essay that recalls the best or most unforgettable
memory of their teenage years. Winners will receive a prize.

Sift through the ideas in your journal and those from Writing Activity 1 on page 226 to select your best or most unforgettable memory as a teenager. If you cannot find a good subject in these sources, write freely about teenage memories until you find the one you will most enjoy writing about. Based on the meaning of that memory for you, write the main idea of your essay. After making sure that your subject is suitable for your audience, brainstorm for a list of specific details you will use to develop your main idea. To make your memory come alive on paper, remember to include sensory details as well. When your list is complete, organize your details in a logical arrangement. Since you will be recalling an experience, you probably will want to use chronological order.

Drafting   As you write the first draft of the introduction and body of your article, you may find it helpful to refer to the guidelines on pages 234 and 236. Keep in mind as you write that your personal essay is for an audience of parents. Therefore, choose an appropriate tone and keep it consistent. Remember there are a variety of tones to choose from for a personal essay, such as reflective, humorous, serious, or even one of alarm. As you conclude your essay, follow the strategies listed on page 237. Be sure to remember to leave your readers with the idea or feeling you wish to convey.

Revising   If possible, read your essay aloud to yourself or to someone else—preferably an adult. Does the listener find your work interesting and entertaining? Is the reader left with any questions? Are any parts of your memory hazy or hard to visualize? After you respond to your reader's comments, go over your essay a couple of times. Each time, check for different points on the Revision Checklist on page 34. Then revise, rearrange, and rewrite until you are proud of your essay and sure that you will win the magazine's prize.

Editing and Publishing   Edit your personal essay, using the Editing Checklists on pages 38 and 241. Then copy it into a neat final form and give it to your teacher, who will submit it to a panel of adult judges.

Independent Writing

Choose one of the quotations on the next page—or one of your own—and relate it to your own experiences and thoughts in some way. Then follow the Checklist for Writing Personal Essays on page 245 as you write a personal essay based on that quotation.

1. Never put off until tomorrow what you can do the day after tomorrow.   MARK TWAIN

2. Never eat more than you can lift.   MISS PIGGY

3. Ya gotta do what ya gotta do.   ROCKY in *Rocky IV*

4. There is nothing permanent except change.   HERACLITUS

5. Don't talk unless you can improve the silence.

Vermont Proverb

6. "If Today Was a Fish, I'd Throw It Back In"   Song Title

7. Humor is emotional chaos remembered in tranquility.

JAMES THURBER

8. I'm a great believer in luck, and I find the harder I work the more I have of it.   THOMAS JEFFERSON

9. "When You Wish Upon a Star"   Song Title

10. This is another fine mess you've gotten us into.   OLIVER HARDY

WRITING
ABOUT THE
THEME

Creative Writing

In her autobiography Agatha Christie explains how she used her memories of real people as the basis for some of her characters and her own experience of working at the dispensary as the basis for the plot of a murder mystery. Follow her example by developing the outline of a plot for a short story or a mystery. Use your own memories and knowledge to develop the plot. When you have finished, save your notes and your outline in your writing folder.

WRITING
ABOUT THE
THEME

Writing about Literature

An *autobiography* is a person's written account of his or her own life. In the form of a paragraph, explain how you think the excerpt from Agatha Christie's autobiography would have been different if the same information had been included in a *biography,* the account of a person's life written by another person.

Writing in Other Subject Areas

Mathematics   The United States is facing a critical shortage of mathematicians. Compared with other industrial nations, this country does not seem to produce students well educated in math. Write a personal essay expressing your thoughts on this subject.

Checklist

Writing Personal Essays

Prewriting

✔ Sift through your memories for experiences, reflections, and observations. *(See page 226.)*

✔ Review your list of possible subjects and choose the one that interests you most. *(See page 226.)*

✔ Decide on the meaning of the experience for you and from that meaning write a main idea. *(See pages 226–228.)*

✔ Focus on the probable audience for this subject and your purpose for writing. *(See pages 228 and 230.)*

✔ Choose a suitable means of developing your subject: narration, description, exposition, or all three. *(See page 233.)*

✔ List the details that best develop your main idea. *(See page 231.)*

Drafting

✔ Introduce your subject in a way that catches the reader's interest and sets the tone of the essay. *(See page 234.)*

✔ Build the body of your essay from the details you have chosen so that you make your point. *(See pages 236–237.)*

✔ Add a conclusion that leaves your readers with the idea or feeling that you wish to convey. *(See pages 237–238.)*

Revising

✔ Revise your essay for adequate development by adding vivid and interesting details where necessary. *(See page 239.)*

✔ Revise your essay for unity, coherence, emphasis, and smooth transitions. *(See pages 33–34.)*

✔ Choose a title that is true to the tone of your essay.

Editing and Publishing

✔ Use the Editing Checklist to polish your grammar, spelling, and mechanics. *(See pages 38 and 241.)*

✔ Refer to the Ways to Publish Your Writing for ideas on how to present your personal essay. *(See page 42.)*

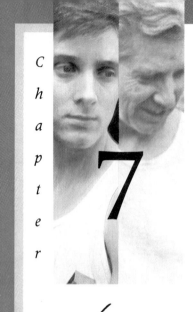

7 Writing Essays about Literature

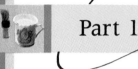

Part 1 — *Reading to Write*

THEME: *Relationships*

When you refer to yourself as a daughter or son, a student, a friend, an employee, or a customer, what you are really doing is naming a relationship. For example, you are a daughter or son in relation to your parents, or you are a student in relation to your teacher. As you move through life, your relationships help you define yourself and those around you.

Relationships, however, can be confusing at certain times and challenging at other times because they are constantly changing. The relationship you now have with your parents, for example, is quite different from the relationship you had with them when you were two or three years old. As you grow older, that relationship will change even more. In fact, somewhere along the way, your relationship with your parents may even seem to reverse itself. You may find that they need care and support from you.

In this chapter you will read about two very different relationships in the stories "Shaving" and "A Nincompoop." As you read, notice whether or not you begin to identify with any of the characters. Consider what you find familiar about the relationship in each story.

Shaving

L e s l i e   N o r r i s

Earlier, when Barry had left the house to go to the game, an overnight frost had still been thick on the roads, but the brisk April sun had soon dispersed it, and now he could feel the spring warmth on his back through the thick tweed of his coat. His left arm was beginning to stiffen up where he'd jarred it in a tackle, but it was nothing serious. He flexed his shoulders against the tightness of his jacket and was surprised again by the unexpected weight of his muscles, the thickening strength of his body. A few years back, he thought, he had been a small, unimportant boy, one of a swarming gang laughing and jostling to school, hardly aware that he possessed an identity. But time had transformed him. He walked solidly now, and often alone. He was tall, strongly made, his hands and feet were adult and heavy, the rooms in which all his life he'd moved had grown too small for him. Sometimes a devouring restlessness drove him from the house to walk long distances in the dark. He hardly understood how it had happened. Amused and quiet, he walked the High Street among the morning shoppers.

He saw Jackie Bevan across the road and remembered how, when they were both six years old, Jackie had swallowed a pin. The flustered teachers had clucked about Jackie as he stood there, bawling, cheeks awash with tears, his nose wet. But now Jackie was tall and suave, his thick, pale hair sleekly tailored, his gray suit enviable. He was talking to a girl as golden as a daffodil.

"Hey, hey!" called Jackie. "How's the athlete, how's Barry boy?"

He waved a graceful hand at Barry.

"Come and talk to Sue," he said.

Barry shifted his bag to his left hand and walked over, forming in his mind the answers he'd make to Jackie's questions.

"Did we win?" Jackie asked. "Was the old Barry Stanford magic in glittering evidence yet once more this morning? Were the invaders sent hunched and silent back to their hovels in the hills? What was the score? Give us an epic account, Barry, without modesty or delay. This is Sue, by the way."

"I've seen you about," the girl said.

"You could hardly miss him," said Jackie. "Four men, roped together, spent a week climbing him—they thought he was Everest. He ought to carry a warning beacon, he's a danger to aircraft."

"Silly," said the girl, smiling at Jackie. "He's not much taller than you are."

She had a nice voice too.

"We won," Barry said. "Seventeen points to three, and it was a good game. The ground was hard, though."

He could think of nothing else to say.

"Let's all go for a frivolous cup of coffee," Jackie said. "Let's celebrate your safe return from the rough fields of victory. We could pour libations all over the floor for you."

"I don't think so," Barry said. "Thanks. I'll go straight home."

"Okay," said Jackie, rocking on his heels so that the sun could shine on his smile. "How's your father?"

"No better," Barry said. "He's not going to get better."

"Yes, well," said Jackie, serious and uncomfortable, "tell him my mother and father ask about him."

"I will," Barry promised. "He'll be pleased."

Barry dropped the bag in the front hall and moved into the room which had been the dining room until his father's illness. His father lay in the white bed, his long body gaunt, his still head scarcely denting the pillow. He seemed asleep, thin blue lids covering his eyes, but when Barry turned away he spoke.

"Hullo, Son," he said. "Did you win?"

His voice was a dry, light rustling, hardly louder than the breath which carried it. Its sound moved Barry to a compassion that almost unmanned him, but he stepped close to the bed and looked down at the dying man.

"Yes," he said. "We won fairly easily. It was a good game."

His father lay with his eyes closed, inert, his breath irregular and shallow.

"Did you score?" he asked.

"Twice," Barry said. "I had a try in each half."

He thought of the easy certainty with which he'd caught the ball before his second try; casually, almost arrogantly he had taken it on the tips of his fingers, on his full burst for the line, breaking the fullback's tackle. Nobody could have stopped him. But watching his father's weakness he felt humble and ashamed, as if the morning's game, its urgency and effort, was not worth talking about. His father's face, fine-skinned and pallid, carried a dark stubble of beard, almost a week's growth, and his obstinate, strong hair stuck out over his brow.

"Good," said his father, after a long pause. "I'm glad it was a good game."

Barry's mother bustled about the kitchen, a tempest of orderly energy.

"Your father's not well," she said. "He's down today, feels depressed. He's a particular man, your father. He feels dirty with all that beard on him."

She slammed shut the stove door.

"Mr. Cleaver was supposed to come up and shave him," she said, "and that was three days ago. Little things have always worried your father, every detail must be perfect for him."

Barry filled a glass with milk from the refrigerator. He was very thirsty.

"I'll shave him," he said.

His mother stopped, her head on one side.

"Do you think you can?" she asked. "He'd like it if you can."

"I can do it," Barry said.

He washed his hands as carefully as a surgeon. His father's razor was in a blue leather case, hinged at the broad edge and with one hinge broken. Barry unfastened the clasp and took out the razor. It had not been properly cleaned after its last use and lather had stiffened into hard yellow rectangles between the teeth of the guard. There were water-shaped rust stains, brown as chocolate, on the surface of the blade. Barry removed it, throwing it in the wastebin. He washed the razor until it glistened, and dried it on a soft towel, polishing the thin handle, rubbing its metal head to a glittering shine. He took a new blade from its waxed envelope, the paper clinging to the thin metal. The blade was smooth and flexible to the touch, the little angles of its cutting clearly defined. Barry slotted it into the grip of the razor, making it snug and tight in the head.

The shaving soap, hard, white, richly aromatic, was kept in a wooden bowl. Its scent was immediately evocative and Barry could almost see his father in the days of his health, standing before his mirror, thick white lather on his face and neck. As a little boy Barry had loved the generous perfume of the soap, had waited for his father to lift the razor to his face, for one careful stroke to take away the white suds in a clean revelation of the skin. Then his father would renew the lather with a few sweeps of his brush, one with an ivory handle and the bristles worn, which he still used.

His father's shaving mug was a thick cup, plain and serviceable. A gold line ran outside the rim of the cup, another inside, just below the lip. Its handle was large and sturdy, and the face of the mug carried a portrait of the young Queen Elizabeth II, circled by a wreath of leaves, oak perhaps, or laurel. A lion and unicorn balanced precariously on a scroll above her crowned head, and the Union Jack, the Royal Standard, and other flags were furled each side of the portrait. And beneath it all, in small black letters, ran the legend: "Coronation June 2nd 1953." The cup was much older than Barry. A pattern of faint translucent cracks, fine as a web, had worked itself haphazardly, invisibly almost, through the white glaze. Inside, on the bottom, a few dark bristles were lying, loose and dry. Barry shook them out, then held the cup in his hand, feeling its solidness. Then he washed it ferociously, until it was clinically clean.

Methodically he set everything on a tray, razor, soap, brush, towels. Testing the hot water with a finger, he filled the mug and put that, too, on the tray. His care was absorbed, ritualistic. Satisfied that his preparations were complete, he went downstairs, carrying the tray with one hand.

His father was waiting for him. Barry set the tray on a bedside table and bent over his father, sliding an arm under the man's thin shoulders, lifting him without effort so that he sat against the high pillows.

"You're strong," his father said. He was as breathless as if he'd been running.

"So are you," said Barry.

"I was," his father said. "I used to be strong once."

He sat exhausted against the pillows.

"We'll wait a bit," Barry said.

"You could have used your electric razor," his father said. "I expected that."

"You wouldn't like it," Barry said. "You'll get a closer shave this way."

He placed the large towel about his father's shoulders.

"Now," he said, smiling down.

The water was hot in the thick cup. Barry wet the brush and worked up the lather. Gently he built up a covering of soft foam on the man's chin, on his cheeks and his stark cheekbones.

"You're using a lot of soap," his father said.

"Not too much," Barry said. "You've got a lot of beard."

His father lay there quietly, his wasted arms at his sides.

"It's comforting," he said. "You'd be surprised how comforting it is."

Barry took up the razor, weighing it in his hand, rehearsing the angle at which he'd use it. He felt confident.

"If you have prayers to say . . ." he said.

"I've said a lot of prayers," his father answered.

Barry leaned over and placed the razor delicately against his father's face, setting the head accurately on the clean line near the ear where the long hair ended. He held the razor in the tips of his fingers and drew the blade sweetly through the lather. The new edge moved light as a touch over the hardness of the upper jaw and down to the angle of the chin, sliding away the bristles so easily that Barry could not feel their release. He sighed as he shook the razor in the hot water, washing away the soap.

"How's it going?" his father asked.

"No problem," Barry said. "You needn't worry."

It was as if he had never known what his father really looked like. He was discovering under his hands the clear bones of the face and head; they became sharp and recognizable under his fingers. When he moved his father's face a gentle inch to one side, he touched with his fingers the frail temples, the blue veins of his father's life. With infinite and meticulous care he took away the hair from his father's face.

"Now for your neck," he said. "We might as well do the job properly."

"You've got good hands," his father said. "You can trust those hands, they won't let you down."

Barry cradled his father's head in the crook of his left arm, so that the man could tilt back his head, exposing the throat. He brushed fresh lather under the chin and into the hollows alongside the stretched tendons. His father's throat was fleshless and vulnerable, his head was a hard weight on the boy's arm. Barry was filled with unreasoning protective love. He lifted the razor and began to shave.

"You don't have to worry," he said. "Not at all. Not about anything."

He held his father in the bend of his strong arm and they looked at each other. Their heads were very close.

"How old are you?" his father said.

"Seventeen," Barry said. "Near enough seventeen."

"You're young," his father said, "to have this happen."

"Not too young," Barry said. "I'm bigger than most men."

"I think you are," his father said.

He leaned his head tiredly against the boy's shoulder. He was without strength, his face was cold and smooth. He had let go all his authority, handed it over. He lay back on his pillow, knowing his weakness and his mortality, and looked at his son with wonder, with a curious humble pride.

"I won't worry then," he said. "About anything."

"There's no need," Barry said. "Why should you worry?"

He wiped his father's face clean of all soap with a damp towel. The smell of illness was everywhere, overpowering even the perfumed lather. Barry settled his father down and took away the shaving tools, putting them by with the same ceremonial precision with which he'd prepared them: the cleaned and glittering razor in its broken case; the soap, its bowl wiped and dried, on the shelf between the brush and the coronation mug; all free of taint. He washed his hands and scrubbed his nails. His hands were firm and broad, pink after their scrubbing. The fingers were short and strong, the little fingers slightly crooked, and soft dark hair grew on the backs of his hands and his fingers just above the knuckles. Not long ago they had been small bare hands, not very long ago.

Barry opened wide the bathroom window. Already, although it was not yet two o'clock, the sun was retreating and people were moving briskly, wrapped in their heavy coats against the cold that was to come. But now the window was full in the beam of the dying sunlight, and Barry stood there, illuminated in its golden warmth for a whole minute, knowing it would soon be gone. ◆

A Nincompoop

A n t o n   C h e k h o v

A few days ago I asked my children's governess, Julia Vassilyevna, to come into my study.

"Sit down, Julia Vassilyevna," I said. "Let's settle our accounts. Although you most likely need some money, you stand on ceremony and won't ask for it yourself. Now then, we agreed on thirty rubles a month . . ."

"Forty."

"No, thirty. I made a note of it. I always pay the governess thirty. Now then, you've been here two months, so . . ."

"Two months and five days."

"Exactly two months. I made specific note of it. That means you have sixty rubles coming to you. Subtract nine Sundays . . . you know you didn't work with Kolya on Sundays, you only took walks. And three holidays . . ."

Julia Vassilyevna flushed a deep red and picked at the flounce of her dress, but—not a word.

"Three holidays, therefore take off twelve rubles. Four days Kolya was sick and there were no lessons, as you were occupied only with Vanya. Three days you had a toothache and my wife gave you permission not to work after lunch. Twelve and seven—nineteen. Subtract . . . that leaves . . . hmm . . . forty-one rubles. Correct?"

Julia Vassilyevna's left eye reddened and filled with moisture. Her chin trembled; she coughed nervously and blew her nose, but —not a word.

"Around New Year's you broke a teacup and saucer; take off two rubles. The cup cost more, it was an heirloom, but—let it go. When didn't I take a loss! Then, due to your neglect, Kolya climbed a tree and tore his jacket; take away ten. Also due to your heedlessness the maid stole Vanya's shoes. You ought to watch everything! You get paid for it. So that means five more rubles off. The tenth of January I gave you ten rubles . . ."

"You didn't," whispered Julia Vassilyevna.

"But I made a note of it."

"Well . . . all right."

"Take twenty-seven from forty-one—that leaves fourteen."

Both eyes filled with tears. Perspiration appeared on the thin, pretty little nose. Poor girl!

"Only once was I given any money," she said in a trembling voice, "and that was by your wife. Three rubles, nothing more."

"Really? You see now, and I didn't even make a note of it! Take three from fourteen . . . leaves eleven. Here's your money, my dear. Three, three, three, one and one. Here it is!"

I handed her eleven rubles. She took them and with trembling fingers stuffed them into her pocket.

"Merci," she whispered.

I jumped up and started pacing the room. I was overcome with anger.

"For what, this—*'merci'?"* I asked.

"For the money."

"But you know I've cheated you, for God's sake—robbed you! I have actually stolen from you! *Why* this *'merci'?"*

"In my other places they didn't give me anything at all."

"They didn't give you anything? No wonder! I played a little joke on you, a cruel lesson, just to teach you . . . I'm going to give you the entire eighty rubles! Here they are in an envelope all ready for you . . . Is it really possible to be so spineless? Why don't you protest? Why be silent? Is it possible in this world to be without teeth and claws— to be such a nincompoop?"

She smiled crookedly and I read in her expression: "It is possible."

I asked her pardon for the cruel lesson and, to her great surprise, gave her the eighty rubles. She murmured her little *"merci"* several times and went out. I looked after her and thought: "How easy it is to crush the weak in this world!" ◆

Responding to the Theme
Relationships

■ ***Responding in Your Journal*** How would you describe the relationships in "Shaving" and in "A Nincompoop"? What does each person get out of the relationship? What does each bring to it? What do you learn about the characters, based on the way they relate to the other characters? Today, in your journal, freewrite your answers to these questions as well as your other reactions to the stories. Then let your thoughts travel to your own relationships. Which relationships are in the process of changing? Can you see the changes as they occur or do you become aware of them only later as you look back? What relationships have ended? Which ones have disappointed you? Enriched you? Surprised you? Every day this week write in your journal about relationships you encounter: in your own life, in the lives of those around you, and in your reading.

■ ***Speaking and Listening*** Imagine you are looking out your bedroom window at an apple tree in the front yard. Then you look at the same apple tree from your kitchen window. From there you notice many more apples on the tree. What happened is that you changed your point of view. You see the same apple tree, but you see it differently. Similarly, a story has a point of view from which it is told. For example, the story "Shaving" is told through the eyes of Barry. How would the story differ if it were told through the eyes of his mother or father? With your teacher's permission, select a partner and write a version of the shaving scene from the perspective of Barry's mother or father. Then share your scene with your classmates.

■ ***Critical Thinking: Extending*** The author of "Shaving," Leslie Norris, uses a single incident to illustrate the relationship between Barry and his father. How would you describe this father-son relationship? What does the act of shaving symbolize? *Extend* the story further by imagining another incident that shows Barry taking on an adult responsibility.

■ ***Extending Your Vocabulary*** In "Shaving" the author appeals to your sense of smell by describing the odor of the shaving soap and later through the "smell of illness" that even the soap cannot overcome. Using a thesaurus, find at least five words that you could use to describe both of those smells.

255

Razor, Gerald Murphy, 1924, Oil on Canvas, 32⅝" × 36½", Dallas Museum of Art, Foundation for the Arts Collection, gift of the artist

Part 2   *Writing*

As Barry gave his father a shave, "He was discovering under his hands the clear bones of the face and head . . . he touched with his fingers the frail temples, the blue veins of his father's life." Until he felt the bones and veins under his fingers, "It was as if he had never known what his father really looked like." Through these details from the story "Shaving," Leslie Norris shows readers that Barry is discovering things about his father that he had never noticed before.

Reading literature is much the same way. Many insights about a piece of literature may remain undiscovered until you write an analysis of it. Yet, before you analyze and evaluate a work of literature, you need to understand that literature can be divided into three major divisions, or genres: *poetry, prose,* and *drama;* and each of these major genres can be subdivided into smaller genres. For example, prose can be divided into *fiction* (short stories and novels) and *nonfiction* (biography, autobiography, essays, and reports).

256

In this chapter you will write a critical essay in which you will analyze and evaluate some aspect of a short story. *Analyzing* means breaking something down into its parts and examining each part. By looking at the different parts of a story, you are able to understand it better. As a result, you are also able to evaluate it better and to judge its effectiveness as a piece of literature.

Analyzing and evaluating are not new to you. Consciously or unconsciously, you use these techniques frequently, especially when you are making a choice. When you select a sweater to buy, for example, you probably consider such features as fit, style, color, washability, and price. Then you judge the sweater according to how well it meets your standards for each feature. What you are doing is analyzing and evaluating—breaking the item down into its parts and then judging each part on the basis of a set of standards.

You will use similar techniques when you write a critical essay. During the process you will expand and refine the techniques as you apply them to a short story. As you compose your essay, you will also make use of your expository and persuasive writing skills.

Writing Term

A **critical essay** presents an interpretation of a work of literature and supports that interpretation with appropriate responses, details, and quotations.

The structure of a critical essay is shown in the following chart. As you will see, it has the same basic structure as other kinds of essays.

Structure of a Critical Essay	
TITLE	Identifies which aspect of the work the writer will focus on
INTRODUCTION	Names the author and the work
	Contains a thesis statement expressing an interpretation of some aspect of the work
BODY	Supports the thesis statement with details from the work and quotations from respected, recognized sources
CONCLUSION	Summarizes, clarifies, or adds an insight to the thesis statement

Prewriting

Sir Francis Bacon (1561–1626) stated in his essay "Of Studies" that some books are to be tasted, others to be swallowed, and some few to be chewed and digested. No matter what portion of a literary work you, the reader, taste or digest, you will not find the meaning of that literary work simply on the pages alone. Part of its meaning is to be found in you—in the experiences and knowledge you bring to whatever you read.

In this way reading is a two-way process. The author makes a statement and you respond. The degree and quality of your response depend on the feelings that the statement stirs up in you. Because your background, knowledge, and personal experiences are unique, the meaning of a work to you will also be unique. To uncover that meaning, you need to look inside yourself as you read—to become aware of your reactions and the reasons for them.

Responding from Personal Experience

When have you been affected by a story or poem you read? Perhaps you were moved by characters or situations that reminded you of your own life. Perhaps you were intrigued by strange, faraway worlds in which people's feelings turned out to be surprisingly familiar. Perhaps you were disturbed by a conflict that was resolved in a way that you found disappointing or unreal.

Reading sets up a special relationship between you and the writer. A writer's words can leap off the page into your mind and memory, where they take on a meaning that is special to you. At the same time, you contribute your own responses and become a part of what you read. Your response will not always be positive, however; you may even feel annoyed, angered, or uninterested. Still, both negative and positive responses serve as starting points for expressing your ideas about a work of literature. Reading, as a result, becomes a richer experience.

Strategies for Responding from Personal Experience   The strategies on the following page will help you identify feelings and memories that can enrich your reading. When you refer to these strategies, you should record your responses in your journal.

Personal Response Strategies

1. Freewrite answers to the following questions:
   a. Which character do you identify with most closely? Why? Do your feelings about the character stay the same? Do they change? If so, when and why do they change?
   b. What characters remind you of people you know? How are the characters like the people? How are they different?
   c. If you were the character you most identify with, would you behave the same way? Why or why not? What actions or reactions puzzle you?
   d. What situations make you think of situations in your own life? How are these sitiuations alike? How are they different? What feelings do you associate with the experiences?
   e. What feelings does the work evoke? Why?
   f. What moved you in some way? How and why?
2. Write a personal response statement, explaining what the work means to you. Use any form that allows you to express your response comfortably.
3. In small discussion groups, share your reactions to the questions in item 1 above. Listen carefully to the reactions of others and compare and contrast them with your own. Be open to changing your responses. Afterward write freely about whether your ideas changed and why.

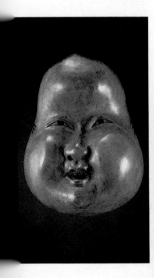
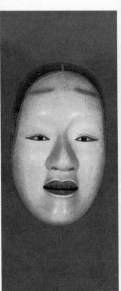

WRITING ACTIVITY *Responding from Personal Experience*

Use your journal to complete the following activity. Be sure to save your writing for future use.

I. Review the story "Shaving" by Leslie Norris on pages 247–252. Read to the end of the fourteenth paragraph on page 248. Then freewrite answers to these questions.

    a. Do you see yourself in any character? Why or why not?

    b. Choose a character. If you were that character, how would you feel? How would you behave?

    c. Which character reminds you of someone you know? How?

    d. What events in your own life come to mind? Do you remember a sudden spurt of growth, for example, or the sickness of a close relative? How was your experience similar? Different?

    e. Based on your own experience, what might happen next?

2. Continue reading to the end of the third paragraph on page 250. Again, freewrite answers to these questions.

    a. How do you feel about what is happening? Why?

    b. Does either of the two new characters—the mother and father—remind you of anyone you know? Why or why not? If so, how are the character and the person similar? How are they different?

    c. Have your feelings toward Barry changed? Why or why not?

    d. Does any new situation touch something familiar in your life?

    e. Would you have acted and reacted the same way as Barry? Why or why not?

    f. What do you think will happen next? How do you think the story will end?

3. Finish reading the story. Then freewrite answers to these questions.

    a. How do you feel about the ending?

    b. How closely did you predict what would happen?

    c. How do you feel about the characters now? How closely can you identify with Barry's actions and feelings? What helps you understand the father's feelings?

    d. Do any situations in your own life come to mind? Do they help you understand what happened? Why or why not?

4. Write a personal response stating what the story means to you.

Responding from Literary Knowledge

In a sense you already are a literary critic, for you usually approach a piece of literature with certain expectations. You base these expectations on your past experience and on your knowledge from reading other stories, poems, or plays.

When you respond to literature on the basis of your literary knowledge, you analyze the elements—the parts and characteristics—of a literary work. The way you approach a work, of course, will depend on the type of work it is—fiction, poetry, or drama. Although each type has its own set of elements, there is much that overlaps. For example, plot is critical in fiction, but it is also important in drama and some poetry. Dialogue is basic to drama, but it also has a place in fiction and sometimes in poetry.

The following chart lists the main elements and their functions according to fiction, poetry, and drama. Since drama shares many of the same elements as fiction, the elements listed under *drama* pertain only to the reading of a dramatic work.

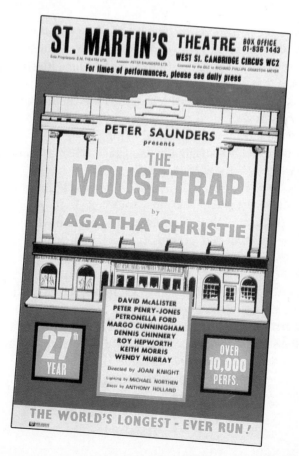

Elements of Literature

FICTION

plot—the events that lead up to a *climax,* or high point, and resolve a central *conflict* or explain the outcome

setting—when and where the story takes place

characters—the people who advance the story through their thoughts and actions

dialogue—conversations among characters, which reveal personalities, actions, and motivations or reasons characters behave as they do

tone—the author's attitude toward his or her characters

mood—the *atmosphere* that prevails throughout a piece of literature

irony—the occurrence of the opposite of what is expected—can be verbal, dramatic, or situational

point of view—the "voice" telling the story: first person *(I)* or third person *(he* or *she)*

theme—the main idea or message of the story

POETRY

persona—the person whose "voice" is saying the poem

meter—the pattern of stressed and unstressed syllables in each line

rhyme scheme—the pattern of rhymed sounds in the poem or at the ends of lines

sound devices—ways in which sounds are used to create certain effects, such as *alliteration (See pages 400–401.)*

imagery—expressions that appeal to the senses

figures of speech—imaginative language, such as *similes* and *metaphors (See pages 402–403.)*

symbols—objects, events, or creatures that stand for other things

shape—the way a poem looks; may contribute to the poem's meaning

theme—the overall feeling or underlying meaning of the poem

allusions—references to persons or events in the past or in literature

DRAMA

setting—the time and place of the action, the lighting, and the stage sets, as described in the stage directions

characters—the people who participate in the action of a play

plot—the story of the play, which is divided into acts and scenes and developed through action and dialogue

theme—the meaning of a play, revealed through the setting and the characters' words and actions

How Literary Elements Contribute to Meaning   Plot, character, dialogue, setting—these and other literary elements contribute to the meaning of a work. Therefore, when you analyze a work, you break it down into various elements. In poetry, for example, you would examine how the rhyme scheme, figures of speech, and certain other elements contribute to the meaning of a poem. The following groups of questions will help you to explore the meaning of a short story or a novel, a poem, or a play.

Questions for Finding Meaning in Fiction

PLOT

1. What is the significance of each main event in the development of the plot? How does each event in the plot affect the main characters?
2. What do details in the plot reveal about the central conflict? What do the climax and the ending reveal about the theme?

SETTING

3. How does the setting contribute to the tone or mood of the story? How do details of the setting help define the characters?
4. Which details of the setting are most important in the development of the plot? How do these details relate to the theme?

CHARACTERS

5. How do the characters respond to their setting?
6. How does each character contribute to the development of the plot? Who or what does each character represent? How do the details reveal the character?
7. What does the dialogue reveal about the characters' personalities and motivations? How does the point of view of the story affect the characterization? What does the point of view contribute to the theme?

THEME

8. What passages and details in the story best express the main theme? Are there other, recurring ideas that contribute to the meaning?
9. How effectively do you think the author communicates the theme through the setting, characters, and plot?
10. How does this theme have meaning for you? What else have you read that has the same or a similar theme?

La Lecture (The Reading), Berthe Morisot (French 1841–1895), 1888, Oil on Canvas, 29¼ x 36½"

Questions for Finding Meaning in Poetry

1. What is the poet's persona? How does the persona relate to the subject, mood, and theme of the poem?
2. How does the meter affect the rhythm of the poem? How does that rhythm express the mood?
3. How does the rhyme scheme affect the expression of thoughts and feelings?
4. What sounds do the sound devices create? What images do those sounds suggest?
5. What images do figures of speech create? What feelings do those images suggest?
6. How do symbols and allusions contribute to the theme?
7. How does the shape of the poem relate to the subject, mood, or theme?
8. What feeling, theme, or message do you think the poem expresses?
9. What effect does the poem have on you?

Questions for Finding Meaning in Drama

1. What details of setting and character do the stage directions emphasize? How do those details contribute to the meaning?
2. What are the key relationships among the characters? How do those relationships reveal the central conflict? What changes in the relationships help resolve the conflict?
3. How does the dialogue alone advance the plot? What developments in the plot occur with each act and scene?
4. What subject and theme does the play treat?

Evaluating a Literary Work When you analyze a piece of literature, you make judgments about the work. You set standards for each element and judge how well those standards are met. To evaluate a work, you do not simply ask, "Is it good?" Instead, you use the standards for each literary element to break the question down into more specific questions, such as "Does the plot build to a high point?" and "Does the setting fit the story?" As you build your evaluating skills, you will gain an increased appreciation not only of the literature but also of the techniques that go into its creation. Because there are different standards of evaluation, you may find it helpful to know the following criteria by which great literature—a classic—is usually judged.

Some Characteristics of Great Literature

1. Explores great themes in human nature and the human experience that many people can identify with—such as growing up, family life, or war.
2. Expresses universal meanings—such as truth or hope—that people from many different backgrounds and cultures can appreciate.
3. Conveys a timeless message that remains true for many generations of readers.
4. Creates vivid impressions of characters and settings that many generations of readers can treasure.

If a literary work you are reading is not regarded as a classic, you can apply other standards of evaluation. For example, when you are making judgments about a work, use the questions on the following page to help you evaluate it.

Questions for Evaluating Literature

1. How effectively does the writing achieve the purpose?
2. How vividly and believably are the characters, settings, dialogue, actions, and feelings portrayed? In fiction how well structured is the plot? Does it have a satisfying resolution of the central conflict?
3. How strongly did you react to the work? Did you identify with a character, situation, or feeling? Did the work evoke any memories or emotions?
4. Did the work have meaning for you? Will you remember anything about it a year from now?

WRITING ACTIVITY *Analyzing a Literary Work*

Review the story "Shaving" on pages 247–258 and write answers to the following questions in your journal.

1. What is the central conflict? How does the main character deal with it? What are the key events? How is the conflict resolved?
2. What is the main setting? In what way is it a suitable backdrop for the events? What does it add to the story?
3. What is the main character like? Why does he behave as he does?
4. How would you describe the father? Who are the other characters? What functions do they serve?
5. From whose point of view is the story written? Why might the author have chosen that point of view? How would the story have been different if it had been written from another point of view?
6. What is the underlying theme of the story?
7. How do the different elements fit together? How do they convey the meaning? What is the meaning for you?

Writing Is Thinking

Making Inferences about Character

When you write about literature, you will find that there are a variety of elements about which to write. For example, from the story "Shaving," you could focus on the motivation of the main character, Barry. But to figure out Barry's motivation, you would have to make *inferences*. That is, you would have to make reasonable guesses about his motivation, basing your guesses on clues in the story.

A reliable method of making inferences is to recall and apply your own experience. For instance, suppose you read in a story, "The man's bushy eyebrows gathered in a frown." In your own experience, you have seen people gather their eyebrows together in a frown. Using that experience, you can infer that the character is displeased.

The following chart shows how you can make inferences to understand the motivation of Barry in the story "Shaving."

Inference Chart	
TYPE OF CLUE	**CLUE**
Description of the character	Barry "was tall, strongly made, his hands and feet were adult and heavy . . ."
Statements about the character	The sound of his father's voice "moved Barry to a compassion that almost unmanned him."
Character's own words	Knowing his father needs to be shaved, Barry says, "I'll shave him . . . I can do it."
Other characters' words	"You're strong," his father said.

Inference: Barry is motivated by love to shave his father, but he has also developed a new maturity and self-assurance that allow him to perform this compassionate act.

Thinking Practice   Read the story "Quality" by John Galsworthy on pages 373–378. Then make an inference chart like the one above to explain the motivation of the bootmaker.

Choosing a Subject

By the time you have explored your personal and literary responses, you have not only become familiar with the work, but you have also accumulated some writing ideas. Your next task is to review your ideas and focus on one that seems especially suitable as a subject for a critical essay.

Unless you have been assigned a subject by your teacher, you will have a wide choice of possible subjects. To narrow the choice, first determine what subjects appeal to you personally. By asking yourself the following questions, you may be able to locate ideas that spark your interest.

Questions for Choosing a Subject

1. What parts of the work puzzle me? What would I like to understand better?
2. What parts of the work do I find moving? Surprising? Disappointing? Why do they have that effect on me?
3. What details or images made a strong impression on me? What do they contribute to the overall work?
4. With which character do I most identify? Why?
5. How do the characters differ from one another? What motivates each one?
6. What does the work "say" to me? What message does it convey? What insight or understanding have I gained from it?
7. What other works does this remind me of? How are the works similar? How are they different?

Since you probably have dealt with some of these questions in your previous responses, review your answers to the questions together with all your other notes. As you do, search for subjects that catch your interest. Be on the lookout especially for ideas that come up more than once. These are apt to be topics that strike a chord and that are probably worth exploring further.

A helpful procedure as you search for a topic is to synthesize, or combine, your personal and literary responses. First zero in on some strong personal reaction. Which response struck you most forcefully in your answers to the questions for Writing Activity 1 on page 260? In your personal response statement?

For example, suppose that the story "Shaving" brought to mind a time when you and someone you had always depended on were forced to reverse roles. Perhaps, for instance, you had to help an older brother or sister work out a problem—a type of role reversal. This personal response to the story can provide the beginning of an essay subject.

To make this idea for a subject more specific, you need to synthesize, or bring together, your personal response with your literary response to the story. To do so, think about the elements of the story that have to do with the reversal of roles. Some elements from "Shaving" related to this theme are as follows.

- Barry carefully prepared the razor, showing his feelings of responsibility. (characterization)
- Barry's father's cup is cracked and showing wear. (symbolism)
- Barry's father is too weak to get out of bed. (plot)
- Barry has the strength to lift his father. (plot)
- Barry's father says, "I used to be strong once." (dialogue)

As can be seen, the theme of the reversal of roles is developed in the story through several elements, including plot, characterization, dialogue, and symbolism. Thus, your subject for this literary essay would be the theme of the reversal of roles between Barry and his father, and to develop that subject you would analyze how the role-reversal theme is dramatized through several different elements of the story.

Finally for a critical essay—as for everything you write—you need to consider not only your own background and interests but also those of your audience. In this case you can assume you are writing for an audience familiar with the work, usually your classmates or teacher.

WRITING ACTIVITY *Choosing Subjects*

For each of the elements shown below, think of a possible subject for a critical essay on the story "Quality." *(See pages 373–378.)*

               EXAMPLE   theme
POSSIBLE ANSWER   what the story says about the changing view of quality

I. character   **3.** plot   **5.** tone
2. mood   **4.** point of view

WRITING ACTIVITY *Writing on Your Own*

WRITING
ABOUT THE
THEME

Prepare to write a critical essay about the short story "Shaving," which begins this chapter. Your essay will deal with what the story has to say about the theme of relationships, but the specific approach and focus will be your decision.

Begin your search for that focus by reviewing your personal and literary responses to the story and the Questions for Choosing a Subject on page 268. Then synthesize your two sets of responses to help direct you toward a subject. Save your work in your writing folder for later use.

Limiting a Subject

After you have chosen a subject, you will probably have to narrow its scope to one that you can handle adequately in an essay. The first step in limiting your subject is to decide on the approach you want to take. Do you want to focus on content by analyzing one or more elements of the work or do you want to focus on the author's presentation, analyzing some aspect of the writing style or technique? Once you have decided on the approach you want to take, start limiting your subject.

Usually the more you qualify a subject, the narrower you make it. Begin, then, by turning a one-word subject into a phrase or a short phrase into a longer one. As you work, ask yourself, "What do I want to say about the subject?" Your answers will lead you to an appropriately limited subject.

The student model on the following page is an abbreviated version of the steps a student went through to narrow the subject of an essay on the story "Quality."

Student Model: *Limiting a Subject*

TOO GENERAL   How the theme is carried out

ASK   What do I want to say about how the theme is carried out?

POSSIBLE ANSWER   The writer uses the failure and death of the old bootmaker to show how society's interest in real quality is declining.

LIMITED SUBJECT   The author uses the decline of the bootmaker to portray the decline of standards in society.

WRITING ACTIVITY **5** *Limiting Subjects for a Critical Essay*

The subjects below are too broad for a critical essay on the story "Quality." Narrow each one to a suitably limited subject.

EXAMPLE   setting

POSSIBLE ANSWER   how the writer uses details about the shop to help portray the bootmaker

1. honesty   **3.** the tone   **5.** the bootmaker
2. dialogue   **4.** the narrator

WRITING ACTIVITY **6** *Writing on Your Own*

WRITING ABOUT THE THEME   Limit the subject you chose for your essay about the story "Shaving" in Writing Activity 4 by asking yourself, "What do I want to say about the subject?"

Developing Your Thesis

A critical essay is based on a thesis, or proposition, that states your interpretation of some aspect of a piece of literature. Because you bring your own experiences and reactions to a work, your interpretation may be different from someone else's. Your task, therefore, is to defend your proposition by presenting evidence that will convince the reader your interpretation is valid. A critical essay, then, is not just a collection of reactions to a work but a carefully reasoned set of arguments.

Once you have limited your subject, you are well on the way toward stating your thesis. In fact, if your limited subject is clear and specific, all you may have to do is rephrase it as a sentence. If you need to narrow your thesis further, you can use a technique like the one you used for your limited subject. Keep asking, "What *exactly* do I want to say about the subject?" until you arrive at a statement that you can defend convincingly.

The thesis you develop in the prewriting stage is a working thesis only. It should be clear and specific enough to guide your thoughts, but it can be revised and even rewritten as you move deeper into the process of writing. For an essay on the story "Quality," one student moved from the limited subject to the thesis shown below.

Student Model: *Developing a Thesis*

LIMITED SUBJECT   How the author uses the decline of the bootmaker to help portray the decline of standards in society

THESIS   In the short story "Quality," John Galsworthy uses the decline of a skilled bootmaker to show the general decline of standards in society.

WRITING ACTIVITY *Writing on Your Own*

WRITING ABOUT THE THEME   Use your limited subject from Writing Activity 6 to develop a thesis statement for your critical essay about the short story "Shaving." This thesis should state exactly what you want to say about the story.

Gathering Evidence

As you read, you automatically gather details and fit them into a pattern in your mind, basing that pattern on your own store of memories and facts. It is this pattern that allows you to make sense of what you read and that helps you form an impression of a work. Thus, the first time you read "Shaving," whether or not you were aware of it, you were already noting details that eventually led you to your thesis. Now you need to return to the story to collect those details and gather others that can back up your thesis. This time go through the story with your thesis in mind and systematically look for supporting material. Dialogue, description, events, thoughts—anything you find in the story can be used as evidence.

While your arguments should be based on the story, you may want to seek additional support from works such as literary histories, author biographies, and collections of reviews. For outside sources use recognized and respected experts only. Furthermore, credit each source in your essay and always use quotation marks when you quote a source directly. *(See pages 278–279 for information on citing sources.)* The following steps will help you gather evidence for a critical essay.

Gathering Details for a Critical Essay

1. Scan the work, looking for quotations and other details that support your interpretation. Details can include events, descriptions, and any other ingredients of the work.
2. Write each detail on a note card or piece of paper. If it is a quotation, indicate who said it and write the page number on which it appears. If it is from a reference work, write the source. (In drama, note the act and scene; in poetry, the line number.)
3. Add a note telling how the detail supports your interpretation.
4. Use a separate card or piece of paper for each detail.

The following pages show some of the note cards prepared by one student for an essay on the story "Quality." The note cards appear on the right. On the left are the portions of the story from which the notes were made. The details were chosen by the student to support the thesis that Galsworthy used the physical decline of the bootmaker to show the decline of standards in society.

Student Model: *Gathering Evidence*

I knew him from the days of my extreme youth, because he made my father's boots; inhabiting with his elder brother two little shops let into one, in a small by-street—now no more, but then most fashionably placed in the West End.

"Id 'urds you dere," he said. "Dose big virms 'ave no self-respect. Drash!" And then, as if something had given way within him, he spoke long and bitterly. It was the only time I ever heard . . . him discuss the conditions and hardships of his trade.

"Dey get id all," he said, "dey get id by adverdisement, nod by work. Dey dake id away from us, who lofe our boods. Id gomes to this—bresently I haf no work. Every year id gets less—you will see."

And looking at his lined face I saw things I had never noticed before, bitter things and bitter struggle—and what a lot of gray hairs there seemed suddenly in his red beard!

As best I could, I explained the circumstances of the purchase of those ill-omened boots. But his face and voice made a so deep impression that during the next few minutes I ordered many pairs!

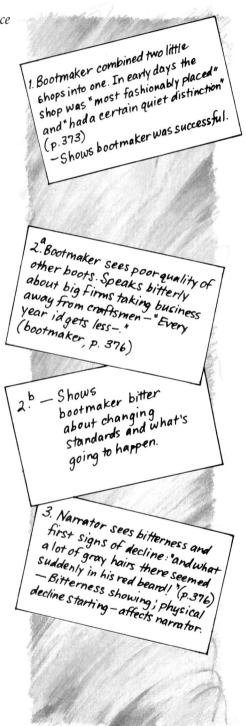

1. Bootmaker combined two little shops into one. In early days the shop was "most fashionably placed" and "had a certain quiet distinction" (p. 373)
   —Shows bootmaker was successful.

2.ᵃ Bootmaker sees poor quality of other boots. Speaks bitterly about big firms taking business away from craftsmen—"Every year id gets less—." (bootmaker, p. 376)

2.ᵇ —Shows bootmaker bitter about changing standards and what's going to happen.

3. Narrator sees bitterness and first signs of decline: "and what a lot of gray hairs there seemed suddenly in his red beard!"(p.376)
   —Bitterness showing; physical decline starting—affects narrator.

It was over a year before I was again in London. And the first shop I went to was my old friend's. I had left a man of sixty, I came back to find one of seventy-five, pinched and worn and tremulous, who genuinely, this time, did not at first know me.

When at last I went I was surprised that outside one of the two little windows of his shop another name was painted, also that of a bootmaker—making, of course, for the Royal Family. The old familiar boots, no longer in dignified isolation, were huddled in the single window. Inside, the now contracted well of the one little shop was more scented and darker than ever.

"That may be a bit flowery, as the sayin' is, but I know myself he was sittin' over his boots day and night, to the very last . . . Never gave 'imself time to eat; never had a penny in the house. All went in rent and leather. How he lived so long I don't know. He regular let his fire go out."

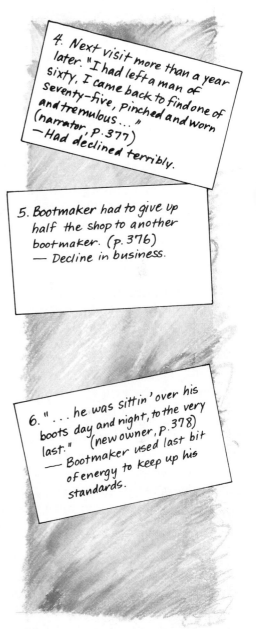

4. Next visit more than a year later. "I had left a man of sixty, I came back to find one of seventy-five, pinched and worn and tremulous..." (narrator, p.377) — Had declined terribly.

5. Bootmaker had to give up half the shop to another bootmaker. (p.376) — Decline in business.

6. "... he was sittin' over his boots day and night, to the very last." (new owner, p.378) — Bootmaker used last bit of energy to keep up his standards.

WRITING ACTIVITY 8 *Writing on Your Own*

On note cards or paper, collect evidence from "Shaving" to support the thesis you developed in Writing Activity 7.

Organizing Details into an Outline

Once you have the details to support the thesis of your essay, you need to organize them. As the following chart illustrates, your method of organization will depend on the nature of your thesis.

Primary Methods of Organization	
THESIS	**METHOD**
To show how a character changes over time	Chronological order *(See pages 101–102.)*
To show similarities and differences between characters or to compare two different works	Comparison and contrast, the *AABB* or the *ABAB* pattern of development *(See pages 153–155.)*
To analyze a character's motivation or the significance of the setting	Order of importance *(See pages 100–102.)*
To draw conclusions about the theme	Developmental order *(See pages 101–102.)*

Comparison and Contrast   One common method of organization in a literary essay is comparison and contrast. With this type of organization, you examine the similarities and the differences between two works of literature. The organization of the information follows one of two patterns—the *AABB* pattern or the *ABAB* pattern.

For instance, you could compare and contrast the bootmaker in "Quality" with the father in "Shaving," focusing on three points: illness, relationships, and values. In the *AABB* pattern, you would first discuss your three points about the bootmaker in "Quality" (selection *A*). Then you would discuss these same three points about the father in "Shaving" (selection *B*), explaining how selection *B* is similar to or different from selection *A*. This approach is called whole by whole because you discuss one whole work before the other.

In the *ABAB* pattern, you would discuss selections *A* and *B* according to each of your three points. For example, you would first discuss how the effects of the father's illness in "Shaving" are similar to or different from those of the bootmaker's decline in "Quality." Then you would discuss the similarities and the differences of the other points.

Outlining   After choosing a method of organization, arrange your details in an outline you can use to guide your writing. The outline should be formal, with several levels of topics. *(See pages 148–152.)* One student prepared the following formal outline for the body of a critical essay about the short story "Quality." To suit the thesis about the decline of a bootmaker and the decline of standards in society, he arranged the ideas chronologically.

THESIS   In the short story "Quality," John Galsworthy uses the decline of a skilled bootmaker to show the general decline of standards in society.

Student Model: *Outline*

MAIN TOPIC   I. Successful bootmaker
SUBTOPICS   A. Combined two shops into one
            B. Located in fashionable neighborhood
            C. Considered bootmaking "an Ardt"

MAIN TOPIC   II. First sign of decline
SUBTOPICS   A. Narrator wearing low-quality boots
            B. Big firms taking business away
            C. Bootmaker beginning to age

MAIN TOPIC   III. Two years later
SUBTOPICS   A. Narrator's return to shop
            B. Shop's division

MAIN TOPIC   IV. Aged bootmaker
SUBTOPICS   A. Bootmaker's physical decline
            B. Brother's death
            C. Bootmaker's ideals

MAIN TOPIC   V. Last encounter with bootmaker
SUBTOPICS   A. Bootmaker shows extreme decline
            B. Narrator orders boots
            C. Bootmaker dies

WRITING ACTIVITY   9   *Writing on Your Own*

WRITING
ABOUT THE
THEME

First, review the notes from Writing Activity 8 that support your thesis for your critical essay about the story "Shaving." Next, organize your notes by category, or topic, and decide on an appropriate order for the topics. Then, using your notes, prepare your outline. Be sure you save your outline in your writing folder for future use.

Drafting

Writing Process

Now that you have organized your ideas into an outline, you should begin to draft your essay. Adjust your outline as needed to accommodate new ideas or new directions that come up as you write. You should also consult your notes so that you do not forget important details. Use the following guidelines to help you draft your essay.

Guidelines for Drafting a Critical Essay

1. Do not retell the story. You can assume that your readers have read the work you are analyzing.
2. Keep yourself and your feelings out of the essay. Use the third person point of view and avoid *I.* Be objective and serious, not subjective or casual.
3. Use the present tense to discuss the work. (For example, write, *"The character is respected at first . . .* or *In the third stanza, the poet speaks about . . ."*)
4. In the introduction identify the title of the work and the author.
5. Revise your thesis statement as needed and work it into the introduction as smoothly as possible.
6. In the body of your essay, present your supporting details in a clearly organized form.
7. Put each subtopic into its own paragraph. Use transitions to show how one detail relates to another.
8. In the conclusion draw together your details to reinforce the main idea of your essay. You may want to restate the thesis in a slightly different form.
9. Throughout your essay use direct quotations from the work to strengthen the points you want to make. *(See page 279.)*
10. Add a title that suggests the focus of your essay.

Using Quotations

When you planned your essay, you took notes to use as evidence to support your thesis. These notes included descriptive details, lines of dialogue, narrative details, and other types of details. When you draft your essay, you should work this evidence into your essay as convincingly as possible. One way to do so is to quote directly from the work. Therefore, you should use quotations to support a point.

You should not just drop the quotations randomly into your essay, however. Instead, work them smoothly into your writing and punctuate them correctly. The following guidelines will help you.

Guidelines for Writing Direct Quotations

1. Always enclose direct quotations in quotation marks.

2. Follow the examples below when writing quotations in different positions in the sentence. Notice that quotations in the middle or end of a sentence are not ordinarily capitalized.

BEGINS SENTENCE
"**T**he old familiar boots, no longer in dignified isolation," were added to the pile of shoes in the window.

INTERRUPTS SENTENCE
Noting their low quality, "**h**e spoke long and bitterly" about big firms. The bootmaker is shockingly "**a**ged and wan," with thinning hair.

ENDS SENTENCE
The shop has "**a**n air of distinction."

3. Use an *ellipsis*—a series of three dots—to show that words have been left out of a quotation.

His "hair had suddenly. . . gone thin."

4. If the quotation is two lines or longer, set it off by itself, without quotation marks. Indent it and leave space above and below it.

I had left a man of sixty, I came back to find one of seventy-five, pinched and worn and tremulous, who genuinely, this time, did not at first know me.

5. After each quotation cite the page number of the source in parentheses. The citation should precede punctuation marks such as periods, commas, colons, and semicolons. For plays or long poems, also give the act and scene of the play or part of the poem, plus line numbers. *(For further information about citing sources, see pages 356–363.)*

On the following page is a sample of a critical essay. Since it has already been revised and edited, it is considerably more polished than your first draft will be. Nevertheless, you should use it as a model of what to aim for as you draft your own essay.

Student Model: *Critical Essay*

TITLE:
IDENTIFIES FOCUS

A Double Decline in "Quality"

INTRODUCTION:
IDENTIFIES
AUTHOR AND
TITLE

**THESIS
STATEMENT**

In "Quality" John Galsworthy tells the story of an aging bootmaker in a changing society. After spending his life making boots of the highest quality, Mr. Gessler cannot fit into a world that cares more about doing things quickly than doing them well. Through the physical decline of the boot-maker, Galsworthy shows the decline of standards in society.

**FIRST BODY
PARAGRAPH:**
DESCRIBES
MR. GESSLER AS
A RESPECTED
BOOTMAKER

At the beginning of the story, Mr. Gessler is a respected craftsman. He is successful enough to have combined two little shops into one, which is "most fashionably placed" and has "a certain quiet distinction" (373). The young narrator is impressed by the dignity of the bootmaker and the wonder of his craft. "For to make boots—such boots as he made—seemed to me then, and still seems to me, mysterious and wonderful" (373). To Mr. Gessler bootmaking is "an Ardt" (374), and he is completely devoted to that art. The joy of working with a beautiful piece of leather and shaping it into a perfect boot—that is his entire life.

SECOND BODY PARAGRAPH: USES SPECIFIC DETAILS TO SHOW FIRST SIGN OF DECLINE

For a while people appear to appreciate Mr. Gessler and the remarkable boots he creates. However, the first sign of decline comes when the narrator enters the shop wearing boots bought somewhere else. "Dose are nod my boods" (375), the bootmaker recognizes immediately. Noting their low quality, "he spoke long and bitterly" (376) about big firms who use advertising, not quality, to take business away from real craftsmen. He predicted what was happening: "Id gomes to this—bresently I haf no work. Every year id gets less—you will see." As Mr. Gessler gives his bitter speech, the narrator notices "what a lot of gray hairs there seemed suddenly in his red beard!" The bootmaker is beginning his decline, along with the standards he holds so high.

THIRD BODY PARAGRAPH: OFFERS DETAILS TO SHOW FURTHER DECLINE

Two years later the narrator returns and is surprised to see that the shop has been divided. "And it was longer than usual, too, before a face peered down" (376) and the bootmaker appeared. Things are obviously getting worse, and "beople do nod wand good boods, id seems" (376).

FOURTH BODY PARAGRAPH: SHOWS PROGRESSION OF DECLINE— AFFECTS BOOTMAKER PHYSICALLY

The decline continues. When the narrator visits the shop again many months later, he finds the bootmaker shockingly "aged and wan" (377), and his "hair had suddenly gone . . . thin" (377). Mr. Gessler has lost his brother and half his shop, and he is obviously falling apart physically. Still, he takes joy in a beautiful piece of leather and fashions boots that "were better than ever" (377). The struggle to hold onto to his ideals is aging him, but he is not giving them up.

FIFTH BODY PARAGRAPH: SETS OFF DIRECT QUOTATION TO EMPHASIZE DECLINE

It is more than a year before the narrator returns, and this time the bootmaker's decline is extreme.

> I had left a man of sixty, I came back to find one of seventy-five, pinched and worn and tremulous, who genuinely, this time, did not at first know me (377).

The narrator orders boots and hurries away, for "To watch him was quite painful, so feeble had he grown" (377). When the boots finally arrive, however, "they were the best he had ever made me" (378). The bootmaker seems to have used up his last bit of energy, "sittin' over his boots day and night, to the very last" (378), for then he died.

CONCLUSION:
RESTATES THESIS

At the end of the story, the new young bootmaker explains that even though "not a man in London made a better boot" (378), there is no place in the modern world for someone who does all his own work, who takes time to do a job right, who insists on the best leather, and who never advertises for customers. The old bootmaker himself knows he no longer fits in a changed world, and so he leaves it. Do his precious values die with him? Galsworthy seems to say that they do.

WRITING ACTIVITY *Writing on Your Own*

WRITING
ABOUT THE
THEME

Draft your critical essay about the story "Shaving." After you use your work from Writing Activity 9 and your notes, follow the guidelines on page 278. Be sure to save your work so that you can revise it.

Revising

Writing Process

Rework your draft until you are reasonably satisfied with it. Then do not look at it for a day or two so that you can return to it with a critical eye. If possible, give your draft to another student to read and comment on in the meantime. Then use your classmate's suggestions and the checklist below to make your revisions.

Revision Checklist

CHECKING YOUR ESSAY

1. Do you have a strong introduction that identifies the author and the work you will discuss?
2. Does your introduction contain a clearly worded thesis?
3. Does the body of your essay provide ample details from the work to support your thesis?
4. Have you quoted from the work to strengthen your points?
5. Are your major points organized in a clear, appropriate way?
6. Does your conclusion synthesize the details in the body of the essay and reinforce the thesis statement?
7. Is there unity and coherence? *(See page 166.)*
8. Do you have an interesting title? *(See page 165.)*

CHECKING YOUR PARAGRAPHS

9. Does each paragraph have a topic sentence? *(See pages 94–95.)*
10. Is each paragraph unified and coherent? *(See pages 99–102.)*

CHECKING YOUR SENTENCES AND WORDS

11. Are your sentences varied and concise? *(See pages 63–71.)*
12. Are your words specific and lively? *(See pages 56–59.)*

WRITING ACTIVITY 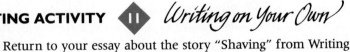 *Writing on Your Own*

WRITING
ABOUT THE
THEME

Return to your essay about the story "Shaving" from Writing Activity 10. With your teacher's permission, exchange papers with a partner and check to see how strongly the supporting details "prove" the proposition stated in your partner's thesis. Then, using your partner's comments and the guidelines above, revise your own draft. Save your work.

Editing and Publishing

Grammar in the Writing Process

At one point in "Shaving," Leslie Norris writes, "He [Barry] sighed as he shook the razor in the hot water, washing away the soap." In this sentence the group of words *washing away the soap* is called a phrase because it has no subject and verb. In particular *washing away the soap* is a *verbal phrase* because it begins with a form of a verb called a *verbal*. Verbal phrases can contribute much to your writing style. You can use them at the beginning of a sentence for variety in your sentence structure, and you can eliminate choppiness in your writing by using them to combine sentences. Because verbals begin with a verb form, they—by their very nature —also add a liveliness to your writing.

Participial Phrases   A participial phrase is one kind of verbal phrase. A *participle* is a verb form that is used as an adjective to describe a noun or a pronoun. *Present participles* end in *-ing,* and *past participles* end in *-ed, -n, -t,* and *-en.* A participle plus its modifiers and complements forms a *participial phrase.* In the following examples, the participial phrases add a certain action, or energy, to the sentences. In addition, the participial phrase that comes at the beginning of the first example sentence creates sentence variety. (*For other examples and for practice in correctly using participial phrases and other kinds of verbal phrases, see pages 591–600.*)

PARTICIPIAL   **Hoping to help his father,** Barry offered to shave
PHRASES   him.

Barry pleased his father, **telling him about the game.**

Punctuation with Participial Phrases   When a participial phrase comes at the beginning of a sentence—as in the first example above— it is separated from the rest of the sentence with a comma. You should also use commas to enclose a nonessential participial phrase. A *nonessential participial phrase* is one that can be removed from a sentence without changing the meaning of that sentence. (*For more information about punctuating nonessential phrases and for practice in writing them correctly, see pages 593–594.*)

NONESSENTIAL PARTICIPIAL PHRASES   The father, **knowing his son won the game,** felt proud. [You could remove the participial phrase without changing the meaning of the sentence: *The father felt proud.*]

Combining Sentences by Using Participial Phrases   Your ability to recognize participial phrases gives you the option of using them to combine short, choppy sentences to form more concise sentences. When you combine sentences, you are also able to show important relationships between two ideas. *(For other examples of sentences combined with phrases and for practice in combining sentences, see pages 602–603.)*

TWO SENTENCES   Barry used hot water to clean the razor. He then polished it with a soft towel.

COMBINED   **Using hot water to clean the razor,** Barry then polished it with a soft towel.

TWO SENTENCES   Barry stood in the afternoon sunlight. He enjoyed its warmth.

COMBINED   Barry stood in the afternoon sunlight, **enjoying its warmth.**

Editing Checklist

1. Have verbal phrases been used to add liveliness and sentence variety? *(See pages 591–598.)*
2. Are all verbal phrases punctuated correctly? *(See pages 593–594.)*
3. Could verbal phrases be used to combine any sentences? *(See page 602.)*

WRITING ACTIVITY ◆ 12 ▶ *Writing on Your Own*

WRITING ABOUT THE THEME

Editing   When you are alone, read aloud your critical essay about the story "Shaving." Listen especially for any verbal phrases. Make sure your words flow smoothly and watch for any sentence fragments or run-on sentences. *(See pages 631–635.)* Then use the checklist above and the Editing Checklist on page 38 to find any usage, mechanics, or spelling errors.

Publishing   When your essay is the best that it can be, write a neat final copy and share it with your classmates.

A Writer Writes

A Critical Essay

PURPOSE: to analyze the short story "A Nincompoop" by Anton Chekhov

AUDIENCE: people who are familiar with the story, especially your classmates and teacher

Prewriting   Relationships are not always easy. In fact, some can be extremely uncomfortable, particularly those that are out of balance. Anton Chekhov, a nineteenth-century Russian writer, tells of such a relationship in the story "A Nincompoop" on pages 253–254. Prepare to write a critical essay about the relationship described there.

After you reread the story "A Nincompoop," pause to explore your personal and literary reactions. Were you able to identify with either of the characters? Why or why not? Did your feelings about either of the characters change at the end of the story? If so, when and why?

Next, write your personal responses in your journal, using the Personal Response Strategies on page 259. Then, tapping into your literary responses, use the Questions for Finding Meaning in Fiction on page 263. As you write your responses in your journal, give special attention to the theme of relationships.

Then, look for a subject for your essay by referring to the Questions for Choosing a Subject on page 268 and your journal notes. Try to synthesize your personal and literary responses. If you need to limit your subject, ask yourself, "What do I want to say about the subject?" Then transform your limited subject into a thesis by rephrasing it as a sentence. If it needs further focusing, ask, "What *exactly* do I want to say about the subject?"

For additional support for your thesis, scan the story. You may find it helpful to use the steps for Gathering Details for a Critical Essay on page 273. Finally, decide on an appropriate way to arrange your supporting details. Put them together in an outline you can use to guide you as you write.

Drafting   Draft your critical essay. Then follow the Guidelines for Drafting a Critical Essay on page 278.

Revising *Peer Conferencing:*   With your teacher's permission, exchange papers with a partner. After you have read your partner's essay, answer the following questions. Then, when you are finished, use your partner's comments and the Revision Checklist on page 283 to revise your essay.

1. Is the thesis clearly and appropriately stated?
2. Do the details include ample evidence from the work?
3. Do the details support the thesis?
4. Does the essay have unity? Coherence?

Editing and Publishing   Check your revised essay for any errors, paying particular attention to the styling of quotations and the consistent use of the present tense. You also may benefit from using the checklists on pages 38 and 285 to look for any other errors. When you are pleased with your essay, make a neat final copy. Your teacher may then want to collect the essays to combine them in a book of critical essays for the school or class library.

Independent Writing

Write an essay analyzing some aspect of what William Butler Yeats says about relationships in the following poem.

When You Are Old

When you are old and gray and full of sleep,
And nodding by the fire, take down this book,
And slowly read, and dream of the soft look
Your eyes had once, and of their shadows deep;

How many loved your moments of glad grace,
And loved your beauty with love false or true,
But one man loved the pilgrim soul in you,
And loved the sorrows of your changing face;

And bending down beside the glowing bars,
Murmur, a little sadly, how Love fled
And paced upon the mountains overhead
And hid his face amid a crowd of stars.

WILLIAM BUTLER YEATS, "When You Are Old"

Creative Writing

There is an old saying that "a picture paints a thousand words." Look at the photograph on page 399 and write a story to accompany it.

Writing about Literature

The *protagonist,* the main character in a literary work, is always involved in the major conflict. The protagonist is also the character with whom most readers sympathize. In an essay explain why Barry is the protagonist in the story "Shaving."

Writing in Other Subject Areas

Government   Write an essay analyzing the views of power suggested in the poem "Ozymandias" on page 52. Use as many present-day examples to support your ideas as possible.

Sociology   Select a literary work, either past or present, and write an essay explaining how the literature reflects the attitudes and concerns of the society of its day. Cite appropriate sources.

7 Checklist

Writing Essays about Literature

Prewriting

✔ Read the work carefully and respond to it from both personal experience and literary knowledge. *(See pages 258–266.)*

✔ Choose and limit a subject for your essay by synthesizing your personal and literary responses. *(See pages 268–271.)*

✔ Shape your limited subject into a thesis statement that will provide a focus as you write. *(See pages 271–272.)*

✔ Scan the work, looking for details that will support your thesis statement. On separate note cards, write each detail, the page reference, and a note explaining its significance. *(See pages 273–275.)*

✔ Decide on an appropriate order for your details and use it to organize them into an outline. *(See pages 276–277.)*

Drafting

✔ Draft your essay, using the Guidelines for Drafting a Critical Essay. *(See page 278.)*

Revising

✔ Use the Revision Checklist to help you revise your essay. *(See page 283.)*

Editing and Publishing

✔ Use the Editing Checklists to check grammar, spelling, usage, and mechanics. *(See pages 38 and 285.)* Pay special attention to the punctuation of direct quotations. *(See page 279.)*

✔ Follow standard manuscript form and prepare a neat final copy of your essay. Then present it to an interested reader. *(See pages 42–43.)*

Chapter

8 Writing Summaries

Part 1 *Reading to Write*

THEME: *Perspectives*

Before the 1400's, painted scenes looked flat and unreal. Then painters learned how to add perspective by creating an illusion of depth. With this added dimension, painted scenes came alive. Likewise, when you examine a scene, an object, or an idea, you give it depth by adding your own insights. Any subject is flat and meaningless until you bring to it the added dimension of a personal perspective.

It is this subject of perspectives that E. M. Forster discusses in "The Beauty of Life," the next selection. In the essay he explains his belief that different people have different perspectives on life. Their perspectives can range from extremely positive to extremely negative views of the world. While some believe that all the world is beautiful, others believe that there is more beauty than ugliness. There are also those who believe that life has a few beautiful parts, or scraps. Finally, there are those who grumble that all of life is dull and there is no beauty in the world at all. As you read the selection, think about your perspective on life. Do you have a perspective similar to one of those described by Forster?

The Beauty of Life

E. M. F o r s t e r

The subject of this article—a magnificent subject—was suggested by the editor.[1] "Would it not be possible," he wrote, "to illustrate the beauty and the wonder of life, to show that they are always manifest wheresoever and howsoever life and force are manifested?" But unfortunately it is a subject that could only be treated by a poet—by a poet who was at the same time a man of action; whose enthusiasm had stood the test of hard facts; whose vision of things as they ought to be had been confirmed and strengthened by his experience of things as they are—by such a poet as Walt Whitman.[2]

> *I believe a leaf of grass is no less than the*
> * journey-work of the stars,*
> *And the pismire[3] is equally perfect, and a*
> * grain of sand, and the egg of the wren,*
> *And the tree toad is a chef-d'oeuvre[4] for the*
> * highest,*
> *And the running blackberry would adorn*
> * the parlors of heaven.*

Whitman knew what life was. He was not praising its beauty from an armchair. He had been through all that makes it hideous to most men—poverty, the battlefield, the hospitals—and yet could believe

---

1. **editor:** Editor of the publication called *The Working Men's College Journal* where this essay was first published.
2. **Walt Whitman:** American poet (1819–1892).
3. **pismire** [pis'mire']: An ant.
4. **chef–d'oeuvre** [she dœ'vrə]: French word for "masterpiece."

that life, whether as a whole or in detail, was perfect, that beauty is manifest wherever life is manifested. He could glorify the absurd and the repulsive; he could catalog the parts of a machine from sheer joy that a machine has so many parts; he could sing not only of farming and fishing, but also of "leather-dressing, coach-making, boiler-making, rope-twisting, distilling, sign-painting, lime-burning, cotton-picking . . . one of the lines in one of his poems runs thus! He went the "whole hog," in fact, and he ought to be writing this article.

But most of us have to be content with a less vigorous attitude. We may follow the whole-hogger at moments, and no doubt it is our fault and not his when we don't follow him; but we cannot follow him always. We may agree that the egg of the wren is perfect, that the running blackberry would adorn the parlors of heaven; but what about the pismire and the tree toad? Do they seem equally perfect? Farming is wonderful because it probes the mystery of the earth; fishing, because it probes the sea . . . To most of us life seems partly beautiful, partly ugly; partly wonderful, partly dull; there is sunshine in it, but there are also clouds, and we cannot always see that the clouds have silver linings. What are we to do? How is the average man to make the best of what he does see? For it is no good him pretending to see what he doesn't.

One might define the average educated man as optimist by instinct, pessimist by conviction. Few of us are thorough optimists; we have seen too much misery to declare glibly that all is for the best in the best of all possible worlds. Nations arming to the teeth; the growing cleavage between rich and poor; these symptoms, after nineteen hundred years of Christianity, are not calculated to comfort an intelligent person. But we are not thorough pessimists either. We are absolutely certain, though we cannot prove it, that life is beautiful. Fine weather—to take what may seem a small example; fine weather during the whole of a day; the whole city cheered by blue sky and sunshine. What a marvelous blessing that is! The thorough pessimist may reply that city weather is more often wet, and that a fine day is only a scrap in the midst of squalor. Possibly. But it is a scrap that glows like a jewel. If we hope for a great deal of beauty in life, we may be disappointed; nature has not cut her stuff thus; she cannot be bothered about us to this extent. But we may hope for *intensity* of beauty; that is absolutely certain, and never, since the beginning of time, has a man gone through life without moments of overwhelming joy. Perhaps, Mr. X., you will contradict this. But can you contradict it from your own experience? Can you sincerely say, "Never since I was born have I had one moment of overwhelming joy"? Don't reply, "I've been happy, but think of poor Mr. Y." It's no answer; for if Mr. Y. is questioned, he too will assuredly reply, "I've been happy," perhaps adding, "but think of poor Mr. X."

Here then is what one may call the irreducible minimum, the inalienable dowry of humanity: Beauty in scraps. It may seem a little thing after the comprehensive ecstasies of Whitman, but it is certain; it is for all men in all times, and we couldn't avoid it even if we wanted to. The beauty of the fine day amid dingy weather; the beauty of the unselfish action amid selfishness: the beauty of friendship amid indifference: we cannot go through life without experiencing these things, they are as certain as the air in the lungs. Some people have luck, and get more happiness than others, but every one gets something. And therefore, however pessimistic we are in our convictions, however sure we are that civilization is going to the dogs on account of those abominable—(here insert the name of the political party that you most dislike)—we yet remain optimists by instinct; we personally have had glorious times, and may have them again.

That is the position, as it appears to the average modern man. To him life is not all gold, as Whitman would have it; it is not even strung on a golden thread, as the great Victorian poets would have it, but it is pure gold in parts—it contains scraps of inexpressible beauty. And it is in his power to make a great deal of the scraps. He can, in the first place, practice cheerfulness. He can dwell on the wonderful moments of his existence, rather than on the dull hours that too often separate those moments. He can realize that quality is more precious than quantity. He can—to put it in plain English—stop grumbling. Grumbling is the very devil. It pretends that the whole of life is dull, and that the wonderful moments are not worth considering. Dante, a man of the soundest sense, puts grumblers deep into Hell.[5] They lie at the bottom of a dirty pond, and their words bubble to the surface saying, "Once we were sullen in the sweet sunlit air. Now we are sullen in the mud." Of course grumbling springs from a very real outside evil—from all the undoubted sorrow that there is in the world, and that no optimism can explain away. But it always flows far from its source. It pretends that the whole world is sorrow, a view that is as false as it is depressing; and if we sometimes resent the shallow optimist, who calls "peace" where there is no peace, we may equally

---

5. **Dante . . . Hell:** Reference to the Italian poet Dante Alighieri (1265–1321) and his work *The Divine Comedy*.

resent the shallow grumbler, who complains of war before war is declared, and who is either regretting the disasters of the past or expecting disaster in the future. To such a man, life can have no beauty. He can never open his eyes and look at the present, which may be full of sweet air and sunlight. If it is night, he cannot remember that the sun set yesterday and may rise tomorrow. He goes through existence pretending that he is at the bottom of a mud pond, as indeed he is, but it is a pond of his own digging. One must distinguish between such a man and the pessimist. The pessimist denies that life as a whole is beautiful, but he never denies the existence of beauty . . . But the grumbler denies everything, and no grumbler ever became a great man; he would not think it worthwhile.

If cheerfulness is one great help toward seeing the beauty in life, courage is certainly another. The average man needs to be just a little braver. He loses so much happiness through what might be termed "minor cowardices." Why are we so afraid of doing the "wrong thing," of wearing the "wrong clothes," of knowing the "wrong people," of pronouncing the names of artists or musicians wrongly? What in the name of Beauty does it matter? Why don't we trust ourselves more and the conventions less? If we first of all dress ourselves appropriately

Two Perspectives of *La Grenouillère*

La Grenouillère, Claude Monet (1840–1926), 1869, Oil on Canvas, 29⅜ x 39¼"

and fashionably, and then fill our minds with fashionable thoughts, and then go out in search of Romance with a fashionable and appropriate friend, is it likely that we shall find Romance? Is it likely that Life will give herself away to us, unless we also give ourselves away? There are occasions when one must be conventional—one's bread and butter often depends upon it; but there are occasions when one need not be, and on those occasions life opens her wonder-house. That is why one's happiest moments usually come on holidays. It is not that the surroundings are different. It is that we are different. We have not to pretend that we are valuable members of society . . . We have not to impress people by our ability or taste. We have merely to be ourselves, and like what we like. A little courage does the trick. The world is touched at once with a magical glow; the sea, the sky, the mountains, our fellow creatures, are all transfigured, and we return to work with unforgettable memories.

To sum up. A few great men—mostly poets—have found life absolutely beautiful, in all its aspects. Other great men have found it threaded, as it were, on a beautiful chain. But the average man finds that it is beautiful in parts only, and it is his attitude that is touched upon in this article. No definition of the Beauty of Life is offered, because it is

La Grenouillère, Pierre Auguste Renoir (1841–1919), 1869, Oil on Canvas, 26 × 31⅞"

"this to me and that to thee." Some people find it reflected in pictures and poems; others, going to life direct, find it in human interaction or in scenery; while a few have even found it in the higher truths of mathematics. But everyone, except the grumbler and perhaps the coward, finds it somewhere; and if the article contains anything, it contains a few tips which may make beauty easier to find. Be cheerful. Be courageous. Don't bother too much about "developing the aesthetic sense," as books term it, for if the heart and the brain are kept clean, the aesthetic sense will develop of itself. In your spare time, never study a subject that bores you, however important other people tell you it is; but choose out of the subjects that don't bore you, the subject that seems to you most important, and study that. You may say, "Oh, yes, it's jolly easy to preach like this." But it's also jolly easy to practice. The above precepts contain nothing heroical, nothing that need disturb our daily existence or diminish our salaries. They aren't difficult, they are just a few tips that may help us to see the wonders, physical and spiritual, by which we are surrounded. Modern civilization does not lead us away from Romance, but it does try to lead us past it, and we have to keep awake. We must insist on going to look round the corner now and then, even if other people think us a little queer, for as likely as not something beautiful lies round the corner. And if we insist, we may have a reward that is even greater than we expected, and see for a moment with the eyes of a poet— may see the universe, not merely beautiful in scraps, but beautiful everywhere and for ever.

> *The sun and stars that float in the open air,*
> *The apple-shaped earth and we upon it,*
>   *surely the drift of them is something*
>   *grand.*
> *I do not know what it is except that it is*
>   *grand, and that it is happiness.*

One final tip; read Walt Whitman. He is the true optimist—not the professional optimist who shuts his eyes and shirks, and whose palliatives do more harm than good, but one who has seen and suffered much and yet rejoices. He is not a philosopher or a theologian; he cannot answer the ultimate question, and tell us what life is. But he is absolutely certain that it is grand, that it is happiness, and that "wherever life and force are manifested, beauty is manifested." ◆

Responding to the Theme

Perspectives

■ ***Responding in Your Journal*** In your journal briefly describe what Forster sees as the perspective of a pessimist, an optimist, and a grumbler. Then explain what he thinks is the perspective of most educated people. Forster suggests that you have the option to change your perspective if you do not like or want the one you have. Do you agree with him? Do you think, for example, that if you are a grumbler, you can become a person who maximizes the "scraps of beauty"? Also, do you agree or disagree with Forster that having the courage to be yourself and to like what you like will make you happier? Throughout the rest of this week, jot down in your journal your thoughts and ideas about these questions—along with any other responses you have to "The Beauty of Life."

■ ***Speaking and Listening*** In the essay, "The Beauty of Life," E. M. Forster describes Walt Whitman as a person who knew what life was all about. As Forster states, Whitman "... had been through all that makes [life] hideous to most men ... yet [he] could believe that ... beauty is manifest wherever life is manifested." To Forster Whitman was a true optimist.

In the library find a copy of Walt Whitman's *Leaves of Grass* or some other poetry by Whitman. Select a poem or an excerpt that expresses Whitman's perspective on the beauty of life and practice reading it with expression and conviction. You may be called on to read your piece to the class.

■ ***Critical Thinking: Evaluating*** Which of the different perspectives on life that Forster proposed in "The Beauty of Life" do you subscribe to? After you evaluate the facts, examples, and illustrations he gives to support each perspective, explain in a paragraph which perspective seems most realistic, useful, or inspiring to you.

■ ***Extending Your Vocabulary*** In the dictionary look up the words *optimist* and *pessimist* to determine their exact meaning. Also find out what the origin of each word is and how the origin relates to the meaning. Then look up the meaning of the following *-ist* words that apply to different views of life: *realist*, *pragmatist*, *idealist*, *materialist*, and *fatalist*. Keep this list of words and their meanings in your journal to refer to later in this chapter.

297

Paris, Rue de Moscou and Rue de Turin, 1990

Paris, A Rainy Day, Gustave Caillebotte, 1876/77, Oil on Canvas, 212.2 × 276.2 cm
Charles H. and Mary F. S. Worcester Collection, 1964.336

Part 2 | *Writing*

To present Walt Whitman's view of life, Forster did not reproduce Whitman's writings word for word. Instead, he extracted some key ideas and expressed them in his own words, or summarized them. Although he did not prepare a formal summary, as you will do in this chapter, he condensed and paraphrased Whitman's ideas to allow you to grasp them more easily.

As a student, you will frequently use the skill of summarizing. For example, when you prepare a research paper, you summarize information to take notes. When you prepare for a test, you summarize information to study. When you explain other people's ideas to an audience, you summarize the ideas, as Forster did.

To write a concise summary, or précis, you should first learn how to identify the main ideas of a piece and how to restate them in your own words. In this chapter you will practice these skills as you follow the steps for writing a formal summary.

Writing Term

A **summary** is a condensation of a longer piece of writing, covering only the main points of the original.

Analyzing a Summary

Your main task when you write a summary is to restate the original ideas accurately and in your own words. Unlike an essay, a summary does not include personal comments, interpretations, or insights. Its purpose is to state clearly the most important ideas of a work by omitting the unnecessary details. The ideas are presented in the same order as in the original and with the same meaning. Writing a good summary takes some skill, then, for you must remain true to the original as you restate the main ideas and condense the details.

Features of a Summary

I. A summary is usually no more than one third the length of the original.

2. A summary extracts the main ideas of the original, omitting all but vital details.

3. A summary presents the main ideas in the same order as in the original.

4. A summary restates the main ideas of the original in the writer's own words.

WRITING ACTIVITY *Analyzing a Summary*

Read the original piece of writing and the summary that follows it. Then write answers to the numbered questions.

ORIGINAL   John Napier was a sixteenth-century Scottish mathematician whose neighbors feared he was a magician practicing the black arts. Fearful that Spain would invade the British Isles, he drew plans for all manner of strange defenses, from solar mirrors for burning ships at a distance to submarines and primitive tanks. However, his true fame rests on two great mathematical inventions: the decimal point and logarithms.

        Today mathematicians take for granted these handy exponents of numbers that make it possible to multiply and divide by simple addition and sub-traction. In Napier's day calculations were done

laboriously in the old-fashioned way, and he fret-
ted many hours over the time such arithmetic took.
. . . In 1594, the thought struck Napier that all
numbers could be written in exponential form, or
as powers of a certain base number. For instance,
4 is 2^2, and 8 is 2^3. This alone is not startling, but
Napier saw beyond it to a simple way of multiplying 4 times 8 without really multiplying. 2^2 plus
2^3 equaled 2^5 in Napier's new arithmetic, and 2^5
equals 32, the same as the product of 4 times 8.
The same principle applies to exponents of all
numbers, although there was a fantastic amount
of work involved in computing these exponents
extensively. In fact, it was not until 1614, twenty
years after his revelation of the basic idea, that
Napier published his logarithm tables. The result
was something like the introduction of the electronic computer in our time. Logarithms drasti-
cally reduced the amount of work involved in
mathematics and relieved scientists, particularly
astronomers, from a great burden of mental
drudgery.   DAN HALACY
Charles Babbage: Father of the Computer

SUMMARY

John Napier, an eccentric Scottish mathematician of the sixteenth century, invented the decimal
point and logarithms. Napier was concerned about
the time-consuming calculations needed to mul-
tiply and divide. In 1594, Napier realized that if
numbers were expressed with exponents, the sim-
pler tasks of addition and subtraction could be used
instead of multiplication and division, with the same
results. Twenty years of testing followed this discovery. When Napier finally published his logarithm tables in 1614, the time savings were similar
to the efficiency offered by electronic computers
in the present age.

1. Is the summary no longer than one third the length of the original?
2. The first paragraph in the original is reduced to how many sentences in the summary?

0–9, Jasper Johns, 1959, Encaustic and Collage on Canvas, 20⅛ x 35", Ludwig Collection

3. What two details about Napier from the first paragraph are omitted in the summary?

4. What adjective in the summary sums up those omitted details?

5. The second paragraph in the original is reduced to how many sentences in the summary?

6. Is the specific example in the third paragraph of the original retained in the summary?

7. Are all the dates from the original included in the summary?

8. Consider your answers to questions 3, 6, and 7. What is the difference between the details omitted in the summary and those retained?

9. What detail about the effect of the logarithm tables has been left out of the summary?

10. How are the main ideas of the original ordered in the summary?

WRITING ACTIVITY 2 *Writing on Your Own*

WRITING
ABOUT THE
THEME
Prepare to write a summary of E. M. Forster's "The Beauty of Life" by rereading the essay to remind yourself of Forster's main ideas about perspectives on life. After you have finished, note the main ideas in your journal for future reference.

Prewriting

For most types of writing, you begin with a main idea and then develop that idea by adding details. When writing a summary, however, you begin with a detailed composition and reduce it to its main ideas by omitting details. Before you write a summary, then, you need to understand the work thoroughly. The following steps will help you.

Preparing to Write a Summary

1. Read the original work to get the main idea.
2. Read the work again, writing down unfamiliar words.
3. Write a synonym or a simple definition for each word.
4. Read the work a third time, writing down the main ideas in the order in which they are presented.
5. Determine the length of the original. Count the words if the original is short; count the lines or pages if it is long.

Recognizing Main Ideas

After you are certain you understand the selection, you can move on to the most important task in summarizing: distinguishing between main ideas and supporting ideas. To find the main ideas, ask, "Which idea is more general than all the others?" In many cases the sentence expressing the most general idea will be the topic sentence of a paragraph or the thesis statement of an essay or article. Sometimes, however, the main idea will be implied, not stated. In such cases phrase a statement of your own expressing the main idea. Study these examples.

Model: *Main Idea Stated*

Weight-Lifting Goals

Despite its apparent simplicity, or perhaps because of it, people have different ideas about what the sport of weight lifting should be. Some confine themselves to seeing how many pounds they can lift. Others feel that strength should be combined with speed. Still others think that what's most important is not what they lift but how their muscles look after they lift it.

WILLIAM F. ALLMAN
"Weight Lifting: Inside the Pumphouse"

The main idea of the preceding paragraph is stated directly in the first sentence, or topic sentence. Now look for the implied main idea in the paragraph that follows.

Model: *Implied Main Idea*

Teenagers and Gulls

An outsider might look at a group of teenagers standing in front of a school and see only a confused and apparently random grouping of individuals. This interpretation, however, would be misleading, just as misleading as it would be to describe a colony of herring gulls as a bunch of birds. The gullery is, in reality, a highly structured society with leaders and followers, defined territories, and a whole host of subtle but very powerful symbols that keep each gull in its place. It is the same with the teenagers standing in front of their school. Generally everybody in the group knows who the leaders are, and a careful observer might be able to spot the leaders by the particular confidence in the way that they walk or stand and by the way others in the group act toward them.

DANIEL COHEN

Human Nature, Animal Nature:
The Biology of Human Behavior

In this paragraph there is no stated idea that is more general than the others. The main idea is quite clear, nevertheless, and could be expressed as follows: *However random they may seem, certain groups of people, like certain groups of animals, are highly structured.* All the other sentences support this idea.

WRITING ACTIVITY *Recognizing Main Ideas*

Write the main idea of each paragraph that follows. If the main idea is stated directly, copy it from the paragraph. If it is implied, write your own sentence expressing the idea.

I.

Some of the most important movies to come from postwar Europe were the Neo-Realist films from Italy. These films show life as it is lived, not as film studios imagine it to be. They show the streets, the houses, the vital everyday people of a struggling world; they neglect glamour, fancy houses and clothes, and movie stars. They argue against poverty, unemployment, inadequate housing, and the moral chaos caused by the war; and they offer realistic approaches, if not solutions, to realistic problems. The postwar Neo-Realist movement was short-lived, but it contributed some film masterpieces and left a distinct influence on future film-making.

2.

The producer works closely in the selection of actors and actresses, and he or she makes sure that the length of their contracts fits the overall shooting schedule. He or she goes over the shooting script (the screenplay broken down into shots, scenes, and locations) to plan indoor sound-stage settings and outdoor shooting locations. The locations must be scouted for such all-important variables as weather, geography, local facilities, transportation, and accessibility. The shooting schedule must be planned around another set of variables, which includes shooting "out of continuity" (in other words, a film in which the last scene might be shot before the first) and weather (when the script calls for sun, the schedule must be planned for a time of year when the sun is likely to shine). When the movie is completed, the producer is in charge of selling it to distributors, of planning advertising and publicity, and of other agreements, such as sales to television. If the film is successful at the box office, the producer takes a large share of the profits. If it wins awards, such as the Academy Award for the best picture, it is the producer, not the director, who receives it.

3.

Movie photography is the responsibility of two people: the director of photography and the camera operator. The director of photography (also called the cinematographer) attends the story conference and plans the shots to be filmed in consultation with the director, writer, and other members of the unit. The camera operator is the person responsible for overseeing the lighting and operating the camera used in shooting the film. In many films the two roles are performed by the same person.

4.

Some actors and actresses are famous for their low-keyed approach to roles; others are popular because they overact (or "chew up the scenery," as such a performance is known). Some are famous for their singing (Elvis Presley), swimming (Esther Williams), or dancing (Fred Astaire). Still others, like Henry Fonda, have become stars for their association with certain historical

Katharine Hepburn and Henry Fonda, from the Movie, *On Golden Pond*

persons whose lives they have portrayed. Some, like Katharine Hepburn, are popular for the simple reason that they perform year after year, in movie after movie, and always give a good performance. There are no easy rules and no easy answers in the subject of acting.

5.

When Robert Redford gets into a fight in *Butch Cassidy and the Sundance Kid* (1969), the chances are that he is not in the fight at all but that a "double" is performing for him. Stunt performers act as doubles for actors and actresses when the action called for in the script is dangerous. Other stunt performers are experts at various sports or at driving fast cars or at falling off horses without getting hurt. Great skill is used in photographing these performers so that the audience sees their work but not their faces. When the film is edited, we are fooled into thinking that the stars of a picture are also excellent skiers or boxers or motorcyclists.

Preceding Excerpts by RICHARD MERAN BARSAM
In the Dark: A Primer for the Movies

WRITING ACTIVITY *Writing on Your Own*

WRITING
ABOUT THE
THEME
Using the essay "The Beauty of Life" on pages 291–296, complete the following tasks to help you fully understand the work. Then save your work in your writing folder.

1. Reread the passage and make a list of unfamiliar words.
2. For each word, write a synonym or a definition in your own words.
3. Read the passage a third time and list the main ideas in order.
4. Determine the length of the work.

Critical Thinking   *Writing Is Thinking*

Using Criteria to Make Evaluations

When you plan a party, you do not invite everyone you know. Instead, you select people who know one another and who fit the occasion for the party. When you pack for a trip, you likewise do not take everything you own. Instead, you select only those things that will meet your needs on the trip. In each case you select items by *evaluating*, or judging, them according to a particular set of *criteria*, or standards. This is exactly the procedure you should follow when you select ideas to include in a summary.

As you gain practice in writing summaries, you are likely to develop criteria of your own. The list below, however, will help you get started evaluating ideas. If you find you answer *yes* to one or more of the questions, you will probably want to include the idea in your summary.

Evaluating Ideas to Include in a Summary

1. Does the idea support the main thesis of the work?
2. Is the idea needed for the reader to understand the work? Does the thesis become unclear if the idea is omitted?
3. Does the idea provide new information, rather than repetitious information?
4. Is the idea necessary to the understanding of another idea, rather than just helpful or interesting as an example or anecdote?
5. Is the idea needed as a logical bridge connecting other ideas?
6. As you sum up the work in your mind, do you find yourself including the idea?

Thinking Practice   Use the criteria listed in the chart above to help you evaluate the main ideas you listed in Writing Activity 4. Once you have evaluated each idea, put a check mark next to those ideas that you will include in your summary of "The Beauty of Life." Then save your work in your writing folder.

Drafting

After you are certain you understand all the words in the selection and have listed the main ideas, you are ready to write the first draft of your summary. The draft should include all the important ideas of the original, restated in your own words and presented in a shortened form. The following steps will help you draft a summary that restates the important ideas in your own words.

Strategies for Drafting a Summary

1. Present the main ideas in the same order in which they appear in the original.
2. Condense the original by
- omitting unnecessary details.
- combining ideas from several sentences into one.
- replacing long phrases, clauses, and sentences with shorter phrases or even single words.
3. Paraphrase (restate the original ideas) by
- using synonyms.
- varying sentence structure.

Condensing

Condensing means shortening the information in a passage. You can do this by eliminating repetitious ideas and other unnecessary details such as examples and descriptions. In addition you can combine ideas and reduce long phrases and clauses into shorter expressions. Study the following examples of an original passage and its summary to see just how these techniques are applied. The sentences in both the original passage and the summary are numbered for easy reference.

Model: *Condensing*

Mount Rushmore

ORIGINAL   (1) Rushmore got a great deal of free publicity in 1934 when the Hearst newspapers sponsored a contest for a six-hundred-word history to be carved on Mount Rushmore. (2) An inscription had been part of Gutzon Borglum's design for a long time. (3) At one point he had asked Coolidge to write the inscription, but he and Coolidge disagreed over the wording, so nothing came of that. (4) Eight hundred thousand entries were submitted in the Hearst contest, and many cash prizes were given. (5) No entries were ever used because eventually Gutzon abandoned the inscription idea in favor of a great Hall of Records to be cut in the stone of the canyon behind the faces. (6) Gutzon felt that records carved or placed in a room in the mountain would last much longer than any identifying inscription on the surface of the mountain.

SUMMARY

(1) In 1934, the Hearst newspapers sponsored a contest for an inscription for Mount Rushmore, which had been part of artist Gutzon Borglum's original plan. (2) Eight hundred thousand people responded. (3) Although many won cash prizes, their inscriptions were abandoned when Borglum decided instead to create a Hall of Records, a room carved into the stone, which he felt would be more permanent than a carved inscription.

The following chart shows how the sentences from the original were condensed in the summary.

Original Sentence	Summary Sentence
1 & 2 ⟶	1 (main idea)
3 ⟶	omitted (unnecessary detail)
4 ⟶	2
5 & 6 ⟶	3

Writing Tip **Condense** information by omitting repetitious and unnecessary details and by combining ideas from two or more sentences into one sentence. Present the ideas in the same order as the original.

WRITING ACTIVITY *Condensing*

Condense each of the following paragraphs to no more than two sentences. Write those sentences next to the number of the paragraph.

(1) Writers exclaim over the coast of Maine so often that their descriptions lose meaning. "Rugged," "rockbound," and "pine-clad" generally fail to stir up any visions of this northeastern shore. Yet the Maine coast is all of them and much more, too. It is a splendid part of the country—shaped and hammered by vast natural forces, softened by forests, haunted by human history. People cannot visit these coves and harbors without falling hopelessly in love with the feeling of morning fog burning off under a warm sun, the scent of pine needles in the cool shade of the forest, the taste of wild blueberries, the muffled thunder of waves, the crisp hue of sunset on a cool evening. The best example of the 3,478-mile Maine coast (including the islands) is Acadia National Park, which became the first great park in the East.

Coast Scene, Mount Desert, Frederic E. Church, 1863, Oil on Canvas

(2) During the last Ice Age, this shoreline was pressed down by the huge weight of ice and snow. Glaciers scraped the rocky land, smoothed the hills, cracked loose rock away from parent ledges. The result is a sunken coast where what were once valleys are now sounds and inlets, where little granite islands jut from the ocean, where tumbled boulders clog the shore. Most of Maine is like this: Acadia typifies it. For here rise the heights of Mount Desert Island, the round-sculptured remnants of the pre-Ice Age mountain ridge. Its tallest summit is the highest point in the United States that overlooks the Atlantic, and one of the first to catch the rising sun's rays.

(3) A deep, narrow sound cuts Mount Desert Island almost in two: Somes Sound, the only true fjord on the New England coast. On either side the hills rise, covered with tough, stunted pine and spruce and rich with wildflowers. Cadillac Mountain, 1,530 feet, marks the high point. Below it spreads Frenchman Bay and the old summer resort of Bar Harbor.

(4) The history of Mount Desert Island portrays a long struggle for ownership. Samuel de Champlain, a French explorer, discovered the island and named it L'Isle des Monts Deserts (the Isle of Bare Mountains). A French colony, later founded on the island, was taken over by English colonists from Virginia. Subsequently, the island was owned privately by several British and French aristocrats including Antoine de la Cadillac, who founded the city of Detroit, and Sir Francis Bernard, the last English governor of Massachusetts. After the Revolutionary War the land was sold to settlers in Maine. By 1900, Mount Desert Island was discovered by thousands of summer visitors.

(5) Acadia was donated to the Federal government by the summer residents (once called "rusticaters" by the locals) who, between them, owned most of Mount Desert Island. That's why the park boundaries are strangely uneven—they follow the property lines. Most of the 48-square-mile park lies on Mount Desert Island; some is across Frenchman Bay on the Schoodic Peninsula; some occupies part of the Isle au Haut, an offshore island southwest of Mount Desert. All these park lands contain choice elements of scenery. Fresh-water ponds and lakes gleam among the dark evergreens on Mount Desert. Trout, salmon, and bass flirt with the angler, while salt-water fishing invites visitors to brave the gray Atlantic in chartered vessels.

PAUL JENSEN, *National Parks* (Adapted)

Paraphrasing

Another valuable technique when summarizing material is *paraphrasing*—that is, using your own words to express the main ideas and essential details. Two techniques will help you paraphrase information: using synonyms to replace the original words and varying the sentence structure of the original.

Writing Tip   **Paraphrase,** or restate ideas in your own words, by using synonyms and by varying the sentence structure of the original.

The following example of paraphrasing shows you how the same ideas are stated in different words.

Model: *Paraphrasing*

ORIGINAL   Ralph Bunche was awarded the Nobel Peace Prize in 1950 for negotiating a resolution to the Israeli-Egyptian conflict of 1948 and 1949.

PARAPHRASE   For his success in mediating a peace agreement between warring Israel and Egypt in 1949, Ralph Bunche won the Nobel Peace Prize in 1950.

The synonyms in the paraphrase are *mediating* for *negotiating, peace agreement* for *resolution,* and *warring* for *conflict.* The passive *was awarded* in the original has been changed to the active *won* in the paraphrase. In addition, the paraphrase begins with a prepositional phrase, while the original begins with the subject.

WRITING ACTIVITY   **6**   *Paraphrasing*

Read the following passage about the camel. Then paraphrase each sentence in the excerpt by using synonyms and a different sentence structure. Look up any unfamiliar words.

(1) The camel has long had a reputation for being able to go for long periods of time without drinking any water. (2) Ancient writers believed that the camel had some mysterious internal water reservoir—a story that was told for so many centuries that it came to be believed. (3) No such reservoir, however, has ever been found. (4) Nevertheless, the camel is remarkably suited to getting along well on a minimum of water.

(5) Even in the Sahara's dry summer, when little natural food is available, camels can go for a week or more without water and for ten days without food. (6) Camels accomplish this feat by drawing on water from their body tissues and on water produced chemically as a breakdown product of fat. (7) The camel's hump contains up to 50 pounds of fat, which is accumulated when food and water are plentiful. (8) As the fat is used up to supply the camel's energy needs, about 1.1 pounds of water are produced for every pound of fat used up. (9) This is made possible because hydrogen is given off as a by-product in the breakdown of fat. (10) Oxygen from breathing is then combined with the hydrogen to produce water.

(11) With the help of this water-producing system, a camel can function well for a good many days, even when carrying a load. (12) When water is again available, the camel gulps down as much as 25 gallons at one time to compensate for the water lost during the period of deprivation.

WILLIAM C. VERGARA, *Science in the World Around Us*

WRITING ACTIVITY 7 *Writing on Your Own*

WRITING
ABOUT THE
THEME

Using your notes from Writing Activity 4 and the Thinking Practice on page 306, write a first draft of a summary of E. M. Forster's perspectives as stated in "The Beauty of Life." Follow the Strategies for Drafting a Summary on page 307. Then save your work for future revision.

Revising

As you revise your summary, check for accuracy and conciseness. Reread the original to make sure you have represented the ideas accurately. Also try to reduce your summary to the fewest words possible. The following checklist will help you.

Revision Checklist

1. Compare your summary to the original. Have you represented the ideas accurately?
2. Are the ideas in your summary presented in the same order as in the original?
3. Estimate the length of your summary. Is your summary no more than one third as long as the original? If it is too long, condense your work further by repeating step 2 in the Strategies for Drafting a Summary. *(See page 307.)*
4. Did you use synonyms and vary the sentence structure to paraphrase?
5. Did you use transitions and other connecting devices to make your summary flow smoothly? *(See pages 101–102.)*

WRITING ACTIVITY *Revising a Summary*

Use the Revision Checklist to revise the following first draft of a summary. The original piece, which you will need to refer to as you revise, appears on page 303.

> A group of teenagers in front of a school is as confused and random a group as a colony of herring gulls. Everybody in the group knows who the leaders are, and outsiders can spot the leaders by their confidence and the way others act toward them. Both are organized groups—with directors and followers, their own turf, and private signals.

WRITING ACTIVITY *Writing on Your Own*

WRITING
ABOUT THE
THEME

Use the Revision Checklist to revise the first draft of your summary of "The Beauty of Life" from Writing Activity 7. Save your work for later use.

Editing and Publishing

Grammar in the Writing Process

If there were no subordinate clauses in English, E. M. Forster would have written short, choppy sentences such as those that follow.

> The thorough pessimist may have a reply. The city weather is more often wet. A fine day is only a scrap in the midst of squalor. Possibly. But it is a scrap. The scrap glows like a jewel. We hope for a great deal of beauty in life. We may be disappointed.

A *subordinate clause* is a group of words that has a subject and verb but that cannot stand alone. With the underlined subordinate clauses, the sentences that Forster actually wrote flow smoothly.

> The thorough pessimist may reply <u>that the city weather is more often wet</u>, and <u>that a fine day is only a scrap in the midst of squalor</u>. Possibly. But it is a scrap <u>that glows like a jewel</u>. <u>If we hope for a great deal of beauty in life</u>, we may be disappointed; nature . . . cannot be bothered about us to this extent.

Adverb Clauses   One kind of subordinate clause—which begins with such words as *after, although, since,* and *when*—is an adverb clause. An *adverb clause* is used just like a single adverb or an adverb phrase, usually to modify a verb. In the following examples, the adverb clauses reduce unnecessary repetition and provide sentence variety. *(For other examples and for practice in using adverb clauses correctly, see pages 612–615.)*

ADVERB
CLAUSES
If we resent the shallow optimist, we may equally resent the shallow grumbler.

No grumbler ever became a great man **because he would not think it worthwhile.**

Although people experience difficult times, people remain optimistic by nature.

(For information about adjective clauses and noun clauses, two other kinds of subordinate clauses, and for practice in using them correctly, see pages 616–621.)

314

Punctuation with Adverb Clauses Place a comma after an introductory adverb clause. If, however, an adverb clause interrupts the main sentence, enclose it in commas. *(For practice in writing adverb clauses correctly, see pages 612–614.)*

ADVERB CLAUSES   Optimists are absolutely certain**, although they cannot prove it,** of life's beauty.

Combining Sentences with Adverb Clauses By changing a sentence into an adverb clause and combining it with another sentence, you can express the relationship between two ideas. Combining sentences is also a good way to eliminate unnecessary words. *(For practice in combining sentences using adverb clauses, see pages 69–70.)*

TWO SENTENCES   Beauty means different things to different people. I cannot give a definition of beauty.

ONE SENTENCE   **Since beauty means different things to different people,** I cannot give a definition of beauty.

TWO SENTENCES   One could look at life with the eyes of a poet. One would see beauty everywhere.

ONE SENTENCE   **If one could look at life with the eyes of a poet,** one would see beauty everywhere.

Editing Checklist

1. Have any subordinate clauses been used for sentence variety? *(See pages 69–71.)*
2. Are all subordinate clauses punctuated correctly? *(See pages 613 and 617.)*
3. Have sentences been combined with subordinate clauses to show the relationship between ideas? *(See pages 612–616.)*

WRITING ACTIVITY 10  *Writing on Your Own*

WRITING ABOUT THE THEME

Editing Using the Editing Checklist on page 38 and the checklist above, edit your summary of E. M. Forster's essay "The Beauty of Life" from Writing Activity 9.

Publishing Write a final copy of your summary. Then, if your teacher permits, form small groups and compare your summaries.

A Writer Writes

A Summary

PURPOSE: to summarize "Shakespeare's Sister" by Virginia Woolf
AUDIENCE: classmates and other peers

Prewriting   Today there are many celebrated and talented women writers—poets, novelists, short-story writers, journalists, essayists, screenwriters, lyricists, speechwriters. This abundance of women writers is a modern phenomenon, however. Not very long ago women writers were rare indeed. Some women writers, like George Eliot and George Sand, even felt it necessary to assume male pseudonymns. Sixteenth-century England—Shakespeare's time—was an especially difficult time for women writers. Why? Virginia Woolf offers her perspective on the question in "Shakespeare's Sister" on pages 131–134.

Doris Lessing

Toni Morrison

Nadine Gordimer
Ruth Prawer Jhabuala

To prepare to write a formal summary of this selection, read or reread "Shakespeare's Sister," pages 131–134, to understand the main thesis. Then complete the following prewriting tasks.

- Read the work again, listing any unfamiliar words. Look up each word and write a synonym for it or a definition in your own words.
- Read the work a third time, jotting down the main ideas in order. Evaluate the various ideas and details to determine which are basic to the main thesis of the selection. In particular, keep in mind that the imaginary story of Shakespeare's sister is used by Virginia Woolf as an example to convey certain ideas. It is Woolf's ideas, rather than the details of the example, that you should summarize.
- Determine the approximate length of the work by counting the pages.

Drafting   Begin to draft your summary by presenting the main ideas in order and condensing and paraphrasing the information. To condense the information, leave out minor details such as examples and descriptions. In addition, combine several sentences into one using phrases and clauses. Reduce the wordiness of the original by leaving out long expressions and unnecessary words. As you paraphrase the main ideas, use your own words by supplying synonyms for the original words and by varying the sentence structure.

Revising   *Peer Conferencing:*   With your teacher's permission, compare your summary with that of a partner. Discuss how each of you condensed and paraphrased Virginia Woolf's essay in your summaries. Then use the following questions to evaluate your partner's summary. Finally, use your partner's comments and the Revision Checklist on page 313 to revise your own summary.

- Are all the important ideas of the original essay represented accurately in the summary?
- Are the ideas in the summary presented in the same order as in the original?
- Does the summary use concise language?

Editing and Publishing   Edit your revised summary carefully, using the Editing Checklists on pages 38 and 315. To make corrections use the proofreading symbols on page 39. Then make a neat final copy to share with an interested reader. You may want to read about and summarize the lives of some women writers, including Virginia Woolf and George Eliot, and collect your summaries into a classroom reference.

Independent Writing

Look through the poetry section of your literature anthology or skim collections of poetry in the library to find a poem in which the author conveys directly or indirectly his or her perspective on life. For example, a poem filled with despair and hopelessness might reflect the perspective of a grumbler as described in Forster's "The Beauty of Life." Once you have found an appropriate poem, write a summary of it.

  # Creative Writing

In your journal you have written about different perspectives on life. Review your journal notes and choose two or three perspectives that spark your interest and imagination. Then write a poem about them, devoting a stanza to each of the views and ending with a stanza presenting your own perspective on life. Publish your poem along with those of your classmates in a class literary magazine.

  # Writing about Literature

Allusion is a reference a writer makes to a person, place, or event that is easily recognized by the reader. For example, an allusion may be made to a historical figure like Julius Ceasar, a literary character like Charles Dickens's Oliver Twist, or to a painting like Leonardo DaVinci's *Mona Lisa*. In the essay "The Beauty of Life," E.M. Forster makes an allusion to Dante. Find this allusion in his essay. Then write a paragraph identifying the allusion and explaining what purpose Forster achieves by including it in his essay.

  # Writing in Other Subject Areas

World History   Use the card catalog in the library to find a book about a historical period that interests you. Then read an article or chapter giving a perspective on an event in history and write a summary of the work.

Foreign Language   Read a newspaper or magazine article in a foreign language that you are studying and write a summary of the article in English. Share your summary with a reader who is unfamiliar with the foreign language used in the original.

8 Checklist

Writing Summaries

Prewriting

✔ Read the original work once to understand the general idea.

✔ Read the work a second time and make a list of unfamiliar words.

✔ Look up each unfamiliar word and write a synonym for it or define it in your own words.

✔ Read the work a third time, jotting down the main ideas in order. *(See pages 302–303.)*

✔ Determine the length of the original work. Count the words if the original is short; count the lines or pages if it is long.

Drafting

✔ Present the main ideas in the same order in which they appeared in the original. *(See page 307.)*

✔ Condense the original to approximately one third its length by omitting unnecessary details, combining ideas from several sentences into one, and replacing long phrases, clauses, and sentences with shorter phrases or even single words. *(See pages 307–308.)*

✔ Restate the original ideas in your own words by using synonyms and by varying sentence structure. *(See page 311.)*

Revising

✔ Use the Revision Checklist to check for accuracy and length. *(See page 313.)*

Editing and Publishing

✔ Use the Editing Checklists to check the accuracy of your grammar, usage, spelling, and mechanics. *(See pages 38 and 315.)*

✔ Use proofreading symbols to mark corrections. *(See page 39.)*

✔ Follow standard manuscript form and make a neat final copy. Then select a way to share your summary. *(See pages 42–43.)*

9 Writing Research Papers

Part 1 | *Reading to Write*

THEME: *Countries of the World*

After seeing a movie that took place in another country, have you ever gone home, wishing that you could pack up and move to that country—or at least go there for a two-week vacation? Perhaps you have even imagined how your life might have been different if you had been born in that country. These wishes and daydreams are common to many people because most countries of the world have a mysterious fascination about them, probably because the majority of people know so little about them. In geography classes in school, you read about a country's geographical features, its imports and exports, and a little about its history. Although information like this is useful, it seldom gives you the feeling of having been there—of having known and talked to the people there.

In the following selection, entitled "Shooting an Elephant," you will read about an experience British writer George Orwell had while working in Burma as a police officer. In that capacity he had to develop an understanding of the Burmese way of thinking, their customs, and their values in order to perform his job effectively. As you read this account, consider what it would be like to live and work in another country.

Shooting an Elephant

G e o r g e   O r w e l l

In Moulmein, in lower Burma, I was hated by large numbers of people—the only time in my life that I have been important enough for this to happen to me. I was sub-divisional police officer of the town, and in an aimless, petty kind of way anti-European feeling was very bitter. No one had the guts to raise a riot, but if a European woman went through the bazaars alone somebody would probably spit betel juice over her dress. As a police officer I was an obvious target and was baited whenever it seemed safe to do so. When a nimble Burman tripped me up on the football field and the referee (another Burman) looked the other way, the crowd yelled with hideous laughter. This happened more than once. In the end the sneering yellow faces of young men that met me everywhere, the insults hooted after me when I was at a safe distance, got badly on my nerves. The young Buddhist priests were the worst of all. There were several thousands of them in the town and none of them seemed to have anything to do except stand on street corners and jeer at Europeans.

All this was perplexing and upsetting. For at that time I had already made up my mind that imperialism was an evil thing and the sooner I chucked up my job and got out of it the better. Theoretically—and secretly, of course—I was all for the Burmese and all against their oppressors, the British. As for the job I was doing, I hated it more bitterly than I can perhaps make clear. In a job like that you see the dirty work of Empire at close quarters. The wretched prisoners huddling in the stinking cages of the lock-ups, the grey, cowed faces of the long-term convicts, the scarred buttocks of the men who had been flogged with bamboos—all these oppressed me with an intolerable sense of guilt. But I could get nothing into perspective. I was young and ill-educated and I had had to think out my problems in the utter silence that is imposed on every Englishman in the East. I did not even know that the British Empire is dying, still less did I know that it is a great deal better than the younger empires that are going to supplant it. All I knew was that I was stuck between my hatred of the empire I served and my rage against the evil-spirited little beasts who tried to make my job impossible. With one part of my mind I thought of the British Raj[1] as an unbreakable tyranny, as something clamped down, in *saecula saeculorum,*[2] upon the will of prostrate peoples; with another part I thought that the greatest joy in the world would be to drive a bayonet into a Buddhist priest's guts. Feelings like these are the normal by-products of imperialism; ask any Anglo-Indian official, if you can catch him off duty.

One day something happened which in a roundabout way was enlightening. It was a tiny incident in itself, but it gave me a better glimpse than I had had before of the real nature of imperialism—the real motives for which despotic governments act. Early one morning the sub-inspector at a police station the other end of the town rang me up on the 'phone and said that an elephant was ravaging the bazaar. Would I please come and do something about it? I did not know what I could do, but I wanted to see what was happening and I got on to a pony and started out. I took my rifle, an old .44 Winchester and much too small to kill an elephant, but I thought the noise might be useful *in terrorem.*[3] Various Burmans stopped me on the way and told me about the elephant's doings. It was not, of course, a wild elephant, but a tame one which had gone "must."[4] It had been chained up, as tame elephants always are when their attack of "must" is due, but on the previous night it had broken its chain and escaped. Its mahout,[5] the only person who could manage it when it was in that state, had set out in pursuit, but had taken the wrong direction and was now twelve hours' journey away, and in the morning the elephant had suddenly reappeared in the town. The Burmese population had no weapons and were quite helpless against it. It had already destroyed somebody's bamboo hut, killed a cow and raided some fruit-stalls and devoured the stock; also it had met the municipal

1. **Raj** [räj]: Rule or sovereignty in India.
2. *saecula saeculorum* [sē′k͞oo lə sē′k͞oo lôr′əm]: Phrase meaning "forever and ever" (Latin).
3. *in terrorem:* Phrase meaning "for terror" (Latin).
4. **"must":** In a state of frenzy.
5. **mahout** [mə hout′]: Person who is the keeper and driver of an elephant.

rubbish van and, when the driver jumped out and took to his heels, had turned the van over and inflicted violences upon it.

The Burmese sub-inspector and some Indian constables were waiting for me in the quarter where the elephant had been seen. It was a very poor quarter, a labyrinth of squalid bamboo huts, thatched with palm-leaf, winding all over a steep hillside. I remember that it was a cloudy, stuffy morning at the beginning of the rains. We began questioning the people as to where the elephant had gone and, as usual, failed to get any definite information. That is invariably the case in the East; a story always sounds clear enough at a distance, but the nearer you get to the scene of events the vaguer it becomes. Some of the people said that the elephant had gone in one direction, some said that he had gone in another, some professed not even to have heard of any elephant. I had almost made up my mind that the whole story was a pack of lies, when we heard yells a little distance away. There was a loud, scandalized cry of "Go away, child! Go away this instant!" and an old woman with a switch in her hand came round the corner of a hut, violently shooing away a crowd of naked children. Some more women followed, clicking their tongues and exclaiming; evidently there was something that the children ought not to have seen. I rounded the hut and saw a man's dead body sprawling in the mud. He was an Indian, a black Dravidian[6] coolie, almost naked, and he could not have been dead many minutes. The people said that the elephant had come suddenly upon him round the corner of the hut, caught him with its trunk, put its foot on his back and ground him into the earth. This was the rainy season and the ground was soft, and his face had scored a trench a foot deep and a couple of yards long. He was lying on his belly with arms crucified and head sharply twisted to one side. His face was coated with mud, the eyes wide open, the teeth bared and grinning with an expression of unendurable agony. (Never tell me, by the way, that the dead look peaceful. Most of the corpses I have seen looked devilish.) The friction of the great beast's foot had stripped the skin from his back as neatly as one skins a rabbit. As soon as I saw the dead man I sent an orderly to a friend's house nearby to borrow an elephant rifle. I had already sent back the pony, not wanting it to go mad with fright and throw me if it smelt the elephant.

The orderly came back in a few minutes with a rifle and five cartridges, and meanwhile some Burmans had arrived and told us that

6. **Dravidian:** Race of people who inhabit southern India.

the elephant was in the paddy fields below, only a few hundred yards away. As I started forward practically the whole population of the quarter flocked out of the houses and followed me. They had seen the rifle and were all shouting excitedly that I was going to shoot the elephant. They had not shown much interest in the elephant when he was merely ravaging their homes, but it was different now that he was going to be shot. It was a bit of fun to them, as it would be to an English crowd; besides they wanted the meat. It made me vaguely uneasy. I had no intention of shooting the elephant—I had merely sent for the rifle to defend myself if necessary—and it is always unnerving to have a crowd following you. I marched down the hill, looking and feeling a fool, with the rifle over my shoulder and an ever-growing army of people jostling at my heels. At the bottom, when you got away from the huts, there was a metalled[7] road and beyond that a miry waste of paddy fields a thousand yards across, not yet ploughed but soggy from the first rains and dotted with coarse grass. The elephant was standing eight yards from the road, his left side towards us. He took not the slightest notice of the crowd's approach. He was tearing up bunches of grass, beating them against his knees to clean them and stuffing them into his mouth.

I had halted on the road. As soon as I saw the elephant I knew with perfect certainty that I ought not to shoot him. It is a serious matter to shoot a working elephant—it is comparable to destroying a huge and costly piece of machinery—and obviously one ought not to do it if it can possibly be avoided. And at that distance, peacefully eating, the elephant looked no more dangerous than a cow. I thought then and I think now that his attack of "must" was already passing off; in which case he would merely wander harmlessly about until the mahout came back and caught him. Moreover, I did not in the least want to shoot him. I decided that I would watch him for a little while to make sure that he did not turn savage again, and then go home.

But at that moment I glanced round at the crowd that had followed me. It was an immense crowd, two thousand at the least and growing every minute. It blocked the road for a long distance on either side. I looked at the sea of yellow faces above the garish clothes—faces all happy and excited over this bit of fun, all certain that the elephant was going to be shot. They were watching me as they would watch a conjurer about to perform a trick. They did not like me, but with the

---

7. **metalled:** Paved using broken stones.

magical rifle in my hands I was momentarily worth watching. And suddenly I realized that I should have to shoot the elephant after all. The people expected it of me and I had got to do it; I could feel their two thousand wills pressing me forward, irresistibly. And it was at this moment, as I stood there with the rifle in my hands, that I first grasped the hollowness, the futility of the white man's dominion in the East. Here was I, the white man with his gun, standing in front of the unarmed native crowd—seemingly the leading actor of the piece; but in reality I was only an absurd puppet pushed to and fro by the will of those yellow faces behind. I perceived in this moment that when the white man turns tyrant it is his own freedom that he destroys. He becomes a sort of hollow, posing dummy, the conventionalized figure of a sahib.[8] For it is the condition of his rule that he shall spend his life in trying to impress the "natives," and so in every crisis he has got to do what the "natives" expect of him. He wears a mask, and his face grows to fit it. I had got to shoot the elephant. I had committed myself to doing it when I sent for the rifle. A sahib has got to act like a sahib; he has got to appear resolute, to know his own mind and do definite things. To come all that way, rifle in hand, with two thousand people marching at my heels, and then to trail feebly away, having done nothing—no, that was impossible. The crowd would laugh at me. And my whole life, every white man's life in the East, was one long struggle not to be laughed at.

But I did not want to shoot the elephant. I watched him beating his bunch of grass against his knees, with that preoccupied grandmotherly air that elephants have. It seemed to me that it would be murder to shoot him. At that age I was not squeamish about killing animals, but I had never shot an elephant and never wanted to. (Somehow it always seems worse to kill a *large* animal.) Besides, there was the beast's owner to be considered. Alive, the elephant was worth at least a hundred pounds; dead, he would only be worth the value of his tusks, five pounds, possibly. But I had got to act quickly. I turned to some experienced-looking Burmans who had been there when we arrived, and asked them how the elephant had been behaving. They all said the same thing: he took no notice of you if you left him alone, but he might charge if you went too close to him.

It was perfectly clear to me what I ought to do. I ought to walk up to within, say, twenty-five yards of the elephant and test his behavior.

8. **sahib** [sä'ib]: Term meaning "sir" or "master." During the colonial period in India, the Indians used this term when addressing Europeans.

If he charged, I could shoot; if he took no notice of me, it would be safe to leave him until the mahout came back. But also I knew that I was going to do no such thing. I was a poor shot with a rifle and the ground was soft mud into which one would sink at every step. If the elephant charged and I missed him, I should have about as much chance as a toad under a steam-roller. But even then I was not thinking particularly of my own skin, only of the watchful yellow faces behind. For at that moment, with the crowd watching me, I was not afraid in the ordinary sense, as I would have been if I had been alone. A white man mustn't be frightened in front of "natives"; and so, in general, he isn't frightened. The sole thought in my mind was that if anything went wrong those two thousand Burmans would see me pursued, caught, trampled on and reduced to a grinning corpse like that Indian up the hill. And if that happened it was quite probable that some of them would laugh. That would never do. There was only one alternative. I shoved the cartridges into the magazine and lay down on the road to get a better aim.

The crowd grew very still, and a deep, low, happy sigh, as of people who see the theatre curtain go up at last, breathed from innumerable throats. They were going to have their bit of fun after all. The rifle was a beautiful German thing with cross-hair sights. I did not then know that in shooting an elephant one would shoot to cut an imaginary bar running from ear-hole to ear-hole. I ought, therefore, as the elephant was sideways on, to have aimed straight at his ear-hole; actually I aimed several inches in front of this, thinking the brain would be further forward.

When I pulled the trigger I did not hear the bang or feel the kick—one never does when a shot goes home—but I heard the devilish roar of glee that went up from the crowd. In that instant, in too short a time, one would have thought, even for the bullet to get there, a mysterious, terrible change had come over the elephant. He neither stirred nor fell, but every line of his body had altered. He looked suddenly stricken, shrunken, immensely old, as though the frightful impact of the bullet had paralysed him without knocking him down. At last, after what seemed a long time—it might have been five seconds, I dare say—he sagged flabbily to his knees. His mouth slobbered. An enormous senility seemed to have settled upon him. One could have imagined him thousands of years old. I fired again into the same spot. At the second shot he did not collapse but climbed with desperate slowness to his feet and stood weakly upright, with legs sagging and head drooping. I fired a third time. That was the shot that did for him. You could see the agony of it jolt his whole body and knock the last remnant of strength from his legs. But in falling he seemed for a moment to rise, for as his hind legs collapsed beneath him he seemed to tower upward like a huge rock toppling, his trunk reaching skywards like a tree. He trumpeted, for the first and only time. And then down he came, his belly towards me, with a crash that seemed to shake the ground even where I lay.

I got up. The Burmans were already racing past me across the mud. It was obvious that the elephant would never rise again, but he was not dead. He was breathing very rhythmically with long rattling gasps, his great mound of a side painfully rising and falling. His mouth was wide open—I could see far down into caverns of pale pink throat. I waited a long time for him to die, but his breathing did not weaken. Finally I fired my two remaining shots into the spot where I thought his heart must be. The thick blood welled out of him like red velvet, but still he did not die. His body did not even jerk when then the shots hit him, the tortured breathing continued without a pause. He was dying, very slowly and in great agony, but in some world remote from me where not even a bullet could damage him further. I felt that I had got to put an end to that dreadful noise. It seemed dreadful to see the great beast lying there, powerless to move and yet powerless to die, and not even to be able to finish him. I sent back for my small rifle and poured shot after shot into his heart and down his throat. They seemed to make no impression. The tortured gasps continued as steadily as the ticking of a clock.

In the end I could not stand it any longer and went away. I heard later that it took him half an hour to die. Burmans were bringing dahs[9] and baskets even before I left, and I was told they had stripped his body almost to the bones by the afternoon.

Afterwards, of course, there were endless discussions about the shooting of the elephant. The owner was furious, but he was only an Indian and could do nothing. Besides, legally I had done the right thing, for a mad elephant has to be killed, like a mad dog, if its owner fails to control it. Among the Europeans opinion was divided. The older men said I was right, the younger men said it was a damn shame to shoot an elephant for killing a coolie, because an elephant was worth more than any damn Coringhee coolie. And afterwards I was very glad that the coolie had been killed; it put me legally in the right and it gave me a sufficient pretext for shooting the elephant. I often wondered whether any of the others grasped that I had done it solely to avoid looking a fool. ◆

9. **dahs** [däz]: Large, heavy knives.

Responding to the Theme

Countries of the World

Responding in Your Journal   Choose a foreign country that you would like to visit one day. Then test your knowledge of that country by answering the following questions. What are the advantages and disadvantages of living in that country? How has the history of the country affected present-day life? What objects are most important to the people? What are some of their customs and traditions? This week do some reading and writing about the country you chose. Read parts of books or magazine articles about the country you have chosen—skimming past the standard information and focusing on the aspects of the country that make it unique. Also look for answers to the questions above. As you read, write in your journal. Jot down any interesting information you find as well as your reactions to what you are reading. What, for example, do you find most interesting about the country or its people? By the end of the week, you should have written a substantial amount about the country.

Speaking and Listening   With your teacher's permission, work with another student to prepare a speech about Burma: its history, geography, government, culture, and any unique features. *(See the steps for preparing a speech on pages 430–437.)* Then be ready to present your speech to the class or a small group of students.

Critical Thinking: Analyzing   "Shooting an Elephant" is not simply a story about a police officer who kills an elephant; it is an essay about the effects of *imperialism*—one country controlling another country. According to Orwell what are the effects of imperialism? Analyze the essay "Shooting an Elephant." Then write a paragraph explaining Orwell's viewpoint. Back up your statements with examples from his essay.

Extending Your Vocabulary   Among the many countries of the world are many different languages from which English has acquired some words. Use a dictionary to find the origin of each of the following animal names:

elephant	rhinoceros	giraffe	goose	raccoon
kangaroo	chimpanzee	alligator	panda	coyote

Part 2 / *Writing*

The research paper is an important tool in gaining knowledge on any subject, including the unique features of different countries in the world. When you read about a subject of interest, you often learn something new. When you go further and analyze and evaluate what you have read, you learn even more. However, if you go still further and write a research paper about what you have learned, you have made the information your own.

Writing Term   A **research paper** is a composition based on research drawn from from books, periodicals, and interviews.

When you write research papers, you draw on many different skills. For example, to find information in books and magazines, you exercise your library skills and study skills. *(See pages 481– 491 and 500–504.)* As you gather information and take notes, you use the skills of summarizing and paraphrasing. *(See Chapter 8, Writing Summaries.)* Finally, since the purpose of a research paper is to convey information, you use the skills developed in expository writing to help you present the information clearly and concisely. *(See Chapter 4, Writing Essays to Inform, on pages 130–173.)*

Prewriting

Writing Process

Your main goals in the prewriting stage of a research paper are to choose your subject and then gather information about it. As you collect information, you will need a good system for keeping track of notes from different sources. Index cards, paper clips, rubber bands, and a folder with pockets will make your job easier.

Discovering Subjects

When you search for ideas to write about, you can explore two avenues. One is inside you—your experiences and thoughts. The other is outside—the classes you take, the books you enjoy, the news stories you read. Therefore, to find an interesting subject, ask yourself questions such as those in the following activities.

WRITING ACTIVITY *Finding Ideas from Personal Experience*

Ask yourself the following questions and write answers to them.

1. What hazardous situation have I found myself in? What could I tell others to help them avoid similar situations?
2. Who are my personal heroes? Why? What function do heroes serve?
3. What careers interest me? What are some of the interesting aspects of the careers? What are some drawbacks?
4. What hobbies or other interests do I have? Who are the experts in these fields? What have they contributed?
5. What information would I like to have about computers and other technological advances?
6. How do I spend my leisure time? How do others my age spend their leisure time?
7. What places have I visited? What places would I like to visit? What places would I like to know more about?
8. What do I do well? What would I like to do well?
9. How are the attitudes of my generation different from those of my parents' generation? What accounts for the differences?
10. How do I take care of my health and safety? What kinds of things do people need to know to prevent illness and injury?

WRITING ACTIVITY **2** *Finding Ideas from Outside Sources*

Ask yourself the following questions and write answers to them.

1. What topics in my classes would I like to know more about?
2. Who are my favorite composers and musicians?
3. What literature have I enjoyed in English class this year?
4. What are some trends in motion pictures today?
5. What changes resulted from the last election?
6. What have I recently learned about from books, magazines, and television and radio shows?
7. What classes or lessons do I take outside of school?
8. What have I learned from an older relative or friend?
9. In what part of the world are dramatic events happening?
10. What noteworthy events have occurred recently?

Choosing and Limiting a Subject

After you have explored your thoughts and experiences, use the following guidelines to help you choose one idea as a subject.

Guidelines for Choosing a Subject

1. Choose a subject you would like to know more about.
2. Choose a subject that would interest your audience.
3. Choose a subject that can be adequately covered in a research paper of about 2,000 words (or 7 typed pages).
4. Choose a subject on which there is likely to be sufficient information in the school or local library.

To see if sufficient information exists, check the card catalog in the library, as well as the *Readers' Guide to Periodical Literature. (See pages 484–490.)* If you cannot find at least two books and two magazine articles on your subject, you should probably think of another one.

When you are satisfied that you can find enough information, your next step is to limit your subject and give it a clear focus. The subject of black holes in space, for example, is broad enough to fill a whole book. Within that subject, though, are more specific subjects such as "how Einstein's work predicted the possibility of black holes"; "how black holes are created"; or "how instruments are used to search for black holes."

One way to limit your subject is to ask yourself a series of "what about" questions. Each question helps you focus on a more specific aspect of a broad subject. The following model shows how to use "what about" questions to narrow down the broad subject of *computers*.

Student Model: *Limiting a Subject*

BROAD SUBJECT	computers
FIRST QUESTION	*What about* computers?
MORE LIMITED	how computers help people with disabilities
SECOND QUESTION	*What about* computers and people with disabilities?
MORE LIMITED	how computers help people with disabilities in language, vision, and motion
THIRD QUESTION	*What about* computers' helping with language, vision, and motion?
SUITABLY LIMITED	recent developments and successes in computers' helping people with disabilities in language, vision, and motion

Continue your "what about" questions until your answer is a phrase. This focused statement will help guide you through the subsequent steps of researching and writing.

Writing Tip  **Limit your subject** by asking, "What about [the subject]?" until you can express the focus of your research paper in a phrase or partial sentence.

WRITING ACTIVITY *Choosing and Limiting a Subject*

For each subject that follows, write *suitable* if the subject is narrow enough for a short research paper. If it is too broad, write a series of "what about" questions and answers until you arrive at a suitably limited subject. Use the model above as a guide.

  I. the Japanese language
  2. American Indian words that have become part of the English language
  3. how the space shuttle serves business and research

4. baseball

5. physical fitness

6. what to do when you encounter potentially dangerous animals while hiking through the wilderness

7. Martin Luther King, Jr.

8. Poland

9. how engineers solved the problems in building the Brooklyn Bridge

10. the Ming dynasty

WRITING ACTIVITY *Writing on Your Own*

WRITING
ABOUT THE
THEME
 Use your journal notes and your answers to the questions in Writing Activities 1 and 2 to generate ideas for a research paper on some aspect of a particular country of the world. After you use the guidelines on page 332 to choose a subject, limit that subject by asking a series of "what about" questions.

Gathering Information

Once you have a suitably limited subject, your next step is to formulate a list of questions your paper should answer. If you have decided to write a paper on current developments in how computers are helping people with disabilities, for example, your guide questions might include the following.

Student Model: *Guide Questions*

- Are there different kinds of computers for different disabilities?
- How do computers help people with language disabilities?
- How do they help people who have lost their ability to speak or have never been able to speak?
- Just how do computers help people who are blind "see"? How do they help them read and write?
- How do computers help people who have limited mobility? How do they help people who are paralyzed? How do they help them move? What tasks do they help them perform?
- What are the costs? What are the benefits?

After you have a list of between five and ten questions, you can turn to appropriate library sources to answer them. The following steps will guide you through the process of collecting appropriate sources in the library.

Steps for Gathering Information

1. Begin by consulting a general reference work such as an encyclopedia or handbook to gain an overview of your subject. Also make a note of any sources that are listed at the end of articles.

2. Use the subject cards in the card catalog to find books on your subject.

3. Consult the *Readers' Guide to Periodical Literature* to find magazine articles on your subject.

4. Use a newspaper index to identify news articles.

5. Make a list of all available sources on your subject. For each book, record the author, title, copyright year, name and location of the publisher, and the call number. If your source is a magazine or newspaper, record the name and date of the publication, the author, the title, and the location (section and page numbers) of the article.

6. Assign each source a number to identify it in your notes.

Conducting an Interview If you are aware of one or more experts who can contribute valuable details to your paper, make an appointment for an interview, either in person or by telephone. The steps on the next page will help you prepare for an interview and conduct it productively.

Connie Chung interviewing Shirley Temple Black, via satellite

Steps for Conducting an Interview

1. Prepare at least five specific questions to ask the person you are interviewing.

2. Go to the interview with your questions in hand. Also take pencils and paper for note-taking and a tape recorder if available.

3. If you are taking notes, summarize the main ideas in your own words.

4. Stay alert for important details and colorful, lively phrases that you might quote directly. Write these word for word and enclose them in quotation marks.

5. If you need extra time to write your notes, politely ask the interviewee to wait for a few moments while you finish writing.

6. If you are recording the interview, follow steps 3 and 4 when you take notes from the recording.

7. Immediately after the interview, review your notes and fill in any details you may not have had time to include.

WRITING ACTIVITY *Gathering Information*

Using the resources in the library, list five sources for three of the following subjects. At least two of your sources should be magazine articles. Be sure to include all the information named in step 5 on page 335.

1. violence on television

2. pros and cons of nuclear power plants

3. improving public housing

4. new car designs

5. fighting air and water pollution

WRITING ACTIVITY *Conducting an Interview*

Interview a classmate in preparation for a research paper on the future plans of today's high school graduates. Follow the steps outlined above in Steps for Conducting an Interview. After the interview write a paragraph or two paraphrasing the interview. Include some direct quotations in your paraphrase. *(See more about paraphrasing on pages 311–312.)*

Writing Is Thinking

Analyzing

Suppose you wanted to know how a car works. How would you find out? You would probably open the hood and start looking at the different parts of the engine to see what they are and what they do. Breaking something down into its various parts is usually the best way to understand it—whether it is a car, a story, or an idea. When you carry out the process systematically, you are *analyzing*.

As you prepare to write a research paper, stop to analyze your subject. Ask yourself how you can break it down into smaller parts. To open your mind and help you analyze the subject, try a cluster. Below, for example, is a cluster made by a student preparing a research paper on computers.

An Analyzing Cluster

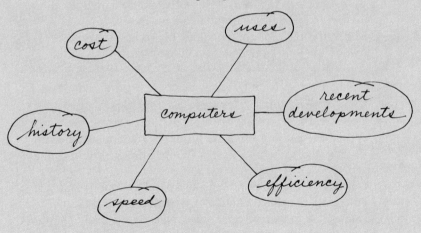

Once you have identified the major parts of a subject, you can use them to limit the subject and also to point out specific directions for your research.

Thinking Practice   Make a cluster to analyze the main parts of your research paper on a nation of the world. Use it to help you limit your subject and decide on specific aspects of that country you should investigate.

Evaluating Sources

Reviewing sources for up-to-dateness, accuracy, and objectivity is an essential part of all research. If a book has an old publication date, for example, it may be missing critical new information. If the author is biased—has a strong leaning toward one viewpoint because of emotion or self-interest—then the book or article may have only information that supports the author's viewpoint. The following checklists will help you evaluate your sources.

Checklist for Evaluating Books

1. Who is the author? What are his or her credentials? You can find these by reading the book jacket or by reading about the author in a biographical reference work. *(See page 488.)*
2. Is there anything in the author's background that might suggest a biased viewpoint?
3. What is the publication date? If the subject requires the most up-to-date information, such as recent medical findings, then avoid books that are more than a few years old.
4. Check the table of contents and the index. Is there information on your limited subject in the book?

Checklist for Evaluating Articles

1. Who is the author? What are his or her credentials? You can usually find these in a note at the beginning or end of the article.
2. Does the magazine or newspaper appeal to a special-interest group that may have a biased viewpoint on your subject? For example, a magazine called *Conserving Energy* would probably try to persuade people to rely less on automobiles. A periodical called *Highways and Byways,* on the other hand, might try to boost tourism by encouraging people to use their automobiles for long trips.
3. When was the article published? If your subject requires the most up-to-date information, then avoid publications that are more than a few years old.
4. Does the article contain specific information on your limited subject?

After using the preceding checklists to evaluate books and articles, use only those sources you can rely on for accuracy and objectivity. Five to ten good sources should supply you with enough information to build a strong research paper.

WRITING ACTIVITY *Evaluating Sources*

Each of the following sources for a report on consumer safety suffers from one of the weaknesses listed below. Write the weakness that applies to each source.

probably outdated   lacks strong author credentials
probably biased   does not relate to subject

1. "Unnecessary Safety Controls Will Raise Prices," article in *Toymaker's Trade*, written by Lara Scranton, director of public relations at Smile-a-While Toy Company, published in 1990.
2. "Consumer Price Index Holds Steady," article in *Today* magazine, written by Manuel Garcia, chief economist at Central State Bank, published in 1990.
3. *Consumer Rights and Safety*, book published in 1963, written by William Stepanian, researcher in the Office of Consumer Affairs in the state of Illinois.
4. "The Need for Warning Labels," article in *Your House* magazine, written in 1991 by Helene Mayer, a magazine writer who writes a regular column on fashion tips.
5. "Harmful Additives," pamphlet published in 1991 by Nature-Foods Industries, written by Kyle Gardner, Executive Vice President of Nature-Foods Industries.

WRITING ACTIVITY *Writing on Your Own*

WRITING
ABOUT THE
THEME

Using your limited topic from Writing Activity 4, make a list of five to ten research guide questions that can help you find more information about the country you have chosen. These are the questions you will want your paper to answer. Then proceed to gather appropriate sources, using the guidelines on page 335 to help you. Finally, use the checklists on page 338 to evaluate each source you find and then eliminate any sources that do not fulfill the criteria. Keep your list of sources in your writing folder as preparation for taking research notes.

Taking Notes and Summarizing

The research guide questions you developed earlier will help you locate relevant information in each source. As you take notes on that information, keep the following goals in mind.

Writing Tip   The goals of **note-taking** are to summarize main points in your own words and record quotations that you might use in your research paper.

Start by taking your index cards out of your folder. As you use each card, write the identifying number of each source in the upper right-hand corner of the note card. *(See page 342.)* Then, in the upper left-hand corner, write the topic of the note. In most cases that topic will correspond to one of your guide questions. For instance, on the subject of computers' helping people with disabilities, notes taken to answer the question "How do computers help people who cannot speak?" might be labeled *loss of speech*. On each card include only notes that relate to a single topic. Then clip the cards from each source together.

As you take notes, include only information that answers a guide question. However, as you acquire more information, you may want to revise your questions to be more specific or to cover different aspects of your subject.

The following paragraphs are from a *Forbes* magazine article. The student who is writing the paper on computers and people with disabilities has assigned this source the identifying number *10*. Read the excerpt and compare it with the sample note card on page 342.

Student Model: *Taking Notes on Note Cards*

Past Cambridge University's King's College, where dozens of bicycles lean against time-blackened, 15th-century walls, a dim courtyard off Silver Street houses the Department of Applied Mathematics and Theoretical Physics.

There, in a cluttered, dank office, one of the true geniuses of 20th-century science quietly goes about his daily work of pondering the universe. He is Stephen Hawking, 45, the world's greatest theoretical physicist.

For more than 20 years this seminal thinker has suffered from amyotrophic lateral sclerosis, a progressively debilitating, ultimately fatal nerve disease that strips its victims of the ability to walk, talk, and eventually move even a finger. For a decade,

Hawking has been wheelchair bound. Two years ago he lost his ability to speak altogether.

But Hawking keeps right on thinking and communicating from within his bodily prison, and for that both he and the world can thank the advances of computer technology and bionic medicine. At the office, Hawking writes and talks through an IBM personal computer equipped with a voice synthesizer and custom-designed communications software. Outside the university, he uses a battery-operated computer with a small, liquid crystal screen and a voice synthesizer that is mounted beneath the seat of his motorized wheelchair.

To start his desktop computer, Hawking moves his thumb [one of the few remaining activities he can perform] to press a button on a box that an assistant places in the palm of his hand. A menu of letters and words appears on the computer screen. Hawking presses another button to move his cursor to the desired words, which then slowly appear as complete sentences at the bottom of the screen. Another movement from his thumb sends the sentence to a built-in voice synthesizer, which generates speech. During a recent interview with *Forbes*, Hawking pressed on his box several times until the disembodied voice asked, "Can I have some tea?"   RICHARD C. MORAIS, *Forbes*

Stephen Hawking at home with his wife Jane

Sample Note Card

TOPIC 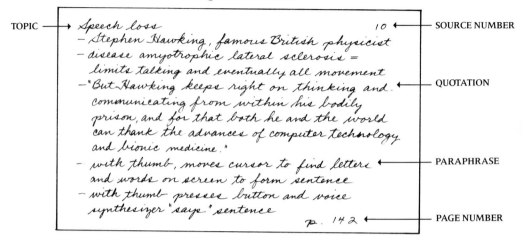 SOURCE NUMBER

QUOTATION

PARAPHRASE

PAGE NUMBER

WRITING ACTIVITY *Taking Notes*

Take notes on the following excerpt about Stonehenge, the ancient arrangement of stones in England through which one can observe celestial activities. The excerpt is from pages 117–118 of the book *Stonehenge Decoded*, written by Gerald S. Hawkins and John B. White. Assume that the work has the identifying number *3*.

The Stonehenge sun-moon alignments were created and elaborated for two, possibly three, reasons: they made a calendar, particularly useful to tell the time for planting crops; they helped to create and maintain priestly power, by enabling the priest to call out the multitude to see the spectacular risings and settings of the sun and moon, most especially the midsummer sunrise over the heel stone[1] and the midwinter sunset through the great trilithon[2] and possibly they served as an intellectual game.

To amplify a little on those three supposed reasons, let me state that it is well known that methods for determining the times of planting were of most vital concern to primitive peoples. Those times are hard to detect. One can't count backwards from the fine, warm days; one must use some other means. What better means could there be for following the seasons than

---

[1] A large stone standing alone outside the circular structure and marked with a heel-shaped nick at the bottom.
[2] A trilithon is a grouping of three rocks in which two tall pillar rocks are connected at the top by a third that spans the distance between them.

observation of those most regular and predictable recurring objects, the heavenly bodies? Even in classic times there were still elaborate sets of instructions to help farmers to time their planting by celestial phenomena. Discussing the "deep question" of the "fit time and season of sowing corn," Pliny[3] declared, "this would be handled and considered upon with exceeding great care and regard; as depending for the most part on Astronomy . . ." Doubtless there are today farmers who time their planting by the sky.

As for the value of Stonehenge as a priestly power enhancer, it seems quite possible that the person who could call the people to see the god of day or night appear or disappear between those mighty arches and over that distant horizon would attract some of the aura of deity. Indeed, the whole people who possessed such a monument and temple must have felt lifted up.

The other possible reason for the astronomical ingenuity . . . of Stonehenge is, I must admit, my own invention. I think that those Stonehengers were true ancestors of ours. I think that the people who designed its various parts, and perhaps even some of the people who helped to build those parts, enjoyed the mental exercise above and beyond the call of duty. I think that when they had solved the problem of the alignments efficiently but unspectacularly, they couldn't let the matter rest. They had to set themselves more challenges, and try for more difficult, rewarding, and spectacular solutions, partly for the greater glory of their pre-Christian gods, but partly for the joy of humans, the thinking animals. I wonder if some day some authority will establish a connection between the spirit which animated the Stonehenge builders and that which inspired the creators of the Parthenon, and the Gothic cathedrals, and the first space craft to go to Mars.

[3] An ancient Roman writer.

WRITING ACTIVITY  *Writing on Your Own*

WRITING ABOUT THE THEME Take out the sources you evaluated in Writing Activity 8 and use your guide questions to take notes on each of your sources. When you have finished, clip your note cards together and save them in your folder for later use.

Developing a Working Thesis Statement

After you have finished taking notes, draft a *working thesis statement* that expresses the main idea of your paper. *(See pages 156–157.)* The following working thesis statement is based on information gathered about computers helping people with disabilities.

Student Model: *Working Thesis Statement*

Computers are able to help people who have language problems, vision problems, and motion problems related to paralysis and loss of limb.

WRITING ACTIVITY *Writing a Working Thesis*

Below are notes on robot sensors, which allow robots to sense objects around them. Write a working thesis statement that covers the information and then save your work.

a. Some robots are programmed to hear and respond to only one human voice giving commands.

b. The sense of touch in some robots is controlled by the machine's receiving an electrical charge when it touches an object.

c. Some robots can be programmed to edit out differences in voice quality so that they can respond to any human voice.

d. The simplest form of robot sight is the ability to detect the presence or absence of light.

e. In some hearing robots, a double entry system is used. The first step is a voice command from its programmer; the second step requires an additional command from the programmer.

f. Some robots can control the amount of pressure they exert on an object through what is called force feedback.

g. Some robots can "see" gradations of light and dark, not merely its presence or absence.

h. TV cameras are used in some robots as a vision device.

i. Some robots do not have to touch things to know they are nearby; proximity sensors tell them when they are near objects.

WRITING ACTIVITY *Writing on Your Own*

WRITING
ABOUT THE
THEME

After you review the notes you took in Writing Activity 10, formulate a working thesis statement that expresses the purpose and main idea of your research paper. Save your work.

344

Organizing Your Notes

Your working thesis statement and your guide questions are all you need to help you sort your note cards into categories. Notice, for example, that the following categories on the subject of computers' helping people with disabilities are directly related to the questions that guided the research. Some questions have been left out, however, to control the length of the paper.

Student Model: *Organizing Note Cards into Categories*

CATEGORY 1	How computers help those with language disabilities
CATEGORY 2	How computers help those with vision-related problems
CATEGORY 3	How computers help those with paralysis or loss of limb
CATEGORY 4	Computer costs versus benefits

Writing Tip **Group your notes** into three or more main categories of information.

After you arrange your note cards by category, clip the cards in each group together. If some notes do not fit a category, put them into a separate group for possible use in your introduction or conclusion.

WRITING ACTIVITY **13** *Creating Categories*

Review the notes on robot sensors in Writing Activity 11. List the three categories into which you can group the details and then, under each category, write the letters of the details that belong in that group. Save your work.

Outlining

Your final prewriting step is to organize your notes into an outline. As the basis for your outline, use the categories into which you grouped your notes. Then look over your notes to determine the overall organization of the paper. If your subject is a historical event, *chronological order* may be appropriate. If you intend to describe something, *spatial order* may be suitable. However, the two most common methods of organizing research papers are *order of importance* and *developmental order. (See pages 28–29 for more about ordering information.)*

Writing Tip   Plan the **outline** of your research paper by deciding on a method of organization and by assigning your categories accordingly, using Roman numerals.

Below is the beginning of the outline for the paper on computers and disabled people. Notice the parallel phrasing.

Student Model: *Categories*

    I. Computers helping people with language disabilities
   II. Computers helping people with vision disabilities
  III. Computers helping people with motion disabilities

The outline omits one category from page 345—*Computer costs versus benefits*—because this material will be covered in the conclusion.

Once you have outlined your main topics, you can use the information on your note cards to add subtopics (listed with capital letters) and supporting points (listed with Arabic numerals). To check that the form of your outline is correct, refer to the checklist on page 152.

The following outline can serve as a model for your own outline. Each group of subtopics and details is phrased in parallel form.

Student Model: *Outlining*

WORKING THESIS STATEMENT	Computers are able to help people who have language problems, vision problems, and motion problems related to paralysis and loss of limb.
MAIN TOPIC	I. Computers helping people with language disabilities
SUBTOPICS	A. Program for children slow in speech development
	B. "Light talkers" for cerebral palsy victims
	C. Computer and speech synthesizer
	II. Computers helping people with vision disabilities
	A. "Seeing Eye" computers
	B. Reading machines
SUPPORTING DETAILS	1. Convert print into vibrating rods
	2. Convert print into speech and Braille
	3. Convert print into electronic impulses
	4. Convert calculator operations into speech
	5. Convert typed messages into speech

346

III. Computers helping people with motion disabilities
    A. Wheelchairs with legs
    B. Voice-operated computers
    C. Eye-operated computers
       1. ERICA
       2. Sutter's work
    D. Work stations

WRITING ACTIVITY *Writing an Outline*

Using your work from Writing Activities 11 and 13, write an outline about robot sensors. Write your working thesis statement at the top of your paper. Then, in your outline, show three main topics with at least three subtopics under each one. List the main topics with Roman numerals and the subtopics with capital letters.

WRITING ACTIVITY *Writing on Your Own*

WRITING
ABOUT THE
THEME

Write an outline for your research paper about a foreign country. Begin by organizing your note cards from Writing Activity 10 into categories and arranging those categories. Then create an outline based on the categories you created. Once you fill in subtopics and details from your notes, check the form of your outline. Finally, save your work for later use.

Three Flags, Jasper Johns, 1958, Encaustic on Canvas, 30⅞ × 45½ × 5″

Drafting

Once you have synthesized, or pulled together, your research to form an outline, you should use that outline as the basis of your first draft. As you draft, you want to flesh out your outline, adding an introduction and conclusion and working the results of your research into the flow of your paper.

Writing the Thesis Statement

A clear, well-worded *thesis statement* expresses your main idea and serves as a guiding beacon to help you keep on track as you write your first draft. Therefore, before you start to write, evaluate your working thesis to ensure that it covers all the topics in your outline—and only those topics. The following guidelines will help you revise your working thesis statement.

Writing a Thesis Statement

1. A thesis statement should make the main point of your research paper clear to a reader.
2. A thesis statement should be broad enough to cover all the main topics listed in your outline.
3. A thesis statement should be narrow enough to cover only the topics listed in your outline.
4. A thesis statement should fit smoothly into your introduction.

Suppose you are doing research on the subject of animal camouflage and have come up with the following main topics.

   I. Creatures with spots resembling eyes that appear threatening to would-be predators
  II. Creatures with coloration that matches the environment
 III. Creatures with coloration that changes with the seasons

You might then start with the following working thesis.

Sample: *Working Thesis Statement*

Many creatures find some protection from predators through coloration that blends into the environment.

The preceding thesis is too narrow because it fails to include the category of creatures with eyespots, whose camouflage does not blend into the environment but instead makes the creature appear threatening. A simple revision, however, can broaden the thesis.

Sample: *Revised Thesis Statement*

> Many creatures adopt a disguise that helps protect them from predators.

WRITING ACTIVITY *Revising Thesis Statements*

Rewrite each of the following numbered thesis statements so that it covers all the main topics in the accompanying outline (shown with Roman numerals).

South of the Border

1. Many of Mexico's most important exports are foodstuffs.
   I. Sugar
   II. Cotton
   III. Coffee
   IV. Forestry products

2. The three climate zones of Mexico are determined by the various altitudes of the lands.
   I. Tierra fria (cold lands), above 1,830 m (6,000 ft.)
   II. Tierra templada (temperate lands), plateau region at 1,830 m
   III. Tierra caliente (hot lands), coastal areas below 900 m (3,000 ft.)
   IV. Shortage of rainfall in all climate zones except in some coastal areas

3. The Social Security System in Mexico is similar to that of the United States.
   I. Benefits for accidents and disability
   II. Retirement pensions
   III. Differences

4. Mexico shows the influences of many different cultures.
   I. Spanish influence on language
   II. Spanish influence on customs
   III. Survival of some ancient Indian languages and customs

5. The site of Mexico City is unusual.
   I. Situated on former lake; land under buildings is sinking
   II. Valley location makes waste disposal a problem
   III. High altitude makes air pollution from cars a problem

WRITING ACTIVITY *Writing on Your Own*

Use the guidelines in the box on page 348 to revise the working thesis statement that you wrote at the top of your outline in Writing Activity 15. Be sure that the thesis statement covers all the information you have gathered in your research.

Structuring the Research Paper

With your thesis statement revised, you can move on to the remainder of your paper. Below is a summary of the parts and special features of research papers.

The Structure of a Research Paper

TITLE	• suggests the subject of the report
INTRODUCTION	• captures attention
	• provides important and interesting background information
	• contains the thesis statement
BODY	• supports the thesis statement with information drawn from research
	• consists of a series of well-developed paragraphs
CONCLUSION	• brings the report to a close by restating the thesis or giving fresh emphasis to ideas stated previously
CITATIONS	• credits appropriate sources of words, facts, and ideas
WORKS CITED	• lists sources used in preparing the report
	• appears at the end of paper

Read the following model research paper, noticing how each element fits into the whole structure. In addition, notice how research details are worked in and cited. When you write your own paper, you will also incorporate words, ideas, and facts from your sources. Each time you use information from a source, write the title, author, and page number in parentheses directly after the detail.

Since the following paper has been revised and edited, you can use it as a model to work toward as you draft and redraft.

Student Model: *Research Paper*

TITLE	New Help for People with Disabilities
INTRODUCTION: BACKGROUND INFORMATION	Computers have proved their usefulness in business, learning, and play. For much of the population, at work and at home, they have made ordinary tasks easier, faster, and often more fun. Computers, however, can do more than make
THESIS STATEMENT	already possible procedures more efficient. For many people with disabilities, computers can make the impossible possible--by providing language for those who cannot speak, vision for those who cannot see, and movement for those who cannot move.
BODY: MAIN TOPIC I FROM OUTLINE	A computer program to help children with language disabilities communicate has been developed by Laura Meyers, a specialist in children's language development. As a child types on the keyboard, each letter, word, and sentence is displayed on the screen and "pronounced" by a voice synthesizer--a device that imitates the sound of a human voice. Meyers
BORROWED WORDS IN QUOTATION MARKS	says, "The children see the thought printed. They hear it repeated, and it becomes psycho-logically real to them because they did it themselves" (Adelson 166). Once the computer has spoken for the children, they find it easier to speak for themselves.

The United Cerebral Palsy Association of Nassau County, New York, holds preschool classes in which children with cerebral palsy use "light talkers." They hit a switch that lights up a picture and sends a spoken message. If a child lights up the Cookie Monster, for example, the computer declares, "I'm hungry" (Cunningham 17). Older children use more complicated light talkers with many more pictures and messages.

351

Adults unable to speak as a result of disease or injury are also using speech synthesizers to communicate. A victim of the disease amyotrophic lateral sclerosis, the world-famous physicist Stephen Hawking is unable to talk or to move, except for his thumb. "But Hawking keeps right on thinking and communicating from within his bodily prison, and for that both he and the world can thank the advances of computer technology and bionic medicine" (Morais). Using his thumb on a keyboard, he selects words and letters and sends them to a voice synthesizer that speaks for him.

BODY:
MAIN TOPIC II
FROM OUTLINE

Computers are also opening new doors for the blind. "Seeing Eye" computers are being developed that can alert people who are sightless to objects in their path. A camera worn on the shoulder takes in images of objects ahead. A computer then processes these images and, with a speech generator, "talks" to the person. "The blind person is told what direction to take and how far away an obstacle is. The computer provides an update on landscape every 1 or 2 feet" (Hintz and Hintz 23).

BORROWED
FACT CITED
WITH NOTE

Devices have also been developed to help people who are blind read. One reading machine converts printed characters into patterns of vibrating rods that can be "read" with the fingertips. Another more sophisticated machine converts a printed text into synthesized speech and also into Braille (Cattoche 59). A computer mouse, or pointer, has been adapted to carry electronic impulses that allow users who are blind to "read" the screen through their fingertips (Bronson 140). New York City's National Technology Center of the American

Foundation for the Blind is working on advanced tools such as talking scientific calculators (Cunningham 16). Finally computers that use speech synthesizers to convert typed messages into "spoken" ones are extremely useful for students and workers who are blind, just as they are for people who are language-impaired.

BODY:
MAIN TOPIC III
FROM OUTLINE

Computers have come to the aid of people who are movement-impaired as well. "Even such familiar devices as wheelchairs are being souped up using microprocessors and sophisticated computer design" (Bronson 143). John Trimble at the Veterans Administration Hospital in Hines, Illinois, is working on a chair with movable legs controlled by a microprocessor. Mechanical devices work hand in hand with computers, even on the simplest level. A program at the University of Illinois produced a mechanical table that lowers a computer screen within the reach of a user who can move only one finger ("Engineers' Devices" 44).

In 1985, a football accident paralyzed Marc Buoniconti from the neck down. Four years later Marc was a college honors student, aided by a voice-operated computer that answered the phone, turned off lights, and performed other tasks (Rogers 66).

Even people who can neither move nor speak can begin to do things on their own. In August 1986, Jamie Mitchell, who was eighteen and had cerebral palsy, looked at a spot on a computer screen to signal that he wanted his back scratched--the first time he was able to communicate a wish. He used ERICA, the Eye-gaze Response Interface Computer Aid developed by Thomas Hutchinson, professor of biomedical engineering at the University of Virginia. "An infrared camera records light from the eye, and the computer indicates which portion of the screen the eye is focused on" (Albrecht 86). Dr. Lance Meagher, a victim of amyotrophic lateral sclerosis, cannot move, talk, or even breathe on his own. Yet one day he hopes "to fly solo around the world," thanks to Erich Sutter of San Francisco's Smith-Kettlewell Institute of Visual Sciences (Ward 30). Electrodes implanted in Meagher's skull pick up brain waves produced when his eyes focus on an object. By staring at a command on a computer screen, Meagher can make the computer carry out that command. Other systems are also being worked on to allow patients "to use their eyes as the sole means of communicating and controlling their environment" (Weiss).

"Robots may be the next logical partners for disabled workers" (Rogers 66). Work stations that combine computers with robot arms enable users to control lights, pick up books, even get things from the refrigerator. As a result, workers with disabilities can be fully productive. Programs like Atlanta's IBM National Support Center are helpful in informing employers on such issues relating to the hiring of workers who are disabled (Lewis).

CONCLUSION:
RESTATES THESIS

Although the costs of developing techno-logical aids are enormous, the rewards are enormous too. Moreover, money that went into long-term care and hospitalization of those with disabilities, as well as lost wages and skills, can now be devoted to research into computer technology for people with disabili-ties. "This is the best chance we've had for those we have left behind to be allowed to catch up" (Rash 130).

Works Cited

Adelson, Suzanne. "Laura Meyers Creates
    Software That Talks Friendly to Help
    Disabled Kids Find Their Voices."<u>People</u>
    <u>Weekly</u> 4 Dec. 1989: 65-66.

Albrecht, Lelia. "With Thomas Hutchinson's
    Marvelous ERICA, a Flick of an Eye Brings
    Help to the Helpless."<u>People Weekly</u>
    20 July 1987: 85-86.

Bronson, Gail. "In the Blink of an Eye."<u>Forbes</u>
    23 Mar. 1987: 140+.

Cattoche, Robert J. <u>Computers for the Disabled</u>
    New York: Watts, 1986.

Cunningham, Ann Marie. "High-Tech Help."
    <u>Technology Review</u> Feb.-Mar. 1989:
    16-17.

"Engineers' Devices Aid the Disabled."<u>New York</u>
    <u>Times</u> 26 Feb. 1989, sec. 1: 43-44.

Hintz, Sandy and Martin Hintz.<u>Computers in Our</u>
    <u>World, Today and Tomorrow</u> New York:
    Watts, 1983.

Lewis, Peter H. "Putting Disabled in Touch."
    <u>New York Times</u> 20 Feb. 1990: C9.

Morais, Richard C. "Genius Unbound."<u>Forbes</u> 23
    Mar. 1987: 142.

Rash, Wayne, Jr. "A Helping Hand."<u>Byte</u> Dec.
    1989: 129-30.

Rogers, Michael. "More Than Wheelchairs."
    <u>Newsweek</u> 24 Apr. 1989: 66-67.

Ward, Darrell E. "Gaze Control."<u>Omni</u> Dec.
    1988: 30.

Weiss, Rick. "Disabled Communication: The Eyes
    Have It." <u>Science News</u> 20 Aug. 1988: 122.

Using Transitions

Transitions help you achieve a smooth flow and a logical progression of ideas. Therefore, in your research paper, use transitional words and phrases such as *first, second, most important,* and *finally. (See page 102 for a list of transitions.)* Other transitional devices are repeated key words or phrases from earlier sentences or paragraphs and pronouns used in place of nouns from earlier sentences.

WRITING ACTIVITY *Recognizing Transitions*

Answer the following questions about the research paper on computers and people with disabilities on pages 351–355.

1. What transitional word showing contrast prepares readers for the thesis statement?
2. What key word from the thesis statement is repeated in the first sentence of the second paragraph?
3. What transitional word leads into the fifth paragraph?
4. What transitional phrase in the sixth paragraph shows the relative sophistication of the vision aid that converts printed text into Braille?

Using and Citing Sources

Because the words and ideas of authors are protected by copyrights, failure to give credit for borrowed words, ideas, and facts is a serious offense, called *plagiarism.* Therefore, give credit to the original authors for any borrowed material by providing parenthetical notes, footnotes, or endnotes. In addition, a list of works cited, which is similar to a bibliography, must appear at the end of your paper.

Using Sources When you have worked hard to find appropriate sources and to obtain sound supporting material, you want to present it as effectively as possible. The following five techniques will help you work borrowed words and ideas smoothly into your writing, particularly when you write a research paper.

Tips for Using Sources

1. Use a quotation to finish a sentence you have started.

EXAMPLE   Other systems are also being worked on using patterns of eye movements to allow patients "to use their eyes as the sole means of communicating and controlling their environment" (Weiss).

2. Quote a whole sentence.

EXAMPLE   "This is the best chance we've had for those we have left behind to be allowed to catch up" (Rash 130).

3. Quote just a few words.

EXAMPLE   Yet one day he hopes "to fly solo around the world," thanks to Erich Sutter of San Francisco's Smith-Kettlewell Institute of Visual Sciences (Ward 30).

4. Paraphrase and summarize information from a source. *(See Chapter 8.)*

5. Quote five or more lines from your source. Start the quotation on a new line after skipping two lines and indenting ten spaces. Single-space the quoted lines. Do not use quotation marks for such an extended quotation. Use a colon in the sentence that introduces the quotation.

EXAMPLE   Stephen Hawking writes and talks by means of his computer and voice synthesizer:

A menu of letters and words appears on the computer screen. Hawking presses another button to move his cursor to the desired words, which then slowly appear as complete sentences at the bottom of the screen. Another movement from his thumb sends the sentence to a built-in voice synthesizer, which generates speech (142).

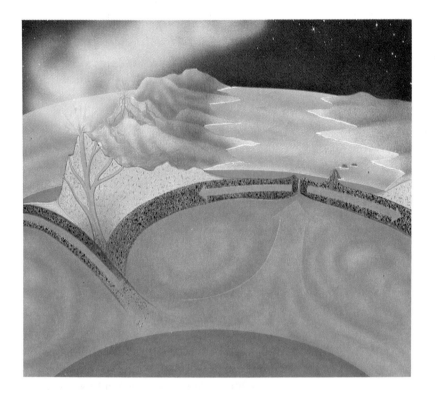

WRITING ACTIVITY *Using Sources*

Read the following article about continental drift and use it as a source to complete the assignment that follows it.

Catching the Drift

The longer you wait to take that trip to Europe, the farther you'll have to go. Researchers at the National Aeronautics and Space Administration say that the continents of Europe and North America may be drifting apart at the rate of as much as two-thirds of an inch a year.

"Not only that," says Goddard Space Flight Center geophysicist David Smith, "but Peru moved two inches away from Hawaii in 1983, while Australia drifted two inches toward it." Smith and his colleagues have been collecting data from laser tracking stations located all over the world. The stations shoot a beam of laser light at a satellite as it flies overhead. The satellite is studded with hundreds of mirrors that are constructed in such a way that they reflect a light beam back at its source. By accurately calculating the orbit of the satellite and timing the laser beam's trip to the satellite and back, Smith and other geophysicists can map the positions of the tracking stations on the Earth to within nearly an inch. The scientists get similar results by clocking radio waves from space as they arrive at various points on Earth.

The research is the first direct measurement of the rate of continental drift. According to the theory of plate tectonics, already widely accepted among geologists on the basis of other geological evidence, the continents and ocean floors are not firmly rooted on the Earth but rather are part of large plates that "float" on the Earth's mantle. As the plates drift and slide into each other they are deformed, creating mountain ranges and deep sea trenches and causing earthquakes along the fault lines where the two plates meet. At one potential earthquake zone, California's San Andreas fault, tracking stations on either side of the fault moved nearly three inches in one year.

Science '84, (Adapted)

I. Write a sentence about the drifts of Europe and North America. End your sentence with a quotation.

2. Write three sentences describing how the laser measurements are taken. One sentence should be a direct quotation.

3. Write a paragraph about continental drift and the theory of plate tectonics. Include an extended quotation of at least five lines. Be sure to indent and space the quoted lines correctly. Remember that quotation marks are not necessary.

4. Write a sentence about land's drifting toward and away from Hawaii, quoting just a few words from the source.

5. Write a paraphrase of the last sentence.

WRITING ACTIVITY 20 *Writing on Your Own*

WRITING
ABOUT THE
THEME

Write a first draft of your research paper about another country in the world. First review your revised thesis statement, note cards, and outline from Writing Activities 15 and 17. When drafting your introduction, rework your thesis statement so that it fits in smoothly. Then follow your outline to draft the body. At this point do not worry about using the correct form for parenthetical citations. Instead, simply identify the source and page number fully enough so that you know which source you are using. After finishing the body, draft your conclusion and save your work for later use.

Citing Sources   The notes in a research paper that show the original sources of borrowed words or ideas are called citations. There are three different types of citations.

Types of Citations	
PARENTHETICAL CITATIONS	appear within parentheses directly following the borrowed material in the paper itself
FOOTNOTES	appear at the bottom of page
ENDNOTES	appear on a separate sheet at the end of the paper, after the conclusion but before the works cited page or bibliography

Writing Tip   Cite the sources of information you include in your  research paper by using **parenthetical citations, footnotes,** or **endnotes.** Use only one type of citation throughout the paper.

The following guidelines will help you determine which information in your paper requires a citation.

Citing Sources
1. Cite the source of a direct quotation. Use direct quotations when the original wording makes the point more clearly.
2. Cite the sources of ideas you gained from your research, even when you express the ideas in your own words.
3. Cite the sources of figures and statistics that you use.
4. Do not cite sources that are common knowledge.

Using Parenthetical Citations   One way to cite sources in research reports is the parenthetical citation, as shown in the model report. In a parenthetical citation, you give the reader just enough information in the paper itself to identify the source. The reader then refers to the list of works cited at the end for more complete information about sources. On the following page are examples showing the correct form for parenthetical citations.

Correct Form for Parenthetical Citations

BOOKS WITH A SINGLE AUTHOR	Give author's last name and page reference: (Cattoche 46).
BOOKS WITH TWO OR MORE AUTHORS	Give both authors' names and a page reference: (Hintz and Hintz 23).
ARTICLE WITH AUTHOR NAMED	Give author's last name and a page reference if article is longer than a page: (Adelson 65).
ARTICLE WITH AUTHOR UNNAMED	Give title or shortened form of title of article and page reference if article is longer than a page: ("Engineers' Devices" 43).
ARTICLE FROM GENERAL REFERENCE WORK, AUTHOR UNNAMED	Give title or shortened form of title; no page number is needed if article is one page or if it is from an alphabetically arranged encyclopedia: ("Speech Synthesis").
WORKS BY SAME AUTHOR	Give author's last name, title of work, and page reference: (Morais, "Genius Unbound" 142).
AUTHOR NAMED IN TEXT	Give only the page reference: (142).

You should place parenthetical citations as close as possible to the words or ideas being credited. In order to avoid interrupting the natural flow of the sentence, place the citations at the end of a phrase, a clause, or a sentence. The following guidelines will tell you specifically where to place the citation in relation to punctuation marks. *(See examples in the sample research paper on pages 351–355 and in the tips on Citing Sources on page 360.)*

Correct Placement of Parenthetical Citations

1. If the citation falls next to a comma or end mark, place the citation before the punctuation mark.
2. If the citation accompanies a long quotation that is set off and indented, place the citation after the end mark.
3. If the citation falls next to a closing quotation mark, place the citation after the quotation mark but before any end mark.

Using Footnotes or Endnotes The correct form for footnotes and endnotes is essentially the same. Both use a *superscript*, unlike parenthetical citations, which do not require one. A *superscript* is a number above the line in the text, to refer readers to the footnote or endnote with the same number. The superscript comes immediately after the borrowed material.

The examples below show the correct form for footnotes and endnotes. In the final copy of your research paper, individual footnotes are single-spaced (with a double space between each footnote), while endnotes are double-spaced.

Correct Form for Footnotes and Endnotes

GENERAL REFERENCE WORKS
[1] George Epstein, "Computer," World Book Encyclopedia, 1988 ed.

BOOKS WITH A SINGLE AUTHOR
[2] Robert J. Cattoche, Computers for the Disabled (New York: Watts, 1986) 46.

BOOKS WITH MORE THAN ONE AUTHOR
[3] Sandy Hintz and Martin Hintz, Computers in Our World, Today and Tomorrow (New York: Watts, 1983) 23.

ARTICLES IN MAGAZINES
[4] Suzanne Adelson, "Laura Meyers Creates Software That Talks Friendly to Help Disabled Kids Find Their Voices," People Weekly 4 December 1989: 65–66.

ARTICLES IN NEWSPAPERS
[5] "Engineers' Devices Aid the Disabled," New York Times 26 Feb. 1989, sec. 1: 43–44.

INTERVIEWS
[6] Dr. Michelle Harper, ophthalmologist, Roseville Hospital, Milwaukee, Wisconsin, personal [or telephone] interview, 31 August 1990.

Notice in number 5 above that if the author of an article is not given, the footnote begins with the title of the article.

For repeated references to a work already cited, you can use a shortened form of footnote. The author's last name and the page number are enough to refer to a work already cited in full. If you have cited more than one work by the author, include a shortened form of the title in the shortened footnote.

REPEATED REFERENCES
[1] Morais 142.
[2] Cattoche, Computers 61.

List of Works Cited All of the sources cited or mentioned in the paper are listed in the works cited section.

Writing Term A **works cited** page is an alphabetical listing of sources used in a research paper. It appears at the end of the paper.

The entries in a list of works cited differ from parenthetical citations, footnotes, and endnotes in four main ways. (1) The first line is not indented, but the following lines are. (2) The author's last name is listed first. (3) Periods are used in place of commas, and parentheses are deleted. (4) No specific page reference is necessary. The following examples show the correct form for the entries in a list of works cited. The entries would be listed in alphabetical order—according to the first word of the entry—on one or more separate pages at the end of the research paper. The entire works cited list should be double-spaced.

Correct Form for a List of Works Cited

GENERAL REFERENCE WORKS	Epstein, George. "Computer." <u>World Book Encyclopedia</u>. 1988 ed.
BOOKS WITH A SINGLE AUTHOR	Cattoche, Robert J. <u>Computers for the Disabled</u>. New York: Watts, 1986.
BOOKS WITH MORE THAN ONE AUTHOR	Hintz, Sandy, and Martin Hintz. <u>Computers in Our World, Today and Tomorrow</u>. New York: Watts, 1983.
ARTICLES IN MAGAZINES	Adelson, Suzanne. "Laura Meyers Creates Software That Talks Friendly to Help Disabled Kids Find Their Voices." <u>People Weekly</u> 4 December 1989: 65–66.
ARTICLES IN NEWSPAPERS	"Engineers' Devices Aid the Disabled." <u>New York Times</u> 26 Feb. 1989, sec. 1: 43–44.
INTERVIEWS	Harper, Michelle. Telephone interview. 31 August 1990.

In addition to or instead of a list of works cited, your teacher may ask you to include a bibliography or a list of works consulted. These lists of sources include all of the sources that you used to research your subject, regardless of whether you cited them in the research paper itself.

WRITING ACTIVITY *Citing Sources*

Use the information in each item to write (1) a parenthetical citation and (2) a footnote. Follow the models on pages 361 and 362.

1. Title of newspaper article: Engineers Fight the Mississippi's Sense of Direction
   Location of article: Section IA, p. 36
   Name and date of newspaper: Chicago Tribune; August 30, 1984
2. Title of book: Mighty Mississippi: Biography of a River
   Publishing company: Ticknor and Fields
   Author: Marquis W. Childs
   Place and date of publication: New Haven; 1982
   Page number: 72
3. Title of article in encyclopedia: Mississippi River
   Edition of encyclopedia: 1980
   Author of article: Johnson E. Fairchild
   Name of encyclopedia: Collier's Encyclopedia
4. Name of magazine: National Geographic
   Page number: 227
   Author of magazine article: Douglas Lee
   Title of article: Mississippi Delta: The Land of the River
   Date of magazine: August 1983
5. Author of magazine article: Susan Tiftt
   Page number: 19
   Name and date of magazine: Time; January 23, 1984
   Title of article: Going with the Floe

WRITING ACTIVITY *Preparing a Works Cited List*

Use the information from Writing Activity 21 to prepare a works cited list for a research paper about the Mississippi River. Alphabetize the entries and follow the format shown on page 363.

WRITING ACTIVITY *Writing on Your Own*

WRITING
ABOUT THE
THEME

Prepare the list of works cited for the research paper, which you drafted in Writing Activity 20. Place the entries in alphabetical order and follow the format on page 363. Then put your parenthetical citations in the correct form, using the examples on page 361. If you need more information, refer to the *MLA Handbook for Writers of Research Papers* by Joseph Gibaldi and Walter S. Achtert. Save your work for later use.

Revising

Writing Process

When you have finished the first draft of your paper, if possible put it away for a day or so. Then come back to it with a fresh eye to find ways to improve it. Keep in mind as you reread the paper that the writing process does not always move in a forward direction. Sometimes you must return to one of the earlier stages and do more work. For example, if you do not have all the information you need, you may have to return to your sources or look for additional sources. The following guidelines will help you as you revise.

Revision Checklist

CHECKING YOUR RESEARCH PAPER

1. Does your introduction contain a well-worded thesis statement? *(See pages 348–349.)*
2. Does your research paper support the thesis statement?
3. Did you use transitional devices? *(See page 356.)*
4. Did you use and cite sources correctly? *(See pages 356–363.)*
5. Does your report have unity, coherence, and emphasis? *(See page 166.)*
6. Does your conclusion add a strong ending?
7. Does your report have a title?

CHECKING YOUR PARAGRAPHS

8. Does each paragraph have a topic sentence? *(See page 94.)*
9. Is each paragraph unified and coherent? *(See pages 99–102.)*
10. Does one paragraph lead smoothly into the next?

CHECKING YOUR SENTENCES AND WORDS

11. Are your sentences varied and concise? *(See pages 63–71.)*
12. Did you avoid faulty sentences? *(See pages 72–79.)*
13. Did you use specific words with appropriate connotations? *(See page 56.)*

WRITING ACTIVITY  *Writing on Your Own*

WRITING
ABOUT THE
THEME

Using the Revision Checklist, revise the research paper you drafted in Writing Activity 20. Then save your revised paper.

Editing and Publishing

Grammar in the Writing Process

When George Orwell started writing his essay "Shooting an Elephant," he commented that "a story always sounds clear enough at a distance, but the nearer you get to the scene of events the vaguer it becomes." One way to make your writing consistently clear and interesting to your readers is to vary your sentence structure. Just as reading the same book over and over again would be dull and boring, so would writing that contained only one kind of sentence.

Kinds of Sentence Structure   The four basic kinds of sentences—simple, compound, complex, and compound-complex—are classified by the number and kind of clauses within each sentence. A *simple sentence*, for example, consists of one independent clause. (An independent clause can stand alone as a sentence.) A *compound sentence* consists of two or more independent clauses. A *complex sentence* consists of one independent clause and one or more subordinate clauses. (A subordinate clause has a subject and verb but cannot stand alone as a sentence.) A *compound-complex sentence* consists of two or more independent clauses and one or more subordinate clauses. *(For more information about independent and subordinate clauses, see pages 611–618.)*

When you revise your writing, always check to see whether you have used a variety of these different kinds of sentences. If you have, your writing will flow smoothly. *(For practice in classifying sentences, see pages 622–623.)*

SIMPLE SENTENCE	I was a police officer of the town.
COMPOUND SENTENCE	I was young, and this job was important.
COMPLEX SENTENCE	One day something happened that in a roundabout way was enlightening.
COMPOUND-COMPLEX SENTENCE	It was a tiny incident, but it gave me a glimpse of the real motives for which despotic governments act.

Punctuation with Compound Sentences   The two independent clauses in a compound sentence can be joined by either a comma and a coordinating conjunction or by a semicolon. *(For other examples and* *for practice in writing compound sentences correctly, see pages 774–775. For information about punctuating complex sentences and for practice in writing them, see pages 775–776 and 782–783.)*

COMMA AND
CONJUNCTION
The elephant had turned over a van, **but** the driver had escaped.

SEMICOLON
The morning was cloudy and stuffy; it was the beginning of the rainy season.

Capitalization and Punctuation of Titles Apply the following rules to the titles in the citations and works cited page in your research paper. *(For more information, see pages 761–764 and 800–803.)*

1. Capitalize the first word, the last word, and all important words in the titles of books, newspapers, magazines, stories, poems, movies, plays, and other works of art.
2. Underline the titles of long written or musical works that are published as a single unit—such as books, newspapers, magazines, full-length plays, and long poems.
3. Use quotation marks to enclose the titles of chapters, articles, stories, one-act plays, short poems, and songs.

TITLES
George Orwell is known for essays such as "Shooting an Elephant" and novels such as <u>Animal Farm</u>.

Editing Checklist

1. Have different sentence structures been included to create variety? *(See pages 622–623.)*
2. Are the sentences punctuated correctly? *(See pages 774–776.)*
3. Are the titles written correctly? *(See pages 761–764 and 800–803.)*

WRITING ACTIVITY   *Writing on Your Own*

WRITING
ABOUT THE
THEME
 Editing Use the checklist above and the one on page 38 to edit your research paper. Also refer to pages 803–806 to check the correct punctuation of all direct quotations.

Publishing After you bind your paper in plastic or cardboard covers, share it with someone interested in your subject.

A Writer Writes

A Research Paper

PURPOSE: to inform about the contributions of a group of people
that immigrated to the United States

AUDIENCE: fellow students and your teachers

Prewriting   The United States, perhaps more than any other nation
in the world, has benefited from the contributions of people who
have emigrated from almost all of the other countries of the world.

Although the United States has been called the melting pot of the world, aspects of the different backgrounds and cultures of all the immigrants have remained, enriching this country with their diversity.

Plan and write a research paper about one immigrant group of people and its contributions to the United States. To find a subject, think about such groups that you have connections to or are interested in. After you choose one by using the guidelines on page 332, make a cluster to help you analyze the various aspects your paper can cover. Then choose a specific subject and limit it by asking "What about" questions.

After writing questions to guide your research, gather information not only from reference books but also from magazines and newspapers and even from interviews with people you know. The steps outlined on page 335 should be helpful in gathering your information. Remember to evaluate your sources, making sure that they are up-to-date, accurate, and objective. When you have enough information, write a working thesis statement that you can use to organize your notes into an outline.

Drafting Following the guidelines on page 348, rewrite your thesis statement—if necessary—as you work it into the introduction of your research paper. Then follow your outline as you write the paragraphs in the body of your paper. Whenever you borrow the exact words or the ideas from a source, remember to add citations. Finally, write your conclusion and prepare your works cited page. You may find it helpful to review pages 356–363 for using and citing sources.

Revising *Peer Conferencing:* The purpose of a research paper is to inform others about your subject. Peer conferencing is a good way to find out whether you are accomplishing your purpose. With your teacher's permission, therefore, exchange papers with a partner. Then use the Revision Checklist on page 365 to comment on your partner's paper and afterward to revise your own paper. If you use the proofreading symbols on page 39, your revising and upcoming editing will be neat and efficient.

Editing and Publishing After you copy your paper into a neat final draft, using the correct manuscript form on page 43, consider writing a summary of your research paper and submitting it to the school or local newspaper for publication.

Independent Writing

Write a research paper on some aspect of one of the following topics or a topic of your own choice. As a guide use the Checklist for Writing Research Papers on page 371.

I. a famous artist   **6.** a recent discovery
2. history of movies   **7.** advances in computers
3. trends in music   **8.** black holes
4. origin of fads   **9.** predicting earthquakes
5. space travel   **10.** endangered species

WRITING
ABOUT THE
THEME
 ## Creative Writing

Historical fiction often includes real settings and is based on real events. In addition, the characters may be actual historical figures or imaginary figures. Material gathered for a research paper, therefore, can often be used as background information for a piece of historical fiction. After you look over the note cards you have made for the research paper assignment on pages 368–369, use some of the cards as the basis for a story about an American teenager who befriends another teenager who just immigrated to the United States. After making an outline of your story, put it and your note cards in your writing folder for later development.

WRITING
ABOUT THE
THEME
 ## Writing about Literature

Style is the characteristic way a writer writes—including his or her word choice, sentence structure, and use of figurative language. Some writers, for example, write precisely and straightforwardly; others use long sentences and many figures of speech to convey their meaning. Write a paragraph that describes George Orwell's style. Support your statements with examples from "Shooting an Elephant."

Writing in Other Subject Areas

Astronomy   Write a research paper that explains what new information was learned about Mercury as a result of *Mariner 10*, a United States satellite that was launched on November 3, 1973.

World History   Write a research paper on the causes of the Industrial Revolution in England.

Checklist

Writing Research Papers

Prewriting

✔ After listing possible subjects, choose one and limit it. *(See pages 332–333.)*

✔ Make a list of questions to guide your research. *(See page 334.)*

✔ Gather information from books, magazines, newspapers, and interviews with experts. *(See pages 334–336.)*

✔ Use note cards for taking notes and summarizing your sources. *(See pages 340–343.)*

✔ Write a working thesis statement. *(See page 344.)*

✔ Organize your notes by finding categories. *(See page 345.)*

✔ Use your working thesis statement and note categories to outline the body of your research paper. *(See pages 345–347.)*

Drafting

✔ Revise your working thesis statement as needed. *(See page 348.)*

✔ Write your first draft, including an introduction, body, and conclusion. *(See page 350.)*

✔ Avoid plagiarism by using and citing sources carefully. *(See pages 356–363.)*

✔ Add a title.

Revising

✔ Using the Revision Checklist, check your report for structure, well-developed paragraphs, unity, coherence, emphasis, and varied and lively sentences and words. *(See page 365.)*

Editing and Publishing

✔ Using the Editing Checklist, check your grammar, spelling, mechanics, manuscript form, and footnote and bibliography form. *(See pages 38 and 367.)*

Creative Writing

Part 1 *Reading to Write*

THEME: *Values*

"They don't make 'em like they used to!" This is what people declare who feel that today's products are not very well made—that instead of crafters' taking pride in their work, they care only about getting things done fast. In fact, this has been called a disposable society, one in which objects and even ideas are tossed away with little thought.

Do you agree with such criticisms or are you all for today's idea of progress? What are the values people actually live by? What are the standards that guide people's work? Are they the values people *should* live by? To share your thoughts on such questions, you need not limit yourself to a form like the essay. As you will learn in this chapter, with a touch of imagination you can deal with serious themes in creative ways—namely, in a short story or a poem.

The following selection, "Quality" by John Galsworthy, is a good example of how a creative mind can explore an important theme. Galsworthy tells the simple story of an old bootmaker who will not compromise his values. While telling this story, Galsworthy is also able to comment on the values of his society. Even though he is dealing with a serious theme, he is able to transport you to another time and place, and even surprise you with an unexpected turn of events.

372

Quality

J o h n   G a l s w o r t h y

I knew him from the days of my extreme youth, because he made my father's boots; inhabiting with his elder brother two little shops let into one, in a small by-street—now no more, but then most fashionably placed in the West End.

That tenement had a certain quiet distinction; there was no sign upon its face that he made for any of the Royal Family—merely his own German name of Gessler Brothers; and in the window a few pairs of boots. I remember that it always troubled me to account for those unvarying boots in the window, for he made only what was ordered, reaching nothing down, and it seemed so inconceivable that what he made could ever have failed to fit. Had he bought them to put there? That, too, seemed inconceivable. He would never have tolerated in his house leather on which he had not worked himself. Besides, they were too beautiful—the pair of pumps, so inexpressibly slim, the patent leathers with cloth tops, making water come into one's mouth, the tall brown riding-boots with marvelous sooty glow, as if, though new, they had been worn a hundred years. Those pairs would only have been made by one who saw before him the Soul of Boot—so truly were they prototypes, incarnating the very spirit of all footwear. These thoughts, of course, came to me later, though even when I was promoted to him, at the age of perhaps fourteen, some inkling haunted me of the dignity of himself and brother. For to make boots—such boots as he made—seemed to me then, and still seems to me, mysterious and wonderful.

I remember well my shy remark, one day, while stretching out to him my youthful foot:

"Isn't it awfully hard to do, Mr. Gessler?"

And his answer, given with a sudden smile from out of the sardonic redness of his beard: "Id is an Ardt!"

Himself, he was a little as if made of leather, with his yellow crinkly face, and crinkly reddish hair and beard, and neat folds slanting down his cheeks to the corners of his mouth, and his guttural and one-toned voice; for leather is a sardonic substance, and stiff and slow of purpose. And that was the character of his face, save that his eyes, which were gray-blue, had in them the simple gravity of one secretly possessed by the Ideal. His elder brother was so very like him—though watery, paler in every way, with a great industry—that sometimes in early days I was not quite sure of him until the interview was over. Then I knew that it was he, if the words, "I will ask my brudder," had not been spoken, and that, if they had, it was the elder brother.

When one grew old and wild and ran up bills, one somehow never ran them up with Gessler Brothers. It would not have seemed becoming to go in there and stretch out one's foot to that blue iron-spectacled face, owing him for more than—say—two pairs, just the comfortable reassurance that one was still his client.

For it was not possible to go to him very often—his boots lasted terribly, having something beyond the temporary—some, as it were, essence of boot—stitched into them.

One went in, not as into most shops, in the mood of: "Please serve me, and let me go!" but restfully, as one enters a church; and, sitting on the single wooden chair, waited—for there was never anybody there. Soon—over the top edge of that sort of well—rather dark, and smelling soothingly of leather—which formed the shop, there would be seen his face, or that of his elder brother, peering down. A guttural sound, and the tip-tap of bast slippers beating the narrow wooden stairs, and he would stand before one without coat, a little bent, in leather apron, with sleeves turned back, blinking—as if awakened from some dream of boots, or like an owl surprised in daylight and annoyed at this interruption.

And I would say: "How do you do, Mr. Gessler? Could you make me a pair of Russia leather boots?"

Without a word he would leave me, retiring whence he came, or into the other portion of the shop, and I would continue to rest in the wooden chair, inhaling the incense of his trade. Soon he would come back, holding in his thin, veined hand a piece of gold-brown leather. With eyes fixed on it, he would remark: "What a beaudiful biece!" When I, too, had admired it, he would speak again. "When do you wand dem?" And I would answer: "Oh! As soon as you conveniently can." And he would say: "Tomorrow fordnighd?" Or if he were his elder brother: "I will ask my brudder!"

Then I would murmur: "Thank you! Good-morning, Mr. Gessler." "Goot-morning!" he would reply, still looking at the leather in his hand. And as I moved to the door, I would hear the tip-tap of his bast slippers restoring him, up the stairs, to his dream of boots. But if it were some new kind of foot-gear that he had not yet made me, then indeed he would observe ceremony—divesting me of my boot and holding it long in his hand, looking at it with eyes at once critical and loving, as if recalling the glow with which he had created it, and rebuking the way in which one had disorganized this masterpiece. Then, placing my foot on a piece of paper, he would two or three times tickle the outer edges with a pencil and pass his nervous fingers over my toes, feeling himself into the heart of my requirements.

I cannot forget that day on which I had occasion to say to him: "Mr. Gessler, that last pair of town walking-boots creaked, you know."

He looked at me for a time without replying, as if expecting me to withdraw or qualify the statement, then said:

"Id shouldn't 'ave greaked."

"It did, I'm afraid."

"You goddem wed before dey found demselves?"

"I don't think so."

At that he lowered his eyes, as if hunting for memory of those boots, and I felt sorry I had mentioned this grave thing.

"Zend dem back!" he said; "I will look at dem."

A feeling of compassion for my creaking boots surged up in me, so well could I imagine the sorrowful long curiosity of regard which he would bend on them.

"Zome boods," he said slowly, "are bad from birdt. If I can do noding wid dem, I dake dem off your bill."

Once (once only) I went absent-mindedly into his shop, in a pair of boots bought in an emergency at some large firm's. He took my order without showing me any leather, and I could feel his eyes penetrating the inferior integument of my foot. At last he said:

"Dose are nod my boods."

The tone was not one of anger, nor of sorrow, not even of contempt, but there was in it something quiet that froze the blood. He put his hand down and pressed a finger on the place where the left boot, endeavouring to be fashionable, was not quite comfortable.

"Id 'urds you dere," he said. "Dose big virms 'ave no self-respect.

Drash!" And then, as if something had given way within him, he spoke long and bitterly. It was the only time I ever heard him discuss the conditions and hardships of his trade.

"Dey get id all," he said, "dey get id by adverdisement, nod by work. Dey dake id away from us, who lofe our boods. Id gomes to this—bresently I haf no work. Every year id gets less—you will see." And looking at his lined face I saw things I had never noticed before, bitter things and bitter struggle—and what a lot of gray hairs there seemed suddenly in his red beard!

As best I could, I explained the circumstances of the purchase of those ill-omened boots. But his face and voice made a so deep impression that during the next few minutes I ordered many pairs! Nemesis fell! They lasted more terribly than ever. And I was not able conscientiously to go to him for nearly two years.

When at last I went I was surprised that outside one of the two little windows of his shop another name was painted, also that of a bootmaker—making, of course, for the Royal Family. The old familiar boots, no longer in dignified isolation, were huddled in the single window. Inside, the now contracted well of the one little shop was more scented and darker than ever. And it was longer than usual, too, before a face peered down, and the tip-tap of the bast slippers began. At last he stood before me, and, gazing through those rusty iron spectacles, said:

"Mr. —, isn'd id?"

"Ah! Mr. Gessler," I stammered, "but your boots are really *too* good, you know! See, these are quite decent still!" And I stretched out to him my foot. He looked at it.

"Yes," he said, "beople do, nod wand good boods, id seems."

To get away from his reproachful eyes and voice I hastily remarked: "What have you done to your shop?"

He answered quietly: "Id was too exbensif. Do you wand some boods?"

I ordered three pairs, though I had only wanted two, and quickly left. I had, I know not quite what feeling of being part, in his mind, of a conspiracy against him; or not perhaps so much against him as against his idea of boot. One does not, I suppose, care to feel like that; for it was again many months before my next visit to his shop, paid I remember, with the feeling: "Oh! well, I can't leave the old boy— so here goes! Perhaps it'll be his elder brother!"

For his elder brother, I knew, had not character enough to reproach me, even dumbly.

And, to my relief, in the shop there did appear to be his elder brother, handling a piece of leather.

"Well, Mr. Gessler," I said, "how are you?"

He came close, and peered at me.

"I am breddy well," he said slowly; "but my elder brudder is dead."

And I saw that it was indeed himself—but how aged and wan! And never before had I heard him mention his brother. Much shocked, I murmured: "Oh! I am sorry!"

"Yes," he answered, "he was a good man, he made a good bood; but he is dead." And he touched the top of his head, where the hair had suddenly gone as thin as it had been on that of his poor brother, to indicate, I suppose, the cause of death. "He could nod ged over losing de oder shop. Do you wand any boods?" And he held up the leather in his hand: "Id's a beaudiful biece."

I ordered several pairs. It was very long before they came—but they were better than ever. One simply could not wear them out. And soon after that I went abroad.

It was over a year before I was again in London. And the first shop I went to was my old friend's. I had left a man of sixty, I came back to find one of seventy-five, pinched and worn and tremulous, who genuinely, this time, did not at first know me.

"Oh! Mr. Gessler," I said, sick at heart; "how splendid your boots are! See, I've been wearing this pair nearly all the time I've been abroad; and they're not half worn out, are they?"

He looked long at my boots—a pair of Russia leather, and his face seemed to regain its steadiness. Putting his hand on my instep, he said:

"Do dey vid you here? I 'ad drouble wid dat bair, I remember."

I assured him that they had fitted beautifully.

"Do you wand any boods?" he said. "I can make dem quickly; id is a slack dime."

I answered: "Please, please! I want boots all round—every kind!"

"I will make a vresh model. Your food must be bigger." And with utter slowness, he traced round my foot, and felt my toes, only once looking up to say:

"Did I dell you my brudder was dead?"

To watch him was quite painful, so feeble had he grown; I was glad to get away.

I had given those boots up, when one evening they came. Opening the parcel, I set the four pairs out in a row. Then one by one I tried them on. There was no doubt about it. In shape and fit, in finish and quality of leather, they were the best he had ever made me. And in the mouth of one of the town walking-boots I found his bill. The amount was the same as usual, but it gave me quite a shock. He had never before sent it in until quarter day. I flew downstairs and wrote a check, and posted it at once with my own hand.

A week later, passing the little street, I thought I would go in and tell him how splendidly the new boots fitted. But when I came to where his shop had been, his name was gone. Still there, in the window, were the slim pumps, the patent leathers with cloth tops, the sooty riding-boots.

I went in, very much disturbed. In the two little shops—again made in one—was a young man with an English face.

"Mr. Gessler in?" I said.

He gave me a strange, ingratiating look.

"No, sir," he said, "no. But we can attend to anything with pleasure. We've taken the shop over. You've seen our name, no doubt, next door. We make for some very good people."

"Yes, yes," I said, "but Mr. Gessler?"

"Oh!" he answered; "dead."

"Dead! But I only received these boots from him last Wednesday week."

"Ah!" he said; "a shockin' go. Poor old man starved 'imself."

"Good God!"

"Slow starvation, the doctor called it! You see he went to work in such a way! Would keep the shop on; wouldn't have a soul touch his boots except himself. When he got an order, it took him such a time. People won't wait. He lost everybody. And there he'd sit, goin' on and on—I will say that for him—not a man in London made a better boot! But look at the competition! He never advertised! Would 'ave the best leather, too, and do it all 'imself. Well, there it is. What could you expect with his ideas?"

"But starvation—!"

"That may be a bit flowery, as the sayin' is but I know myself he was sittin' over his boots day and night, to the very last. You see, I used to watch him. Never gave 'imself time to eat; never had a penny in the house. All went in rent and leather. How he lived so long I don't know. He regular let his fire go out. He was a character. But he made good boots."

"Yes," I said, "he made good boots." ◆

Responding to the Theme

Values

Responding in Your Journal   What does the bootmaker represent in Galsworthy's story? What did *quality* mean to Galsworthy? What standards did Galsworthy value in boots? In people? In life? What did he think was happening to those standards? Write your responses to those questions in your journal today. Then answer the same questions for yourself. What does *quality* mean to you? What standards do you value in people and in life? What, do you think, is happening to those values? Toward the end of the week, reread what you have written and think about how you could turn some of your ideas and experiences into stories. Then jot down any additional ideas in the margins of your journal notes.

Speaking and Listening   With your teacher's permisssion, form groups of three or more students and discuss how the old bootmaker in "Quality" represents one set of values, while the young bootmaker at the end of the story represents another set. Afterward your teacher will call on two students at a time from each group to role-play those two characters. The students in each pair should have a debate, in which each one defends his or her character's set of values.

Critical Thinking: Imagining   Thinking is not just reasoning and judging; it is also imagining. Imagination is essential to a short-story writer, not only in the initial search for a subject and plot but all the way through the writing process. To make the characters real, a writer needs to get inside them—to imagine what they see, what they do, and how they feel. Find and describe five examples in "Quality" in which the characters come to life because Galsworthy has used his imagination in this way.

Extending Your Vocabulary   The following ten words are from the story "Quality." Using a dictionary, define each one and label what part of speech it is. Then write a sentence of your own for each word.

1. divesting
2. guttural
3. incarnating
4. ingratiating
5. integument

6. prototypes
7. rebuke
8. reproachful
9. sardonic
10. tremulous

Dickens's Dream, R. W. Buss

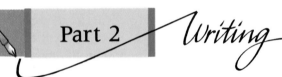

Part 2 — Writing

"It is a delicious thing to write, to be no longer yourself but to move in an entire universe of your own creating," said the French writer Flaubert. This "delicious" experience is open to you when you write a short story or a poem, for you create a universe you can fill with whatever characters, situations, feelings, and images you choose. Your universe may be realistic—a reflection of everyday life. Or it may be fantastic—an extravagant dream world. Whatever kind of world you create through your writing, it will be rooted in your experience, your feelings, and your imagination.

John Galsworthy, for example, apparently had strong feelings about the decline of craftsmanship and pride in one's work. Although he could have expressed those feelings in various ways—as in a persuasive essay or a speech—he chose, instead, to write the short story "Quality." In this chapter you will be given the opportunity to create your own universe in the form of a short story and a poem.

Writing Term

Creative writing uses literary forms such as short stories and poems to allow a writer to invent characters, events, and images.

Writing a Short Story

As you learned in Chapter 3, a piece of writing that tells what happens is called a *narrative.* Short stories are narratives born in the author's imagination. The characters and events can be realistic or fanciful, ordinary or extraordinary. The events all revolve around a conflict faced by the main character. Just how the character deals with this conflict provides the story with its interest and suspense.

Think about stories you have enjoyed reading. They aroused your curiosity with an interesting character and situation, kept you curious about what would happen, and finally satisfied your curiosity by telling you what did happen. Entertaining the reader in this way is the purpose of every story and the goal to aim for as you write a story of your own.

Writing Term   A **short story** is a well-developed fictional account of characters resolving a conflict or problem.

Prewriting

The creative process does not occur all by itself. To create an effective short story, painting, song, or poem, you need to encourage and direct your imagination. The prewriting strategies that follow can help move the creative process along as you plan the conflict, theme, characters, point of view, and plot of your story. Treat the strategies as suggestions only, for as a writer you will work out your own ways of generating ideas. Feel free to move back and forth among the techniques and to select and add as you work your way through them.

Choosing a Conflict or Problem   What will your story be about? All short stories are based on a central conflict or problem. Therefore, deciding what your story will be about actually means deciding what the main conflict or problem will be.

A story can revolve around any kind of conflict, as dramatic as a disabled spaceship or as ordinary as a misplaced homework assignment—or a new way of making boots. Usually the conflict builds between the main character and some other force in the story. The following chart summarizes and gives examples of the most common kinds of conflicts that are at the center of short stories.

Types of Conflicts

1. **Between the main character and another character:**
   A son objects to his mother's limits on his use of her car.
2. **Between the main character and a natural force:**
   An inexperienced surfer faces unusually rough surf.
3. **Between forces or feelings inside the main character:**
   A student is torn between her desire to go to college and the need to help support her family.

You might begin your search for story ideas by brainstorming lists of familiar conflicts or problems, such as those relating to friendships, family situations, school activities, and other areas of your life. Also review your journal, which—if you record thoughts and observations regularly—can be a rich source of ideas. Discuss story ideas with others. A comment from someone else may ignite your imagination.

As you search for story ideas, remember that dramatic stories do not always require extraordinary conflicts. If the events are well-told, a search for a lost book can be as absorbing as a search for a lost planet. Also, hold on to your sense of humor. Problems and their solutions do not always have to be serious.

After you put together a list of possible conflicts, review the list and cross out any conflicts that seem difficult, unfamiliar, or dull. For those that remain, see what ideas come to mind. Put a check next to the conflicts that inspire an interesting character or plot and then choose one you think you would enjoy writing about.

WRITING ACTIVITY *Listing Familiar Conflicts*

Brainstorm a list in answer to each question below, basing the list on your own experiences or the experiences of those around you. Then save your list in your writing folder.

1. What personal values of yours are different from those of a friend or a relative? What conflicts has this caused?
2. If you were writing a situation comedy for television called *Senior Year,* what situations might you use for some of the episodes?
3. When has humor helped you or someone else deal with a problem?
4. What sorts of problems have been caused by the weather, a power failure, illness, or some other event beyond your control?
5. When have you had to struggle to fulfill a dream?

Choosing a Theme   The question "What is the story about?" has
more than one answer. On one level a story is about a particular
conflict. In Galsworthy's "Quality," for example, the conflict has to do
with the bootmaker's inability to keep up with the times. Yet, on a
deeper level, rooted in the conflict is the theme of the story. The *theme*
expresses a particular thought or impression that the writer has about
life. For instance, in "Quality" Galsworthy's focus on the decline of
craftmanship reflects the theme, which concerns the decline of values.

In the following excerpt from "The Doll's House," Katherine Mansfield centers the conflict around a young girl's desire to reach out to
some poorer children, of whom her family and friends disapprove.
Rooted in this conflict is the theme, which is about the cruelties of
differences between social classes. Like many writers Mansfield does
not state her theme directly but leaves clues for the reader to infer it.
In the following excerpt, notice how Mansfield implies the theme.

Model: *Implied Theme*

> "Hullo," she said to the passing Kelveys.
>
> They were so astounded that they stopped. Lil gave her silly
> smile. Our Else started.
>
> "You can come see our doll's house if you want to," said Kezia,
> and she dragged one toe on the ground. But at that Lil turned
> red and shook her head quickly.
>
> "Why not?" asked Kezia.
>
> Lil gasped, then she said, "Your ma told our ma you wasn't
> to speak to us."
>
> "Oh, well," said Kezia. She didn't know what to reply.
>
> KATHERINE MANSFIELD, "The Doll's House"

Before you write a story, you should decide on a theme—a comment that you want your story to make, such as a comment about
growing up. If you do not have a theme in mind, freewrite to generate
possible themes. Keep in mind, however, that the theme should be
an idea you care about, as well as one that fits your story.

WRITING ACTIVITY *Generating Story Themes*

Go back to your notes from Writing Activity 1 and choose three conflicts. First freewrite about each conflict to generate possible story
themes and then choose a suitable theme for each one. Write a statement expressing the theme in each case.

Sketching Characters   Whether you start with real people or work entirely from your imagination, you can make your characters look and behave just as you please. Your only limits are the boundaries of your imagination and the requirements of your story.

Every story has one or more *main characters*—the characters who deal with the central problem. To develop each character, freewrite, brainstorm, or cluster around a detail or idea. You can begin with the smallest detail, such as the name. However, you must go on to sketch the characters fully if you are to bring them to life. Use the following chart to help you develop character sketches.

Character Sketch
Name: Age: Occupation and interests: Family, past history: Physical characteristics: Speech: Mannerisms, expressions, habits: Behavior toward others: Attitude toward self: Reactions of others to character: Strengths and weaknesses:

Feeding the Ducks, Mary Cassatt, 1894, First State, Drypoint over Aquatint Etching

WRITING ACTIVITY *Sketching Characters*

Use three of the details below to sketch three story characters. Free-write about one detail, brainstorm about the second, and cluster around the third. Then, for each character, complete a character sketch like the one on the previous page. Save your sketches.

1. a person with a fringed, red-leather jacket
2. a person with a high-pitched, squeaky voice
3. a person named Ramona DeTromblay
4. a person who is an ambitious young musician
5. a person who is always late

Choosing a Point of View Every story has a narrator—the person who tells the story. When you choose the narrator, you decide not only who will relate the events but also through whose eyes, or from whose *point of view,* the reader will see them. Once you choose a point of view, use it consistently throughout the story. Otherwise your story will be confusing. The following chart outlines the choices you have for point of view.

Point of View	Narrator
FIRST PERSON	Observes or participates in the action personally
	Tells personal observations and thoughts Uses first person pronouns
THIRD PERSON LIMITED	Observes one character who participates in the action
	Tells the words, actions, and feelings of the character and observations about him or her
	Uses third person pronouns
THIRD PERSON OMNISCIENT ("ALL-KNOWING")	Observes but does not participate in the action
	Tells the words, actions, and feelings of all the characters as well as observations about them
	Uses third person pronouns

The first person point of view allows the reader to view the events from inside one of the characters. This adds a personal tone to the story, as shown in the following example.

FIRST PERSON   **I** closed the door softly, wondering if anyone had seen **me.**

When you choose the third person limited point of view, your story has a less personal tone. Yet this point of view allows you to give the reader more information.

THIRD PERSON LIMITED   **Eva** closed the door softly, wondering if anyone had seen **her. She** did not even realize that **she** had held **her** breath all the way down the stairs.

The third person omniscient point of view, on the other hand, balances the disadvantage of being impersonal with the advantage of letting the reader know the thoughts of all the characters.

THIRD PERSON OMNICIENT   **Eva** closed the door softly, wondering if anyone had seen **her.** A block away **David** waited anxiously, hoping that **she** would come.

WRITING ACTIVITY 4   *Using Different Points of View*

The following summary of events can be told in a story of just a few paragraphs. Write three versions of the story, choosing a different point of view each time: (1) the first person as Leonard, (2) the third person limited as Mr. Gomez, and (3) the third person omniscient. Be aware of the different effects the stories have as you write the three versions.

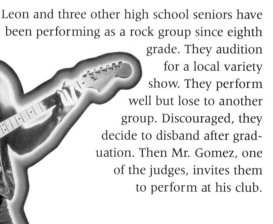

Leon and three other high school seniors have been performing as a rock group since eighth grade. They audition for a local variety show. They perform well but lose to another group. Discouraged, they decide to disband after graduation. Then Mr. Gomez, one of the judges, invites them to perform at his club.

Outlining the Story Always prepare an outline of the important elements of your story to make sure that the story parts fit together. Include the following headings in your outline.

Story Outline

Title:

Setting:

Characters: *(List the characters and include brief descriptions.)*

Conflict:

Plot: *(List the events, one by one, in order of presentation.)*

Resolution:

Title Although the title naturally appears first in the outline, you may want to choose it last, when you have a clearer sense of your story. Select a title that fits the selection in subject and mood and one that will arouse the reader's interest.

Setting The setting is the time and place in which the story occurs. However, it is more than a physical location; it is also an atmosphere and mood that provide a suitable framework for the events. In order to convey these elements to the reader, you need to use *description*. *(See pages 109–110.)* For example, what are the descriptive details used in the following setting? What sorts of events, do you think, might occur?

Model: *Setting*

The room that afternoon was full of such shy creatures, lights and shadows, curtains blowing, petals falling—things that never happen, so it seems, if someone is looking. The quiet old country room, with its rugs and stone chimney pieces, its sunken bookcases and red and gold lacquer cabinets, was full of such nocturnal creatures . . .

But, outside, the looking glass reflected the hall table, the sunflowers, the garden path so accurately and so fixedly that they seemed held there in their reality unescapably. It was a strange contrast—all changing here, all stillness there. One could not help looking from one to the other.   VIRGINIA WOOLF
"The Lady in the Looking Glass: A Reflection"

387

This "strange contrast," as well as the mirror itself, provides an appropriate framework for a story in which the main character herself seems to move into another person—as caught, of course, by the mirror. In the same way, choose a suitable backdrop for the events of your story and describe it briefly in your outline.

Writing Tip   Match the setting of your story to the action, mood, and characters' feelings.

Characters   In your story outline, write a brief description of each character, starting with the main character. *(See page 384.)*

Conflict   Add a sentence or two telling about the conflict or problem that the main character will have to face. *(See pages 381–382.)*

Plot   Next in the outline of the story is the series of events, or *plot*. Most plots begin with an incident that triggers the conflict. Then, as the plot progresses, the conflict becomes more and more serious until it reaches a critical point, or *climax*. After that the conflict is resolved.

In your outline list the events in the order in which you will relate them, such as *chronological order*. Sometimes, to establish the setting or to begin at an exciting point, you may instead use *flashback*—that is, you may interrupt the action to go back to an earlier event and then return to the main action.

Resolution   To complete your outline, write the resolution—the way the conflict or problem is settled. Be sure to tie up the events of the story in a way that will satisfy the reader.

WRITING ACTIVITY ⬥5⬥ *Outlining a Story*

Choose a myth, legend, or other story that you have read and outline it, following the form given on page 387.

WRITING ACTIVITY ⬥6⬥ *Writing on Your Own*

WRITING
ABOUT THE
THEME

Using your journal notes, your responses to Writing Activities 1 through 4, and the prewriting activities discussed in this section, prepare to write a short story on a theme relating to values. First choose a conflict or problem and a point of view. Then, before you sketch your characters and outline your story, add one unexpected element to your plot.

Writing Is Thinking

Implying

An effective way for a writer to engage a reader's attention is to *imply*, or suggest, an idea or fact rather than simply state it outright. By implying information a writer can captivate and involve readers, forcing them to make inferences and draw conclusions, as Katherine Mansfield does in the following excerpt from "The Singing Lesson."

> This little ritual of the flower . . . was as much part of the lesson as opening the piano. But this morning . . . Miss Meadows totally ignored the chrysanthemum, made no reply to her [Mary's] greeting, but said in a voice of ice, "Page fourteen, please . . ."

Through specific details Katherine Mansfield implies that Miss Meadows is not in a good mood. First, Miss Meadows acknowledges neither the flower nor Mary's kind gesture. Second, she continues to direct her class "in a voice of ice."

A chart like the following one can help you imply unstated facts or conclusions. On the left list events, settings, or character traits for your story, and on the right list details to imply those elements.

Trait	Details
considerate	fearful of awakening sister, uses hallway light to guide her, creeps softly into room

Event	Details
graduation	field of blue and gold ribbons, applause fills the stadium, tassled caps tossed in the air

Thinking Practice   Write a passage that implies a setting, event, or character trait from your story or use any of the following suggestions. To help you think of details, use a chart like the one above.

1. traits: kindness, dishonesty, perseverance
2. settings: an amusement park, a university, a mall
3. events: a track meet, a job interview, a car accident

Drafting

Your goal in drafting a story is to produce a workable narrative, one that can be shaped and polished into a solid story. As you draft your story, you can use a variety of types of writing, including *narration, description,* and *exposition. (See pages 106–120.)* This section will show you how to use these types of writing in different parts of your story—the beginning, the middle, and the end.

Drafting the Beginning   As the following examples demonstrate, you can open a story in many different ways.

DIALOGUE	"They say he's worth a million," Lucia said. GRAHAM GREENE, "Across the Bridge"
INTRODUCTION OF THE MAIN CHARACTER	With despair—cold, sharp despair—buried deep in her heart like a wicked knife, Miss Meadows, in cap and gown and carrying a little baton, trod the cold corridors that led to the music hall. KATHERINE MANSFIELD, "The Singing Lesson"
DESCRIPTIVE DETAILS	North Richmond Street, being blind [dead end], was a quiet street except at the hour when the Christian Brothers' School set the boys free. JAMES JOYCE, "Araby"
NARRATIVE DETAILS	Toward the end of her day in London Mrs. Drover went round to her shut-up house to look for several things she wanted to take away. ELIZABETH BOWEN, "The Demon Lover"
GENERAL STATEMENT	People should not leave looking glasses hanging in their rooms any more than they should leave open checkbooks or letters confessing to some hideous crime. VIRGINIA WOOLF "The Lady in the Looking Glass: A Reflection"

Each of these openings sets up a situation that makes the reader curious. Is the man really worth a million? Why is Miss Meadows full of despair? What does the boys' school have to do with the story? Why is Mrs. Drover's house shut up? Why shouldn't people have looking glasses hanging in their rooms? Use your opening sentences, like these sentences, to hook your reader. Then give further details to keep the reader reading. The box on the next page lists some ways to begin a story.

Ways to Begin a Story

1. Set the time and place.
2. Introduce the main character or characters.
3. Provide needed background information.
4. Set the plot in motion with a triggering event.
5. Establish the conflict or problem.

Drafting the Middle As you draft the middle portion of your story, connect the events so that they flow naturally. Transitions— such as *the next day* and *a week later*—help tie events together and show the passage of time. *(See page 102.)* Also try to make every event add to the development and the tension until the climax of the plot is reached. If you include a flashback, use one of these two methods.

SHOWING A
FLASHBACK
WITH SPACING

As Ben walked along the beach, his eyes followed the gulls, but his thoughts were far away.

*　　*　　*　　*　　*　　*　　*

"Ben, wake up! Are you up, Ben?" That day had begun like every other school day, with his mother's voice.

SHOWING A
FLASHBACK
WITH NARRATIVE

As Ben walked along the beach, his eyes followed the gulls, but his thoughts were on that day almost a year ago. It had begun like every other school day, with his mother's voice.

As you develop your characters, give details that tell how they look, what they think, and how they behave. Notice in the following story parts how much livelier the version with the dialogue is. Then use the guidelines below to draft the middle section of your story.

NARRATIVE They stopped talking when they heard a noise.
DIALOGUE "Shhh!" hissed Elena. "I just heard something!"

Guidelines for the Middle of a Story

1. Relate the events either chronologically or with flashbacks.
2. Use transitions to connect the events smoothly and clearly.
3. Use dialogue to make your characters vivid.
4. Use descriptive details to bring your story to life.

Drafting the Ending   A story ending does not need to be positive or happy, nor does it need to solve every problem. It does, however, need to bring the story to a close by tying the events together. In other words it needs to feel like an ending to the reader.

Guidelines for the End of a Story

1. Resolve the conflict and complete the action of the plot.
2. Use dialogue, action, or description to show, not just tell, what happens.
3. Leave the reader feeling satisfied.

WRITING ACTIVITY *Drafting a Story*

Without looking back at the original version, write your own draft of the story you outlined in Writing Activity 5. Resolve the conflict in a surprising way. Then follow the guidelines on pages 391 and 392. Save your draft in your writing folder.

WRITING ACTIVITY  *Writing on Your Own*

WRITING
ABOUT THE
THEME
   Write a draft of your own story about values, using your outline from Writing Activity 6. Then follow the guidelines on pages 391 and 392. Be sure to save your work for later use.

Revising

"I have never thought of myself as a good writer . . ." claimed James A. Michener, "but I'm one of the world's great rewriters." For many writers the revising stage can be the most productive of all.

Improving the Plot   Not every sequence of events is a plot. Compare the two sets of sequences below and notice how they are different.

EVENTS   Mark got dressed. He went for a walk. He walked to the bank. He returned two hours later.

PLOT   Nervously Mark got dressed. He walked to the bank for a job interview. The bank was being robbed. Mark ran for the police. He was a hero. He did not get the job.

In the first sequence, the events are related only chronologically. In the second sequence, every event relates to Mark's job interview. One event leads naturally to the next in a pattern of rising action. To tighten your plot as you revise, ask yourself the following questions.

Guidelines for Improving the Plot

1. Are events arranged chronologically, except for flashbacks?
2. Are flashbacks easily recognizable?
3. Are transitions used to help tie events together and to show the passage of time?
4. Does every event revolve around the central conflict?
5. Is each event clearly linked to the events before and after?
6. Does each event add to the tension and build to the climax?
7. Does the resolution tie up the events?

Improving Characterization   Bland, predictable characters mean that even the most exciting of plots will be dull. As you revise, look for ways to make your characters real and engaging. Read the following story parts and try to identify the techniques D. H. Lawrence uses to draw the picture of a woman so bitter and disappointed that she finds it hard to feel love.

Model: *Improving Characterization*

There was a woman who was beautiful, who started with all the advantages, yet she had no luck. She married for love, and the love turned to dust. She had bonny children, yet she felt they had been thrust upon her, and she could not love them. They looked at her coldly, as if they were finding fault with her . . . Everybody else said of her: "She is such a good mother. She adores her children." Only she herself, and her children themselves, knew it was not so . . .

"Mother," said the boy Paul one day, "why don't we keep a car of our own? Why do we always use uncle's, or else a taxi?"

"Because we're the poor members of the family," said the mother.

"But why *are* we, Mother?"

"Well—I suppose," she said slowly and bitterly, "it's because your father has no luck."   D. H. LAWRENCE

"The Rocking-Horse Winner"

Feeding the Ducks, Mary Cassatt, 1894, Fourth State, Drypoint over Aquatint Etching

Following are characterization techniques that Lawrence and other writers use. Look for places to apply them in your own story.

Guidelines for Improving Characterization

1. Add natural-sounding dialogue that fits the personality.
2. Add descriptive details about appearance and behavior.
3. Show how the character acts and reacts.
4. Show how others react to the character.

WRITING ACTIVITY *Improving Characterization*

Write a scene for a story starring one of your characters from Writing Activity 3. Then revise the scene to improve the characterization.

Improving the Style *Style* refers to the way you use words and sentences. Your style may be simple and spare or lush and complex or somewhere in between. The choice depends upon your personal preference and the needs of your story. Every style, however, demands skillful use of language—the right word connected to the right word to form the right sentence.

Go over your story for style, reading it aloud and listening to the rhythm and flow of the words. As you do, keep the questions listed below in mind.

Guidelines for Improving Style

1. Does your style fit the theme, events, and characters?
2. Is the style appropriate for your audience?
3. Do your words and sentences fit the style and the characters?
4. Does the language fit the tone, or feeling, of the story?
5. Have you maintained the style consistently?
6. Are your words vivid and precise?
7. Have you varied the length and the structure of your sentences?

Using a Revision Checklist The following checklist will help you remember basic points to look for as you revise a short story.

Revision Checklist

1. Does your beginning capture attention and present the conflict, setting, and main characters? *(See pages 390–391.)*
2. In the middle do you present events chronologically or through flashbacks? Do all events relate to the conflict and build to a climax? Do transitions connect the events and show the passage of time? *(See pages 390–391.)*
3. Is your resolution fitting and satisfying? *(See page 392.)*
4. Do you use dialogue and description? *(See page 390.)*
5. Is the theme clearly implied? *(See page 383.)*
6. Is the point of view consistent? *(See pages 385–386.)*

WRITING ACTIVITY *Revising a Story*

Use the guidelines on pages 393, 394, and 395 and the Revision Checklist above to revise the story from Writing Activity 7.

WRITING ACTIVITY *Writing on Your Own*

WRITING
ABOUT THE
THEME

If your teacher permits, read to some classmates the story about values from Writing Activity 8. Then use their comments and the guidelines in this section to revise it.

Editing and Publishing

Grammar in the Writing Process

Mr. Gessler, the old bootmaker, and the narrator have the following conversation in the short story "Quality" by John Galsworthy.

> "Do you wand any boods?" he said. "I can make dem quickly; id is a slack dime."
> I answered: "Please, please! I want boots all round—every kind!"
> "I vill make vresh model. Your food must be bigger."

In fiction such a conversation between two or more characters is called *dialogue*. To make sure that your readers clearly understand the dialogue between your characters, you will need to know which pronouns to use and how to punctuate your dialogue correctly.

Cases of Pronouns   A *pronoun* is a word that takes the place of a noun. Knowing which pronoun to use in a particular sentence involves understanding the different cases of pronouns. *Nominative case pronouns,* used as subjects and predicate nominatives, are *I, you, he, she, it, we,* and *they. Objective case pronouns,* used as objects, are *me, you, him, her, it, us,* and *them. Possessive case pronouns,* used to show ownership or possession, are *my, mine, your, yours, his, her, hers, its, our, ours, their,* and *theirs. (For more information about pronouns in the different cases and for practice in using them correctly, see pages 671–680.)*

NOMINATIVE CASE   When **I** came in, **he** came down the stairs.

OBJECTIVE CASE   The young man in the shop told **me** that there had not been enough work for **him.**

POSSESSIVE CASE   **His** boots were better than any of **my** other boots.

Quotation Marks with Dialogue   Quotation marks enclose only a person's exact words—not a speaker tag, such as *he said,* or any other words.

"What have you done to your shop?" I asked.
He answered, "Id was too exbensif. Do you want some boods?"

Capital Letters with Dialogue   Just like a regular sentence, a direct quotation begins with a capital letter.

> "**W**here is your brother?" I asked.
> "**D**idn't you know," Mr. Gessler answered, "that he is dead? **H**e was a good man." [*That* does not begin with a capital letter because it is in the middle of the sentence.]

Commas and End Marks with Dialogue   Use a comma to separate the direct quotation from the speaker tag. Place the comma inside the closing quotation mark. Also, you should usually place end marks inside the closing quotation mark when the end of the quotation comes at the end of the sentence. *(For more information about punctuating dialogue and writing direct quotations, see pages 803–809.)*

> "The doctor said he died of starvation**,**" the man said.
> I exclaimed**,** "That is so hard to believe**!**"

Indentation with Dialogue   Each time the speaker changes in a dialogue, begin a new paragraph. For an example look at the dialogue at the beginning of the previous page.

Editing Checklist

I. Has the correct case of each pronoun been used? *(See pages 671–679.)*
2. Has all the dialogue been punctuated, capitalized, and indented correctly? *(See pages 803–808.)*

WRITING ACTIVITY   *Editing a Story*

Edit your story from Writing Activity 10, using the Editing Checklist above and the checklist on page 38.

WRITING ACTIVITY    *Writing on Your Own*

WRITING ABOUT THE THEME   **Editing**   Use the checklist above and the one on page 38 to edit your story from Writing Activity 11.

Publishing   Make a neat final copy of your story. Then combine it with your classmates' stories to form a collection of short stories.

Writing a Poem

Dig deeply into your feelings and you may discover not a story but a poem. A poem is a form of imaginative writing that is more tightly structured than a story. To create its special effect, a poem uses words not only to convey meaning but also to paint pictures and produce a kind of music. In this section you will be guided as you express your creativity through poetry.

Writing Term   **Poetry** is a form of writing that encourages the expression of feelings through sound, images, and other imaginative uses of language.

Finding Ideas for Poems

Poetry is not reserved for lofty or romantic subjects such as patriotism, the soaring of an eagle, or a lost love. In fact, any subject can be poetic. W. D. Snodgrass wrote about "Lobsters in the Window," and Pablo Neruda wrote "Ode to My Socks."

To find an idea for a poem, then, you need not look for an imaginative subject. Instead, look for an imaginative response to a subject by searching inside yourself. Probe your emotions and sensations in both ordinary and dramatic situations. For example, what does a traffic jam make you think of? How does it feel to sleep late on a weekend morning? What comes to mind when you look at a particular picture? What do you associate with the color orange? Concentrate on your impressions and sensations as you dig into your thoughts.

Filling out a chart might help you launch some ideas. Begin by listing some general subject areas and then brainstorm or list examples for each one. Use your journal as well as your memory as a source of examples. The following part of a chart may be used as a guide.

Idea Chart	
EVENTS	birthday, football touchdown, first moon landing
SCENES	streets after a rain, bus stop, surface of Venus
SENSATIONS (Smells)	fish frying, shampooed hair, air after a rainstorm

Look over the ideas on your chart and start exploring the most promising ones. Use freewriting, brainstorming, clustering, questioning, and any other technique that will prod your imagination and encourage ideas and images to flow freely.

WRITING ACTIVITY *Charting to Find Ideas for a Poem*

Use item 1 and four others to create a chart like the one on page 398. List at least ten examples for each subject. Keep your chart.

I. some personal values   **6.** sensations: sounds
2. world events   **7.** sensations: textures
3. busy scenes   **8.** sensations: tastes
4. peaceful scenes   **9.** emotions
5. sensations: smells   **10.** hopes and dreams

WRITING ACTIVITY *Focusing to Find Ideas for a Poem*

Write your responses to each of the following questions. Focus on the sensations, emotions, images, and impressions that come to mind.

I. What does a spider bring to mind?
2. Why does a hot shower feel good?
3. What do you associate with the color yellow?
4. What thoughts do you have about free speech?
5. What comes to mind when you look at the photograph below?

Using Sound Devices

Since poems are usually meant to be read aloud, poets use the sounds of words as well as their meanings to achieve an effect. The following chart shows the major sound devices you can use when you write a poem.

Sound Devices

ONOMATOPOEIA Use of words whose sounds suggest their meaning
    snap, howl, hiss, whine, creak, murmur

ALLITERATION Repetition of a consonant sound at the beginning of a series of words
    And in the **pr**etty **p**ool the **p**ike stalks
               STEVIE SMITH, "Pretty"

CONSONANCE Repetition of a consonant sound or sounds with different vowel sounds, usually in the middle or at the end of words
    And where the wate**r** had **dripp**ed **fr**om the ta**p** . . .   D. H. LAWRENCE, "Snake"

ASSONANCE Repetition of a vowel sound within words
    And r**a**diant r**ai**ndrops c**ou**ching in c**oo**l fl**ow**ers . . .
         RUPERT BROOKE, "The Great Lover"

REPETITION Repetition of a word or phrase
    We are the hollow men
    We are the stuffed men . . .
    Remember us—if at all—not as lost
    Violent souls, but only
    As **the hollow men**
    The stuffed men.
         T. S. ELIOT, "The Hollow Men"

RHYME Repetition of accented syllables with the same vowel and consonant sounds
    I was angry with my **friend:**
    I told my wrath, my wrath did **end.**
    I was angry with my **foe:**
    I told it not, my wrath did **grow.**
        WILLIAM BLAKE, "A Poison Tree"

Before you compose a poem, you may want to compile a word-and-phrase list from which you can draw as you write. Begin by listing words and phrases associated with your subject. Then, for each item on your list, think of words and phrases associated with it by sound or by meaning. You can keep an eye and ear out for sound patterns by speaking words aloud as you work. Although you will not include all the listed items in your poem, the act of creating the list will help you focus your thoughts and identify sound patterns.

Rhythm and Meter   A basic part of the sound of a poem is its *rhythm*—the beat created by the arrangement of accented and unaccented syllables. Sense the rhythm as you read the lines below, where ´ marks accented syllables and ˘ marks unaccented syllables.

> Tiger, Tiger, burning bright
>
> In the forests of the night . . .   WILLIAM BLAKE, "The Tiger"

The rhythm of poetry is usually more regular than that of prose, shaping its effect and providing a musical quality. When the rhythm follows a strict pattern, as it does in Blake's lines above, it is called *meter*. The most common meter in English is a line of five accented syllables called *iambic pentameter*, as shown in the following example.

> A thing of beauty is a joy forever . . .   JOHN KEATS, "Endymion"

Not all poems follow a strict meter. Some are written in *free verse*, with a freely moving rhythm that flows from the rhythm of the words. *(See page 405.)* Sometimes the rhythm will emerge naturally as you write a poem; other times you will want to plan the pattern of syllables in advance. Experiment with your subject. A single phrase or image may set the rhythm for an entire poem.

WRITING ACTIVITY   *Developing Sound Devices for a Poem*

Using item 1 and two others for ideas, find three subjects for a poem. For each subject develop word lists and sound devices as suggested above.

1. values you do not admire
2. music
3. big moments in sports
4. someone you would like to meet
5. something you fear

Using Figurative Language

Poetry should appeal to the mind's eye as well as to the ear. Poets use the following major devices to paint pictures with words.

Figurative Language

IMAGERY
Use of concrete details to create a picture and appeal to the senses
And now a gusty shower wraps
The grimy scraps
Of withered leaves about your feet . . .
T. S. ELIOT, "Preludes"

SIMILE
Comparison between unlike things, using *like* or *as*
She walks in beauty like the night . . .
LORD BYRON, "She Walks in Beauty"

METAPHOR
Implied comparison between unlike things
Life's but a walking shadow, a poor player
That struts and frets his hour upon the stage . . .
WILLIAM SHAKESPEARE, *Macbeth*

PERSONIFICATION
Giving human qualities to something nonhuman
As Earth stirs in her winter sleep . . .
ROBERT GRAVES
"She Tells Her Love While Half Asleep"

HYPERBOLE
Use of exaggeration or overstatement
Our hands were firmly cemented . . .
JOHN DONNE, "The Ecstasy"

OXYMORON
Use of opposite or contradictory terms, such as *joyful misery, living death, dark snow*
Beautiful tyrant! fiend angelical!
WILLIAM SHAKESPEARE, *Romeo and Juliet*

SYMBOL
Use of one thing to stand for another, as the sea journey mentioned below stands for death
And may there be no moaning of the bar,[1]
When I put out to sea . . .
ALFRED, LORD TENNYSON,
"Crossing the Bar"

[1] sandbar

Once you have chosen the subject of your poem, find related images, figures of speech, and symbols by closing your eyes and focusing on different aspects of your subject. Put all your senses to work as you dig into your imagination. If you want to take a few notes, try not to interrupt the flow of your thoughts and feelings too much. Then, after your mind has traveled for a while, brainstorm or freewrite. Promising ideas are bound to emerge.

WRITING ACTIVITY *Developing Figurative Language for Poems*

Return to the sound devices you developed in Writing Activity 16. Now use the relaxation technique described above to explore figurative language for each of the three subjects. Save your notes.

Choosing a Form

Most poems have a pattern of sound and rhythm, plus a visual arrangement of words. These patterns help to hold the reader's attention and to strengthen the effect of the poem. The pattern of rhyme, rhythm, and lines determines the form of a poem. At times you may wait for the details of form to reveal themselves as you work. At other times you will decide on these elements in advance, especially if you want the form to help establish a particular mood or tone.

Writing a Rhymed Poem   Usually—but not always—a rhymed poem has a tighter structure than an unrhymed poem does. You can think of rhymes in your head, experiment on paper, or use a rhyming dictionary, in which words are grouped by their endings.

The pattern of rhyme, or *rhyme scheme,* can be shown by letters of the alphabet, each letter standing for a different rhyme. Notice in the following two poems that the rhyme scheme does not dictate a particular meter. The first poem has four accents per line, for example, while the second poem, on the following page, has five.

Had we but world enough, and **time,**	*a*
This coyness lady were no **crime.**	*a*
We would sit down, and think which **way**	*b*
To walk, and pass our long love's **day.**	*b*

ANDREW MARVELL, "To His Coy Mistress"

It is a beauteous evening, calm and **free,**	*a*
The holy time is quiet as a **Nun**	*b*
Breathless with adoration; the broad **sun**	*b*
Is sinking down in its **tranquillity** . . .	*a*

WILLIAM WORDSWORTH
"It Is a Beauteous Evening, Calm and Free"

Lines with similar rhyme schemes and rhythms can be grouped into *stanzas,* as in the poem below, which has yet another rhyme scheme. As you read it, notice the *half rhymes,* which are words that have similar but not identical sounds *(plow/furrow, falling/stumbling).*

My father worked with a horse **plow,**	*a*
His shoulders globed like a full sail **strung**	*b*
Between the shafts and the **furrow.**	*a*
The horses strained at his clicking **tongue** . . .	*b*
I was a nuisance, tripping, **falling,**	*c*
Yapping always. But **today**	*d*
It is my father who keeps **stumbling**	*c*
Behind me, and will not go **away.**	*d*

SEAMUS HEANEY, "Follower"

Cradling Wheat, Thomas Hart Benton (American 1889–1975), 1938, Tempera and Oil on Board, 78.7 x 96.5 cm

You do not need to follow any of the rhyme schemes shown in this section or, in fact, any rhyme scheme at all. As the poet you decide what rhyme scheme to use, if any. Simply try different alternatives and then choose the one that works best for you and your topic.

Writing Free Verse   *Free verse* is verse that does not have a strict meter. Instead, the rhythm flows freely from the natural beats of the spoken language. Lines and stanzas, if any, may vary in length. If there is rhyme, it is usually irregular, as in the following excerpt from the poem "Snake" by D. H. Lawrence.

Snake

A snake came to my water trough
On a hot, hot day, and I in pajamas for the heat,
To drink there.

In the deep, strange-scented shade of the great dark
      carob tree
I came down the steps with my pitcher
And must wait, must stand and wait, for there he was
      at the trough before me.

He reached down from a fissure in the earth-wall in the
      gloom
And trailed his yellow-brown slackness soft-bellied
      down, over the edge of the stone trough
And rested his throat upon the stone bottom,
And where the water had dripped from the tap, in a
      small clearness,
He sipped with his straight mouth,
Softly drank through his straight gums, into his slack
      long body.
Silently.

                                     D. H. LAWRENCE

WRITING ACTIVITY

WRITING
ABOUT THE
THEME

Write two poems on the theme of values, one in rhyme and one in free verse. For ideas refer to your journal, your notes from Writing Activities 14, 15, 16, and 17, and the charts on pages 400 and 402. When you have finished your final drafts, read them aloud to some classmates or friends. Do your listeners prefer one poem over the other? Do you? Why?

A Writer Writes

WRITING
ABOUT THE
THEME

A Short Story

PURPOSE: to entertain with an adventure, a science-fiction story,
or a mystery story

AUDIENCE: your classmates

Prewriting   When you select a piece of fiction to read, what type
of story do you choose? Would you most likely choose a story of
adventure, such as one that involved the exploration of an uncharted
island? Perhaps, on the other hand, a science-fiction story or a good
mystery novel would appeal to you more. Regardless of what type of
story you would choose, you would find at the core of each story a
protagonist who is confronted with a conflict—internal and/or external. For example, in the story "Quality" the bootmaker is faced with
the *internal conflict* of not wanting to compromise his standards of
craftsmanship and the *external conflict* of having to compete with larger
businesses that sell inferior boots.

Prepare to write an adventure story, a science-fiction story, or a mystery story in which the conflict is about values. The negative value of greed, for instance, could be the focus of a story in any of the three genres. You could write a science-fiction story about a greedy scientist who tries to gain control of the resources on a wealthy planet in another galaxy. A mystery story could focus on a greedy but charming business person who cheats a partner to gain control of that partner's share of the company. An adventure story could be about a greed-driven archaeologist who desperately wants to locate and possess a famous lost treasure.

Once you have plenty of ideas and have selected a conflict or problem, choose a theme. Then briefly sketch the characters and setting, choose a point of view, and go on to outline the events of the plot. Make sure that the resolution of your story settles the conflict or problem in a way that will satisfy your readers.

Drafting As you write your first draft, include descriptive words and figurative language to make your setting and characters come alive in the minds of the readers. Also add dialogue to lend realism to your story and to move the plot along. For example, mystery writers sometimes will supply clues in different statements that the characters make.

Revising In addition to the checklists on pages 34 and 395, use the following questions as guides to your revision. Are the events in chronological order? Do all of the events lead to the climax of the story? Have you included sufficient details, figurative language, and sensory words to make your story clearly visible in the minds of your readers?

Editing and Publishing Edit your short story, using the checklists on pages 38 and 397. When you have finished and have made a neat final copy, be prepared to read it to your classmates.

Independent Writing

Sometimes a story is based on a *proverb*—a well-known saying, such as "He who hesitates is lost" or "A stitch in time saves nine." Use one of these proverbs or choose one of your own and write a short story with the proverb as your theme. In the story you should imply the proverb instead of stating it directly. *(See Writing Is Thinking in this chapter on page 389.)*

Creative Writing

As was discussed in Chapter 2, a *sonnet* is a verse form consisting of 14 lines of poetry with 5 beats to the line. It follows a regular rhyme scheme, usually *abab/cdcd/efef/gg* or *abba/abba/abba/cde/cde*. One of the most easily recognized sonnets is "Sonnet 43" by Elizabeth Barrett Browning. After reading this sonnet, write one of your own.

Sonnet 43

How do I love thee? Let me count the ways.	*a*
I love thee to the depth and breadth and height	*b*
My soul can reach, when feeling out of sight	*b*
For the ends of Being and ideal Grace.	*a*
I love thee to the level of everyday's	*a*
Most quiet need, by sun and candle light.	*b*
I love you freely as men strive for Right;	*b*
I love thee purely, as they turn from Praise.	*a*
I love thee with the passion put to use	*c*
In my old griefs, and with my childhood faith.	*d*
I love thee with a love I seemed to lose	*c*
With my lost saints—I love thee with the breath,	*d*
Smiles, tears, of all my life!—and, if God choose,	*c*
I shall but love thee better after death.	*d*

ELIZABETH BARRETT BROWNING

WRITING
ABOUT THE
THEME

Writing about Literature

There are three types of irony an author may use—verbal, situational, or dramatic. In the story "Quality," John Galsworthy uses situational irony. *Situational irony* occurs when an event that takes place contradicts what the characters and you, the reader, believe is going to happen. In the form of an essay, explain what situation or situations in the story "Quality" are ironic.

Writing in Other Subject Areas

European History   Choose a newsmaking event in government that recently occurred in a European country and turn it into a narrative. Use all available facts but round out the incidents and characters with description, dialogue, and narrative. Convey a clear theme.

Physics   Write a poem presenting a personal impression of some phenomenon you have studied in physics.

10 Checklist

Creative Writing

Writing a Short Story

Prewriting

✔ Choose a conflict. *(See pages 381–382.)*
✔ Sketch all the characters. *(See page 384.)*
✔ Choose a point of view. *(See pages 385–386.)*
✔ Match the setting of your story to the action, mood, and characters' feelings. *(See pages 387–388.)*
✔ Plan a plot, including a climax and a resolution. *(See page 388.)*
✔ Present the events in chronological order except for flashbacks. Then prepare a story outline. *(See pages 387–388 and 391.)*

Drafting

✔ Write a beginning that introduces the setting, the main character, and the conflict and that engages the reader. *(See pages 390–391.)*
✔ Use transitions, dialogue, and descriptive details. *(See page 391.)*
✔ Write an ending that ties the events together. *(See page 392.)*

Revising

✔ Improve the plot and characterization. *(See pages 392–394.)*
✔ Match your style to fit the theme, events, and characters. Then use the Revision Checklist. *(See pages 34 and 395.)*

Editing and Publishing

✔ Use the Editing Checklists to correct errors in grammar, spelling, and mechanics. *(See pages 38 and 397.)*
✔ Pay special attention to punctuating, capitalizing, and indenting dialogue. *(See pages 396–397.)*
✔ Prepare and share a final copy of your story. *(See page 42.)*

Writing a Poem

✔ Use sound devices and figurative language. *(See pages 400–402.)*
✔ Write rhymed verse or free verse. *(See pages 403–405.)*

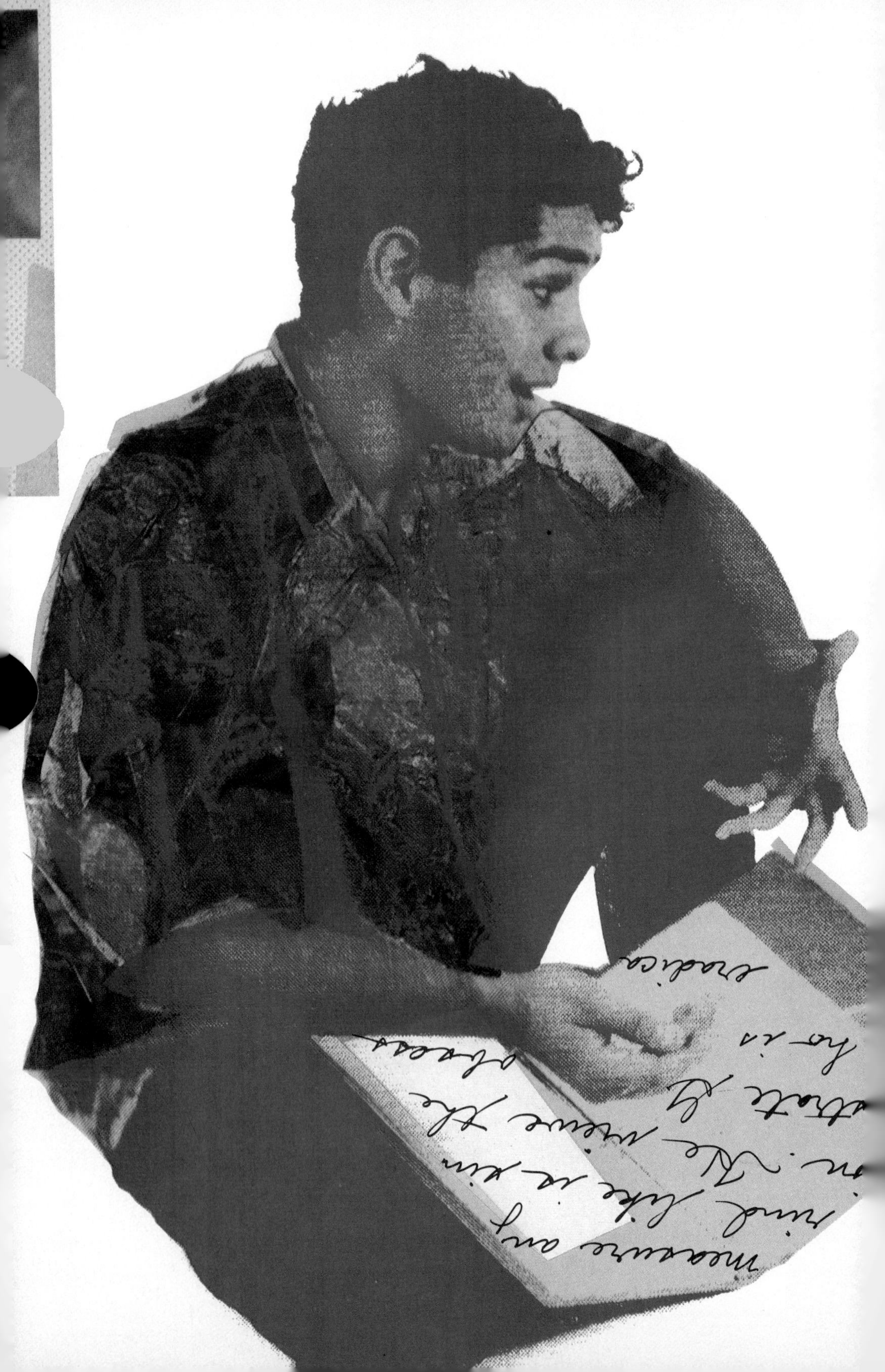

Unit 3
Applying Communication and Study Skills

STUDY

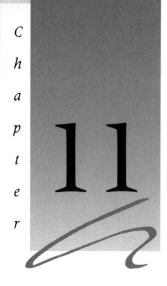

11 Communication for Careers and College

As students pursuing higher education and as future employees seeking jobs, you will be required to communicate information and ideas in business letters, applications, résumés, and interviews. Students use business letters to request catalogs from various colleges or universities and to apply to them for admission. Job seekers use letters, résumés, and applications to present their qualifications to prospective employers.

In this chapter you will learn the correct form for business letters and résumés. In addition, you will practice strategies for preparing college applications and interviewing for both jobs and college admission.

Communication for Careers

Whatever career you decide to pursue, a letter or résumé will often be your first opportunity to communicate information about yourself to a prospective employer. Your goal in writing the letter or résumé is to provide the employer with specific information about your background and experience, encouraging the employer to consider you for the position. Then, during the interview, your manner of communicating and the way you present yourself may be deciding factors in whether you are offered the job.

In this section you will learn the correct form for business letters and résumés. You will also practice strategies for interviewing for a job.

Business Letters

To get the best results, a business letter must express ideas in clear and polite language. In addition, use the correct form. Following is a commonly used form for a business letter called the *modified block style*. The heading, closing, and signature are positioned at the right, and the paragraphs are indented. All sample letters in this chapter use the modified block style.

Modified Block Style

HEADING 45 Mountain Rd
Limestone, ME 28383
April 26, 1992

INSIDE
ADDRESS
Customer Service
Woodland Supplies
Northwoods, ME 07354

SALUTATION
Dear Sir or Madam:

BODY I recently ordered a Cozy Comfort family-size tent, item number T-44783 in your November catalog, from your store in Northwoods, ME. Upon setting up the tent for the first time, however, I found that the center pole was missing from the package. Would you please send this pole to me as soon as possible. I have enclosed a photocopy of my order form and also a copy of the diagram of the tent, with the missing item circled in red. Thank you.

CLOSING Yours truly,

SIGNATURE *Carol Brien*

Carol Brien

All business letters have the same six parts: heading, inside address, salutation, body, closing, and signature.

How to Write a Business Letter

HEADING

- Write your full address, including the ZIP code.
- Write the name of your state in full or use the two-letter postal abbreviation.
- Write the date.

INSIDE ADDRESS

- Write the receiver's address below the heading.
- Include the name of the person if you know it, using *Mr.*, *Ms.*, *Mrs.*, *Dr.*, or some other title.
- If the person has a business title, write it on the next line.
- Use the same way of identifying the state that you used in the heading.

SALUTATION

- Start two lines below the inside address.
- Use *Sir* or *Madam* if you do not know the person's name. Otherwise use the person's last name preceded by *Mr.*, *Ms.*, *Mrs.*, or some other title.
- Use a colon after the salutation.

BODY

- Start two lines below the salutation.
- Double-space a single paragraph. For longer letters single-space each paragraph, skipping a line between paragraphs.

CLOSING

- Start two or three lines below the body.
- Line up the closing with the left-hand edge of the heading. Use a formal closing, such as *Sincerely yours* or *Yours truly,* followed by a comma.

SIGNATURE

- Type your name four or five lines below the closing.
- Then sign your name in the space between the closing and your typed name.

Letters about Employment   When you apply for a job, you may write a letter to the potential employer. Your letter about employment should state specifically the kind of job you desire and should also give information about your qualifications and experiences. In addition, your letter should make a strong favorable impression by being grammatically correct and neat. Include the following information in a letter about employment.

Information in a Letter about Employment	
POSITION SOUGHT	The first paragraph should state the job you are seeking and how you learned about the opening.
EDUCATION	Include both your age and your grade in school. Emphasize courses you have taken that apply directly to the job you are seeking.
EXPERIENCE	State the kinds of work you have done. Although you may not have work experience that relates to the open position, any paid or unpaid positions of responsibility you have held are valuable work experiences.
REFERENCES	Include at least two references, such as a teacher or a former employer, with either an address or a telephone number for each. You should obtain permission in advance from the people you name as references.
REQUEST FOR INTERVIEW	The last paragraph of your letter should ask for an interview. Indicate where and when you can be reached to make an appointment.

In addition to using the correct format for a business letter, apply the following tips for neatness as you prepare the final copy.

Tips for Neatness in Business Letters
1. Use white paper, 8½ by 11 inches in size.
2. Leave margins at least 1 inch wide.
3. Type whenever possible.
4. If you type your letter, type your envelope.
5. Fold your letter neatly to fit the envelope.

The following model illustrates an employment letter written by a student who is seeking employment as a management trainee at a place of business. Note that the letter is typed neatly using the modified block style. In addition, it includes information about the position sought and the applicant's education and work experience. The letter suggests references and ends with a request for an interview.

Employment Letter

```
                                  72 Halsey Avenue
                                  Kilmer, NJ 07800
                                  May 4, 1992


     Mr. William Coles
     Optima Office Supplies, Inc.
     South Suburban Mall
     Kilmer, NJ  07800


     Dear Mr. Coles:

         I would like to apply for the management trainee
     position advertised in this morning's Daily Express.
     Next week I will graduate with honors from Bodes High
     School, where I have taken courses in retailing.

         For the past three years, I have worked as a
     part-time sales clerk for the Monroe Computer Center
     in West Kilmer.  Last summer I was a lifeguard at
     Lenape State Park.

         Ms. Toni Armand, owner of the Monroe Computer
     Center, and Mr. Lance Dooley, staff coordinator at
     Lenape State Park, have agreed to supply references.
     Ms. Armand's business phone number is 663-3886; Mr.
     Dooley's is 947-2431.

         I believe that my background qualifies me for
     the position you have advertised.  I would be pleased
     to come in for an interview at your convenience.  My
     home telephone number is 884-3887.

                                  Very truly yours,

                                  Michael Paci
                                  Michael Paci
```

EXERCISE *Writing an Employment Letter*

Write an employment letter for the following summer job, which a local newspaper has posted in your school guidance office. Use the name and address of your local newspaper, your own address, and today's date.

POSITION AVAILABLE	
Job title:	Landscape architect's assistant
Place:	Lawn & Leaf Landscape Service
Duties:	Assist with mowing, pruning, and landscaping tasks; operate mowers; plant and transplant shrubs, trees and garden plants
Hours:	8:00 A.M. to 5:00 P.M. Mon.-Fri.
Salary:	$5.85 hr.
Requirements:	Person must be dependable, energetic, cooperative, and conscientious.
Apply to:	Mr. Petrini

Using Commas in Dates and Addresses The rules relating to commas that you use in other kinds of writing apply to letters as well. For example, when you write the date, you separate the day and the year with a comma. In addition, when you write an inside address in a letter, you separate the city and the state with a comma. There are, however, a few exceptions to this rule.

Exceptions to Separating Parts of Addresses with Commas

1. Do not use a comma at the end of a line in the heading or inside address but do separate parts of an address on the same line.

EXAMPLE   378 Washington Street, Apartment 235

2. Do not use a comma to separate the state from the ZIP code.

EXAMPLE   Chicago, IL 60616

Edit the employment letter you wrote for Exercise 1 above, checking to make sure you have used commas correctly in the heading and inside address.

Letters of Complaint   If a product or service fails to measure up to its promise, you can write a letter of complaint to try to remedy the problem. Most companies stand behind their goods and services and are willing to make suitable adjustments if there is a problem. If your letter is reasonable and polite, chances are it will bring the desired results. In the following example of a complaint letter, notice that the writer suggests a reasonable solution.

Letter of Complaint

4544 Canyon Drive
Reno, NV 89543
June 11, 1992

Adjustments
Keynote Stationers
435 Pine Street
Salt Lake City, UT 84137

Dear Sir or Madam:

    In a letter dated May 15, I ordered several items from your catalog, including a Norman Rockwell poster. On June 9, I received the other merchandise in the mail, but the poster was not in the package.

    Since I have paid in full for the poster, I request an explanation of the missing merchandise as soon as possible. I am enclosing a copy of the packing slip, which shows that the poster was not included. If for some reason the poster is no longer available, please return my money.

    Thank you very much.

Sincerely,

Susan Lee

Susan Lee

The Envelope   When writing a business letter, use the correct form for the envelope as shown in the following example.

Susan Lee
4544 Canyon Drive
Reno, NV 89543

YOUR NAME
AND ADDRESS

RECEIVER'S
ADDRESS

Adjustments
Keynote Stationers
435 Pine Street
Salt Lake City, UT 84137

EXERCISE   *Writing a Letter of Complaint*

Use the following situation and address to write a letter of complaint. Unscramble the information in the inside address and write it in the proper order. Use your own name and address and today's date.

SITUATION   You ordered several items from a music store, including a Patriot harmonica (in the key of G), #471–12, for $15.00. When the rest of your order arrived, the harmonica was not included.

INSIDE
ADDRESS   Rutger's Music Store; Customer Service Department; Ramsey, New Jersey 07466; 465 Washington Street

Résumés

A *résumé* is a careful summary of your work experience, education, and interests. The purpose of a résumé is to give a potential employer a brief and positive overview of your qualifications for a job.

Always accompany your résumé with a cover letter. The letter should use the correct form for a business letter and should state the job you are applying for and summarize your qualifications for filling it. Your cover letter might end with a statement explaining how the employer can contact you further.

Organize your résumé according to categories of information. The following guidelines and model will help you write your own résumé.

How to Write a Résumé

GENERAL FORM

- Use one sheet of white 8½- by 11-inch paper.
- Use even margins and leave space between sections.
- Center your name, address, and telephone number at the top of the page.

WORK EXPERIENCE

- List your most recent job first.
- Include part-time, summer, and volunteer jobs you have done.
- For each job list the dates you worked, your employer's name, your title, and your primary responsibilities.

EDUCATION

- List the name and address of each school and the years you attended.
- List any special courses you have taken that would help make you a valuable employee.

SKILLS, ACTIVITIES, AWARDS, INTERESTS

- List skills, such as typing, computer programming, or fluency in a foreign language, that relate to the position for which you are applying.
- List school or community activities in which you have participated, such as music lessons, volunteer work, teams, or scouting.
- List awards or certificates of merit you have earned.
- Include your hobbies and special interests.

REFERENCES

- Give the names and addresses of people who have agreed to give you a recommendation or state that references are available on request.
- As references list one previous employer, one teacher or school administrator, and one family friend. Choose people who can attest positively to your character and abilities. Be sure you obtain permission in advance from the people you list as references.

Sample Résumé

Cynthia Klein
21 Bluebonnet Lane
Rayburn, Texas   75295
Telephone: (214) 426-7135

WORK EXPERIENCE

1989--present   Alvis Dance Studio, 945 Main Street,
Rayburn, Texas   75295
<u>Position</u>: Part-time dance instructor
<u>Responsibilities</u>: Teach ballet to
children ages 5 to 12

1986--1988   CRM Store, Ravenswood Mall, Rayburn,
Texas 75295
<u>Position</u>: Cashier
<u>Responsibilities</u>: Ring up and bag
purchases at variety store

EDUCATION

1989--present   Lone Star High School, Fassett
Highway, Rayburn, Texas 75295
<u>Special Courses</u>: Fundamentals of
business, history of dance, modern
dance

1987--1989   Nimitz Junior High School,
350 Route 17, Rayburn, Texas 75295

SPECIAL SKILLS   Word processing, type 70 words per
minute, speak Spanish

ACTIVITIES   Tenth-grade class president,
Computer Club and Drama Club member

AWARDS   Rayburn Fine Arts Achievement Award,
1985

SPECIAL INTERESTS   Dance, drama, computers

REFERENCES   Available on request

Interviewing for a Job

When you apply for a job, the employer will very likely ask you to come to a formal interview. The interview provides an opportunity for both you and the employer to learn more about whether you are well-suited for the job. You will feel more confident during an interview if you take some time to prepare yourself beforehand.

One way to prepare for an interview is to learn as much as possible about the employer's business. The more you know about what the employer does and how the business operates, the better you will be able to discuss the job and your qualifications for filling it. To obtain information about the business, you might talk with people you know who are employed there. In addition, many large companies publish an annual report, which may be available in the library or from the company itself.

The way you present yourself during an interview may determine whether the employer considers you further for the position. The following strategies will help you interview successfully.

Strategies for Interviewing for a Job

1. Prepare a list of questions about the job that you would like to ask the person who interviews you.
2. Be on time for the interview.
3. Present a neat, clean appearance.
4. Be polite to the interviewer.
5. Make eye contact with the interviewer as you speak.
6. Speak clearly and distinctly and use proper grammar.
7. Answer all questions thoughtfully and honestly.
8. Ask questions about the job that display your interest in the business.
9. Thank the interviewer when the interview is finished.
10. Follow up the interview with a letter thanking the interviewer and expressing your interest in the position. Summarize the reasons you think you are a good candidate for the job.

Communication for College

If you plan to continue your education after high school, there are two kinds of letters you will probably write. The first kind is a short request for information, special materials, or a catalog from a professional school or college.

Request for Information from a College

```
                                    339 Wayland Street
                                    Apt. 14-A
                                    Lubbock, TX  74900
                                    September 6, 1992


Director of Admissions
Grand Canyon College
Phoenix, AZ  85061


Dear Sir or Madam:

     I am a senior at Lubbock High School in Lubbock,
Texas.  In the fall I plan to attend college with the
intention of majoring in early childhood education.
I would like to know if Grand Canyon College offers a
degree in early childhood education.

     Please send me your current catalog, an
application for admission, and any information on
scholarships.

     Thank you very much.

                              Sincerely yours,

                              Joyce Inman

                              Joyce Inman
```

The second kind of letter you will write to a college is one requesting an interview. Your letter should express your interest in the college and should suggest a convenient time for your visit to the campus or your meeting with the interviewer. Like the request for information, your letter should be as brief and specific as possible. The following letter is one requesting an interview.

Request for Interview

```
                                      945 Olaf Road
                                      Dorney, MN  56500
                                      February 2, 1992


Mr. Daniel J. Murray
Director of Admissions
Hamline University
St. Paul, MN  55104


Dear Mr. Murray:

     Thank you for sending me the Hamline University
catalog and the applications that I requested.  I
would like to learn more about the university before
I submit my application.  Would it be possible to
visit classes for one day during the week of April 7
through 11?  I will be on vacation from school that
week and can arrive any day that you suggest.  If
possible, I would like to visit music theory and
computer science classes, since I hope to major in
one of these disciplines.

     In addition, I would like to arrange an
interview with someone from your office.  Please let
me know a convenient date and time for my visit.  I
look forward to visiting Hamline University and
learning more about it.

                              Sincerely yours,

                              George Chen
                              George Chen
```

Completing College Applications

Applications enable college admissions officers to learn about your specific qualifications as a potential student. To give the admissions officer a clear and accurate account of your experiences and accomplishments, you should complete the application carefully and thoroughly. The following strategies may help you.

Strategies for Completing College Applications

1. Make one or two copies of each application before you begin to fill it out. Use these copies for practice before you make your final copy.
2. Get an overview of the applications by reading each one thoroughly, including all the directions, before you begin to answer any questions.
3. Type or have someone else type your application if you possibly can. If you cannot type it, print neatly in dark blue or black ink.
4. Make your responses to questions about work, travel, and awards as concise as possible. Use the essay to expand on important information.
5. Do not be modest about your accomplishments but be selective. Instead of listing everything you have ever done, stress your most important activities—the ones you have most contributed to or learned most from.
6. Make sure to answer every question; do not leave any blanks. If a question asks about employment experiences and you have not had any, describe volunteer work you have done. If a question does not apply to you, write *N/A* (for "not applicable"). By doing this you will indicate that you have not skipped any questions by accident.

Writing Essays on College Applications

To become further acquainted with you, many colleges request that you write an essay about a particular subject to be submitted with your application. While the application gives you an opportunity to call attention to your important accomplishments and interests, the essay enables you to demonstrate how well you can organize your thoughts and express your ideas.

As you prepare an essay for a college application, apply the same strategies you have learned for writing a short composition or an essay for a classroom test. *(See pages 527–531.)* In addition, use the following guidelines.

Guidelines for Writing a College-Application Essay

1. Carefully read and interpret the directions. Pay special attention to key words that will help you define your purpose and structure your essay.

2. Note any requirements for the length of the essay. Some instructions may specify that you write a 250- or a 500-word essay. Bear in mind that 250 words is about one and a half pages of typed, double-spaced material. A 500-word essay includes approximately three pages of typed, double-spaced material.

3. Begin by brainstorming or freewriting to generate ideas about the topic. Then decide on your focus, write a thesis statement, and brainstorm for supporting details.

4. Organize your details in a modified outline. *(See page 529.)*

5. Draft your essay, being sure to include an introduction that states the main idea of your essay, supporting details organized in a logical order and connected by transitions, and a strong conclusion.

6. Read your draft and look for ways to improve it. In addition, you might ask a teacher, parent, or friend to read your essay and make suggestions for improvement.

7. Finally, type or neatly copy over your essay, using the form specified in the directions or standard manuscript form. *(See page 43.)*

EXERCISE 3   *Writing a College-Application Essay*

Use the Guidelines for Writing a College-Application Essay to write a 250-word essay on the following topic, which frequently appears on college applications.

> Identify an event that has had a significant influence on you and describe that influence.

Interviewing for College Admission

Some colleges to which you apply may request an interview. In fact, even if an interview is not required by the college, you may find one helpful.

An interview gives a college admissions officer an opportunity to evaluate you firsthand, and it also gives you an opportunity to learn more about the college by asking important questions. As you prepare for an interview, therefore, think about the questions you might be asked and about the questions you want to ask. The following examples may be helpful.

Questions an Interviewer May Ask

- How has high school been a worthwhile educational experience for you? How might it have been improved?
- What have been your best subjects at school? Which have given you the most difficulty?
- How do you spend your time outside of school?
- What hobbies or sports do you especially enjoy?
- What was the last book you read that was not required reading in school?
- Have you decided on a college major yet? If so, what is it going to be?
- In what ways do you expect to benefit from your college experience?

Questions to Ask at College Interviews

- How large are freshman classes?
- Will I have a faculty advisor as a freshman? How many other students will this advisor have?
- At what point must a student decide on a major?
- Are there specific course requirements for freshmen? What are they?
- Are there any foreign or intercollegiate exchange programs offered?
- What is the average total cost of the first year of college?
- What opportunities are there for on-campus part-time employment?

For a successful interview, you should not only prepare ahead, but also do your best to make a favorable impression through the manner in which you conduct yourself during the interview. Apply the following strategies when interviewing.

Strategies for Interviewing

1. Present a neat appearance.

2. Arrive on time or a few minutes early for the interview.

3. Display a courteous manner by introducing yourself and shaking hands.

4. During the interview listen attentively and answer all questions thoughtfully, pausing to think about your answers when necessary.

5. Use proper grammar and syntax in your questions and answers.

6. Maintain eye contact with the interviewer as you speak.

7. Be prepared to ask a few questions that you could not find answers to simply by reading the college catalog.

8. When the interview is over, thank the interviewer.

9. Follow up the interview with a brief business letter expressing interest in the college and thanking the interviewer.

EXERCISE *Writing a Letter to a College*

Find out more about some schools or colleges that you might be interested in attending. Write a business letter to the college admissions offices requesting a catalog. Consult a current college reference book in the library or school guidance department to find the college addresses.

EXERCISE *Practicing for a College Interview*

With your teacher's permission, work with a partner to practice for a college interview. Each partner should prepare several questions to ask first as the interviewer and then as the applicant. Using the Strategies for Interviewing listed above, role-play an interview by having one person act as the interviewer and the other as the applicant. Then switch roles and do another interview.

Chapter

11 Review

A **Letter and Résumé for Employment** Look through the Career Opportunities section of a newspaper and find a job that you would like to apply for. Create a résumé for yourself that you could send to apply for that job. Then write an employment letter to accompany the résumé.

B **Letter of Complaint** Imagine that you have ordered a year's subscription of *Sports Life* but that you have not received your copies for the months of August and September. Write a letter of complaint to the Customer Service Department in which you explain the problem and suggest a reasonable solution. Use your own name and address in the heading and unscramble the following information to include in the inside address.

Lansing, Michigan 22976; Suite 20; 1400 Willard Boulevard

C **Letters to Colleges** Choose a school or college that strongly interests you and write a letter to the college admissions office to request more information or to arrange an interview. Consult a college reference book in the library or school guidance department for the college address.

D **College Application Essay** Write a 250-word essay on the following topic frequently used on college applications:

Discuss a current local, national, or international event or trend and its significance to you.

E **Interview** With a partner plan to role-play a job interview. Decide what the job will be and who will act as the interviewer and who will be the applicant. Then write several questions for each to ask during the interview. With your teacher's permission, present the interview to the class, having your classmates evaluate the interview according to the Strategies for Interviewing on page 428. Be sure to review your classmates' evaluations.

12 Speaking and Listening

"Speech is civilization itself. The word, even the most contradictory word, preserves contact—it is silence which isolates." These words of the great German writer Thomas Mann express the importance of spoken language. The goal of effective speaking is to communicate your thoughts and ideas to your audience in such a way that the members of the audience will be inspired, persuaded, entertained, or better informed about an interesting subject. This chapter will help you become not only a more effective speaker but also a better listener.

Preparing a Speech

It is likely that there will be opportunities during your life when you will be called upon to prepare and deliver a speech. As a student you may have to speak to a class, a special interest group, or a group of parents and teachers. In your career you may have to address formally a group of colleagues at a meeting or seminar or a group of townspeople at a local political rally.

Your experience in writing informative reports and persuasive and creative compositions will be helpful to you as you prepare a speech—no matter whether your purpose is to inform, to persuade, or to entertain. In fact, the steps you follow as you write a speech are similar to the stages of the writing process. *(See Chapter 1, pages 10–37.)* The main difference between a speech and a composition is in the final stages. Instead of editing and publishing your composition, you will practice your speech and then deliver it orally to an audience.

Knowing Your Audience and Purpose

Having your audience clearly in mind as you prepare your speech will help you deliver a speech that addresses the interests and concerns of your audience.

Strategies for Considering Audience and Purpose

1. If possible, find out the interests of your audience. Decide how these interests are similar to or different from yours.
2. Try to determine what your audience will already know about the subject you plan to talk about. Consider what your audience might expect to hear.
3. Decide whether your purpose is to inform your audience, to persuade them, or to entertain them by expressing your thoughts and feelings or by telling a story. *(See Chapter 4, pages 130–173; Chapter 5, pages 174–215; and Chapter 10, pages 381–397 for more information about these purposes.)*

Although the purpose of most speeches you give in school will be to inform others about certain subjects, some speeches may be given to persuade or to entertain an audience. Most speeches, of course, have more than one purpose. For example, a speaker can inform while trying to persuade an audience to follow a certain course of action.

The following examples suggest ways to limit the subject of traveling in a foreign country to suit the purpose of your speech.

Purposes of Speeches

PURPOSE	EXAMPLES
to inform	to explain ways to travel cheaply in Europe
to persuade	to persuade people to visit Greece
to entertain	to tell about the time you toured Paris in one day

---

EXERCISE *Determining a Purpose*

Number your paper 1 to 3. Write an example of a topic for a speech you might give for each of the three purposes.

Choosing and Limiting a Subject

After you decide on an interesting subject for your speech, it will be necessary to limit the subject so that you can cover it effectively in a given amount of time. Follow the strategies below.

Strategies for Choosing and Limiting a Subject

1. Choose a subject that interests you and is likely to interest your audience.

2. Choose a subject that you know well or can research thoroughly.

3. Limit the subject by choosing one aspect of a broader topic. For a 20-minute speech, for example, you could limit the subject "baseball greats" to "Babe Ruth: a great batter and pitcher." To time yourself, keep the following rule of thumb in mind: It takes about as much time to give a 10-minute speech as it does to read aloud slowly a 4-page report or essay typed double-space.

EXERCISE *Finding a Subject*

Number your paper 1 to 10. Then write a subject of a speech for each of the following general categories.

1. personal experiences	**6.** how to make something
2. experiences of others	**7.** jobs or professions
3. current events or issues	**8.** school-related subjects
4. past events or people	**9.** ideas for inventions
5. how to do something	**10.** ideas about the future

EXERCISE *Limiting a Subject*

Number your paper 1 to 10. Then write a limited subject for each topic that would be suitable for a 20-minute speech.

1. air pollution	**6.** football
2. Japan	**7.** careers in medicine
3. education	**8.** John F. Kennedy
4. conserving wildlife	**9.** communism
5. Shakespeare's plays	**10.** history of space travel

Gathering and Organizing Information

To gather information for an informative speech, follow the same procedure you would for a written report. *(See pages 320–371.)* Begin with your own experience by brainstorming a list of everything you already know about the subject. Then consult several other good sources of information—including encyclopedia articles, books, and periodicals in the library. *(See pages 481–491.)* You also might interview people who are knowledgeable about your subject. When you are planning the interview, always make a list of the questions you want to ask.

Taking Notes   Be sure to take notes throughout your research. Note cards are the best way to record information from encyclopedias, periodicals, and books because they can be easily organized later. If you interview someone, take notes in modified outline form or use a tape recorder. Write down any words from the interview you intend to quote, put them in quotation marks, and get permission from the speaker to use the quotations. After gathering your information, organize it by following the strategies below.

Strategies for Organizing Your Speech

1. Arrange your note cards by topics and subtopics in the order you plan to present your information. Use the cards to make a detailed outline of your speech and then draft an introduction and a conclusion.

2. To capture the interest of your audience, begin your speech with an anecdote, an unusual fact, a question, an interesting quotation, or some other attention-getting device. Include a thesis statement that makes clear the main idea and the purpose of your speech. *(See pages 156–157.)*

3. Arrange the supporting points or details in a logical order for the body of your speech. Rearrange your note cards and revise your outline as needed to improve the logical flow of ideas. Think of the transitions you will use to connect your ideas. *(See pages 101–102.)*

4. Write a conclusion for your speech that summarizes your main idea and signals the audience that you have finished. *(See pages 163–165.)*

Audiovisual Aids   Good speakers often use audiovisual aids to give impact to their speeches. Decide which main points to enhance with maps, photographs, slides, artifacts, tapes, records, or any other type of audiovisual aids and collect or create these materials as you prepare your speech.

EXERCISE *Gathering and Organizing Information*

Choose and limit a subject for a 20-minute speech in which your purpose is to inform. Write what you know about the subject on note cards. Next, go to the library and find additional information for at least ten more note cards. Then, organize your cards in the order you will present your information and write an outline of your speech. Gather any audiovisual aids you plan to use. Finally, draft a strong introduction and conclusion.

Practicing Your Speech

Practicing guarantees improvement, whether you play the piano, play tennis, or give a speech. While you should practice your speech, you should not attempt to memorize it, because it will sound stiff and unnatural. Instead, make a set of cue cards from your outline and note cards to remind you of the important points you wish to make. Prepare one cue card for the main topic and one cue card for each subtopic in your outline. On the topic card, write words to remind you of your introductory remarks, anecdote, or facts. On each subtopic card, list examples, reasons, or illustrations about that subtopic.

In addition, as you write your cue cards, include words and phrases that will give impact to your speech, for colorful use of language often distinguishes a good speaker from a dull one. Finally, put your cue cards in order. A model cue card follows.

Subtopic Cue Card

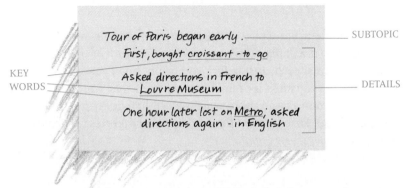

Following are some strategies that will be helpful to use when practicing your speech.

Strategies for Practicing Your Speech
1. Practice in front of a long mirror so that you will be aware of your gestures, posture, and facial expressions.
2. Practice looking at an imaginary audience as you say your speech.
3. Time your speech. Add or cut information if necessary.
4. Practice using your cue cards and any audiovisual aids you plan to use.
5. Practice over a period of several days. Your confidence will grow each time you practice your speech, and as your confidence grows, your nervousness will decrease.

Make revisions in your speech as you practice. You can do this by experimenting with word choice and by adding or deleting information to clarify your main points. In addition, if you practice your speech with a classmate or friend, you can use this listener's comments to improve your speech before you deliver it.

EXERCISE **5** *Practicing and Revising Your Speech*

Prepare cue cards for the speech you developed in Exercise 4. In front of a relative, friend, or classmate, practice the speech. Afterward discuss your speech and revise it, using the listener's comments as a guide. Save your speech for Exercise 6.

435

Delivering Your Speech

Each moment you spent researching your speech, organizing it, and practicing it will pay off when you get up in front of your audience to deliver your speech. Just before you begin, however, you can alleviate your nervousness by reminding yourself that you are now an expert who knows more about your subject than does anyone in your audience. Also, keep in mind these additional strategies for delivering a speech.

Strategies for Delivering a Speech

1. Have ready all the necessary materials, such as your outline or cue cards and audiovisual materials.
2. Wait until your audience is quiet and settled.
3. Relax and breathe deeply before you begin to speak.
4. Stand with your weight evenly divided between both feet. Avoid swaying back and forth.
5. Look directly at the people in your audience, not over their heads. Try to make eye contact.
6. Speak slowly, clearly, and loudly enough to be heard.
7. Be aware of using correct grammar and well-formed sentences.
8. Use gestures and facial expressions to help you emphasize your main points.
9. Since your speech is not over until you have taken your seat, walk to your seat without making comments to people in the audience.

Evaluating an Oral Presentation

Evaluating your own speech and accepting the comments of others about your speech will help you improve your performance on future speeches. When you listen to a speech, try to determine how well the speaker knows and covers the information. Also decide whether the speaker makes a good impression on the audience by speaking clearly, making eye contact, and choosing appropriate words. Be specific in your evaluation and remember that your suggestions should be positive and intended to help. The Oral Presentation Evaluation Form on the next page may be helpful.

Oral Presentation Evaluation Form

Subject: _____

Speaker: _____

Date: _____

Content
Are the subject and purpose of your speech appropriate for the audience?
Is the main point clear?
Are there enough details and examples?
Do all the ideas clearly relate to the subject?
Is the length appropriate (not too long or too short)?

Organization
Does the speech begin with an interesting introduction?
Do the ideas in the body follow a logical order?
Are transitions used between ideas?
Does the conclusion summarize the main points?

Presentation
Does the speaker use good word choice?
Does he/she speak loudly and clearly enough?
Is the rate appropriate (not too fast or too slow)?
Does the speaker make eye contact with the audience?
Are audiovisual aids or other props used effectively?
Are cue cards or an outline used effectively?

Comments _____
_____
_____
_____

EXERCISE *Delivering and Evaluating Your Speech*

With your teacher's permission, present the speech you practiced and revised in Exercise 5. Afterward complete an Oral Presentation Evaluation Form for your speech at the same time that your classmates are evaluating it. In addition, complete an evaluation form for any speeches presented by your classmates. Share your comments with the speaker you evaluated and read the comments your classmates wrote about your speech. Use your listeners' suggestions to note ways that you can improve your future speeches.

437

Listening

Successful listening involves more than merely hearing the words that someone speaks. It often means understanding, evaluating, organizing, remembering, and applying the information.

Listening to Directions

Throughout a normal day, you will be given many sets of directions to follow, from how to do a homework assignment to how to get to a new shopping mall. Whatever kind of directions you hear, always listen carefully—from beginning to end. Do not assume you already know what the speaker is going to say before he or she finishes. In addition, follow the strategies below.

Strategies for Listening to Directions

1. Write down the directions as the speaker gives them.
2. If any part of the directions is unclear, ask specific questions to help you understand.
3. When you finish an assignment, review the directions to make sure you have followed them correctly.

EXERCISE *Following Directions*

Ask someone you know, either a friend or a relative, to give you directions to an unfamiliar place in your area. Then see if you can accurately repeat or write the directions. Explain in your journal why you think the strategies you learned helped or did not help you to listen to directions more accurately.

Listening for Information

Hearing becomes listening only when you are able to understand the information you have heard well enough to evaluate it and apply it. The strategies that follow should help you use listening skills effectively in order to learn new information.

Listening Strategies

1. Try to focus on what the speaker is saying without being distracted by people and noises.

2. Determine whether the speaker's purpose is to inform, to persuade, or to express thoughts and feelings.

3. To identify the speaker's main ideas, listen for verbal clues, such as the points introduced by *most important, remember that, first,* and *finally.*

4. Watch for nonverbal clues such as gestures, pauses, or changes in the pace of speaking. Clues like these can signal important points.

5. Determine the speaker's point of view about the subject. For example, what is the speaker's position? Is the speaker arguing for or against an issue?

6. Take notes to organize your thoughts and to help you remember details. *(See pages 501–503 for information about taking notes.)*

EXERCISE *Listening and Taking Notes*

With your teacher's permission, ask a classmate to explain to a small group how to do something, such as making pottery or using a video camera. If time permits afterward, compare the notes each person took. Try to determine why all members recorded certain points and not others.

Recognizing Propaganda

As you listen to the literal meanings of words, pay attention to any hidden purposes or motives behind those words. Also listen carefully for the speaker's point of view or bias. What is the intent of a commercial, an editorial, or a political speech? Speakers who use *propaganda techniques* misrepresent or distort information or present opinions as if they were facts. Do not confuse propaganda with persuasion. In persuasion the speaker uses facts, evidence, and logical arguments to promote a viewpoint. In propaganda, on the other hand, the speaker uses emotional language, exaggeration, and sometimes even scare tactics to win people over.

439

Confusing Fact and Opinion   A *fact* is a statement that can be proven, but an *opinion* is a personal feeling or judgment about a subject. When opinions are stated as facts, listeners can be confused or misled. Understanding the difference will help you be a more critical listener.

EXERCISE *Distinguishing between Facts and Opinions*

Number your paper 1 to 10. Then label each statement *F* for *fact* or *O* for *opinion*.

I. Shakespeare wrote most of his works during the 1600's.

2. Males are smarter than females in math, but females are smarter than males in English.

3. Acid rain will destroy all our forests before Americans stop polluting the air.

4. Every senior in Mrs. Mason's English classes must write a research paper.

5. The senior year is the best year of high school.

6. Acid rain is destroying valuable forest land in the United States and Canada.

7. Shakespeare was the greatest playwright of all time!

8. Last year every senior—except two—bought a yearbook.

9. Last summer 68 percent of students attending summer school were male.

10. Students who are not going to college should not have to write a research paper in Mrs. Mason's English class.

Bandwagon Appeals   The *bandwagon appeal* tries to get you to do or think the same thing as everyone else. Often bandwagon appeals are used in advertising to make customers feel inadequate if they do not buy a certain product. These appeals are also used in politics to make potential voters feel that they must support a particular candidate or risk being out of step with everyone else.

> Rosemary Filippo has the support of all of our city workers. She has the support of the young, the middle-aged, and the seniors. Rosemary Filippo has the support of all the people! Doesn't she deserve your support too?

Testimonials   A famous person's endorsement of a product is called a *testimonial*. A testimonial, however, can be misleading because it often suggests that because the famous person uses the product or endorses it, the product is so good that everyone else should also use it. A testimonial may also suggest that using the product will give you the same success as the famous person endorsing it. The following testimonial is misleading for both of these reasons.

> Hi, Guys, I'm Jeff Strong. I hope you liked my last movie, *Muscle Head*. When I auditioned for the movie, I made sure to wear my InvisiVision contact lenses. Glasses are a bother when I'm doing all those action shots. So get yourself some InvisiVision lenses if you want to be a star in your own neighborhood!

Unproved Generalizations   A *generalization* is a conclusion that is based on many facts and examples. A generalization is unproved, however, if it is based on only one or two facts or examples. Unproved generalizations usually include words such as *always, never, all,* or *none*. Statements using words such as these can easily be disproved by finding just one exception.

UNPROVED GENERALIZATION	Flowers at Blossom's Blossoms are **always** the freshest you can buy!
ACCURATE GENERALIZATION	Flowers at Blossom's Blossoms are **usually** the freshest you can buy!

EXERCISE *Identifying Propaganda Techniques*

Number your paper 1 to 5. Then label each statement *B* for *bandwagon, T* for *testimonial,* or *U* for *unproved generalization*.

1. Look down! What do you see? Everyone is wearing Prairie Rider cowboy boots. They're in, and you'll be "out" if you don't hurry to get your own pair of Prairie Riders!
2. If your car is sick, take it to Dr. Stan at Stan's Garage, where you always find the latest electronic equipment and the lowest prices in town.
3. Everyone—from Granddad to Junior—is eating Yummy-Oats for breakfast. Don't wait till morning; eat a bowl now. Don't miss out on this great taste-tingling experience!

4. Because I get pushed, kicked, and hit every Sunday on the football field, I always look forward to a good hot shower afterward and the soothing feeling of Chill-Out ointment. Got any tense, tired muscles like me? Relax them away with Chill-Out.
5. All of Dr. Dan's patients look forward to their next appointment. Going to the dentist is always a happy time—no matter who you are!

Analyzing a Misleading Advertisement   Think of a product you have used that you feel was extremely unsatisfactory. Then find or recall an advertisement for the product. Write an analysis of the propaganda techniques that were used in the ad. What misleading information was used to try to get you to buy the product? Was there any information left out of the ad that might have made you hesitate to buy the product? Sometimes what is left out can be as important as what is included!

Group Discussions

One effective way to communicate ideas, exchange opinions, solve problems, and reach conclusions is through a group discussion. Discussions may be informal, as in discussing what movie to see, or formal, as in contributing to a panel discussion or debate. In informal discussion groups, you express your views freely and share your ideas and experiences. In formal discussion groups, you usually present evidence—reasons or facts—to support a point of view.

Group discussions serve a variety of practical purposes. As part of the prewriting stage in the writing process, you may brainstorm in a group or have a roundtable discussion. You may also use discussion skills to prepare a speech or an oral report or to study for a test. As part of a study group, you may discuss assigned readings, help your group to reach agreement on answers to questions, or prepare for a test. Use the strategies that follow to help you participate in group discussions.

Strategies for Participating in Group Discussions

1. Listen carefully and respond respectfully to others' views.
2. Ask questions to make sure you understand others' views and information.
3. Keep in mind that everyone in the group should have an equal opportunity to speak.
4. Make sure your contributions to the discussion are clear, constructive, and relevant to the subject.

Discussion Leaders

The leader, or moderator, of a discussion group has certain additional responsibilities. If you are chosen to lead a group discussion, use the following strategies for meeting these responsibilties.

Strategies for Discussion Leaders

1. Introduce the subject, question, or problem.
2. If the subject or problem is complicated, divide it into manageable tasks and ask or assign group members to take responsibility for each task.
3. With the group's help, state the purpose or goal of the discussion.
4. Keep the discussion on track to help the group achieve its goal.
5. Encourage everyone to participate.
6. Make sure that everyone has an equal opportunity and equal time to speak.
7. Keep a record of the group's main points and decisions or assign this task to a group member.
8. At the end of the discussion, summarize the main points and point out any conclusions or decisions the group has reached.

EXERCISE *Participating in a Group Discussion*

With your teacher's permission, form small groups and conduct a discussion on a topic having to do with careers of interest to the group's members. Choose a leader and set a time limit for the discussion. Afterward evaluate your participation in the group.

Cooperative Learning

Cooperative learning means working together in a group to accomplish a specific purpose or goal. Your group might, for example, be assigned to report on the Soviet Union for your history class. Every group member will have a specific task to do. One member might provide information on climate, for example, and another might research recent changes in the government. Still another student might prepare maps. After doing this individual work, the members of the group coordinate their work, and prepare and present the final report.

Strategies for Cooperative Learning

1. If you have been given a particular task, do not let your group down by coming to the discussion unprepared.

2. Help your group to achieve its goals by taking your fair share of responsibility for the group's success.

3. Cooperate in helping to resolve any conflict, solve any problem, reach a consensus, draw a conclusion, or make a decision.

EXERCISE *Cooperative Learning Project*

With your teacher's permission, form a cooperative learning group with other students to plan a presentation related to a current national issue. Decide together on a topic, choose a leader, and assign tasks. Allow adequate time to prepare and discuss the information. Then coordinate your work and present it to the class. Finally, evaluate your own participation in the group according to the Strategies for Cooperative Learning above.

12 Review

A Giving a Speech Prepare a 20-minute speech about one of the following subjects or one of your own choosing. Decide whether your purpose will be to inform, to persuade, or to entertain. Your teacher may ask you to deliver your speech to the class.

1. applying for a job
2. the Vietnam War
3. cholesterol
4. an outdoor career

B Listening for Directions Create a special place in your notebook for homework assignments. Then, when your teachers give you directions for assignments, listen carefully and write them down in your notebook.

C Listening for Information Find an interesting article in an almanac or some other book of factual information. Then take notes on its major points. Bring the article to class and be prepared to read it to a small group of classmates. As you read it, members of your group should also take notes. Afterward compare notes within your group and discuss their differences.

D Recognizing Propaganda For one week listen to the radio or television for persuasive techniques that are used to convince you to buy or use certain products. Write them down and if time permits, discuss them with other members of your class.

E Group Discussion With your teacher's permission, form small groups to discuss the advantages and disadvantages of using plastics for various products. Each group should select a leader, who will direct the discussion and summarize the group's findings.

F Cooperative Learning Form a cooperative-learning group with the goal of researching and preparing a presentation on using animals for scientific research. Brainstorm about the subject, assign tasks, and choose a leader to help coordinate your work. With your teacher's permission, give your presentation before the class.

13

Vocabulary

Whether you go to college or take a job after high school graduation, you will constantly encounter unfamiliar words. Expanding your vocabulary will help you communicate more effectively, both in school and on the job.

Word Bank for Writing   The more you read, the more your vocabulary is likely to expand. Then as your vocabulary grows, your writing will also improve as you incorporate new words into your compositions and research papers. Begin by jotting down unfamiliar words in a section of your journal. Throughout the year add to this list as you come across new words in your reading. Then when you are revising your writing, look over the list and include as many new words as possible. Begin this process by writing down any unfamiliar words in the following list.

Vocabulary List

aberrant	crypt	intercede	predatory
amorphous	emancipate	meritorious	resolute
beguile	exultation	noncommittal	savory
captivate	feasible	oblique	sequential
cerebral	heretic	orator	symmetry
compatible	imperative	paraphrase	transition
compulsory	inanimate	physiology	vulnerable

The History of English

English—like Latin, Greek, and many other languages—goes back to a parent language called Indo-European. Although Indo-European was an unwritten language, linguists have been able to reconstruct it to some extent. To do so, they have studied words such as the following, which show English to be closely connected with Dutch, German, Irish, Latin, and Greek.

ENGLISH	brother	GERMAN	bruder	LATIN	frater
DUTCH	broeder	IRISH	brathair	GREEK	phrater

The English that people use today has gone through three principal stages, the first of which began about 1,500 years ago.

Old English (450–1150)

This earliest form of English was the language of three German tribes—the Angles, the Saxons, and the Jutes—that invaded England and settled there. These tribes seem to have called their language *Englisc* (from *Engle*, "the Angles"). Although the Old English vocabulary was extensive, only a small fraction of those words have survived. Among them, however, are some of the most common words in the modern English language.

Words from Old English

FAMILIAR OBJECTS	horse, cow, meat, stone, earth, home
FAMILY MEMBERS	father, mother, brother, sister, wife
PRONOUNS	I, you, he, she, we, they, who
NUMBERS	one, two, three, four, five, six, seven
ARTICLES	a, an, the
PREPOSITIONS	in, out, at, by, under, around

447

Middle English (1150–1500)

In 1066, the Normans, who came from what is now northwestern France, invaded England under the command of William the Conqueror. This invasion, known as the Norman Conquest, had far-reaching effects on the language. For centuries afterward the rulers and the upper classes of England spoke French, the Normans' language, although religious and legal documents continued to be written in Latin. During this Middle English period, Old English, French, and Latin gradually became intermixed. Consequently, synonyms for many words came from all three languages. For example, *old* is from Old English; *ancient* is from French; and *venerable* is from Latin.

Modern English (1500 to Present)

By 1500, the assimilation of the contributing languages was largely complete. William Shakespeare wrote his great works early in the Modern English period, and more than 200 years later the documents of the American Revolution were written in Modern English. Changes have continued to occur in English since 1500. Today English is a rich, versatile language with choices and variants that are acceptable in different situations and in different parts of the country.

Knowing how a word was adopted into the English language and what its original meaning was can often help you understand its current meaning. The *etymology* of a word is the history of that word from its earliest recorded use. For example, from the Greek word *koronos*, meaning "curved," came the Latin word *corona*, meaning "wreath or crown." That word became the Old French word *corone* and then the Middle English word *coroune* or *crowne*. Eventually, the word took its present form, *crown*. Many dictionaries include brief etymologies. *(See page 497.)*

Origins of American Words

Although most of the words in use in the United States today were brought to this country by English settlers, other cultural groups have also contributed—and continue to contribute—words to American English. For instance, the various American Indian languages have had a significant influence on place-names in the United States— *Omaha*, *Wichita*, and *Niagara*, for example. Some other Indian contributions include *succotash*, *raccoon*, and *opossum*.

As explorers, settlers, and visitors from other countries came to this country, they brought with them their own contributions to American English. For example, the words *Los Angeles* and *tornado* are Spanish, and *opera* and *spaghetti* are Italian. Following are more examples.

SPANISH	breeze, poncho, mustang, alligator, rodeo
FRENCH	cartoon, dentist, liberty, garage, parachute
GERMAN	hamster, nickel, zinc, noodle, waltz
DUTCH	landscape, skipper, cookie, cruise, iceberg
ITALIAN	zero, candy, magazine, pizza, stanza, opera
AFRICAN	Gullah, banjo, banana, dashiki, okra
CHINESE	tea, kowtow, chow, shanghai, typhoon

Unusual Origins of Words   Although many English words come from Old English, French, Latin, Greek, and other languages, some have more unusual origins. The names of characters in literature and mythology and the names of real people, places, and historical events have occasionally become familiar English words. The word *quixotic*, meaning "idealistic to an impractical degree," derives from the name *Don Quixote,* the hero of the seventeenth-century novel *Don Quixote de la Mancha,* by Miguel de Cervantes. Some words have their origins in mythology: *cereal,* for example, comes from *Ceres,* the Roman goddess of the harvest and grain. The *diesel* engine is named for its inventor, Rudolf Diesel. The word *waterloo,* "decisive defeat," is usually used in the phrase "meet one's waterloo" and derives from the location of the battle that marked Napoleon's defeat in 1815. Following are a few additional examples of words with unusual origins.

Words with Unusual Origins

WORD	MEANING	ETYMOLOGY
malapropism	humorous misuse of a word	from Mrs. *Malaprop*, a character noted for misusing words in Richard Sheridan's 1775 comedy, *The Rivals*
martinet	strict disciplinarian	from Jean *Martinet*, a seventeenth-century French army officer

New words come into use in other ways as well. Some words, called *compound words*, are formed by combining two words. Two examples are *sunglasses* and *birthday*. Other words are a blend of two words; *breakfast* and *lunch* blend to make *brunch*, and *smoke* and *fog* blend to make *smog*. The use of still other words to imitate sounds—for example, *hiss*, *sizzle*, and *swish*—is known as *onomatopoeia*.

EXERCISE *Recognizing Etymologies*

Write the letter of the phrase that matches the etymology of each numbered word. Then check your answers in the dictionary.

I. bunkum

2. saga

3. canyon

4. saxophone

5. cologne

6. mercury

7. Pullman

8. mesmerize

9. succotash

10. utopia

11. calico

12. martial

13. lethargic

14. Socratic

15. watt

a. cotton cloth; named after a city located in India

b. teaching method used by Greek philosopher and his followers

c. chemical element; named for god in Roman myth

d. corn kernels and lima beans; from American Indian word

e. insincere talk; named after North Carolina county

f. comfortable railroad sleeping car; named for its inventor

g. lazy or indifferent; word based on Greek "river of forgetfulness"

h. electrical unit; named for Scottish engineer and inventor

i. narrow valley; from Spanish word for "tube"

j. warlike; from name of god of war in Roman myth

k. long, heroic narrative; from Norse word for "tale"

l. perfumed water; named after a city located in Germany

m. musical instrument; named for French maker of musical instruments

n. to fascinate or hold spellbound; from French doctor who developed a form of hypnotism

o. a perfect, ideal society; from title of English novel by Sir Thomas More

Enriching Your Vocabulary

Because learning and understanding new words is valuable to both your reading and your writing, the rest of this chapter will give you some ways to unlock the meanings of unfamiliar words.

Using Context Clues

The *context* of a word is the sentence, surrounding words, or situation in which the word appears. Usually the context of a word gives only a clue to meaning rather than an actual definition. Following are familiar types of context clues.

RESTATEMENT The sun reached its *zenith*, or **highest point in the sky,** just as we began to eat lunch. [The word *or* introduces an appositive that defines the word *zenith*.]

EXAMPLE *Symmetry* often contributes to the beauty of architecture, as it does, for example, in the **perfect proportions and balanced forms of the Taj Mahal.** [By using the well-known Taj Mahal as an example, the writer makes clear what is meant by *symmetry*.]

COMPARISON A *prodigy* in music, she was **nearly the equal of Mozart, the composer who wrote a sonata at the age of eight.** [The comparison with Mozart shows that *prodigy* means "a highly talented child."]

CONTRAST Mark's **customized purple jeep, with a gilt crown for a hood ornament,** is as *gaudy* as Mr. Foster's gray sedan is plain. [The contrast between Mark's car and Mr. Foster's shows that *gaudy* means just the opposite of *plain*: "showy, garish, and possibly tasteless."]

PARALLELISM She was **determined,** he was **iron-willed,** and I was equally *resolute*. [The parallel sentence structure suggests that *resolute* is a synonym for *determined* and *iron-willed*.]

451

EXERCISE ⟨2⟩ *Using Context Clues*

Number your paper 1 to 20. Then write the letter of the word or words closest in meaning to each underlined word. Use context clues to help you.

  1. Congress passed a <u>statute</u>, or law, to provide for federal enforcement of the Constitutional amendment.
  (A) request (B) written rule (C) sculptured likeness
  (D) book (E) statement

  2. The king decided to <u>abdicate</u>, as King Edward VIII had done when he gave up the throne of England in 1936.
  (A) relinquish power (B) be crowned (C) control
  (D) marry (E) escape

  3. <u>Amity</u> exists between Switzerland and its neighbors, in contrast to the ill will that exists between some other nations of the world.
  (A) rivalry (B) hostility (C) borders (D) friendship
  (E) helplessness

  4. Inquiring about his son's career, the man naturally took a <u>paternal</u> interest in the boy's success.
  (A) brotherly (B) long-term (C) fatherly (D) excessive
  (E) mild

  5. The recent political <u>caucus</u>, unlike those old-time small gatherings, was well reported by the press.
  (A) defeat (B) meeting (C) campaign (D) dinner (E) platform

  6. A referee should be completely <u>impartial</u>, favoring neither one side nor the other.
  (A) businesslike (B) enthusiastic (C) outspoken
  (D) cordial (E) fair

  7. This is a <u>facsimile</u>, or replica, of a five-hundred-dollar bill issued by the Confederate States of America.
  (A) reproduction (B) variety (C) counterfeit
  (D) bonanza (E) display

  8. When the foreman was warned about his <u>laxity</u>, he changed overnight and became a complete perfectionist.
  (A) extravagance (B) appearance (C) negligence
  (D) ignorance (E) temper

  9. Although the candidate failed to win a majority of votes in the primary, he did have a sizable <u>plurality</u> over the first runner-up.
  (A) loss of votes (B) excess of votes (C) celebration
  (D) concern (E) surprise

10. Among the other pleasant smells in the village was the <u>savory</u> odor of chili coming from a small cafe.

(A) appetizing (B) sturdy (C) flowery (D) gracious (E) rural

11. In some countries military service is <u>compulsory</u>; in others it is voluntary.

(A) enjoyable (B) unnecessary (C) disagreeable
(D) required (E) illegal

12. He holds the <u>orthodox</u>, or customary, view of what the company should do to increase sales.

(A) modern (B) religious (C) thoughtful
(D) unpopular (E) traditional

13. Dr. Elroy tried to <u>ascertain</u> the cause of the illness, but he was never sure he was right.

(A) cure (B) destroy (C) treat (D) determine (E) dismiss

14. The lake was <u>placid</u> after the storm, its surface as smooth as a tabletop.

(A) peaceful (B) transparent (C) choppy (D) muddy (E) cold

15. Every <u>recipient</u> of the humanitarian-of-the-year award gives an acceptance speech.

(A) promoter (B) loser (C) receiver (D) giver (E) producer

16. A handwritten note is not enough; you must have an <u>affidavit</u>, a document signed and witnessed.

(A) instruction (B) explanation (C) alibi
(D) oral oath (E) sworn statement

17. Sally is so <u>meticulous</u> in her work that she will rewrite a whole page to correct one small error.

(A) prompt (B) careful (C) excitable (D) remarkable
(E) indifferent

18. Some board games require very little thought or intelligence, but chess is quite <u>cerebral</u>.

(A) simple (B) intellectually demanding (C) thrilling
(D) socially impressive (E) ancient

19. It is almost as hard to <u>decipher</u> Mr. Cook's handwriting as it is to crack a tough foreign code.

(A) study (B) imitate (C) analyze (D) interpret
(E) print

20. Emily Dickinson's <u>renown</u>, or fame, is based on a collection of short, brilliant poems.

(A) pen name (B) gentleness (C) technical mastery
(D) obituary (E) honored status

Prefixes, Suffixes, and Roots

Besides using the context of a word, you can use a word's structure, or parts, to find clues to its meaning. These word parts are prefixes, roots, and suffixes. A *root* is the part of a word that carries the basic meaning. A *prefix* is one or more syllables placed in front of the root to modify the meaning of the root or to form a new word. A *suffix* is one or more syllables placed after the root to affect its meaning and often to determine its part of speech.

The English language contains hundreds of roots, prefixes, and suffixes. With a knowledge of even a few examples of each kind of word part, you should be able to make reasonable guesses about the meanings of words that contain these parts. The following examples illustrate how the meaning of each word part contributes to the meaning of the word as a whole.

Word Parts with Latin Origins

WORD	PREFIX	ROOT	SUFFIX
abrasive	ab- (away)	-rase- (erase)	-ive (toward action)
component	com- (together)	-pon- (put)	-ent (one that performs)
inaccessible	in- (not)	-access- (approach)	-ible (capable of)

Word Parts with Greek Origins

WORD	PREFIX	ROOT	SUFFIX
amorphous	a- (without)	-morph- (form)	-ous (quality of)
ejection	e- (out)	-ject- (throw)	-ion (act or process)
precedence	pre- (before)	-ced- (go)	-ence (act or process)

As you can see, the meanings of prefixes, roots, and suffixes seldom give a complete definition of a word. Rather, they give clues to the meaning of a word. Following are dictionary definitions of the previous examples.

abrasive: tending to rub or wear away

component: simple part or element of a system

inaccessible: not capable of being approached

amorphous: having no definite form, shapeless

ejection: act of throwing out or off from within

precedence: act of going before

Prefixes Many prefixes have clear and familiar meanings. The number prefixes, such as *mono-, bi-,* and *tri-,* are good examples. Other prefixes, however, have more than one meaning and spelling. The prefix *ad-,* for example, may mean "to" or "toward." It may be spelled *ad-* (adjacent), *ac-* (acquire), or *al-* (allure), depending on the first letter of the root to which it is attached. The following charts show common Latin and Greek prefixes.

Prefixes from Latin		
PREFIX	**MEANING**	**EXAMPLE**
ab-, a-	from, away, off	ab + errant: wandering away from the right or normal way
ad-, ac-, af-, ag-, al-, ap-, as-, at-	to, toward	ad + jacent: nearby ac + quire: get as one's own al + lure: entice by charm as + sure: make certain or safe
ante-	forward, in front of, before	ante + chamber: outer room, such as a waiting room
bi-	two, occurring twice	bi + lingual: using two languages with equal skill
circum-	around, about	circum + navigate: sail completely around

PREFIX	MEANING	EXAMPLE
com-, col-, con-	with, together	com + press: squeeze together con + cur: happen together
contra-	opposite, against	contra + dict: resist or oppose in argument
de-	do the opposite of, remove	de + activate: make inactive or ineffective
dis-	opposite of, not	dis + assemble: take apart
ex-	out of, outside	ex + clude: shut out
in-, il-, im-, ir-	not, in, into	in + animate: not spirited im + press: affect deeply
inter-	between, among	inter + stellar: among stars
intra-, intro-	within, during	intra + venous: within or entering by way of a vein
non-	not	non + committal: not giving a clear indication of attitude
ob-	against, in the way	ob + stacle: something that stands in the way
post-	after, behind	post + script: writing added after a completed work
pre-	earlier than, before	pre + determine: decide or establish in advance
re-	again, back	re + organize: arrange or systematize again
retro-	backward, back, behind	retro + spect: review of past events
semi-	half of	semi + circle: half of a circle
sub-	beneath, under	sub + plot: secondary series of events in a literary work
super-	over and above, more than	super + human: exceeding normal human size, capability
trans-	across, beyond, through	trans + atlantic: extending across the Atlantic Ocean
ultra-	beyond in space, beyond limits of	ultra + violet: a violet beyond that visible in the spectrum
vice-	one that takes the place of	vice + principal: person who acts in place of the principal

Prefixes from Greek

PREFIX	MEANING	EXAMPLE
a-, an-	without, not	a + typical: not regular or usual
anti-	against	anti + pathy: dislike, distaste
cata-, cat-, cath-	down	cata + comb: underground passageway or tomb
dia-, di-	through, across	dia + gonal: extending from one edge of a solid figure to an opposite edge
dys-	difficult, impaired	dys + lexia: disturbance of the ability to read
epi-	over, after, outer	epi + dermis: outer layer of skin
hemi-	half	hemi + sphere: half a sphere
hyper-	above, excessive	hyper + tension: abnormally high blood pressure
para-	beside, closely related to	para + phrase: restate a text in another form or in other words
peri-	all around, surrounding	peri + pheral: relating to the outward bounds of something
pro-	earlier than, in front of	pro + logue: introduction to a literary work
syn-, sym-	with, at the same time	syn + thesize: combine to form a new, complex product

EXERCISE *Combining Prefixes and Roots*

Write the prefix with the same meaning as each underlined word or words. Then write the complete word defined after the equal sign.

EXAMPLE <u>between</u> + cede = act as mediator in a dispute
ANSWER inter—intercede

1. <u>two</u> + lingual = using two languages
2. <u>back</u> + active = extending to a prior time or to conditions that existed in the past

3. <u>against</u> + toxin = substance that counteracts poison

4. <u>with</u> + league = associate in a profession

5. <u>opposite of</u> + continue = cease to operate or use

6. <u>not</u> + fallible = not capable of making mistakes

7. <u>before</u> + bellum = existing before a war

8. <u>around</u> + ference = perimeter of a circle

9. <u>excessive</u> + active = excessively energetic

10. <u>after</u> + mortem = occurring after death

11. <u>beside</u> + graph = distinct division in written composition, often shown by indentation

12. <u>again</u> + generate = form or create again

13. <u>across</u> + fuse = cause to pass from one to another

14. <u>down</u> + clysm = momentous event marking demolition

15. <u>remove</u> + moralize = weaken the morale of

Suffixes   There are two kinds of suffixes. One kind, called an *inflexional suffix* (or grammatical suffix), serves a number of purposes. This inflexional suffix changes the number of nouns (*computer, computers*), the possession of nouns (*woman, woman's*), the degree of comparison of modifiers (*soft, softer, softest*), and the form of verbs (*care, cared, caring*). An inflexional suffix does not change either the essential meaning of the word or its part of speech.

A second kind of suffix is the *derivational suffix*, which is more important than the inflectional suffix in vocabulary study. The derivational suffix changes the meaning and very often the part of speech of the word to which it is added. Look at the changes that the derivational suffixes make when they are added to the verb *observe*.

WITH NO SUFFIX   *observe:* verb
WITH *-ance*   *observance:* noun
WITH *-able*   *observable:* adjective
WITH *-ly*   *observably:* adverb (*-ly* added to the adjective form)

As the previous examples show, some suffixes form nouns, some form adjectives, some form verbs, and some form adverbs. (The only common adverb-forming suffix is *-ly.*) The following chart shows a number of suffixes and the part of speech formed by each one.

Suffixes

SUFFIX	MEANING	EXAMPLE
-ance, -ence	action, process, quality, state	exist + ence: state or fact of being
-ard, -art	one that does to excess	bragg + art: one that boasts excessively
-cy	action, state, quality	normal + cy: state of being average or regular
-dom	state, rank, or condition of	free + dom: state of having liberty or independence
-er, -or	one that is, does, makes	retail + er: one who sells directly to consumers
-ion	act, process, result, state	react + ion: act of responding
-ism	act, state, or characteristic of	critic + ism: act of evaluating
-ity	state, quality, degree	moral + ity: doctrine or system of correct conduct
-ness	state, quality	brisk + ness: state of being keenly alert and lively
-ure	act, process, function	post + ure: position or bearing of the body
-able, -ible	capable of, fit for, tending to	expend + able: capable of being consumed by use
-al	characterized by, relating to	tradition + al: relating to the handing down of customs
-en	belonging to, made of	earth + en: made of soil or clay
-ful	full of, having the qualities of	master + ful: having the skill of a qualified worker
-ic	having the character of	hero + ic: being courageous and daring
-ish	characteristic of, inclined to	clown + ish: having characteristics of a clown
-less	not having	purpose + less: lacking goals
-ly	like in appearance, manner, or nature	friend + ly: of, relating to, or befitting a friend

SUFFIX	MEANING	EXAMPLE
-ory	of, relating to, producing	transit + ory: of brief duration
-ous	full of, having the qualities of	clamor + ous: marked by a confused din or outcry
-some	characterized by action or quality	burden + some: character-ized by being a heavy load to bear
-ate	act on, cause to become	captive + ate: influence by special charm
-en	cause to be or have	height + en: cause to have increased amount or degree of
-fy, -ify	make, form into, invest with	spec + ify: make clear and state explicitly
-ize	become like, cause to be	character + ize: cause to be a distinguishing trait of

Some suffixes can form more than one part of speech. The suffix *-ate*, for example, can be used to form verbs (*activate*), nouns (*candidate*), and adjectives (*temperate*).

EXERCISE *Adding Suffixes to Words*

Write the suffix that has the same meaning as each underlined word or words. Then write the complete word defined after the colon.

EXAMPLE   category + <u>cause to be</u>: classify

ANSWER   ize—categorize

  1. zeal + <u>full of</u>: full of eagerness and enthusiasm
  2. convention + <u>characterized by</u>: relating to established customs
  3. survey + <u>doer</u>: one who measures tracts of land
  4. complicate + <u>act of</u>: act of making complex or difficult
  5. enlight + <u>cause to be</u>: cause to receive knowledge
  6. gull + <u>capable of</u>: capable of being easily deceived or cheated
  7. serf + <u>state of</u>: state of being in a servile feudal class
  8. amalgam + <u>act on</u>: merge into a single body
  9. lag + <u>one who does to excess</u>: one who lingers too much
10. flavor + <u>full of</u>: full of pleasant taste
11. tire + <u>characterized by</u>: characterized by being wearisome

12. pleasure + <u>capable of</u>: capable of gratifying
13. daunt + <u>not having</u>: not having fear
14. material + <u>cause to be</u>: cause to come into existence
15. sheep + <u>characteristic of</u>: resembling a sheep in meekness
16. break + <u>capable of</u>: capable of being cracked or smashed
17. orate + <u>one that does</u>: one who delivers a formal, elaborate speech
18. angel + <u>having the character of</u>: having the goodness of an angel
19. malice + <u>full of</u>: full of spite and ill will
20. bounty + <u>full of</u>: characterized by providing abundantly

Roots The root of a word may be well known in English, or it may be less obvious, having come from Latin or Greek. Sometimes a root may stand alone, as in the word *self*. A root may be combined with a prefix (re*tract*), a suffix (*port*able), or even another root (*autograph*). The following charts contain common Latin and Greek roots that are the basic elements of many English words.

Latin Roots		
ROOT	**MEANING**	**EXAMPLES**
-aqua-, -aqui-	water	aquarium, aqueous
-aud-	hear	audience, auditorium
-bene-	good, well	benefit, benevolence
-cred-	believe	credential, credit
-cid-	kill	germicidal, insecticide
-fid-	faith, trust	bona fide, infidel
-fract-, -frag-	break	fraction, refract, fragile, fragment
-grat-	pleasing, thankful	grateful, gratitude, gratuity
-loqu-	speak	eloquent, loquacious
-mor-, -mort-	death	immortal, mortuary
-omni-	all, every	omniscient, omnivorous
-ped-	foot	pedestrian, centipede
-port-	carry	portable, import
-rupt-	break, burst	rupture, interrupt
-scrib-, -script-	write	describe, prescribe, inscription, manuscript

ROOT	MEANING	EXAMPLES
-sequ-	follow	sequel, subsequent
-tort-	twist	distort, tortuous
-tract-	draw, pull	traction, retract
-vert-, -vers-	turn	invert, subvert, versatile, reverse
-vic-, -vinc-	conquer	victory, convince, invincible
-viv-, -vit-	life, live	survive, vivacious

Greek Roots

ROOT	MEANING	EXAMPLES
-anthrop-	man, human	anthropology
-arch-	rule	monarch, hierarchy
-auto-	self	autograph, automobile
-biblio-	book	bibliography
-bio-, -bi-	life	biology, antibiotic
-chrom-	color	chromatic, monochrome
-cosm-	world, order	cosmic, macrocosm
-geo-	earth, ground	geography, geology
-gram-	drawing, writing	grammatical, program
-graph-	write	graph, typography
-log-, -logy-	speech, reason, study, science	catalog, monologue, bacteriology
-micro-	small	microfilm, microwave
-mono-	one, single	monopoly, monograph
-morph-	form	amorphous
-neo-	new	neon, neoclassical
-path-	suffering	pathetic, apathy
-phon-	sound	phonetic, telephone
-pod-	foot	podiatrist, tripod
-poly-	many	monopoly, polytechnic
-psych-	mind	psychology, psychic
-tele-	far off	telescope, telegraph
-therm-	heat	thermal, thermometer

EXERCISE *Recognizing Latin and Greek Roots*

Number your paper 1 to 10. Write the root of each word. Then use the charts in this chapter to write a definition for each word. Refer to the dictionary if necessary.

EXAMPLE   audible
ANSWER   aud—capable of being heard

1. disruption
2. subscription
3. gratify
4. convertible
5. graphic

6. colloquial
7. transport
8. convivial
9. infraction
10. sequential

EXERCISE *Using Roots, Prefixes, and Suffixes*

Number your paper 1 to 10. Then write the letter of the word or phrase closest in meaning to each word in capital letters. (Information in this chapter will help you decide the meaning of each word.)

1. MERITORIOUS: (A) without value
(B) having worthy qualities   (C) wise
2. COMPATIBLE: (A) capable of getting along together
(B) in the manner of a friend   (C) well qualified
3. EMANCIPATE: (A) obey a king   (B) cause to become free
(C) win great acclaim
4. POLYCHROMATIC: (A) science of color   (B) metal alloy
(C) having many colors
5. ILLOGICAL: (A) between reason and knowledge
(B) within reason   (C) not valid, or unskilled in reasoning
6. TRANSITION: (A) secret underground passage
(B) process of going across from one place to another
(C) loss of credibility
7. BIPED: (A) able to walk backward   (B) bicycle
(C) two-footed animal
8. RETROGRESS: (A) lack of progress   (B) in need of repairs
(C) go backward
9. COMMUNICABLE: (A) capable of being transmitted
(B) full of unnecessary information
(C) condition of being infected
10. RECOIL: (A) jump forward suddenly   (B) draw back
(C) lose sight of

463

Synonyms and Antonyms

Another way of expanding your vocabulary is to have a thorough understanding of synonyms and antonyms. A *synonym* is a word that has the same—or nearly the same—meaning as another word. An *antonym* is a word that means the opposite—or nearly the opposite—of another word.

There are often several synonyms for a word. For instance, among the synonyms for the word *candor* are *sincerity* and *forthrightness*. Notice that these words have slightly different shades of meaning. Dictionary entries often explain the slight differences between synonyms. You have probably also used the specialized dictionary for synonyms called a *thesaurus*. Usually a thesaurus is indexed to help users find the synonyms they need.

EXERCISE *Recognizing Synonyms*

Number your paper 1 to 10. Write the letter of the word or words closest in meaning to each word in capital letters. Then check your answers in the dictionary.

1. ADAMANT: (A) skillful   (B) unworthy   (C) unyielding
   (D) distressing   (E) faithful
2. INDICT: (A) accuse   (B) show   (C) imprison   (D) warn
   (E) release
3. ULTIMATE: (A) preliminary   (B) substitute
   (C) rewarding   (D) eventual   (E) concealed
4. NOTORIOUS: (A) legal   (B) fortunate
   (C) unfavorably known   (D) unfamiliar   (E) industrious
5. BESTOW: (A) discard   (B) give   (C) restore   (D) darken
   (E) gamble
6. PREDATORY: (A) entertaining   (B) tragic   (C) corrupt
   (D) preying   (E) lackluster
7. LATERAL: (A) potential   (B) upward   (C) sluggish
   (D) afterward   (E) related to the side
8. ARBITRATION: (A) authority   (B) mystery   (C) concern
   (D) mediation   (E) treatment
9. BEGUILE: (A) deceive   (B) begin   (C) explain   (D) reject
   (E) learn
10. ARABLE: (A) feathery   (B) fashionable   (C) tillable
    (D) windy   (E) livable

EXERCISE *Recognizing Antonyms*

Number your paper 1 to 10. Write the letter of the word most nearly opposite in meaning to each word in capital letters. Then check your answers in the dictionary.

 1. FEASIBLE: (A) faulty   (B) impossible   (C) impoverished
    (D) fatigued   (E) insecure
 2. ACCENTUATE: (A) de-emphasize   (B) protest
    (C) regulate   (D) disagree   (E) relinquish
 3. ERRONEOUS: (A) mistaken   (B) possible   (C) skillful
    (D) tardy   (E) correct
 4. VULNERABLE: (A) unsusceptible   (B) cheerful
    (C) greedy   (D) ridiculous   (E) modest
 5. EMANCIPATE: (A) forget   (B) strengthen   (C) disallow
    (D) enslave   (E) forget
 6. CYNICAL: (A) soothing   (B) stable   (C) trustful
    (D) square   (E) charming
 7. OBLIQUE: (A) brilliant   (B) questionable   (C) direct
    (D) passive   (E) painful
 8. ALLEVIATE: (A) forget   (B) associate   (C) persuade
    (D) improve   (E) aggravate
 9. HERETIC: (A) villain   (B) conformist   (C) saint
    (D) traitor   (E) critic
10. EQUILIBRIUM: (A) disapproval   (B) observation
    (C) hope   (D) imbalance   (E) high pitch

Analogies

You often come across analogy items on standardized tests. Analogy items require you to identify the relationships between given pairs of words. While many kinds of relationships are used in analogy items, synonyms and antonyms are the most frequent.

    HUGE:GIGANTIC   : :   (A) liberate:imprison
    (B) noise:clamor   (C) mature:juvenile

To answer this test item, you first must identify the relationship between the two words in capital letters. Those words, *huge* and *gigantic*, are synonyms because they have similar meanings. The next step is to find the other pair of words among the choices that have the same relationship as this first pair. The answer is *B* because *noise* and *clamor* are also synonyms. The other two answers are not correct, because *liberate* and *imprison* are antonyms, as are *mature* and *juvenile*.

EXERCISE *Understanding Analogies*

Number your paper 1 to 15. Write the letter of the word pair that has the same relationship as the word pair in capital letters. Then write *synonyms* or *antonyms* to identify the relationship.

EXAMPLE   COMPLIMENT:CRITICIZE   : :   (A) kidnap:abduct
          (B) guard:protect   (C) bravery:cowardice
ANSWER   C—antonyms

1. INFINITE:LIMITLESS   : :   (A) disorganized:orderly
   (B) inaccessible:available   (C) placid:calm
2. PURGE:CLEANSE   : :   (A) ornate:plain
   (B) privacy:seclusion   (C) impartial:biased
3. MALICIOUS:KIND   : :   (A) gaudy:flashy
   (B) harmony:discord   (C) adage:proverb
4. AUSPICIOUS:FAVORABLE   : :   (A) saga:epic
   (B) retreat:advance   (C) savory:bland
5. LUSTROUS:DULL   : :   (A) gobble:devour
   (B) faultless:perfect   (C) infallible:unreliable
6. CRYPT:TOMB   : :   (A) covetous:desirous   (B) dictate:obey
   (C) fictitious:factual
7. DECREPIT:ROBUST   : :   (A) indictment:charge
   (B) jovial:gloomy   (C) hospitable:friendly
8. CURRENCY:MONEY   : :   (A) charitable:stingy
   (B) compatible:agreeable   (C) mandatory:optional
9. HAGGLE:BARGAIN   : :   (A) occasionally:never
   (B) courteous:rude   (C) fatherly:paternal
10. ORTHODOX:UNCONVENTIONAL   : :   (A) lament:mourn
    (B) trinket:ornament   (C) acquire:forfeit
11. SECLUDED:EXPOSED   : :   (A) parched:wet
    (B) paraphrase:reword   (C) rousing:lively
12. OBSCURE:OBVIOUS   : :   (A) brave:dauntless
    (B) decrease:maximize   (C) famous:renowned
13. TOLERANT:LENIENT   : :   (A) jovial:merry
    (B) inopportune:convenient   (C) hollow:full

14. SUITABLE:COMPATIBLE　： ：　(A) exclude:boycott
(B) diminish:increase　(C) loyalty:infidelity
15. LIBERAL:CONSERVATIVE　： ：　(A) precious:valuable
(B) retrieve:salvage　(C) compulsory:voluntary

EXERCISE *Understanding Analogies*

Number your paper 1 to 15. Write the letter of the word pair that has
the same relationship as the word pair in capital letters. Then write
synonyms or *antonyms* to identify the relationship.

1. PASSIVE:RESPONSIVE　： ：　(A) essential:necessary
(B) isolate:group　(C) pursue:follow
2. DISSENT:AGREEMENT　： ：　(A) increase:dwindle
(B) surmise:guess　(C) lustrous:shiny
3. ZENITH:PEAK　： ：　(A) continuation:extension
(B) invasion:retreat　(C) partial:complete
4. JUDICIOUS:DISCREET　： ：　(A) lucrative:profitable
(B) mirth:sadness　(C) tranquil:agitated
5. COHERENT:IRRATIONAL　： ：　(A) homage:respect
(B) swell:shrink　(C) fringe:border
6. LETHARGIC:ENERGETIC　： ：　(A) reliable:dependable
(B) smug:conceited　(C) scarcity:abundance
7. COMPULSORY:NECESSARY　： ：　(A) stalk:pursue
(B) serene:moody　(C) decease:continue
8. COLLOQUIAL:FORMAL　： ：　(A) thoroughbred:pedigreed
(B) unusual:ordinary　(C) leanness:spareness
9. FEASIBLE:WORKABLE　： ：　(A) flatter:compliment
(B) plunge:withdrawal　(C) extinguish:revive
10. DECIPHER:TRANSLATE　： ：　(A) persist:discontinue
(B) ruthless:merciful　(C) gargantuan:gigantic
11. DISRUPT:AGITATE　： ：　(A) revert:progress
(B) detect:discover　(C) restrict:free
12. SIMILARITY:DIFFERENCE　： ：　(A) acclaim:praise
(B) empty:replenish　(C) negotiate:bargain
13. TURMOIL:ORDER　： ：　(A) unanimous:unified
(B) skeptic:doubter　(C) auspicious:ominous
14. MAINTAIN:ADJUST　： ：　(A) affected:genuine
(B) stingy:miserly　(C) specify:enumerate
15. REVENUE:INCOME　： ：　(A) candid:deceitful
(B) contrary:consistent　(C) revelation:disclosure

13 Review

A Recognizing Synonyms   Number your paper 1 to 10. Then write the letter of the word or words closest in meaning to each word in capital letters.

1. EMANCIPATE: (A) free   (B) jeopardize   (C) uphold
   (D) revise   (E) penalize
2. ULTIMATE: (A) fussy   (B) initial   (C) hidden
   (D) eventual   (E) amusing
3. ALLEVIATE: (A) depart   (B) raise   (C) undertake
   (D) relieve   (E) assign
4. RECIPIENT: (A) receiver   (B) improvement
   (C) appearance   (D) revival   (E) critic
5. STATUTE: (A) equation   (B) likeness   (C) law
   (D) prestige   (E) stable
6. NONCOMMITTAL: (A) trivial   (B) disturbed
   (C) unlikely   (D) indefinite   (E) unreliable
7. OMNISCIENT: (A) impressive   (B) sympathetic
   (C) stylish   (D) resentful   (E) all-knowing
8. FACSIMILE: (A) writing   (B) reproduction
   (C) understanding   (D) code   (E) reply
9. BEGUILE: (A) annoy   (B) disappear   (C) advance
   (D) deceive   (E) explain
10. LAXITY: (A) negligence   (B) legality   (C) genius
    (D) insistence   (E) worth

B Recognizing Antonyms   Number your paper 1 to 10. Then write the letter of the word or words most nearly opposite in meaning to each word in capital letters.

1. METICULOUS: (A) unusual   (B) kindly   (C) careless
   (D) violent   (E) mischievous
2. IMPERATIVE: (A) fading   (B) unessential
   (C) mysterious   (D) eminent   (E) tactless
3. FEASIBLE: (A) casual   (B) repeatable   (C) impossible
   (D) praiseworthy   (E) sensible

4. MALICIOUS: (A) charitable   (B) spiteful
(C) foul-smelling   (D) gaudy   (E) lazy

5. CONVENTIONAL: (A) extravagant   (B) handy
(C) talkative   (D) invaluable   (E) untraditional

6. ADAMANT: (A) yielding   (B) exciting   (C) flavorful
(D) reasonable   (E) obscure

7. ZEALOUS: (A) fertile   (B) difficult   (C) upset
(D) unforgiving   (E) unenthusiastic

8. AMITY: (A) generosity   (B) talent   (C) hostility
(D) purity   (E) coolness

9. INANIMATE: (A) leafy   (B) forgotten   (C) partial
(D) foolhardy   (E) lively

10. RESOLUTE: (A) unfamiliar   (B) undecided
(C) defensive   (D) outdated   (E) lethal

C **Understanding Analogies**   Number your paper 1 to 10. Then write the letter of the word pair that has the same relationship as the word pair in capital letters.

1. TRANSITION:PASSAGE   : :   (A) shortage:deficit
(B) procrastinate:hasten   (C) mediocre:peerless

2. NUISANCE:PEST   : :   (A) colossal:slight
(B) moderate:excessive   (C) beginner:novice

3. MINIMIZE:ENLARGE   : :   (A) gaze:gawk
(B) accumulate:disperse   (C) extraction:removal

4. CHAMPION:VICTOR   : :   (A) wisdom:ignorance
(B) unique:ordinary   (C) baffle:confuse

5. RESTRAINED:BOUNDLESS   : :   (A) origin:source
(B) ornament:decoration   (C) selfish:generous

6. INTENTIONAL:ACCIDENTAL   : :   (A) unify:divide
(B) recede:shrink   (C) rowdy:boisterous

7. SOLICIT:REQUEST   : :   (A) qualified:incompetent
(B) illusion:fantasy   (C) unpredictable:foreseeable

8. OBTRUSIVE:RESTRAINED   : :   (A) scrawny:lean
(B) pretentious:simple   (C) retreat:withdrawal

9. PROSPER:SUCCEED   : :   (A) deserving:worthy
(B) unveiled:closed   (C) peculiar:curious

10. SUBSTANTIATE:REFUTE   : :   (A) robust:vigorous
(B) unrealistic:feasible   (C) stamina:endurance

14

Spelling

Learning to spell correctly is an ongoing process. Even the best spellers continue to find words that give them difficulty. You can become a better speller if you follow the strategies in this chapter.

Recognizing Commonly Misspelled Words   In the editing section of your journal, record words in the following list of *spelling demons*, commonly misspelled words, that are a particular problem for you. Then, each time you edit your work, refer to your list of spelling demons. It is also a good idea to add to this list each time you come across a misspelled word.

Spelling Demons

abundance	crystal	mammoth	rendezvous
accuracy	descendant	melancholy	sacrifice
allege	dilettante	mosquito	severely
ambiguous	extraordinary	naive	sieve
apparent	financier	obsolete	simultaneous
bankruptcy	gauge	overture	succession
bizarre	hypocrisy	parallelism	symmetrical
catastrophe	incessant	phenomenon	testimonial
chassis	interference	plagiarism	thesaurus
colossal	liaison	prophecy	transcend
convalescent	livelihood	rehearsal	unwieldy

Spelling Improvement

The strategies in the box will help you to improve your spelling.

Strategies for Improving Your Spelling

1. In a section of your journal, list the words you find difficult to spell and review that list often.
2. When editing, use the dictionary to check your spelling.
3. Carefully proofread all your written work.
4. Sound out each syllable to avoid dropping letters.
   ac ces so ry   com fort a ble   lab o ra to ry
5. Use memory tricks to master some difficult words. Following is an example.
   biscuits: **U** and **I** like bis**cui**ts.

EXERCISE *Recognizing Misspelled Words*

Number your paper 1 to 10. Write the letter preceding the misspelled word in each group. Then write the word, spelling it correctly.

1.	(A)	occurrence	(B)	neice	(C)	stretch
2.	(A)	fiery	(B)	drought	(C)	arial
3.	(A)	condemn	(B)	weight	(C)	interupt
4.	(A)	courtesy	(B)	milage	(C)	regrettable
5.	(A)	assistence	(B)	biscuit	(C)	carriage
6.	(A)	immigrant	(B)	fasinate	(C)	pitiful
7.	(A)	business	(B)	bargain	(C)	campain
8.	(A)	ilustrate	(B)	seize	(C)	reference
9.	(A)	chord	(B)	luxury	(C)	napsack
10.	(A)	analyze	(B)	orindery	(C)	cooperate

Spelling Rules

If you know certain spelling rules, your spelling should improve as soon as you apply them. The following rules apply to a large number of words.

Spelling Patterns

The best-known rule of spelling is probably the "*i* before *e*, except after *c*" rule. The second rule, almost as familiar, covers the spelling of the "seed" sound at the end of words.

Words with *ie* or *ei* When the sound is long *e* (e), the spelling is usually *ie*. After the letter *c*, however, the spelling is *ei*.

Put *i* before *e*:	chief	fierce	piece	relieve
Except after *c*:	ceiling	deceit	perceive	receive
or when				
sounded like *a*:	feign	freight	heinous	reign

Although this *ie/ei* rule covers most words, there are a number of exceptions, such as the following words.

ancient	counterfeit	height	seize
conscience	either	leisure	sovereign
efficient	foreign	neither	their

Note: This rule does not apply if the *i* and *e* are in different syllables.   be ing   de ice   pi ety   sci ence

Words with the "Seed" Sound The "seed" sound is spelled three ways: *-sede*, *-ceed*, and *-cede*.

1. Only one word in English ends in *-sede: supersede.*
2. Only three words in English end in *-ceed: exceed, proceed,* and *succeed.*
3. All other words that end in the "seed" sound have the ending *-cede: accede, concede, precede, recede,* and *secede.*

Note: There is no *-seed* ending except in words derived from the noun *seed,* such as *reseed,* "to sow again."

472

EXERCISE  *Using Spelling Patterns*

Number your paper 1 to 20. Write each word, adding either *ie* or *ei*.

I. br_f	**6.** p_ce	**11.** s_ge	**16.** dec_ve
2. for_gn	**7.** l_sure	**12.** hyg_ne	**17.** n_ther
3. th_r	**8.** perc_ve	**13.** s_zure	**18.** med_val
4. n_ce	**9.** w_gh	**14.** rec_ve	**19.** rel_ve
5. rec_pt	**10.** y_ld	**15.** conc_t	**20.** counterf_t

EXERCISE 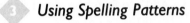 *Using Spelling Patterns*

Number your paper 1 to 10. Then write each word, adding -*sede*, -*ceed*, or -*cede*.

I. re____	**3.** ex____	**5.** pro____	**7.** ac____	**9.** super____
2. con____	**4.** inter____	**6.** se____	**8.** suc____	**10.** pre____

Plurals

There are a number of useful rules that will help you spell the plural form of most nouns.

Regular Nouns   To form the plural of most nouns, add *s*.

SINGULAR	geologist	frog	bicycle	rose
PLURAL	geologist**s**	frog**s**	bicycle**s**	rose**s**

To form the plural of nouns ending in *s*, *ch*, *x*, or *z*, add *es*.

SINGULAR	moss	clutch	dish	tax	waltz
PLURAL	moss**es**	clutch**es**	dish**es**	tax**es**	waltz**es**

Nouns Ending in *y*   Add *s* to form the plural of a noun ending in a vowel and *y*.

SINGULAR	payday	journey	alloy	monkey
PLURAL	payday**s**	journey**s**	alloy**s**	monkey**s**

For a noun ending in a consonant and *y*, change the *y* to *i* and add *es*.

SINGULAR	baby	fallacy	category	supply
PLURAL	bab**ies**	fallac**ies**	categor**ies**	suppl**ies**

EXERCISE *Forming Plurals*

Number your paper 1 to 20. Then write the plural of each noun.

1. family	**6.** fox	**11.** casualty	**16.** birthday
2. editor	**7.** ally	**12.** bench	**17.** melody
3. latch	**8.** phrase	**13.** caddy	**18.** sketch
4. thistle	**9.** hoax	**14.** railway	**19.** melee
5. tragedy	**10.** blueberry	**15.** grass	**20.** query

Nouns Ending in *o*   Add *s* to form the plural of a noun ending in a vowel and *o*.

SINGULAR	curio	ratio	stereo	rodeo	cuckoo
PLURAL	curio**s**	ratio**s**	stereo**s**	rodeo**s**	cuckoo**s**

Also add *s* to form the plural of a musical term ending in *o*.

SINGULAR	alto	piano	maestro	trio	piccolo
PLURAL	alto**s**	piano**s**	maestro**s**	trio**s**	piccolo**s**

Plurals of nouns ending in a consonant and *o* follow no regular pattern. They may end in either *s* or *es*.

SINGULAR	burro	credo	echo	potato	tornado
PLURAL	burro**s**	credo**s**	echo**es**	potato**es**	tornado**es**

Note: Since a number of words ending in a consonant and *o* can form their plurals with either *s* or *es*, consult a dictionary when you are in doubt about the spelling. If the dictionary shows more than one plural form, use the first form listed. It is the preferred form. If no plural is shown for the word as a noun, simply add *s* or *es*.

Nouns Ending in *f* or *fe*   To form the plural of some nouns ending in *f* or *fe*, simply add *s*.

SINGULAR	chef	staff	roof	waif	fife
PLURAL	chef**s**	staff**s**	roof**s**	waif**s**	fife**s**

For other nouns, change the *f* to *v* and add *s* or *es*.

SINGULAR	shelf	leaf	hoof	wife	knife
PLURAL	shel**ves**	lea**ves**	hoo**ves**	wi**ves**	kni**ves**

When you are in doubt about how to form the plural of a noun ending in *f* or *fe*, consult a dictionary.

Foreign Plurals To form the plural of some foreign words, change their form.

SINGULAR	alga	alumnus	bacterium	ellipsis
PLURAL	algae	alumni	bacteria	ellipses

Plurals of Numbers, Letters, Symbols, and Words Used as Words Add an apostrophe and an *s* to form the plural of numbers, letters, symbols, and words used as words.

NUMBERS	The *7*'s in this particular column of figures should be *4*'s.
LETTERS	If *e*'s are closed at the top, they look like *i*'s.
SYMBOLS	Ampersands—that is, *&*'s—are used in some company names.
WORDS AS WORDS	When used, these ampersands replace *and*'s.

EXERCISE *Forming Plurals*

Number your paper 1 to 20. Then write the plural of each noun. Use a dictionary if necessary.

1. scenario	**6.** stereo	**11.** belief	**16.** gulf
2. cello	**7.** hero	**12.** half	**17.** proof
3. tomato	**8.** soprano	**13.** sheriff	**18.** self
4. *the*	**9.** pimiento	**14.** basis	**19.** *12*
5. analysis	**10.** folio	**15.** alumna	**20.** chief

Other Plural Forms A number of familiar nouns form their plurals in irregular ways.

Irregular Plurals

child, children	woman, women	tooth, teeth
foot, feet	mouse, mice	goose, geese

Same Form for Singular and Plural

sheep	moose	corps	scissors	Chinese
Swiss	cattle	salmon	species	series

Compound Nouns   The plurals of most compound nouns are formed in the same way that other plural nouns are formed.

SINGULAR	stepchild	wristwatch	musk-ox
PLURAL	step**children**	wristwatch**es**	musk-**oxen**

In hyphenated compounds and in nouns of more than one word, the main word is often made plural.

SINGULAR	mother-in-law	knight-errant	bill of sale
PLURAL	mother**s**-in-law	knight**s**-errant	bill**s** of sale

EXERCISE   6   *Forming Plurals*

Number your paper 1 to 15.
Then write the plural of each noun.

1. buildup
2. attorney-at-law
3. teaspoonful
4. headquarters
5. rosebush
6. sergeant at arms
7. eyetooth
8. day lily
9. chairperson
10. notary public
11. Sioux
12. Portuguese
13. midwife
14. pliers
15. onlooker

Prefixes and Suffixes

A *prefix* is one or more syllables placed in front of a root to modify the meaning of the root or to form a new word. When you add a prefix, do not change the spelling of the root.

anti + toxin = antitoxin	pre + industrial = preindustrial
co + ordinate = coordinate	re + enact = reenact
over + rule = overrule	il + literate = illiterate

A *suffix* is one or more syllables placed after a root to help shape its meaning. The spelling of the root usually does not change when the suffixes *-ness* and *-ly* are added.

even + ness = evenness   usual + ly = usually

When you add a suffix other than *-ness* and *-ly,* you may have to change the spelling of the root.

Words Ending in *e* Drop the final *e* before adding a suffix that begins with a vowel.

care + ing = caring   note + able = notable
imagine + ary = imaginary   refuse + al = refusal

Retain the final *e* before adding any suffix that begins with a consonant.

excite + ment = excitement   tame + ness = tameness

Also keep the final *e* in a word that ends in *ce* or *ge* if the suffix begins with *a* or *o*. The *e* keeps the sound of the *c* or *g* soft.

advantage + ous = advantageous   notice + able = noticeable
manage + able = manageable   trace + able = traceable

Note: Following are some exceptions to these rules.

true, truly   judge, judgment   die, dying   awe, awful

EXERCISE *Adding Prefixes and Suffixes*

Number your paper 1 to 15. Then write each word, adding the prefix or the suffix shown. Make any necessary spelling changes to add the prefix or suffix.

1. dis + appear
2. re + elect
3. nerve + ous
4. operate + ion
5. argue + ment
6. grieve + ous
7. ir + regular
8. use + able
9. im + mobile
10. smile + ing
11. final + ly
12. true + ly
13. co + operate
14. tribe + al
15. under + rate

Words Ending in *y* When adding a suffix to most words ending in a vowel and *y,* keep the *y.*

display + ing = displaying   repay + ment = repayment

For most words ending in a consonant and *y,* change the *y* to *i* before adding a suffix.

ally + ance = alliance   merry + ly = merrily

Note: Following are some exceptions to these rules.

| SUFFIX BEGINNING WITH *i* | relying | hobbyist | gratifying |
| ONE-SYLLABLE ROOT WORDS | daily | paid | shyness |

EXERCISE *Adding Suffixes*

Number your paper 1 to 15. Then write each word, adding the suffix shown. Make any necessary spelling changes.

1. ally + ance	**6.** deny + al	**11.** sunny + er
2. shy + ness	**7.** worry + er	**12.** thirty + eth
3. gray + est	**8.** scary + est	**13.** early + ness
4. study + ing	**9.** lazy + ly	**14.** supply + ed
5. toy + like	**10.** rely + able	**15.** tray + ful

Doubling the Final Consonant   Sometimes you double the final consonant when adding a suffix beginning with a vowel. Do so only if the root word has *both* of the following characteristics.

- The word has only one syllable or is stressed on the final syllable.
- The word ends in one consonant preceded by one vowel.

ONE-SYLLABLE WORD	tap + ing = tapping	run + er = runner
FINAL SYLLABLE STRESSED	upset + ing = upsetting	omit + ed = omitted

Words Ending in *c*   There is a special rule for words that end in *c* preceded by a single vowel. If the suffix begins with *e* or *i*, do not double the final *c*. Instead, add *k* before the suffix to keep the *c* sound hard.

    picnic, picnicking   shellac, shellacked   frolic, frolicking

EXERCISE 9 *Adding Suffixes*

Number your paper 1 to 20. Write each word, adding the suffix shown. Make any necessary spelling changes.

1. lobby + ist	**8.** regret + able	**15.** knit + ed
2. offer + ed	**9.** politic + ing	**16.** amateur + ish
3. grace + ous	**10.** bag + age	**17.** deter + ence
4. vary + ance	**11.** plan + er	**18.** clamor + ous
5. imply + ing	**12.** profit + able	**19.** drift + ing
6. transmit + al	**13.** apply + ance	**20.** admit + ance
7. clear + ance	**14.** concur + ent	

14 Review

Spelling Words Correctly   Number your paper 1 to 15. Write the letter preceding the misspelled word in each group. Then write the word correctly.

1. (A) proceed   (B) sharing   (C) stereos   (D) acurracy
   (E) rendezvous
2. (A) deceive   (B) occurred   (C) managable   (D) eyeglasses
   (E) forgettable
3. (A) piece   (B) excede   (C) feign   (D) fifes
   (E) echoes
4. (A) thesaurus   (B) usualy   (C) descendant   (D) gauge
   (E) notaries public
5. (A) rarity   (B) chefs   (C) alloys   (D) rein
   (E) rehersal
6. (A) apparant   (B) concede   (C) referral   (D) patios
   (E) outrageous
7. (A) releive   (B) seize   (C) veil   (D) wives
   (E) thesis
8. (A) leisure   (B) overrule   (C) alumnuses   (D) obedient
   (E) bizarre
9. (A) changeable   (B) disimilar   (C) loneliness   (D) mosquito
   (E) bushes
10. (A) recurence   (B) license   (C) overture   (D) sieve
    (E) neither
11. (A) believing   (B) sopranos   (C) mistatement   (D) hooves
    (E) superintendent
12. (A) rustiest   (B) onlookers   (C) allegiance   (D) accede
    (E) sacrafice
13. (A) prestige   (B) supplier   (C) location   (D) heinous
    (E) bill of sales
14. (A) thier   (B) alga   (C) trios   (D) naive
    (E) corps
15. (A) dryness   (B) advantageous   (C) financier   (D) dilemna
    (E) plentiful

15 Reference Skills

When you are on your own a short time from now, where will you look for help when it comes time to buy a car, rent an apartment, or get a full-time job? A library holds information that can help you handle these and many other tasks you will encounter throughout life. Now, however, is the time to learn your way around a library and become familiar with all of its valuable resources.

Personal Reference File for Writing A problem that you may have from time to time is finding subjects to write about. One solution to this problem is to accumulate a personal reference file in your writer's notebook.

Copy, duplicate, or summarize every article, story, poem, advertisement, or picture you see that catches your interest at home or in the library. Of course, there is no need to stop there. Include photographs of your friends and family, a copy of the school newspaper, a flyer announcing a car wash, or a catalog of sports clothes that you received in the mail. Any and all of these entries could ultimately serve as a jumping-off point for a writing idea. Begin today. Writing ideas are all around you. All you need to do is reach out and find them.

The Library

The library is an unequaled resource for information and ideas. Books, magazines, newspapers, and pamphlets contain information on an almost limitless number of subjects. Most libraries also provide nonprint materials such as records, compact discs, films, videotapes, and computer software. Understanding the library's arrangement and the wide variety of sources available will help you efficiently locate the materials you need.

Library Arrangement

For many years the most popular system of organizing books was the Dewey decimal system. As library collections grew to include more than 30,000 titles, another system became necessary. As a result, the Library of Congress system, which can be used to classify millions of books, was developed. Today large libraries, such as those at colleges and universities, use the Library of Congress system.

The Dewey Decimal Classification System Most school and local libraries use the Dewey decimal system. In this system works of fiction, such as short stories and novels, are kept separate from non-fiction works. Works of fiction are arranged alphabetically by the authors' last names. When searching for a work of fiction, remember the following guidelines for alphabetizing.

Guidelines for Finding Works of Fiction

- Two-part names are alphabetized by the first part of the name. (**De** Soto, **O'**Connor, **Van** Buren)
- Names beginning with *Mc* and *St.* are alphabetized as if they began with *Mac* and *Saint*.
- Books by authors with the same last name are alphabetized by the authors' first names.
- Books by the same author are alphabetized by title, skipping *a, an,* and *the.*
- Numbers in titles are alphabetized as if they were written out. (40,000 = forty thousand)

In the Dewey decimal classification system, nonfiction books are assigned a number according to their subjects, as shown in the following chart.

Main Subject Areas in the Dewey Decimal System	
000–099	General Works (reference works)
100–199	Philosophy
200–299	Religion
300–399	Social Sciences (law, education, economics)
400–499	Language
500–599	Science (mathematics, biology, chemistry)
600–699	Technology (engineering, medicine)
700–799	Fine Arts (painting, music, theater)
800–899	Literature
900–999	History (biography, geography, travel)

For each main subject area, there are ten smaller divisions. The following subdivisions show how the main subject *Science* is classified by number.

500–599 Science			
500–509	Pure sciences	550–559	Earth sciences
510–519	Mathematics	560–569	Paleontology
520–529	Astronomy	570–579	Anthropology
530–539	Physics	580–589	Botany
540–549	Chemistry	590–599	Zoology

Note: These subdivisions are divided further with the use of decimal points and other identifying symbols. The shelves are also marked with numbers so that books can be easily located.

The numbers identifying a book make up the *call number.* Every book has a different call number. In addition to the call number, some books carry a special label to show the section of the library in which they are shelved. Biographies, for example, are often marked with a *B* or *92* (short for *920* in the Dewey decimal system).

The following chart shows some other special labels.

CATEGORIES	SPECIAL LABELS
Juvenile books	J or X
Reference works	R or REF
Records	REC
Filmstrips	FS

Biographies and autobiographies are often in a section of their own. They are arranged in alphabetical order according to the name of the person they are about. Books about the same person are arranged within themselves according to the author's last name.

EXERCISE *Understanding the Dewey Decimal System*

Number your paper 1 to 10. Then, using the list of classifications on page 482, write the subject numbers for each book. If the title is marked with an asterisk (*), also write the science subdivision listed on page 482.

EXAMPLE   *Beyond the Galaxy**
ANSWER   500−599, 520−529

 1. *This Chemical Age**
 2. *Engineering Technology*
 3. *Drawing Portraits*
 4. *New Church Programs for the Aging*
 5. *Basic Principles of Geometry**
 6. *Twentieth-Century French Literature*
 7. *The British Empire before the American Revolution*
 8. *Guide to Philosophy*
 9. *Mineral Wealth in Mountains**
10. *Principles of Political Economy*

The Library of Congress Classification System   This system assigns letters, rather than numbers, to books and uses 20 subject divisions instead of 10. The Library of Congress system also does not separate fiction and biography from other kinds of works. On the next page are the 20 main subject categories found in the Library of Congress system.

Main Categories in the Library of Congress System			
A	General works	L	Education
B	Philosophy, religion	M	Music
C	Sciences of history	N	Fine arts
D	Non-American history and travel	P	Language and literature
		Q	Science
E	American history	R	Medicine
F	U.S. local history	S	Agriculture
G	Geography, anthropology	T	Technology
		U	Military science
H	Social sciences	V	Naval science
J	Political science	Z	Library science

These 20 main categories can be further divided by using a second letter. *QB*, for example, refers to the general category of science with a focus on philosophy. Further subdivisions are made by using numbers and letters.

EXERCISE 2 *Understanding the Library of Congress System*

Number your paper 1 to 10. Using the list of classifications above, write the first letter of the call number for each of the books listed in Exercise 1.

EXAMPLE *Beyond the Galaxy*
ANSWER Q

The Card Catalog

The card catalog contains cards for every book in the library. Most books have three cards in the card catalog: the *author card, title card,* and *subject card.* These cards are arranged either alphabetically or in separate file cabinets.

The author card is sometimes called the *main entry* because it contains the most information. When you need a particular book by an author, look under the author's last name in the catalog.

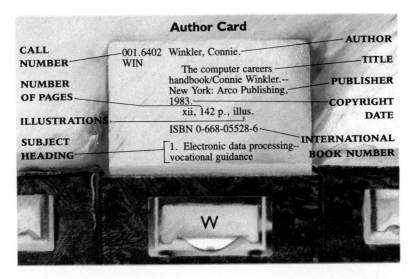

Title cards list the title of the book at the top of each card. Title cards are alphabetized by the first word in the title except for the words *a, an,* and *the.*

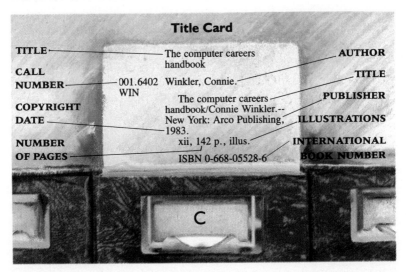

Subject cards are especially useful if you do not know the title or author of a specific book or if you do not even have a specific book in mind. These cards are arranged alphabetically according to the first main word in the subject heading. Subject headings under history, however, are filed in chronological order.

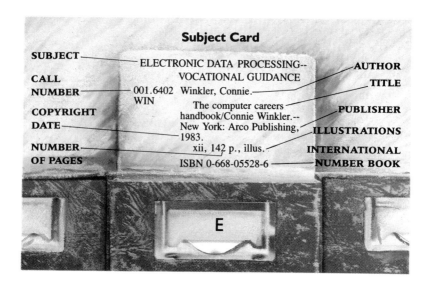

Subject Card

SUBJECT — ELECTRONIC DATA PROCESSING-- — AUTHOR
VOCATIONAL GUIDANCE — TITLE
CALL NUMBER — 001.6402 Winkler, Connie.
WIN
COPYRIGHT DATE — The computer careers — PUBLISHER
handbook/Connie Winkler.--
New York: Arco Publishing, — ILLUSTRATIONS
1983.
NUMBER OF PAGES — xii, 142 p., illus. — INTERNATIONAL NUMBER BOOK
ISBN 0-668-05528-6

E

In addition to the author, title, and subject cards for each book, the catalog contains "see" and "see also" cards. These are called *cross-reference cards* because they refer you to other listings in the catalog. A "see" card tells you that the subject you have looked up is under another heading. A "see also" card refers you to additional headings you could look up to find relevant titles about your subject.

If you are searching for a work that is part of a collection, an *analytic card* will help you find it. These cards are alphabetized according to the specific work you are seeking. They also, however, list all the other pieces contained within the collection.

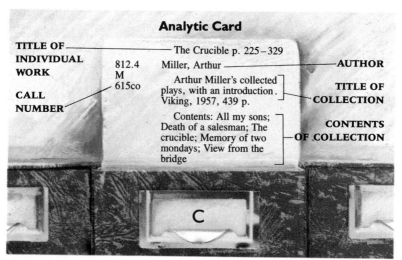

Analytic Card

TITLE OF INDIVIDUAL WORK — The Crucible p. 225–329
812.4 Miller, Arthur — AUTHOR
M
615co Arthur Miller's collected
CALL NUMBER — plays, with an introduction. — TITLE OF COLLECTION
Viking, 1957, 439 p.
Contents: All my sons; — CONTENTS OF COLLECTION
Death of a salesman; The
crucible; Memory of two
mondays; View from the
bridge

C

Note: Most card catalogs are alphabetized word by word rather than letter by letter. The entry *car safety,* for example, would come before the entry *Caracas.*

EXERCISE *Understanding the Card Catalog*

Number your paper 1 to 10. Then, using the catalog card below, write the answer to the following questions.

1. Is this catalog card an author, subject, or title card?
2. Who is the author of this book?
3. What is the call number for this book?
4. How do you know that this book is a biography?
5. Who is the publisher?
6. Does this book contain illustrations?
7. Books about this subject are listed under what headings?
8. What is the book's copyright date?
9. What is the international code number for this book?
10. What do the letters *Ha* stand for in the call number?

BW
276
Ha 2

Harlan, Louis R.

Booker T. Washington: the wizard of Tuskegee, 1901–1915/Louis R. Harlan.-- New York: Oxford Univ. Press, 1983.

xiv, 548 p.

ISBN 0-19-503202-0

1. Washington, Booker T., 1856–1915
2. Afro-Americans-- Biography
3. Educators-- United States --Biography

Reference Materials

In most libraries reference materials are kept in a separate room or area. Since these materials cannot be removed from the library, a study area is usually provided. Following are some of the reference materials you may find most helpful in the reference section of your library.

Reference Materials

REFERENCE	INFORMATION THAT IT CONTAINS	EXAMPLES
general encyclopedia	general information about many subjects, arranged from *A* to *Z* by subject	*Encyclopaedia Britannica, The New Columbia Encyclopedia*
specialized encyclopedias	detailed information that is concentrated on a specific subject or discipline	*The Encyclopedia of Chemistry, The Encyclopedia of Dance and Ballet*
biographical references	information about famous people, arranged alphabetically	*Who's Who, Current Biography, Who's Who of American Women*
atlases	maps and related information about geography	*Goode's World Atlas, The World Book Atlas, Hammond Medallion World Atlas*
almanacs or yearbooks	various facts such as world records; published once a year with current information	*Information Please Almanac, Guinness Book of World Records, Collier's Yearbook*
specialized dictionaries	entries of only one type or on only one subject or discipline	*Dictionary of Science and Technology, Harvard Dictionary of Music*
vertical file	file folders by subject, containing newspaper clippings, pamphlets, catalogs, and other sources of information	located in a file cabinet—usually in the reference section of the library

Readers' Guide to Periodical Literature Each year indexes help readers locate thousands of newspaper and magazine articles by naming the author, title, date, and periodical. Most indexes are arranged alphabetically by subject matter and author. The *Readers' Guide to Periodical Literature* is one of the most useful and popular indexes. It indexes articles, short stories, and poems published in more than 175 magazines. It is issued in paperback form once in February, July, and August and twice during all other months. Notice the numerous cross-references and abbreviations in the following excerpt.

ALPHABETICAL
SUBJECT
LISTINGS

College education, Value of
Education's earning power [how college education relates to salaries for men and women] S. Guinzburg. *Psychol Today* 17:20-1 O'83
College enrollment *See* Colleges and universities—Attendance
College Entrance Examination Board
The Educational Equality Project: focus on results. A. Y. Bailey. *Phi Delta Kappan* 65:22-5 S'83
College fraternities
New wave networkers [black fraternities and sororities] P. King. *Black Enterp* 14:89-90+ D'83
College graduates
See also
Business schools and colleges—Graduates
College education, Value of
Colleges and universities—Graduate work
For 10,000 sons of Harvard and Yale, the schools' 100th football reunion will, as always, be more than a game. R. Drake. il *People Wkly* 20:179+ N 21'83
The reunion [male college friends] P. Gottlieb. il *N Y Times Mag* p25 D 25/'83
Employment
College graduates and the market. S. M. Ehrenhalt. *Current* 257:15-24 N'83
Turn for better in job prospects for '84 grads. C. W. English. il map *U S News World Rep* 95:32-3 D 12'83
Dismissal
The president who did not leave [dismissal of H. J. Perkins from Manitoba's Brandon University] E. Mills. *Macleans* 96:14-15 D 19'83
College sports *See* **College athletics**
College students
See also
Black students
College fraternities
College graduates
Foreign students
College students in the 1990s: a demographic portrait. H. L. Hodgkinson. *Educ Dig* 49:28-31 N'83
What they should have told me when I was a senior [address, September 13, 1983] R. C. Jann. *Vital Speeches Day* 50:51-2 N 1'83

ABBREVIATIONS
EXPLAINED
AT FRONT
OF BOOK

MAGAZINE
ISSUE

CROSS-
REFERENCES

Some large newspapers like the *New York Times* and the *Chicago Tribune* publish indexes to articles that have appeared in their own pages only. A more general index that includes articles from many newspapers is called *The Newspaper Index*.

EXERCISE *Understanding the* Readers' Guide

Number your paper 1 to 10. Then, using the excerpt from the *Readers' Guide* on the previous page, write the answers to the following questions.

1. What three subheadings are under the heading *College Graduates?*
2. Who wrote about the College Entrance Examination Board?
3. Under what heading would be articles about college sports?
4. What are the titles of the two articles about employment for college graduates?
5. Which magazine published an article about the 100th Harvard-Yale football reunion?
6. Who is the author of the article "College Students in the 1990's: A Demographic Portrait"?
7. What is the title of the article about the dismissal of H. J. Perkins from Manitoba's Brandon University?
8. What year were all of the articles published?
9. Under what other subject headings would articles about college students be found?
10. What is the title of the article listed under the heading *College Education* about?

EXERCISE *Using Specialized References*

Write one kind of reference work other than a general encyclopedia that would contain information about each of the following.

1. newspaper articles about space shuttles
2. information about a senator's life
3. how ocean currents affect climate
4. pamphlet on obtaining a lifesaver's certificate
5. the meaning of the computer term *interface*
6. the highest mountain peak in the Himalayas
7. synonyms for the word *imagination*
8. pamphlets on windsurfing or board sailing
9. magazine articles about job opportunities in Alaska
10. college and university catalogs

Reference Materials about Language and Literature The following reference works, which are usually shelved with the general works of the same type, provide information about language and literature.

SPECIALIZED DICTIONARIES
Webster's Dictionary of Synonyms
A Dictionary of Literary Terms

SPECIALIZED ENCYCLOPEDIAS
Cassell's Encyclopedia of World Literature
Encyclopedia of World Literature in the 20th Century

BIOGRAPHICAL REFERENCES
Contemporary Authors
British Authors of the Nineteenth Century

The handbook is another kind of literary reference work. A *handbook* explains literary terms, gives plot summaries, and/or describes characters.

HANDBOOKS
The Oxford Companion to American Literature
The Oxford Companion to English Literature

A book of quotations can tell you the source of a particular quotation. In addition to printing the complete quotation, it will list other quotations about the same subject.

BOOKS OF QUOTATIONS
Bartlett's Familiar Quotations
Dictionary of Quotations

Indexes are useful references when you are looking for a specific poem, short story, or play. An *index* lists the books that contain the particular selection you are looking for.

INDEXES
Ottemiller's Index to Plays in Collections
Short Story Index

EXERCISE   6   *Understanding Literary Reference Works*

Number your paper 1 to 5. Then write the name of one source listed above that you could use to answer each question.

1. In what year did Leo Tolstoy write *War and Peace?*
2. Where could you find a short story called "Flowering Judas" by Katherine Anne Porter?
3. What American novelists were at work during the Civil War period?
4. Which poem begins, "The time you won your town the race"?
5. What does the term *picaresque* mean in literature?

The Dictionary

The dictionary is a valuable resource tool. As you read, the dictionary can help you define unfamiliar words. As you write, it can help you make accurate word choices. Whatever your purpose, you can usually find a dictionary that contains the information you need.

Information in an Entry

All words listed in a dictionary are called *entry words*. Entry words are printed in heavy type and are broken into syllables to show how the word is divided. In addition to the entry word itself, the dictionary includes the part of speech of the word, other forms of the word, the meaning of the word, the history of the word, and often synonyms and antonyms. All of this information about each word is called a *main entry*. The following list shows different types of entry words and how they would be listed in the dictionary in alphabetical order.

SINGLE WORD	mercy
SUFFIX	-mere
PREFIX	meso-
COMPOUND WORD	mess kit
ABBREVIATION	Messrs.

Preferred and Variant Spellings   Some words have more than one correct spelling. The spelling most commonly used, called the *preferred spelling*, is usually listed first. Less common spellings, called *variants*, usually follow the preferred spelling.

PREFERRED SPELLING ⌐

caddie *also*, caddy.

VARIANT SPELLING ⌐

EXERCISE *Finding Preferred Spellings*

Number your paper 1 to 5. Find each of the variant spellings in the dictionary. Then write the preferred spelling for each word.

I. pilaff   **3.** sulphur   **5.** dialog
2. cooky   **4.** chlorophyl

Syllable Division of Words Sometimes when you write a composition, you may need to divide a word at the end of a line with a hyphen. The dictionary shows the correct division of syllables for each entry word. *(See page 812 for the rules for dividing words.)*

re·sus·ci·tate   ret·i·cence   re·vers·i·ble

Pronunciation Following the entry word is the phonetic spelling of the word, which shows how the word is pronounced.

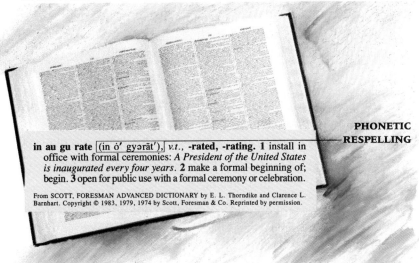

PHONETIC
RESPELLING

in au gu rate [(in ô′ gyərāt′),] *v.t.*, **-rated, -rating. 1** install in office with formal ceremonies: *A President of the United States is inaugurated every four years.* **2** make a formal beginning of; begin. **3** open for public use with a formal ceremony or celebration.

From SCOTT, FORESMAN ADVANCED DICTIONARY by E. L. Thorndike and Clarence L. Barnhart. Copyright © 1983, 1979, 1974 by Scott, Foresman & Co. Reprinted by permission.

A chart at the front of the dictionary contains a complete list of phonetic symbols. Most dictionaries also provide a partial pronunciation key on each right-hand page.

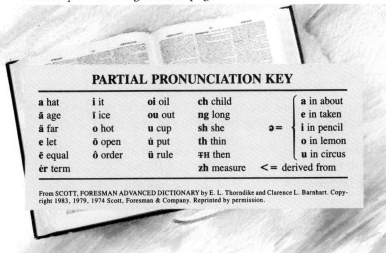

PARTIAL PRONUNCIATION KEY

a hat	**i** it	**oi** oil	**ch** child	**a** in about
ā age	**ī** ice	**ou** out	**ng** long	**e** in taken
ä far	**o** hot	**u** cup	**sh** she ə =	**i** in pencil
e let	**ō** open	**ù** put	**th** thin	**o** in lemon
ē equal	**ô** order	**ü** rule	**ŦH** then	**u** in circus
ėr term			**zh** measure < = derived from	

From SCOTT, FORESMAN ADVANCED DICTIONARY by E. L. Thorndike and Clarence L. Barnhart. Copyright 1983, 1979, 1974 Scott, Foresman & Company. Reprinted by permission.

To find out how to pronounce the vowel sound in the last syllable of *inaugurate*, for example, find the symbol *ā* in the key. You can see that it is pronounced like the *a* in *age*.

To distinguish vowel sounds, dictionaries use diacritical marks above the vowels. *Webster's Ninth New Collegiate Dictionary*, for instance, shows two different ways to pronounce the letter *o*.

DIACRITICAL
MARKS   ō as in *go*   ȯ as in *law*

All vowels can sometimes be pronounced *uh*. This sound is represented by a symbol called the *schwa* (ə). In the word *inaugurate*, for example, the third syllable contains the schwa sound.

SCHWA   in ȯ′ gyə rāt′

Phonetic spellings also show which syllables are stressed. A heavy accent mark, called a *primary stress*, shows which syllable receives more emphasis. A *secondary stress* is marked with a lighter accent mark.

PRIMARY STRESS   SECONDARY STRESS
in ȯ′ gyə rāt′

If a word can be pronounced in more than one way, the dictionary will show each pronunciation. The first one shown, however, is preferred. In some dictionaries only those parts of an alternate pronunciation that differ will be given.

ALTERNATE   **ro·de·o** (rō′dē ō′, rō dā′ ō)
PRONUNCIATIONS   **en·ve·lope** (en′və lōp, än′—)

Check the front of your dictionary to learn the phonetic symbols that are used.

EXERCISE 8 *Using a Pronunciation Key*

Using the pronunciation key on page 493, write the word in Column B that matches each phonetic spelling in Column A.

COLUMN A	COLUMN B
1. fyü′ dl iz′əm	a. pterodactyl
2. ter′ə dak′təl	b. pseudonym
3. süd′ən im	c. feudalism
4. sib′ə lənt	d. fustian
5. fus′ chən	e. sibilant

Parts of Speech Labels   An entry also contains one of the following abbreviations that indicates the word's part of speech. If the word can be used as more than one part of speech, its most common usage will usually be listed first.

PARTS OF SPEECH LABELS			
n.	noun	*v.*	verb
pron.	pronoun	*prep.*	preposition
adj.	adjective	*conj.*	conjunction
adv.	adverb	*interj.*	interjection

Multiple Meanings   Many words have more than one meaning. Dictionaries will usually list the most common meaning first. A few dictionaries, however, list meanings in historical order, showing the oldest meaning first.

Dictionaries use labels to indicate these differences in meaning. These are called *restrictive labels,* since they restrict the meaning of a word to a certain geographic area, a certain subject area, or a certain level of usage (informal, slang, etc.). Meanings also vary according to the part of speech a word is being used as. Notice the various meanings of the word *quarter.*

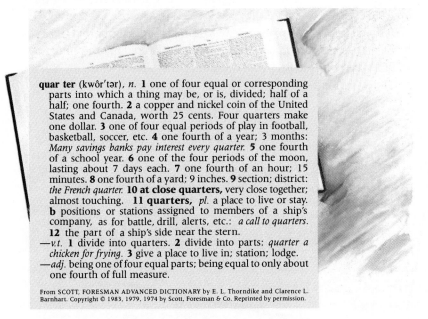

quar ter (kwôr′tər), *n.* **1** one of four equal or corresponding parts into which a thing may be, or is, divided; half of a half; one fourth. **2** a copper and nickel coin of the United States and Canada, worth 25 cents. Four quarters make one dollar. **3** one of four equal periods of play in football, basketball, soccer, etc. **4** one fourth of a year; 3 months: *Many savings banks pay interest every quarter.* **5** one fourth of a school year. **6** one of the four periods of the moon, lasting about 7 days each. **7** one fourth of an hour; 15 minutes. **8** one fourth of a yard; 9 inches. **9** section; district: *the French quarter.* **10 at close quarters,** very close together; almost touching.   **11 quarters,** *pl.* a place to live or stay. **b** positions or stations assigned to members of a ship's company, as for battle, drill, alerts, etc.: *a call to quarters.* **12** the part of a ship's side near the stern.
—*v.t.* **1** divide into quarters. **2** divide into parts: *quarter a chicken for frying.* **3** give a place to live in; station; lodge.
—*adj.* being one of four equal parts; being equal to only about one fourth of full measure.

The last part of an entry is often a list of synonyms with an explanation of their different shades of meaning.

EXERCISE ❾ *Recognizing Multiple Meanings*

Number your paper 1 to 5. Then use the entry for *quarter* on the previous page to write the part of speech and the number of the definition that suits the use of the word *quarter* in each sentence.

1. My favorite family restaurant is in the Italian *quarter* of the city.
2. Would you lend me a *quarter?*
3. My grade in physics this *quarter* should be a B +, giving me an A − for the entire year.
4. We are going to *quarter* our friends' Great Dane for two weeks this summer.
5. Business for the Acme Shoe Company was brisk during the first *quarter.*

Inflected Forms and Derived Words *Inflections* are endings that change the form of the word but not its part of speech. Verbs, for example, can be inflected with the endings *-ed* or *-ing* to show a change from one principal part to another. Adjectives can be inflected with *-er* or *-est* to show degrees of comparison. Nouns can be inflected by adding *-s* or *-es* to make them plural. Most dictionaries show the inflected forms only when they are formed irregularly.

Derived words are also formed by adding endings, but in such cases the part of speech of the word also changes. For example, adding the suffix *-ly* turns the adjective *hungry* into the adverb *hungrily*. Such derived words are listed at the end of a main entry.

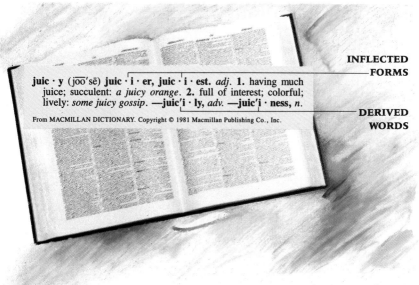

INFLECTED FORMS

juic · y (jo͞o′sē) **juic · i · er, juic · i · est.** *adj.* **1.** having much juice; succulent: *a juicy orange*. **2.** full of interest; colorful; lively: *some juicy gossip*. —**juic′i · ly,** *adv.* —**juic′i · ness,** *n.*

From MACMILLAN DICTIONARY. Copyright © 1981 Macmillan Publishing Co., Inc.

DERIVED WORDS

Etymologies   The *etymology* of a word is an explanation of its origin and history. In an etymology abbreviations are used to stand for the different languages from which a word has developed. Symbols are also used to stand for such words as *derived from* (<) or *equal to* (=). A chart at the beginning of the dictionary lists all the abbreviations and symbols used in the etymology of a word. Notice in the following etymology that the most recent source of the word is listed first.

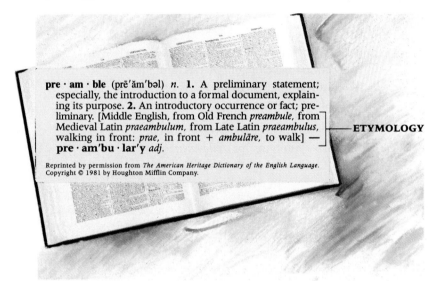

pre · am · ble (prē′ăm′bəl) *n.* **1.** A preliminary statement; especially, the introduction to a formal document, explaining its purpose. **2.** An introductory occurrence or fact; preliminary. [Middle English, from Old French *preambule*, from Medieval Latin *praeambulum*, from Late Latin *praeambulus*, walking in front: *prae*, in front + *ambulāre*, to walk] — pre · am′bu · lar′y *adj.* —————ETYMOLOGY

Reprinted by permission from *The American Heritage Dictionary of the English Language.*
Copyright © 1981 by Houghton Mifflin Company.

The etymology for *preamble* can be translated as follows: The word *preamble* comes from the Middle English, which came from the Old French *preambule*. *Preambule* came from the Medieval Latin word *praeambulum*, which was taken from the Late Latin word *praeambulus*, which meant "walking in front." *Praeambulus* was from the Latin prefix *prae*, meaning "in front," and *ambulare*, meaning "to walk."

EXERCISE   *Tracing Word Origins*

Number your paper 1 to 10. Use your dictionary to find the etymology of each word. Then choose one etymology and write its translation. (Use the example of *preamble* as a model.)

1. bellicose
2. chromosome
3. forceps
4. geranium
5. guitar

6. hominy
7. menace
8. nightmare
9. philodendron
10. verdict

15 Review

A **Choosing Reference Materials** Number your paper 1 to 20. Then, using the following list of library resources, write the best resource for finding the answer to each question.

A card catalog
B general encyclopedia
C specialized encyclopedia
D biographical reference
E specialized dictionary

F *Readers' Guide*
G atlas
H almanac
I vertical file
J index

1. In what year was Ernest Hemingway born?
2. What are two synonyms for *ambivalent?*
3. When was Richard Wright's novel *Native Son* published?
4. What three European countries begin with the letter *A?*
5. Who won the Pulitzer Prize for fiction in 1932?
6. How many moons does Jupiter have?
7. Who wrote the poem "Ozymandias"?
8. Through what three states does the Snake River flow?
9. Which work by American playwright Eugene O'Neill is said to be autobiographical?
10. What four food groups are part of good nutrition?
11. What are the entrance requirements for Florida State University?
12. Who holds the world record for the high jump?
13. What events led up to statehood for Hawaii?
14. How many plays by T. S. Eliot does your library have?
15. What is the name of one recent magazine article published on the subject of airplane safety?
16. Miss Havisham appears in which of Charles Dickens's novels?
17. In the game of tennis, what does the word *love* mean?
18. Who said, "Beware of false knowledge; it is more dangerous than ignorance"?
19. Which South American nation is larger, Columbia or Ecuador?
20. Where in the library would you find a catalog describing local tourist attractions?

B **Using Reference Sources** Use the resources of your library to answer the first ten questions in part A.

C **Using the Dictionary** Number your paper 1 to 15. Then, using the following entries, write the answer to each question.

1. What is the variant spelling of *epilogue?*
2. What parts of speech can the word *epidemic* be used as?
3. How many meanings does the word *epitomize* have?
4. How many syllables are there in the name *Epicurus?*
5. What syllable receives the primary stress in *epidemic?*
6. How many schwas are in the phonetic spelling of *Epicurus?*
7. What are the inflected forms of the word *epitomize?*
8. What is the meaning of the prefix *epi-?*
9. What is the etymology of *epinephrine?*
10. What were the teachings of Epicurus?
11. What do the letters *EPA* stand for?
12. What definition of the word *epilogue* suits the meaning in the following sentence?
  When the actor finished the *epilogue*, the audience clapped.
13. What are the two noun forms of the verb *epitomize?*
14. How would you write the adverb form of the word *epidemic?*
15. What is a translation for the etymology of *epidemic?*

EPA, Environmental Protection Agency.

epi-, *prefix.* on; upon; above; among: *Epicalyx = on the calyx. Epidermis = upon or above the dermis.* [<Greek *epi*]

Ep i cur us (ep′ i kyür′ə s), *n.* 342?–270 B.C., Greek philosopher who taught that pleasure is the highest good, but that true pleasure depends on self-control, moderation, and honorable behavior.

ep i dem ic (ep′ ə dem′ik), *n.* **1** the rapid spread of a disease so that many people have it at the same time: *a flu epidemic.* **2** the rapid spread of an idea, fashion, etc.—*adj.* affecting many people at the same time; widespread: *an epidemic disease.* [<Greek *epidēmia* a stay, visit, prevalence (of a disease) <*epi*-among + *dēmos* people]—**ep′i dem′i cal,** *adj.*—**ep′i dem′i cal ly,** *adv.*

ep i logue or **ep i log** (ep′ə lôg, ep′ə log), *n.* **1** a concluding section added to a novel, poem, etc., that rounds out or interprets the work. **2** speech or poem, addressed to the audience by one of the actors at the end of a play. **3** any concluding act or event. [<Greek *epilogos,* ultimately <*epi*-above + *legein* speak]

ep i neph rine (ep′ə nef′ rən, ep′ə nef′ rēn′), *n.* adrenalin. [<*epi* + Greek *nephros* kidney]

e pit o mize (i pit′ə mīz), *v.t.,* **-mized, -mizing. 1** give an epitome of; summarize. **2** be typical or representative of: *Helen Keller epitomizes the human ability to overcome handicaps.*—**e pit′o mi za′tion,** *n.*—**e pit′o miz′er,** *n.*

16 Study and Test-Taking Skills

Success in school is often measured by how well you perform on tests, both in your daily classes and in standardized testing situations. Developing good study skills and test-taking strategies, therefore, may be your key to success as a student. This chapter will discuss strategies and provide practice that will help prepare you for important tests, especially standardized tests.

Learning Study Skills

Tests are designed to evaluate how much you know about certain subjects. How well you do on these tests, however, often reflects how effectively you study and prepare assignments on a daily basis. How effective are your study habits?

Strategies for Effective Studying
1. Choose an area that is well lighted and free from noise and other distractions.
2. Equip your study area with everything you need for reading and writing, including, if possible, a dictionary, a thesaurus, and other reference books.
3. Keep a notebook for recording assignments and due dates.
4. Allow plenty of time for studying. Begin your reading and writing assignments early.

Adjusting Reading Rate to Purpose

Whenever you read, it is important to understand your purpose for reading the material. Reading a story for entertainment requires different kinds of reading strategies than reading a textbook to learn important information. Reading textbooks requires an organized approach that enables you to focus your attention and achieve your purpose. The following strategies can help you read textbook material most effectively.

Scanning   *Scanning* is reading to get a general impression and to prepare for learning about a subject. Scan a chapter or section first by reading the title, headings, subheadings, picture captions, words and phrases in boldface and italics, and any focus questions. This technique helps you to determine quickly what the reading is about and what questions to keep in mind as you read.

Skimming   After scanning a chapter, section, or article, skim the introduction, the topic sentence and summary sentence of each paragraph, and the conclusion. *Skimming* is reading to identify quickly the purpose, thesis, main ideas, and supporting ideas of a selection.

Close Reading   After skimming a selection to learn the main ideas, read it more slowly to learn the details. *Close reading* is for locating specific information, following the logic of an argument, or comprehending the meaning or significance of information.

Taking Notes

Note-taking is an important skill for helping you remember what you have read in a textbook or heard in a lecture. Two methods for taking notes are the modified outline and the summary.

In a *modified outline*, words and phrases are used to record main ideas and important details. When studying for an objective test such as a multiple-choice test, a modified outline will help you easily see and review the important facts and details.

In a *summary* sentences are used to express important ideas in your own words. Writing summaries is useful in preparing for an essay test because you must think about the information, see relationships between ideas, and draw conclusions.

In the following passage from a textbook, the essential information is underlined. Following the passage are examples of notes in both modified-outline form and summary form.

Thomas Hardy had two distinct literary careers, the first as a novelist and the second as a poet. His deepening pessimism in *Jude the Obscure,* coupled with the public burning of the book by an Anglican bishop, turned him away from novel writing and toward poetry.

Until the age of fifty-eight, Hardy was known only as a novelist. Among his best-known novels are *The Return of the Native* and *The Mayor of Casterbridge.* These novels show Hardy's pervasive gloominess, yet his rustic characters also reveal an underlying sense of humor. Hardy considered himself a meliorist, one who believes that things tend to improve.

For the last 30 years of his life, Hardy wrote nothing but poetry. His great epic drama, *The Dynasts,* is less well-known than his shorter poems, such as "The Man He Killed," "Channel Firing," and "In Time of 'The Breaking of Nations.' " These poems tend to be *sad and pessimistic,* like his novels, but they also suggest the heroic dignity of humanity's struggle.

MODIFIED OUTLINE

Thomas Hardy

1. Two writing careers—novelist and poet
2. Until age fifty-eight—known only as a novelist
   a. Novels show gloominess but also humor
   b. Reflect Hardy's belief that things tend to improve
3. Last 30 years of life—wrote only poetry
4. Short poems most familiar
   a. Display sadness and pessimism
   b. Reveal heroic dignity of human beings

SUMMARY

Thomas Hardy

Hardy had two different writing careers: he was a novelist until age fifty-eight and a poet thereafter. His most well-known novels are gloomy but show an underlying sense of humor. Hardy believed that things tend to improve.

Hardy's short poems, for which he is best known, display sadness and pessimism but also reveal the heroic dignity of human beings.

"Mr. Osborne, may I be excused? My brain is full."

The strategies below will help you take well-organized notes.

Taking Notes

1. Label your notes with the title and page numbers of the chapter or section, or the topic and date of the lecture.
2. Record only the main ideas and important details.
3. Use the titles, subtitles, and words in special type or color to help you select the most important information.
4. Use your own words; do not copy word for word.
5. Use as few words as possible.

MODIFIED OUTLINE

- Use words and phrases.
- Use main ideas for headings.
- List any supporting details under each heading.

SUMMARY

- Write complete sentences, using your own words.
- Show the relationship between ideas, being careful to use only the facts stated in the textbook or lecture.

EXERCISE *Taking Notes*

Read the selection "Shakespeare's Sister," by Virginia Woolf, on pages 131–134. Then take notes on this selection using either a modified outline or a summary. If time permits, divide into small groups and compare your results.

Preparing Subject-Area Assignments

While using the strategies you have learned for reading textbooks, taking notes, and preparing for tests can be valuable when doing assignments in any subject area, using those study aids specific to various subject areas can be of special help. Mathematics and science texts often list important rules, formulas, charts, graphs, equations, or models. Consequently you may spend much of your study time in these areas, applying rules and practicing your analytical and computational skills. Social studies materials, on the other hand, often emphasize such skills as reading and interpreting maps, charts, graphs, chronologies, time lines, documents, and statistical data, which you will use in preparing assignments. Use the following study tips to help you prepare assignments for whatever subject area you are studying.

Strategies for Preparing Subject-Area Assignments

1. Carefully read and follow all directions. *(See page 527.)*
2. Adjust your reading rate to suit your purpose. *(See page 501.)*
3. Take notes from both readings and lectures. In reviewing notes, use the technique of highlighting to help you remember important information, such as names, dates, terms, or facts. *(See pages 501–503.)*
4. Be organized. For example, you will find it helpful to keep your reading notes and lecture notes on the same topic together in your notebook.
5. For review keep a separate list of vocabulary words, key terms and concepts, or rules and equations.
6. Keep a running list of questions that arise as you read, listen, or review. Seek answers promptly. If there is anything you do not understand, get help.
7. Participate in study groups, following the principles of cooperative learning. *(See Strategies for Cooperative Learning on page 444.)*
8. In preparing for tests, leave ample time for study. Focus on anticipating and answering the questions you will be asked by your teacher.
9. Practice applying what you have learned using the specialized learning aids and skills for the particular subject area you are working in.

Taking Standardized Tests

By asking different kinds of questions, a standardized test measures your abilities, skills, progress, and achievement. One kind of standardized test measures your understanding of the meaning of words and the way they are used in sentences. Tests within this category often contain analogy questions, which test your ability to understand word relationships, and sentence-completion questions which require you to use the context to complete a sentence.

Standardized tests also include reading comprehension tests and tests of writing ability. Your ability to write clearly and effectively is often checked with objective questions about usage and mechanics, as well as with a sample of a spontaneously written essay within a limited time period.

The best way to prepare for taking a standardized test, as for any other kind of test, is to work conscientiously on all classwork all along, to read widely, and to become familiar with standard testing formats.

The following strategies can help you succeed at taking standardized tests.

Strategies for Taking Standardized Tests

1. Read the test directions carefully. Answer sample questions to be sure you understand what the test requires.
2. Relax. Although you can expect to be a little nervous, concentrate on doing the best you can.
3. Preview the whole test by quickly skimming. This will give you an overview of the kinds of questions on the test.
4. Plan your time carefully, allotting a certain amount of time to each part of the test.
5. Answer first the questions you find easiest. Skip those you find too hard, coming back to them later if you have enough time.
6. Read all choices before you choose an answer. If you are not sure of the answer, eliminate any choices that are obviously wrong. Making an educated guess is usually wise in such a case.
7. If you have time, check your answers. Look for omissions and careless errors on your answer sheet.

Analogies

Analogy questions test your skill at figuring out word relationships. Your first step is to decide how the first two words in capital letters are related. In the following analogy *HAND:FINGER*, for example, the relationship of the two words is whole-to-part. The hand (the whole) includes the finger (the part). Your next step is to find the pair of words among the choices that shows the same kind of relationship as that of the first pair. Determine the correct answer in the following analogy.

> HAND:FINGER   : :   (A) author:story   (B) top:bottom
> (C) state:city   (D) handle:mug   (E) joke:laughter

The answer is *(C) state:city* because it contains the only whole-to-part relationship among the choices. The other choices are incorrect. The relationship of *author:story* is *worker-to-product,* not whole-to-part. *Top:bottom* is a word-to-antonym relationship, and *joke:laughter* is a cause-to-effect relationship. *Handle:mug* is a part-to-whole relationship, not a whole-to-part relationship. Remember, the word order must be exactly the same in the answer as it is in the question.

Sometimes analogies are written in sentence form and require you to select the word that best completes the analogy.

> *Decipher* is to *decode* as *proclaim* is to
> (A) influence   (B) acknowledge   (C) announce   (D) annoy
> (E) encode

The first two italicized words, *decipher* and *decode*, are synonyms. Therefore, the correct answer is *(C) announce*, a synonym for *proclaim*.

Knowing some common types of analogies, such as those in the chart below, will help you figure out word relationships.

Common Types of Analogies	
ANALOGY	**EXAMPLE**
word:synonym	evade:escape
word:antonym	feasible:impossible
part:whole	caboose:train
cause:effect	exercise:fitness
worker:tool	mason:trowel
worker:product	publisher:magazine
item:purpose	bus:transport

EXERCISE 2 *Completing Analogies*

Number your paper 1 to 10. Then write the letter of the word that best completes the analogy.

EXAMPLE   *Plumber* is to *wrench* as *architect* is to _____.
(A) symmetry   (B) builder   (C) blueprint   (D) office
(E) easel

ANSWER   (C)

1. *Purpose* is to *intention* as *surplus* is to _____.
(A) excess   (B) equipment   (C) storage   (D) discussion
(E) determination
2. *Heat* is to *expansion* as *wind* is to _____.
(A) erosion   (B) donation   (C) dismissal   (D) breeze
(E) temperature
3. *Talent* is to *achievement* as *genius* is to _____.
(A) innovation   (B) prodigy   (C) underachievement
(D) shrewdness   (E) failure
4. *House* is to *frame* as *body* is to _____.
(A) skin   (B) torso   (C) joint   (D) skeleton   (E) brain
5. *Merge* is to *separate* as *flippant* is to _____.
(A) swimming   (B) unbalanced   (C) talkative   (D) thrown
(E) respectful
6. *Corrode* is to *metal* as *decay* is to _____.
(A) organism   (B) erosion   (C) statement   (D) rust
(E) plastic
7. *Zealous* is to *eager* as *specific* is to _____.
(A) ambiguous   (B) lengthy   (C) morose   (D) gaudy
(E) precise
8. *Buyer* is to *merchandise* as *accountant* is to _____.
(A) formality   (B) success   (C) calendar   (D) precision
(E) ledgers
9. *Splendid* is to *elegant* as *dubious* is to _____.
(A) authentic   (B) sincere   (C) doubtful   (D) similar
(E) strong
10. *Penal* is to *punishment* as *regal* is to _____.
(A) lecture   (B) laughter   (C) royalty   (D) exercise
(E) truth

EXERCISE *Recognizing Analogies*

Number your paper 1 to 15. Then write the letter of the word pair that has the same relationship as the word pair in capital letters.

1. PATERNAL:MATERNAL : : (A) precise:accurate
(B) numerous:many (C) frequent:seldom (D) brave:fearless
(E) descended:related

2. VERTEBRATE:MAMMAL : : (A) crustacean:snake
(B) money:bank (C) fog:precipitation (D) element:copper
(E) silver:ore

3. TIRED:EXHAUSTED : : (A) alike:dissimilar (B) won:lost
(C) firmed:fixed (D) constructed:built (E) fear:dislike

4. WRISTWATCH:DIGITAL : : (A) soles:shoes
(B) camera:tripod (C) school:book (D) tree:cypress
(E) steel:iron

5. INSPECT:EXAMINE : : (A) condemn:encourage
(B) cease:begin (C) attempt:try (D) lead:inspire
(E) inform:confuse

6. TRIVIAL:IMPORTANT : : (A) windy:wet (B) patron:client
(C) lazy:tired (D) complete:finished (E) stale:fresh

7. CONVENE:DELEGATES : : (A) students:dismiss (B) yes:no
(C) round up:horses (D) voters:booth (E) lower:reduce

8. PETITE:HUGE : : (A) calm:peaceful (B) gazing:staring
(C) minuscule:tiny (D) key:lock (E) meager:abundant

9. CURE:REMEDY : : (A) agree:decide (B) ask:answer
(C) protect:shield (D) dampen:lighten (E) seek:solve

10. BRUSH:PAINTER : : (A) sports:competitor
(B) jeweler:gem (C) stonecutter:chisel (D) shirt:price
(E) bowl:chef

11. EPITAPH:TOMBSTONE : : (A) poem:verse
(B) prose:speech (C) radio:music (D) inscription:monument
(E) story:plot

12. CARDINAL:BIRD : : (A) wren:hawk (B) burlap:cloth
(C) fish:mackerel (D) flag:country (E) duck:drake

13. FOYER:HOTEL : : (A) room:closet (B) house:apartment
(C) lobby:theater (D) tent:barracks (E) door:window

14. IRRELEVANT:UNIMPORTANT : : (A) honest:deceitful
(B) prior:former (C) arrogant:humble (D) pointless:active
(E) humorous:serious

15. MAST:SHIP : : (A) rowboat:oar (B) dentist:drill
(C) sedan:car (D) string:violin (E) igloo:house

Sentence-Completion Tests

Sentence-completion questions assess your ability to use the context to complete a sentence. *(See page 451.)* These questions ask you to figure out what word or words make the most sense in the blanks of a sentence. Although the sentences in these tests cover a wide variety of subjects, they do not require that you have a prior knowledge of those subjects. By using key words that appear in the sentences, you should be able to determine the answers from the context alone. First read the following sentence from beginning to end. Then choose the most appropriate word from the list of choices below it to complete the sentence.

> Because you failed to meet the April 30 deadline and have since refused to say when or whether you will complete the work, we are forced to ———— our contract with you.
>
> (A) honor (B) discuss (C) terminate (D) negotiate
> (E) extend

The answer is *(C) terminate.* The rest of the sentence, including its tone, clearly suggests that the contract has not been honored and that the time for negotiating or granting an extension of time has passed. The other choices—*honor, discuss, negotiate,* and *extend*—do not make sense in the context of the sentence.

Sentence-completion questions, like the one that follows, sometimes have two blanks in the same sentence. Find the correct answer in this example.

> Despite ———— to the contrary, the detective was ————
> that Mrs. Arnold had mislaid her jewels.
>
> (A) suspicions . . . pleased
> (B) evidence . . . convinced
> (C) feelings . . . certain
> (D) confessions . . . depressed
> (E) furor . . . surprised

The answer is *(B) evidence . . . convinced.* The key words in the sentence that help you determine this answer are *contrary* and *mislaid. Feelings . . . certain* contains a contradiction, while the other choices simply do not make good sense in the context of the sentence. When you answer an item like this, read the sentence to yourself with the words in place to be sure the sentence makes sense.

EXERCISE *Sentence-Completion Tests*

Number your paper 1 to 10. Then write the letter of the word or words that best complete each of the following sentences.

1. Since we had to meet at the Lincoln Memorial at exactly 2:35 P.M., we decided to _____ our watches.
   (A) synchronize (B) ignore (C) wind (D) consider (E) hide

2. His use of short sentences and contractions made his speech seem _____ rather than formal.
   (A) unacceptable (B) hilarious (C) slurred (D) colloquial
   (E) pompous

3. Jill came so close to winning many of the track events that she was awarded a special _____ prize.
   (A) academic (B) financial (C) unsuitable (D) patronizing
   (E) consolation

4. The crowd at the international convention heard a number of _____ speakers demanding that war be outlawed.
   (A) bored (B) pacifist (C) natural (D) inactive (E) war-mongering

5. An economist stated that the _____ of foreign currency could stimulate the small country's economy.
   (A) influx (B) suppression (C) study (D) suitability
   (E) lack

6. After auditioning unsuccessfully for more than a dozen roles, the actor remarked that _____ is as important as talent.
   (A) unselfishness (B) perseverance (C) timidity
   (D) brutality (E) underhandedness

7. The giraffe is _____, feeding only on plants.
   (A) quadruped (B) hoofed (C) herbivorous (D) huge
   (E) endangered

8. King Edward VIII said he would _____ the throne of England in order "to marry the woman I love."
   (A) ruin (B) climb (C) decorate (D) abdicate (E) examine

9. Her acceptance speech was so long that we can print only an _____ of it in the newspaper.
   (A) extension (B) array (C) excerpt (D) overture
   (E) understatement

10. As a young man, the actor was slim and lithe; but as the years passed, he became a _____ character actor.
    (A) loose-limbed (B) portly (C) well-paid (D) forgotten
    (E) lackluster

EXERCISE *Sentence Completion with Two Blanks*

Number your paper 1 to 10. Then write the letter of the pair of words that best completes each of the following sentences.

I. It was quite a moment when he _____ into the room and casually _____ he had been signed by the Celtics, a professional basketball team.
(A) stormed . . . growled   (B) strode . . . snapped
(C) walked . . . shouted
(D) sauntered . . . announced
(E) rushed . . . trumpeted

2. The detective claimed that the suspect, in his _____ to leave the scene, _____ left a laundry ticket behind.
(A) reluctance . . . surprisingly
(B) haste . . . inadvertently
(C) plot . . . absentmindedly
(D) decision . . . foolishly   (E) anger . . . purposely

3. Great Britain, with its long coastline and _____ ports, is one of the leading _____ nations in the world.
(A) many . . . agricultural
(B) outstanding . . . industrial
(C) excellent . . . nautical   (D) crowded . . . financial
(E) overabundant . . . debtor

4. Ted was far ahead in the game and was _____ to win, but his opponent refused to _____.
(A) likely . . . play   (B) demanding . . . agree
(C) playing . . . reason
(D) doubtful . . . lose
(E) certain . . . yield

5. The _____ dictionary is about a foot thick; the _____ edition is only about one quarter as large.
(A) unabridged . . . concise
(B) enormous . . . other
(C) modern . . . recent   (D) paperback . . . recognized
(E) children's . . . old-fashioned

6. When the _____ was cut to 18 players, Phil was retained despite his _____ playing.
(A) team . . . superb
(B) management . . . unsatisfactory
(C) staff . . . improved   (D) roster . . . inconsistent
(E) choice . . . exuberant

7. By the terms of the will, Marie's _____ was to be invested, and she was to receive _____ payments.
(A) future . . . limited   (B) inheritance . . . periodic
(C) account . . . spectacular   (D) income . . . no
(E) property . . . worthwhile

8. The good news made Freddie's _____ brighter, and he smiled _____.
(A) expression . . . enthusiastically
(B) outlook . . . solemnly   (C) aspect . . . grimly
(D) afternoon . . . thoughtlessly
(E) well-being . . . happily

9. After a lengthy discussion, the _____ of the group was that our _____ affairs should be handled by an experienced accountant.
(A) disagreement . . . legal   (B) intent . . . basic
(C) equality . . . fund-raising   (D) vote . . . important
(E) consensus . . . budgetary

10. We agreed that any _____ who could play both Juliet and Lady Macbeth had to be very _____.
(A) woman . . . elderly   (B) performer . . . tricky
(C) actress . . . versatile   (D) stagehand . . . flexible
(E) amateur . . . professional

Reading Comprehension Tests

Reading comprehension tests assess your ability to understand and analyze written passages. The information you need to answer the questions may be either directly stated or implied in the passage. You must study, analyze, and interpret a passage in order to answer the questions. The following strategies can help you answer such questions.

Strategies for Comprehension Questions

1. Begin by skimming the questions that follow the passage.
2. Read the passage carefully and closely. Notice the main ideas, organization, style, and key words.
3. Study all possible answers. Avoid choosing one answer the moment you think it is a reasonable choice.
4. Use only the information in the passage when you answer the questions. Do not rely on your own knowledge or ideas on this kind of test.

Most reading comprehension questions will ask you to interpret or evaluate one or more of the following characteristics of a written passage.

- **Main idea** At least one question will usually focus on the central idea of the passage. Remember that the main idea of a passage covers all sections of that passage, not just one section or paragraph.
- **Supporting details** Questions about supporting details test your ability to identify the statements in the passage that back up the main idea.
- **Implied meanings** In some passages not all information is directly stated. Some questions ask you to interpret information that the author has merely implied.
- **Tone** Questions on tone require that you interpret or analyze the author's attitude toward his or her subject.

The following passage is an example of the kind you will often find on reading comprehension tests. Study it and then answer the questions that follow the passage using the strategies recommended in this chapter.

One of the most fascinating institutions in American history was the short-lived Pony Express, established in 1860. The plan seemed brilliant at the time. The Pony Express, a relay system of horseback riders, would carry mail between Missouri and California in the breathtaking time of just 10 days. The feat required the building of 190 way stations at 10-mile intervals between St. Joseph, Missouri, and San Francisco, California. As work on the way stations progressed, 500 horses were chosen, and a group of adventurous, experienced, rough-and-ready riders were hired.

April 3, 1860, was the day this new, lightning-fast mail service began operations. Cheering crowds in St. Joseph and San Francisco sped the first two riders on their way. Each rider raced at full gallop for 10 miles, then thundered into a way station where another mount was saddled and waiting. The rider would leap on the fresh horse, flinging the *mochila*, or mail pouch, onto the new saddle, and dash off again. Each rider put in 70 miles of this grueling work at breakneck speed before turning his mail over to the next rider.

The Pony Express made Americans proud. It cut a full 10 days off the usual stagecoach schedule, and it was the stuff of romance. Eighty riders were always traveling, day and night, winter and summer, rain or shine, 40 of them racing east, 40 flying west. They braved open prairies, twisting mountain trails, and ever-present threats of Indian attacks.

Alas, the glory of the Pony Express exceeded its profits, and technology soon made it obsolete. Despite rates of $4 to $10 per ounce and a steady increase in letters carried, each piece of mail cost the company $38 to transport. The venture was already losing money when, on October 24, 1861, an unbeatable competitor entered the field. On that date the wires of a new transcontinental telegraph company were joined, and communication time between the coasts dropped from 10 days to a fraction of a second. Then, if not earlier, the Pony Express was doomed.

1. The best title for this passage is
  (A) A Dangerous Gamble.
  (B) How the Pony Express Operated.
  (C) Early Communication.
  (D) The Ill-Fated Pony Express.
  (E) Technology and the Pony Express.
2. The Pony Express failed because
  (A) its rates were too high.
  (B) the telegraph was invented.
  (C) the trip was too dangerous.
  (D) service was too slow.
  (E) operating costs and competition made it unprofitable.
3. It seems to be true that the Pony Express
  (A) made money at first but not later on.
  (B) experienced many disasters on the trail.
  (C) appealed to the Americans of that time.
  (D) might have succeeded with better management.
  (E) was an unworkable scheme because of its organization.
4. This passage would most likely appear in
  (A) a western novel.
  (B) a textbook on the American westward movement.
  (C) a local history of St. Joseph, Missouri.
  (D) a concise history of nineteenth-century economics.
  (E) a book on the telegraph in America.

You should have chosen the following answers.

1. *(D) The Ill-Fated Pony Express.* Choices *(A)* and *(C)* are too broad, *(B)* is too narrow, and *(E)* does not reflect the main idea.

2. *(E) operating costs and competition made it unprofitable.* These reasons are stated directly in the passage. Choice *(A)* is untrue, *(B)* is only partly true, and *(C)* and *(D)* are not accurate statements.

3. *(C) appealed to the Americans of that time.* Although this is an inference, it is a very clear one. There is nothing to support the inferences in choices *(A)*, *(B)*, or *(D)*.

4. *(B) a textbook on the American westward movement.* Because of all the facts, choice *(A)* is unlikely, and *(C)*, *(D)*, and *(E)* are either too specific or unrelated to the topic.

EXERCISE *Reading Comprehension Questions*

Number your paper 1 to 4. Read the following passage and write the letter of each correct answer.

Although Edgar Allan Poe was a demon-haunted man who made many enemies in his brief lifetime, he is also the honored father of the detective story, a genre that has been continuously popular ever since "The Murders in the Rue Morgue" first appeared in print in 1841. In that one story, Poe introduced a number of features that have since become traditional for this type of fiction, such as the eccentric private detective, the relatively dull-witted but admiring narrator, the locked room, the unjustly suspected person, and the presentation of clues to the reader.

Had Poe stopped with "The Murders in the Rue Morgue," his place in the long history of the mystery genre would already have been secure, but he did not stop there. With his second story, "The Mystery of Marie Roget," he added to his achievement. By bringing back his imaginative and keenly observant C. Auguste Dupin as the detective, he created the first series fictional detective, as well as the first armchair detective, since in this case Dupin never leaves his quarters. The last Dupin case, "The Purloined Letter," introduces psychological detection, the clue in plain sight, the staged diversion, and the long and condescending explanation at the end—all elements familiar to readers of detective stories.

Even though some critics argue otherwise, with these three short stories, Poe furnished future generations of mystery writers, from Baroness Orczy to Agatha Christie, from Arthur Conan Doyle to Ellery Queen, with the essential features of their tales.

1. The main idea of this passage is that
  (A) Poe deserves to be remembered as a great writer.
  (B) Poe created features of the traditional mystery.
  (C) Poe was not a well-liked man.
  (D) Poe wrote formula stories, which others have copied.
  (E) only three of Poe's stories should be remembered.
2. Whenever a modern detective story uses an obvious clue, the writer owes a debt of gratitude to
  (A) "The Purloined Letter."
  (B) Agatha Christie.
  (C) "The Mystery of Marie Roget."
  (D) Arthur Conan Doyle.
  (E) "The Murders in the Rue Morgue."
3. The selection states Poe is the father of the detective story rather than of the mystery story because
  (A) "The Murders in the Rue Morgue" is not a mystery.
  (B) mystery stories do not have detectives.
  (C) Sherlock Holmes appeared earlier than Dupin.
  (D) mystery stories existed before Poe.
  (E) detective stories and mystery stories are the same.
4. This passage contains many facts, and its intent seems to be both to inform and to
  (A) amuse.   (B) disprove.   (C) argue.   (D) irritate.
  (E) persuade.

The Double Passage   Some tests may also ask you to read two passages together and then answer questions about each passage individually and about similarities and differences between the two passages. The questions about the individual passages are typically just like single-passage questions. The questions about both passages ask you to compare and contrast such issues as viewpoints, tone, and implied meanings. A short introduction that precedes the passages may help you anticipate the ways in which the passages may contrast with or complement one another.

On these tests, both reading passages are presented first, followed by questions about Passage 1, then questions about Passage 2, and finally the comparison questions. You may find it helpful to read Passage 1 first and immediately answer the questions related to that passage before you read Passage 2. When you have finished the Passage 1 questions, you can return to read the second passage and then answer the remaining questions.

EXERCISE *Double Passage Reading Comprehension*

The following passages present two views of heroes and heroism. The first passage is from the introduction of a popular book about heroes and heroines in our time. The second is from a book on mythology by Edith Hamilton.

Passage 1

In a simple society such as the Greeks' of three thousand years ago, the heroes' world was straightforward and uncomplicated. It was, in the words of Joseph Campbell, a world of "monomyths": it had single goals, definite and clear purposes. The heroes and heroines of that society spoke for and perpetuated humankind's goals and purposes. In more complicated societies, such as our own, heroes and heroines wear many faces because of their numerous responses to the varied needs of individuals, groups of people, and national purposes.

As a society's needs become more complicated, so too do the heroes and heroines; as people become more sophisticated, the heroes and heroines become less modeled on the conventional demi-gods of the past, less clear-cut and obvious. In a swiftly moving society like America today, heroes and heroines undergo rapid transformation. They frequently develop in ways and for purposes that are not immediately apparent. Twentieth-century American heroes and heroines, existing in a highly technological society and driven by the electronics of mass communication, change quickly. They often are hailed as heroic today and forgotten tomorrow. But though they may disappear rapidly, they serve useful and needed purposes while they endure. So we continue to create heroes and heroines because they can concentrate the power of a people—of a nation—and serve as the driving force for the movement and development of individuals and society.

Passage 2

The world of Norse mythology is a strange world. Asgard, the home of the gods, is unlike any other heaven men have dreamed of. No radiancy of joy is in it, no assurance of bliss. It is a grave and solemn place, over which hangs the threat of an inevitable doom. The gods know that a day will come when they will be destroyed. Sometime they will meet their enemies and go down beneath them to defeat and death. Asgard will fall in ruins. The cause the forces of good are fighting to defend against the forces of evil is hopeless. Nevertheless, the gods will fight for it to the end.

Necessarily the same is true of humanity. If the gods are finally helpless before evil, men and women must be more so. This is the conception of life which underlies the Norse religion, as somber a conception as the mind of man has ever given birth to. The only sustaining support possible for the human spirit, the one pure unsullied good men can hope to attain, is heroism; and heroism depends on lost causes. The hero can prove what he is only by dying. The power of good is shown not by triumphantly conquering evil, but by continuing to resist evil while facing certain defeat.

1. According to the author of Passage 1, which of the following factors best explains why heroes in Greek society differed from heroes of today?
(A) lack of monomyths
(B) mass communication
(C) technological advancements
(D) simple versus complicated societies
(E) development of nations

2. In relation to paragraph 1 in Passage 1, the purpose of paragraph 2 is mainly to
(A) define heroes.
(B) trace the development of heroes through the centuries.
(C) contrast contemporary heroes with ancient heroes.
(D) elaborate the point made in sentence 1.
(E) illustrate the concept of monomyth.

3. The tone of Passage 1 is
(A) lighthearted.   (B) neutral.   (C) sarcastic.
(D) ironic.   (E) emotional.

4. According to the author of Passage 2, heroism in Norse mythology is achieved by

(A) overcoming the forces of evil.

(B) triumphing over death.

(C) fighting to the death against forces of evil.

(D) accomplishing great deeds.

(E) mastering god-like powers.

5. According to the author of Passage 2, which best describes mythology's sphere of influence in Norse culture?

(A) spiritual

(B) social

(C) political

(D) intellectual

(E) artistic

6. Which of the following ideas from Passage 1 about heroes and heroism in contemporary life hold true for the Norse idea of heroism as described in Passage 2?

(A) Heroes undergo rapid transformation.

(B) Heroes may disappear rapidly.

(C) Heroes are not clear-cut and obvious.

(D) Heroes can concentrate the power of a people.

(E) Heroes are varied to reflect cultural diversity.

Tests of Standard Written English

An objective test of standard written English contains sentences with underlined words, phrases, or punctuation. The underlined parts may contain errors in grammar, usage, mechanics, vocabulary, and spelling. You must find the error in each sentence or, on some tests, identify the best way to revise a faulty sentence or passage.

Error Recognition   This kind of question tests grammar, usage, capitalization, punctuation, word choice, and spelling. As a rule, each item consists of a sentence with five underlined parts. Four of these underlined parts suggest possible errors in the sentence. The fifth indicates that there is no error. No sentence has more than one error. Read the following sentence and identify the error, if there is one.

The Pacific <u>Ocean</u> is 36,198 feet deep in the Mariana
         A

Trench<u>,</u> even deeper <u>then</u> Mount Everest or the mountain
  B   **C**

K2 <u>is</u> high. <u>No error</u>
 D   **E**

The answer is *C*. Standard usage requires *than* rather than *then* in this sentence. Sometimes you will find a sentence that contains no error. Be careful, however, before you choose *E* as the answer. The errors included in this kind of test are often common errors that are hard to notice. Remember that everything not underlined in a sentence is correct; you can often use these correct parts to help identify the errors.

EXERCISE 8 *Recognizing Errors in Writing*

Number your paper 1 to 10. Then write the letter of the underlined word or punctuation mark that is incorrect. If the sentence contains no error, write *E*.

1. The <u>Reverend</u> William Spooner, <u>who's</u> last name became
       A   **B**

   a common noun, <u>had</u> <u>an</u> unusual quirk of speech. <u>No error</u>
           C **D**   **E**

2. <u>Spooners'</u> quirk was <u>to</u> transpose the initial sounds of
    A   **B**

   <u>two</u> or <u>more</u> words. <u>No error</u>
    C   **D**   **E**

3. <u>There</u> <u>are</u> a great many examples of <u>his</u> odd<u>,</u> humorous
    A **B**   **C**   **D**

   mistakes. <u>No error</u>
          E

4. When Spooner <u>spoke</u>, "a well-oiled bicycle<u>,</u>" for example, would
           A   **B**

   come out <u>as</u> "a well-boiled icicle<u>".</u> <u>No error</u>
        C   **D**   **E**

Calvin & Hobbes © 1990 Universal Press Syndicate. Reprinted with permission.

5. Spooner was an experienced, <u>knowledgeable</u> teacher
                                           A

   <u>who</u> <u>his</u> students liked and respected. <u>No error</u>
    B   C   D   E

6. If you <u>was</u> to ask most of his students, they would <u>say</u>
          A   B   C

   he <u>was</u> unforgettable. <u>No error</u>
      D   E

7. After all, how could <u>anyone</u> forget a man who said, "Let
         A   B

   me sew you to your sheet," when he <u>intends</u> to show you
                                    C

   to your seat? <u>No error</u>
          D   E

8. Everyone <u>who</u> knew Reverend Spooner <u>had</u> <u>their</u> own
          A   B   C

   story to tell about <u>him</u>. <u>No error</u>
               D   E

9. Still, as time went by, the old <u>man's</u> long service at
                                A

   New <u>College</u>, Oxford, was all but <u>forgotten</u>. <u>No error</u>
       B   C   D   E

10. Spoonerisms, however, are remembered to this day, and <u>are</u> the
                                        A   B

    classic examples <u>used</u> in all dictionary definitions of the word
                   C

    based on <u>his</u> name. <u>No error</u>
         D   E

Sentence Correction These questions test your ability to recognize appropriate phrasing. Instead of locating an error, you must select the best way to write a sentence. In this kind of question, part of the sentence is underlined. Following the sentence are five different ways of writing the underlined part. The first way shown, *A*, is the same as the underlined part. The other four ways, *B* through *E*, present alternatives. The choices may involve questions of grammar, usage, capitalization, punctuation, or diction. Your answer must not change the meaning of the sentence.

We all agreed that the guest lecturer was well-informed, articulate, and <u>he had a nice personality.</u>

(A) he had a nice personality.
(B) he had a pleasant personality.
(C) a nice personality.
(D) likable.
(E) nice personality wise.

The answer is *(D)*. The problem with the original sentence, as well as with choices *(B)* and *(C)*, is lack of parallelism. *(See page 77.)* Choice *(E)* is parallel but contains an awkward verbal construction. Notice that *(D)* includes a new adjective, *likable*, although *personable* would have been satisfactory. This answer also makes the sentence parallel in construction.

EXERCISE *Correcting Sentences*

Number your paper 1 to 10. Then write the letter of the correct way, or the best way, of phrasing each underlined part.

 1. Walking through the unfamiliar park at noon, <u>a statue of Thoreau was visible to me.</u>
    (A) a statue of Thoreau was visible to me.
    (B) a statue of Thoreau caught my eye.
    (C) I saw a statue of Thoreau.
    (D) Thoreau's statue became visible.
    (E) my eyes caught a glimpse of a statue of Thoreau.
 2. Each <u>of us in the audience hopes</u> to learn your views on the bond issue.
    (A) of us in the audience hopes
    (B) of we in the audience hopes
    (C) of us in the audience hope
    (D) of we in the audience hope
    (E) member of the audience hope
 3. The prince, along with all <u>his supporters, were observed coming toward</u> the village.
    (A) his supporters, were observed coming toward
    (B) his supporters were observed, coming toward
    (C) his supporters, was observed coming toward
    (D) his supporters, was observed, coming toward
    (E) his' supporters, was observed coming toward
 4. Was it Jacqueline who said, <u>Its not too late to get a collar for your puppy?</u>
    (A) Its not too late to get a collar for your puppy?
    (B) "Its not to late to get a collar for your puppy"?
    (C) "It's not too late to get a collar for you're puppy?"
    (D) It's not to late to get a collar for your puppy.
    (E) "It's not too late to get a collar for your puppy"?

5. The <u>alarm should of begun</u> ringing by now.
   (A) alarm should of begun
   (B) alarm, it should of begun
   (C) alarm should have begun
   (D) alarm should have began
   (E) alarm should of began

6. Begin by stating what your occupation is, where you come from, and <u>your reason for deciding to enter the contest.</u>
   (A) your reason for deciding to enter the contest.
   (B) you're reason for deciding to enter the contest.
   (C) your reason for deciding too enter the contest.
   (D) why you decided to enter the contest.
   (E) your reason to decide to enter the contest.

7. "It seems," Joanne said, <u>"As if they're pleased with the results."</u>
   (A) "As if they're pleased with the results."
   (B) "as if they're pleased with the results."
   (C) "as if they're pleased with the results".
   (D) "like there pleased with the results."
   (E) "like they're pleased with the results".

8. Mr. Ferragamo spoke very <u>angry about losing the women's tickets.</u>
   (A) angry about losing the women's tickets.
   (B) angry about loosing the women's tickets.
   (C) angrily about losing the women's tickets.
   (D) angrily about losing the womens' tickets.
   (E) angrily about loosing the women's tickets.

9. Her popular books on European <u>history made the Middle Ages</u> come alive.
   (A) history made the Middle Ages
   (B) History made the Middle Ages
   (C) history made the middle ages
   (D) History made the Middle ages
   (E) History made the middle ages

10. The editor <u>hadn't hardly given him</u> the assignment when a new story broke.
   (A) hadn't hardly given him
   (B) hadn't hardly gave him
   (C) had hardly give him
   (D) had hardly given him
   (E) had hardly gave him

Revision-in-Context   Another type of question you may encounter on a standardized test is *revision-in-context*. You will be asked to read a brief essay, one that represents an early draft of a student's work. In the questions that follow the essay, you will be asked to choose the best revision of a sentence, group of sentences, or the essay as a whole and to demonstrate your understanding of the writer's intention. The following example shows the types of questions and the correct answers.

(1) Recently, a questionnaire was developed that asked people to give their opinions. (2) What they were to give their opinions about was the value of leisure time. (3) Most people said that their favorite pastime was watching television. (4) Commenting on the quality of the shows, however, the programs were not very satisfying. (5) Most people felt that their time would be better spent if they pursued physical activities such as sports and athletics. (6) They felt such activities would make a noticeable difference in the way they felt. (7) Unfortunately, they also felt there was little likelihood that they would take up exercise on a regular basis. (9) Many people, it seems, are willing to settle for so-so pastimes despite the fact that they know other pastimes might enhance the quality of their lives.

I. In relation to the rest of the passage, which of the following best describes the writer's intention in sentence (9)?
  (A) To restate the opening sentence
  (B) To draw a conclusion
  (C) To provide examples
  (D) To contrast active versus passive pastimes
  (E) To offer contradictory evidence

The correct answer is (B). You can eliminate all the others; sentence 9 does not restate the opening sentence, which simply tells about the questionnaire; it offers no examples or evidence, and it does not mention active versus passive activities.

2. Which of the following is the best revision of the underlined portion of sentence (4) below?

(4) Commenting on the quality of the shows, however, the programs were not very satisfying.

(A) , however; the programs were not very satisfying.

(B) however the viewers reported that the programs were not very satisfying.

(C) , however, the viewers reported that the programs were not very satisfying.

(D) ; however, the programs were not very satisfying.

(E) , however, the viewers reported that, the shows were not very satisfying.

The correct answer is (C). The sentence as written contains a misplaced modifier; the word *commenting* incorrectly modifies the word *programs*. Answer (C) addresses that problem effectively, while (A) and (D) do not. (B) and (E), while fixing the problem with the modifier, contain punctuation errors.

3. Which of the following is the best way to combine sentences (1) and (2)?

(A) Recently, a questionnaire was developed that asked people to give their opinions, and what they were to give their opinions about was the value of leisure time.

(B) Recently, a questionnaire was developed that asked people to give their opinions on the value of leisure time.

(C) Recently, people were asked to give their opinions on the value of leisure time.

(D) Recently, a questionnaire was developed, it asked people to give their opinions on the value of leisure time.

(E) A recent questionnaire developed to ask people to give their opinions on the value of leisure time.

The correct answer is (B). (A) is wordy, (C) omits mention of the questionnaire, and (D) contains a comma splice, and (E) is grammatically incomplete.

EXERCISE *Revision-in-Context*

Number your paper 1 to 3. Carefully read the passage, and then write the letter of the correct answer next to each number.

(1) The impact of computers on the productivity of business has been well documented. (2) Now there is also information about how having a computer at home affects family life. (3) A study of 130 computer users in California showed how it changed their family activities. (4) For example, television viewing dropped by about 75% after people acquired a home computer. (5) Time spent on hobbies dropped by about 40%. (6) People also spent about 37% less time sleeping. (7) Leisure time spent with family decreased by about 20%. (8) The amount of time people spent working or studying increased by about 28%, and time spent alone increased by about 40%. (9) In short, home computers tend to promote isolated, work-related activities, perhaps at the expense of valuable family interactions.

1. The purpose of sentence (9) is mainly to:
(A) summarize the study.
(B) provide examples.
(C) restate the main idea of sentence (2).
(D) interpret the data in the study.
(E) offer contradictory evidence.

2. Which of the following is the best revision of the underlined portion of sentence (3) below?
A study of 130 computer users in California <u>showed how it changed their family activities.</u>
(A) showed, how it changed their family activities.
(B) showed the way in which it changed their family activities.
(C) showed how a computer changed they're family activities.
(D) showed how computers changed their family activities.
(E) , showed how it changed their family activities.

3. Which of the following transitions would be the most effective way to begin sentence (8)?
(A) Additionally,
(B) As a matter of fact,
(C) On the other hand,
(D) Meanwhile,
(E) Nonetheless,

Taking Essay Tests

The main difference between a classroom writing assignment and an essay test is time. Since you have a limited amount of time on a test, you must organize and express your ideas quickly, clearly, and logically.

Kinds of Essay Questions

Before you begin to write your answers on an essay test, plan the amount of time you should spend on each part of the test. (The time you spend should be in proportion to the number of points allotted to each part.) Then, when it comes time to begin your first question, look for key words, such as those listed in the box below. Such key words will tell you precisely what kind of question you are being asked to answer.

Kinds of Essay Questions	
Analyze	Separate into parts and examine each part.
Compare	Point out similarities.
Contrast	Point out differences.
Define	Clarify meaning.
Discuss	Examine in detail.
Evaluate	Give your opinion.
Explain	Tell how, what, or why.
Illustrate	Give examples.
Summarize	Briefly review main points.
Trace	Show development or progress.

As you read the instructions, jot down everything that is required in your answer or underline key words and circle instructions. For instance, the key words are underlined and the instructions are circled in the following example.

When Francisco Pizarro first landed <u>in 1531</u> on the coast of what is now Ecuador, <u>the Inca Empire was larger than any European city of the time</u>. Nevertheless, <u>within only several years, the Spanish were able to destroy this mighty empire</u>. (Analyze) <u>three possible reasons</u> for the <u>rapid collapse of the Inca Empire</u>. (Include specific details) to support each point.

527

EXERCISE *Interpreting Essay Test Questions*

Number your paper 1 to 10. Write the key word in each question. Then write one sentence that explains what the question is asking you to do.

EXAMPLE Trace the development of a butterfly.
POSSIBLE ANSWER Trace—Show the stages from egg to full-grown butterfly.

 1. Explain how carbon-14 is used to date objects.
 2. Based on your study of literature, explain and illustrate either *alliteration* or *onomatopoeia.*
 3. Briefly contrast a myth and a fable.
 4. How does the working of a gasoline engine compare with that of an electric engine?
 5. In his *Dictionary of the English Language,* Samuel Johnson defines youth as "The part of life succeeding to childhood and adolescence; the time from fourteen to twenty-eight." Do you agree? Discuss Johnson's definition.
 6. Briefly summarize the plot of *Silas Marner,* a novel by George Eliot.
 7. Trace the development of a tornado.
 8. Briefly analyze the scientific contributions of lasers.
 9. In your own words, define *market economy.*
10. Evaluate one of William Wordsworth's poems.

Writing an Effective Essay Answer

Since the procedures for writing an essay for a test are basically the same as those for a typical writing assignment, you should recall and apply all that you have learned about using the writing process for writing an essay. *(See pages 141–169.)* However, because you will be restricted in the amount of time you have in a test situation, you first must do some extra preplanning.

You should first decide how much time you will work on each question and how much time you will spend on each step in the writing of each answer. One general guideline is that you should allow two minutes of planning and one minute of revising and editing for every five minutes of writing. As you calculate according to this timetable, plan to give more time to the essay answers worth the most points.

Prewriting   Knowing what you are going to write—and in what order you are going to write it—is essential before you begin to write your essay answer. Your first step, therefore, should be to organize your answer by writing a simple modified outline. Study the following example.

MODIFIED   Reasons for the collapse of the Inca Empire
OUTLINE   1. (thesis statement) 1st reason: weapons
        2. 2nd reason: transportation
        3. 3rd reason: internal war (conclusion)

Your next step is to write a thesis statement that states the main idea of your essay and covers all of your major supporting ideas. A helpful hint when writing an essay answer is to reword the test question itself—if possible—into a thesis statement. Read the following example.

ESSAY   When Francisco Pizarro first landed in 1531 on the coast
QUESTION   of what is now Ecuador, the Inca Empire was larger than any European city at the time. Nevertheless, within only several years, the Spanish were able to destroy this mighty empire. Analyze three reasons for the rapid collapse of the Inca Empire.

THESIS   Although the Inca Empire was larger than any Euro-
STATEMENT   pean city in 1531, the Spanish were able to destroy this mighty empire for three reasons.

Writing   As you write your essay answer, keep the following strategies in mind.

Strategies for Writing an Essay Answer

1. Begin with a thesis statement that states the main idea of your essay and covers all of your major supporting ideas.
2. Follow the order of your outline, writing one paragraph for each main point.
3. Provide adequate support for each main point—using specific facts, examples, and/or other supporting details.
4. Use transitions to connect ideas and/or examples.
5. End with a strong concluding statement that summarizes the main idea of the essay.
6. Write clearly and legibly.

Model: *Essay Test Answer*

Although the Inca Empire was larger than any European city in 1531, the Spanish were able to destroy this mighty empire for three reasons—or, more likely, the combined effect of three reasons. Perhaps the most obvious reason was the discrepancy in the weapons that the Spanish and the Incas used. Having no knowledge of iron, the Incas fought mainly with bronze-edged spears and slingshots. The Spanish returned such attacks with muskets, crossbows, and full-sized cannons.

The Spanish were able to transport themselves, their cannons, and their supplies into the interior of the Inca Empire because they not only had horses, but they also had the use of the wheel. Even though they had built a sophisticated system of roads, the Incas traveled only by foot. They did not have horses, and they could only carry, not pull, things, since the wheel was unknown to them.

When Pizarro entered the empire, Atahuallpa had successfully captured the throne from his half-brother. Realizing the threat from the Spanish, Atahuallpa had his brother killed. However, shortly afterward the Spanish killed Atahuallpa himself. As a result the Incas, greatly divided and lacking a strong leader, became easy prey for the Spanish. At the time the combination of these three factors were too much for the Incas. Could the course of history have taken a different turn, however, if someone like Pizarro had come only 20 or 30 years later?

Revising   Always leave yourself a few minutes to revise and edit your essay answer. As you revise your work, ask yourself the questions that follow.

- Did you thoroughly follow the instructions?
- Did you begin with a thesis statement?
- Did you include supporting details and examples?
- Did you use transitions to connect ideas and/or examples?
- Did you end with a strong concluding statement that summarized your essay?

Editing   Once you have made any necessary revisions, quickly read your essay for any mistakes in spelling, usage, or punctuation. To keep your paper as neat as possible, use proofreading symbols to make any corrections. *(See page 39.)* If time permits, you may want to look for the following specific problems:

- proper agreement between subjects and verbs *(See pages 694–713).*
- correct form of adjectives and adverbs in the comparative and superlative forms *(See pages 715–717.)*
- correct capitalization of proper nouns and proper adjectives *(See pages 754–763.)*
- correct use of commas *(See pages 772–785.)*
- correct use of apostrophes *(See pages 789–794.)*
- correct division of words at the end of a line *(See page 812.)*

EXERCISE *Answering an Essay Test Question*

Choose any subject area you are currently studying, including English. Write an essay test question that is likely to be included on an upcoming test and then answer the question, using the strategies discussed in this chapter.

Timed Writing The more you practice writing within a limited time period, the more confident you will feel as you enter a test situation in which you must complete a timed writing assignment. You will have a chance to get some of that helpful practice now. When your teacher tells you to begin, you will have 20 minutes to write an essay on the following topic:

> Keeping yourself informed of national and world news is an important part of each day. Compare and contrast the strengths and weaknesses of the two major news media, television news programs and newspapers. Give specific examples from your own experience.

You may want to plan your time by spending approximately 8 minutes working on prewriting tasks, 9 minutes writing your essay answer, and 3 minutes revising and editing. Remember, do not write anything until your teacher tells you to begin.

16

Review

A **Understanding Analogies** Number your paper 1 to 15. Then write the letter of the word pair that has the same relationship as the word pair in capital letters.

1. PLACARD:SLOGAN : : (A) acceptance:rejection
(B) fish:haddock (C) microscope:scientist
(D) keyboard:computer (E) postcard:message

2. DISPUTE:ARGUE : : (A) organize:divide (B) sing:dancc
(C) propose:demand (D) originate:initiate
(E) replenish:empty

3. NAUTICAL:SHIP : : (A) maneuvers:military
(B) quarterback:athletic (C) theatrical:stage
(D) secretary:executive (E) book:binding

4. LOATHE:ADMIRE : : (A) accuse:decide (B) love:adore
(C) experiment:research (D) confirm:deny (E) retreat:fail

5. MOLLUSK:CLAM : : (A) bird:blue jay
(B) extinction:dinosaur (C) camera:shutter
(D) horse:mammal (E) mammal:fish

6. STETHOSCOPE:DOCTOR : : (A) wrench:mechanic
(B) technician:surgeon (C) employee:employer
(D) baseball:bat (E) entertainer:microphone

7. RESOLUTE:WAVERING : : (A) patient:calm
(B) honest:straightforward (C) protecting:sheltering
(D) vivid:dull (E) springlike:rainy

8. GRANITE:ROCK : : (A) rain:hail (B) beach:ocean
(C) limestone:sandstone (D) typewriter:paper
(E) fir:evergreen

9. CABOOSE:TRAIN : : (A) steamship:paddle wheel
(B) finale:opera (C) igloo:ice (D) currency:coins
(E) bicycle:tricycle

10. ENTERTAINING:DRAMA : : (A) effort:rewarding
(B) travel:broadening (C) milk:healthful
(D) clever:comedian (E) painting:artistic

11. EXERTION:EFFORT : : (A) work:plans (B) loyalty:fidelity (C) election:votes (D) latch:key (E) flight:kite
12. PARTISAN:NEUTRAL : : (A) sink:wash (B) slim:sparse (C) expand:contract (D) dollar:penny (E) precise:exact
13. FAWN:DEER : : (A) cow:bull (B) mutton:sheep (C) leather:suede (D) hog:pig (E) gosling:goose
14. SPOUSE:WIFE : : (A) husband:in-law (B) cousin:uncle (C) nephew:aunt (D) mother:father (E) sibling:sister
15. DAWN:DUSK : : (A) stamp:letter (B) star:light (C) preface:conclusion (D) knee:injury (E) planet:Earth

B Understanding Tests of Standard Written English

Number your paper 1 to 5. Then write the letter that is below the underlined word, group of words, or punctuation mark that is incorrect. If the sentence contains no error, write *E*.

1. Charles Dickens <u>was</u> one of <u>those</u> writers who <u>seems</u> born
      A   B   C
   to create memorable <u>stories</u>, settings, and characters.
                        D
   <u>No error</u>
     E

2. Born on February 7, 1812<u>,</u> he <u>had</u> to go <u>to</u> work at the
                             A   B   C
   age of twelve to help support <u>his</u> family. <u>No error</u>
                                  D   E

3. Dickens then <u>goes</u> to school again briefly<u>,</u> <u>quitting</u> at
                 A   B   C
   the age of fifteen to become an office boy in a firm of <u>attorneys</u>.
                                                            D
   <u>No error</u>
     E

4. As a young <u>parliamentary</u> reporter, he began <u>writing</u>
               A   B
   fiction<u>,</u> and soon the *Monthly Magazine* published one
          C
   of his <u>Stories</u>. <u>No error</u>
           D   E

5. <u>His</u> first great triumph came with the publication of
   A
   Pickwick Papers, <u>which</u> <u>acheived</u> bestseller status.
         B   C   D
   <u>No error</u>
     E

Unit 4
Language Skills Resource

Grammar

Usage

Mechanics

GRAMMAR

17 The Parts of Speech

Diagnostic Test

Number your paper 1 to 10. First write the underlined words in each sentence. Then, beside each word, write its part of speech: *noun, pronoun, verb, adjective, adverb, preposition, conjunction,* or *interjection.*

EXAMPLE   <u>Someone</u> called <u>but</u> didn't leave a message.
ANSWER   someone — pronoun   but — conjunction

1. No part <u>of</u> the state of Maine is as far north as <u>England</u>.
2. Have you seen <u>this</u> review of the new action <u>movie</u> at the Plaza Theater?
3. <u>Which</u> of the toasters is a <u>better</u> buy?
4. Romanoff <u>was</u> the family name of the very last <u>Russian</u> czar in power.
5. David <u>never</u> told <u>anyone</u> the ending of the story he started last night.
6. A lost person often <u>travels</u> in a circle <u>or</u> in a spiral.
7. The earliest <u>possible</u> time <u>for</u> dinner is 5:00 P.M.
8. <u>Where</u> will I find the <u>movie</u> projector?
9. <u>Yes!</u> <u>This</u> is his correct telephone number.
10. The gymnast <u>suddenly</u> lost his balance <u>and</u> fell, but he was all right.

Nouns and Pronouns

The grammatical elements covered in this chapter include the eight parts of speech: *noun, pronoun, verb, adjective, adverb, preposition, conjunction,* and *interjection.* The part of speech of a word can vary, depending upon its use in a sentence.

Understanding the function of grammatical elements can help you as a writer. For example, if you can identify an adverb clause, you will be able to include adverb clauses in your writing. By doing that, you will add variety to your writing. As a writer, you also need to know, for example, when a word is a noun and when a word is a verb. Then you can diagnose any problems—such as incorrect agreement between a subject and a verb—in your writing as you edit.

Nouns

There are more nouns in our language than any other part of speech. Nouns are words that name persons, places, things, and ideas. Pronouns are words that replace nouns.

Rule 17a   **A noun** is the name of a person, place, thing, or idea.

Nouns can be classified in several ways.

Common and Proper Nouns   A *common noun* names any person, place, or thing. Always beginning with a capital letter, a *proper noun* names a particular person, place, or thing.

COMMON NOUNS   quarterback, state, car
PROPER NOUNS   Sam Levin, New Jersey, Chrysler

Note: Some proper nouns, such as *Sam Levin* and *New Jersey,* include more than one word; but they are still considered one noun. *Sam Levin* is one person, and *New Jersey* is one state.

Concrete and Abstract Nouns   A *concrete noun* names a person or an object that can actually be seen, touched, tasted, heard, or smelled. An *abstract noun* names qualities, conditions, and ideas that cannot be perceived through the senses.

CONCRETE NOUNS   table, feather, lemon, salt, bells, roses
ABSTRACT NOUNS   courage, joy, friendship, loyalty, freedom

Compound and Collective Nouns A *compound noun* is made up of more than one word. Since a compound noun can be written as one word, written hyphenated, or written as two or more separate words, it is always best to check the dictionary for the correct, up-to-date form. A *collective noun* names a group of people or things.

COMPOUND NOUNS peacemaker, falsehood [one word]
sister-in-law, bird-watcher [hyphenated]
life jacket, city hall [two words]

COLLECTIVE NOUNS squadron, quartet, flock, orchestra, crew

EXERCISE *Finding Nouns*

Number your paper 1 to 33. Then write the nouns in the following paragraphs. (A date should be considered a noun.)

The Eiffel Tower

The Eiffel Tower is perhaps the most familiar human-made land-mark on Earth. It was designed for the Paris Exposition in 1889. The tower can now accommodate 10,000 visitors annually. Some people, however, go there for publicity, not for enjoyment. A man once climbed 363 steps on stilts, and a stuntman came down on a unicycle.

The tower is repainted every seven years, requiring thousands of gallons of paint. As part of one cleanup, nearly 1,000 tons of rust and dirt were shaved off. This kind of effort signifies the tremendous pride the city takes in its famous structure — even if only a very small percentage of its visitors are Parisians.

Pronouns

Rule 17b A **pronoun** is a word that takes the place of one or more nouns.

The word that the pronoun replaces or refers to is called its *antecedent*. The antecedent of a pronoun can be in the same sentence or in another sentence. In the following examples, an arrow has been drawn from each pronoun to its antecedent.

Stephen wore **his** new jacket to school today.

Rob and Beth are at the library. **They** have **their** history exam tomorrow.

Occasionally the antecedent will follow the pronoun.

"That ten-speed bicycle is **mine,**" Heather said.

Personal Pronouns   Personal pronouns, the most commonly used type of pronoun, are divided into the following groups.

Personal Pronouns	
FIRST PERSON	(The person speaking)
SINGULAR	I, me, my, mine
PLURAL	we, us, our, ours
SECOND PERSON	(The person spoken to)
SINGULAR	you, your, yours
PLURAL	you, your, yours
THIRD PERSON	(The person or thing spoken about)
SINGULAR	he, him, his, she, her, hers, it, its
PLURAL	they, them, their, theirs

FIRST PERSON   **We** want to sell **our** old car.
SECOND PERSON   Did **you** ever find **your** watch?
THIRD PERSON   **He** told **them** to call **him** if **they** needed help.

EXERCISE ◆2▶ *Finding Personal Pronouns and Their Antecedents*

Number your paper 1 to 10. Write the personal pronoun(s) in each sentence. Then beside each one, write its antecedent.

1. "Are the pictures yours?" Megan asked Robert.
2. Danny lost his book in the subway when he was going home.
3. "Mr. Sanchez read my term paper and wrote comments on it," Michael told Harold.
4. "Did Pat tell you that she would be there?" Sue asked Bart.
5. Lorraine, where have you put your copy of *Life* magazine?
6. Ian told Rosa, "I will save a seat for you at the assembly."
7. The Morgans will be taking their retriever with them.
8. "Our duet was the hit of the show!" Jan exclaimed to Pat.
9. "We should take ours with us," Zachary told Yvonne.
10. Pam said, "When I gave Mia her award, she thanked me."

Reflexive and Intensive Pronouns   Reflexive and intensive pronouns are formed by adding *-self* or *-selves* to personal pronouns.

Reflexive and Intensive Pronouns	
SINGULAR	myself, yourself, himself, herself, itself
PLURAL	ourselves, yourselves, themselves

A *reflexive pronoun* refers to the noun or the pronoun that is the subject of the sentence. It is an essential part of the sentence. An *intensive pronoun* is included in a sentence to add emphasis—or intensity—to a noun or another pronoun. Because an intensive pronoun is not a necessary part of a sentence, it can be removed without affecting the meaning of the sentence.

REFLEXIVE PRONOUN   Rob taught **himself** to speak French.
[*Himself* cannot be removed from the sentence without changing the meaning.]

INTENSIVE PRONOUN   Rob volunteered his help **himself.**
[*Himself* can be removed from the sentence: Rob volunteered his help.]

Indefinite Pronouns   Indefinite pronouns often refer to unnamed persons or things and usually do not have specific antecedents.

Common Indefinite Pronouns	
SINGULAR	another, anybody, anyone, anything, each, either, everybody, everyone, everything, much, neither, nobody, no one, one, somebody, someone, something
PLURAL	both, few, many, others, several
SINGULAR/PLURAL	all, any, most, none, some

Few attended the meeting.
Most of the students did **something** to help the **many** who were homeless after the flood.

Demonstrative and Interrogative Pronouns A *demonstrative pronoun* is used to point out a specific person, place, or object in the same sentence or in another sentence. An *interrogative pronoun* is used to ask a question.

Demonstrative Pronouns		Interrogative Pronouns	
this	these	what	whom
that	those	which	whose
		who	

DEMONSTRATIVE PRONOUNS	**This** is the perfect place for a picnic.
	Of all the pears, **these** were the ripest.
INTERROGATIVE PRONOUNS	**What** is the best film playing tonight?
	Who wrote that song?

Note: *Relative pronouns* are used to introduce adjective clauses. *(See pages 616–618.)*

EXERCISE 3 *Finding Pronouns*

Number your paper 1 to 15. Then write each pronoun. There are 30 pronouns.

1. Who will be riding with them in the parade?
2. She is someone I have wanted to meet for a long time.
3. Did you find yourself something to eat?
4. I will lead the orchestra myself.
5. Many of the team members will need new equipment.
6. That is the place most of us like best.
7. What do you want for your birthday?
8. Anybody can run in the Fourth of July marathon.
9. Both of the candidates know everything about the issues.
10. Each of the compact-disc players is a good buy.
11. Which did Ellen say is the road to her house?
12. Tomás himself selected those.
13. Some of the spinach salad was left, but none of the dessert.
14. Whom has everybody chosen?
15. He didn't like either of the proposed plans.

Verbs

A verb is an essential part of a sentence because it tells what the subject does, is, or has.

Action Verbs

Rule 17c   An **action verb** tells what action a subject is performing.

Action verbs can show several types of action.

PHYSICAL ACTION	drive, march, soar, sing, talk, paint
MENTAL ACTION	believe, think, dream, imagine, wish
OWNERSHIP	have, own, possess, keep, control

Transitive and Intransitive Verbs   An action verb is *transitive* if it has an object. You can find an object by asking the question *What?* or *Whom?* after the verb. *(See pages 569–570 for more information about objects.)* An action verb is *intransitive* if it has no object.

TRANSITIVE   I **found** a dollar the other day. [*Found* what?]

INTRANSITIVE   We **met** only yesterday. [*Met* what or whom?]

Some action verbs may be either transitive or intransitive.

TRANSITIVE   He **writes** mystery stories in his spare time.

INTRANSITIVE   He often **writes** to me.

EXERCISE *Identifying Transitive and Intransitive Verbs*

Number your paper 1 to 10. Write each action verb. Then label each one *transitive* or *intransitive*.

Fishy Facts
1. Rings on the scales of some fish show the age of the fish.
2. The electric eel throws a charge of 600 volts.
3. Rays live on the ocean bottom.
4. The Nile catfish swims upside down.
5. Minnows have teeth in their throat.
6. The female marine catfish hatches her eggs in her mouth.
7. The trout belongs to the salmon family.

8. The flounder changes its color.
9. Some fish thrive in underground streams and caves.
10. Sharks, despite their reputation, rarely attack humans.

Linking Verbs

Rule 17d A **linking verb** links the subject with another word in the sentence. The other word either renames or describes the subject.

A linking verb serves as a bridge between the subject and another word in the sentence.

Football **is** my favorite sport. [*Sport* renames *football*.]

This winter **has been** exceptionally warm. [*Warm* describes the subject *winter.*]

The most common linking verbs are the various forms of *be*.

Common Forms of *Be*		
be	can be	has been
is	could be	had been
am	should be	could have been
are	would be	should have been
was	may be	would have been
were	might be	might have been
shall be	must be	must have been
will be	have been	

Diane **may be** my new neighbor.

These mushrooms **will be** delicious in the salad.

Note: The forms of *be* are not always linking verbs. Only a verb that links the subject with another word in the sentence that renames or describes the subject can be a linking verb. In the following examples, the verbs simply make a statement or describe a state of being.

Her coat **is** here.   She **was** in Memphis on Tuesday.

Forms of *be* are not the only linking verbs. The verbs listed below may also be used as linking verbs.

Additional Linking Verbs			
appear	grow	seem	stay
become	look	smell	taste
feel	remain	sound	turn

Jonathan **became** my best friend last year. [*Friend* renames the subject *Jonathan*.]

The barbecued chicken **looks** very tasty. [*Tasty* describes the subject *chicken*.]

Most of the additional linking verbs, listed in the preceding box, can be linking verbs in some sentences and action verbs in other sentences.

LINKING VERB   That plan **sounded** perfect. [*Perfect* describes the subject *plan*.]

ACTION VERB   The woman quickly **sounded** the alarm. [No word describes the subject *woman*.]

EXERCISE ◆ 5 ▸ *Finding Linking Verbs*

Number your paper 1 to 10. Then write each linking verb. If a sentence does not have a linking verb, write *none* after the number.

 1. George III was the king of England during the American Revolution.
 2. The hardest natural substance in the world is a diamond.
 3. You looked much older with short hair.
 4. He could have been the best runner in the history of our school.
 5. I felt a hole in my pocket.
 6. Indira Gandhi became the prime minister of India in 1966.
 7. Luella will become a lab technician after her graduation from Mercer High School.
 8. For an hour we looked for the extra set of keys.
 9. In 1900, many automobiles were electric cars, with battery-operated engines.
 10. For about a month after my surgery, I felt quite weak.

Verb Phrases

When one or more *helping verbs,* or auxiliary verbs, are added to either an action verb or a linking verb, a *verb phrase* is formed.

Rule 17e A **verb phrase** is a main verb plus one or more helping verbs.

Common Helping Verbs	
be	am, is, are, was, were, be, being, been
have	has, have, had
do	do, does, did
others	may, might, must, can, could, shall, should, will, would

In the following examples, the helping verbs are in heavy type.

┌──────verb phrase──────┐
Jeff **has been** throwing our newspaper into the bushes.

┌──────────verb phrase──────────┐
You **should have been** notified of the change.

A verb phrase is often interrupted by other words.

Marvin **will** soon **apply** for that job.
Have you always **taken** the bus to school?
I **don't want** any dessert.

Note: Throughout the rest of this book, the term *verb* will refer to the whole verb phrase.

EXERCISE 6 *Finding Verb Phrases*

Number your paper 1 to 10. Then write the verb in each sentence. Include all helping verbs.

1. At dinnertime Sheila was still practicing her scales.
2. The committee has held several productive meetings.
3. The group will not return for several hours.
4. The number of galaxies in the universe has been estimated at over a billion.
5. New basketball courts are being installed in the gym.
6. With his new job at the health club, George must always work on Saturdays.

7. I should never have eaten a second helping!
8. The runners have now reached the midpoint of the race.
9. The earth is traveling through space at the rate of 66,600 miles per hour.
10. Rebecca isn't working at Franklin Market anymore.

EXERCISE ⬖**7** *Cumulative Review*

Number your paper 1 to 10. Write the verb in each sentence. Then label each verb *action* or *linking*. Be sure to include all helping verbs.

1. That antique jar can hold three gallons of water.
2. Leslie should be proud of her performance.
3. Stone walls and fences are favorite spots for poison ivy.
4. A redwood tree can often grow to a height of 275 feet.
5. Both Bach and Beethoven were German composers.
6. All the leaves on our oak tree have already fallen.
7. I have grown too tall for these jeans.
8. Picnics have always been part of summer vacations.
9. A lightning bolt does not move at the speed of light.
10. Lee exercises, at one sport or another, about an hour each afternoon.

Adjectives and Adverbs

An adjective and an adverb have similar functions in a sentence. They both modify or describe other parts of speech. Adjectives and adverbs improve the style of sentences by adding vividness and exactness.

Adjectives

Rule 17f An adjective is a word that modifies a noun or a pronoun.

An adjective answers one of the following questions about a noun or a pronoun.

WHAT KIND?	**fresh** muffins	**plaid** shirt	
WHICH ONE(S)?	**red** pencil	**those** few	
HOW MANY?	**six** potatoes	**many** pages	
HOW MUCH?	**extensive** damage	**much** publicity	

An adjective may come in one of three places.

BEFORE A NOUN OR A PRONOUN	The **young, eager** reporter worked for the *Daily News*.
AFTER A NOUN OR A PRONOUN	The reporter, **young** and **eager,** worked for the *Daily News*.
AFTER A LINKING VERB	The reporter for the *Daily News* was **young** and **eager.**

Proper and Compound Adjectives

Proper and Compound Adjectives   Because a *proper adjective* is formed from a proper noun, it begins with a capital letter. A *compound adjective* is made up of more than one word. Since a compound adjective may be one word, a hyphenated word, or two or more separate words, check the dictionary for the correct form.

PROPER ADJECTIVES	**Roman** emperor	**Hawaiian** island
	French cuisine	**Shakespearean** play
COMPOUND ADJECTIVES	**seaworthy** vessel	**long-term** loan
	spellbound child	**two-piece** outfit
	high school student	**ice cube** tray

Note: The words *a, an,* and *the* form a special group of adjectives called *articles*. The article *a* comes before words that begin with a consonant sound, and *an* comes before words that begin with a vowel sound. You will not be asked to list articles in the exercises in this book.

Other Parts of Speech Used as Adjectives

Other Parts of Speech Used as Adjectives   Sometimes a word will be used as a noun in one sentence and as an adjective in another sentence.

NOUNS	flower, glass, refrigerator, cold
ADJECTIVES	**flower** garden, **glass** vase, **refrigerator** door, **cold** spell

The same word may also be a pronoun in one sentence and an adjective in another sentence. The words listed at the top of the next page are adjectives when they come in front of a noun or a pronoun and modify that noun or pronoun. They are pronouns when they stand alone.

Words Used as Pronouns or Adjectives			
DEMONSTRATIVE	**INTERROGATIVE**	**INDEFINITE**	
that	what	all	many
these	which	another	more
this		any	most
those		both	neither
		each	other
		either	several
		few	some

ADJECTIVE	**These** records must be yours.
PRONOUN	**These** must be yours.
ADJECTIVE	**Each** player was given a new uniform before the first game of the season.
PRONOUN	**Each** of the players was given a new uniform before the first game of the season.

Note: The possessive pronouns *my, your, his, her, its, our,* and *their* are sometimes called *pronominal adjectives* because they answer the adjective question *Which one(s)?* Throughout this book, however, these words will be considered pronouns.

EXERCISE ❽ *Finding Adjectives*

Number your paper 1 to 25. Then write the adjectives in the following paragraph.

The Eyes
Have It

    According to the ancient Greeks, eyes could reveal a personality. The Greeks compared the eyes of people to the eyes of various animals. Then they attributed the personality traits of those animals to people. Lion eyes, for example, are almondlike. In a person they signified a sense of fairness, a sense of justice, and leadership skills. Monkey eyes are small in relation to the face, but they have large irises. The Greeks thought that people with these eyes were unpredictable and shy. Elephant eyes are long and narrow with several folds of skin on the upper and lower eyelids. People with elephant eyes, it was believed, could handle difficult problems and solve them in a thoughtful, methodical manner. This unusual list of eye types also included the eyes of sheep, horses, wolves, hogs, snakes, and fish.

Adverbs

Rule 17g   An **adverb** is a word that modifies a verb, an adjective, or another adverb.

An adverb answers the question *Where? When? How?* or *To what extent?*

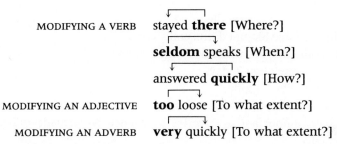

MODIFYING A VERB   stayed **there** [Where?]

seldom speaks [When?]

answered **quickly** [How?]

MODIFYING AN ADJECTIVE   **too** loose [To what extent?]

MODIFYING AN ADVERB   **very** quickly [To what extent?]

Note: Adverbs that describe verbs modify all parts of a verb phrase.

Occasionally we have met **here.**

Although many adverbs end in *-ly,* the following common adverbs do not end in *-ly: almost, also, always, here, just, later, never, not (n't), now, quite, rather, so, soon, then, too, very,* and *yet.* The words *when, where,* and *how* are also adverbs.

Note: Do not confuse an adverb that ends in *-ly* with an adjective that ends in *-ly.*

ADVERB   We meet **weekly** with her. [When?]

ADJECTIVE   That **weekly** magazine is available at any newsstand. [What kind?]

Nouns Used as Adverbs   The same word may be used as a noun in one sentence and an adverb in another sentence.

NOUN   **Tomorrow** is the day my braces will be removed.

ADVERB   I will see the dentist **tomorrow.** [When?]

NOUN   **Uptown** is a good location for the new vegetarian restaurant.

ADVERB   We will build the restaurant **uptown.** [Where?]

EXERCISE **9** *Finding Adverbs*

Number your paper 1 to 10. Write the adverbs in the following sentences. Then beside each one, write the word or words each adverb modifies. There are 20 adverbs.

 1. The playful porpoises will not swim away.
 2. Where and when did you meet him?
 3. The winner had run fast and steadily.
 4. I always drive very carefully.
 5. The zinnias have bloomed unusually early.
 6. That friendly dog is constantly wagging its tail.
 7. Don't make any plans today.
 8. Here I could live happily.
 9. I had an early appointment yesterday.
 10. Some very important discoveries in science were made quite accidentally.

EXERCISE **10** *Cumulative Review*

Number your paper 1 to 10. Make two columns on your paper. Label the first column *adjectives* and the second column *adverbs*. Then under the proper column, write each adjective and each adverb.

The Sand
Swimmer

 1. Southwest deserts appear totally empty of life.
 2. Many animals, birds, and insects survive very well in this barren land.
 3. An unusual denizen, or inhabitant, of these bleak areas is one type of lizard.
 4. This lizard can swiftly skim along the sandy surface and can easily burrow into the sand.
 5. You have probably watched swimmers at the ocean or a lake on a hot summer day.
 6. These bathers often run quickly to the water, dive in, and then disappear beneath the surface.
 7. In the same way, this lizard runs very fast, dives into the sand, and disappears without a trace.
 8. During the course of this swift run, the lizard may actually fly for a few seconds.
 9. The body of the lizard is perfectly suited for this incredible stunt.
 10. During the dive a group of scales cleverly protects the eyes of the lizard.

Other Parts of Speech

Prepositions, conjunctions, and interjections are the three remaining parts of speech. A *preposition* shows a relationship between words, a *conjunction* connects words or groups of words, and an *interjection* shows strong feeling or emotion.

Prepositions

Rule 17h A **preposition** is a word that shows the relationship between a noun or a pronoun and another word in the sentence.

In the following example, the words in heavy type are prepositions. Notice how the different prepositions change the relationship between the plant and the table.

The plant $\left\{\begin{array}{l}\textbf{on}\\ \textbf{beside}\\ \textbf{near}\end{array}\right.$ the table is a geranium.

Following is a list of common prepositions. Prepositions of two or more words are called *compound prepositions*.

Common Prepositions			
about	below	in front of	outside
above	beneath	in place of	over
according to	beside	inside	past
across	besides	in spite of	prior to
after	between	instead of	through
against	beyond	into	throughout
ahead of	by	in view of	to
along with	despite	like	toward
among	down	near	under
apart from	during	next to	underneath
around	except	of	until
aside from	for	off	up
at	from	on	upon
because of	in	on account of	with
before	in addition to	opposite	within
behind	in back of	out, out of	without

A preposition is always part of a group of words called a *prepositional phrase*. A prepositional phrase begins with a preposition and ends with a noun or a pronoun called the *object of a preposition*. One or more modifiers may come between the preposition and its object. The prepositional phrases in the following examples are in heavy type.

> **During English class** we watched a film **about Shakespeare.**

> **On account of the snowstorm,** traffic was snarled **throughout the city.**

Preposition or Adverb? The same word may be a preposition in one sentence and an adverb in another sentence. A word is a preposition if it is part of a prepositional phrase. An adverb stands alone.

PREPOSITION	I saw the cat *outside the house.*
ADVERB	I saw the cat **outside.**
PREPOSITION	Greg speaks well *before an audience.*
ADVERB	Have you heard this story **before?**

EXERCISE *Finding Prepositional Phrases*

Number your paper 1 to 20. Then write the prepositional phrases in the following paragraph.

The First Airmail Service   In a sense the French were the originators of airmail service. During the siege of Paris in the Franco-Prussian War of the 1870's, mail was sent from the capital by balloon, along with hundreds of homing pigeons. Return letters were photo-reduced on thin film, which held an average of 2,500 letters. Then pigeons delivered the letters to the capital. Approximately 300 pigeons carrying the mail were dispatched. Some of these got past the Prussian pigeon snipers. In Paris the messages were enlarged on a projection screen, copied by clerks, and delivered to addresses within the city.

EXERCISE *Writing Sentences*

Write two sentences for each word. The first sentence should use the word as a preposition, and the second sentence should use the word as an adverb.

1. around   **2.** below   **3.** near   **4.** by   **5.** down

Conjunctions and Interjections

Rule 17i   A **conjunction** connects words or groups of words.

Coordinating conjunctions are single connecting words, and *correlative conjunctions* are pairs of connecting words.

Conjunctions	
COORDINATING	**CORRELATIVE**
and nor yet but or for so	both/and not only/but also either/or whether/or neither/nor

Following are some uses of a conjunction.

> **Either** *write* her a note **or** *call* her. [connect verbs]
>
> That evergreen is *tall* **but** *full.* [connects adjectives]
>
> *I can't wait any longer,* **for** *I have an appointment.* [connects sentences]

Note: *Subordinating conjunctions are used to introduce adverb clauses. (See pages 612–613.)*

Rule 17j   An **interjection** is a word that expresses strong feeling or emotion.

Fear, anger, surprise, and happiness are just some of the emotions expressed by interjections. A comma or an exclamation point always separates an interjection from the rest of the sentence, depending on whether strong or mild feeling is being expressed.

> **Ouch!** Don't touch my sunburn.   **Yes,** I agree with you.

EXERCISE 13   *Finding Conjunctions and Interjections*

Number your paper 1 to 10. Then write the coordinating and correlative conjunctions and the interjections in the following sentences.

1. I can swim or float more easily in salt water than in fresh water.

2. Whew! I just finished a short but difficult exam.

3. Oliver Wendell Holmes, Sr., was both an author and a physician.

4. Gosh! I ate just an hour ago, yet I'm hungry now.

5. Slowly and carefully she began to open the box.

6. You'll find a pen either on the desk or in the top drawer.

7. Gertrude Stein encouraged not only young authors like Ernest Hemingway but also young painters like Picasso.

8. The beautiful cape was handwoven and made entirely of alpaca wool.

9. Mom rises early every morning, for she has to go to work.

10. Neither your clock nor my watch was correct.

EXERCISE **14** *Cumulative Review*

Number your paper 1 to 25. Write the numbered, underlined words in the following paragraphs. Then beside each one, write its part of speech: *noun, pronoun, verb, adjective, adverb, preposition, conjunction,* or *interjection.*

More for
Your Money

(1)Anyone who visits the Bureau of Engraving and Printing in (2)Washington can buy one hundred fifty dollars' worth of (3)United States currency (4)for seventy-five cents. (5)Oh, there (6)is a catch. The money is (7)real, (8)but it has been shredded. Every day the bureau shreds (9)tons (10)of new, misprinted (11)currency, stamps, (12)and (13)other items that are not fit for (14)circulation. (15)At the bureau's visitor center, machines (16)automatically dispense seventy-five-cent packets of shredded currency.

(17)Each of the 12 Federal Reserve district banks is also authorized to dispose of old, worn, (18)or soiled currency as (19)it sees fit. For the sum of (20)eighty-three dollars, the (21)Los Angeles branch will deliver an entire day's output—up to 5,550 pounds—to your door if (22)you live closer than the nearest dump. (23)Some of this currency (24)later (25)appears in novelty stores in one form or another.

Application to Writing

If you received a million dollars as an unexpected legacy, what would you do with the money? Brainstorm for a list of possibilities. Then arrange the items in that list from most important to least important. Finally, write a short essay explaining what you would do with the money and why you would use it this way.

Parts of Speech Review

Most creatures are born a certain color and remain that color throughout their entire lives. A chameleon, on the other hand, can instantly change its color to blend with its surroundings. Many words in English are something like chameleons. They can become different parts of speech, depending upon how they are used in different sentences. The word *last,* for example, can be used as four different parts of speech.

NOUN	The **last** of the guests has finally gone.
VERB	The heat spell will **last** two more days.
ADJECTIVE	The **last** bus to Chicago just left.
ADVERB	Our relay team finished **last.**

To find out what part of speech a word is, read the sentence carefully. Then ask yourself, *What is each word doing in this sentence?* The following summary of the eight parts of speech will help you determine how a word is used in a sentence.

NOUN   Is the word naming a person, place, thing, or idea?

The **friendship** between **Ramón** and my **brother** has lasted for 15 **years.**

PRONOUN   Is the word taking the place of a noun?

Everything they said to **you** is true.

VERB   Is the word either showing action or linking the subject with another word in the sentence?

I **read** the book. It **was** fascinating.

ADJECTIVE   Is the word modifying a noun or a pronoun? Does it answer the question *What kind? Which one(s)? How many?* or *How much?*

That soft, comfortable chair is very **old.**

ADVERB   Is the word modifying a verb, an adjective, or another adverb? Does it answer the question *How? When? Where?* or *To what extent?*

The leaves from that **rather** large oak tree are falling **very fast.**

PREPOSITION Is the word showing a relationship between a noun or a pronoun and another word in the sentence? Is it part of a phrase?

In spite of the rain, we walked **until** *dark.*

CONJUNCTION Is the word connecting words or groups of words?

See **either** Ben **or** Jason, **for** they are in charge of the refreshment committee.

INTERJECTION Is the word expressing strong feeling?

Hurrah! We won.

EXERCISE *Determining Parts of Speech*

Write the underlined word in each sentence. Then beside each one, write its part of speech: *noun, pronoun, verb, adjective, adverb, preposition, conjunction,* or *interjection.*

1. Where is the <u>stop</u> sign?
2. <u>Both</u> men saw the accident.
3. Come <u>over</u> this afternoon.
4. <u>Well</u>, that's a surprise.
5. Turn off that <u>loud</u> music!
6. <u>What</u> answer did you give?
7. Read the <u>rest</u> of the book.
8. Did he <u>stop</u> at the blinking light?
9. <u>Oh</u>! I forgot my lunch.
10. Don't drink the <u>well</u> water.
11. <u>What</u> is that?
12. You should <u>rest</u>.
13. Don't sing too <u>loud</u>.
14. <u>This</u> is your color.
15. <u>Both</u> are here.
16. Your <u>ring</u> is lovely.
17. Do you like <u>this</u> hat?
18. Can you jump <u>over</u> the fence?
19. He swims so <u>well</u>.
20. Did the phone <u>ring</u>?

EXERCISE *Identifying Parts of Speech*

Number your paper 1 to 20. Write each numbered, underlined word in the following paragraph. Beside each one write its part of speech: *noun, pronoun, verb, adjective, adverb, preposition,* or *conjunction.*

Adam Bede

Adam Bede, considered a (1)<u>masterpiece</u> by (2)<u>some</u>, was written (3)<u>by</u> George Eliot (4)<u>and</u> published in 1859. (5)<u>Today</u> this book (6)<u>is</u> (7)<u>still</u> (8)<u>one</u> of the (9)<u>most</u> (10)<u>widely</u> read (11)<u>Victorian</u> novels. Eliot's (12)<u>purpose</u> in telling (13)<u>this</u> story (14)<u>was</u> to show (15)<u>her</u> readers what (16)<u>ordinary</u> (17)<u>life</u> was like. The setting is (18)<u>not</u> any more colorful (19)<u>or</u> the characters any more heroic than readers of her day were likely to find (20)<u>in</u> their own experience.

USING YOUR TEXT

*Vivid Words
(55 – 61)
Creative Writing
(372 – 409)*

Grammar: Substituting Specific Words

Anyone who reads the sports pages knows that teams never *win*. They may *crush, stomp, trounce,* or *outclass*—but they never just *win*. Sportswriters use different words to avoid repetition. Follow the example of these writers and look for specific, lively substitutes for general, overused words.

	GENERAL	SPECIFIC, LIVELY
NOUN	accident	casualty, mishap, catastrophe
VERB	fall	sink, plummet, plunge, topple
ADJECTIVE	small	minuscule, trivial, minute, tiny

Checking Your Understanding Write at least two fresh alternates for each of the following words. Then write sentences that use two of the livelier words from each column. If possible, use a thesaurus or the dictionary.

NOUNS	VERBS	ADJECTIVES
1. boss	**1.** run	**1.** lively
2. friend	**2.** smell	**2.** slow
3. meal	**3.** rush	**3.** brave
4. ditch	**4.** demand	**4.** eager
5. top	**5.** give	**5.** fancy

Writing a Narrative Imagine that a heavy mist settles over you for a moment and then passes. Suddenly you begin to shrink. . . Write freely for several minutes, jotting down all the things that may happen next. Be as creative as you can. When you have finished, choose the most interesting ideas you have and arrange them in a chronological sequence. Then write the first draft of a narrative in which you explain what happened after you began to shrink. Write your narrative from a first-person point of view. *(See pages 381–395.)* **Application:** As you revise your draft, replace any general words with specific, lively alternatives. If possible, use a thesaurus or the dictionary to help you find substitutes for any overused words. Then edit your narrative and write a neat final copy.

17 Review

A Determining Parts of Speech

Number your paper 1 to 20. Then write the underlined word in each sentence. Beside each word, label its part of speech, using the following abbreviations.

noun = *n.*   adjective = *adj.*   conjunction = *conj.*
pronoun = *pron.*   adverb = *adv.*   interjection = *interj.*
verb = *v.*   preposition = *prep.*

1. It was very cold <u>outside</u> last night.
2. Did she buy a new <u>iron</u>?
3. <u>Oh</u>! We ran out of tape.
4. Look on the <u>top</u> shelf.
5. The picture fell <u>suddenly</u>.
6. They're in <u>that</u> box.
7. That's a new <u>stop</u> sign.
8. The <u>top</u> of the mountain was covered with snow.
9. <u>Those</u> tomatoes are ripe.
10. Don't run <u>down</u> the hill.
11. He owns the <u>fish</u> market on May Road.
12. What on earth is <u>that</u>?
13. He is <u>in</u> the store.
14. Come <u>in</u>.
15. I usually <u>fish</u> there.
16. Did you <u>iron</u> it?
17. I caught three <u>fish</u>.
18. It was cold <u>outside</u> the house.
19. <u>Those</u> are mine.
20. I can't <u>stop</u> this.

B Identifying Parts of Speech

Number your paper 1 to 20. Write each numbered, underlined word in the following paragraph. Then beside each one, write its part of speech, using the abbreviations in Part A.

Adam Bede, which takes place in the early nineteenth (1)<u>century,</u> (2)<u>chronicles</u> the lives of (3)<u>several</u> people who live in a small village. (4)<u>Readers</u> witness the intertwining (5)<u>of</u> these stories (6)<u>and</u> can eavesdrop on the characters as (7)<u>they</u> make fateful decisions. These choices, of course, (8)<u>drastically</u> change the course of their lives. The two central characters (9)<u>are</u> Adam Bede, a local carpenter, and Dinah Morris, a (10)<u>Methodist</u> preacher and missionary. Having suffered bitter (11)<u>disappointment</u> in an (12)<u>early</u> (13)<u>love</u> affair, Adam is (14)<u>cautious</u> during (15)<u>his</u> initial meetings (16)<u>with</u> Dinah. Though attracted to Adam, Dinah cannot reconcile (17)<u>her</u> religious calling with her love (18)<u>for</u> him. (19)<u>Both</u> struggle as they search for (20)<u>happiness.</u>

C   Determining Parts of Speech   Copy the following sentences, skipping a line after each one. Then above each word, label its part of speech, using the abbreviations in Part A. Remember that articles are adjectives.

EXAMPLE   Soccer matches usually last for ninety minutes.

                      adj.   n.   adv.   v. prep. adj.   n.
ANSWER   Soccer matches usually last for ninety minutes.

1. Houston is one of the largest cities in Texas.
2. My uncle will visit us today.
3. Have you ever been to Gettysburg?
4. Eighteen holes are played in a round of golf.
5. The history test was rather long and difficult.
6. Rome was originally built on seven hills.
7. Anyone can attend the meeting, but the room holds only 60 people.
8. The diameter of a basketball hoop is 18 inches.
9. Wow! Did you see that long, high drive down the field?
10. The third Sunday in June is Father's Day.

Mastery Test

Number your paper 1 to 10. Write the underlined words in each sentence. Then beside each one, write its part of speech: *noun, pronoun, verb, adjective, adverb, preposition, conjunction,* or *interjection.*

1. The mudskipper, an <u>African</u> fish, can <u>actually</u> skip along the ground outside the water.
2. <u>Many</u> people have asked for reservations on the first commercial flight into <u>space</u>.
3. The <u>excitement</u> <u>of</u> the crowd lining the streets downtown was contagious.
4. The pan on the stove <u>is</u> <u>very</u> hot.
5. <u>When</u> do wisdom teeth <u>usually</u> appear?
6. <u>I</u> couldn't do without my old <u>but</u> comfortable shoes.
7. We need a <u>space</u> divider <u>between</u> the two offices.
8. <u>Oh!</u> You just dropped <u>something</u> on the stairs.
9. Don't give <u>me</u> that <u>many</u>!
10. <u>What</u> are you going to do with all <u>these</u> coins?

18 The Sentence Base

Diagnostic Test

Number your paper 1 to 10. Write the subject, the verb, and the underlined complement in each sentence. (A subject or a verb may be compound.) Then label each complement, using the following abbreviations.

direct object = *d.o.*   predicate nominative = *p.n.*
indirect object = *i.o.*   predicate adjective = *p.a.*
objective complement = *o.c.*

EXAMPLE   Nelson threw a 60-yard <u>pass</u> for a touchdown.
ANSWER   Nelson, threw   pass—d.o.

1. The United States produces approximately 62 billion <u>cans</u> a year.
2. *Newsweek* has become my favorite <u>magazine</u>.
3. The wind rattled the windows and swirled <u>leaves</u> along the streets.
4. Several test scores were remarkably <u>high</u>.
5. Jamie built <u>me</u> a cabinet for my tapes and VCR.
6. We will paint the walls in this room light <u>yellow</u>.
7. A house in the city is quite <u>safe</u> from lightning.
8. Marcy sent <u>us</u> an announcement of her graduation.
9. Canada and the United States share the longest unguarded <u>border</u> in the world.
10. Is Jonathan the <u>one</u> in the middle?

Subjects and Predicates

A well-constructed house has a foundation, which basically holds all the other parts of the house together. Like a house a sentence must also have a foundation. The foundation, or *sentence base*, of a sentence is composed of a subject, a verb, and sometimes a complement. It is to this foundation that all other words in the sentence are added.

Rule 18a   A **sentence** is a group of words that expresses a complete thought.

A group of words that does not express a complete thought is called a *fragment*. In many cases a group of words is a fragment because it does not have a subject or a predicate. *(See pages 631–635 for more information about fragments.)*

FRAGMENT	SENTENCE
Under the mat.	**The house key is** under the mat.
To get a job.	**I want** to get a job.

To express a complete thought, a group of words must have both a subject and a predicate.

Rule 18b   A sentence has two main parts: a **subject** and a **predicate**. A *subject* names the person, place, thing, or idea the sentence is about. The *predicate* tells something about the subject.

COMPLETE SUBJECT	COMPLETE PREDICATE
My aunt from Alabama	is living in Alaska now.
The box on the counter	contains coupons for the store.
Hailstones	fell for ten minutes today.

Simple Subjects and Predicates

Each complete subject and predicate can usually be narrowed down to a single word or phrase.

Rule 18c   A **simple subject** is the main word in the complete subject.

Rule 18d   A **simple predicate,** or **verb,** is the main word or phrase in the complete predicate.

In the following examples, the simple subjects and the verbs are in heavy type.

```
┌── complete subject ──┐ ┌────── complete predicate ──────┐
```
The narrow dirt **road took** a sudden turn into a clearing.

```
┌── complete subject ──┐ ┌──── complete predicate ────┐
```
Two valuable **reporters** recently **resigned** from the *Chronicle*.

```
┌────── complete subject ──────┐ ┌── complete predicate ──┐
```
Memorial Hospital in Acton **is raising** money for a new wing.

In the last example, *Memorial Hospital* is a single proper noun; therefore, both words make up the simple subject. Notice also that the verb phrase *is raising* is considered the verb of the sentence. *(See pages 545–546 for more information about verb phrases.)*

Note: Throughout the rest of this book, the term *subject* will refer to a simple subject, and the term *verb* will refer to a simple predicate, which may be a single verb or a verb phrase.

Finding Subjects and Verbs   To find the subject of an action verb, ask yourself *Who?* or *What?* before the verb. The answer to either question will be the subject of the sentence. In the following examples, each subject is underlined once, and each verb is underlined twice.

Mandy has taken French for two years. [The action verb is *has taken*. Who has taken? The subject is *Mandy.*]

His temperature is rising rapidly. [The action verb is *is rising*. What is rising? The subject is *temperature.*]

To find the subject of a linking verb, ask yourself, *About whom or what is the statement being made?* When you have answered that question, you will have identified the subject. *(See pages 543–544 for lists of linking verbs.)*

My brother is a freshman at Colorado College. [The linking verb is *is*. About whom is the statement being made? The subject is *brother.*]

The velvet jacket feels exceptionally soft. [The linking verb is *feels*. About what is the statement being made? The subject is *jacket.*]

Note: When you look for a subject and a verb, it is often helpful to eliminate all modifiers and prepositional phrases from the sentence. *A subject is never part of a prepositional phrase. (See page 585 for more information about prepositional phrases.)*

~~Numerous~~ masterpieces ~~by Michelangelo~~ are located ~~throughout Florence~~. [*Masterpieces* is the subject; *are located* is the verb.]

EXERCISE *Finding Subjects and Verbs*

Number your paper 1 to 10. Then write the subject and the verb in each sentence.

Will's Will
1. William Shakespeare lived from 1564 to 1616.
2. At his death this famous playwright left a most unusual will.
3. Considerable real-estate holdings in and near Stratford went to his two daughters, Susanna and Judith.
4. Shakespeare did, however, make some curious bequests.
5. The following line from his will is still confusing many historians.
6. "I give unto my Wiffe my 2nd-best bed with the furniture."
7. He apparently had just scribbled these words into the will as an additional note.
8. His will also never mentions his plays.
9. This omission has raised serious doubts in some historians' minds.
10. The writer of this will may not have been the author of the Elizabethan dramas.

Compound Subjects and Verbs A sentence can have more than one subject and more than one verb.

Rule 18e **A compound subject** is two or more subjects in one sentence that have the same verb and are joined by a conjunction.

Use the method in the "Finding Subjects and Verbs" section on page 562 to find a compound subject.

The <u>hamburgers</u> and <u>corn</u> <u>tasted</u> delicious.

<u>Maria</u>, <u>Barry</u>, and <u>Martin</u> <u>attended</u> the meeting.

Rule 18f   A **compound verb** is two or more verbs that have the same subject and are joined by a conjunction.

<u>You</u> <u>can join</u> the swim team or <u>sing</u> in the school chorus.

A <u>diamond</u> <u>will cut</u> all other substances and <u>will resist</u> even the strongest acids.

A sentence can have both a compound subject and a compound verb.

<u>Paul</u> and his <u>sister</u> <u>fed</u> the horses and <u>cleaned</u> the stable.

EXERCISE *Finding Subjects and Verbs*

Number your paper 1 to 20. Then write the subjects and the verbs in the following sentences.

Hunting for
Buried
Treasure

1. For centuries the *Atocha*, with tons of gold and silver, lay on the bottom of the sea and tempted treasure hunters.
2. In 1622, the ship was bound for Spain but during a hurricane sank in the waters off the Florida coast.
3. Because of a second hurricane, other vessels could not rescue the *Atocha's* treasure.
4. The position of the ship either was never recorded or was finally forgotten.
5. Eventually ocean currents covered the ship with sand.
6. The legend of the *Atocha* and the promise of great wealth brought many treasure hunters to Florida.
7. Mel Fisher and his family joined the others and became full-time treasure hunters.
8. Mel had once run a chicken farm and then had operated a diving shop.
9. He had some original ideas about the possible location of the ship and used clever techniques in the search.
10. Mel and members of his family continued their search in the face of many hardships and much scorn.
11. Critics constantly laughed at their efforts.
12. Finally, in June 1975, Fisher's crew found a cannon from the *Atocha* and silenced the critics.
13. The joy of the Fisher party was intense but soon ended because of a tragedy.
14. On the night of July 18, 1975, Fisher's son, his daughter-in-law, and another diver drowned.

15. Mel and his wife did not stop their work.
16. The tragedies would then have been meaningless.
17. They continued and salvaged more and more objects.
18. They could not keep all of the treasure.
19. The state of Florida claimed a portion of the treasure and held much of it for a long period of time.
20. Perhaps some day you will see some of the *Atocha*'s treasures in a museum.

Position of Subjects

When a sentence is in its natural order, the subject comes before the verb. For various reasons a sentence may also be written in *inverted order,* with the verb or part of the verb phrase coming before the subject. Subjects in inverted order are sometimes more difficult to find.

Questions   Questions are often phrased in inverted order. To find the subject and the verb in a question, turn the question around to make a statement.

QUESTION   Have you seen Luis tonight?
STATEMENT   You have seen Luis tonight.

There and **Here**   A sentence beginning with *there* or *here* is always in inverted order. To find the subject and the verb, place the words in the sentence in their natural order. Sometimes the word *there* or *here* must be dropped before the sentence can be put in its natural order.

INVERTED ORDER   Here is an extra sock.
NATURAL ORDER   An extra sock is here.

INVERTED ORDER   There will be a test given on Friday.
NATURAL ORDER   A test will be given on Friday. [Drop *there*.]

Emphasis or Variety   To create emphasis or variety, you may sometimes deliberately write a sentence in inverted order. To determine the subject and the verb, put the sentence in its natural order.

INVERTED ORDER   Across the snow lay the black shadows of tree trunks.
NATURAL ORDER   The black shadows of tree trunks lay across the snow.

Understood *You*   The subject of most commands and requests is the pronoun *you*. Although *you* seldom appears in such sentences, it is still understood to be there. In the following examples, *you* is the understood subject of each sentence.

Set the alarm for six. [*You* is the understood subject.]

Cathy, call Luis now. [*You* is the understood subject—even though the person receiving the command is named.]

EXERCISE ◀ 3 ▶ *Finding Subjects and Verbs in Inverted Sentences*

Number your paper 1 to 15. Then write the subject and the verb in each sentence. If the subject is an understood *you,* write it in parentheses.

1. There are no snakes in New Zealand or in Ireland.
2. Look at this advertisement in the Sunday paper for free compact discs!
3. What kind of special equipment does a well-prepared scuba diver need?
4. Over the heads of the crowd soared the Blue Angels in perfect formation.
5. Here are the names of the five finalists in the high school art show.
6. Have you ever angled for brook trout?
7. Wanda, please hand me that handmade pot holder on the kitchen counter.
8. Around medieval castles there was usually a moat for defense purposes.
9. When will the county fair open this year?
10. Across Virginia, from the northeast to the southwest, stretch the beautiful Blue Ridge Mountains.
11. How tall do giraffes usually grow?
12. There is an excellent whale and dolphin show at Sea World in Orlando, Florida.
13. From the oven on Thanksgiving morning came the delicious aroma of turkey.
14. Do wait for us at the airport for at least half an hour.
15. Here is a list of the exotic fruits and vegetables at a nearby gourmet-foods store.

EXERCISE ◆4◆ *Cumulative Review*

Number your paper 1 to 15. Then write the subjects and the verbs in the following sentences.

Bits about
the Body

1. The average three-pound human brain is very complex.
2. During the first six months of a baby's life, the brain doubles in size.
3. Each second the brain receives and translates 100 million nerve messages from your body.
4. With increased age men and women hear fewer high-pitched sounds.
5. The human eye can discriminate among several million gradations of color.
6. At sea level there are 2,000 pounds of air pressure on each square foot of your body.
7. The nose, the windpipe, and the lungs form the respiratory system.
8. The respiratory system provides the body with oxygen and rids the body of carbon dioxide.
9. The nose cleans, warms, and humidifies over 500 cubic feet of air every day.
10. In the lungs there are millions of tiny air sacs.
11. During a lifetime an average person could consume about 60,000 pounds of food, a weight equivalent to that of six elephants.
12. Nerve signals may travel through nerve or muscle fibers at speeds up to 200 miles per hour.
13. Most heat from the body escapes through the head.
14. There are 9,000 taste buds on a person's tongue.
15. Through your circulatory system flow 680,000 gallons of blood a year.

Application to Writing

Choose one system of the body—such as the respiratory system, the circulatory system, or the central nervous system—and write a short expository essay about some aspect of it. (You may first want to do some research in the library.) The main point of your essay should be the remarkable functions that system has. As you edit, make sure each sentence has a subject and a verb.

USING YOUR TEXT

Letters (412 – 429)
Subject and Verb
Agreement
(694 – 713)

Grammar: Combining Sentences

Combining sentences that have the same subject but different verbs or the same verb but different subjects prevents needless repetition in your writing.

TWO SENTENCES	Before the Constitution each <u>state</u> <u>coined</u> money. Some private <u>citizens</u> also <u>coined</u> money.
ONE SENTENCE WITH A COMPOUND SUBJECT	Before the Constitution each <u>state</u> and some private <u>citizens</u> <u>coined</u> money.
TWO SENTENCES	The <u>government</u> now <u>coins</u> money. The <u>government</u> also <u>regulates</u> its value.
ONE SENTENCE WITH A COMPOUND VERB	The <u>government</u> now <u>coins</u> money and <u>regulates</u> its value.

Checking Your Understanding Combine each pair of sentences into one sentence with a compound subject or a compound verb, using *and* or *but*.

Minting
Coins

1. Many coins are minted each year. They are then put into circulation.
2. From time to time, certain coins are needed in a hurry. They are produced under an emergency schedule.
3. A new sales tax may create a sudden demand for a particular coin. A change in bus fares may also create a demand.
4. Pennies are always in demand. Dimes are also very popular.
5. Quarters represent a relatively small percentage of the total production of coins. So do half-dollars.

Writing a Letter Choose the one place in the world you would most like to go to for a vacation. Then write the first draft of a letter to the tourist bureau of that place, stating the reasons for your interest and then asking for further information. *(Follow the form for a business letter on page 414.)* **Application:** As you revise, combine short sentences wherever possible. Then make a final copy and send your letter.

Complements

Sometimes a sentence needs more than a subject and a verb to sound complete. Such a sentence also needs a completer, or *complement*. None of the following sentences, for example, would be complete without the complements in heavy type.

Todd made **breakfast.**   Kate has become a **painter.**
Dan gave **me** a **key.**   Our car is **old.**

There are five kinds of complements. *Direct objects, indirect objects,* and *objective complements* complete the meaning of action verbs. *Predicate nominatives* and *predicate adjectives,* which are called *subject complements,* complete the meaning of linking verbs.

Direct Objects and Indirect Objects

Rule 18g A **direct object** is a noun or a pronoun that receives the action of the verb.

To find a direct object, ask yourself *What?* or *Whom?* after an action verb. Notice in the third example below that a direct object can be compound.

d.o.
Leo removed the **lint** from his suit. [Leo removed what? *Lint* is the direct object.]

d.o.
I drove **Heather** to school. [I drove whom? *Heather* is the direct object.]

d.o.   d.o.
Earl makes leather **belts** and **wallets.** [Earl makes what? *Belts* and *wallets* make up the compound direct object.]

Each part of a compound action verb can have its own direct object.

d.o.   d.o.
Larry focused his **camera** and snapped the **picture.** [*Camera* is the direct object of *focused,* and *picture* is the direct object of *snapped.*]

If a sentence has a direct object, the same sentence may also have an indirect object.

Rule 18h An **indirect object** answers the question *To or for whom?* or *To or for what?* after an action verb.

To find an indirect object, first find the direct object by asking *What?* or *Whom?* after the action verb. Then ask *To or for whom?* or *To or for what?* after the direct object. An indirect object always comes before a direct object in a sentence.

 i.o.   d.o.
I bought **Paul** a new catcher's mitt.
[*Mitt* is the direct object of the verb *bought.* I bought a mitt for whom? *Paul* is the indirect object. Notice that the indirect object comes before the direct object.]

                     i.o.   ┌─d.o.─┐
The coach gave the **team** a pep talk.
[*Pep talk* is the direct object of the verb *gave.* The coach gave a pep talk to whom? *Team* is the indirect object. Notice that the indirect object comes before the direct object.]

As you study the following example, notice that an indirect object may be compound.

              i.o.   i.o.   d.o.
Pepita is teaching **Lee** and **Kelly** Spanish.
[*Spanish* is the direct object of the verb *is teaching.* Pepita is teaching Spanish to whom? *Lee* and *Kelly* make up the compound indirect object.]

Note: Neither a direct object nor an indirect object is ever part of a prepositional phrase. *(See pages 585 and 552 for more information about prepositional phrases.)*

            i.o.   d.o.
We gave **Roger** an album for his birthday.
[*Roger* is the indirect object. It comes before the direct object *album* and is not part of a prepositional phrase.]

                  d.o.
We gave an album to Roger for his birthday.
[In this sentence *Roger* is *not* the indirect object, because it follows the direct object *album* and is the object of the preposition *to.*]

EXERCISE *Finding Indirect Objects and Direct Objects*

Number your paper 1 to 20. Write the indirect objects and the direct objects in the following sentences. Then label each one *indirect object* or *direct object*.

1. Some centipedes have 31 to 180 pairs of legs.
2. The hyena has powerful jaws and long forelegs.
3. Mr. Roland showed Martin and me the difference between wheat and oats.
4. Lloyd sent my cousin a record of Portuguese folk songs.
5. Yesterday Jessie gave the dogs a bath.
6. Show Angie and Peter your pictures from the dance.
7. Give that book to Howard this afternoon.
8. Robert Louis Stevenson first dreamed the plot of *Dr. Jekyll and Mr. Hyde* and then wrote it.
9. Our neighbors brought us a spaghetti dinner and an apple pie.
10. The pianist acknowledged the applause but did not give the audience an encore.
11. Which computer do you recommend for me?
12. Mr. Tanner sprayed our fruit trees from the helicopter.
13. Will you give the desk a second coat of paint?
14. Tell Craig the joke about the elephant.
15. In 1883, Buffalo Bill organized his famous Wild West show.
16. Did you set the alarm for six o'clock?
17. During homeroom Amy will show us the yearbook.
18. A hummingbird usually lays two eggs during the nesting period.
19. Did you buy Mittens some catnip?
20. Emotional strain may cause an increase in blood pressure.

Objective Complements

Rule 18i   An **objective complement** is a noun or an adjective that renames or describes the direct object.

To find an objective complement, first find the direct object. Then ask the question *What?* after the direct object. An objective complement will always follow the direct object. Notice the compound objective complement in the third example on the next page.

The team chose Calvin **captain.** [*Calvin* is the direct object. The team chose Calvin what? *Captain* is the objective complement. It follows the direct object and renames it.]

We consider our parakeet the perfect **pet** for any family. [*Parakeet* is the direct object. We consider our parakeet what? *Pet* is the objective complement. It follows the direct object and renames it.]

The award made Juanita **happy** and **proud.** [*Juanita* is the direct object. The award made Juanita what? The words *happy* and *proud* make up the compound objective complement. These words follow the direct object and describe it.]

EXERCISE *Finding Complements*

Number your paper 1 to 15. Write each complement in the following sentences. Then label each one *direct object, indirect object,* or *objective complement.*

 1. Chlorophyll makes grass green.
 2. Wish me luck in the swim meet.
 3. Have you already given the two cats their dinners?
 4. Nancy recently did a favor for Mrs. Ellis.
 5. In most urban areas, buses have made trolleys obsolete.
 6. Did Leroy ever show you his new watch?
 7. Dad built the bookcase tall and narrow.
 8. Some people once actually raised spiders and sold the silk.
 9. The lack of trail markers made me unsure of the way out of the woods.
10. The judges declared Sebastian the winner.
11. The American people elected Franklin Delano Roosevelt president four times.
12. Carolyn took our ripest tomatoes to the people next door.
13. More and better insulation in the attic will undoubtedly make the house warmer.
14. The uniformed doorman at the hotel called us a cab for the trip to the airport.
15. Bring a towel with you.

Subject Complements

Two kinds of complements, called *subject complements,* complete the meaning of linking verbs. *(See pages 543–544 for lists of linking verbs.)*

Rule 18j   **A predicate nominative** is a noun or a pronoun that follows a linking verb and identifies, renames, or explains the subject.

To find a predicate nominative, first find the subject and the linking verb. Then find the noun or the pronoun that follows the verb and identifies, renames, or explains the subject. Notice in the second example that a predicate nominative can be compound.

p.n.
Bart will become a **mechanic**. [mechanic = Bart]

p.n.———p.n.
The winners of the scholarships are **Bryan** and **Julie**. [Bryan and Julie = winners]

Like the other complements, a predicate nominative is never part of a prepositional phrase.

p.n.
Pamela is **one** of the tellers at the First National Bank. [*One* is the predicate nominative. *Tellers* is the object of the preposition *of.*]

The other subject complement is a predicate adjective.

Rule 18k   **A predicate adjective** is an adjective that follows a linking verb and modifies the subject.

To find a predicate adjective, first find the subject and the linking verb. Then find an adjective that follows the verb and modifies, or describes, the subject. Notice in the second example that a predicate adjective can be compound.

p.a.
That movie was **weird**. [*Weird* describes the subject: *the weird movie.*]

p.a.———p.a.
The clothes smelled **clean** and **fresh**. [*Clean* and *fresh* describe the subject: clean, fresh clothes.]

Note: Remember that a predicate adjective *follows* a linking verb and modifies, or describes, the subject. Do not confuse a predicate adjective with a regular adjective.

PREDICATE ADJECTIVE Carlos is **brilliant.** [*Brilliant* describes the subject *Carlos.*]

REGULAR ADJECTIVE Carlos is a **brilliant** student. [*Brilliant* describes the word *student.*]

EXERCISE *Finding Subject Complements*

Number your paper 1 to 20. Write each subject complement in the following sentences. Then label each one *predicate nominative* or *predicate adjective.*

1. Benjamin Franklin was the inventor of bifocals.
2. The sting of the Portuguese man-of-war is always serious and sometimes fatal.
3. That's he over there with the blue baseball cap.
4. Nitrogen is the main component of air.
5. Hot apple cider tastes good on a cold afternoon.
6. Some of the products of the peanut are margarine, soap, and cosmetics.
7. Was Davy Crockett one of the defenders of the Alamo?
8. The chili tastes particularly spicy.
9. Mrs. Hanover is a tireless and unselfish person.
10. My favorite colors have always been blue and purple.
11. Air masses from Canada are often cold and dry.
12. The shore of Crater Lake in Oregon is the rim of an extinct volcano.
13. With a yearly average of less than 20 inches of rainfall, Australia is the world's driest continent.
14. The winners of the door prize were she and Lisa.
15. Heather is scared but optimistic about the test.
16. After graduation my sister became a newspaper writer for the *Regional Review.*
17. The mushroom is actually a type of fungus.
18. At the end of our hike through the White Mountains, we were tired and hungry.
19. Hydrogen is the most abundant element in the universe.
20. Maria was tired after jogging three miles.

EXERCISE ◆8◆ *Cumulative Review*

Number your paper 1 to 20. Write each complement. Then label each one, using the following abbreviations.

direct object = *d.o.*   predicate nominative = *p.n.*
indirect object = *i.o.*   predicate adjective = *p.a.*
objective complement = *o.c.*

 1. Your body makes approximately one and a half million blood cells every second.
 2. Before 8:30 A.M., the large lounge in the east wing is open to all students.
 3. George Washington appointed John Jay Chief Justice of the United States.
 4. Lloyd became enthusiastic about speaking in the debate.
 5. Ms. Williams gave the class a list of research topics.
 6. Leslie can swim 50 laps in 20 minutes.
 7. Birds' feathers are actually a kind of scale, like the scales of reptiles.
 8. The students elected Melissa president of the class with more than 86 percent of the vote.
 9. The typical American black bear can be black, white, brown, or gray-blue.
10. On February 20, 1962, John Glenn orbited the earth in the spacecraft *Friendship 7*.
11. Advertising agencies have given the English language many new words, such as *glamorize* and *personalize*.
12. The original color of that old colonial house was red.
13. Last night I reread my journal.
14. Some respected nutritionists consider vitamin C an effective cold preventive.
15. Our apartment is very close to public transportation.
16. Early in his junior year, Tomás became captain of the high school lacross team.
17. Henry Perkey of Denver, Colorado, and William Ford of Watertown, New York, gave consumers their first breakfast cereal in 1893.
18. Some icebergs appear blue or green in the sun.
19. For her birthday we gave Marcy a box of stationery and an album for her photographs.
20. The two longest rivers on the earth are the Amazon and the Nile.

USING YOUR TEXT

Expository
Paragraphs
114–120

Grammar: Using Sentence Patterns

Each sentence you write seems unique—like the patterns and shapes of snowflakes. Looking more closely at the sentences you write, however, you will see that each falls into one of six basic sentence patterns. You can vary your writing style by expanding these basic sentence patterns. They can be expanded by adding modifiers, appositives, prepositional phrases, and verbal phrases. Any of these patterns can also be expanded by making the subject, the verb, or any of the complements compound. In this way you create many variations within a particular pattern itself.

PATTERN 1: S-V (subject-verb)

S   V
Cattle graze.

S   V
Cattle belonging to Matt always graze in the far pasture.
|_____||_____|

PATTERN 2: S-V-O (subject-verb-direct object)

S   V   O
Girls swam laps.

        S   V   O
The girls on the swim team effortlessly swam many laps.
|_____||_____||_____|

PATTERN 3: S-V-I-O (subject-verb-indirect object-direct object)

S   V   I   O
Todd sent me tickets.

S   V   I   O
Todd unexpectedly sent me tickets to the Ice Capades.
|__||_____||__||_____|

PATTERN 4: S-V-N (subject-verb-predicate nominative)

S   V   N
Campers are hikers.

        S   V   N
Many campers in this group are enthusiastic hikers.
|_____||__||_____|

PATTERN 5: S-V-A (subject-verb-predicate adjective)

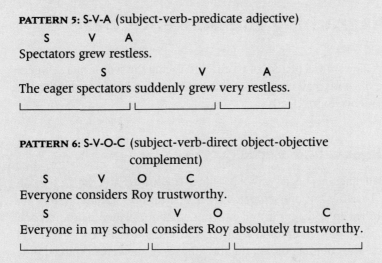

S   V   A

Spectators grew restless.

S   V   A

The eager spectators suddenly grew very restless.

PATTERN 6: S-V-O-C (subject-verb-direct object-objective
complement)

S   V   O   C

Everyone considers Roy trustworthy.

S   V   O   C

Everyone in my school considers Roy absolutely trustworthy.

Checking Your Understanding   Number your paper 1 to 5. Then write the sentence pattern that each sentence follows.

1. Freshly cut hay always smells clean and sweet.
2. Many historians consider Harriet Tubman a major personality in United States history.
3. The coach of the field hockey team gave each member a certificate of achievement.
4. Fallen meteors have been discovered by scientists in various parts of the world.
5. The correct answer to the question is the last one.

Writing an Expository Paragraph   Have you ever wondered how food is canned—or how the Olympics were started—or how the ancient Egyptians built the pyramids? Brainstorm for a list of questions you would like answered. Then choose the one question you are most curious about. Research the answer in reference books at school or at the library. Take notes on the information you find that will answer your question. After taking notes, organize your details in a logical order.

Write a topic sentence for your paragraph. Then write the first draft of an expository paragraph that answers the *How?* question you chose. *Application:* As you revise and edit your paragraph, make certain it includes a variety of sentence patterns. Then write a final copy.

Diagraming the Sentence Base

A *diagram* is a picture of words. By placing the words of a sentence in a diagram, you can often see the relationship between the parts of a sentence more clearly.

Subjects and Verbs

All diagrams begin with a baseline. The subject and the verb go on the baseline but are separated by a vertical line. Capital letters are included in a diagram, but not punctuation. Notice in the second diagram how compound subjects and verbs are placed on parallel lines. The conjunction joining the subjects or the verbs is placed on a broken line between them.

He is working.

He	is working

Lupe and Carl both sang and danced.

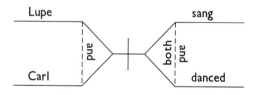

Inverted Order and Understood Subjects An inverted sentence is diagramed like a sentence in natural order. The understood subject *you* is diagramed in the subject position with parentheses around it.

Have you eaten?

you	Have eaten

Listen!

(you)	Listen

Adjectives and Adverbs

Adjectives and adverbs are connected by a slanted line to the words they modify. Notice that a conjunction joining two modifiers is placed on a broken line between them. Notice, too, how an adverb that describes another adverb is written parallel to the word it modifies.

Her small but valuable diamond sparkles quite brilliantly.

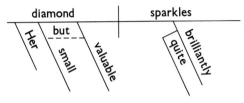

Note: Possessive pronouns, such as *her* in the example above, are diagramed like adjectives.

Complements

All complements except the indirect object are diagramed on the baseline with the subject and the verb.

Direct Objects   A short vertical line separates a direct object from the verb. Notice in the second example that the parts of a compound direct object are placed on parallel lines. The conjunction is placed on a broken line.

I have already seen that movie.

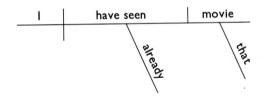

Buy four oranges and six bananas.

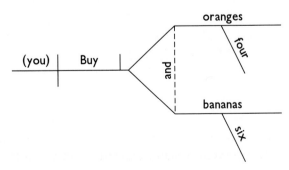

Indirect Objects   An indirect object is diagramed on a horizontal line that is connected to the verb by a slanted line. Notice in the second example that the parts of a compound indirect object are diagramed on horizontal parallel lines. The conjunction is placed on a broken line between them.

Send them an invitation.

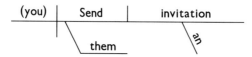

Aunt May bought David and me identical sweaters.

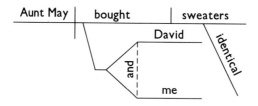

Objective Complements   Since an objective complement renames or describes the direct object, it is placed to the right of the direct object on the baseline. A slanted line that points toward the direct object separates the two complements. Notice in the second example that a compound objective complement is placed on horizontal parallel lines. The conjunction is placed on a broken line between them.

We named our dog King.

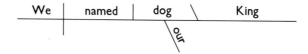

Mom will paint the kitchen yellow or green.

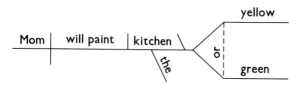

Subject Complements   A predicate nominative and a predicate adjective are diagramed in exactly the same way. They are placed on the baseline after the verb. A slanted line that points back toward the subject separates a subject complement from the verb. Notice in the second example that a compound subject complement is placed on horizontal parallel lines. The conjunction is placed on a broken line between them.

This camera was a birthday present.

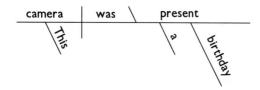

This lecture was not only interesting but also informative.

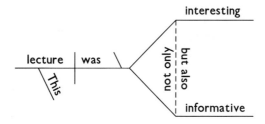

EXERCISE *Diagraming Sentences*

Diagram the following sentences or copy them. If you copy them, draw one line under each subject and two lines under each verb. Then label each complement, using the following abbreviations.

direct object = *d.o.*   predicate nominative = *p.n.*
indirect object = *i.o.*   predicate adjective = *p.a.*
objective complement = *o.c.*

1. Our newspaper subcription should have been canceled.
2. Did you find your coat and his scarf?
3. Michael gave the officer his name.
4. Charlene became a new member yesterday.
5. The weather has been cold and dreary.
6. Read this short but humorous article.
7. The club named Paul chairman.
8. Very quietly the snake slithered away.
9. The lonely guard walked back and forth.
10. Stacy and Rico swam and floated.

18 Review

A **Finding Subjects and Verbs** Number your paper 1 to 20. Write the subjects and the verbs in the following sentences. If the subject is an understood *you,* write it in parentheses.

1. The giant tortoise of the Galápagos Islands may weigh as much as 500 pounds and may live up to 150 ycars.
2. In Spain every large city and nearly every large town has a bull ring.
3. Did you contact the Better Business Bureau about the problem with your new television set?
4. Most people remember Paul Revere's patriotism but forget his work as a silversmith and engraver.
5. Over the horizon that August day sailed the ships of Columbus's small fleet.
6. Revise your report carefully.
7. There are hundreds of inlets and bays along the coast of Nova Scotia.
8. There are over 200 tapes of classical and popular music in the cabinet.
9. Have you seen the exciting new computers on sale at Murphy's Hi-Tech?
10. Brad, take these shirts back to the store for a refund or a credit toward a future purchase.
11. There is no living descendant of William Shakespeare.
12. Hasn't he answered your letter yet?
13. American Indians do not pay taxes on their land.
14. John Adams, John Quincy Adams, John F. Kennedy, and George Bush were all born in Norfolk County, Massachusetts.
15. Slowly over the mountain rose the morning sun.
16. The most common word in English conversation is *I.*
17. Here are the balloons and streamers.
18. Postage stamps were first used in the United States in 1847.
19. Take notes for me during the lecture.
20. A male emperor moth can detect and find a female of his species a mile away.

B **Finding Complements** Number your paper 1 to 10. Write each complement. Then label each complement, using the following abbreviations.

direct object = *d.o.*   predicate nominative = *p.n.*
indirect object = *i.o.*   predicate adjective = *p.a.*
objective complement = *o.c.*

1. The Puritans considered buttons a sign of vanity.
2. At first the old trunk in the basement appeared empty.
3. Michelle showed Mom a copy of the yearbook.
4. Many early settlers found the Indians friendly and helpful.
5. In Williamsburg, Virginia, we visited several shops and explored the old jail.
6. Their grandfather clock is quite old and very valuable.
7. James Monroe was the fourth president from Virginia.
8. Tell Alma and James that funny story about your uncle.
9. From the top of Mount Irazu in Costa Rica, a person can see the Atlantic Ocean and the Pacific Ocean.
10. Centuries ago a collection of books was a sign of wealth.

Mastery Test

Number your paper 1 to 10. Write the subject, the verb, and the underlined complement in each sentence. (A subject or a verb may be compound.) Then label each complement, using the following abbreviations.

direct object = *d.o.*   predicate nominative = *p.n.*
indirect object = *i.o.*   predicate adjective = *p.a.*
objective complement = *o.c.*

1. The state flower of Kentucky is the <u>goldenrod</u>.
2. This cereal has a low sugar <u>content</u>.
3. Tell <u>Marcy</u> the score of last night's game.
4. There are many apartments in the complex still <u>vacant</u>.
5. I dyed the sweater <u>maroon</u>.
6. Kim grabbed an <u>apple</u> and raced to the bus stop.
7. Food and oxygen sweep in with the ocean tides and nourish the <u>organisms</u> on the rocks along the shore.
8. Is this his business <u>address</u>?
9. Our lawn and shrubs never looked <u>greener</u>.
10. The obedience trainer gave the dog's <u>leash</u> a quick snap.

19

Phrases

Diagnostic Test

Number your paper 1 to 10. Write the phrases in the following sentences. Then label each one *prepositional, appositive, participial, gerund,* or *infinitive.*

EXAMPLE   Raising beef cattle is a scientific process.
ANSWER   Raising beef cattle—gerund

1. George Washington, a great politician, was also a prosperous Virginia farmer.
2. On our front doorstep stood a bedraggled, forlorn dog without a collar.
3. Finding one's way through the enormous new high school is not easy.
4. At parties Leslie is always willing to play her guitar.
5. Climbing the foremast, the sailor sighted dangerous coral reefs in the distance.
6. Before tomorrow morning I have to find a ride to school.
7. The bagpipe, Scotland's national instrument, can be traced back to ancient Mesopotamia.
8. My older brother doesn't like waiting more than ten minutes for anyone.
9. We finally found Christopher studying in the library.
10. Delaware was the first state to ratify the Constitution.

Prepositional Phrases

The subject, the verb, and sometimes a complement are the foundation of a sentence. Once you are familiar with the basic structure of a sentence, you can build on it. In a way, you become an architect. Instead of adding rooms, however, you are adding grammatical elements, such as phrases. The rooms in a house have specific purposes, and their different shapes and sizes make the house interesting and unique. Similarly, different phrases have different purposes. Some phrases are used to expand or to qualify an idea, while others are used to show relationships between ideas. Using different kinds of phrases will make your writing more varied and more interesting.

Rule 19a | A **phrase** is a group of related words that functions as a single part of speech. A phrase does not have a subject or a verb.

This chapter will first review prepositional phrases and appositive phrases. Then it will review the three kinds of verbal phrases: *participial, gerund,* and *infinitive.*

A prepositional phrase is a group of words that begins with a preposition and ends with a noun or pronoun. That noun or pronoun is called the *object of the preposition. (See page 551 for a list of common prepositions.)* The prepositional phrases in the following sentences are in heavy type.

> **Before midnight** the candidate **from Canton** conceded the election **to his opponent.**

> **In spite of the forecast,** she is proceeding **with her plans for the barbecue.**

Prepositional phrases are used like single adjectives and adverbs to modify other words in a sentence.

Adjective Phrases

Rule 19b | An **adjective phrase** is a prepositional phrase that is used to modify a noun or a pronoun.

The examples on the next page show how an adjective phrase works exactly like a single adjective.

SINGLE ADJECTIVE Did you read **this** letter? [*This* tells which letter.]

ADJECTIVE PHRASE Did you read the letter **on the table?** [*On the table* also tells which letter.]

A single adjective and an adjective phrase answer the same questions: *Which one(s)?* and *What kind?*

WHICH ONE(S)? The horse **in the first stall** is a Morgan.

WHAT KIND? I like broccoli **with cheese sauce.**

An adjective phrase usually follows the word it modifies. That word may be the object of a preposition of another prepositional phrase.

Millions *of* **acres** *of* **the earth's surface** are still unexplored.

Two adjective phrases occasionally will modify the same noun or pronoun.

Put away the bag *of* **groceries** *on* **the counter.**

Adverb Phrases

Rule 19c An **adverb phrase** is a prepositional phrase that is used to modify a verb, an adjective, or an adverb.

An adverb phrase works exactly like a single adverb. Notice in the following examples that an adverb phrase, like a single adverb, modifies the whole verb phrase.

SINGLE ADVERB The senior choir will perform **soon.** [*Soon* tells when the choir will perform.]

ADVERB PHRASE The senior choir will perform **on Friday.** [*On Friday* also tells when the choir will perform.]

A single adverb and an adverb phrase answer the same question: *Where? When? How? To what extent?* or *To what degree?* An adverb phrase also answers the question *Why?*

WHERE?   I left my sneakers **in my locker.**

WHEN?   The rehearsal lasted **until ten o'clock.**

HOW?   I planted the shrubs **according to his instructions.**

WHY?   **Because of the heavy traffic,** we missed the plane.

Two or more adverb phrases may modify one verb.

For three days all the flags were flying **at half-mast.**

Over the weekend I put my records **into the cabinet.**

Although most adverb phrases modify a verb, some modify adjectives and adverbs.

MODIFYING AN ADJECTIVE   Margo is kind **to everyone.**

MODIFYING AN ADVERB   We arrived late **in the afternoon.**

Punctuation with Adverb Phrases

Do not place a comma after a short introductory adverb phrase—unless it is needed for clarity. You should, however, place a comma after an adverb phrase of four or more words or after several introductory phrases.

NO COMMA   **From the tree** I can see the lake.
COMMA   **From the tree on the hill,** I can see the lake.

EXERCISE *Recognizing Prepositional Phrases as Modifiers*

Number your paper 1 to 10. Write the prepositional phrases in the following sentences. Then beside each phrase, write the word it modifies.

The First Modern Olympic Champion

1. The first champion of the modern Olympic Games was James Brendan Connolly.
2. In 1896, when he was a 27-year-old undergraduate at Harvard, he read about the revival of the ancient Greek games.
3. At that time Connolly was the triple-jump champion of the United States.

4. Connolly left school and went to Athens in March.
5. Ten American athletes and one trainer spent 16½ days on a ship to Naples and another day on a train to Athens.
6. On the following day, the Olympics began with the triple jump.
7. Before his turn Connolly surveyed the mark of the leader on the ground and threw his cap beyond it.
8. He then jumped beyond his cap and became the first champion of the modern Olympics.
9. He later became a journalist and the author of 25 novels.
10. Connolly died in 1957 at age 88.

EXERCISE *Identifying Prepositional Phrases*

Number your paper 1 to 10. Write the prepositional phrases in the following sentences. Then beside each phrase, label it *adjective* or *adverb*.

A Future
Space
Station

1. In the near future, a United States space station may be orbiting around the earth.
2. One plan of the scientists foresees a modular station with canisterlike components.
3. These components would be ferried to the station by a space shuttle and assembled in orbit.
4. One of the many components would provide living quarters for eight crew members.
5. Electric power would be generated by huge solar panels.
6. The size of the station would totally eclipse present facilities in space.
7. The initial cost of this huge undertaking would be approximately ten billion dollars.
8. Over the following years, another fifteen billion dollars would be needed for additional modules.
9. The space station might perform experiments like those of a space shuttle.
10. Unfortunately the space station will not be ready by the 500th anniversary of Columbus's discovery of the New World.

 Application to Writing

In a paragraph describe a rainstorm as vividly as possible. Be prepared to identify each prepositional phrase.

Appositives and Appositive Phrases

An **appositive** is a noun or a pronoun that identifies or explains another noun or pronoun in the sentence.

An appositive usually follows the word or words it identifies or explains.

My friend **Bart** is moving to Kansas.

I enjoyed my favorite meal, **spaghetti.**

Most often an appositive is used with modifiers to form an *appositive phrase.* Notice in the second example that one or more prepositional phrases may be part of an appositive phrase.

New Bedford, **once the world's largest whaling port,** is located on Buzzards Bay in Massachusetts.

I just bought *Modern Poetry,* a **collection of poems by American authors.**

Punctuation with Appositives and Appositive Phrases

If an appositive contains information essential to the meaning of a sentence, no punctuation is needed. Information is essential if it identifies a person, place, or thing. If an appositive or an appositive phrase contains nonessential information, a comma or commas should be used to separate it from the rest of the sentence. Information is nonessential if it can be removed from the sentence without changing the basic meaning. An appositive that follows a proper noun is usually nonessential.

ESSENTIAL	The famous artist **Manet** was born in 1832. [No commas are used because *Manet* is needed to identify which artist.]
NONESSENTIAL	Manet**, a famous French artist,** was born in 1832. [Commas are used because the appositive could be removed from the sentence: Manet was born in 1832.]

EXERCISE *Finding Appositives and Appositive Phrases*

Write the following sentences and underline each appositive or appositive phrase. Then add a comma or commas where needed.

1. Josie my golden retriever often swims at the nearby pond.
2. At the picnic Dad used Grandmother's chicken recipe a family secret.
3. Stainless steel a valuable alloy of iron is noted for its ability to resist rust and tarnish.
4. Georgia O'Keeffe an American abstract painter was famous for her paintings of the desert region of the Southwest.
5. Naomi Uemura a Japanese explorer was the first person to reach the North Pole alone by dogsled.
6. *Romeo and Juliet* a beautiful ballet was performed last evening at the Cultural Center.
7. The painting *Sunflowers* is one of Van Gogh's most recognized masterpieces.
8. March the first month of the Roman Year was named for Mars the Roman god of war.
9. Did you check the thesaurus a good source of antonyms as well as synonyms?
10. Cheese a food rich in protein is also an excellent source of vitamins and minerals.

EXERCISE *Cumulative Review*

Number your paper 1 to 10. Write the prepositional phrases and the appositive phrases in the following sentences. Then label each one *adjective*, *adverb*, or *appositive*.

Facts about
Sports
1. In 1936, Jesse Owens, a famous track star, beat a horse in the hundred-yard race.
2. During the following year, Forest Towns, an Olympic hurdler, beat a horse in the hundred-yard hurdles.
3. Micki King, a gold-medal winner in the 1972 Olympics, became a diving coach at the U.S. Air Force Academy.
4. O. J. Simpson once had a severe case of rickets and wore leg braces.
5. Later Simpson set ground-gaining records in the National Football League.

6. Cathy Rigby, the first American winner in women's international gymnastics, had a lung ailment during her youth.
7. For six years Hugh Daily played baseball for several major-league teams.
8. As a pitcher he held a long-standing record of 19 strikeouts in a single game.
9. Hugh Daily was a man with only one arm.
10. Fourteen-year-old Nadia Comaneci had seven perfect scores in gymnastics at the Montreal Olympics.

Verbals and Verbal Phrases

Verbals are part of your everyday speech. If you have ever apologized for your *unmade* bed or told someone that you would be ready *to leave* at six o'clock, you have used verbals. A *verbal* is a verb form that is used not as a verb, but as a noun, an adjective, or an adverb. Because verbals are verb forms, they are usually lively words that add action and vitality to your writing. The three kinds of verbals are *participles, gerunds,* and *infinitives.*

Participles and Participial Phrases

Rule 19e A **participle** is a verb form that is used as an adjective.

Used like an adjective, a participle modifies a noun or a pronoun and answers the adjective question *Which one(s)?* or *What kind?* The participles in the examples are in heavy type. An arrow points to the word each participle modifies.

The **rising** sun was reflected on the **frozen** pond.

Broken tree branches lay across the **winding** road.

There are two kinds of participles: a present participle and a past participle. A *present participle* ends in *-ing,* while a *past participle* has a regular ending of *-ed* or an irregular ending of *-n, -t,* or *-en.*

PRESENT PARTICIPLES   spinning, shrinking, ringing, winning
PAST PARTICIPLES   buried, defeated, worn, bent, stolen

Note: Do not confuse a participle, which is used as an adjective, with the main verb of a sentence. A participle will have one or more helping verbs if it is used as a verb.

PARTICIPLE   Our **reserved** seats are in the sixth row of the mezzanine.

VERB   We **have reserved** a room in the hotel.

PARTICIPLE   The **broken** clock on the mantel in the living room belonged to my grandfather.

VERB   During my lab period in chemistry, a glass beaker **was broken.**

Participial Phrases   Because a participle is a verb form, it may have modifiers and complements. Together these words form a *participial phrase.*

> **Rule 19f**   A **participial phrase** is a participle with its modifiers and complements—all working together as an adjective.

The following examples show three variations of a participial phrase. As you can see, a participle may be followed by an adverb, a prepositional phrase, or a complement.

PARTICIPLE WITH AN ADVERB   **Bought early,** her presents had to be hidden until her birthday.

PARTICIPLE WITH A PREPOSITIONAL PHRASE   Our dog, **barking at the back door,** wants to come in.

PARTICIPLE WITH A COMPLEMENT   Who is that young man **raising his right hand?**

The present participle *having* is sometimes followed by a past participle.

Having seen the flashing lights ahead, we slowed down.

Note: Sometimes an adverb that modifies a participle may come before the participle. The adverb in this position is still part of the participial phrase.

A hurricane is a tropical cyclone **usually accompanied by heavy rains.**

Punctuation with Participial Phrases

Always place a comma after an introductory participial phrase.

Charging up the center, he streaked for a touchdown.

Participial phrases that come in the middle or at the end of a sentence may or may not need commas. If the information in a phrase is essential to identify the noun or the pronoun it describes, no commas are needed. If the information is nonessential, commas are needed to separate it from the rest of the sentence. A phrase is nonessential if it contains information that can be removed from the sentence without changing the basic meaning. A phrase that follows a proper noun is usually nonessential.

ESSENTIAL   The player **pitching for the Hornets** is Jason Sands. [No commas are used because the phrase is needed to identify which player.]

NONESSENTIAL   Jason Sands**, pitching for the Hornets,** has ten wins to his credit. [Commas are used because the phrase can be removed: Jason Sands has ten wins to his credit.]

EXERCISE *Finding Participial Phrases*

Number your paper 1 to 10. Write each participial phrase. Then beside each one, write the word or words it modifies.

EXAMPLE   Having assumed new roles in all aspects of society, women have become increasingly successful in the political arena.

ANSWER   Having assumed new roles in all aspects of society
              women

Women Mayors

1. Winning the confidence of many voters, women have become the mayors of several large cities in the United States.
2. One report identifies some of the women elected in recent years.
3. Jane Byrne of Chicago captured the office held by Mayor Richard J. Daley for 21 years until his death.
4. Isabelle Cannon, having won the support of young people, became the mayor of Raleigh in a major upset.
5. Having complained unsuccessfully about a dangerous intersection, Janet Gray Hayes ran for mayor of San Jose.

6. Gaining prominence in a nonpartisan campaign, she went on to win the election.

7. Demonstrating her leadership abilities, Mayor Margaret Hance of Phoenix won a second term.

8. Mayor Carole McClellan of Austin, gathering 79 percent of the vote, also won a second term.

9. Effectively governing San Francisco, Dianne Feinstein became nationally prominent.

10. All of these outstanding women led the way for other women entering politics.

EXERCISE *Identifying and Punctuating Participial Phrases*

Write the following sentences and underline each participial phrase. Then add a comma or commas where needed.

1. A device used as a crude steam engine about 2,000 years ago is today's lawn sprinkler.

2. Having been sewn by my great-great grandmother the patchwork quilt was a treasure.

3. Homing pigeons used as messengers fly at an average speed of 45 miles per hour.

4. The Hawthorne High School Athletic Club formed in 1980 has raised thousands of dollars for new equipment.

5. The boys rowing steadily appeared around the bend of the river.

6. Seeing the warblers in the tree Stanley stood perfectly still with his camera.

7. The light shining from the streetlight kept me awake all night.

8. We found a record of our family history written in an old Bible.

9. Winding down the steep mountain road Ted drove very slowly.

10. Indians living high in the Andes have larger lungs than almost everyone else.

EXERCISE *Distinguishing between Verbs and Participles*

Write two sentences for each of the following words. The first sentence should use the word as a verb. The second sentence should use the word as a participle in a participial phrase. Use punctuation where needed.

EXAMPLE cracked
POSSIBLE Her voice cracked on the high notes.
ANSWER Cracked in three places, the vase couldn't be used.

1. barking		**6.** dating	
2. built		**7.** found	
3. written		**8.** chiming	
4. dashing		**9.** riding	
5. lost		**10.** confused	

Gerunds and Gerund Phrases

Rule 19g A **gerund** is a verb form that is used as a noun.

Because a gerund ends in *-ing,* it looks like a present participle. A gerund, however, is used as a noun. The gerunds in the following examples are in heavy type.

> **Reading** does not strain your eyes. [subject]
> I thoroughly enjoy **painting.** [direct object]

Gerund Phrases   Like other verbals, a gerund may be combined with modifiers and complements to form a phrase.

Rule 19h A **gerund phrase** is a gerund with its modifiers and complements—all working together as a noun.

A gerund or a gerund phrase may be used in all the ways in which a noun may be used. As you can see from the following examples, a gerund phrase may take several forms. A gerund may be followed by an adverb, a prepositional phrase, or a complement.

SUBJECT	**Walking vigorously** is excellent exercise.
DIRECT OBJECT	I like **riding on roller coasters.**
INDIRECT OBJECT	My dad gave **cleaning the garage** his full attention last Saturday.
OBJECT OF A PREPOSITION	We drove to Philadelphia from Richmond without **making a single stop.**
PREDICATE NOMINATIVE	His greatest achievement was **making the Olympic team.**
APPOSITIVE	Heather's dream, **getting the lead in the play,** came true last November.

Note: The possessive form of a noun or a pronoun comes before a gerund and is considered part of the gerund phrase.

What do you think of **Eric's winning the high jump?**
Her finding that contact lens was fortunate.

EXERCISE *Finding Gerund Phrases*

Number your paper 1 to 10. Write each gerund phrase. Then underline each gerund.

1. You can get a good seat by arriving early.
2. I couldn't understand her refusing the award.
3. Throwing a Frisbee competitively began in 1971.
4. The average grasshopper is capable of jumping a distance up to 20 times its body length.
5. My major fault is leaving everything until the last minute.
6. Abner Doubleday is generally credited with originating the game of baseball.
7. After jogging early in the morning, Leroy studied for his math exam.
8. Writing in her journal every day is a practice Jan started this year.
9. Joel's parents were delighted with his winning the art contest.
10. Doubling the diameter of a pipe increases fourfold its capacity for conveying liquids.

EXERCISE *Determining the Uses of Gerund Phrases*

Number your paper 1 to 10. Write each gerund phrase. Then label the use of each one, using the following abbreviations.

subject = *subj.*   object of a preposition = *o.p.*
direct object = *d.o.*   predicate nominative = *p.n.*
indirect object = *i.o.*   appositive = *appos.*

1. Collecting tiny china dogs is Julie's hobby.
2. My exercise schedule includes doing 50 push-ups each morning.
3. In 1874, Thomas Edison improved the typewriter by substituting metal parts for wooden ones.
4. For a change of pace, give baking bread a try.
5. One distinction of Franklin Pierce's administration was his retaining the same cabinet for four years.

6. Several students succeeded in finishing the marathon.
7. Julia has an unusual job, taking three dogs for their morning walk.
8. Sarah's plans for riding her new bicycle were delayed by the storm.
9. Being a good athlete involves training the mind as well as the body.
10. The highlight of my day was seeing my article in the school newspaper.

EXERCISE *Distinguishing between Gerunds and Participles*

Write two sentences for each of the following words. The first sentence should use the word as a gerund. The second sentence should use the word as a participle. Use punctuation where needed.

EXAMPLE   taking
POSSIBLE   Karen was nervous about taking the math test.
ANSWER   The students taking the math test in room 401 should not be disturbed.

1. holding   2. collecting   3. finding   4. thawing   5. studying

Infinitives and Infinitive Phrases

Rule 19i An **infinitive** is a verb form that usually begins with *to*. It is used as a noun, an adjective, or an adverb.

Infinitives do not look like the other verbals because they usually begin with the word *to*. An infinitive has several forms. The infinitives of *change*, for example, are *to change, to be changing, to have changed, to be changed,* and *to have been changed*. The infinitives in the following examples are in heavy type.

I hope **to be invited.** [noun—direct object]
Pat couldn't think of anything **to say.** [adjective]
That unexpected compliment was nice **to hear.** [adverb]

Note: Do not confuse a prepositional phrase that begins with *to* with an infinitive. A prepositional phrase ends with a noun or a pronoun; an infinitive ends with a verb form.

PREPOSITIONAL PHRASE   I'll drive you **to school.**

INFINITIVE   When is it time **to eat?**

Infinitive Phrases   An infinitive may be combined with modifiers and complements to form an *infinitive phrase.*

Rule 19j   An **infinitive phrase** is an infinitive with its modifiers and complements—all working together as a noun, an adjective, or an adverb.

The following examples show how an infinitive phrase may be used as a noun, an adjective, or an adverb. Notice that like other verbals, an infinitive phrase may also take several forms. An infinitive, for example, may be followed by an adverb, a complement, or a prepositional phrase.

NOUN   **To sew well** requires patience. [subject]
I tried **to get two tickets.** [direct object]

ADJECTIVE   These are the letters **to be mailed by tomorrow.**

ADVERB   We printed the story **to create public awareness.**

Note: *To* is occasionally omitted when an infinitive follows such verbs as *dare, feel, help, make, let, need, see,* or *watch.* It is, nevertheless, understood to be there.

We helped **collect litter from the park.** [to collect]

EXERCISE *Finding Infinitive Phrases*

Number your paper 1 to 10. Write each infinitive phrase. Then underline each infinitive.

1. Jason was the first freshman to play on the varsity team.
2. To be brave from a distance is easy.—AESOP
3. Joshua helped serve the refreshments.
4. Paula was the first person to see the fire.
5. Dad wanted to raise vegetables in containers on the roof.
6. Grandfather is happy to have found an apartment.
7. Zora's plan was to jog daily.
8. Approximately 46,000 pounds of earth must be mined and sifted to produce a half-carat diamond.
9. The mechanic promised to service our car today.

10. It is about ten times easier to shoot a hole in one in golf than it is to roll a perfect 300 game in bowling.

EXERCISE ◆ **12** *Determining the Uses of Infinitive Phrases*

Number your paper 1 to 10. Write the infinitive phrases in the following sentences. Then label how each one is used—*noun, adjective,* or *adverb.*

  1. Balboa was the first explorer to see the Pacific Ocean.
  2. The early years of your life are the best time to learn a foreign language.
  3. Beth hopes to enter the Air Force Academy in September.
  4. The students hurried to reach their classrooms on time.
  5. To become a veterinarian is my sister's chief ambition.
  6. Charlene was eager to start her new job.
  7. Dad suggested books to use as references for our term papers.
  8. My grandmother attends the local night school to improve her Spanish.
  9. Have you tried to find a summer job?
10. Jeffrey's hope is to study fashion design after high school.

EXERCISE ◆ **13** *Writing Sentences*

Write sentences that follow the directions below.

  1. Use an infinitive phrase as a subject.
  2. Use an infinitive phrase as a direct object.
  3. Use an infinitive phrase as an adjective.
  4. Use an infinitive phrase as an adverb.
  5. Use two infinitive phrases.

EXERCISE ◆ **14** *Cumulative Review*

Number your paper 1 to 20. Write the verbal phrases in the following sentences. Then label each one *participial, gerund,* or *infinitive.*

Firsts for Women
  1. Born in New York in 1856, Louise Blanchard Bethune is considered the first woman architect.
  2. After designing many buildings, she became the first woman to gain membership in the American Institute of Architects.

3. The first woman canoeist to make a solo trip down the Mississippi River was Rebecca Johnson.
4. Starting in Minnesota, Johnson finally arrived in New Orleans 96 days later.
5. Making her first ascent in 1880, Mary H. Myers became the first woman balloon pilot.
6. She is credited with developing better balloon fabrics and designing portable hydrogen generators.
7. In 1886, Myers ascended to an altitude of four miles in a balloon filled with natural gas.
8. Making such an ascent was remarkable because the aircraft was not equipped with oxygen.
9. The first American woman to receive the Nobel Peace Prize was Jane Addams.
10. In 1931, she was recognized for establishing a center for social reform in Chicago.
11. Changing her name to Dale, Dalia Messick submitted her comic strip "Brenda Starr" to the *Chicago Tribune* in 1940.
12. "Brenda Starr," read by 7.5 million people today, was also the first comic strip to feature a woman.
13. The first woman to be pictured on a United States coin in circulation was suffragist Susan B. Anthony.
14. Treasury officials had first considered picturing only a representative female figure such as Miss Liberty.
15. Feminists, however, lobbied for honoring a real individual.
16. Anthony, appearing later on a one-dollar coin, was selected over Jane Addams and Eleanor Roosevelt.
17. Long before Sarah Walker became the first black woman millionaire, she supported herself by taking in laundry.
18. In 1905, after 18 years as a laundress, she decided to create a line of hair products especially for black women.
19. Working at home, she formulated shampoos and oils.
20. Concerned for other black women, Walker created many college scholarships.

Misplaced and Dangling Modifiers

The meaning of a sentence sometimes gets confused because a modifier is placed too far away from the word it describes. When that happens, the modifier appears to describe some other word. Such modifiers are called *misplaced modifiers.* Remember to place phrases used as modifiers as close as possible to the word or words they describe.

MISPLACED   Rob will answer this ad for a typist **in the *Globe.***

CORRECT   Rob will answer this ad **in the *Globe*** for a typist.

MISPLACED   I found my keys looking through my jacket.

CORRECT   **Looking through my jacket,** I found my keys.

Another problem sometimes arises when a phrase that is being used as a modifier does not have a word to describe. This kind of phrase is called a *dangling modifier.*

DANGLING   **To be a good quarterback,** calm under pressure is needed. [*Calm* cannot be a good quarterback.]

CORRECT   **To be a good quarterback,** you need to be calm under pressure.

EXERCISE *Correcting Misplaced and Dangling Modifiers*

Write the following sentences, correcting the error in each one. Either place a phrase closer to the word it modifies or add words and change the sentence around so that the phrase has a noun or a pronoun to modify. Use punctuation where needed.

1. Rummaging through the trash can, we saw the raccoon.
2. I followed Lisa as she ran around the pond on my bike.
3. Booming in the distance, I was awakened by the thunder.
4. To win a medal in the Olympics, dedication as well as training is essential.
5. I could see Mr. Blake mowing his lawn through the upstairs window.
6. Walking through the mall, Kate's eyes fell on a red coat.
7. As the plane descended, we no longer could see the sun blazing brightly in the sky through the dark clouds.
8. Rowing steadily, the boat was brought to the dock.
9. To do well in the SAT's, a solid foundation in English and math is necessary.
10. Roaring loudly, Juan took a picture of the lion.

USING YOUR TEXT

*Persuasive Essays
(174–215)*

Grammar: Combining Sentences

An old cliché states, "Variety is the spice of life." Using phrases—particularly verbal phrases—will add variety and spice to your writing. One way to include phrases in your writing is by using them to combine two sentences. Combining sentences will make your writing smoother.

TWO SENTENCES	The Manx is an extremely rare breed of cat. It has no tail.
ONE SENTENCE	The Manx is an extremely rare breed of cat **with no tail.** [prepositional phrase]
TWO SENTENCES	Yesterday in English we read "Jabberwocky." It is a poem by Lewis Carroll.
ONE SENTENCE	Yesterday in English we read "Jabberwocky," **a poem by Lewis Carroll.** [appositive phrase]
TWO SENTENCES	We heard something outside the tent. We became alarmed.
ONE SENTENCE	**Hearing something outside the tent,** we became alarmed. [participial phrase]
TWO SENTENCES	Gary walked the first two batters. That was the way he started the inning.
ONE SENTENCE	**Walking the first two batters** was the way Gary started the inning. [gerund phrase]
TWO SENTENCES	We hung a dozen Japanese lanterns outside. They lighted the patio.
ONE SENTENCE	We hung a dozen Japanese lanterns outside **to light the patio.** [infinitive phrase]

Checking Your Understanding   Combine each pair of sentences by using phrases. Use punctuation where needed.

I. Henry Thoreau lived in a cabin. It was by Walden Pond in Concord, Massachusetts.

2. Dad made a fruit salad. He planned to take it to the company picnic.

3. Black Labradors have webbed feet. They are skilled at retrieving objects from the water.

4. We climbed to the top of the Statue of Liberty. It was an exhausting experience.

5. The Nobel Peace Prize was first awarded in 1901. It is one of the world's greatest honors.

6. Todd lay awake most of the night. He was worried about his final exams the next day.

7. David Scott was the first person to drive a vehicle on the moon. He is an American.

8. Last night there was an informative debate. The debate was between the two Democratic candidates.

9. The desert Arabs wrap thick layers of wool around their heads. This keeps out the heat.

10. Patty Berg is a member of the World Golf Hall of Fame. She works tirelessly to help people with cerebral palsy.

Writing a Persuasive Essay   Over the next few weeks, study the cartoons on the editorial page of a daily newspaper. Discuss any that puzzle you with a family member, a teacher, or a friend. After you have looked at five to ten of the cartoons, write freely for several minutes, jotting down your impressions as to why these cartoons are featured on the editorial page. (Is there something they can accomplish better than a written editorial can?)

Then make a list, based on your notes, of reasons why you think cartoons are—or are not—valuable tools for expressing opinions. When you have finished, arrange the reasons on your list in order of importance, putting the most important reason first.

Write the first draft of a persuasive essay in which you argue that editorial cartoons are—or are not—an important means of expressing views. As you write, include some specific examples of cartoons that you have seen. *Application:* As you read over your essay, look specifically for opportunities to combine sentences by using phrases. Then, with your teacher's permission, read your essay to someone else in your class and discuss whether your arguments are strong and convincing. Finally, edit and write the final copy. Your teacher may want to put the finished essays in an editorial collection.

Diagraming Phrases

The way a phrase is used in a sentence determines how and where the phrase is diagramed.

Prepositional Phrases An adjective phrase or an adverb phrase is connected to the word it modifies. The preposition is placed on a connecting slanted line. The object of a preposition is placed on a horizontal line that is attached to the slanted line. The following example includes two adjective phrases and one adverb phrase. Notice that an adjective phrase can modify the object of the preposition of another adjective phrase.

The assignment for Mr. Marshard's class in English literature must be completed by tomorrow.

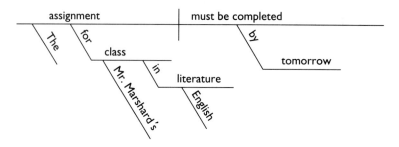

An adverb phrase that modifies an adjective or an adverb needs an additional horizontal line that is connected to the word modified.

The two trophies stood close to each other on the mantel.

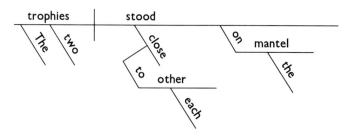

Appositives and Appositive Phrases An appositive is diagramed in parentheses next to the word it identifies or explains. Its modifiers are placed directly underneath it.

The appetizer, egg rolls with hot mustard, arrived before a huge meal of several Chinese dishes.

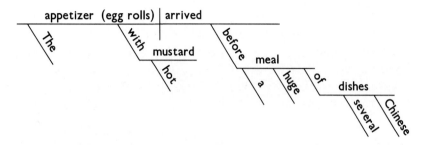

Participial Phrases   Like an adjective, a participle is always dia-gramed under the word it modifies. The participle, however, is written in a curve. In the first example below, the participial phrase modifies *Marcy,* the subject of the sentence. In the second example, the parti-cipial phrase modifies the direct object, *tree.*

Seeing the time on the kitchen clock, Marcy rushed out the door.

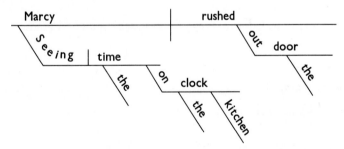

I transplanted the maple tree growing in our backyard.

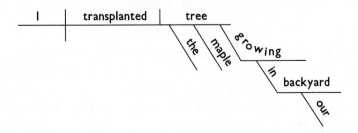

Gerund Phrases A gerund phrase is diagramed in any position in which a noun is diagramed. In the next diagram, the gerund phrase is used as a direct object. In the diagram after that, a gerund phrase is used as a subject, and another gerund phrase is used as an object of a preposition. Notice how an adverb, a prepositional phrase, and a complement may be part of a gerund phrase.

> During my summer vacation, I enjoy sitting quietly by the lake.

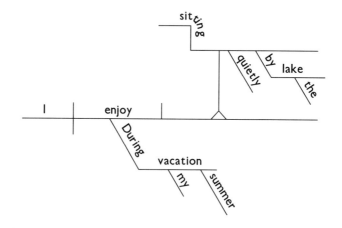

> Studying hard is a sure way of guaranteeing a good grade.

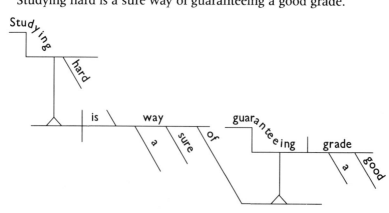

Infinitive Phrases Because an infinitive phrase may be used as a noun, an adjective, or an adverb, it is diagramed in several ways. The following example shows one infinitive phrase used as an adjective and one used as a predicate nominative. Both infinitive phrases have complements.

The only way to have a friend is to be one. EMERSON

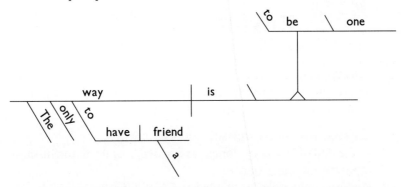

If the *to* of an infinitive is omitted from the sentence, it is diagramed in parentheses. The infinitive phrase in the following example is used as a direct object.

Do you dare interview the mayor?

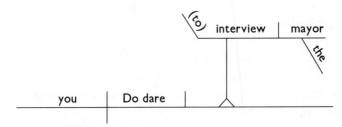

EXERCISE *Diagraming Phrases*

Diagram the following sentences or copy them. If you copy them, draw one line under each subject and two lines under each verb. Put parentheses around each phrase. Then label each phrase *prepositional, appositive, participial, gerund,* or *infinitive.*

1. The costume from the wardrobe collection is perfect.
2. We arrived later in the evening.
3. Riding a surfboard requires skill.
4. At the fair we saw Theresa riding a unicycle.
5. My neighbors own Fix It, the nearby hardware store.
6. Michael hopes to finish his report soon.
7. Kim, the captain of the gymnastics team, won a medal.
8. Finding her notebook, Sandy sighed with relief.
9. Tom saves money by taking his lunch to school.
10. Joshua did not dare contradict the referee.

19 Review

A **Identifying Phrases** Number your paper 1 to 20. Write the phrases in the following sentences. Then label each one *prepositional, appositive, participial, gerund,* or *infinitive.*

1. Seaweed sometimes grows to 200 feet in length.
2. At the end of February, Jonathan decided to apply to the Institute of Electronics near Denver.
3. Carrying pollen back to the beehive is the worker bees' job.
4. Meteors, known as shooting stars, may be seen on almost any clear night.
5. Cervantes and Shakespeare, two of the foremost writers in history, both died on April 23, 1616.
6. Scoring five runs in the first inning, the Red Sox took command of the game.
7. I enjoy swimming laps every morning.
8. An old game, played since ancient times, is marbles.
9. Do you want to frame your diploma?
10. Running the bases clockwise was the custom during the early days of baseball.
11. Joan, my aunt from Tulsa, was an Olympic swimmer.
12. The club's secretary handed me the minutes, written in shorthand.
13. Dan's father enjoys restoring antique cars.
14. The President, planning a new appointment to the cabinet, studied the list of possible candidates.
15. In some places in the world, geese are trained to tend sheep.
16. Dad and Mom stopped to admire the laurel, the state flower of Connecticut.
17. Jimmy Carter was the first president of the United States to have been born in a hospital.
18. The sun, containing 99.8 percent of the total mass of the solar system, is truly colossal in size.
19. On Career Day Susan plans to attend the dental and nursing talks.
20. At the recital Marilyn's triumph was playing the entire sonata from memory.

B **Identifying Phrases** Number your paper 1 to 12. Write each phrase in the following paragraph. Then label each one *prepositional, appositive, participial, gerund,* or *infinitive.*

Little is known about the early life of William Shakespeare, the playwright. There are, however, many legends like these. Abandoning his family to pursue a more carefree life, Shakespeare became a soldier, lawyer, or teacher. Joining a troupe of actors, Shakespeare left his home on Stratford-upon-Avon and went to London. After stealing Sir Thomas Lucy's deer, Shakespeare left his birthplace to avoid prosecution. Little or no proof exists, though, to support any of these legends.

Mastery Test

Number your paper 1 to 10. Write the phrases in the following sentences. Then label each one *prepositional, appositive, participial, gerund,* or *infinitive.*

1. Banging the gavel for order, the moderator began the annual meeting.
2. It is very difficult to play the French horn correctly.
3. West Point, the United States Military Academy in New York, was established in 1892.
4. Photographing old buildings is my sister's hobby.
5. Working tirelessly for three days, Dennis wallpapered the upstairs bedroom.
6. The coach didn't like your missing Saturday's practice.
7. Every person must swim 25 full laps to qualify for the swim team.
8. Mrs. Grayson, my history teacher, is president of the Historical Society.
9. One of Pepe's goals is making the Jefferson High School varsity football team.
10. Travelers driving from Los Angeles to Reno, Nevada, will have to travel northwest.

20

Clauses

Diagnostic Test

Number your paper 1 to 10. Then label each sentence *simple, compound, complex,* or *compound-complex.*

EXAMPLE   We just found the front-door key that was missing.
ANSWER   complex

1. The average number of solar eclipses in a year is two.
2. Either the electricity is off, or we blew a fuse.
3. Ann explained why she chose Fisher Junior College to attend next year.
4. Although whales usually bear only one offspring, baby twin whales have been reported.
5. Grove Street and Kendall Avenue will be closed for repaving next week.
6. Bentley High, which you predicted would win, lost by 36 points.
7. I heard the alarm clock but didn't get out of bed.
8. My first choice was the Mexican restaurant that had just opened down the road, but Elizabeth wanted Chinese food.
9. As we entered the room, we immediately noticed that the meeting had already started.
10. I wrote to the city's new mayor, but he has not answered my letter yet.

Independent and Subordinate Clauses

You could paint a landscape with just one color, but it would be a dull, unrealistic picture when you finished. You could also write only simple sentences in a composition or a report. People would certainly understand what you wrote. Like the picture painted all in one color, however, your written work would be a dull, unrealistic representation of ordinary speech.

You can add color and interest to your writing by varying the structure of your sentences. One way to do this is to include various combinations of clauses within your sentences.

Rule 20a **A clause is a group of words that has a subject and a verb.**

This chapter will cover independent and subordinate clauses and show you how a subordinate clause can be used as an adverb, an adjective, or a noun. This chapter will also show you how clauses form different kinds of sentences.

The two kinds of clauses are *independent clauses* and *subordinate clauses.*

Rule 20b **An independent (or main) clause can usually stand alone as a sentence because it expresses a complete thought.**

When an independent clause stands alone, it is called a *sentence.* When it appears in a sentence with another clause, it is called a *clause.* In the following examples, each subject is underlined once, and each verb is underlined twice. Notice that each independent clause can stand alone as a separate sentence.

┌── independent clause ──┐   ┌── independent clause ──┐
Greg waited a long time, but his mail order never arrived.

┌──── sentence ────┐ ┌──── sentence ────┐
Greg waited a long time. His mail order never arrived.

Rule 20c **A subordinate (or dependent) clause cannot stand alone as a sentence, because it does not express a complete thought.**

A subordinate clause has a subject and a verb; nevertheless, it does not express a complete thought. It can never stand alone as a sentence. A subordinate clause is dependent upon an independent clause to complete its meaning.

┌──── subordinate clause ────┐ ┌──── independent clause ────┐
When <u>we</u> <u>saw</u> the game, <u>we</u> <u>sat</u> in the bleachers.

┌──── independent clause ────┐ ┌──── subordinate clause ────┐
<u>We</u> <u>found</u> some blue paint <u>that</u> <u>matches</u> the wallpaper.

┌──── independent clause ────┐ ┌──── subordinate clause ────┐
<u>No one</u> at the meeting <u>knew</u> that <u>you</u> <u>were</u> a newcomer.

Uses of Subordinate Clauses

Like a phrase, a subordinate clause can be used in a sentence as an adverb, an adjective, or a noun. Keep in mind, however, the basic difference between a clause and a phrase. A clause has a subject and a verb; a phrase does not.

Adverb Clauses

Rule 20d An **adverb clause** is a subordinate clause that is used as an adverb to modify a verb, an adjective, or an adverb.

An adverb clause is used just like a single adverb or an adverb phrase. In the following examples, the single adverb, the adverb phrase, and the adverb clause all modify the verb *arrived*.

SINGLE ADVERB   The train arrived **late.**
ADVERB PHRASE   The train arrived **at five o'clock.**
ADVERB CLAUSE   The train arrived **before we reached the station.**

In addition to the questions *How? When? Where? How much?* and *To what extent?* adverb clauses also answer *Under what condition?* and *Why?* Although most adverb clauses modify verbs, some modify adjectives and adverbs.

MODIFYING   **After Rusty had eaten,** I took him for a walk.
A VERB   [The clause answers *When?*]

MODIFYING AN ADJECTIVE	Your chili tastes spicier **than mine does.** [The clause answers *How much?*]
MODIFYING AN ADVERB	I worked harder **than I had ever worked before.** [The clause answers *To what extent?*]

Subordinating Conjunctions An adverb clause usually begins with a *subordinating conjunction*. Notice in the following list such words as *after, before, since,* and *until,* which can also be used as prepositions. Notice also that subordinating conjunctions can be phrases, such as *even though.*

Common Subordinating Conjunctions		
after	because	though
although	before	unless
as	even though	until
as far as	if	when
as if	in order that	whenever
as long as	since	where
as soon as	so that	wherever
as though	than	while

An adverb clause that describes a verb modifies the whole verb phrase.

You may watch the photo session **as long as you are quiet.**

As soon as you hear from the college, you must call us.

Punctuation with Adverb Clauses
Always place a comma after an adverb clause that comes at the beginning of a sentence.

    Since Jay was sick, I took his place.

If an adverb clause interrupts an independent clause, place a comma before it and after it.

    The guests**, after they had eaten the wonderful meal,** applauded the cook.

EXERCISE *Finding Adverb Clauses*

Number your paper 1 to 10. Write each adverb clause. Then write the word or words the adverb clause modifies.

1. When a thunderstorm strikes on a hot day, hail may fall.
2. As soon as you finish your homework, call me.
3. We went to the dance so that we could hear the band.
4. We waited for them longer than we should have.
5. After the snowstorm ended, we shoveled the walk and the driveway.
6. We ate dinner later than we had originally planned.
7. We can fill all these orders if we get more help.
8. Before William Butler Yeats wrote plays for the Abbey Theater, he had written many poems celebrating Ireland.
9. Complete the employment application after you read the directions.
10. Because tuna need a flow of water across their gills in order to breathe, they would suffocate if they ever stopped swimming.

EXERCISE *Identifying and Punctuating Adverb Clauses*

Write the following sentences and underline each adverb clause. Then add a comma or commas where needed.

1. When the storm began we ran for shelter.
2. All day we acted as though we had forgotten his birthday.
3. Because Judy studied she did well on the French test.
4. Magnesium when it is ignited burns with a white light.
5. Even though we were cold we played hockey for an hour.
6. The circumference of the earth is about 42 miles greater around the equator than it is around the poles.
7. The mayor of San Francisco left after he had completed his speech.
8. A blue whale gains about 200 pounds a day until it is fully grown.
9. Niagara Falls since their origin 10,000 years ago have moved seven miles upstream.
10. If our basketball team wins we will celebrate.

Elliptical Clauses Words in an adverb clause are sometimes omitted to streamline a sentence and to prevent unnecessary repetition. Even though the words are omitted, they are still understood to be there. An adverb clause in which words are missing is called an *elliptical clause*. Notice in the following examples that the elliptical clauses begin with *than* or *as* and are missing only the verb. *(See pages 683–684 for information about using the correct case of a pronoun in an elliptical clause.)*

> Alvin understands the rules better **than I.** [The completed elliptical clause reads *than I do.*]

> A hippopotamus may weigh as much **as a medium-sized truck.** [The completed elliptical clause reads *as a medium-sized truck weighs.*]

Sometimes the subject and the verb, or just part of the verb phrase, may be omitted in an elliptical clause.

> I sold more tickets to the spring concert this weekend **than last weekend.** [The completed elliptical clause reads *than I sold last weekend.*]

> **When sighted,** the plane had already lost one engine and was in distress. [The completed elliptical clause reads *When it was sighted.*]

EXERCISE *Recognizing Elliptical Clauses*

Number your paper 1 to 10. Then write the completed version of each elliptical clause.

1. Water has more uses than any other single substance on this earth.
2. Dirty snow melts faster than clean snow.
3. My father is as fine a cook as my mother.
4. When told about the project to raise money for the homeless, Charlene volunteered.
5. Helium weighs about one seventh as much as air.
6. The kind of boot with air cushioning is better for hiking than this kind.
7. *David Copperfield*, though not a biography, includes many details of Dickens's life.
8. On July 8, 1835, the Liberty Bell cracked while tolling the death of Chief Justice John Marshall.
9. Christopher and Michael did more push-ups and sit-ups today than yesterday.
10. I like football more than baseball.

Adjective Clauses

Rule 20e An **adjective clause** is a subordinate clause that is used like an adjective to modify a noun or a pronoun.

An adjective clause is used like a single adjective or an adjective phrase. In the following examples, the single adjective, the adjective phrase, and the adjective clause all modify *fire.*

SINGLE ADJECTIVE   The **intense** fire destroyed the building.

ADJECTIVE PHRASE   The fire, **with billowing flames and thick smoke,** destroyed the building.

ADJECTIVE CLAUSE   The fire, **which raged out of control,** destroyed the building.

Like a single adjective, an adjective clause answers the question *Which one(s)?* or *What kind?*

WHICH ONE(S)?   The teachers **who chaperoned the dance last night** enjoyed themselves.

WHAT KIND?   He bought himself running shoes **that have extra support for his arches.**

Relative Pronouns   *A relative pronoun* usually begins an adjective clause. A relative pronoun relates an adjective clause to its antecedent. *Where* and *when* also introduce adjective clauses.

Relative Pronouns				
who	whom	whose	which	that

Lakeview's football team, **which won the championship last year,** hasn't won a single game so far this year.

The Dalys moved here from Miami, **where they had lived all their lives.**

Note: The relative pronoun *that* will occasionally be omitted from an adjective clause. It is still understood to be there.

Poison ivy is something **everyone should avoid.** [*That everyone should avoid* is the complete adjective clause.]

Punctuation with Adjective Clauses

No punctuation is used with an adjective clause that contains information essential to the identification of a person, place, or thing in the sentence. The relative pronoun *that* usually begins an essential clause. A comma or commas, however, should set off an adjective clause that is nonessential. A clause is nonessential if it can be removed from the sentence without changing the basic meaning of the sentence. A clause is usually nonessential if it modifies a proper noun.

ESSENTIAL The person **who became the first woman Supreme Court justice** was Sandra Day O'Connor. [No commas are used because the clause is needed to identify which woman.]

NONESSENTIAL Sandra Day O'Connor, **who became the first woman Supreme Court justice,** had served as majority leader in the Arizona state senate. [Commas are used because the clause can be removed from the sentence.]

EXERCISE *Identifying and Punctuating Adjective Clauses*

Write the following sentences and underline each adjective clause. Then add a comma or commas where needed.

1. Judo which was first included in the Olympic Games in 1964 is now an international sport.
2. The only state that borders only one other state is Maine.
3. Panama is a country where one can see the sun rise over the Pacific Ocean and set over the Atlantic Ocean.
4. The McGee Company which makes engine parts is hiring.
5. Helen Keller whose sight and hearing were destroyed by an early illness eventually conquered her handicaps.
6. I enjoyed reading the novel Mrs. Johnson assigned me.
7. In Paris the Louvre which houses one of the world's largest art collections has eight miles of galleries.
8. Did you meet my Uncle Harry who is a coast pilot?
9. The penguin has an apparatus above its eyes that enables it to get rid of excess salt.
10. Yesterday was a day when everything seemed to go well.

Functions of a Relative Pronoun A relative pronoun functions in several ways in a sentence. It usually introduces an adjective clause and refers to another noun or pronoun in the sentence. A relative pronoun also has a function within the adjective clause itself. It can be used as a subject, a direct object, or an object of a preposition. A relative pronoun can also show possession.

SUBJECT
: Amy Berger, **who lives next door,** is now a vice president at the bank. [*Who* is the subject of *lives.*]

DIRECT OBJECT
: The photographs **you saw** were taken by Rob. [The understood relative pronoun *that* is the direct object of *saw.* You saw *that.*]

OBJECT OF A PREPOSITION
: The article **from which you took this material** must be quite old. [*Which* is the object of the preposition *from.*]

POSSESSION
: Jan is the person **whose broad-jump record was broken at last night's meet.** [*Whose* shows possession of *record.*]

EXERCISE **5** *Determining the Function of a Relative Pronoun*

Number your paper 1 to 10. Write each adjective clause. Then label the use of each relative pronoun, using the following abbreviations. If an adjective clause begins with an understood *that,* write *understood* and then write the use of *that.*

subject = *subj.*   object of a preposition = *o.p.*
direct object = *d.o.*   possession = *poss.*

1. Our dog, which is frisky and intelligent, is a poodle.
2. The camera that you want is on sale at Hailey's.
3. The person to whom this package is addressed has left.
4. Aerobic dancing is an exercise many people enjoy.
5. Robert Frost, whose poetry was awarded the Pulitzer Prize, first published his poems at age thirty-eight.
6. My sister, who is an accountant, has just been promoted.
7. The deli, which my neighbor owns, has good food.
8. He is the man from whom I bought the plants.
9. Janet Guthrie, who was once an aerospace physicist, has driven in the Indianapolis 500.
10. The person whose wallet you found is in the office now.

Misplaced Modifiers

To avoid confusion, place an adjective clause as near as possible to the word it describes. Like a phrase a clause placed too far away from the word it modifies can cause confusion and is called a *misplaced modifier.*

MISPLACED   Timothy discovered an old coin near his house that was worth about five dollars.

CORRECT   Near his house Timothy discovered an old coin **that was worth about five dollars.**

MISPLACED   Dennis ran to take the meat off the grill, which was burned to a crisp.

CORRECT   Dennis ran to take the meat, **which was burned to a crisp,** off the grill.

EXERCISE *Correcting Misplaced Modifiers*

Write the following sentences, correcting each misplaced modifier. Use a comma or commas where needed.

1. Nancy had to mail a package at the post office that was being sent to Michigan.
2. This Ponderosa tomato was grown by my father that weighs nearly a pound.
3. For several weeks a car stood in my neighbor's driveway that had a flat tire.
4. In *Poor Richard's Almanac,* Benjamin Franklin described the construction of a lightning rod which was published for 25 years.
5. I showed the yellow-striped cotton sweater to my sister that you gave me.
6. O. Henry's story "The Gift of the Magi" has a surprise ending which is included in many short-story anthologies.
7. Angelo left his goggles by the pool that he had received for his birthday.
8. The bicycle belongs to my neighbor that has the new white rims.
9. The teddy bear was created by Morris Michton which was named after President Theodore Roosevelt,
10. Large plants lent a bright touch to the room which filled the bay window.

Noun Clauses

Rule 20f **A noun clause** is a subordinate clause that is used like a noun.

A noun clause is used in the same ways in which a single noun can be used. The examples show some of the uses.

SUBJECT	**What Jenny suggested** makes sense.
DIRECT OBJECT	Julian knows **that he was wrong.**
INDIRECT OBJECT	Give **whoever volunteers** this manual.
OBJECT OF A PREPOSITION	People are often influenced by **what they see in commercials.**
PREDICATE NOMINATIVE	A good hot meal is **what I could use most right now.**

The following list contains words that often introduce a noun clause. *Who, whom, whose, which,* and *that* can also be used as relative pronouns to introduce adjective clauses.

Common Introductory Words for Noun Clauses

how	what	where	who	whomever
if	whatever	whether	whoever	whose
that	when	which	whom	why

EXERCISE **7** *Finding Noun Clauses*

Number your paper 1 to 10. Then write the noun clause in each sentence.

1. Mexican food is what I like best.
2. That our pitcher was tiring was obvious to everyone.
3. The Plaza will give a half-price ticket to whoever wins.
4. I just learned that Charles Dickens first published most of his books in installments in magazines.
5. No one knows who actually made the first American flag.
6. That Jody was the best candidate was apparent.
7. Give whomever you wish an invitation to our party.
8. How people live in other countries interests me.
9. His reason was that his alarm didn't go off.
10. I read that the cost of cars will increase.

EXERCISE *Determining the Uses of Noun Clauses*

Number your paper 1 to 10. Write each noun clause. Then label the use of each one, using the following abbreviations.

> subject = *subj.*   object of a preposition = *o.p.*
> direct object = *d.o.*   predicate nominative = *p.n.*
> indirect object = *i.o.*

1. That she works late on Saturday is common knowledge.
2. Did you know that certain species of trees have been in existence for 60 million years?
3. One explanation is that someone forgot to lock the door.
4. Send whoever answers the ad this brochure.
5. Be ready to take responsibility for what you do.
6. The coach gave whoever practiced daily his attention.
7. His reason for being late was that he took the wrong bus.
8. Where the new gym will be built is the latest news.
9. Do you know why plants need light?
10. A prize will be given to whoever raises the most money.

EXERCISE *Cumulative Review*

Number your paper 1 to 10. Write the subordinate clauses in the following sentences. (There may be more than one in a sentence.) Then label the use of each one—*adverb, adjective,* or *noun.*

1. When the earth, moon, and sun are in line, an eclipse occurs.
2. What distinguished the Spartan soldiers of ancient Greece was their almost inhuman discipline.
3. The coach predicted that the game would be canceled.
4. The four-ton stegosaurus dinosaur that lived 150 million years ago was about 20 feet long and 8 feet tall.
5. As a baby bird hatches, it uses a toothlike structure that enables it to break out of the egg.
6. Fishing is what I often do on the weekends.
7. Although the sun shone brightly, the weather forecasters maintained that the weekend would be rainy.
8. Community gardens, which are numerous in our city, offer people in urban areas the chance to be self-sufficient.
9. Honey is one of the few foods that do not spoil.
10. We arrived at South Dakota's Black Hills as the sun was sinking below the horizon.

Kinds of Sentence Structure

A sentence can be *simple, compound, complex,* or *compound-complex,* depending on the number and the kind of clauses in it.

Rule 20g / **A simple sentence** consists of one independent clause.

Certain <u>lizards</u> <u>can climb</u> trees.

A simple sentence can have a compound subject, a compound verb, or both.

During the early 1800's, <u>hunters</u> and <u>trappers</u> <u>went</u> west of the Mississippi and <u>explored</u> new territory in America.

Rule 20h / **A compound sentence** consists of two or more independent clauses.

A compound sentence should be composed of only closely related independent clauses joined by a coordinating conjunction such as *and, but, for, nor, or, so,* or *yet.*

⌐────── independent clause ──────┐   ⌐independent clause─┐
We went to a movie last night, but it was rather boring.

⌐── independent clause ──┐ ⌐──independent clause──┐   ⌐──
The stew is in the oven, the salad is on the counter, and the

⌐── independent clause ──┐
dessert is in the freezer.

Note: See pages 774–775 and 794 for the punctuation of a compound sentence.

Rule 20i / **A complex sentence** consists of one independent clause and one or more subordinate clauses.

⌐── independent clause ──┐ ⌐──subordinate clause──┐
We bought him a wallet that has his initials on it.

⌐─── independent clause ───┐ ⌐──subordinate clause──┐ ⌐──
We took Ann to the hospital because we were worried that

⌐── subordinate clause ──┐
her injury might be serious.

Note: See pages 775–776 and 782–783 for the punctuation of a complex sentence.

Rule 20j A **compound-complex sentence** consists of two or more independent clauses and one or more subordinate clauses.

┌──────independent clause──────┐ ┌──────independent clause──────┐
I have tried to lose ten pounds, but up to now I have failed

┌──────────────subordinate clause──────────────┐
because fattening foods taste too good to me.

EXERCISE *Classifying Sentences*

Label each sentence *simple, compound, complex,* or *compound-complex.*

Eating in
Space

1. In 1984, Byron Lichtenberg, who is a biomedical engineer, became a member of a spacecraft crew.
2. Lichtenberg discovered that dealing with zero gravity was difficult.
3. The other two astronauts were able to control their movements, but at first Lichtenberg kept bouncing off the walls.
4. Lichtenberg found that eating wasn't easy either.
5. He ate with only a spoon because he had to hold on to his food with his other hand.
6. Once he tried to make a sandwich, but this task was much harder than he had expected.
7. The beef and cheese floated around, but then he clamped them together with the bread.
8. Peanuts were the most fun to eat.
9. When Lichtenberg tried to pour them down his throat, they escaped and floated around the cabin.
10. Eventually he chased them down like Pac Man.

EXERCISE *Writing Sentences*

Number your paper 1 to 8. Then write two simple sentences, two compound sentences, two complex sentences, and two compound-complex sentences. Use proper punctuation.

 Application to Writing

Write an essay that describes how you felt the last time you were sick. Include specific examples, perhaps by making comparisons. Make sure that your essay contains at least one compound sentence and three complex sentences: one with an adjective clause, one with an adverb clause, and one with a noun clause.

Grammar: Combining Sentences

A paragraph with all simple sentences eventually becomes dull and monotonous to read. On the other hand, a paragraph with all complex or compound-complex sentences can become confusing. A paragraph that includes a combination of different kinds of sentences is by far the most interesting.

As part of your editing, analyze the structure of your sentences. If most of your sentences run two, three, and four lines long, divide some of them into shorter, simple sentences. If most of your sentences are simple sentences, combine some of them into compound or complex sentences.

TWO SIMPLE SENTENCES	The mayor favored the proposal. She could not attend the meeting.
A COMPOUND SENTENCE	The mayor favored the proposal, **but she could not attend the meeting.**
TWO SIMPLE SENTENCES	The hummingbird hovers in the air. Its weak feet cannot support it on a flat surface.
A COMPLEX SENTENCE	The hummingbird hovers in the air **because its weak feet cannot support it on a flat surface.** [adverb clause]
TWO SIMPLE SENTENCES	The high-wheeler bicycle had an enormous front wheel. The wheel was almost six feet high.
A COMPLEX SENTENCE	The high-wheeler bicycle had an enormous front wheel **that was almost six feet high.** [adjective clause]
TWO SIMPLE SENTENCES	A sheep dog does the work of three or four men. All ranchers agree on this.
A COMPLEX SENTENCE	All ranchers agree **that a sheep dog does the work of three or four men.** [noun clause]

Checking Your Understanding   Combine the first five pairs of sentences into compound sentences. Then combine the second ten pairs of sentences into complex sentences. Use punctuation where needed.

1. A human being continually sheds skin. An entire new outer layer of skin is replaced once every 28 to 38 days.
2. Last summer I worked at the supermarket. This summer I have a job on a farm.
3. A solar eclipse can be seen in a narrow band across the earth. A lunar eclipse can be seen over very large areas.
4. Oysters are an expensive delicacy today. In medieval England they were among the cheapest foods available.
5. Carl enjoys working with wood. He is not as interested in working with metal.
6. Earl took typing for six months. He can type 75 words per minute.
7. The rays of the setting sun pass through miles of dense lower air. This air absorbs all colors except red and green.
8. Sandra will not pass the history quiz. She memorizes all the important dates.
9. e. e. cummings did not use capital letters in his poetry or in his name. Our teacher told us this.
10. Tomorrow will be hazy and overcast. We will not go to the beach.
11. Amateur astronomers can tell a star from a planet. Only stars twinkle.
12. The first wristwatch appeared in 1571. It was made by Royal Clockmaker Bartholomew Newsam for Queen Elizabeth of England.
13. Rehearsal has been canceled this afternoon. Susan told me that.
14. The longest reign of an English monarch was that of Queen Victoria. She ruled over 63 years.
15. Absenteeism is far lower in air-conditioned offices and factories. Studies have shown this.

Writing a Personal Essay Experiences that are unnerving when they occur may turn into good stories to tell afterward. Brainstorm for a list of such experiences of your own. From your list choose the one experience that now seems the most amusing. Next freewrite about it, jotting down all the details you can remember. Finally, arrange your notes in chronological order.

Write the first draft of a personal essay about the traumatic experience that now strikes you as humorous. Include details, sense impressions, figurative language, and any other devices that will make your essay descriptive and realistic. *Application:* As you revise your essay, look for places where combining sentences would improve your writing. Then, after you have someone else read and comment on your essay, edit it and make a final copy.

Diagraming Sentences

Each clause—whether independent or subordinate—is diagramed on a separate baseline like a simple sentence.

Compound Sentences   Each independent clause is diagramed like a simple sentence. The clauses are joined at the verbs with a broken line on which the conjunction is written.

The cafeteria food is good, but I still take my lunch.

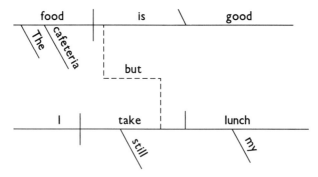

Complex Sentences   An adverb or an adjective clause in a complex sentence is diagramed beneath the independent clause it modifies. The following diagram contains an adverb clause. The subordinating conjunction goes on a broken line that connects the verb in the adverb clause to the modified verb, adjective, or adverb in the independent clause.

Before I begin my article, I must do more research.

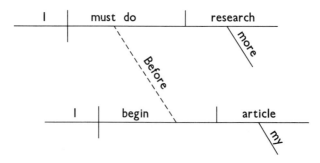

The relative pronoun in an adjective clause is connected by a broken line to the noun or the pronoun the clause modifies.

We recently bought a clock that chimes on the hour.

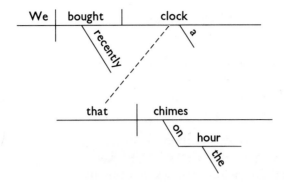

A noun clause is diagramed on a pedestal in the same position as a single noun with the same function. In the following diagram, the noun clause is used as a direct object.

Tell us what you want for your birthday.

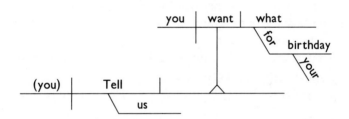

Compound-Complex Sentences To diagram these sentences, apply rules for diagraming compound and complex sentences.

EXERCISE *Diagraming Sentences*

Diagram the following sentences or copy them. If you copy them, draw one line under each subject and two lines under each verb. Then put parentheses around each subordinate clause and label each one *adverb, adjective,* or *noun.*

1. The gorilla may look fierce, but it is a gentle animal.
2. When the key broke in the door, we used the window.
3. Many roads that the Romans built are still used.
4. You should tell the reporter whatever you saw.
5. She turned the key, but the car wouldn't start because the battery was dead.

20 Review

Understanding Uses of Clauses Number your paper 1 to 30. Write the subordinate clauses in the following sentences. (There may be more than one subordinate clause in a sentence.) Then label the use of each one—*adverb, adjective,* or *noun.*

1. Although many tornadoes occur throughout the United States, they are quite rare west of the Rockies.
2. Several champion ice-hockey teams have come from Canada, where ice-skating is a very popular sport.
3. I heard that trucks can no longer travel on Grove Street.
4. Wrap that meat in foil before you put it into the freezer.
5. Because I wanted to do better in Spanish, I decided that I would go to the language lab for help.
6. The microphone that he used had a cord attached to it.
7. If you take a trip to Mount Vernon, you will be taken back two centuries into the past.
8. Parachutists often fall a considerable distance before they pull the cord that opens the parachute.
9. Someone once said that an egotist is a person who is "me-deep" in conversation.
10. My mother, who seemed happy and relieved, reported that she had found a new apartment for us.
11. Don ran when he saw a huge bull approaching him.
12. Whoever is qualified for the job will have an interview.
13. Early schoolhouses were always red because red paint was the cheapest paint available.
14. The oldest fossils date back to a time when seas covered large areas that have long since become dry land.
15. Since I wasn't there, I don't know what happened.
16. Margaret Mead, who was an anthropologist, was famous for her studies of cultural influences.
17. Leroy and I talked before we went to football practice.
18. Melissa was pleased with what she had accomplished.
19. The person whose ring you found is offering a reward.
20. When the power was out for two days, we learned that life without electricity is extremely inconvenient.
21. Sebastian picks strawberries faster than Matthew.

22. The painting that hangs in the cafeteria is a gift from the senior class.
23. What he told you actually happened.
24. Christina claimed that this summer she read every book on the reading list.
25. If all the blood vessels in a single human body were stretched end to end, they would form a rope that is 60,000 miles long.
26. Scientists believe that the porpoise is the most intelligent animal next to humans.
27. Tom is much stronger than I.
28. It was Christopher Columbus who brought pickles to the Americas.
29. Sing the song that you wrote.
30. As ants build their colonies, they sometimes move up to 40 tons of dirt.

Mastery Test

Number your paper 1 to 10. Then label each sentence *simple, compound, complex,* or *compound-complex.*

1. Look at a drop of water under a microscope, and you will see a very busy world.
2. The mule deer's coat, which is rusty red in summer, changes to grayish brown in winter.
3. The newspaper reported that most citizens of our town support the bill for a new library.
4. We wallpapered the living room in our new house but painted the kitchen.
5. Any volunteer who gives an oral report as well as a written one will receive extra credit.
6. Deck tennis is a game similar to court tennis, but it requires rope or rubber rings instead of rackets and balls.
7. Although the dandelion is considered chiefly a pest, it is cultivated for both food and medicine.
8. We fished all day but didn't catch anything.
9. I took some pictures at the dance; and after they were developed, two of them appeared in the school paper.
10. Grass clippings that are allowed to remain on the ground soon decompose and return valuable nutrients to the soil.

21

Sound Sentences

Number your paper 1 to 10. Then label each group of words *sentence, fragment,* or *run-on.*

EXAMPLE   Two skaters racing and circling the rink.
ANSWER   fragment

1. When Barry heard about the new job opening, he applied for the position.
2. The Abyssinian cat, a breed thought to come from a cat of India or Africa.
3. The seed of a cacao tree looks somewhat like an almond, it has a bitter taste.
4. From a plane one can see the huge underwater portions of icebergs that are not visible from the water.
5. When some people answer the telephone.
6. The picture hanging above the fireplace.
7. The federal government has classified the wolf as an endangered species in every state except Alaska and Minnesota.
8. Dolphins make a wide variety of noises, their sound effects include whistling, chirping, and squeaking.
9. The streams froze twelve inches of snow covered everything in sight.
10. To make the best possible use of your time.

Sentence Fragments and Run-on Sentences

In recent years several books have been written about how to create the right impression when you apply for a job. These books include everything from how to dress appropriately to how to shake hands after an interview. Employers, teachers, college entrance boards, and admissions officers also form impressions of people from their written work. Negative impressions are often formed of students who submit written work filled with sentence fragments, or incomplete sentences, and sentences that run together. This chapter will show you how to recognize and correct these two kinds of sentence errors, so that the first impression you make will be your best.

A *sentence fragment* is not a sentence at all. It is an incomplete thought that usually leaves a reader with unanswered questions, asking for more information. A *run-on sentence* is the exact opposite of a sentence fragment. It is two or more sentences that run together with only a comma to separate them or no punctuation at all. A run-on sentence gives a reader too much information too fast.

Sentence Fragments

Rule 21a A **sentence fragment** is a group of words that does not express a complete thought.

You can correct a fragment in one of two ways. You can add words to it to make a complete sentence, or you can attach it to the sentence next to it. Sometimes when you attach a fragment to a sentence, you may have to add or drop words.

There are several kinds of sentence fragments. All sentence fragments, however, have one thing in common. They all are missing one or more of the elements needed to make them sentences.

Phrase Fragments Since a phrase is a group of words that does not have a subject and a verb, it can never express a complete thought. The fragments in the examples on the next two pages are in heavy type.

PREPOSITIONAL PHRASE FRAGMENT — After 1945, many new words and expressions came into our language. **Like *baby-sit, cutback, rat race*, and *soap opera*.**

CORRECTED — After 1945, many new words and expressions, like *baby-sit, cutback, rat race,* and *soap opera,* came into our language.

PARTICIPIAL PHRASE FRAGMENT — The Navaho are the most populous Indian tribe in the United States. **Numbering over 130,000.**

CORRECTED — The Navaho, numbering over 130,000, are the most populous Indian tribe in the United States.

GERUND PHRASE FRAGMENT — **Making the honor roll during second semester.** This was Kenneth's goal.

CORRECTED — Making the honor roll during second semester was Kenneth's goal.

INFINITIVE PHRASE FRAGMENT — **To provide healthful living and working conditions.** This is one important objective of medical researchers.

CORRECTED — To provide healthful living and working conditions is one important objective of medical researchers.

APPOSITIVE PHRASE FRAGMENT — The first woman veterinarian was Dr. Elinor McGrath. **A 1910 graduate of the Chicago Veterinary College.**

CORRECTED — The first woman veterinarian was Dr. Elinor McGrath, a 1910 graduate of the Chicago Veterinary College.

Clause Fragments   Even though a subordinate clause has both a subject and a verb, it does not express a complete thought. *(See pages 610–621.)*

ADVERB CLAUSE FRAGMENT — The Nile River would stretch farther than the distance between New York and Los Angeles. **If it were straightened out.**

CORRECTED — If it were straightened out, the Nile River would stretch farther than the distance between New York and Los Angeles.

ADJECTIVE At the career workshop, she visited the booths.
CLAUSE FRAGMENT **That featured journalism.**

CORRECTED At the career workshop, she visited the booths that featured journalism.

Other Fragments   There are other kinds of fragments besides phrase and clause fragments.

PART OF A Walter Hunt patented the safety pin in 1849. **And**
COMPOUND **gave the world a very useful product.**
PREDICATE

CORRECTED Walter Hunt patented the safety pin in 1849 and gave the world a very useful product.

ITEMS IN Many flowers grow from bulbs. **Daffodils, tulips,**
A SERIES **and irises.**

CORRECTED Many flowers—such as daffodils, tulips, and irises— grow from bulbs.

EXERCISE *Correcting Sentence Fragments*

Number your paper 1 to 15. Then correct each sentence fragment. Add capital letters and punctuation where needed. If both groups of words in an item are sentences, write *C* after the number.

  1. The pouter pigeon puffs out its chest. When anyone pays attention to it.
  2. Sheepskin is a spongy leather. And is often used for gloves and other light garments.
  3. The warm morning sunshine shone brightly. Into the small, dreary hotel room.
  4. Sequoya was a Cherokee Indian. The giant sequoia tree is named after him.
  5. On the hike we carried all the supplies we needed. Food, water, tents, rain gear, and sleeping bags.
  6. In the Sonoran Desert is found the saguaro cactus. Which grows to a height of 15 feet before producing its first branches.
  7. Reacting against the status of women in the nineteenth century. Charlotte Brontë wrote the novel *Jane Eyre.*
  8. The calliope was first used on a riverboat. Now it can be heard under the big top.
  9. Yesterday I had a flat tire. At the end of Meriden Road.
 10. To be an astronaut. This is Andrea's ambition.

11. The Americans lost the Battle of Bunker Hill. Because they ran out of gun powder.

12. When camping, we should take warm clothes. Such as sweaters.

13. The average lead pencil has enough lead to draw a line 35 miles long. Or write approximately 50,000 words.

14. Gaining independence from England. This was the goal of the American Revolutionary War.

15. The Oscar trophy given at the Academy Awards is named after Oscar Pierce. A wealthy Texas rancher.

Run-on Sentences

Rule 21b A **run-on sentence** is two or more sentences that are written as one sentence and are separated by a comma or no mark of punctuation at all.

Run-on sentences result either from writing too fast or from the mistaken idea that very long sentences sound more scholarly. A run-on sentence is usually written in either of the following two ways.

WITH A COMMA   Buoys are the guideposts of the sea, they mark out channels.

WITH NO PUNCTUATION   In the winter some animals migrate others hibernate.

A run-on sentence can be corrected in several ways. (1) It can be written as two separate sentences. (2) It can be written as a compound sentence with a comma and a conjunction or with a semicolon. (3) It can be written as a complex sentence by changing one part of the run-on sentence into a subordinate clause.

RUN-ON SENTENCE   The continent of Europe covers over four million square miles, it is the second smallest continent.

SEPARATE SENTENCES   The continent of Europe covers over four million square miles. It is the second smallest continent.

COMPOUND SENTENCE   The continent of Europe covers over four million square miles, and it is the second smallest continent. [with a comma and a conjunction]

The continent of Europe covers over four million square miles; it is the second smallest continent. [with a semicolon]

COMPLEX   The continent of Europe, which covers over four
SENTENCE   million square miles, is the second smallest continent.
[adjective clause]

Although the continent of Europe covers over four
million square miles, it is the second smallest
continent. [adverb clause]

EXERCISE **2**   *Correcting Fragments and Run-on
Sentences*

Number your paper 1 to 10. Then correct each fragment or run-on
sentence. If a group of words is a sentence, write *C* after the number.
Add capital letters and punctuation.

Facts and
Figures

 1. In professional football the quarterback is the key player on the
    offense, the linebacker is the pivot of the defense.
 2. The finch belongs to the largest family of birds and is considered
    the most highly developed of all birds.
 3. Across Florida Bay lies Cape Sable, here giant turtles nest each
    summer.
 4. A skunk will not bite and throw its scent simultaneously.
 5. Handel wrote many musical compositions. His best-known work
    being the *Messiah.*
 6. The chow is the only dog that has a black tongue, the tongues of
    all other dogs are pink.
 7. There are many familiar legal holidays in the United States, two
    unfamiliar ones are Fast Day and Arbor Day.
 8. A python can swallow a rabbit whole and may eat as many as
    150 mice in a six-month period.
 9. Many kinds of birds migrate to the South during the winter some
    species of butterflies also fly south.
10. The woolly mammoth has been extinct since the Ice Age, it had
    tusks almost 16 feet long.

 Application to Writing

Write a newspaper article that describes the sighting of a woolly
mammoth near the Arctic Circle. Include an eyewitness account.
As you edit your article, check for any sentence fragments or run-
on sentences.

EXERCISE *Cumulative Review*

Correct each sentence fragment or run-on sentence. Add capital letters and punctuation where needed.

When the Martians Invaded

1. Once people believed that life existed on Mars, many authors encouraged this belief through their books.
2. One such book was a novel by H. G. Wells. Called *The War of the Worlds*.
3. In this book Martians invade Earth humans seem defenseless against them.
4. When the world appears doomed. It is discovered that the Martians have a hidden weakness.
5. They die of a human ailment. The common cold.
6. Their bodies unable to fight off the attacks of Earth's bacteria that humans are used to.
7. A radio program presented a dramatization of *The War of the Worlds*. On October 30, 1938.
8. Aired less than a year before the start of World War II.
9. At that time many Americans were apprehensive, news bulletins were not uncommon.
10. The scene of the program was set in the United States, the Martians landed in New Jersey.
11. The program started with an ordinary weather report. To provide realism.
12. Then came a special bulletin. About a huge metal cylinder that had landed in a farmer's field.
13. Some people only half listened. And missed the fact that the program was about a fictitious invasion.
14. Most people believed the invasion was real, they became frantic and desperate.
15. People rushing out into the streets and making desperate telephone calls.
16. People's imaginations played tricks on them, some saw a fire in the distance, others smelled poisonous gas.
17. A local power failure finally persuaded listeners. That the situation was hopeless.
18. People got into cars and headed west. To try to escape the attack of the Martians.
19. Calm was eventually restored. When people realized that the invasion was just a radio program.
20. No one forgot *The War of the Worlds*. For a long time.

Grammar: Editing for Sentence Errors

First drafts often contain sentence fragments and run-on sentences because writers are primarily thinking about subject matter, not accuracy or style. After you have written your first draft, however, you should always edit your work for sentence errors. One way to do this is by reading your written work aloud. The inflection of your voice will often detect many of your errors for you. For instance, if a sentence seems long and does not have a break, it may be a run-on.

Checking Your Understanding   Rewrite the following paragraphs, correcting all sentence fragments and run-on sentences. Correct the errors in a variety of ways; otherwise, you will have all short, choppy sentences. Add capital letters and punctuation where they are needed.

> While it is true that Mark Twain was a great writer, He was also an inventor. Twain hoped to make millions on his ideas, he lost a fortune, And had to earn a living by writing.
>
> Long before they came into being, Twain predicted such innovations as microfilm, data storage and retrieval, and television. He had great ideas, he was not a good businessman. He lost $300,000, for example, on an automatic typesetting machine, Because it had 18,000 moving parts and seldom worked. Twain did make a small profit on one of his ventures. Which was called Mark Twain's Self-Pasting Scrapbook.

Writing a Summary   Skim the table of contents of a current almanac or other book of interesting information. Find a topic that is particularly interesting to you, read it, and take notes. *(See pages 501–503.)* Then write the first draft of a paragraph that summarizes the topic you chose. Remember to put the information in the article into your own words.   *Application:* After you have revised your summary, edit it, correcting any sentence fragments or run-on sentences. When you have finished, write a final copy. Be prepared to read your summary aloud to the class.

21 Review

Correcting Sentence Errors   Rewrite the following sentences, correcting each sentence fragment or run-on sentence. Add capital letters and punctuation where needed.

1. Captain James Cook named the Sandwich Islands after an English noble. The fourth Earl of Sandwich.
2. Riding down the rapids of the Colorado River was exciting, twice the raft nearly capsized.
3. Ultrasound employs sound waves of high frequency, doctors use it to see within a person's body.
4. Oliver High's football team won the championship, now the baseball team is making a strong showing.
5. The tiny glass prism slowly turned on the string. And created beautiful rainbows on the wall.
6. Our subway stop is being repaired, we had to walk six blocks to the next one.
7. The human body has 70,000 miles of blood vessels, the heart pumps blood through these vessels and back again once every minute.
8. During the early part of the game, Predictions were that South High would win by ten points.
9. The last of the Florida Keys disappeared from sight, we headed for the open sea.
10. Eskimos sometimes buy refrigerators. To keep their food from freezing in the cold Arctic temperatures.
11. There are many community merchants. Who may want to advertise in the school newspaper.
12. We watched the campfire. Growing dimmer and dimmer in the darkness.
13. The Siamese is one of the most popular breeds of cats, most experts believe that it originated in Thailand.
14. Our halfback dodged to the left. To avoid the Tigers' swift backfield.
15. Storm clouds lay over the Allegheny Mountains to the west of us. occasionally we could see flashes of lightning.
16. Sarah read one novel a week. During the first two months of the school year.
17. Edward swung, the ball bounced past the third baseman for a double.

18. Water makes up about three fifths of your body weight, even your bones are about one-quarter water.
19. Horses were originally transported to North America by the Spaniards. Who brought them into Mexico.
20. Patrick raced unsteadily down the muddy field. Clutching the slippery football.
21. By the time you are 65 years old. Your heart will have beaten about 2½ billion times.
22. The bark of the redwood tree is fireproof, during a forest fire, the tree burns on the inside.
23. The ancient Romans occasionally filled the Colosseum with water once an entire naval battle was staged there.
24. Victoria Park is the perfect place. To hold the company softball team's picnic.
25. In the city of Washington, D.C. No building may be built taller than the Capitol building.

Mastery Test

Number your paper 1 to 10. Then label each group of words *sentence*, *fragment*, or *run-on*.

1. The rain stopped, sunlight fell across the wet leaves.
2. To put the roast in the oven and to set the timer.
3. I hit the cold, dark water feet first and plunged down to the bottom of the lake.
4. The distinguished man wearing the immaculate blue pin-striped suit.
5. Illinois is a great producer of corn Kansas is a great producer of wheat.
6. The moon is an airless and waterless world that has extremes of temperatures.
7. Waiting for the light to change at the intersection of Evergreen Avenue and Highland Road.
8. As graduation draws near, I've noticed that attendance at class meetings has increased.
9. Although the neighborhood grocery store is only two blocks away from here.
10. The French horn is a brass instrument, the English horn is a woodwind instrument.

22 Using Verbs

Diagnostic Test

Number your paper 1 to 10. Then write the past or the past participle of each verb in parentheses.

EXAMPLE   Yesterday I (swim) the length of the pool six times.
ANSWER   swam

1. Many early explorers reported that they had (see) mermaids on their voyages.
2. Has the bell (ring) for third period yet?
3. Five minutes after the downpour, the sun (come) out.
4. By the time Brad and Sunny arrived in their car, Kaya had already (go).
5. Wendy (break) the school's high-jump record by two inches last week.
6. The art class (make) very appealing advertising posters for the school play.
7. No one (know) what animal had made the strange tracks in the woods.
8. Before I could stop her, Mittens had (eat) most of the hamburger meat.
9. Joshua has (choose) that small mare to ride today.
10. The drum major (lead) the band onto the field during halftime.

Principal Parts

This is the first chapter in a unit on usage. The next three chapters will show you how to use pronouns correctly, how to make a verb agree with its subject, and how to determine which form of a modifier to use. These chapters on using the grammar that you have learned are extremely important. Knowing grammar without knowing proper usage is like buying a new car and leaving it parked in the driveway because you never learned to drive!

This first chapter covers verbs. Why should you know what a verb is? If you know which word in a sentence is a verb, you can consciously substitute a specific, colorful verb for a dull, general one. Once you have chosen a particular verb, however, you must know which form of that verb to use. In this chapter you will learn to use the correct forms of verbs.

The four basic forms of a verb are called its *principal parts*. The six tenses of a verb are formed from these principal parts.

Rule 22a   The **principal parts** of a verb are the *present,* the *present participle,* the *past,* and the *past participle.*

In each of the following examples, one of the four principal parts of *eat* is used as the main verb of the sentence. Notice that helping verbs are needed with the present participle and the past participle of the verb.

PRESENT	I usually **eat** lunch at noon.
PRESENT PARTICIPLE	I am **eating** lunch earlier this week.
PAST	I **ate** lunch an hour ago.
PAST PARTICIPLE	I have already **eaten** lunch.

Regular and Irregular Verbs

Verbs are sometimes classified in two categories—*regular verbs* and *irregular verbs.* How a verb forms its past and past participle will determine how it is classified.

Regular Verbs   Most verbs are classified as regular verbs because they form their past and past participle in the same way.

Rule 22b A **regular verb** forms its past and past participle by adding *-ed* or *-d* to the present.

Because a spelling change sometimes occurs when certain endings are added to the present, you should always check a dictionary if there is any doubt in your mind.

Note: *Have* is not part of the past participle. It has been added to all the following examples, however, to help you remember the past participle form. A past participle must have a *helping verb* when it is used as a verb.

PRESENT	PRESENT PARTICIPLE	PAST	PAST PARTICIPLE
talk	talking	talked	(have) talked
cook	cooking	cooked	(have) cooked
equip	equipping	equipped	(have) equipped
commit	committing	committed	(have) committed

Note: Occasionally the *-ed* or *-d* is incorrectly dropped from such frequently used verb forms as *asked, helped, looked, seemed, supposed, talked, used,* and *walked.*

INCORRECT   Every spring we **use** to plant a vegetable garden.
CORRECT   Every spring we **used** to plant a vegetable garden.

EXERCISE *Determining the Principal Parts of Regular Verbs*

Make four columns on your paper. Label them *present, present participle, past,* and *past participle.* Then write the four principal parts of the following verbs.

1. wish	**3.** turn	**5.** use	**7.** wave	**9.** seem
2. drop	**4.** dine	**6.** offer	**8.** stop	**10.** occur

Irregular Verbs Some common verbs are classified as irregular because they form their past and past participle in different ways and do not add *-ed* or *-d* to the present.

Rule 22c An **irregular verb** does not form its past and past participle by adding *-ed* or *-d* to the present.

The following irregular verbs have been divided into groups according to the way they form their past and past participle.

Group 1

These irregular verbs have the same form for the present, the past, and the past participle.

PRESENT	PRESENT PARTICIPLE	PAST	PAST PARTICIPLE
burst	bursting	burst	(have) burst
cost	costing	cost	(have) cost
hit	hitting	hit	(have) hit
hurt	hurting	hurt	(have) hurt
let	letting	let	(have) let
put	putting	put	(have) put
set	setting	set	(have) set

Group 2

These irregular verbs have the same form for the past and the past participle.

PRESENT	PRESENT PARTICIPLE	PAST	PAST PARTICIPLE
bring	bringing	brought	(have) brought
buy	buying	bought	(have) bought
catch	catching	caught	(have) caught
feel	feeling	felt	(have) felt
find	finding	found	(have) found
get	getting	got	(have) got or gotten
hold	holding	held	(have) held
keep	keeping	kept	(have) kept
lay	laying	laid	(have) laid
lead	leading	led	(have) led
leave	leaving	left	(have) left
lose	losing	lost	(have) lost
make	making	made	(have) made
say	saying	said	(have) said
sell	selling	sold	(have) sold
send	sending	sent	(have) sent
sit	sitting	sat	(have) sat
teach	teaching	taught	(have) taught
tell	telling	told	(have) told
win	winning	won	(have) won

EXERCISE *Using the Correct Verb Form*

Number your paper 1 to 25. Then write the past or the past participle of each verb in parentheses.

 I. The note (say) that Sean was staying after school for football practice.
 2. Under the pressure of the water, the levee (burst).
 3. I think I (leave) my raincoat in homeroom.
 4. Marjorie (lay) the mat on the porch.
 5. After several hours Martin finally (catch) a striped bass.
 6. I should have (send) this coat to the cleaners.
 7. Have you (find) the answer to the last math problem?
 8. Where have you (put) the paper towels?
 9. At the bake sale, the Drama Club (make) ninety dollars.
10. We should have (win) the state championship in soccer.
11. I just (sell) my old bicycle.
12. So far this year Miguel has (hit) two home runs.
13. I haven't (feel) well all day.
14. Yesterday Gary (get) a letter telling him about the hockey season.
15. How long have you (sit) here?
16. The park ranger (tell) us that the trails were open.
17. Has the table been (set) for dinner?
18. While I was shopping, I (buy) a poster for my brother.
19. I (hold) on to the bar of the roller coaster as tightly as I could.
20. Carmen (teach) me how to use the computer at school.
21. How long have you (keep) this scrapbook?
22. Have you (lose) your contact lens again?
23. You should have (bring) your tapes to the party.
24. Has anyone (let) the dog outside?
25. Two police officers on motorcycles (lead) the motorcade.

EXERCISE *Determining the Principal Parts of Irregular Verbs*

Make four columns on your paper. Label them *present, present participle, past,* and *past participle.* Then write the four principal parts of the following verbs.

I. lose	**3.** sit	**5.** let	**7.** feel	**9.** teach
2. keep	**4.** put	**6.** find	**8.** cost	**10.** leave

Group 3

These irregular verbs form the past participle by adding -*n* to the past.

PRESENT	PRESENT PARTICIPLE	PAST	PAST PARTICIPLE
break	breaking	broke	(have) broken
choose	choosing	chose	(have) chosen
freeze	freezing	froze	(have) frozen
speak	speaking	spoke	(have) spoken
steal	stealing	stole	(have) stolen

Group 4

These irregular verbs form the past participle by adding -*n* to the present.

PRESENT	PRESENT PARTICIPLE	PAST	PAST PARTICIPLE
blow	blowing	blew	(have) blown
draw	drawing	drew	(have) drawn
drive	driving	drove	(have) driven
give	giving	gave	(have) given
grow	growing	grew	(have) grown
know	knowing	knew	(have) known
rise	rising	rose	(have) risen
see	seeing	saw	(have) seen
take	taking	took	(have) taken
throw	throwing	threw	(have) thrown

EXERCISE 4 *Using the Correct Verb Form*

Number your paper 1 to 10. Then write the past or the past participle of each verb in parentheses.

1. Willis has (throw) three balls through the hoop.
2. Brian (steal) three bases during the sixth inning.
3. The musician stood and (blow) a few notes on the clarinet.
4. Every day at the camp, we (draw) water from a well.
5. The heater in our car has been (break) for a week.
6. Last night we (see) the school's production of *Camelot*.
7. We have (grow) corn for the first time this year.
8. Suki had never (speak) before such a large group.
9. The flag slowly (rise) on the flagpole.
10. Chris asked if we had (choose) a captain yet.

EXERCISE 5 *Determining the Correct Verb Form*

Number your paper 1 to 20. Then write the correct form of each underlined verb. If the verb is correct, write *C* after the number. (This exercise includes verbs from the first four groups.)

   1. Have you <u>took</u> any pictures with your new camera?
   2. Ever since she went to obedience school, Princess has <u>brung</u> in the newspaper each morning.
   3. I <u>seen</u> her on the school bus this morning.
   4. Has everyone already <u>left</u> for the game?
   5. Ann and Paul have <u>drove</u> to the beach with Luis.
   6. My dog Hank has <u>stole</u> my shoe again.
   7. Dad has <u>chose</u> a watch for Barry's graduation present.
   8. You should have <u>known</u> about the new regulations.
   9. I have never <u>drew</u> her portrait.
  10. Alison has often <u>spoke</u> about her plans for the future.
  11. For an hour the winds have <u>blew</u> steadily with gale force.
  12. Mom has <u>growed</u> the biggest and most beautiful geraniums you have ever seen!
  13. Without your help we would never have <u>made</u> it this far.
  14. I should have <u>sent</u> the package by express mail.
  15. We <u>losed</u> the basketball game by only two points.
  16. The bread dough has <u>rose</u> high in the pan.
  17. Oh, no! I have just <u>broke</u> the meat platter.
  18. We should have <u>froze</u> those extra strawberries.
  19. Why have you <u>given</u> your new jacket to Tracy?
  20. I have <u>keeped</u> every receipt from our purchases.

Group 5

These irregular verbs form the past and the past participle by changing a vowel.

PRESENT	PRESENT PARTICIPLE	PAST	PAST PARTICIPLE
begin	beginning	began	(have) begun
drink	drinking	drank	(have) drunk
ring	ringing	rang	(have) rung
shrink	shrinking	shrank	(have) shrunk
sing	singing	sang	(have) sung
sink	sinking	sank	(have) sunk
swim	swimming	swam	(have) swum

Group 6

These irregular verbs form the past and the past participle in other ways.

PRESENT	PRESENT PARTICIPLE	PAST	PAST PARTICIPLE
come	coming	came	(have) come
do	doing	did	(have) done
eat	eating	ate	(have) eaten
fall	falling	fell	(have) fallen
go	going	went	(have) gone
lie	lying	lay	(have) lain
ride	riding	rode	(have) ridden
run	running	ran	(have) run
tear	tearing	tore	(have) torn
wear	wearing	wore	(have) worn
write	writing	wrote	(have) written

EXERCISE *Using the Correct Verb Form*

Number your paper 1 to 15. Write the past or the past participle of each verb in parentheses. Then read each sentence aloud to check your answer.

1. Before anyone knew what had happened, Edward had (run) 20 yards for a touchdown.
2. Andy (shrink) back into the doorway to surprise his friend.
3. Some critics feel that William Wordsworth had (write) his best poetry by the time he was thirty.
4. I have already (ring) the doorbell twice.
5. The tenor (sing) the aria magnificently.
6. Have you ever (tear) a shirt the first day you (wear) it?
7. I (ride) in a train for the first time last week.
8. I (lie) down after dinner for half an hour.
9. As the canoe (sink), we (swim) to shore.
10. The dinner was delicious, but we should have (eat) earlier.
11. Felicia (run) a mile to try out her new running shoes.
12. I have (do) the dishes and have (come) to see if you want me to do anything else.
13. In colonial days a shoe could be (wear) on either foot.
14. After Bart (eat) breakfast, he (begin) to paint the porch.
15. Have you ever (ride) on a subway?

EXERCISE *Supplying the Correct Verb Form*

Number your paper 1 to 10. Then complete each pair of sentences by supplying the past or the past participle of the verb in parentheses at the beginning of the sentence.

1. (begin) The play _____ 15 minutes ago. It should have _____ a half hour ago.
2. (do) Have you _____ your homework? I _____ mine at school.
3. (run) Matthew _____ for Student Council president last year. He should have _____ again this year.
4. (drink) We _____ some ice water after running the marathon. We should never have _____ it so fast.
5. (go) Have you _____ to the supermarket yet? Yes, I _____ this afternoon.
6. (lie) After dinner Connie _____ down because she wasn't feeling well. She has _____ on the couch for two hours.
7. (write) I _____ the first draft of my essay last night. Have you _____ yours?
8. (swim) Kelly _____ from the dock to the pier. I have _____ that distance many times.
9. (sing) Have you ever _____ in public before? Once I _____ a solo in a chorus concert.
10. (eat) I just _____ an artichoke for the first time. Have you ever _____ one?

EXERCISE *Using the Correct Verb Form*

Number your paper 1 to 20. Then write the past or the past participle of each verb in parentheses. (This exercise includes verbs from all six groups.)

1. Diane (make) two loaves of bread for the picnic.
2. As the wheels (begin) to turn, the riverboat moved away.
3. Chester (write) his essay on a word processor.
4. Uncle Barney has (drive) a truck for 30 years now.
5. Last week the mayor (lay) the cornerstone for the museum.
6. Melba carefully (set) the vase of flowers on the table.
7. The bells in the church steeple (ring) after the wedding.
8. Many of the world's lemons are (grow) in California.
9. Who (win) first place in the poetry contest?
10. Last summer we (eat) fresh fruit every day.
11. I have not (wear) my new jacket yet.

12. At 1:32 A.M., we (see) the comet streak across the horizon.

13. I haven't (do) all the research for my report yet.

14. In 1962, in his first year as a pro, Jack Nicklaus (win) the U.S. Open in a playoff against Arnold Palmer.

15. The puma leaped from the branch and (run) swiftly.

16. You should have (give) your car a good waxing.

17. Last night Mario (go) to see a play at the outdoor theater.

18. The coach (speak) to the team about sportsmanship.

19. Rita was unanimously (choose) to be the editor.

20. Somehow the dog (lose) its identification tag.

EXERCISE 9 *Cumulative Review*

Number your paper 1 to 15. Then write the past or the past participle of each verb in parentheses. (This exercise includes regular and irregular verbs.)

The Harlem Globetrotters

1. For over six decades, the Harlem Globetrotters have (bring) an unusual dimension to basketball.

2. They have (draw) some of the largest crowds in basketball history.

3. In 1926, the Globetrotters (begin) as a serious team.

4. They (play) some of their first games in the Savoy Ballroom in Chicago.

5. When the dance hall (fall) on hard times, the team (go) on the road.

6. Since that time the Globetrotters have never (leave) the touring circuit.

7. Abe Saperstein, who (form) the first team, always (choose) the best players he could find.

8. As a result his team eventually (get) so good that no one (want) to play them.

9. That's when Saperstein (make) an important decision.

10. He (break) from tradition and (add) comedy routines.

11. The fans had never (see) anything like it before.

12. Saperstein (expand) the clowning, and the popularity of the Globetrotters (grow).

13. Eventually the comedy routines (become) a permanent part of the team's show.

14. In 1940, the "Trotters" (get) a big boost when they (win) a world professional basketball tournament in Chicago.

15. Since then they have (give) the world a unique and wonderful game of basketball.

Verb Tense

All the tenses of a verb are formed from the principal parts. Different verb forms express the *tense,* or time, of a verb. The six tenses are *present, past, future, present perfect, past perfect,* and *future perfect.* The six tenses of the verb *drive* express action at different times.

PRESENT	Bart **drives** Tad to school.
PAST	Bart **drove** Tad to school yesterday.
FUTURE	Bart **will drive** Tad to school tomorrow.
PRESENT PERFECT	Bart **has driven** Tad to school all month.
PAST PERFECT	Bart **had** never **driven** Tad to school before March.
FUTURE PERFECT	By June Bart **will have driven** Tad to school for four months.

Conjugation of a Verb

A *conjugation* lists all the singular and plural forms of a verb in its various tenses. Following is a conjugation of the irregular verb *eat.*

CONJUGATION OF *EAT*

Principal Parts

PRESENT	PRESENT PARTICIPLE	PAST	PAST PARTICIPLE
eat	eating	ate	eaten

Present

This tense expresses action that is going on now.

SINGULAR	PLURAL
I eat	we eat
you eat	you eat
he, she, it eats	they eat

Past

This tense expresses action that took place in the past.

SINGULAR	PLURAL
I ate	we ate
you ate	you ate
he, she, it ate	they ate

Future

This tense expresses action that will take place in the future. It is formed by adding *shall* or *will* to the present.

SINGULAR	PLURAL
I shall/will eat	we shall/will eat
you will eat	you will eat
he, she, it will eat	they will eat

Present Perfect

This tense expresses action that was completed at some indefinite time in the past or action that started in the past and is still going on. It is formed by adding *has* or *have* to the past participle.

SINGULAR	PLURAL
I have eaten	we have eaten
you have eaten	you have eaten
he, she, it has eaten	they have eaten

Past Perfect

This tense expresses action that took place before some other past action. It is formed by adding *had* to the past participle.

SINGULAR	PLURAL
I had eaten	we had eaten
you had eaten	you had eaten
he, she, it had eaten	they had eaten

Future Perfect

This tense expresses action that will be completed at some specific time in the future. It is formed by adding *shall have* or *will have* to the past participle.

SINGULAR	PLURAL
I shall/will have eaten	we shall/will have eaten
you will have eaten	you will have eaten
he, she, it will have eaten	they will have eaten

EXERCISE *Conjugating a Verb*

Using *eat* above as a model, conjugate the following verbs.

1. give, giving, gave, given
2. go, going, went, gone

Progressive Forms   Each tense has additional forms called the *progressive forms*. They are used to express continuing action. Progressive forms are formed by adding a form of the verb *be* to the present participle. Following are the progressive forms of the verb *eat.*

PRESENT PROGRESSIVE	am, is, are eating
PAST PROGRESSIVE	was, were eating
FUTURE PROGRESSIVE	shall/will be eating
PRESENT PERFECT PROGRESSIVE	has, have been eating
PAST PERFECT PROGRESSIVE	had been eating
FUTURE PERFECT PROGRESSIVE	shall/will have been eating

Emphatic Forms   The present and past tenses of a verb have additional forms called the *emphatic forms,* which can be used to show emphasis. They are formed by adding *do, does,* or *did* to the present. Following are the emphatic forms of the verb *eat.*

PRESENT EMPHATIC	do, does eat
PAST EMPHATIC	did eat

EXERCISE *Forming the Progressive and the Emphatic*

Using the two preceding models of *eat,* write the progressive and emphatic forms of the verb *give.*

Conjugation of the Irregular Verb *Be*   The principal parts of the verb *be* are highly irregular. As a result the conjugation of that verb is very different from those of other irregular verbs.

CONJUGATION OF *BE*

Principal Parts

PRESENT	PRESENT PARTICIPLE	PAST	PAST PARTICIPLE
am	being	was	been

Present

SINGULAR	PLURAL
I am	we are
you are	you are
he, she, it is	they are

Past

SINGULAR	PLURAL
I was	we were
you were	you were
he, she, it was	they were

Future

SINGULAR	PLURAL
I shall/will be	we shall/will be
you will be	you will be
he, she, it will be	they will be

Present Perfect

SINGULAR	PLURAL
I have been	we have been
you have been	you have been
he, she, it has been	they have been

Past Perfect

SINGULAR	PLURAL
I had been	we had been
you had been	you had been
he, she, it had been	they had been

Future Perfect

SINGULAR	PLURAL
I shall/will have been	we shall/will have been
you will have been	you will have been
he, she, it will have been	they will have been

EXERCISE *Identifying Verb Tenses*

Number your paper 1 to 20. Then write the tense of each underlined verb.

EXAMPLE   I <u>have taken</u> Spanish for three years.

ANSWER   present perfect

1. At dinner tonight we <u>ate</u> fresh corn from our garden.
2. Pilar <u>will be attending</u> the press conference.
3. A male fox <u>will mate</u> for life.
4. We <u>have been</u> here for over an hour.
5. I <u>drink</u> tomato juice every day.

6. <u>Have</u> you <u>been practicing</u> your chords and scales on the guitar lately?

7. I <u>had</u> never <u>tasted</u> swordfish before last night.

8. A prairie dog <u>is</u> a rodent, not a dog.

9. I <u>was taking</u> a nap when you called.

10. There <u>was</u> neither cranberry sauce nor pumpkin pie at the first Thanksgiving.

11. Diana <u>is waiting</u> for you at the library.

12. Too much rain and too little sunshine <u>have caused</u> the tomato plants to fail.

13. <u>Will</u> you <u>be</u> ready at seven o'clock?

14. Joe DiMaggio's batting average <u>fell</u> below 0.300 only twice in his career.

15. Our senator <u>will have visited</u> 16 cities by the time he returns from his latest trip.

16. I <u>did put</u> my books on the kitchen table.

17. Before today she <u>had been</u> my choice for class president.

18. Andrew <u>has written</u> several songs, and they're great!

19. Before Kevin joined the Raiders, he <u>had been singing</u> with another group.

20. You <u>did answer</u> his letter.

Uses of the Tenses

The six tenses and their various forms have particular uses. Clearly communicating your ideas will sometimes depend upon knowing the distinctions among these tenses.

The Present Tense This tense mainly expresses action (or state of being) that is taking place at the present time. The present tense is also used to express customary or habitual action and general truths.

PRESENT ACTION   This small car **rides** smoothly.

HABITUAL ACTION   I **jog** a mile each day.

A GENERAL TRUTH   Haste **makes** waste.

The present progressive form expresses present, ongoing action; and the present emphatic form emphasizes present action.

PRESENT PROGRESSIVE   Hannah **is working** at Lamont's Market.

PRESENT EMPHATIC   Yes, he **does own** a bicycle.

Another use of the present tense is called the historical present. The *historical present* is used to express past action when you want to give a certain historical event even greater impact or make it seem more immediate.

HISTORICAL PRESENT   Paul Revere **sees** the two lights in the church belfry, **jumps** onto his horse, and **heads** toward Lexington and Concord to warn the people.

The Past Tense   This tense expresses action (or state of being) that occurred at a definite time in the past. Words such as *yesterday, a week ago,* and *last winter* often indicate that the action took place at a definite time. The past progressive expresses continuous action that was completed in the past, and the emphatic past emphasizes action that occurred in the past.

PAST   Last week I **made** an important decision about my future.

PAST PROGRESSIVE   Yesterday Danny **was watching** the children at the playground.

PAST EMPHATIC   Your package **did arrive.**

The Future Tense   This tense expresses action (or state of being) that will take place in the future. The future progressive expresses a continuous action that will take place in the future.

FUTURE   I **will call** Betsy tonight.

FUTURE PROGRESSIVE   He **will be thinking** about your recommendations all summer.

Note: Sometimes the present or the present progressive is used to express future action as well.

Janice **goes** to the lake next Saturday.
Janice **is going** to the lake next Saturday.

The Present Perfect Tense   This tense expresses action (or state of being) that ended at some indefinite time in the past. The present perfect tense also expresses action that started in the past and is still going on. All the progressive forms of the perfect tenses show continuing action.

PRESENT PERFECT   Sheila **has written** two prizewinning poems. [She wrote them at some indefinite time in the past.]

The Rosens **have been** our neighbors for six years. [The Rosens became our neighbors six years ago and are still our neighbors.]

PRESENT PERFECT PROGRESSIVE   Recently I **have been taking** swimming lessons at the YMCA.

The Past Perfect Tense   This tense expresses action (or state of being) that took place before some other event in the past.

PAST PERFECT   The *Herald* sent its most informed reporter to interview the senators who **had toured** Poland. [The touring occurred before the *Herald* sent its reporter.]

The young child was found several hours after he **had been reported** missing. [The reporting came before the child was found.]

One day after Peggy **had applied** for the job at the bakery, she started working. [The applying came before she started to work.]

PAST PERFECT PROGRESSIVE   Wilma **had been studying** for two hours before she made dinner.

The Future Perfect Tense   This tense expresses action (or state of being) that will be completed at some future time before some other future event.

FUTURE PERFECT   The plane **will have landed** by the time we get to the airport.

FUTURE PERFECT PROGRESSIVE   By April 10, we **will have been living** here for five years.

EXERCISE *Choosing the Correct Tense*

Number your paper 1 to 25. Then write the correct form of the verb in parentheses. Be prepared to identify the tense you chose and tell why that tense is correct.

1. Dennis (applied, has applied) for that job yesterday.
2. I realized too late that I (left, had left) my keys at home.
3. For a month now, Carol (waited, has been waiting) for the first snowfall.
4. So far this week King (chewed, has chewed) three socks, a pair of slippers, and my science book.
5. After Roberta (read, had read) the best-seller, she gave the book to me.
6. Before taking off for our first parachute jump, we carefully (checked, have checked) our equipment.
7. Ever since 1914, the Panama Canal (is, has been) a shortcut between New York and California.
8. Before he retired in June, Coach Randolph (was, had been) coaching football for 15 years.
9. Last Thursday we (make, made) Mexican food for dinner.
10. My mother (is, has been) working at the same company for eight years.
11. Tanya (needs, needed) to use the phone now.
12. Halfway to the lake, we remembered that we (forgot, had forgotten) to bring the picnic basket.
13. Larry (met, had met) us at the stadium.
14. Ever since 1791, the Bill of Rights (was, has been) the safeguard of our civil liberties.
15. When the waiter brought the check, Dan realized that he (left, had left) his wallet at home.
16. Many relatives and friends (come, came) to our Fourth of July party last summer.
17. Two hours after Muffin (ran, had run) away, we found her.
18. Lionel (received, has received) two letters for varsity track and basketball at the awards banquet last night.
19. Tomorrow we finally (meet, will meet) Senator Abrams.
20. I (called, have called) their apartment every half hour since noon.
21. All summer long I (take, have been taking) tennis lessons.
22. Last month Henry (buy, bought) a car.
23. After he (cleaned, had cleaned) out the basement, he took a load of junk to the dump.
24. The meeting (will start, will have started) by the time we get there.
25. Until yesterday the committee (worked, had been working) on the membership drive.

EXERCISE *Understanding Tenses of Verbs*

Number your paper 1 to 10. Label the tense of each sentence. Then write the difference in meaning between the sentences in each pair.

EXAMPLE   **a.** Colin owned the garage for two years.
           b. Colin has owned the garage for two years.

ANSWER   **a.** past **b.** present perfect
          Sentence *a* means that Colin no longer owns the garage. Sentence *b* means that he still owns the garage after two years.

1. a. Why has Howard been learning Spanish?
   b. Why had Howard been learning Spanish?
2. a. They will take lifesaving training on Saturday.
   b. They will have taken lifesaving training on Saturday.
3. a. He has been very tired lately.
   b. He had been very tired lately.
4. a. What happened in chemistry?
   b. What has been happening in chemistry?
5. a. Catherine was resting when the fire alarm rang.
   b. Catherine had been resting when the fire alarm rang.
6. a. I volunteered at the animal shelter for three years.
   b. I have been volunteering at the animal shelter for three years.
7. a. Rover eats dinner in the kitchen.
   b. Rover is eating dinner in the kitchen.
8. a. By spring Nancy will have applied to several colleges in the United States and Canada.
   b. Before spring Nancy will apply to several colleges in the United States and Canada.
9. a. Tammy was the treasurer for the past two years.
   b. Tammy has been the treasurer for the past two years.
10. a. He is taking skiing lessons.
   b. He will be taking skiing lessons.

Problems with Tenses

Knowing the tenses of verbs and their uses will eliminate most of the verb errors you may have been making. There are, however, a few special problems you should keep in mind when you edit your writing.

Shifts in Tense When you write, avoid shifting from one tense to another. Use the same tense for a compound verb in simple sentences and for all verbs in compound and complex sentences *when the actions occur at the same time.*

Rule 22d Avoid shifting tenses when relating events that occur at the same time.

INCORRECT	┌─ past ─┐ The small plane **developed** engine trouble and ┌ present ┐ **returns** immediately to the field.
CORRECT	┌─ past ─┐ The small plane **developed** engine trouble and ┌─ past ─┐ **returned** immediately to the field.
INCORRECT	┌ past ┐ ┌ present ┐ I **wrote** the invitations, and Marcy **prepares** the refreshments.
CORRECT	┌ past ┐ ┌─ past ─┐ I **wrote** the invitations, and Marcy **prepared** the refreshments.
INCORRECT	┌ present ┐ When I **practice** the piano every morning, I ┌─ past ─┐ always **repeated** the scales.
CORRECT	┌ present ┐ When I **practice** the piano every morning, I ┌ present ┐ always **repeat** the scales.

EXERCISE 15 *Correcting Shifts in Tense*

If the second verb in a sentence incorrectly shifts in tense, write it correctly. If a sentence is correct, write *C* after the number.

1. The fire fighters left the station and arrive at the burning house five minutes later.
2. The forest rangers found the lost hiker and call his parents.
3. Sarah walked to the library, but Nathan rides his bicycle.
4. I reached the station just as the train left.
5. Carl wrapped the presents while I decorate the dining room.

6. The movie ended, but the audience remains seated.

7. Donna bought the book for Jody and gives it to her yesterday.

8. The ballerina bowed and accepts a bouquet of flowers.

9. When the quarterback raced down the field, we roared.

10. Dad stripped the old varnish from the chair and sands it.

11. Mom planned the camping trip, but Dad buys all the equipment.

12. When I find old coins, I polish them and keep them.

13. After we ate dinner, we leave immediately for the theater.

14. When I finally found the key, the door remained stuck.

15. As Jake started the car, Tony hops in.

Sequence of Tenses In complex sentences some changes in tense are correct. They are made to show precisely when the actions occur in a sequence of events. For example, if the action in the independent clause occurs in the present, use the past tense to express the dependent clause's earlier action—if that action was completed at a definite time in the past.

> ┌ present ┐   ┌ past ┐
> I **believe** that she **went** to the game with Harold yesterday.
> [*Believe* is present because the action is occurring now. *Went* is past because it was completed at a definite time in the past.]

If two events occur at different times in the past, use the past perfect tense to express the event that occurred first.

> ┌— past perfect —┐
> After Mandy **had completed** the requirements for her
> ┌— past —┐
> lifesaving certificate, she **applied** for a job as a lifeguard.
> [*Had completed* is past perfect and *applied* is past to show that the completing came before the applying.]

Note: When you want to emphasize the closeness in the time of two events, use the past tense for both events.

> When the whistle **blew,** the workers **stopped** for lunch.

EXERCISE *Selecting Verbs in a Sequence*

Number your paper 1 to 15. Then write the correct verb form in parentheses.

  1. The guests congratulated the cook who (prepared, had prepared) the delicious dinner.

2. After Sol (heard, had heard) the joke, he laughed loudly.

3. When I got to school, class already (begun, had begun).

4. The lawyer said that his client (stopped, had stopped) working.

5. I think that she (makes, made) a big mistake yesterday.

6. After he (baked, had baked) the birthday cake, he decorated it.

7. We feel that he (is, was) going too fast at the time.

8. Isabel is relaxed because she (swam, has swum) 20 laps this afternoon.

9. When Al started upstairs, he (tripped, had tripped).

10. The coach canceled the game because most of the team (caught, had caught) the flu.

11. I know that Ralph (scored, had scored) 26 points in last night's basketball game.

12. There is an office building where our house (was, had been).

13. Dad thinks that Joseph already (picked, has picked) some corn.

14. When Chuck Murdock (fell, had fallen) into Horn Pond, Marie Montey rescued him.

15. She is the sophomore who (wrote, has written) the editorial about the need for longer gym classes.

Tenses of Participles and Infinitives Participles and infinitives have present and perfect tenses to express specific time.

	PARTICIPLE	INFINITIVE
PRESENT	talking	to talk
PERFECT	having talked	to have talked

Note: Add *having* to the past participle to form the perfect participle; add *to* plus *have* to the past participle to form the perfect infinitive.

Always use the present participle or the present infinitive to express an action that happens at the same time as the main verb.

Talking intensely, the couple walked through the park.
Corey started **to talk** just as the bell rang.

Remember to use the perfect participle or perfect infinitive to express action that happened before the time of the main verb.

Having talked with his father about the plans for the evening, Mark left with his friends.

Julie was relieved **to have talked** with her doctor just before the surgery.

EXERCISE **17** *Using the Correct Participle or Infinitive*

Number your paper 1 to 10. Then write the correct verbal form in parentheses.

1. Mavis expected (to see, to have seen) you at the track meet on Saturday.
2. (Speaking, Having spoken) before the PTA, Claudia was extremely nervous.
3. (Buying, Having bought) a map, we set out to explore San Francisco.
4. I intended (to go, to have gone) to the museum exhibit last week.
5. Amy was delighted (to become, to have become) the new class president.
6. (Hearing, Having heard) the principal's welcoming remarks, we waited for the senator to address us.
7. (To help, To have helped) with the picking, David joined his brothers in the orchard.
8. (Watching, Having watched) the news on TV, Pearl recognized her history teacher.
9. Lynn hoped (to finish, to have finished) her report by six.
10. I'm proud (to participate, to have participated) in the conference in Washington, D.C., last month.

Active and Passive Voice

All verbs have tense, but some action verbs also have voice. Transitive verbs can be in the *active voice* or the *passive voice. (See page 542 for an explanation of transitive verbs.)*

Rule 22e The **active voice** indicates that the subject is performing the action.

Rule 22f The **passive voice** indicates that the action of the verb is being performed upon the subject.

In the following examples, the verb in the active voice has a direct object, but the verb in the passive voice has no direct object.

ACTIVE VOICE	The referee **called** a strike. [d.o.]
PASSIVE VOICE	A strike **was called** by the referee. [no direct object]

ACTIVE VOICE   Marie **sent** the le̅t̅t̅e̅r̅ by express mail.

PASSIVE VOICE   The letter **was sent** by express mail. [no direct object]

Notice in the preceding examples that when the active voice is changed to the passive voice, the direct object becomes the subject. Notice also that both verbs in the passive voice consist of a form of the verb *be* plus the past participle—*was called* and *was sent.*

EXERCISE *Recognizing Active and Passive Voice*

Number your paper 1 to 10. Write the verb in each sentence. Then label each one *active* or *passive.*

Money
Matters

1. The early American colonists used currencies from several different countries.

2. America once issued a five-cent bill.

3. The first Continental coin was designed by Benjamin Franklin.

4. The dies for that coin were engraved by Abel Buell.

5. Tobacco, in great demand, was used as money in Virginia and Maryland.

6. Martha Washington may have donated several of her silver forks and spoons for the minting of a series of half dimes.

7. The buffalo nickel was designed by James Earle Fraser, a famous sculptor.

8. Fraser's model for the nickel had been borrowed from the Bronx Zoo.

9. Nickels contain mostly copper.

10. The average United States dollar bill has a life span of less than one year.

 Application to Writing

When told in the present tense, historical events seem more immediate or more timely. Choose a historical event that you know about in some detail, such as the Boston Tea Party or the California Gold Rush. Write an account of it in the present tense—as if you were recording the events in an ongoing diary. As you edit your account, make sure you have used the active voice and have maintained the present tense where appropriate.

Use of Voice

Because verbs in the active voice are more forceful and have greater impact than verbs in the passive voice, you should use the active voice as much as possible. The passive voice, however, should be used in the following situations: (1) when the doer of the action is unknown or unimportant and (2) when you want to emphasize the receiver of the action or to emphasize the results.

Two extra innings **were played** in yesterday's game. [doer unknown or unimportant]

The first iron tools **were** probably **made** by the Hittites. [emphasis on the results]

EXERCISE **19** *Using the Active and Passive Voices*

Number your paper 1 to 15. Then write each sentence, changing the passive voice to the active voice—if appropriate. If a sentence is better in the passive voice, write *C* after the number.

1. The earth was circled by the first satellite about once every 95 minutes.
2. This year corn was planted in the far field.
3. The new pitcher was given his instructions by Coach Santos.
4. I was sent my favorite video game by my aunt.
5. The Acropolis in Athens was originally used for a fortress.
6. During yesterday's terrible storm, our maple tree was struck by lightning.
7. The report on solar heating will be completed by Tim on Thursday, if everything goes as he hopes it will.
8. In 1980, President Jimmy Carter was defeated in his bid for a second term in office.
9. The banks of the river are being cleaned of litter by some high school students.
10. Tropical fruits are often flown to northern cities by jet.
11. Fruit and cottage cheese were eaten by the dieters.
12. On Sundays breakfast is prepared by Dad.
13. New lockers for students in the ninth and tenth grades were installed at the high school.
14. *Gulliver's Travels* was written by Jonathan Swift.
15. The leading part in the senior play was played by Martin.

Mood

The *mood* of a verb is the way in which the verb expresses an idea. The three moods in English are the indicative, the imperative, and the subjunctive. Because the *indicative mood* is used to state a fact or to ask a question, it is used most often. The *imperative mood* is used to give a command or to make a request.

INDICATIVE   The sky **looks** very blue today.
                  What **makes** the sky blue?

IMPERATIVE   **Look** at this article in the newspaper.

The *subjunctive mood* has two main uses.

Rule 22g   The **subjunctive** mood is used to express (1) a condition contrary to fact, which begins with words like *if, as if,* and *although* or (2) a wish.

CONTRARY TO FACT   If I **were** you, I'd enter the art contest. [I am not you.]

A WISH   I wish I **were** a rich and famous athlete.

To form the subjunctive mood in conditions contrary to fact and in wishes, change *was,* the past indicative, to *were.*

If Kerry ~~was~~ **were** here, she could fix the TV picture.
I wish I ~~was~~ **were** a few inches taller.

EXERCISE *Using the Subjunctive Mood*

Number your paper 1 to 10. Write each verb that should be in the subjunctive mood. Then write it correctly.

 1. I wish I was brave enough to ski the steep slopes.
 2. Tom talks as if he was the athletic director.
 3. I wish Earl was here.
 4. If I was you, I'd learn to type.
 5. You make me feel as if I was the Queen of England.
 6. Lisa wished she was at the beach right now.
 7. If Marnie was smaller, she could play the part of Peter Pan.
 8. We played the exhibition game as if it was a league contest.
 9. If I was you, I'd order my class ring now.
10. He wishes he was as good a batter as you.

EXERCISE ◀21▶ *Writing Sentences*

Write sentences that follow the directions below.

1. Include an indicative-mood verb that makes a statement.
2. Include an indicative-mood verb that asks a question.
3. Include a verb in the imperative mood.
4. Include a subjunctive-mood verb that is used to express an idea contrary to fact.
5. Include a subjunctive-mood verb that is used to express a wish.

EXERCISE ◀22▶ *Cumulative Review*

Write the correct verb form or verbal in parentheses.

1. Ben ran into the house and (heads, headed) for the phone.
2. I'm sorry (to cause, to have caused) you so much worry yesterday.
3. I wish I (was, were) president of a big corporation.
4. Since noon Matthew (is, has been) at the pool.
5. Stephanie just remembered that she (promised, had promised) to pick up Claire.
6. You act as though I (was, were) the only person who voted.
7. Elaine (goes, will go) to her music lesson this afternoon.
8. (Losing, Having lost) a leg in an encounter with Moby Dick, Captain Ahab vowed revenge.
9. Ted wondered if he (earned, had earned) a pay increase.
10. If James (was, were) playing, we'd have a chance to win.
11. Last night Lee intended (to make, to have made) dinner.
12. I (started, have started) working yesterday.
13. My grandmother paints landscapes, and my grandfather (makes, made) the frames for them.
14. (Running, Having run) the electric mixer, Lester blocked out the sound of the doorbell.
15. Leslie went to the library and (looks, looked) for some reference books for her report.
16. If Courtney (was, were) here, she'd know how to start the car.
17. Leroy is very relieved that he (found, has found) his notebook before class.
18. Ever since my freshman year, Ms. Rivera (was, has been) my guidance counselor.
19. Charlene was happy (to hear, to have heard) the good news.
20. I think that Joyce (wrote, has written) her essay last night.

USING YOUR TEXT

*Using Verbs
(640–669)
Personal Essays
(216–245)*

Usage: *Editing for Verb Errors*

When editing your written work, carefully check for any errors in verb usage. Check, for example, for the correct use of the tenses of verbs and verbals and for any shifts in tense. Look also for weak passive verbs. By reading your work aloud, you also should be able to find most incorrect verb forms.

Checking Your Understanding   Edit the following paragraphs. Correct each incorrect verb form. Then, if a sentence is incorrectly written in the passive voice, rewrite it correctly in the active voice.

In 1956, several professional football teams try something new. From the sidelines a coach speaked through a microphone. Through a wireless receiver in his helmet, the coach's instructions could be heard by the quarterback on the field. The Cleveland Browns first use this idea in a game against the Detroit Lions. Even though the quarterback heard all the coach's plays, the Browns lost 31–14.

Having believed the system would work, Coach Paul Brown took to the airwaves again the following week. This time the radio dies mid-game. The Browns, nevertheless, winned by ten points. In a game between the Browns and the New York Giants, the Browns' radio signals were intercepted by a Giants' reserve end with a receiver of his own. The Browns once again lost, 21–9. On October 18, 1956, the National Football League's commissioner come to a decision: All radio helmets were banned.

Writing a Personal Essay   Brainstorm for a list of times when you were a teacher. For example, you may have taught a brother or sister how to ride a bicycle or taught a friend how to change a tire. After you have thought of three or four such experiences, choose the best one.

Write the first draft of a personal essay that describes that time when you instructed someone else. Write the essay in the present tense, as if the events were happening now. *Application:* Before writing a final copy, edit your essay, looking specifically for verb errors.

Chapter 22 Review

C h a p t e r

22 Review

A **Using the Correct Verb Form**   Number your paper 1 to 10. Then write the past or the past participle of each verb in parentheses.

1. We (speak) to her before she (drive) to New York.
2. I should have (know) his name because we (grow) up together in Park Ridge.
3. She (write) to the manufacturer after the boat had (sink) for the second time.
4. Grandmother (make) two blueberry pies and (take) them to the fair.
5. I (begin) thinking about entering the race because I have (ride) a bicycle for ten years.
6. He has (begin) a letter that he should have (write) months ago.
7. I (rise) at 6:00 A.M. and (run) around the reservoir.
8. After I (send) him a telegram, I (speak) to him on the phone.
9. Paulo has (catch) the ball and has (throw) it to first.
10. I have (do) most of my homework and have (come) to watch some TV now.

B **Choosing the Correct Tense**   Number your paper 1 to 10. Then write the correct verb form or verbal in parentheses.

1. Ever since 1787, the bald eagle (was, has been) this country's national bird.
2. When the game was almost over, the quarterback (throws, threw) a pass into the end zone for a touchdown.
3. If that dog (was, were) mine, I'd train him to heel.
4. Michael suddenly realized that he (left, had left) his books in Leroy's car.
5. Pamela wants (to work, to have worked) on the senator's reelection campaign.
6. Since my youth I (was, have been) afraid of bees.
7. (Sleeping, Having slept) late, Karen missed the bus.
8. I wish I (was, were) already graduated from college.
9. Roy realized where he (saw, had seen) the sloop before.
10. Dad knows that I (worked, have worked) at the garage this afternoon.

C **Determining Active and Passive Voice**   Number your paper 1 to 10. Label the verb in each sentence *active* or *passive*. Then rewrite any sentence in the passive voice that should be in the active voice.

1. In 1863, Abraham Lincoln made Thanksgiving a national holiday for the first time.
2. Because of the storm, school was closed for the day.
3. An interesting experiment was performed by Margaret in chemistry.
4. The mayor began his speech with a joke.
5. The first copy of the Declaration of Independence with the signers' names was printed by Mary Katherine Goddard.
6. The initial flight of Alan Shepard, the first United States astronaut, lasted only 15 minutes 22 seconds.
7. A diamond can be shattered by a sharp blow.
8. During the past two decades, great interest in outer space has been shown by the United States.
9. My brother Mark pitched a no-hitter today.
10. The SAT's were taken by many seniors on Saturday.

Mastery Test

Number your paper 1 to 10. Then write the past or the past participle of each verb in parentheses.

1. Nikki (do) a great job finding costumes for our drama group's play.
2. I have never (ride) on a Ferris wheel before.
3. Last winter many of the orange trees in Florida (freeze) when the temperature fell below 20 degrees.
4. Tomatoes are (grow) in desert sand at the Epcot Center in Orlando, Florida.
5. I have (write) for six college catalogs.
6. Yesterday my youngest brother (throw) a football 40 yards in a game against Denner High.
7. Our dog has (lie) in front of the heater all day.
8. Daniel never (go) to the meeting last night.
9. Who (teach) world history last year?
10. Have you (begin) to think about what plans you'll make for after graduation?

23

Using Pronouns

Diagnostic Test

Number your paper 1 to 10. Then write the correct form of the pronoun in parentheses.

EXAMPLE   Kate and (I, me) have joined the yearbook staff.
ANSWER   I

1. Are Joel and (he, him) trying out for the varsity football team this fall?
2. For answering questions about history, there's no one like Ramón or (she, her).
3. (We, Us) club officers should discuss the agenda.
4. With (who, whom) are you sharing a locker?
5. Let's keep the fact of (me, my) passing the driving test a surprise from everyone.
6. The two people sitting in the front row of the auditorium are Kita and (he, him).
7. The seniors (who, whom) won the special scholarships are Gary and Sasha.
8. Within the past year, my younger brother has become as tall as (I, me).
9. Have you seen (their, they're) new Irish setter?
10. Some of the girls haven't taken (her, their) swimming tests yet.

The Cases of Personal Pronouns

As a child you learned that the colors of traffic lights are signals to motorists and pedestrians. You also learned another set of signals. You learned, for example, that you should use the pronoun *he* in one situation but *him* in another situation.

He, him, and *his* send out different signals because they indicate the case of a pronoun. A pronoun has a different form and a different function for each case. When you use a particular form of a pronoun, therefore, you are signaling to a reader or a listener how that pronoun is being used in a sentence. (Nouns change form only in the possessive case. For example, *girl* becomes *girl's* in the possessive case.)

Rule 23a **Case** is the form of a noun or a pronoun that indicates its use in a sentence.

English has three cases: the *nominative case,* the *objective case,* and the *possessive case.* Many pronouns change form for each of the cases.

Nominative Case
(Used for subjects and predicate nominatives)

SINGULAR   I, you, he, she, it
PLURAL   we, you, they

Objective Case
(Used for direct objects, indirect objects,
objects of prepositions, and objects of verbals)

SINGULAR   me, you, him, her, it
PLURAL   us, you, them

Possessive Case
(Used to show ownership or possession)

SINGULAR   my, mine, your, yours, his, her, hers, its
PLURAL   our, ours, your, yours, their, theirs

Note: *You* and *it* are the same in both the nominative and the objective cases.

The Nominative Case

I, you, he, she, it, we, and *they* are the personal pronouns in the nominative case.

Rule 23b The **nominative case** is used for subjects and predicate nominatives.

Pronouns as Subjects A pronoun can be used as a subject of an independent clause or a dependent clause.

INDEPENDENT CLAUSE **We** enjoyed the play.
DEPENDENT CLAUSE As soon as **he** had washed the car, the rain started.

The case of a pronoun that is part of a compound subject is sometimes not as obvious as a single-subject pronoun. That is why it is important to double-check any pronoun in a compound subject to make sure that it is in the nominative case. To do this, say the nominative and the objective pronouns separately—to find out which one is correct.

Jason and (he, him) entered the art contest.
He entered the art contest.
Him entered the art contest.

The nominative case *he* is the correct form to use.

Jason and **he** entered the art contest.

This method of checking for the correct case also works if both subjects are pronouns.

Pronouns as Predicate Nominatives A predicate nominative follows a linking verb and identifies, renames, or explains the subject. *(See pages 543–544 for lists of common linking verbs.)*

That was **I** who answered the telephone.

The preceding example probably sounds extremely formal—or even incorrect—to you. However, while *That was me* or *It's me* is common usage in conversation, it should be avoided in written work.

It was **she.**   That is **he.**   The winners are **they.**

To check to see if the pronoun in a compound predicate nominative is in the correct case, turn the sentence around to make the predicate nominative the subject. Then say the nominative and the objective pronouns separately to find out which one is correct.

The two nominees for treasurer are Ben and (she, her).
Ben and (she, her) are the two nominees for treasurer.
She is a nominee.   **Her** is a nominee.
The two nominees for treasurer are Ben and **she.**

Note: Sometimes the wording of a sentence becomes awkward when pronouns are used as predicate nominatives. Such awkwardness can be avoided by turning the sentence around.

AWKWARD   The leads in the school play are Bart and **she.**

TURNED AROUND   Bart and **she** are the leads in the school play.

Appositives with *We*   An appositive is a noun or a pronoun that renames or identifies another noun or pronoun in the sentence. Occasionally when *we* is used as a subject or a predicate nominative, a noun or a pronoun is in apposition with *we*. The noun appositive that follows *we* never affects the case of *we*. The best way to check whether you have used the correct pronoun is to drop the appositive mentally from the sentence.

We *cross-country skiers* thoroughly enjoy winter. [We thoroughly enjoy winter.]

The most relaxed people in the group were **we** *joggers*. [The most relaxed people in the group were we.]

Nominative Case Pronouns as Appositives   An appositive is in the same case as the noun or pronoun to which it refers. Occasionally a pronoun itself will be part of an appositive to a subject or a predicate nominative. Then the pronoun should be in the nominative case.

The exchange students, *Yuri and he*, spoke at the meeting.

Yuri and *he* are appositives to the subject *students*. Since the subject is in the nominative case, an appositive to the subject is also in the nominative case.

EXERCISE *Using Pronouns in the Nominative Case*

Number your paper 1 to 10. Then write the correct form of the pronoun in parentheses.

  1. Rayna and (she, her) haven't received their invitations.
  2. (He, Him) and (she, her) plan to try out for the play.
  3. The officers in charge were (they, them).
  4. The captain of the team is either Patrick or (he, him).
  5. Ruth knew that Jay or (she, her) would be at the game.
  6. The persons most concerned are (we, us) average citizens.
  7. It wasn't (I, me) who answered the telephone.
  8. The cocaptains, Sarah and (she, her), graduate this year.
  9. (We, Us) survivors of the flood will rebuild our homes.
 10. Neither Ava nor (I, me) have a part-time job.

EXERCISE *Finding Errors in the Nominative Case*

Number your paper 1 to 10. If an underlined pronoun is in the wrong case, write it correctly. If it is in the correct case, write *C* after the number.

  1. Mom said that Monica and <u>him</u> would be home in an hour.
  2. The witnesses to the accident were Charles and <u>her</u>.
  3. <u>We</u> guides directed the group of visitors through the school.
  4. During practice today Miguel and <u>him</u> threw passes for a total of 106 yards.
  5. When Gloria and Michael left, <u>we</u> left also.
  6. The people surprised by the awards were Sabrina and <u>me</u>.
  7. Their children and <u>them</u> are camping this weekend.
  8. The finalists in the state swimming competition are <u>us</u> Central High students.
  9. Two quarterbacks, Joe Montana and <u>him</u>, appeared on a talk show.
 10. The two babies in the photograph are <u>him</u> and <u>me</u>.

EXERCISE *Writing Sentences*

Write a sentence for each of the following groups of words. Use one group as a compound subject, one as a compound predicate nominative, and one as a compound appositive. Then label each one.

  1. you and I   **2.** he and she   **3.** Julio and they

The Objective Case

Me, you, him, her, it, us, and *them* are the personal pronouns in the objective case.

Rule 23c The **objective case** is used for direct objects, indirect objects, objects of prepositions, and objects of verbals.

Pronouns as Direct and Indirect Objects   A pronoun that is used as a direct object will follow an action verb and answer the question *Whom?* A pronoun that is used as an indirect object will answer the question *To whom?* or *For whom?* after the direct object.

DIRECT OBJECTS   Dad will drive **us** to school.
                        The mayor will see **her** now.

                                  d.o.
INDIRECT OBJECTS   The usher gave **me** a program.

                           d.o.
                        Tell **him** that joke.

To check for the correct case of a compound direct object, say the nominative and the objective case pronouns separately.

     Jason saw the Dyers and (they, them) at the horse show.
     Jason saw **they** at the horse show.
     Jason saw **them** at the horse show.

The objective case *them* is the correct form to use.

     Jason saw the Dyers and **them** at the horse show.

Compound indirect objects can be checked in the same way.

     Fred made Beth and (I, me) turquoise earrings.
     Fred made **I** turquoise earrings.
     Fred made **me** turquoise earrings.

The objective case *me* is the correct form to use.

     Fred made Beth and **me** turquoise earrings.

Pronouns as Objects of Prepositions   A prepositional phrase begins with a preposition and ends with a noun or a pronoun called the *object of a preposition. (See page 551 for a list of common prepositions.)* As examples on the following page show, a pronoun that is used as an object of a preposition is in the objective case.

You can ride with **us.** [*With us* is the prepositional phrase.]

Is this note for **me?** [*For me* is the prepositional phrase.]

You can check to see that a pronoun in a compound object of a preposition is in the objective case by saying the nominative and objective case pronouns separately.

Rachel left a message for David or (she, her).
Rachel left a message for **she.**
Rachel left a message for **her.**

The objective case *her* is the correct form to use.

Rachel left a message for David or **her.**

EXERCISE 4 *Using Pronouns in the Objective Case*

Number your paper 1 to 20. Write the correct form of the pronoun in parentheses. Then write how the pronoun is used: *d.o.* for direct object, *i.o.* for indirect object, or *o.p.* for object of a preposition.

 I. The coach chose Tim and (he, him) for the team.
 2. Dad called Megan and (I, me) for dinner.
 3. You should talk to Rebecca and (she, her).
 4. For an hour Roy waited for the Ryans and (they, them).
 5. Give the principal and (we, us) a copy of your speech.
 6. Between you and (I, me), I plan to join the army.
 7. Mrs. Samuelson will pay (they, them) or (we, us) fifteen dollars to rake the leaves on her property.
 8. Would you like to go to the rodeo with Tom and (we, us)?
 9. Why did you disagree with Clare and (he, him)?
10. Ask Janice or (she, her) about the assignment.
11. You will be seated near the Kents and (they, them).
12. Ms. Randolph gave Alma and (I, me) extra tickets to the show.
13. The board will notify Andrea or (she, her) of its decision.
14. After school yesterday Neal showed (he, him) and (I, me) the new outboard skiffs.
15. Nobody showed up except Jacqueline and (he, him).
16. Please bring Dad and (she, her) their sweaters.
17. Like you and (I, me), Yvonne is looking for a job.
18. That present is from David and (we, us).
19. Danielle will meet Scott and (they, them) at the gym.
20. Leave your keys with Heather or (she, her).

Pronouns as Objects of Verbals   Because participles, gerunds, and infinitives are verb forms, they can take objects. The direct object of a verbal is in the objective case. *(See pages 591– 600 for an explanation of verbals.)*

PARTICIPIAL
PHRASE
   Seeing **her** in the restaurant, Jeff asked the beautiful movie star for her autograph. [The phrase is *seeing her in the restaurant. Her* is the object of the participle *seeing.*]

GERUND
PHRASE
   I don't recall meeting **him** at school. [The phrase is *meeting him at school. Him* is the object of the gerund *meeting.*]

INFINITIVE
PHRASE
   I want to visit **them** soon, but I am very busy. [The phrase is *to visit them soon. Them* is the object of the infinitive *to visit.*]

A pronoun in a compound object of a verbal can be checked by saying the nominative and objective case pronouns separately.

I hope to see Philip and (she, her) at the game.
I hope to see **she** at the game.
I hope to see **her** at the game.
I hope to see Philip and **her** at the game.

Appositives with *Us*   An appositive of *us* does not affect the case of *us*. To check whether you have used the correct pronoun, mentally drop the appositive from the sentence.

Take **us** *taco lovers* to the Mexican restaurant with the fastest service. [*Us* is used as a direct object. Take *whom* to the Mexican restaurant?]

Objective Case Pronouns as Appositives   Occasionally a pronoun itself is part of an appositive to a direct object, an indirect object, or an object of a preposition. Then the pronoun should be in the objective case.

We found two volunteers, *Gladys and **him**,* to work at the refreshment stand.

Gladys and *him* are the appositives to the direct object *volunteers.* Since a direct object is in the objective case, an appositive to the direct object is also in the objective case.

EXERCISE *Using Pronouns in the Objective Case*

Number your paper 1 to 10. Then write the correct form of the pronoun in parentheses.

 1. Making (he, him) the shortstop was a wise decision.
 2. The principal asked (we, us) computer users for a demonstration
    of the new software.
 3. Finding (he, him) in the old shack, the police officers took the
    lost boy home.
 4. Be sure to tell Carrie and (she, her) about the meeting after school.
 5. At the awards ceremony, the coach gave special recognition to
    two athletes, Pedro and (he, him).
 6. It was a great disappointment to (we, us) fans when Mason struck
    out.
 7. Alex tried in vain to find Sarah and (he, him) in the crowd.
 8. I don't recall seeing Nat and (they, them) at the game.
 9. They interviewed two of our neighbors, Mrs. Sousa and (she,
    her), for the evening newscast.
10. Watching Liz and (they, them) on stage, Mom was very proud.

EXERCISE *Finding Errors in the Objective Case*

Number your paper 1 to 15. If an underlined pronoun is in the wrong
case, write it correctly. If it is in the correct case, write *C* after the
number.

 1. Please save seats for Sharon and <u>him</u>.
 2. Will you show Marcia and <u>I</u> your canoe over the weekend?
 3. Dad had warned you and <u>she</u> about that thin ice!
 4. The engineer explained the procedure to <u>we</u> architects.
 5. Will Roger be able to drive <u>us</u> home after the game?
 6. We heard the speeches of the two finalists, Pat and <u>he</u>.
 7. He should never have taken <u>him</u> along.
 8. We saw Dad watching <u>them</u> on the balance beams.
 9. Mom sent Harold and <u>I</u> to the store for some milk.
10. Be sure to call <u>us</u> when you get home.
11. Dad saved some turkey for Leslie and <u>I</u>.
12. Timing <u>her</u> during the race is my job.
13. Mrs. Vargas gave <u>we</u> workers some lunch.
14. I wanted to invite <u>them</u> to the party.
15. Mr. Vernon took Valerie and <u>he</u> through the factory.

The Possessive Case

My, mine, your, yours, his, her, hers, its, our, ours, their, and *theirs* are the personal pronouns in the possessive case.

Rule 23d The **possessive case** is used to show ownership or possession.

Possessive case pronouns are used before a noun, before a gerund, or by themselves.

BEFORE A NOUN   This is **my** notebook.

BEFORE A GERUND   We were surprised at **his** entering the race.
["We were surprised at *him* entering the race" is *not* correct.]

BY THEMSELVES   These are **mine,** but which are **his?**

Note: Do not confuse certain possessive pronouns with contractions. A personal pronoun in the possessive case never includes an apostrophe. *Its, your, their,* and *theirs* are possessive pronouns. However, *it's, you're, they're,* and *there's* are contractions.

EXERCISE *Using Pronouns in the Possessive Case*

Number your paper 1 to 10. Then write the correct word in parentheses.

 1. Is there any chance of (you, your) winning an athletic scholarship?
 2. (Theirs, There's) is the two-door navy sedan.
 3. We were surprised at (them, their) setting out to cross the bay in the heavy fog.
 4. (Him, His) completing that forward pass to the ten-yard line was a lucky break for Windsor High.
 5. That portable radio must be (ours, our's).
 6. Coach Morgan was surprised at (me, my) losing so much weight over the summer.
 7. I hadn't heard about (him, his) getting chosen for the varsity team.
 8. The car and (its, it's) owner were taken down the highway to the nearest garage.
 9. Dad appreciated (you, your) explaining the insurance benefits to him.
 10. My parents were pleased at (me, my) doing so well on the last math exam.

EXERCISE **8**   *Cumulative Review*

Number your paper 1 to 25. Find and write each pronoun that is in the wrong case. Then write it correctly. If a sentence is correct, write *C* after the number.

1. They showed Alicia and me the programs for the musical.
2. Leave some of the strawberries for Leon and she.
3. Them must have been difficult for Paulo to make.
4. During the storm him and me were in a rowboat.
5. Notifying them of the change in plans will take time.
6. The sets for the play were painted by two people, Carmen and I.
7. In the car, dressed and ready to go, were Nelson and her.
8. Everyone was glad to hear of me joining the track team.
9. We want to give her luggage for graduation.
10. Us climbers started up Mount Washington at 5:00 A.M.
11. Ask the librarians, Mr. Omori and she, about a job.
12. The best students in the class are Beverly and him.
13. Eva was in the bus with John and they.
14. Taking him by the hand, she led the crying child home.
15. This spring vacation will give we boys a chance to work on restoring Oliver's 1934 Buick.
16. Jim and him have soccer practice every afternoon.
17. Give your dues to a class officer—Ted, Maya, or she.
18. Scott's mother doesn't like him playing football.
19. Please find us something to eat.
20. Us girls are forming a softball team.
21. Did they mind you practicing the tuba?
22. The only witnesses to the automobile accident were he and I.
23. There's a chance of him winning the prize for the best invention.
24. A police officer gave Rico and I our driving tests.
25. Seeing her all alone, they invited her to join them.

Application to Writing

Imagine that you are a small child again—or even a small household pet. Write a brief descriptive essay that tells how the world looks from your particularly low vantage point. Write from the first person point of view. *(See page 107.)* As you edit your essay, make sure you have used the correct form of each pronoun.

Pronoun Problems

Has anyone at the other end of the telephone ever said to you, "Whom may I say is calling"? The next time you hear that expression, you will know that the speaker has just made a pronoun error. This section will cover the cases of the pronouns *who* and *whoever* as well as the correct use of pronouns in elliptical clauses.

Who and Whom

Like personal pronouns, the pronouns *who* and *whoever* change their forms—depending upon how they are used within a sentence.

NOMINATIVE CASE   who, whoever

OBJECTIVE CASE   whom, whomever

POSSESSIVE CASE   whose

Who and *whoever* and their related pronouns are used in questions and in subordinate clauses.

Rule 23e   The correct case of *who* is determined by how the pronoun is used in a question or a clause.

In Questions   Frequently *who* and *whoever* or one of their related pronouns is used in questions. The case you should use depends upon how the pronoun is used.

NOMINATIVE CASE   **Who** found her contact lens? [subject]

OBJECTIVE CASE   **Whom** did you invite? [direct object]
To **whom** did you speak? [object of the preposition *to*]

When deciding which case to use, turn a question around to its natural order.

QUESTION   **Whom** did you invite?

NATURAL ORDER   You did invite **whom.**

Note: In casual conversation you might hear people say, *Who did you invite?* This informal use of *who,* however, should be avoided in formal, written work.

In Clauses *Who* and *whoever* or one of their related pronouns is also used to introduce adjective and noun clauses. The case you use depends, once again, upon how the pronoun is used in a clause. The following examples show how forms of *who* are used in adjective clauses.

NOMINATIVE CASE   Heather is one of those people **who excel in any sport.** [*Who* is the subject of *excel.*]

OBJECTIVE CASE   Mr. Jenkins is the man **whom the theater group consulted about the spring musical.** [*Whom* is the direct object of *consulted.* The theater group *consulted* whom.]

Peg is the person **from whom I bought this tape recorder.** [*Whom* is the object of the preposition *from. From* is part of the clause.]

The following examples show how forms of *who* and *whoever* are used in noun clauses.

NOMINATIVE CASE   **Whoever sells 50 magazine subscriptions** will receive a portable radio. [*Whoever* is the subject of *sells.*]

In the dark hallways, Jerry couldn't tell **who the girl was.** [*Who* is a predicate nominative. The girl was who.]

OBJECTIVE CASE   Invite **whomever you want.** [*Whomever* is the direct object of *want.* You want whomever.]

Ray persuaded **whomever he talked to.** [*Whomever* is the object of the preposition *to.* He talked to whomever.]

Note: An interrupting expression such as *I believe, we know, do you suppose,* and *I hope* sometimes appears in a question or a clause. Before you decide the case of a pronoun, mentally drop this expression to avoid any confusion.

Who *do you suppose* will win the track meet? [Who will win the track meet? *Who* is the subject of *will win.*]

Otis, **who** *I think* is the best player on the team, is now a senior. [Otis, who is the best player on the team, is now a senior. *Who* is the subject of *is.*]

EXERCISE *Using* **Who** *and Its Related Pronouns*

Number your paper 1 to 15. Write the correct form of the pronoun in parentheses. Then, using the following abbreviations, write how each pronoun is used in the question or the clause.

subject = *subj.*   direct object = *d.o.*
predicate nominative = *p.n.*   object of a preposition = *o.p.*

I. (Who, Whom) will pitch against Kenneth on Saturday?
2. On Friday I met Joyce Roth, (who, whom) is an engineer.
3. Did they say (who, whom) the finalists are?
4. Tell (whoever, whomever) you see about the meeting.
5. With (who, whom) did you sit at the concert?
6. (Who, Whom) did you nominate?
7. Do you know (who, whom) the bearded man is?
8. The members of the school board will give fifty dollars to (whoever, whomever) writes the best school song.
9. With (who, whom) did you study for the test?
10. Mr. Davis is the expert (who, whom) everyone respects.
II. Aaron usually likes (whoever, whomever) he works for.
12. From (who, whom) should we lease a trailer?
13. It was John Marshall (who, whom) historians agree did the most to establish the authority of the Supreme Court.
14. (Who, Whom) did he think should have the lead in the play?
15. Do you know (who, whom) the trainer of the horse is?

Elliptical Clauses

An adverb clause that is only partially expressed is called an *elliptical clause*. Although words are missing from the clause, they are understood to be there by both the writer and the reader. An elliptical clause often begins with *than* or *as*.

Mr. Lee coached Eric more **than I.**
Mr. Lee coached Eric more **than me.**

Depending upon what meaning is intended, both of the preceding examples are correct.

Mr. Lee coached Eric more **than I coached Eric.** [*I* is correct because it is the subject of *coached*.]

Mr. Lee coached Eric more **than he coached me.** [*Me* is correct because it is the direct object of *coached*.]

Rule 23f / In an **elliptical clause,** use the form of the pronoun you would use if the clause were completed.

To decide which pronoun to use in an elliptical clause, mentally complete the clause. Then choose the form of the pronoun that expresses the meaning you want. An elliptical clause, however, can sometimes express only one meaning.

> Do you think David is as tall as (I, me)?
> Do you think David is as tall **as I am?**

EXERCISE *Using Pronouns in Elliptical Clauses*

Number your paper 1 to 10. Complete and write each elliptical clause. Then underline the pronoun you chose.

EXAMPLE   Sally is twice as energetic as (he, him).
ANSWER   as <u>he</u> is

1. Amy made a better score on the test than (I, me).
2. In the tryouts I think Susannah did better than (she, her).
3. When working with children, Barry has more patience than (he, him).
4. Andrea is as experienced an actress as (I, me).
5. Martha likes Shirley more than (we, us).
6. At the fair Anna earned more money than (I, me).
7. Mr. Ferguson trained him better than (she, her).
8. Ben is not as tall as (she, her), but he is much heavier.
9. My sister was always better in sports than (I, me).
10. Mary praised Melissa more than (he, him).

EXERCISE *Cumulative Review*

Number your paper 1 to 15. Find and write each pronoun that is used incorrectly. Then write it correctly. If a sentence is correct, write *C* after the number.

1. With whom is Anita dancing?
2. A reward was promised to whomever found the necklace.
3. Maria and I have belonged to the club longer than him.
4. She is the teacher whom I believe should be hired.
5. Wayne, who everyone had chosen, declined the offer.

6. They're as fast on their skates as we.
7. Do you think Joe pitches better than me?
8. Whom do you think will win the writing contest?
9. Is the governor as concerned about acid rain as them?
10. Did he tell you who the nominees are?
11. Has anyone heard whom the new principal will be?
12. No one can draw cartoons better than her.
13. Gail is the girl with who I always study.
14. You did better on the English test than I.
15. Who do you imagine could play that role?

Pronouns and Their Antecedents

A pronoun's *antecedent* is the word that the pronoun refers to, or replaces. A pronoun and its antecedent must agree in number and gender, since they both are referring to the same person, place, or thing.

Number is the term used to indicate whether a noun or a pronoun is singular or plural. *Singular* indicates one; *plural* indicates more than one. *Gender* is the term used to indicate whether a noun or a pronoun is *masculine, feminine,* or *neuter.*

Masculine	Feminine	Neuter
he, him, his	she, her, hers	it, its

Rule 23g A **pronoun** must agree in number and gender with its antecedent.

To make a pronoun agree with its antecedent, first find the antecedent. Then determine its number and gender. Making a pronoun agree with a single-word antecedent usually is not a problem.

Nancy must take **her** final exams early. [*Nancy* is singular and feminine; therefore, *her* is correct because it also is singular and feminine.]

Members of the prom committee presented **their** ideas to the seniors at a special meeting. [*Members* is plural; therefore, *their* is plural.]

If the antecedent of a pronoun is more than one word, you need to remember two rules.

Rule 23h If two or more singular antecedents are joined by *or, nor, either/or,* or *neither/nor,* use a singular pronoun to refer to them.

All the conjunctions listed in this rule indicate a choice—one *or* the other. In the following example, Harold *or* Cliff signed his name—not both of them. As a result the pronoun must be singular.

Either Harold or Cliff signed **his** name to the petition.

Note: When one antecedent is singular and the other is plural, the pronoun agrees with the closer antecedent.

Neither Sue nor the other two actors brought **their** costumes to rehearsal.

Neither my brothers nor my father brought **his** skis on our trip to the mountains.

Rule 23i If two or more singular antecedents are joined by *and* or *both/and,* use a plural pronoun to refer to them.

The conjunctions *and* and *both/and* indicate more than one. In the following example, both Greta and Mavis—two people—turned in term papers early. Because the antecedent is plural, the plural pronoun must be used.

Both Greta and Mavis turned in **their** term papers early.

The gender of most antecedents is obvious. *Harold* and *Cliff* are masculine; *Greta* and *Mavis* are feminine. The gender of some antecedents, however, is not so obvious. Standard English solves the agreement problem in such cases by using *his* or *his or her* to refer to antecedents of unknown gender.

Each senior should rent **his** cap and gown.

Each senior should rent **his or her** cap and gown.

You can avoid this awkward wording by rewriting such sentences, using the plural form.

All seniors should rent **their** caps and gowns.

EXERCISE **12** *Making Pronouns and Antecedents Agree*

Number your page 1 to 20. Then write the pronoun that correctly completes each sentence.

1. Each boy on the soccer team must have _____ picture taken for the yearbook.
2. Leaving the bus from London, the tourists carried _____ own luggage to the hotel.
3. Sheila and Rubina had a hard time finding _____ jackets on the crowded coat rack.
4. All cats in the pet store have had _____ shots.
5. Neither King Arthur nor _____ knights suspected the enemy's plan.
6. The workers at the plant must show _____ identification badges before entering.
7. Each member of the League of Women Voters contributed _____ time to the debate.
8. Whenever Larry catches a good-sized flounder or striped bass, _____ gives _____ away.
9. Both Andrew and Mark need two new tires on the rear wheels of _____ cars.
10. Neither Clara nor Sally remembered to bring _____ ticket to the play.
11. Mom and Dad wanted to attend the concert, but _____ were too busy.
12. Either José or Don left _____ glasses on one of the tables.
13. The baseball team and the softball team held _____ annual banquet at the Regis Hotel.
14. Neither Paula nor _____ sister has received _____ invitation to the party yet.
15. Both Devon and Maria said that _____ would join us after the game.
16. Either Harry Elroy or the Wilsons will lend you _____ saw.
17. Baby birds digest _____ food very rapidly.
18. Neither Andrea nor _____ brothers will have _____ vacations in August this year.
19. Marshall is taking _____ parents out to dinner for _____ anniversary.
20. If you have a rubber band or some paper clips, please give _____ to me for my index cards.

Indefinite Pronouns as Antecedents

Based on their number, the common indefinite pronouns have been divided into the following three groups.

Common Indefinite Pronouns	
SINGULAR	anybody, anyone, each, either, everybody, everyone, neither, nobody, no one, one, somebody, someone
PLURAL	both, few, many, several
SINGULAR/PLURAL	all, any, most, none, some

A personal pronoun must be singular if its antecedent is one of the singular indefinite pronouns.

Each of the girls is hiking during **her** vacation.

A personal pronoun must be plural if its antecedent is one of the plural indefinite pronouns.

Both of the men donated **their** time to the paper drive.

If the antecedent of a personal pronoun is one of the singular/plural indefinite pronouns, the personal pronoun agrees in number and gender with the object of the preposition that follows the indefinite pronoun.

Some of the dirt has mulch mixed into **it.** [singular]

Some of the teachers have graded **their** exams. [plural]

Note: The gender of a singular indefinite pronoun sometimes is not indicated by other words in the sentence. Standard English solves this problem by using *his* or *his or her.* The best solution, however, is to rewrite the sentence, using the plural form.

Each of the members must pay **his** dues by Monday.

Each of the members must pay **his or her** dues by Monday.

All of the members must pay **their** dues by Monday.

EXERCISE *Making Pronouns Agree*

Number your paper 1 to 10. Then write the pronoun that correctly completes each sentence.

1. Neither of the parakeets has had _____ dinner.
2. All of the applicants had to put _____ names on a roster.
3. Both of my grandmothers recently attended _____ high school reunions.
4. Most of the sheets had a flaw in _____.
5. Each of the men in the glider class got _____ license.
6. If any of your shirts need buttons on _____, don't throw _____ into the laundry.
7. Several of my friends have lost the keys to _____ lockers.
8. One of the boys said that _____ would see if there were any openings at the supermarket.
9. Most of the front page of the paper had mud smeared across _____.
10. Either of the women should submit _____ résumé.

EXERCISE 14 *Cumulative Review*

Number your paper 1 to 15. Then write the pronoun that correctly completes each sentence.

1. All of my sisters received bonuses with _____ pay.
2. Both Ray and Otis forgot _____ keys today.
3. Most of these books will be claimed by _____ owners.
4. Somebody in the male quartet has forgotten _____ music.
5. Some of the women are taking _____ vacations now.
6. Many of the boys on the swim team have already bought _____ summer passes for the public pool.
7. Susan and Julie asked _____ father for a ride to the library.
8. Neither of my brothers could find _____ boots in the basement.
9. Everyone on the girls' hockey team will introduce _____ to the members on the other team.
10. One of the boxes should have a note inside _____.
11. Some pieces of the cheese had mold on _____.
12. Either Ted or his neighbor will loan you _____ tools.
13. Somebody in the quintet left _____ gloves in the auditorium.
14. Both of the farmers near us planted _____ corn early this year.
15. Several of my friends drive _____ cars to school every day.

USING YOUR TEXT

*Pronouns
(538–541)
Creative Writing
(372–409)*

Usage: Editing for Pronoun Errors

Whenever you edit your written work, check to see if the pronouns are in the right case and if they agree with their antecedents in number and gender. There are four other common errors to look for as well: pronoun shifts, vague antecedents, missing antecedents, and the unclear use of *it, you,* or *they.*

Avoid shifting person between a pronoun and its antecedent.

PRONOUN SHIFT	**I** like running because **you** feel invigorated. [There is a shift from the first person *I* to the second person *you.*]
CORRECT	**I** like running because **I** feel invigorated.

Avoid using a pronoun that could refer to two antecedents.

VAGUE ANTECEDENT	Mom bought two puppies for my sisters when **they** were only six weeks old. [Does *they* refer to the *puppies* or the *sisters?*]
CORRECT	Mom bought two puppies for my sisters when the **puppies** were only six weeks old.
CORRECT	Mom bought two six-week-old puppies for my sisters.

Avoid using a pronoun that does not have an antecedent.

MISSING ANTECEDENT	Mr. Case is a successful lawyer, but none of his sons chose **it** as a career. [*It* has no antecedent.]
CORRECT	Mr. Case is a successful lawyer, but none of his sons chose **law** as a career.

Avoid using a pronoun without a *clear* antecedent.

UNCLEAR PRONOUN	**It** asks for three references on the application. [The antecedent of *it* is not clearly stated.]
CORRECT	The application asks for three references.

Checking Your Understanding   Rewrite each sentence to make its meaning clear.

1. I bought ice skates because it is so much fun to do in the winter.
2. Rick is intelligent, but he doesn't always use it.
3. In the Carlsbad Caverns in New Mexico, they have one huge cave that covers 14 acres.
4. I like to edit my work on the word processor because you can do it so quickly.
5. Tom wanted Mark to sing because he has such a fine baritone voice.
6. In the movie they seem to take you instantly into the farthest reaches of outer space.
7. My sister Anna is studying to be a nurse, and she likes it very much.
8. I opened the package cautiously because you never can tell when you'll get one of Uncle Frank's practical jokes.
9. After the art students had made several sketches, Mr. Botts evaluated them.
10. In the spring they're beginning to offer lifesaving courses at the YMCA.

Writing a Short Story   Create a fantasy adventure in which you and your best friend get involved. While thinking about familiar science-fiction stories and movies like *Star Trek—The Movie,* write freely, creating an imaginary world of strange surroundings and bizarre creatures. Then work out the important events of the story: How did you and your friend get to this peculiar place? Where are you going or what is your goal? What is the first obstacle you meet? How do you overcome that obstacle?

Write the first draft of your fantasy adventure, using the first person point of view. *(See pages 381–395.)* As you revise your story, notice in particular whether you have included specific details and references to the senses when describing the land and its inhabitants. Would readers be able to picture the images clearly in their own minds? *Application:* As you edit your story, check especially for pronoun errors. Make any necessary corrections; then write a final copy and read your story to your best friend or to a family member.

23 Review

A Using Pronouns in the Correct Case

Number your paper 1 to 10. Then write the correct form of the pronoun in parentheses.

1. Mom told Kate that the hats and scarves were for Ben and (she, her).
2. (Who, Whom) do you think will win the award?
3. Roy knows more about both folk music and country music than (she, her).
4. Was it Kevin or (she, her) who saved that man's life at the beach yesterday?
5. Daniel, (who, whom) the coach promoted from junior varsity, has become one of Reading's best players.
6. The mayor promised three seniors—Carla, Chester, and (he, him)— summer jobs at City Hall.
7. Is Spencer older than (she, her)?
8. Show your pass to (whoever, whomever) is at the entrance to the estate.
9. Three of (we, us) boys volunteered to help load the moving van for Mr. Rodriguez.
10. Dad was surprised at (me, my) offering to clean the garage.

B Correcting Pronoun Problems

Number your paper 1 to 10. Then write the correct pronoun in parentheses.

1. With (who, whom) are you going to the senior prom Friday night?
2. Daniel talks to Beth more than he talks to (she, her).
3. (Who, Whom) do you suppose will replace Mrs. Bennett?
4. Tony is more confident than (he, him).
5. Yolanda asked (who, whom) the man in the blue seersucker suit was.
6. Gretchen is one person (who, whom) I think will succeed.
7. Maura collected more contributions than (she, her).
8. (Who, Whom) did you see at the track meet with Parker High School?
9. The coach praised Michael more than she praised (I, me).
10. Give this message to (whoever, whomever) telephones.

C Making Pronouns Agree with Antecedents Number your paper 1 to 10. Then write the pronoun that correctly completes each sentence.

1. All of the girls on the softball team have packed _____ gear into the bus.
2. Every duck in the pond next to the town hall had a piece of bread in _____ beak.
3. Neither Jerry nor Vincenzo submitted _____ monthly history report on time.
4. One of the girls must have sold _____ bicycle.
5. Dogs perspire through _____ paw pads.
6. Both Anna and Jean have had _____ eye examinations.
7. A few of the seniors haven't ordered _____ yearbooks.
8. Each of the ballerinas knew _____ steps perfectly.
9. Either Tim or Scott bought _____ track shoes at the new mall in Farmington.
10. All of the food had mold on _____.

Mastery Test

Number your paper 1 to 10. Then write the correct form of the pronoun in parentheses.

1. (Who, Whom) did you visit in Albany?
2. Neither the blue jay nor the sparrow abandoned (its, their) nest during the storm.
3. The only ones in the store were Kim and (he, him).
4. Both Lynn and Donna brought (her, their) umbrellas to the baseball game.
5. When am I going to ride in (your, you're) new car?
6. The yearbook photographers—Carlotta, Lionel, and (she, her)—should be at the gym tonight.
7. Did the shop teacher approve of (him, his) project?
8. The person (who, whom) I thought was the senator turned out to be a television newscaster.
9. Is Lee's brother as blond as (she, her)?
10. Between you and (I, me), I can't wait until the next summer vacation.

24 Subject and Verb Agreement

Diagnostic Test

Number your paper 1 to 10. Write the subject in each sentence. Then next to each one, write the form of the verb in parentheses that agrees with the subject.

EXAMPLE   The last two pages of the book (is, are) missing.
ANSWER   pages—are

1. Neither the shortstop nor the second baseman (was, were) able to catch the grounder.
2. (Doesn't, Don't) those fresh strawberries in the fruit salad look absolutely delicious?
3. Only two thirds of the lawn (has, have) been mowed so far this week.
4. There (is, are) two letters on the table for you.
5. The song currently at the top of the charts (has, have) been there for six weeks.
6. One of my neighbors (is, are) a helicopter pilot.
7. (Wasn't, Weren't) you notified of the change?
8. The hammer and nails (is, are) in the toolbox.
9. People riding bicycles on the sidewalk (is, are) a hazard to pedestrians.
10. Both of my brothers (has, have) weekend jobs to give them some pocket money.

Agreement of Subjects and Verbs

How many times have you seen the "perfect" pair of jeans, tried them on, and then discovered to your great disappointment that they were either too loose or too short? "Perfect" as they are, you cannot wear them because they do not fit. In a way, subjects and verbs are like people and jeans. Some fit together; others do not. When words do fit together, they are said to have *agreement*. This chapter will review the different types of subjects and verbs. Then it will show you which agree and which do not.

A subject and a verb agree when they have the same number. *Number* determines whether a word is singular or plural. *Singular* indicates one, and *plural* indicates more than one.

Rule 24a A verb must agree with its subject in number.

In order to understand agreement, you must know the singular and plural forms of nouns, pronouns, and verbs. The plurals of most nouns are formed by adding *-s* or *-es* to the singular form. Some nouns, however, form their plurals irregularly. For example, *children* is the plural of *child*. Certain pronouns form their plurals by changing form.

Nouns		Pronouns	
SINGULAR	**PLURAL**	**SINGULAR**	**PLURAL**
light	lights	I	we
dress	dresses	he, she, it	they
goose	geese		

Verbs also have singular and plural forms, but only present tense verbs change endings. The third person singular of present tense verbs ends in *-s* or *-es*. However, most plural forms of present tense verbs do *not* end in *-s* or *-es*.

THIRD PERSON SINGULAR   he, she, it **sits**

OTHERS   I, you, we, they **sit**

Notice that *I* and *you* take the plural form of the verb.

In the following box are the singular and the plural forms of the irregular verbs *be, have,* and *do* in the present tense. Notice that *be* also has irregular forms for both the singular and the plural in the past tense.

Present Tense	Past Tense
SINGULAR	**SINGULAR**
I **am, have, do**	I **was**
you **are, have, do**	you **were**
he, she, it **is, has, does**	he, she, it **was**
PLURAL	**PLURAL**
we **are, have, do**	we **were**
you **are, have, do**	you **were**
they **are, have, do**	they **were**

Since a subject and a verb both have number, they must agree in a sentence.

Rule 24b A singular subject takes a singular verb.

Rule 24c A plural subject takes a plural verb.

The **light shines.**	The **lights shine.**
The **dress wrinkles.**	The **dresses wrinkle.**
The **goose flies.**	The **geese fly.**
He is my brother.	**They are** my brothers.

Be, have, and *do* are often used as helping verbs. When they are, they must agree in number with the subject.

Rule 24d The helping verb must agree in number with its subject.

Pamela is marching in the Memorial Day parade on Saturday.
The **rakes were** found in the cellar.
The **birds have** flown away.
Mark does know the answer to the question on the application form.

Interrupting Words

Often a subject and a verb are side by side in a sentence. When they are, agreement between them is usually easy to recognize. Many times, however, a phrase or a clause modifying a subject separates it from the verb. In such sentences a mistake in agreement sometimes occurs. The error one tends to make is to have the verb agree with the word closest to it—rather than with its subject. To avoid making this mistake in agreement, first find the subject and then make the verb agree with it.

Rule 24e The agreement of a verb with its subject is not changed by any interrupting words.

Notice in each of the following examples that the subject and the verb agree in number—regardless of any interrupting words.

The **posters** on the wall **were** bought at the art museum.
[The plural helping verb *were* agrees with the plural subject *posters,* even though the singular noun *wall* is closer to the verb.]

The **couch,** covered with throw pillows, **was** very attractive.
[*Was* agrees with *couch,* not *pillows.*]

Students who finish the test early **are** allowed to leave.
[*Are* agrees with *students,* not *test.*]

Note: Make the verb agree with the positive subject, not with an interrupting negative subject.

A good **band,** not fancy decorations, **makes** a prom a success.
[*Makes* agrees with the positive subject *band,* not with the negative subject *decorations.*]

Occasionally a parenthetical expression—beginning with a word (or words) such as *like, as well as, in addition to, including,* or *together with*—will interrupt a subject and a verb. Be careful to make the verb agree with the subject, not with a word in the parenthetical expression.

Gail, together with her sisters, **is** running an errand service.
[*Is* agrees with *Gail,* not *sisters.*]

The **boys,** as well as my uncle, **are** going to the barbecue.
[*Are* agrees with *boys,* not *uncle.*]

EXERCISE *Making Interrupted Subjects and Verbs Agree*

Number your paper 1 to 15. Write the subject in each sentence. Beside each one write the form of the verb in parentheses that agrees with the subject.

1. Several students at graduation (was, were) honored for their academic achievement.
2. The whale, unlike most other sea creatures, (needs, need) to surface in order to live.
3. The costumes that we wore in the play (was, were) rented.
4. The square-bottomed brown paper bag, so essential to supermarkets, (was, were) invented in 1872.
5. The loaf of bread, not the rolls, (is, are) for the bake sale.
6. The average age of the signers of the Declaration of Independence (was, were) forty-five.
7. The beaver, as well as other small animals, (is, are) quite common in Grand Teton National Park.
8. The horns of a bighorn sheep may (weighs, weigh) 30 pounds.
9. Water, as well as sunlight, (is, are) needed for healthy plants.
10. The last page of the yearbook, totally filled with photographs, (has, have) brought back many memories.
11. Louisa May Alcott, author of *Little Women,* (was, were) a nurse during the Civil War.
12. The return of the red-winged blackbirds (is, are) a sure sign of spring.
13. The people standing by the door (is, are) members of the church choir.
14. The flowers that were in Karen's bridal bouquet (was, were) miniature orchids.
15. A list of lost-and-found articles (has, have) been posted on the main bulletin board.

Compound Subjects

When you make two or more subjects agree with a verb, you should remember two rules.

Rule 24f When subjects are joined by *or, nor, either/or,* or *neither/nor,* the verb agrees with the closer subject.

Either Joe or Lola **writes** the sports column each week. [*Writes* agrees with the closer subject, *Lola*.]

A pencil or a pen **is** fine for the test. [*Is* agrees with the closer subject, *pen*.]

The same rule applies when one subject is singular and the other subject is plural.

Neither the umbrella nor our raincoats **were** enough to keep us dry. [*Were* agrees with the closer subject, *raincoats*—even though *umbrella* is singular.]

When compound subjects are joined by other conjunctions, however, a different rule applies.

Rule 24g When subjects are joined by *and* or *both/and*, the verb is plural.

These conjunctions always indicate more than one. Since more than one is plural, the verb must be plural also.

The stapler and the glue **are** in the top drawer. [Two items— the stapler and the glue—are in the top drawer. The verb must be plural to agree with both of them.]

Both those magazines and that book **were** left in the study hall. [Even though *book* is singular, the verb is still plural because the book and the magazines—together—were left.]

The second rule has certain exceptions. Two subjects joined by *and* occasionally refer to only one person or one thing. In such a case, the verb must be singular.

Fruit and cheese **is** my mom's favorite dessert. [*Fruit and cheese* is considered *one* dessert.]

Bacon and eggs **is** also very good. [*Bacon and eggs* is considered one food.]

Another exception involves the words *every* and *each*. If one of these words comes before a compound subject that is joined by *and*, each subject is being considered separately. As a result, the verb must be singular to agree with a singular subject.

Every athlete and coach **attends** the athletic banquet at the end of the school year.

Each chair and table **looks** freshly painted.

EXERCISE 2 *Making Verbs Agree with Compound Subjects*

Number your paper 1 to 15. Then write the correct form of the verb in parentheses.

1. Neither Bolivia nor Paraguay (has, have) a seacoast.
2. Each car and truck in the lot (was, were) towed away.
3. Paint and crayon (blends, blend) well in the portrait.
4. Either the mountains or the seashore (is, are) enjoyable.
5. In a democracy every man, woman, and child (is, are) guaranteed certain rights.
6. Neither rain nor snow (is, are) supposed to prevent mail delivery.
7. Wheat and corn (grows, grow) on my uncle's farm.
8. Spaghetti and meatballs (is, are) an easy meal to make.
9. Neither the gym nor the cafeteria at our school (is, are) large enough for the graduation ceremonies.
10. Every door and window in the cottage (was, were) bolted.
11. Both Kansas and Missouri (has, have) a Kansas City.
12. The soccer coach and athletic director at Henderson High (is, are) Mr. Robertson.
13. Pancakes and sausage (is, are) my favorite breakfast.
14. Every mountain, hill, and trail (was, were) familiar.
15. Hornets and yellow jackets (is, are) two kinds of wasps.

EXERCISE 3 *Cumulative Review*

Number your paper 1 to 15. Find and write the verbs that do not agree with their subjects. Then write them correctly. If a sentence is correct, write *C* after the number.

EXAMPLE   Every mosquito and gnat seem to be out tonight.
ANSWER   seem—seems

1. The location of the volcanic islands are not marked on this map.
2. Ivy and geraniums covers most of the area around the school's courtyard.
3. Either Steve or Maggie have decided to become a doctor.
4. The beautiful curtains in Katherine's room is handmade.
5. Neither *Othello* nor *Richard III* were presented at the Shakespeare Festival this year.
6. Six members of the team were able to compete in the relay.

7. Cheese, lettuce, and tomato are my favorite sandwich for lunch.
8. Mandarin, the tongue of millions of Chinese, top the list of the ten most widely spoken languages.
9. Every girl and boy in the athletic program has promised to help with the fund-raising drive.
10. Lake Superior, with an area of 31,700 square miles, is the largest freshwater lake in the world.
11. The Grand Canyon and Sunset Crater is located in Arizona.
12. The daffodils that the Garden Club planted around the library are in full bloom.
13. Bread and butter were served with the meal in the hotel restaurant where we ate.
14. Either the dictionary or the thesaurus are a good place to look for colorful verbs.
15. The secretary and treasurer of the photography club are Marvin Goldenberg.

Special Agreement Problems

There are several other situations in which agreement between a subject and a verb may present a problem.

Indefinite Pronouns as Subjects   When an indefinite pronoun is used as a subject, the verb must agree with the number of that particular indefinite pronoun.

Rule **24h**   **A verb must agree in number with an indefinite pronoun used as a subject.**

The indefinite pronouns in the following chart have been grouped according to number.

Common Indefinite Pronouns	
SINGULAR	anybody, anyone, each, either, everybody, everyone, neither, no one, one, somebody, someone
PLURAL	both, few, many, several
SINGULAR/PLURAL	all, any, most, none, some

A singular verb agrees with a singular indefinite pronoun, and a plural verb agrees with a plural indefinite pronoun.

SINGULAR   **One** of my tapes **is** broken.

PLURAL   **Many** of my tapes **are** broken.

The number of an indefinite pronoun in the singular/plural group is determined by the object of the preposition that follows it.

SINGULAR
OR PLURAL   **Some** of the paint **is** on sale.

Some of the tires **are** on sale.

EXERCISE **4** *Making Verbs Agree with Indefinite Pronoun Subjects*

Number your paper 1 to 20. Write the subject in each sentence. Next to each one, write the form of the verb in parentheses that agrees with the subject.

1. All of the players (has, have) received their letters.
2. Both of the books (includes, include) illustrations.
3. Neither of those buses (stops, stop) at the mall.
4. Some of the guests (has, have) arrived.
5. All of the book (is, are) very interesting.
6. Everyone, including the musicians, (was, were) lined up for the final curtain call.
7. Several of the books (was, were) damaged.
8. All of the performers' jewelry (was, were) imitation.
9. Each of those lamps (needs, need) a new bulb.
10. None of the washing machines (is, are) on sale.
11. All of the bread in this bakery (contains, contain) oat bran.
12. Some of the streams (is, are) about to overflow their banks.
13. Many of those shirts (is, are) priced too high.
14. One of my sisters (has, have) just visited Gettysburg.
15. Most of the world's diamonds (comes, come) from Africa.
16. None of my homemade applesauce (is, are) left.
17. Few of those suntan lotions (gives, give) much protection.
18. Most of the voters in our town (has, have) rejected the new property tax.
19. Some of the detergent (was, were) spilled on the floor.
20. Most of the photos in the magazine (is, are) in full color.

Subjects in Inverted Order   A sentence is said to be in *inverted order* when the verb or part of the verb phrase comes before the subject. Even though a verb may precede a subject, it still must agree with the subject in number.

Rule 24i   The subject and the verb of an inverted sentence must agree in number.

There are several types of inverted sentences. *(See pages 565–567.)* When you are looking for the subject in an inverted sentence, turn the sentence around to its natural order. To have the sentence make sense, you must occasionally drop *here* or *there* when putting the sentence into its natural order.

INVERTED ORDER	In the hall closet **were** two unfinished model **ships.** [Two unfinished model *ships were* in the hall closet.]
QUESTIONS	**Have** the **finalists** been announced? [The *finalists have* been announced.]
SENTENCES BEGINNING WITH *HERE* OR *THERE*	Here **are** the attendance **records.** [The attendance *records are* here.]
	There **are** only two **mistakes** in your report. [Drop *there*. Only two *mistakes are* in your report.]

EXERCISE **5** *Making Verbs Agree with Subjects in Inverted Order*

Number your paper 1 to 20. Write the subject in each sentence. Next to each one, write the form of the verb in parentheses that agrees with the subject.

1. There (is, are) over one million different species of animals on Earth.
2. Deep in the waters of the Spanish Main (lies, lie) the treasure chests of several pirate ships.
3. There (is, are) seven poodles in the show.
4. (Has, Have) they gone downtown?
5. Throughout the West (is, are) the ruins of once prosperous mining towns.
6. There (is, are) about ten million bricks in the Empire State Building.

7. On the walls (hang, hangs) chains of scarlet chili.
8. Here (is, are) the tickets for the Rose Bowl game.
9. Which (was, were) the last state to join the Union?
10. There (is, are) no lefties on our baseball team.
11. (Is, Are) the milk in these cartons sour?
12. On the birthday cake (was, were) a picture of a shiny sports car.
13. Here (is, are) your registration and your driver's license.
14. (Has, Have) anyone applied to the Morrison Technical School yet?
15. (Does, Do) each of the lamps need a new bulb?
16. (Does, Do) *TV Guide* really have more than ten million subscribers?
17. Here (is, are) my only copy of the school newspaper.
18. On the water (was, were) beautiful reflections of the trees.
19. There (is, are) 206 bones in the human body.
20. Here (was, were) the location of the pirates' treasure.

Collective Nouns   A *collective noun*—such as *choir, family, herd, jury, series, majority,* and *team*—names a group of people or things. Depending on how it is used in a sentence, it may be either singular or plural.

Rule 24j   Use a singular verb with a collective-noun subject that is thought of as a unit. Use a plural verb with a collective-noun subject that is thought of as individuals.

The **class is** presently holding elections. [The class is working together as a whole unit in this sentence. As a result, the verb is singular]

The **class are** casting their ballots today. [The members of the class are acting independently—each one casting his or her own ballot. As a result, the verb is plural.]

Words Expressing an Amount   Words that express amounts, measurements, or weights usually have a plural form but are often considered to be a singular unit.

Rule 24k   A subject that expresses an amount, a measurement, or a weight is usually considered singular and takes a singular verb.

Five dollars is the membership fee. [*Five dollars is one amount of money.*]

Six months is needed to complete the project. [*Six months is one period of time.*]

If an amount, measurement, or weight is being thought of in its individual parts, then the verb must be plural.

> **Five dollars were** tucked under the vase. [The five dollars are being thought of as five individual dollars.]

> **Six months have** passed since school began. [The six months are being thought of as six individual months.]

When the subject is a fraction or a percent, the verb agrees with the object of the preposition that follows the subject.

> **Three fourths** of my salary **goes** to the bank.

> **Three fourths** of the seniors **are** going to the prom.

The Number of, A Number of   Although these expressions are very similar, one expression takes a singular verb and one takes a plural verb.

Rule 24l   Use a singular verb with *the number of* and a plural verb with *a number of.*

> **The number of** students considering college **increases** each year. [singular]

> **A number of** high school students **intend** to go on to vocational schools. [plural]

Singular Nouns That Have a Plural Form   Even though a word ends in *-s,* it may not take a plural verb. Some nouns are plural in form but singular in meaning because they name a single thing—one area of knowledge or one type of disease, for example.

USUALLY SINGULAR   civics, economics, gymnastics, mathematics, measles, molasses, mumps, news, physics, social studies, the United States

Rule 24m   Use a singular verb with certain subjects that are plural in form but singular in meaning.

> **Measles is** a very contagious disease.

> The local **news is** on from six to seven o'clock every weekday evening.

A second group of similar nouns are usually plural, as their form indicates. A third group can be either singular or plural—depending on how they are used in a sentence. Since it is impossible to tell what number verb these words take by looking at them, it is always best to check the dictionary.

USUALLY PLURAL   barracks, data, eyeglasses, media, pliers, scissors, shears, slacks, thanks, trousers

SINGULAR/PLURAL   acoustics, athletics, headquarters, ethics, politics, tactics

Your **eyeglasses were** found in the cafeteria. [plural]

The **headquarters** for the United Nations **is** located in New York City. [singular—an administrative center]

The **headquarters were** located on the outskirts of the town. [plural—a group of buildings]

Note: If the word *pair* precedes a word that is usually plural, the verb is nevertheless singular because the verb then agrees with the singular noun *pair.*

PLURAL   Those **scissors are** dull.
SINGULAR   That **pair** of scissors **is** dull.

EXERCISE *Making Subjects and Verbs Agree*

Number your paper 1 to 20. Then write the correct form of the verb in parentheses.

1. A large number of the books (is, are) bound in suede.
2. Gymnastics (takes, take) up most of my sister's spare time.
3. Two thirds of the people in the world (does, do) not get enough to eat.
4. A number of the trees (was, were) struck in the storm.
5. Ten minutes after the end of the opera, the audience (was, were) still applauding.
6. Sixty percent of the student body (has, have) never missed a single day of school this year.
7. Three miles (is, are) the distance from here to Glen Cove.
8. The jury (was, were) in complete disagreement throughout the deliberations.
9. Almost three fourths of the apples in the basket (was, were) bruised.

10. Mumps (is, are) preventable with a vaccine.

11. A number of students in the creative-writing class (has, have) entered a national writing contest.

12. Approximately four cents (was, were) paid for each acre of land in the Louisiana Territory.

13. At the end of the first quarter, the Jefferson High team (was, were) leading by six points.

14. The number of candidates for the Student Council (is, are) surprisingly large.

15. The jury (was, were) arguing about the value of the circumstantial evidence.

16. Two gallons of gasoline (is, are) enough to get us to the nearest service station.

17. That brand-new pair of pliers (belongs, belong) to my Uncle Roberto.

18. Economics (is, are) Kevin's major at the University of Florida in Gainesville.

19. Forty-one percent of the moon (is, are) not visible from the earth at any time.

20. The number of students attending the soccer matches (has, have) increased this year.

Doesn't and Don't   *Doesn't* and *don't* are contractions. When checking for agreement with a subject, say the two words of a contraction separately. Also keep in mind which contractions are singular and which are plural.

SINGULAR   **does**n't, **has**n't, **is**n't, **was**n't
  PLURAL   **do**n't, **have**n't, **are**n't, **were**n't

Rule 24n   The verb part of a contraction must agree in number with the subject.

This cold **weather does**n't bother me at all.
These **directions do**n't make sense.

Subjects with Linking Verbs   A predicate nominative follows a linking verb and identifies, renames, or explains the subject. *(See pages 543–544 for lists of linking verbs.)* Occasionally, however, a subject and its predicate nominative will not have the same number. The verb, nevertheless, agrees with the subject.

Rule 24o A verb agrees with the subject of a sentence, not with the predicate nominative.

> An important **crop** in Florida **is** oranges. [The singular verb *is* agrees with the singular subject *crop*—even though the predicate nominative *oranges* is plural.]
>
> **Oranges are** an important crop in Florida. [In this sentence *are* agrees with the plural subject *oranges*—not with the singular predicate nominative *crop*.]

Note: For better sentences, avoid writing any in which the subject and the predicate nominative do not agree in number.

> The orange **crop** in Florida **is** an important **one.**

Titles   Some titles may *seem* plural because they are composed of several words. A title, nevertheless, is the name of only one book, poem, play, work of art, or the like. As a result, a title is singular and takes a singular verb. Most multiword names of businesses and organizations are also considered singular.

Rule 24p A title is singular and takes a singular verb.

> **"The Planters" is** a poem by Margaret Atwood.
> **Barrett's Yard Goods is** having a sale on fabric.

EXERCISE *Making Subjects and Verbs Agree*

Number your paper 1 to 10. Then write the correct form of the verb in parentheses.

  1. Active volcanoes (is, are) a great attraction in Hawaii.
  2. This (doesn't, don't) seem to be the road to the apple orchard.
  3. *Great Expectations* (was, were) written in 1861 by Charles Dickens.
  4. The result of my gardening efforts (was, were) bigger weeds.
  5. (Doesn't, Don't) the buses run on the hour?
  6. *Romeo and Juliet* (was, were) recently performed on PBS.
  7. The committee (isn't, aren't) meeting tonight.
  8. A snake's fangs (is, are) a special kind of teeth.
  9. Murphy's Fruits and Vegetables (is, are) my favorite market.
 10. (Doesn't, Don't) daylight saving time start tonight?

Who, Which, and That *Who, which,* and *that* are often used as relative pronouns to begin an adjective clause. When one of these words is the subject of the clause, the number of its verb will depend upon the number of the pronoun's antecedent.

Rule 24q In an adjective clause in which the relative pronoun *who, which,* or *that* is used as the subject, make the verb agree with the antecedent of the relative pronoun.

Bart caught a **trout** that **was** 18 inches long. [The antecedent of *that* is *trout.* Since *trout* is singular, *was* is also singular.]

Find the titles of three **books** that **deal** with space exploration. [The antecedent of *that* is *books.* Since *books* is plural, *deal* is also plural.]

If an adjective clause is preceded by the expression *one of,* the verb in the clause is usually plural.

Soapstone was *one of* the **rocks** that **were** highly prized by the Indians. [The antecedent of *that* is *rocks,* not *one.*]

EXERCISE **8** *Making Verbs Agree with Relative Pronouns*

Number your paper 1 to 10. Then write the correct form of the verb in parentheses.

1. Did you see the magazines that (was, were) sitting by the door?
2. *Time* quoted people who (was, were) homeless after the flood.
3. One of the fliers who (was, were) honored yesterday has flown over a hundred test flights for the Air Force.
4. Jamie copied the words that (was, were) written on the board.
5. Pat is a person who (seems, seem) naturally artistic.
6. *Christina's World* is one of the paintings that (has, have) been selected for the Andrew Wyeth exhibition.
7. Have you seen the old records that (is, are) on display in the store?
8. The bobwhite is a songbird that (lives, live) in the same part of the country all year.
9. Helen Keller was one of the many persons who (has, have) triumphed over physical handicaps.
10. Is it Amy or Doreen who (wants, want) to go to Italy?

EXERCISE ❾ *Cumulative Review*

Number your paper 1 to 20. Find and write the verbs that do not agree with their subjects. Then write them correctly. If a sentence is correct, write *C* after the number.

1. The magazines on the shelf has good reference material.
2. Almost one third of these bulbs come from Holland.
3. One of the most extensive coral reefs that extends for over a thousand miles is off the coast of Australia.
4. Many of the fine old houses in our town dates back to colonial days.
5. *The Adventures of Tom Sawyer* were the first novel ever to be written on a typewriter.
6. Doesn't the sound of the roosters crowing in the morning wake you up?
7. There are approximately 200 geysers and 10,000 hot springs in Yellowstone National Park.
8. All continents, with the exception of Antarctica and Australia, is wider in the north than in the south.
9. The pillow, as well as the comforter, are filled with down.
10. *Stars and Bars* was the name of the first Confederate flag.
11. New England scenery and the change in seasons has greatly influenced my parents' decision to live in Maine.
12. Seventy-five percent of the nation's blueberries are grown in Michigan, New Jersey, and North Carolina.
13. Was any nineteenth-century stamps printed in two colors?
14. There is one hamburger and one ear of corn left.
15. There are sand dunes in Colorado that is over 500 feet high.
16. At the fair fifty cents were charged for each ride.
17. About one fourth of the land in the state of Alaska is part of the National Park system.
18. Only one president out of the first 36 were left-handed—James A. Garfield.
19. The red cedar is one of the few conifers that doesn't have needles.
20. Several samples of yarn were available at the craft show.

⚜ *Application to Writing*

Write a personal essay that begins, "Everything takes longer than you expect." Check for correct subject and verb agreement.

USING YOUR TEXT

*Subjects and Verbs
(694–713)
Descriptive Writing
(109–113)*

Usage: *Editing for Errors in Agreement*

Always check for subject and verb agreement when revising.

Checking Your Understanding Find and write the verbs that do not agree with their subjects. Then write those verbs correctly.

What does you know about trees? Do you know, for example, that the leaves on a tree has several functions? One of these functions are to make food for the tree. Carbon dioxide from the air is taken in by the leaves. Water and minerals from the soil is taken in by the root system. The chlorophyll in leaves also absorb energy from the sun. The chlorophyll then change the carbon dioxide and water into glucose. The glucose made in leaves are a tree's basic food.

Leaves also give off enormous quantities of water. Some of the water that flows from the roots to the leaves are used to make food. Most of the rest of the water in leaves evaporate through millions of tiny holes on the surface of the leaves.

In much of North America, the water supply of all trees are cut off in winter. After the ground freezes, trees needs more water than they can get from the ground. To prevent water loss, many trees "lock up" by shedding their leaves. In this way evaporation through the leaves don't occur.

Certain trees, however, has different kinds of leaves. Pine, fir, and hemlock has narrow needlelike leaves with a thick, waxy outer covering. The covering on these leaves prevent the evaporation of water. As leaves, or needles, falls off, new ones grow in at the same time. Because the branches never look bare, these trees are called evergreens.

Writing a Personal Essay When you read the excerpt from Agatha Christie's autobiography on pages 217–222, you learned how she created Hercule Poirot, one of her famous detectives. If you were going to write a detective story, what would your detective be like? Go through the same type of process that Agatha Christie did in developing her detective. Then write a short essay that describes your detective. *Application:* After you revise your essay, edit it for correct subject and verb agreement. Then write a final copy.

24 Review

A Making Subjects and Verbs Agree   Number your paper 1 to 25. Then write the correct form of the verb in parentheses.

1. New Orleans—with its ornate grillwork, marvelous food, and fascinating history—(attracts, attract) many tourists.
2. One of my presents (was, were) a gift certificate from the huge video store on Madison Avenue.
3. (Was, Were) many world records broken in the 1984 Olympics in Los Angeles?
4. Both the hockey team and the baseball team (has, have) won state championships this year.
5. Mathematics (is, are) a special kind of language.
6. (Is, Are) ten dollars too much for that book?
7. My uncle, not my cousins, (was, were) visiting at the end of August.
8. A grouping of millions of stars (is, are) called a galaxy.
9. Ham and eggs (makes, make) a hearty breakfast.
10. In the basket (was, were) two apples, a pear, and a bunch of grapes.
11. There (is, are) some traffic signs that are understood in all countries.
12. (Doesn't, Don't) Richard play on the varsity basketball team anymore?
13. The number of honor students (is, are) growing.
14. Neither my brother nor his friends (wants, want) to dance.
15. Amy is one of the people who (supports, support) me.
16. (Has, Have) most of the audience been seated?
17. There (is, are) more than 19 species of buzzards.
18. Neither the center nor the guard (knows, know) that play well.
19. A gift and a card (was, were) on the table.
20. All of today's newspaper (is, are) wet.
21. Both Tennessee and Missouri (touches, touch) eight other states.
22. One of our country's First Ladies (was, were) a former newspaper photographer: Jacqueline Kennedy.
23. These old cans of paint (is, are) a fire hazard.
24. Every toaster and mixer (was, were) on sale at the hardware store.
25. Because of a defect, five dollars (was, were) deducted from the price of the sweater.

B **Editing for Correct Subject and Verb Agreement**

In the following paragraphs, find and write the verbs that do not agree with their subjects. Then write them correctly.

There is about 250 different kinds of sharks. The size of these sharks vary greatly—from 2 feet up to 50 or 60 feet long. Only a small percentage of these sharks are known to attack humans. The white shark, the hammerhead, and the tiger is among those that is dangerous. Each of these sharks have been known to kill humans. (Haven't everyone seen the movie *Jaws*?) All of these kinds of sharks, however, prefer other food—such as bony fishes, squid, and shrimp. A turtle or a dolphin make a good dinner as well. The largest sharks—for example, the whale shark—is different. They prefer only the smallest food, such as the tiny animals that feeds on seaweed. To find its food, a shark—similar to human beings—rely a lot on its nose. In fact, the hungrier a shark, the more sensitive its nose will be.

Even though some of the sharks prefers tiny animals, their teeth are very sharp. In a shark's mouth is several rows of pointed teeth. What happens if a shark loses some of its teeth? Are there a clinic with very brave dentists? Actually, sharks need patience, not dentists. In time a new row of teeth grow in to take the place of the old ones.

Mastery Test

Number your paper 1 to 10. Write the subject in each sentence. Then next to each one, write the form of the verb in parentheses that agrees with the subject.

 1. Either a bookcase or some shelves (is, are) needed.
 2. Two thirds of the students (has, have) voted.
 3. (Has, Have) all the applicants been interviewed?
 4. This week there (has, have) been several warm days.
 5. (Doesn't, Don't) the movie start at 5:30?
 6. Neither of these reports (has, have) any footnotes.
 7. Barry's voice and acting ability (is, are) exceptional.
 8. The number of boys who have jobs (is, are) growing.
 9. Most of those cantaloupes (is, are) too soft.
10. Sam, along with members of his family, (is, are) here.

25 Using Adjectives and Adverbs

Diagnostic Test

Number your paper 1 to 10. Then write the correct form of the modifier in parentheses.

1. Through Carlos's small telescope, you can see the rings of Saturn almost (perfect, perfectly).
2. Monday has always been my (less, least) favorite day of the entire week.
3. Alaska is larger by far than (any, any other) state in the United States.
4. Though the quarterback tried both line plunges and pass plays, there wasn't (nothing, anything) that worked.
5. Which type of tree grows (taller, tallest), the redwood or the sequoia?
6. Karla is the (older, oldest) of the two Smith sisters, who live next door.
7. Richard's car has run (good, well) since he completely overhauled the motor.
8. Elena is the (smartest, most smartest) person I know at Swampscott High School.
9. Which is (fresher, freshest), the bread or the rolls?
10. Of the three skaters in the competition, Tina has the (more, most) original routine.

Comparison of Adjectives and Adverbs

Everyone has preferences. You may feel, for example, that meat loaf tastes *good* and spaghetti tastes *better;* but a thick, juicy steak tastes the *best* of all. Adjectives and adverbs have more than one form to express such preferences. This chapter will review the different forms of comparison, as well as some problems with comparisons.

The three forms that most adjectives and adverbs take to show the degrees of comparison are the *positive,* the *comparative,* and the *superlative.*

Rule 25a   Most modifiers show the degree of comparison by changing form.

The basic form of an adjective or an adverb is the *positive* form. It is used when no comparison is being made—when you simply are making a statement about a person or a thing.

ADJECTIVE   This route to school is **quick.**

ADVERB   Brad can run **fast.**

When two people, things, or actions are being compared, the *comparative* degree is used. Notice that *-er* has been added to *quick* and *fast.*

ADJECTIVE   Of the two routes to school, this one is **quicker.**

ADVERB   Of the two runners, Brad can run **faster.**

When more than two people, things, or actions are being compared, the *superlative* degree is used. Notice that *-est* has been added to *quick* and *fast.*

ADJECTIVE   Of the three routes to school, this one is the **quickest.**

ADVERB   Of all the runners in the race, Brad can run the **fastest.**

Regular and Irregular Comparison

Most adjectives and adverbs form their comparative and superlative degrees in the same way, following a few simple rules. A few modifiers, however, form their comparative and superlative degrees irregularly.

Regular Comparison   The comparative and superlative forms of most adjectives and adverbs are determined by the number of syllables in them.

Rule 25b   Add *-er* to form the comparative degree and *-est* to form the superlative degree of one-syllable modifiers.

POSITIVE	COMPARATIVE	SUPERLATIVE
young	younger	youngest
hot	hotter	hottest
soon	sooner	soonest
green	greener	greenest

Note: A spelling change sometimes occurs when an ending is added to a modifier. If you are not sure how to form the comparative or superlative degree of a modifier, check the dictionary.

Most two-syllable words form their comparative degree by adding *-er* and their superlative degree by adding *-est*. Some of these words, however, use *more* and *most* because the words would sound awkward—or be impossible to pronounce—if *-er* or *-est* was added. You would never say, for example, "carefuler" or "famouser." *More* and *most* are also used with all adverbs that end in *-ly*.

Rule 25c   Use *-er* or *more* to form the comparative degree and *-est* or *most* to form the superlative degree of two-syllable modifiers.

POSITIVE	COMPARATIVE	SUPERLATIVE
quiet	quieter	quietest
graceful	more graceful	most graceful
early	earlier	earliest
slowly	more slowly	most slowly

Note: If you are unsure how to spell the comparative and superlative degrees of a two-syllable modifier, check the dictionary.

Modifiers with three or more syllables always form their comparative and superlative degrees by using *more* and *most*.

Rule 25d   Use *more* to form the comparative degree and *most* to form the superlative degree of modifiers with three or more syllables.

POSITIVE	COMPARATIVE	SUPERLATIVE
dangerous	more dangerous	most dangerous
rapidly	more rapidly	most rapidly

Less and *least* are used to form the negative comparisons of all modifiers.

POSITIVE	COMPARATIVE	SUPERLATIVE
tasty	less tasty	least tasty
steadily	less steadily	least steadily

Irregular Comparison A few adjectives and adverbs change form completely for the comparative and superlative degrees.

Positive	Comparative	Superlative
bad/badly/ill	worse	worst
good/well	better	best
little	less	least
many/much	more	most

Note: The endings *-er* and *-est* should never be added to the comparative and superlative forms of these irregular modifiers. For example, you should never use "worser" as the comparative form of *bad*.

EXERCISE *Forming the Comparison of Modifiers*

Number your paper 1 to 15. Then copy each modifier and write its comparative and superlative forms.

1. weak	**6.** light	**11.** little
2. hurriedly	**7.** different	**12.** quickly
3. good	**8.** bad	**13.** clever
4. horrible	**9.** great	**14.** many
5. busy	**10.** unsafe	**15.** swift

EXERCISE *Using the Correct Form of Comparison*

Number your paper 1 to 20. Then write the correct form of the modifier in parentheses.

 1. Of the three boys, Colin wrote the (better, best) essay.
 2. Rita's, not Amy's, kite flew (higher, highest).
 3. Ellen swam to the dock (more, most) rapidly than Juan.
 4. Which subject do you like (better, best): English, history, or math?
 5. Which has the (more, most) beautiful song, the nightingale or the hermit thrush?
 6. Of your two friends, which one is (more, most) sincere?
 7. Which city has the (larger, largest) population: Chicago, Detroit, or Miami?
 8. Since there are two acceptable candidates for the job, the manager has to choose the (better, best) one.
 9. I don't know which I like (less, least), washing the dishes or drying them.
10. Alex is the (shyer, shyest) of all my friends.
11. Which is (longer, longest), a yard or a meter?
12. Which one—Washington, Jefferson, or Kennedy—do you think was the (better, best) president?
13. Since there were three math problems on the test, I did the (easier, easiest) one first.
14. Leroy's essay was (more, most) informative than Maria's.
15. Who do you think was the (better, best) poet, Tennyson or Shelley?
16. This shirt comes in small, medium, and large; but I think the medium one would fit you (better, best).
17. Which is (taller, tallest): the Chrysler Building, the Empire State Building, or the World Trade Center?
18. I find Bianca the (more, most) able writer on the staff.
19. Which costs (less, least), the disc or the cassette?
20. Of the several rivers in Virginia that wind to the ocean, which one is the (longer, longest)?

Problems with Modifiers

The following special problems sometimes arise when you write comparisons.

Double Comparisons   Use only *one* method of forming the comparative and superlative degrees at the same time. Using both methods simultaneously results in a *double comparison.*

Rule 25e Do not use both -er and *more* to form the comparative degree, or both -est and *most* to form the superlative degree.

DOUBLE COMPARISON   That book is **more longer** than this one.
CORRECT   That book is **longer** than this one.

DOUBLE COMPARISON   This is the **most nicest** picture of you.
CORRECT   This is the **nicest** picture of you.

***Other* and *Else* in Comparisons**   Very often one or more people or things will be compared with other people or things in the same group. When you make such a comparison, however, be sure you do not appear to compare a person or a thing with itself.

Rule 25f   Add *other* or *else* when comparing a member of a group with the rest of the group.

INCORRECT   Dyer Road has more potholes than any road in town. [Since Dyer Road is a road in the town, it is being compared with itself.]

CORRECT   Dyer Road has more potholes than any **other** road in town. [By adding the word *other,* Dyer Road is now being compared *only* with the other roads in town.]

INCORRECT   Mandy can sing higher than anyone in the choir. [Since Mandy is a member of the choir, she is being compared with herself.]

CORRECT   Mandy can sing higher than anyone **else** in the choir. [By adding the word *else,* Mandy is now being compared *only* with the other members of the choir.]

EXERCISE 3   *Correcting Mistakes in Comparisons*

Number your paper 1 to 20. Then write the following sentences, correcting each mistake.

1. Alvin jumps higher and farther than any member of the track team.
2. A loosely packed campfire will burn more quicker than a tightly packed one.
3. Nathan DePietro has more wins than anyone on this year's wrestling team.
4. Though not the highest waterfalls in the world, the falls of the Niagara River are perhaps more famous than any waterfalls.

5. I think a rabbit's fur is more softer than even a cat's fur.

6. The force of gravity is more greater near the poles than at the equator.

7. Andrew worked harder than any person on the work crew.

8. The African elephant probably has larger eyes than any animal in the world.

9. This party was the most wonderfulest surprise of my life!

10. Chu plays more sports than anyone in his family.

11. Yellow and green can be seen more readily by the human eye than any colors.

12. Is the humidity more higher today than it was yesterday?

13. Except for Pluto, the outer planets are more larger than the inner planets, including Earth.

14. Kim plays the flute better than anyone in music class.

15. That test was more harder than any test this year.

16. There are more lawyers in Washington, D.C., than in any community in the United States.

17. I think Lee is smarter than anyone I know.

18. These redwoods are the most tallest trees I have ever seen.

19. This pup is friendlier than any dog in the pet shop.

20. The cheetah can run more faster than any four-legged animal.

Illogical Comparisons   When you write a comparison, be sure you compare two or more similar things. When you compare different things, the comparison becomes illogical.

Rule 25g   Compare only items of a similar kind.

ILLOGICAL COMPARISON	A dachshund's **legs** are shorter than other **dogs.** [*Legs* are being compared with *dogs.*]
LOGICAL COMPARISON	A dachshund's **legs** are shorter than other dogs' **legs.** [*Legs* are being compared with *legs.*]
LOGICAL COMPARISON	A dachshund's **legs** are shorter than other **dogs'.** [With the possessive *dogs',* *legs* is understood; therefore, *legs* are being compared with *legs.*]
LOGICAL COMPARISON	A dachshund's **legs** are shorter than **those** of other dogs. [The demonstrative pronoun *those* takes the place of *legs;* therefore, *legs* are being compared with *legs.*]

ILLOGICAL COMPARISON	**Roy's bread** looked quite different from the **picture.** [*Bread* is being compared with a picture.]
LOGICAL COMPARISON	Roy's **bread** looked quite different from the **bread** in the picture. [Now Roy's *bread* is being compared with *bread* in a picture.]

Note: See pages 789–790 for information about the use of an apostrophe with possessives.

Double Negatives   Some words are considered *negatives.* In most sentences two negatives, called a *double negative,* should not be used together.

Rule 25h   Avoid using a double negative.

Common Negatives	
but (meaning "only")	none
barely	no one
hardly	not (and its contraction *n't*)
neither	nothing
never	only
no	scarcely

DOUBLE NEGATIVE	Sue does**n't** have **no** choice in this matter.
CORRECT	Sue does**n't** have any choice in this matter.

DOUBLE NEGATIVE	There is**n't hardly** any reason to meet.
CORRECT	There is**n't** any reason to meet.
CORRECT	There is **hardly** any reason to meet.

EXERCISE ◆4◆ *Correcting Mistakes in Comparisons*

Number your paper 1 to 20. Then write the following sentences, correcting each mistake.

1. There isn't hardly any part of the world that is entirely free of mosquitoes.
2. Tuitions in private colleges are higher than state colleges.
3. We hadn't gone barely a mile when we ran out of gas.
4. Our apartment has less space than the Jacksons.

5. Because of Don's confusing directions, we couldn't hardly find his house.

6. When the fuse blew, we hadn't but one small candle remaining in the house.

7. I think William Butler Yeats's poetry is more difficult to understand than Robert Frost.

8. The women's sweatshirts are more expensive than the men.

9. When Buzz throws a fastball, a batter has hardly no chance of getting a hit.

10. Two ocelots don't never have the same markings.

11. A dog's affection often seems more obvious than a cat.

12. Her schedule is busier than her husband.

13. The first practical submarine wasn't nothing but a leather-covered rowboat that could submerge for about 10 to 15 hours.

14. We don't have no portable television sets in stock.

15. Denise's opinions are quite different from her sister.

16. The brain of an ant isn't scarcely as big as the head of a pin.

17. Are a hare's ears longer than any other animal?

18. The fog is so thick that I can't hardly see the road.

19. This movie isn't nothing like what I expected.

20. Monday's crowd at the baseball game was much larger than Thursday.

Adjective or Adverb? An adjective modifies a noun or a pronoun, and sometimes an adjective follows a linking verb. An adverb modifies a verb, an adjective, or another adverb.

ADJECTIVE   That test was **easy.** [*Easy* is a predicate adjective that follows a form of the linking verb *be* and modifies the noun *test.* It tells *which* test was easy.]

ADVERB   Tad runs five miles **easily.** [*Easily* is an adverb that modifies the verb *runs.* It tells *how* Tad runs.]

The verbs *appear, feel, look, remain, smell, sound, stay, taste*, and *turn* are common linking verbs. These same verbs, however, can also be action verbs. An adjective follows a linking verb, but an adverb follows an action verb.

If you are not sure whether one of the verbs listed above is being used as a linking verb or as an action verb, substitute the verb *is.* If the sentence makes sense, the verb is a linking verb. If it does not make sense, the verb is an action verb.

ADJECTIVE   He looked **handsome** in his tuxedo. [*He is handsome* makes sense. *Looked* is used as a linking verb; therefore, *handsome* is a predicate adjective.]

ADVERB   He looked **carefully** through the files for the missing report. [*He is carefully through the files* does not make sense. *Looked* is used as an action verb; therefore, *carefully* is an adverb.]

ADJECTIVE   In the crowd the small child appeared **nervous.** [*In the crowd the small child is nervous* makes sense. *Appeared* is used as a linking verb; therefore, *nervous* is a predicate adjective.]

ADVERB   The bear appeared **suddenly.** [*The bear is suddenly* does not make sense. *Appeared* is used as an action verb; therefore, *suddenly* is an adverb.]

Good is always an adjective. *Well* is usually used as an adverb. *Well* is used as an adjective, however, when it means "in good health" or "satisfactory."

ADJECTIVE   Sally is a **good** writer.

ADVERB   Sally writes **well.**

ADJECTIVE   Sally doesn't feel **well** today. [in good health]

EXERCISE 5 *Choosing an Adjective or an Adverb*

Number your paper 1 to 10. Write the correct form of the modifier in parentheses.

1. Everyone did (good, well) on the final exam.
2. Jeff looked (hungry, hungrily) at the leftover drumstick on the platter.
3. That perfume smells rather (strong, strongly).
4. Adrienne can (easy, easily) beat Tim at racquetball.
5. You presented your ideas (good, well) at the Student Council meeting yesterday.
6. Don't you think Peter looks exceptionally (good, well) after his operation?
7. If you say your lines too (rapid, rapidly), no one will understand you.
8. I did rather (good, well) in the marathon yesterday.
9. That orange tastes very (bitter, bitterly).
10. Christopher felt (good, well) after getting an extra hour's sleep.

EXERCISE **6** *Cumulative Review*

Number your paper 1 to 20. Rewrite the following sentences, correcting each mistake. If a sentence is correct, write *C* after the number.

1. Of all the cities in the United States, I think New York City would be the more exciting place to live.
2. Is gold more valuable than any metal?
3. Of the two teams, I think the Braves have the best chance of winning the World Series this year.
4. Prepare your speech carefully before you present it at the class meeting.
5. This year's senior play was better than last year.
6. Jaime thinks that history is more interesting than his other subjects.
7. Are beagles more friendlier than basset hounds?
8. The band performed that difficult number perfect.
9. Isn't there no one you can talk to?
10. Scott likes soccer better than any sport.
11. I think the dogwood is the more beautiful of the two trees in your yard.
12. Terry's graduation ring looks different from Janice.
13. The lilies of the valley in that vase smell sweetly.
14. That was the most scariest movie I have ever seen!
15. That cocker spaniel has won more ribbons than any dog in the show.
16. I don't know which is worse, taking a test or waiting to hear the grade.
17. I think Army will beat Navy easily this year.
18. There wasn't no reason given for his resignation.
19. Those were the most tastiest strawberries that I have ever eaten.
20. This clam chowder tastes particularly well.

Application to Writing

As dark as night is a simile that has turned into a cliché. The phrase has been used so often that it no longer creates any special image in a reader's mind. Think of a new way to write the simile. Then explain how the two things in your new comparison are similar. *Application:* When you have finished, make sure you have used the correct forms of any adjectives and adverbs.

Usage: Editing for Correct Use of Modifiers

When you write a comparison, always check to see that you have used the correct forms of comparison and that you have avoided all the problems with comparisons that have been explained in this chapter.

Checking Your Understanding   Find and write each error in the comparison of modifiers in the following paragraphs. Then correct each error.

Venus has been called Earth's twin. Second in distance from the sun, Venus comes more nearer to Earth than any planet. Venus's diameter, density, mass, and gravity are all close to Earth. Venus's year is about three fifths as long as Earth's. Venus's rotation, however, is from east to west, while Earth and most other planets rotate from west to east.

Venus is masked by dense, pale yellow clouds. Astronomers knew hardly nothing about Venus's atmosphere and surface until radar and unpiloted spacecraft penetrated the clouds. Despite Venus's clouds, the surface gets much more hotter than Earth. The temperature on Venus can reach 460°C.

Because Venus is more closer to the sun than Earth is, you can see it only when you face in the general direction of the sun. During most of the daytime, the sun shines too vivid to allow you to see Venus. When Venus is east of the sun, however, the sun sets before it. Then Venus can be seen clear in the twilight of the western sky. It is then called the evening star.

Writing a Persuasive Essay   What sport do you like more than any other? Is it a team sport? An individual sport? A sport in which you participate? Brainstorm for a list of reasons why you find this sport superior. Then write the first draft of an essay intended to persuade your classmate that *your* favorite sport is better than all others. Include facts, examples, and details to support your major points. *Application:* After you revise your essay, be sure to edit it, correcting any errors in the use of modifiers. Then write a final copy.

25 Review

Correcting Errors with Modifiers Number your paper 1 to 30. Then write the following sentences, correcting each mistake. If a sentence is correct, write *C* after the number.

1. We couldn't go swimming this morning because there wasn't no lifeguard on duty.
2. Who finished the newspaper's crossword puzzle fastest, Theresa or Miguel?
3. On the rooftop two robins sang cheerfully.
4. Do you know that Jupiter is larger than any planet in the solar system?
5. I hope my picture of the Clydesdale horses will do good in the photography contest.
6. Before I got my new glasses, I couldn't hardly see the chalkboard at the front of the classroom.
7. The eldest of the two Thornton children is going to Illinois State in the fall.
8. That kind of ice skate is more better for hockey than for figure skating.
9. Which of the two performances of *Romeo and Juliet* did you like better?
10. Some beetles can run very rapidly when they are searching for food.
11. How was China's early civilization different from Egypt?
12. An ordinary tennis racket is more larger than a paddle-tennis racket.
13. Christina McLaughlin plays the harpsichord better than anyone I know.
14. During your speech speak distinct and try to pause once in a while.
15. Women's fashions do change from year to year more quickly than men.
16. Venus is more brighter than any celestial body except the sun and the moon.
17. Did Manuel do well in the finals of the swimming meet last Saturday?
18. The fog was so thick around us this morning that I couldn't see nothing.

19. The cheetah is different from members of the cat family because it cannot hide its claws.
20. That shirt comes in blue, green, or yellow; but I think the blue looks better on you.
21. Steven is the most wittiest reporter on the school newspaper.
22. Which would you like best, a week at a dude ranch or a trip to Alaska?
23. His sweater and pants match well.
24. Next week I won't have no time to work extra hours at the music shop.
25. I think Yori's acting ability is better than Jason.
26. Rich Campbell can paint both figures and landscapes better than anyone I know.
27. After her argument with Michael, Marsha felt badly.
28. Why haven't you never learned to swim?
29. Today I feel the bestest I have felt in over a week.
30. Which tastes worse, that cough medicine or warm milk?

Mastery Test

Number your paper 1 to 10. Then write the correct form of the modifier in parentheses.

1. The heart performs (good, well) for the average person, beating 2½ billion times during a lifetime.
2. Which is (taller, tallest), the cypress or the elm?
3. A kangaroo's head is small and resembles a (deer, deer's).
4. Ever since Lucia took lessons, she has danced (beautiful, beautifully).
5. Basketball is more popular than (any, any other) sport at our school.
6. The temperature today is (cooler, more cooler) than it was yesterday.
7. Who has the (more, most) beautiful voice, Carl or Ramón?
8. I (have, haven't) never seen the ocean.
9. Of the two routes, this one seems (less, least) hilly.
10. Which of the following cities has the (better, best) climate: Tallahassee, San Francisco, or Boulder?

A Writer's Glossary of Usage

Part of the growing process is learning that some behavior is appropriate and some is not. Everyone quickly learns as a child, for example, that throwing food on the floor is definitely *not* acceptable or appropriate behavior.

As children grow older, most learning becomes more complicated. No longer is everything either good or bad, right or wrong. Some behavior is appropriate in some situations but inappropriate in others. Using your fingers, for example, to eat fried chicken may be appropriate behavior at home, but it may become inappropriate at a fancy restaurant.

Different expressions of the English language are somewhat like certain types of behavior; they may be appropriate with one audience but not with another. Using contractions in your conversations, for example, is standard and acceptable, but using contractions in a research paper may not be appropriate.

Levels of Language

Professor Higgins in *My Fair Lady* prided himself on his ability to name the towns where people were born by analyzing their dialects. *Dialect* is a regional variety of language that includes grammar, vocabulary, and pronunciation. Like the English, Americans have different dialects. The accents and expressions of people from parts of Texas, for example, are quite different from the accents and expressions of people from parts of Massachusetts. In spite of these variations in dialect, though, people from Texas and people from Massachusetts can easily understand one another.

The place of your birth, however, is not the only influence on the way you speak. Your ethnic and educational backgrounds, as well as other factors, also contribute to the particular way you speak. All of these combined factors add a richness and a vibrant diversity to the English language. These factors have also created the need for different levels of expression. Traditionally these levels are recognized as *standard* and *nonstandard* English.

Standard English

Almost all professional people—such as writers, television and radio personalities, government officials, and other notable figures—use in public what is known as *standard English*. Standard English uses all the rules and conventions of usage that are accepted most widely by English-speaking people throughout the world. (They are the same rules and conventions that are taught in this text.) The use of standard English varies, nevertheless, in formal and informal situations.

Formal English   Formal English, which follows the conventional rules of grammar, usage, and mechanics, is the standard for all written work. It is used mainly in such written work as formal reports, essays, scholarly writings, research papers, and business letters. Formal English may include some words that are not normally used in everyday conversation and frequently may employ long sentences with complex structures. To maintain a formal tone of writing, most writers avoid contractions, colloquialisms, and certain other common verbal expressions. The following example of formal English is the last paragraph of Samuel Johnson's essay "On Spring."

> He that enlarges his curiosity after the works of nature multiplies the inlets to happiness. Therefore, the younger part of my readers, to whom I dedicate this speculation, must excuse me for calling upon them to make use at once of the spring of the year and the spring of life—to acquire, while their minds may be yet impressed with new images, a love of innocent pleasures and an ardor for useful knowledge. A blighted spring makes a barren year; and the vernal flowers, however beautiful, are only intended by nature as preparation to autumnal fruits.
>
> S<small>AMUEL</small> J<small>OHNSON</small>, "On Spring"

Informal English   *Informal English* does *not* mean "inferior English." Just like formal English, informal English follows the rules and the conventions of standard English; however, it is less rigid. It includes some words and expressions, such as contractions, that would sound out of place in formal writing. English-speaking people around the world generally use informal English in their everyday conversation. It is also used in magazines, newspapers, advertising, and much of the fiction that is written today. The following example of informal English is a diary entry that was written by Admiral Byrd during one of his expeditions to Antarctica.

> Something—I don't know what—is getting me down. I've been strangely irritable all day, and since supper I have been depressed. . . This would not seem important if I could only put my finger on the trouble, but I can't find any single thing to account for the mood. Yet it has been there; and tonight, for the first time, I must admit that the problem of keeping my mind on an even keel is a serious one.   RICHARD E. BYRD, *Alone*

Nonstandard English

The many variations produced by regional dialects, slang, and colloquial expressions are incorporated into *nonstandard English.* Since nonstandard English lacks uniformity from one section of the country to the next and from year to year, you should always use standard English when you write. Some fiction authors use nonstandard English, however, to re-create the conversation of people from a particular locale or time period. This, for example, was O. Henry's purpose when he wrote the following passage from the short story "The Ransom of Red Chief."

> "I was rode," says Bill, "the ninety miles to the stockade, not barring an inch. Then, when the settlers was rescued, I was given oats. Sand ain't a palatable substitute. And then, for an hour I had to try and explain to him why there was nothin' in holes, how a road can run both ways, and what makes the grass green. I tell you, Sam, a human can only stand so much. So I takes him by the neck of his clothes and drags him down the mountain. On the way he kicks my legs black-and-blue from the knees down . . ."   O. HENRY, "The Ransom of Red Chief"

A Writer's Glossary of Usage

Some of the entries in the following glossary of usage make reference to standard and nonstandard English, the terms discussed in the previous section. Since the glossary has been arranged alphabetically, you can use it easily.

a, an   Use *a* before a word beginning with a consonant sound. Use *an* before a word beginning with a vowel sound. Always keep in mind that this rule applies to sounds, not letters. For example, *an hour ago* is correct because the *h* is silent.

A house on our street has just been sold.
He asked for **an** honest evaluation of his work.

accept, except   *Accept* is a verb that means "to receive with consent." *Except* is usually a preposition that means "but" or "other than." *Acceptance* and *exception* are the noun forms.

The football players will **accept** all the new regulations **except** one.

adapt, adopt   Both of these words are verbs. *Adapt* means "to adjust." *Adopt* means "to take as your own." *Adaption, adaptation,* and *adoption* are the noun forms.

If we **adopt** the dress code suggested by the report, we'll have to **adapt** it to the locale of our school.

advice, advise   *Advice* is a noun that means "a recommendation." *Advise* is a verb that means "to recommend."

What **advice** would you give to a freshman?
I **advise** everyone to wear sturdy boots for the hike.

affect, effect   *Affect* is a verb that means "to influence" or "to act upon." *Effect* is usually a noun that means "a result" or "an influence." As a verb *effect* means "to accomplish" or "to produce."

Eastern Kansas was seriously **affected** by the storm.
The **effects** of the storm cost the state millions of dollars.
The fear of mud slides **effected** a change in the hikers' plans.

ain't   This contraction is nonstandard and should be avoided in your writing.

NONSTANDARD   This **ain't** my first choice.
STANDARD   This **isn't** my first choice.

all ready, already   *All ready* means "completely ready." *Already* means "previously."

Are the children **all ready** to go?
We have **already** eaten dinner.

all together, altogether   *All together* means "in a group." *Altogether* means "wholly" or "thoroughly."

The members of our team were **all together** at the game.
The concert was **altogether** enjoyable.

allusion, illusion   Both of these words are nouns. An *allusion* is "an implied or indirect reference; a hint." An *illusion* is "something that deceives or misleads."

Many literary **allusions** can be traced to the Bible, Shakespeare, or mythology.

You can see motion in motion pictures only because of an optical **illusion.**

a lot   These words are often written as one word. There is no such word as "alot." *A lot* should be avoided in formal writing. (Do not confuse *a lot* with *allot,* which is a verb that means "to distribute by shares.")

INFORMAL   Do you miss them **a lot?**
FORMAL   Do you miss them very much?
The rations should be **allotted** evenly.

among, between   Both of these words are prepositions. *Among* is used when referring to three or more people or things. *Between* is usually used when referring to two people or things.

Shaking hands, the distinguished senator moved **among** the people.

Mario planted flowers **between** the shrubs and the walk.

amount, number   *Amount* refers to a quantity. *Number* refers to things that can be counted.

> A small **number** of students raised a large **amount** of money for the athletic program.

any more, anymore   Do not use *any more* for *anymore*. *Any more* refers to quantity. The adverb *anymore* means "from now on" or "at present."

> Is there **any more** lettuce in the garden?
> No, I don't raise lettuce **anymore.**

anywhere, everywhere, nowhere, somewhere   Do not add *s* to any of these words.

NONSTANDARD   I lost my wallet **somewheres.**
   STANDARD   I lost my wallet **somewhere.**

as far as   This expression is sometimes confused with "all the farther," which is nonstandard.

NONSTANDARD   This is **all the farther** I can drive.
   STANDARD   This is **as far as** I can drive.

at   Do not use *at* after *where*.

NONSTANDARD   Ask the attendant **where** we're **at.**
   STANDARD   Ask the attendant **where** we are.

a while, awhile   *A while* is an expression made up of an article and a noun. It must be used after the prepositions *for* and *in*. *Awhile* is an adverb and is not used after a preposition.

> You won't get your test results for **a while.**
> I think you should wait **awhile** before calling again.

bad, badly   *Bad* is an adjective and often follows a linking verb. *Badly* is used as an adverb and often follows an action verb. In the first two examples, *felt* is a linking verb.

NONSTANDARD   Bart has felt **badly** all day.
   STANDARD   Bart has felt **bad** all day.
   STANDARD   He was so nervous that he did the job **badly.**

EXERCISE *Determining the Correct Word*

Number your paper 1 to 20. Then write the word or group of words in parentheses that correctly completes each sentence.

1. The train station is (all the farther, as far as) I can take you.
2. Do you have to take (any more, anymore) final exams before graduation?
3. The lawn mower works so (bad, badly) that I refuse to use it anymore.
4. Can you stay for (awhile, a while) longer?
5. In her report Jill made interesting (allusions, illusions) to some of Shakespeare's plays.
6. If I had to choose (among, between) swimming and jogging, I'd choose swimming.
7. A large (amount, number) of squawking chickens got out of the coop.
8. I'm sure the doctor will (advice, advise) you to get a week's more rest.
9. I don't think that hat looks (bad, badly) on you.
10. Do you think that the new entrance requirements at the college will (affect, effect) your acceptance?
11. A large (amount, number) of sunlight is needed to keep that plant healthy.
12. The doctors had to divide the serum (among, between) their many patients.
13. How does (a, an) honeybee (adapt, adopt) to the cold weather in the North?
14. We were (all ready, already) to go, but Dad couldn't find the tickets (anywhere, anywheres).
15. This (ain't, isn't) the best time for us to be (altogether, all together).
16. (Accept, Except) all parcels from the mail carrier—(accept, except) any that are damaged.
17. I think you should wait for (a while, awhile) before you (adapt, adopt) another dog.
18. The choir feels (all together, altogether) pleased with the (amount, number) of people who attended the concert.
19. (Between, Among) the six of us, I was the only one who had (all ready, already) eaten.
20. (Accept, Except) for one point, I thought Joyce's (advice, advise) made good sense.

because   Do not use *because* after *the reason*. Use one or the other.

NONSTANDARD   The **reason** he joined the exercise class was **because** he wanted to feel more energetic.

STANDARD   He joined the exercise class **because** he wanted to feel more energetic.

STANDARD   The **reason** he joined the exercise class was **that** he wanted to feel more energetic.

being as, being that   These expressions should be replaced with *because* or *since*.

NONSTANDARD   **Being as** it rained on Saturday, I didn't have to mow the lawn.

STANDARD   **Since** it rained on Saturday, I didn't have to mow the lawn.

beside, besides   *Beside* is always a preposition that means "by the side of." As a preposition, *besides* means "in addition to." As an adverb, *besides* means "also" or "moreover."

Sit **beside** me in homeroom. [by the side of]

Besides the theater tickets, we also won a free dinner for four. [in addition to]

The school has a swimming pool, tennis courts, and an indoor track **besides.** [also]

both   Never use *the* before *both*.

NONSTANDARD   We saw **the both** of you at the mall.

STANDARD   We saw **both** of you at the mall.

both, each   *Both* refers to two persons or objects together, but *each* refers to an individual person or object.

Although **both** office buildings were designed by the same architect, **each** one is quite different.

bring, take   *Bring* indicates motion toward the speaker. *Take* indicates motion away from the speaker.

Bring me a stamp and then **take** this letter to the mailbox.

can, may *Can* expresses ability. *May* expresses possibility or permission.

> **Can** you see the third line of the eye chart?
> **May** I have the next dance?

can't help but In this expression use a gerund instead of *but*. *(See pages 595–597 for more information about gerunds.)*

NONSTANDARD	I **can't help but notice** your attractive new haircut.
STANDARD	I **can't help noticing** your attractive new haircut.

capital, capitol A *capital* is the chief city of a state. Also, names are written with *capital* letters, people invest *capital,* and a person can suffer *capital* punishment. A *capitol* is the building in which the legislature meets.

> The **capitol** in Tallahassee, the **capital** of Florida, has a mural painted on the outside.

coarse, course *Coarse* is an adjective that means "loose or rough in texture" or "crude and unrefined." *Course* is a noun that means "a way of acting or proceeding" or "a path, road, or route." Also, people play golf on a *course;* an appetizer is one *course* of a meal; and students take *courses* in school. *Course* is also the word used in the parenthetical expression *of course.*

> Many people objected to his **coarse** remarks after the tennis match.
> What **course** of action do you recommend in order to get the project done on time?

continual, continuous Both of these words are adjectives. *Continual* means "frequently repeated." *Continuous* means "uninterrupted."

> Because of the **continual** ringing of the phone, I didn't get much done.

> The rain was **continuous** for over ten hours.

different from Use this form instead of *different than. Different than,* however, can be used informally when it is followed by a clause.

INFORMAL   My sweater is **different than** the one Gram knitted for Maureen.

FORMAL   My sweater is **different from** the one Gram knitted for Maureen.

FORMAL   His jacket is **different from** mine.

discover, invent   Both of these words are verbs. *Discover* means "to find or get knowledge for the first time." *Invent* means "to create or produce for the first time." Something that is discovered has always existed, but it was unknown. Something that is invented has never existed before. The noun forms of these words are *discovery* and *invention*.

Isaac Newton **discovered** the law of gravity.

Who first **discovered** oil in Alaska?

Who **invented** the first computer?

doesn't, don't   *Doesn't* is singular and should be used only with singular nouns and the personal pronouns *he, she,* and *it. Don't* is plural and should be used only with plural nouns and the personal pronouns *I, you, we,* and *they.*

NONSTANDARD   He **don't** need any help.

STANDARD   He **doesn't** need any help.

NONSTANDARD   An apple a day **don't** keep the doctor away.

STANDARD   An apple a day **doesn't** keep the doctor away.

done   *Done* is the past participle of the verb *do.* Therefore, when *done* is used as a verb, it must be used with one or more helping verbs.

NONSTANDARD   I **done** what I thought was right by taking the abandoned bike to the police.

STANDARD   I **have done** what I thought was right by taking the abandoned bike to the police.

double negative   Words such as *hardly, never, no, not,* and *nobody* are considered negatives. Do not use two negatives to express one negative meaning. *(See page 721 for a complete list of negative words.)*

NONSTANDARD   I do**n't hardly** have any spare time.

STANDARD   I do**n't** have any spare time.

STANDARD   I **never** have any spare time.

emigrate, immigrate Both of these words are verbs. *Emigrate* means "to leave a country to settle elsewhere." *Immigrate* means "to enter a foreign country to live there." A person emigrates *from* a country and immigrates *to* another country. *Emigrant* and *immigrant* are the noun forms.

> Kin Fujii **emigrated** from Japan ten years ago.
> He **immigrated** to the United States.

etc. *Etc.* is an abbreviation for a Latin phrase, *et cetera,* that means "and other things." Never use *and* with *etc.* If you do, what you are really saying is *"and and* other things." It is best, however, not to use this abbreviation at all in formal writing.

INFORMAL   For the salad we need grapes, **etc.**
 FORMAL   For the salad we need grapes **and other fruits.**

EXERCISE ◆2◆ *Determining the Correct Word*

Number your paper 1 to 25. Then write the word or group of words in parentheses that correctly completes each sentence.

1. I hope Manuel (doesn't, don't) dive from the high board.
2. A proper diet recommends grapefruit and oranges because (both, the both) are rich in vitamin C.
3. We should wear long pants and long-sleeved shirts and take mosquito repellent (beside, besides).
4. How is an orange different (from, than) a tangerine?
5. Please tie up the papers and (bring, take) them down to me.
6. (Because, Being that) the Canadian lynx has unusually large, broad feet, it can move easily over the snow.
7. My bicycle is the one (beside, besides) the fence.
8. That (coarse, course) material caused a rash on my arms.
9. Thomas Edison (discovered, invented) the Dictaphone.
10. (Don't, Doesn't) he know the name of that building?
11. My parents (emigrated, immigrated) from India in 1972.
12. (Both, The both) of us attended the concert.
13. What is the (capital, capitol) of Oregon?
14. (Because, Being as) we got a late start, we arrived late.
15. (Beside, Besides) three inches of much-needed rain, the storm brought a welcome drop in temperature.
16. There is hardly (any, no) reason for his resignation.

17. I (done, have done) only half of the math assignment.

18. (Can, May) Hannah run the mile faster than Susan?

19. I don't know of (any, no) reason why I can't go to the game.

20. (Can, May) I (bring, take) the attendance report to the office?

21. We must (discover, invent) a way to stop the (continual, continuous) showers of acid rain.

22. When my family (emigrated, immigrated) to the United States, they settled in the (capital, capitol) of Kentucky.

23. My brother (can, may) usually finish the 18 holes of a golf (coarse, course) under par.

24. How is the (capital, capitol) in Albany different (from, than) the one in Harrisburg?

25. (Beside, Besides) the (continual, continuous) honking of horns, I've been distracted by the hammering next door.

fewer, less   *Fewer* is plural and refers to things that can be counted. *Less* is singular and refers to quantities and qualities that cannot be counted.

> I received **fewer** birthday cards this year than last year.
> You should have put **less** water in the stew.

former, latter   *Former* is the first of two people or things. *Latter* is the second of two people or things. (Use *first* and *last* when referring to three or more.)

> For the main course, we had a choice of roast beef or pork chops. I chose the **former;** Ben chose the **latter.**

good, well   *Good* is an adjective and often follows a linking verb. *Well* is an adverb and often follows an action verb. However, when *well* means "in good health" or "satisfactory," it is used as an adjective.

> The flannel shirt feels **good.** [adjective]
> I work **well** in the morning. [adverb]
> Pat doesn't feel **well.** [adjective—"in good health"]

had of   Do not use *of* after *had*.

NONSTANDARD	If I **had of** listened to the weather forecast, I would have taken my umbrella.
STANDARD	If I **had** listened to the weather forecast, I would have taken my umbrella.

have, of   Never substitute *of* for the verb *have*. When speaking, many people make a contraction of *have*. For example, someone might say, "You should've called first." Because *-ve* sounds like *of, of* is often incorrectly substituted for *have*.

NONSTANDARD   You should **of** roasted the potatoes.
STANDARD   You should **have** roasted the potatoes.

hear, here   *Hear* is a verb that means "to perceive by listening." *Here* is an adverb that means "in this place."

Stand over **here** so you can **hear** the speech.

hole, whole   A *hole* is an opening. *Whole* means "complete" or "entire."

The **whole** time I watched the **hole,** no animal went in or came out of it.

imply, infer   Both of these words are verbs. *Imply* means "to suggest" or "to hint." *Infer* means "to draw a conclusion by reasoning or evidence." A speaker implies; a hearer infers. *Implication* and *inference* are the noun forms.

Grandmother **implied** that she might be visiting soon.
We **inferred** from what she said that she wouldn't be staying very long.

in, into   Use *into* when you want to express motion from one place to another.

The mixture **in** the bowl should be put **into** the blender.

irregardless   Do not substitute this word for *regardless*.

NONSTANDARD   **Irregardless** of anything you say, I still think he was telling the truth.
STANDARD   **Regardless** of anything you say, I still think he was telling the truth.

its, it's   *Its* is a possessive pronoun. *It's* is a contraction for *it is*.

The committee will announce **its** findings on Friday.
It's going to be a controversial report.

kind, sort, type   These words are singular and should be preceded by *this* and *that. Kinds, sorts,* and *types* are plural and should be preceded by *these* and *those.*

> **This kind** of computer is very expensive.
> **These kinds** of computers are very expensive.

kind of, sort of   Do not substitute these expressions for *rather* or *somewhat* in formal writing.

NONSTANDARD	Those financial statements are **kind of** hard to understand.
STANDARD	Those financial statements are **rather** hard to understand.

knew, new   *Knew,* the past tense of the verb *know,* means "was acquainted with." *New* is an adjective that means "recently made" or "just found."

> We **knew** all along that a **new** gym would be built.

learn, teach   Both of these words are verbs. *Learn* means "to acquire knowledge." *Teach* means "to instruct."

NONSTANDARD	Pamela **learned** me how to water-ski.
STANDARD	Pamela **taught** me how to water-ski.
STANDARD	I **learned** how to water-ski last summer.

leave, let   Both of these words are verbs. *Leave* means "to depart." *Let* means "to allow" or "to permit."

NONSTANDARD	**Leave** me get you a glass of water.
STANDARD	**Let** me get you a glass of water.
STANDARD	Did the train **leave** on time?

lie, lay   *Lie* means "to rest or recline." *Lie* is never followed by a direct object. Its principal parts are *lie, lying, lay,* and *lain. Lay* means "to put or set (something) down." *Lay* is usually followed by a direct object. Its principal parts are *lay, laying, laid,* and *laid.*

LIE	If you feel faint, **lie** down.
	I **lay** awake all last night, worrying about final exams.
	Mopsy has **lain** by the fire all evening.

LAY   **Lay** only the living-room carpet.

        Why are you **laying** your coat over the chair?

        As soon as David **laid** the book down, he fell asleep.

        The workers have already **laid** the foundation.

EXERCISE *Determining the Correct Word*

Number your paper 1 to 25. Then write the word or words in parentheses that correctly complete each sentence.

1. We might (have, of) gone camping if it hadn't rained.
2. (Leave, Let) me answer that question.
3. Mr. Davis has (implied, inferred) that he will retire.
4. Did you (hear, here) the echo?
5. That article was (kind of, rather) funny.
6. How did that baby bird fall from (its, it's) nest?
7. You should (have, of) mentioned that sooner.
8. Is the dog (lying, laying) on the sofa again?
9. I just noticed that I have a huge (hole, whole) in my sleeve!
10. The lifeguard jumped (in, into) the pool to cool off.
11. Mr. Barnes (learned, taught) me a valuable lesson.
12. I don't wish to (imply, infer) that I am running again.
13. The vacuum works (good, well) since Mom fixed it.
14. Nancy gently (lain, laid) the blanket over the baby.
15. These (kind, kinds) of potatoes are good for baking.
16. From her remarks we (implied, inferred) that she might be moving soon.
17. (Fewer, Less) people use the park during the winter.
18. (Irregardless, Regardless) of the weather, we must continue until we reach the cabin.
19. If everything turns out (good, well), we should be able to get a (knew, new) television set.
20. Did you (hear, here) that Mr. Sherman will be (learning, teaching) us fencing after school?
21. We (implied, inferred) from her silence that she didn't do (good, well) in the tryouts.
22. (Irregardless, Regardless) of what the clerk said, (its, it's) the wrong color.
23. (Its, It's) impossible to know if he will (leave, let) us play.
24. I (knew, new) something was wrong the (hole, whole) time.
25. You could (have, of) stopped (hear, here) on your way home.

EXERCISE 4 *Using* Lie *and* Lay *Correctly*

Number your paper 1 to 10. Then complete each sentence by writing the correct form of *lie* or *lay*.

 1. Sandy _____ her handmade mittens on a pile of snow beside the car.
 2. The spare tire was _____ on the floor of the garage.
 3. For a month after his gallbladder operation, Dad _____ down each afternoon.
 4. Two thirds of Alaska _____ below the Arctic Circle.
 5. _____ the pieces of the puzzle right side up.
 6. Her ring must have _____ on the floor all week.
 7. In Yorktown on October 19, 1781, the British _____ down their arms and surrendered to George Washington.
 8. For what seemed like hours, the snake had _____ coiled on the driveway.
 9. I have _____ the clean laundry in a pile at the foot of your bed, Amanda.
 10. He shouldn't be _____ those tools on a glass tabletop.

like, as *Like* can be used as a preposition to introduce a prepositional phrase. *As* is usually a subordinating conjunction that introduces an adverb clause. Although *like* is sometimes used informally as a conjunction, it should be avoided in formal situations. *(See pages 612–615 for more information about adverb clauses.)*

INFORMAL   I think the room is perfect just **like** it is. [clause]
  FORMAL   I think the room is perfect just **as** it is.
  FORMAL   Gloria's cat is gray-striped **like** mine. [prepositional phrase]

loose, lose *Loose* is usually an adjective that means "not tight." *Lose* is a verb that means "to misplace" or "not to have any longer."

I will sew on those **loose** buttons.
If I leave, I'll **lose** my turn at bat.

may be, maybe *May be* is a form of the verb *be. Maybe* is an adverb that means "perhaps."

This **may be** the chance of a lifetime.
Maybe he didn't see you.

most   *Most* is a noun, a pronoun, or an adjective that modifies a noun or a pronoun. *Almost,* which means "nearly," is an adverb. Do not substitute *most* for *almost.*

NONSTANDARD   I finished **most** all of my term paper last night.
STANDARD   I finished **almost** all of my term paper last night.
STANDARD   I keep busy **most** of the time.

nor, or   Use *neither* with *nor* and *either* with *or.*

Neither Fred **nor** Jane is coming to the party.
I will take **either** the red one **or** the blue one.

of   Prepositions such as *inside, outside,* and *off* should not be followed by *of.*

NONSTANDARD   The ball rolled **off of** the lawn into the gutter.
STANDARD   The ball rolled **off** the lawn into the gutter.

ought   Never use *have* or *had* with *ought.*

NONSTANDARD   You **had**n't **ought** to arrive so late.
STANDARD   You **ought** not to arrive so late.

passed, past   *Passed* is the past tense of the verb *pass.* As a noun *past* means "a time gone by." As an adjective *past* means "just gone" or "elapsed." As a preposition *past* means "beyond."

In the **past** she always **passed** her courses with *A*'s. [*past* as a noun]

For the **past** several mornings, I have walked **past** the park on my way to school. [*past* as an adjective and then as a preposition]

precede, proceed   Both of these words are verbs. *Precede* means "to be, go, or come ahead of something else." *Proceed* means "to move along a course; to advance" or "to continue after a pause or an interruption."

These instructions **precede** the ones from yesterday.
Proceed down the mountain with great caution because the incline is steep.

principal, principle   As an adjective *principal* means "main" or "chief." As a noun *principal* means "the head of a school" or "a leader." *Principle* is a noun that is synonymous with *law, truth, doctrine,* or *code of conduct.*

> The **principal** part in the drama was played by Mr. Rogers, the **principal** of Canton High School.

> Roberto lives by a strict set of **principles.**

respectfully, respectively   *Respectfully* is related to the noun *respect,* which means "high regard or esteem." *Respectively* means "in the order given."

> Everyone spoke **respectfully** to the elderly man.
> Jan and Bob are from Detroit and Cleveland, **respectively.**

rise, raise   *Rise* means "to move upward" or "to get up." *Rise* is never followed by a direct object. Its principal parts are *rise, rising, rose,* and *risen. Raise* means "to lift up," "to increase," or "to grow something." *Raise* is usually followed by a direct object. Its principal parts are *raise, raising, raised,* and *raised.*

> The sun **rises** an hour later now that daylight saving time has begun.
> When should we **raise** the flag?

says   Do not use *says,* the present tense of the verb *say,* when you should use the past tense *said.*

NONSTANDARD	Then she **says,** "I want to go with you."
STANDARD	Then she **said,** "I want to go with you."

-self, -selves   A reflexive or an intensive pronoun that ends in *-self* or *-selves* should not be used as a subject. (Never use *hisself* or *theirselves.*)

NONSTANDARD	Ken and **myself** were chosen.
STANDARD	Ken and **I** were chosen.
NONSTANDARD	They made **theirselves** sandwiches.
STANDARD	They made **themselves** sandwiches.

shall, will   Formal English uses *shall* with first person pronouns and *will* with second person pronouns and third person pronouns. Today, however, *shall* and *will* are used interchangeably with *I* and *we*—except that *shall* is still used with first person pronouns for questions.

Shall I meet you at the mall?
Will you meet me at the mall?

sit, set   *Sit* means "to rest in an upright position." *Sit* is never followed by a direct object. Its principal parts are *sit, sitting, sat,* and *sat. Set* means "to put or place (something)." *Set* is usually followed by a direct object. Its principal parts are *set, setting, set,* and *set.*

Sit down and rest for a while.
Set the dishes on the shelf.

so   *So* should not be used to begin a sentence.

NONSTANDARD	**So** when you are leaving on your vacation?
STANDARD	The plane lands in five minutes, **so** we must hurry! [coordinating conjunction]
STANDARD	The dance was **so** wonderful! [adverb]

some, somewhat   *Some* is either a pronoun or an adjective that modifies a noun or a pronoun. *Somewhat* is an adverb.

NONSTANDARD	School enrollment has declined **some.**
STANDARD	School enrollment has declined **somewhat.**

EXERCISE 5 *Determining the Correct Word*

Number your paper 1 to 20. Then write the word or group of words in parentheses that correctly completes each sentence.

1. Nicholas caught that sailfish (himself, hisself).
2. The rain is (some, somewhat) heavier now.
3. Tim will (precede, proceed) with his plans for the party.
4. Denver, Boise, and Helena are the capitals of Colorado, Idaho, and Montana, (respectfully, respectively).
5. Mom and Dad enjoyed (theirselves, themselves) in Tampa.
6. Your sweater is blue (as, like) mine.
7. This will, dated 1978, (preceded, proceeded) the other one.
8. Today (may be, maybe) my lucky day!
9. We pulled (off, off of) the road to let the ambulance pass.

10. In the (passed, past), life was less complicated.

11. (Almost, Most) everyone at the school picnic had a wonderful time.

12. Charlie and (I, myself) are going to work the spotlights at the concert Saturday night.

13. How did the dog get (loose, lose)?

14. Do (as, like) I say, not (as, like) I do.

15. (Almost, Most) all of the arrivals from the Midwest (may be, maybe) slightly delayed because of a storm.

16. Two weeks (passed, past) before I felt (some, somewhat) better.

17. (Shall, Will) we (precede, proceed) to the dining room?

18. Jay (says, said), "I haven't had time to swim for the (passed, past) several days."

19. (May be, Maybe) you will (loose, lose) the nomination.

20. The (principal, principle) issue that (shall, will) be discussed at the meeting is safer streets.

EXERCISE 6 *Using* Rise/Raise *and* Sit/Set *Correctly*

Number your paper 1 to 15. Complete each sentence by writing the correct form of *rise/raise* or *sit/set*.

1. Thao _____ to question the speaker.

2. Please _____ in that large, comfortable chair.

3. The price of clothing is constantly _____.

4. I _____ nervously in the dentist's waiting room for almost 45 minutes.

5. _____ the flag slowly.

6. Have you been _____ there long?

7. Tracy _____ the box on the counter.

8. In about 15 minutes, the dough for the pita bread will have _____ enough.

9. Should I be _____ the napkins to the right of the plates?

10. Who _____ the blinds this morning?

11. The elevator started to _____ before I pushed the button.

12. I have _____ in the back row all year long.

13. The cat has been _____ on the new sofa again!

14. The temperature has been _____ steadily during the day.

15. Our dog _____ his head alertly as the mail carrier approached our house.

than, then   *Than* is usually a subordinating conjunction and is used for comparisons. *Then* is an adverb that means "at that time" or "next."

I have lived in Salt Lake City longer **than** you.
Finish your homework and **then** call me.

that, which, who   These words are often used as relative pronouns to introduce adjective clauses. *(See page 617 for more information about essential and nonessential clauses.) That* refers to people, animals, or things and always begins an essential clause. *Which* refers to animals and things. *Who* refers to people.

The movie **that** was on TV last night is my favorite.
Gone with the Wind, **which** was shown on TV last night, is my favorite movie.

Anyone **who** responds to the ad may fill out an application.

their, there, they're   *Their* is a possessive pronoun. *There* is usually an adverb, and sometimes it will begin an inverted sentence. *They're* is a contraction for *they are.*

Their car is parked over **there.**
They're moving to Mobile in September.

theirs, there's   *Theirs* is a possessive pronoun. *There's* is a contraction for *there is.*

There's a car; is it **theirs?**

them, those   Never use *them* as a subject or an adjective.

| NONSTANDARD | **Them** are from my garden. [subject] |
| STANDARD | **Those** are from my garden. |

| NONSTANDARD | **Them** tomatoes are from my garden. [adjective] |
| STANDARD | **Those** tomatoes are from my garden. |

this, that, these, those   *This* and *that* are singular and should modify singular nouns. *These* and *those* are plural and should modify plural nouns.

NONSTANDARD	Does the Sport Shop sell **those** kinds of bats?
STANDARD	Does the Sport Shop sell **that** kind of bat?
STANDARD	The Sport Shop sells **those** bats.

this here, that there   Avoid using *here* or *there* in addition to *this* or *that.*

NONSTANDARD   **That there** dog looks ferocious!
STANDARD   **That** dog looks ferocious!

threw, through   *Threw* is the past tense of the verb *throw. Through* is a preposition that means "in one side and out the other."

Who **threw** Sunday's newspaper away?
We turned our lights on when we drove **through** the tunnel.

to, too, two   *To* is a preposition. *To* also begins an infinitive. *Too* is an adverb that modifies an adjective or another adverb. *Two* is a number.

Two more people are **too** many **to** take in our car.

try to   Use *try to* instead of *try and,* which is nonstandard.

NONSTANDARD   I will **try and** be there on time.
STANDARD   I will **try to** be there on time.

unique   *Unique* is an adjective that means "the only one of its kind." Because of its meaning, *unique* should not be written in the comparative or superlative degree.

NONSTANDARD   That horse has the **most unique** markings.
STANDARD   That horse has **unique** markings.

way, ways   Do not substitute *ways* for *way* when referring to a distance.

NONSTANDARD   We have a long **ways** to go yet.
STANDARD   We have a long **way** to go yet.

weak, week   *Weak* is an adjective that means "not strong" or "likely to break." *Week* is a noun that means "a period of seven days."

For the first **week** after your surgery, you'll feel quite **weak.**

what   Do not substitute *what* for *that.*

NONSTANDARD   The car **what** I want is very expensive.
STANDARD   The car **that** I want is very expensive.

when, where   Do not use *when* or *where* directly after a linking verb in a definition. *(See page 543 for a list of linking verbs.)*

NONSTANDARD   In the North October is **when** you should plant tulip bulbs.

STANDARD   In the North October is the month in which you should plant tulip bulbs.

NONSTANDARD   The Hall of Mirrors is **where** the Treaty of Versailles was signed.

STANDARD   The Hall of Mirrors is the room in which the Treaty of Versailles was signed.

where   Do not substitute *where* for *that.*

NONSTANDARD   I read **where** bowling is the number one participant sport in the United States.

STANDARD   I read **that** bowling is the number one participant sport in the United States.

who, whom   *Who,* a pronoun in the nominative case, is used as a subject or a predicate nominative. *Whom,* a pronoun in the objective case, is mainly used as a direct object, an indirect object, or an object of a preposition. *(See pages 681–682 for more information about* who *and* whom.*)*

Who is coming to our party? [*Who* is the subject of the sentence.]
Howard is someone **whom** I have known all my life.
[*Whom* is the direct object of the verb *have known* in the adjective clause]

whose, who's   *Whose* is a possessive pronoun. *Who's* is a contraction for *who is.*

Whose suitcase is that?
Who's going with you?

your, you're   *Your* is a possessive pronoun. *You're* is a contraction for *you are.*

You're sure you put **your** baseball glove in the car?

EXERCISE ⬧ 7 ⬧ *Determining the Correct Word*

Number your paper 1 to 25. Then write the word or group of words in parentheses that correctly completes each sentence.

1. (Them, Those) watches are extremely accurate.
2. You should try (and, to) get a good night's sleep.
3. The praying mantis is an insect (that, who) is entirely beneficial to people.
4. Which store in town sells (that, these) kind of paint?
5. The basketball game (that, what) I saw last night was extremely exciting.
6. Mom got Sally (them, those) earrings for her birthday.
7. I couldn't sell (this here, this) old radio for any price!
8. Tree-ripened fruit is usually sweeter (than, then) fruit picked green.
9. I read (that, where) the U.S. Postal Service processes approximately 50 percent of the world's mail.
10. Ever since Elizabeth sprained her left ankle, it has been (weak, week).
11. Who (threw, through) the clean clothes into the hamper?
12. (Who, Whom) is sitting with Jason?
13. I want a bike (that, what) is very lightweight.
14. Earl is taller (than, then) most other boys in his class.
15. (Theirs, There's) is the house with the green shutters.
16. In a magazine I read (that, where) Anne Murray earned her college degree as a physical-education teacher.
17. (Whose, Who's) taking care of (your, you're) dog?
18. (Theirs, There's) an easy way (to, too) open that jar.
19. (This, These) kind of brass key ring costs about (to, too, two) dollars.
20. In the Brontë family, (their, there) were six children, three of (which, whom) became famous novelists.
21. They went (threw, through) (their, they're) files, but they couldn't find the birth certificates.
22. Don't try (to, and) stay awake because we have a long (way, ways) to go yet.
23. (Your, You're) the one they want (to, too) nominate.
24. (Their, There) are streets in Quebec that are (to, too) narrow for large cars to pass each other easily.
25. I can't forget (this, these) kind of horror movie for at least a (weak, week).

26 Capital Letters

Diagnostic Test

Number your paper 1 to 10. Then write each word that should begin with a capital letter.

EXAMPLE   last summer we visited niagara falls.
ANSWER   Last, Niagara, Falls

1. as we drove to memphis, we saw the mississippi river to our left.
2. did judge gershen speak at the rally on the fourth of july?
3. linda attended a school in pennsylvania before entering wild-wood high school this year.
4. while searching for a northeastern route around north america, henry hudson discovered hudson bay.
5. until this year i had never read john keats's poem "ode to a grecian urn."
6. during christmas vacation we traveled from seattle to portland on mountain railroad to visit my grandparents.
7. to get to victoria park, go south on route 74.
8. during my junior year, my favorite courses were american history and art.
9. we saw the play the phantom of the opera at the shubert theater on forty-fourth street.
10. georgia's family is moving to the southwest next month.

Rules for Capital Letters

Until the advent of printing in the fifteenth century, words were written in all capital letters, and no punctuation was used. When scribes wrote, they ran words TOGETHERLIKETHIS.

Fortunately along with the printing press came specific uses for capital letters and the introduction of punctuation. As a result, not only could people read faster, but they could also understand more easily what they read. The correct use of capital letters and punctuation will add clarity to your writing and will prevent any misunderstanding of your meaning.

When lowercase letters were first introduced, capital letters were used only in special situations. Today, however, a capital letter marks the beginning of certain constructions and emphasizes the importance of certain words. This chapter will review the uses of capital letters.

First Words

Capital letters draw a reader's attention to the beginning of a new sentence or a new line of poetry.

Rule 26a Capitalize the first word of a sentence or in a line of poetry.

SENTENCE **T**eenagers in our community have become increasingly involved in political campaigns.

POETRY **T**he splendor falls on castle walls
And snowy summits old in story:
The long light shakes across the lakes,
And the wild cataract leaps in glory.
ALFRED, LORD TENNYSON

Capitalize the first word when a direct quotation is used. *(See pages 803–804.)*

Marvin asked, "**W**ill you call me when you get home?"

Capitalize the first word of each heading in an outline. *(See page 152.)*

I. **A**rgument for a new gym
   A. **A**dditional space

Capitalize the first word in a formal resolution.

> *Resolved,* **T**hat this school should permit seniors to leave school assemblies before other students.

Capitalize the first word of a formal statement that follows a colon.

> The question was this: **C**ould a runner break the four-minute-mile record?

Note: For capitalization in business letters and social letters, see pages 413–419.

I and *O*

Always capitalize these single-letter words.

Rule 26b   Capitalize the pronoun *I*, both alone and in contractions. Also capitalize the interjection *O.*

> *I*   **I**'m sure **I** saw her at the game.
> *O*   **O** hark, **O** hear! how thin and clear,
>   And thinner, clearer, farther going!
>   ALFRED, LORD TENNYSON

Note: *Oh* is not capitalized unless it comes at the beginning of a sentence.

Proper Nouns

Beginning a noun with a capital letter tells a reader that the noun may be a proper noun—that it names a particular person, place, or thing.

Rule 26c   Capitalize proper nouns and their abbreviations.

Since there are so many proper nouns, they have been divided into the following groups to help you remember them easily.

Names of Persons and Animals   Capitalize the names of particular persons and animals.

PERSONS   James, Jocelyn **W**eiss, **A**llison, **R**. **F**errara
ANIMALS   **R**ex, **F**elix, **M**orris, **D**ancer, **T**hunderbolt

Surnames that begin with *De, Mc, Mac, O',* or *St.* usually contain two capital letters. However, since such names do vary, it is always best to ask individual people how their names are spelled and capitalized.

DeJon, McGuire, MacInnis, O'Hara, St. James

Capitalize a descriptive name, title, or nickname that is used as a proper noun or as part of a proper noun.

Calamity Jane, **H**onest **A**be, the **C**ornhusker **S**tate

Capitalize abbreviations that follow a person's name.

Stephanie Wong, **M.D.**, will be tonight's guest speaker.

Capitalize common nouns that are clearly personified.

O **M**emory! thou fond deceiver.   OLIVER GOLDSMITH

Geographical Names   Capitalize the names of particular places, bodies of water, and celestial bodies.

STREETS, HIGHWAYS	Tremont Street, Meridan Turnpike, Route 77, Thirty-second Street [The second part of a hyphenated numbered street is not capitalized.]
CITIES, STATES	Rapid City, South Dakota; Terre Haute, Indiana; Washington, D.C.
TOWNSHIPS, COUNTIES	Pottsville Township, Broward County
COUNTRIES	Saudi Arabia, Thailand, the Soviet Union, Ireland, Canada
SECTIONS OF A COUNTRY	the Northwest, New England, the South [Words that are used as sections of the country are often preceded by *the*. Compass directions do not begin with a capital letter: *Go east on Route 23.*]
CONTINENTS	South America, Africa, Australia
ISLANDS	Long Island, the Philippine Islands
MOUNTAINS	Mount Hood, the Allegheny Mountains, the White Mountains
PARKS	Bryce Canyon National Park
BODIES OF WATER	Pacific Ocean, South China Sea, Persian Gulf, Niagara Falls, Merrimack River, Cedar Lake

STARS	**S**irius, **N**ova **H**ercules, **N**orth **S**tar
	Canopus, **V**ega
CONSTELLATIONS	**B**ig **D**ipper, **U**rsa **M**inor, **O**rion
PLANETS	**V**enus, **N**eptune, **S**aturn, **E**arth [Do not
	capitalize *sun* or *moon*. Also, do not
	capitalize *earth* if it is preceded by *the*.]

Note: Capitalize words such as *street, mountain,* or *island* only when they are part of a proper noun.

Which lake is larger, **L**ake **S**uperior or **L**ake **M**ichigan?

EXERCISE *Using Capital Letters.*

Number your paper 1 to 20. Then write the following items, using capital letters only where needed.

1. the columbia river
2. jackson park
3. the milky way
4. fifty-third street
5. a trip to the southwest
6. the city of louisville
7. the earth and mars
8. north on hayes highway
9. his horse dusty
10. alfred moses, jr.

11. the state of ohio
12. lake victoria
13. the new york turnpike
14. the indian ocean
15. mountains in the east
16. the gulf of suez
17. madrid, spain
18. newport news, virginia
19. a country in africa
20. the bluegrass state

EXERCISE *Using Capital Letters*

Number your paper 1 to 10. Then write each word that should begin with a capital letter.

1. woodrow wilson had a pet ram named old ike.
2. sparrows are not native to north america.
3. if you look directly to the east, i will be able to show you the little dipper.
4. before they were known as the rocky mountains, they were called the stony mountains.
5. the first woman to swim the english channel in both directions was florence chadwick of california.
6. paul revere's family name originally was de rivoire.

7. the gasoline station at morgan avenue and twenty-first street has the lowest prices in town.

8. the capital of texas was changed 15 times before austin was finally chosen.

9. address the invitation to rachel r. bliss, d.d.s., 8 highland road, birmingham, england.

10. the time is out of joint; o cursèd spite, that ever i was born to set it right! WILLIAM SHAKESPEARE

Names of Groups and Businesses Capitalize the names of organizations, businesses, institutions, government bodies, and political parties.

ORGANIZATIONS	the American Red Cross, the Boy Scouts of America, the National Guard
BUSINESSES	Eastern Airlines, Polaroid Corporation, G. Fox and Company, Jacobs and Associates, Arborway Natural Foods
INSTITUTIONS	Hawthorne High School, Lakeview Hospital, the University of Pennsylvania [Words such as *school, hospital,* and *university* are not capitalized unless they are part of a proper noun.]
GOVERNMENT BODIES	the United States Supreme Court, Congress, the Senate, the Veterans Administration, the House of Commons, Parliament
POLITICAL PARTIES	the Democratic party, a Republican

Specific Time Periods, Events, and Documents Capitalize days of the week, months of the year, civil and religious holidays, and special events. Also capitalize the names of historical events, periods, and documents.

DAYS, MONTHS	Tuesday, Wednesday, February, March [Do not capitalize the seasons of the year.]
HOLIDAYS	Memorial Day, Thanksgiving, Hanukkah
SPECIAL EVENTS	the Orange Bowl Parade, the Olympic Games, the Boston Marathon
HISTORICAL EVENTS	the Trojan War, the Boston Tea Party, the Louisiana Purchase, D-Day

PERIODS	the **Middle Ages**, the **Age** of **Reason**, the **Great Depression, Reconstruction**
DOCUMENTS	the **Truman Doctrine**, the **Treaty** of **Paris**, the **First Amendment**, the **Civil Rights Act**, the **Voting Rights Act**

Note: Prepositions are not capitalized in such cases.

Nationalities, Races, Languages, and Religions Capitalize the names of nationalities, races, languages, religions, and religious references.

NATIONALITIES	the **Chinese**, the **Mexicans**, a **Scandinavian**
RACES	**Caucasian, Oriental, Mongoloid**
LANGUAGES	**Spanish, Greek, Russian, English, French**
RELIGIONS	**Roman Catholic, Judaism, Lutheran**
RELIGIOUS REFERENCES	the **Bible**, the **Old Testament**, the **Torah**, the **Koran, God** [Capitalize pronouns referring to the Diety: *They prayed to God for His direction.* Do not capitalize *god* when it refers to a mythological god.]

Other Proper Nouns Capitalize other nouns that name specific places and things.

VEHICLES	*Explorer I, Lusitania, California Zephyr* [Names of vehicles are also italicized.]
AWARDS	the **Nobel Prize**, the **Davis Cup**
BRAND NAMES	**Apple** computer, **Dove** soap, **Ford** sedan [The product itself is not capitalized.]
MONUMENTS, MEMORIALS	**Washington Monument, Vietnam Memorial, Mount Rushmore**
BUILDINGS	**Metropolitan Opera House, Sears Tower, Eiffel Tower**
PARTS OF A BOOK	**Chapter** II, **Vol.** V, **No.** 4, **Part** IV
SPECIFIC COURSE NAMES	**Chemistry** II, **Drafting** I, **English**

Unnumbered courses such as *history, science,* and *art* are not capitalized. Also, do not capitalize class names such as *freshman* or *senior* unless they are part of a proper noun, such as *Senior Class Picnic.*

Note: For capitalization in business letters and social letters, see pages 413–419.

EXERCISE *Using Capital Letters*

Number your paper 1 to 10. Then write the following items, using capital letters only where needed.

1. math and spanish

2. the eiffel tower in paris

3. turkey on thanksgiving

4. spring and summer

5. the stone age

6. nabisco crackers

7. the supreme court

8. the god zeus

9. a hardware store in town

10. a college in the midwest

EXERCISE *Using Capital Letters*

Number your paper 1 to 15. Then write each word that should begin with a capital letter.

1. the cease-fire on palm sunday, april 9, 1865, ended the civil war.

2. during several months last winter, we were able to skate on the lake near our home.

3. dolley madison was voted a seat in the house of representatives on january 9, 1844.

4. john adams was a member of the federalist party.

5. chili con carne originated among mexicans living in what is now texas.

6. last year, when i was a junior, i enjoyed french, creative writing, art II, and mechanical drawing.

7. when my sister graduated from purdue university, she got a job in a computer company.

8. the fourth amendment to the constitution protects citizens from unreasonable search.

9. my first job was assembly-line work at the costello and morand company of portland, delaware.

10. the *mayflower* first touched land at the tip of cape cod on november 11, 1620.

11. have you ever visited mount vernon, george washington's home?

12. the industrial revolution started in england and spread to europe and america.

13. ty cobb of the detroit tigers made 4,191 base hits during his career.

14. the lutheran minister read a passage from genesis at the dedication ceremony.

15. edith wharton won a pulitzer prize for her fiction.

EXERCISE ◀ 5 ▶ *Cumulative Review*

Number your paper 1 to 10. Then write each word that should begin with a capital letter.

Facts and
Figures

1. in an average year, santa fe, new mexico, receives 17 more inches of snow than fairbanks, alaska.
2. the first college for women, which opened in 1834, was wheaton college in norton, massachusetts.
3. andrew jackson fought in the revolutionary war when he was only thirteen years old.
4. the largest natural history museum in the world is the american museum of natural history in new york.
5. the closest planet to the sun, mercury, is about one third the size of earth.
6. john glenn's space capsule, *friendship* 7, was picked up by the recovery ship *noah*.
7. the people of philadelphia first celebrated the fourth of july a year after the declaration of independence had been adopted by the continental congress.
8. the kodak camera was invented in 1888 in new york by george eastman.
9. the philadelphia eagles started playing in the national football league in 1933.
10. the last state to join the union before alaska and hawaii was arizona, admitted on valentine's day in 1912.

Proper Adjectives

Because proper adjectives are formed from proper nouns, they should be capitalized—as proper nouns are.

Rule 26d / Capitalize most proper adjectives.

PROPER NOUNS **S**pain, **I**daho, the **W**est
PROPER ADJECTIVES **S**panish rice, **I**daho potatoes

Note: When adjectives are formed from the words that refer to the compass directions, such as *east,* no capital letters are used.

The wind was blowing from an **e**asterly direction.

Some proper adjectives derived from proper nouns are so familiar that they are no longer capitalized.

china plates, **p**asteurized milk, **q**uixotic vision

When a proper adjective is part of a hyphenated adjective, capitalize only the part that is a proper adjective.

all-**A**merican team   trans-**S**iberian journey

Sometimes both of the parts of a hyphenated adjective will be proper adjectives.

Indo-**E**uropean languages   **A**frican-**A**merican literature

EXERCISE *Using Capital Letters*

Number your paper 1 to 10. Then write each word that should begin with a capital letter.

1. several of our neighbors fly the american flag outside their houses on state and national holidays.
2. the artifacts on exhibit at our local museum are believed to be pre-columbian.
3. a majority of the republican senators have voted for the appropriations.
4. the first non-indian visitor to arizona arrived in 1539.
5. my father and mother have driven their american-made car for 15 years.
6. is *X* the roman numeral for ten?
7. the verrazano-narrows bridge in new york city was designed by othmar a. ammans, a swiss-american engineer.
8. many of the numerous french-speaking people in canada live in quebec.
9. the friday afternoon traffic is quite heavy.
10. the sinking of the *maine* in havana harbor touched off the spanish-american war.

Titles

Capital letters signal the importance of titles of people and works of art.

Rule 26e Capitalize the titles of people and works of art.

Titles Used with Names of People   Capitalize a title showing office, rank, or profession when it comes before a person's name.

BEFORE A NAME   Is **J**udge **G**oodell in his chambers?
USED ALONE   Who was the **j**udge at the trial?

BEFORE A NAME   I worked on **S**enator **A**mes's reelection campaign.
USED ALONE   The **s**enator from our district is running for reelection.

Note: Do not capitalize the prefix *ex-* or the suffix *-elect* when either is connected to a title.

ex-**S**enator Hill   **G**overnor-elect Baray

Titles Used Alone   Capitalize a title that is used alone when it is being substituted for a person's name in direct address or when it is being used as a name. The titles for the current United States *President* and *Vice President,* for the *Chief Justice,* and for the *Queen of England* are always capitalized when they are being substituted for the person's name.

USED AS A NAME   How is the patient, **D**octor?
NOT USED AS A NAME   The **d**octor will speak to you soon.
HIGH GOVERNMENT OFFICIAL   The **P**resident and the **V**ice **P**resident will attend the summit meeting.

Note: *President* and *vice president* are capitalized when they stand alone only if they refer to the current president and vice president.

Was John F. Kennedy the youngest **p**resident?

Titles Showing Family Relationships   Capitalize a title showing family relationship when it comes before a person's name, when it is used as a name, or when it is substituted for a person's name.

BEFORE A NAME   When did **U**ncle Ron and **A**unt Mary leave?
USED AS A NAME   Please tell **M**om that she has a telephone call.
DIRECT ADDRESS   I'll help you paint the porch, **D**ad.

Titles showing family relationships should not be capitalized when they are preceded by a possessive noun or pronoun—unless they are considered part of a person's name.

NO CAPITAL   My **a**unt lives in California.

Aaron is taking Phil's **s**ister to the prom.

CAPITAL   When does your **U**ncle Ralph get home from work?

[*Uncle* is part of Ralph's name.]

Titles of Works of Art   Capitalize the first word, the last word, and all important words in the titles of books, newspapers, periodicals, stories, poems, movies, plays, musical compositions, and other works of art. Prepositions, coordinating conjunctions, and articles should not be capitalized—unless they are the first or last words in a title.

Last night I read the poem "**T**he **R**ime of the **A**ncient **M**ariner" in my anthology, *Our Literary Heritage.*

Read this headline in the *New York Daily News:* "**A**lligator **F**ound in **S**ewer." [The word *the* before the title of a newspaper or a periodical is usually not capitalized.]

EXERCISE ◆7▸ *Capitalizing Titles*

Number your paper 1 to 10. Then write each word that should begin with a capital letter.

   1. appointed by president john f. kennedy in 1961, dr. janet g. travell served as white house physician.
   2. did dad remember to buy the eggs we needed or will your sister get them?
   3. napoleon I was the emperor of france's first republic.
   4. i'm very glad to meet you, sir.
   5. one of the stars of *the barretts of wimpole street,* a hit play of 1931, was a spaniel named flush.
   6. is ex-mayor myers planning to run for office again?
   7. when is your grandmother moving to kansas?
   8. ernest hemingway helped supply films of fishers for the film version of his book *the old man and the sea.*
   9. in the summer of 1981, prince charles of england married lady diana spencer.
   10. "the successes of the space shuttle" was an article in the *earlville herald* last week.

EXERCISE **8** *Cumulative Review*

Number your paper 1 to 20. Then write each word that should begin with a capital letter.

Do You
Know?

1. was alan b. shepard, jr., or john glenn the first american to orbit the earth?
2. was it the pilgrims or the puritans who landed at plymouth rock in 1620?
3. which is the most westerly state in the u. s., alaska or hawaii?
4. who is the author of *great expectations,* a novel written during queen victoria's reign in England?
5. do muslims face mecca or izmir when they pray?
6. in what country were the first olympic games held?
7. was william mckinley or theodore roosevelt the first president elected in the twentieth century?
8. what was the name of dorothy's dog in *the wizard of oz?*
9. is the geyser old faithful in wyoming or nevada?
10. "i want to hold your hand" was the first american number-one single of what british group?
11. did world war II end in 1942 or 1945?
12. is the cy young award given in baseball or football?
13. is sacramento or los angeles the capital of california?
14. general lee surrendered to general grant at the appomattox court house. in what state did this occur?
15. did clark kent work for the *metropolis journal* or the *daily planet?*
16. what is the russian equivalent of the central intelligence agency in the united states?
17. is the lincoln memorial or the washington monument the tallest structure in washington, d.c.?
18. the parliament of england consists of the house of commons and what other governmental body?
19. is the astrodome in chicago or houston?
20. the united kingdom consists of england, scotland, northern ireland, and what other country?

 Application to Writing

In a short essay, describe what changes you would make in your town if you were the mayor. Check for proper capitalization.

USING YOUR TEXT

*Descriptive Writing
(109–113)*
Synonyms (464)

Mechanics: Editing for Capital Letters

An important part of editing your own writing is searching for errors in the use of capital letters.

Checking Your Understanding Number your paper 1 to 50. Then write all the words in the following paragraphs that should begin with a capital letter. Do not include any words already capitalized.

On april 25, 1979, at harper dry lake, california, young bryan allen piloted the longest human-powered flight that had ever been made—1 hour 9 minutes 3 seconds. The pilot supplied muscle power for the *gossamer albatross*, a tiny craft invented and designed by dr. paul d. maccready, jr.

The next challenge for the american flight team was a european journey across the english channel. Pilot allen accomplished the mission by pedaling the aircraft *gossamer albatross II* from manston, kent, england, to a french beach. Although the flight had been far behind schedule halfway across, the total flying time was 2 hours 49 minutes.

On july 7, 1981, the program's 210-pound plane flew 165 miles, between england and france. This unique aircraft, called the *solar challenger*, used no fuel except sunlight.

The story of dr. maccready's accomplishments is highlighted in *the flight of the gossamer condor*, a film that won an academy award in 1979. This unusual flight project is the subject of the book *gossamer odyssey*, of allen's article "winged victory of *gossamer albatross*" in the *national geographic magazine*, and of numerous other publications.

Writing a Description Imagine that you are an ad writer preparing a magazine ad to lure visitors to your city—in the year 2100. Brainstorm for ideas about things that will be the same as now and things that will have changed. Next write the first draft of the ad. Include your city's location and major attractions. *Application:* Revise and edit your ad. Before making a final copy, check for the correct use of capital letters.

26 Review

A Using Capital Letters Correctly Number your paper 1 to 20. Then write each word that should begin with a capital letter.

1. dalia's address is 43 thirty-third street, kokomo, indiana.

2. school usually starts on the wednesday after labor day.

3. the mediterranean is one of the most polluted seas on earth.

4. mount desert island, off the coast of maine, was discovered in 1604 by champlain, a french explorer.

5. have you any tickets for the chicago white sox game?

6. when i was a junior, my favorite course was biology, but this year i like english best.

7. the oscar weighs 7 pounds and is 10 inches high.

8. minnesota is called the land of 10,000 lakes, but it actually contains more than 11,000 lakes.

9. there really was a molly pitcher, but her real name was mary hayes mccauley.

10. during the battle of monmouth, she carried water in a pitcher to thirsty american soldiers.

11. when my parents went to canada last summer, they visited the small nova scotian town where mother was born.

12. have you ever read elizabeth jennings's poem "in memory of anyone unknown to me"?

13. last month the vice president represented the president on a tour of the far east.

14. the *andrea doria* collided with a swedish ship off the coast of nantucket in 1956.

15. if you sail through the panama canal from the atlantic to the pacific, you will actually be going from northwest to southeast, not east to west.

16. i enjoy watching the television series *masterpiece theatre.*

17. we asked nurse jahan when the doctor would see mother.

18. i saw the ballet *romeo and juliet,* based on shakespeare's play.

19. during the middle ages, few people, including kings, could read or write.

20. the first american novel, *the power of sympathy,* was published in boston in 1789.

B   **Editing for the Correct Use of Capital Letters**   Number your paper 1 to 20. Then write all the words in the following paragraph that should begin with a capital letter. Do not include any words that are already capitalized.

How did the state of idaho get its name? Some believe it is a shoshoni indian word meaning "gem of the mountains." The idaho state historical society, though, insists that the state's name does not have any meaning. It was first coined by a mining lobbyist in 1860 as a good name for a new territory in the pikes peak mining country. However, just before congress voted in washington, d.c., the hoax was discovered. That territory was then named colorado. The word *idaho,* nevertheless, kept popping up in the pacific northwest. For example, a steamboat that carried prospectors up and down the columbia river was named the *idaho.* As a result, three years later the name was again suggested to congress; but this time it was accepted.

Mastery Test

Number your paper 1 to 10. Then write each word that should begin with a capital letter.

1. the statue of liberty stands in new york harbor.
2. zachary taylor's horse, old whitey, was allowed to graze on the white house lawn.
3. did mom say that uncle ricardo will visit us this winter?
4. hot springs, new mexico, is my favorite city.
5. john steinbeck's novel *the grapes of wrath* takes place during the great depression.
6. graham mcnamee did the first play-by-play broadcast of a world series game in 1921.
7. jean transferred from central high school in kalamazoo, michigan.
8. joan payson, owner of the new york mets, wanted to call her team the meadowlarks.
9. who was the 16th president?
10. in 1931, emperor haile selassie began to rule ethiopa.

27 End Marks and Commas

Diagnostic Test

Number your paper 1 to 10. Write each sentence, adding a comma or commas where needed. Then add an appropriate end mark.

EXAMPLE   No Howard I haven't seen Susan all day
ANSWER   No, Howard, I haven't seen Susan all day.

1. Send your donations to the American Red Cross 107 Spencer Highway New Haven Connecticut 06520
2. Well I'm glad you made that suggestion
3. Two-dollar bills are seldom seen for they have never been printed in great quantities
4. Wouldn't you like to live in a warm dry climate
5. Janice Flemming the captain of our debating team has won a college scholarship
6. Do you want to go to the dance to an amusement park or to the movies
7. At three o'clock in the morning the telephone rang
8. Facing the jury the lawyer gave his closing arguments
9. Gerty Cori who won a Nobel Prize in 1947 was both a physician and a biochemist
10. Following Mary Ann cleared the pole at 12 feet

Kinds of Sentences and End Marks

A sentence has one of four different functions. It can make a statement, give a command, ask a question, or express strong feeling. Depending on its function, a sentence is either *declarative, imperative, interrogative,* or *exclamatory.* The end mark you use with a particular sentence is determined by the function of that sentence.

The first function of a sentence is to make a statement or to express an opinion. The majority of sentences fall into this category.

Rule 27a A **declarative sentence** makes a statement or expresses an opinion and ends with a period.

The following examples are both declarative sentences, even though the second example contains an indirect question.

Hail is usually produced during the passing of a cold front.

I don't remember where the receipt is. [The direct question would be *Where is the receipt?*]

The second function of a sentence is to give directions, make requests, or give commands. Generally *you* is the understood subject of these sentences.

Rule 27b An **imperative sentence** gives a direction, makes a request, or gives a command. It ends with either a period or an exclamation point.

If a command is given in a normal tone of voice, it is followed by a period when written. If it expresses strong feeling, it is followed by an exclamation point.

Follow the signs to the fairgrounds. [normal tone of voice]

Don't leave without me! [emotional tone of voice]

Occasionally an imperative sentence is stated as a question, but no reply is expected. Since the purpose of the sentence remains the same—to make a request—the sentence is followed by a period or by an exclamation point.

Will you please open the window a little wider.

The third function of a sentence is to ask a question—whether it is completely or incompletely expressed.

Rule 27c An **interrogative sentence** asks a question and ends with a question mark.

Have you ever visited San Francisco**?**

Where**?** I don't see any empty seats.

The fourth function of a sentence is to express strong feeling, such as excitement or anger. Avoid overusing this type of sentence, for it can very quickly lose its impact.

Rule 27d An **exclamatory sentence** expresses strong feeling or emotion and ends with an exclamation point.

What a busy day this has been**!**

Note: An interjection, such as *wow* or *oh,* may also be followed by an exclamation point. *(See page 553.)*

Ouch**!** Don't touch my sunburn.

EXERCISE *Classifying Sentences*

Number your paper 1 to 10. Write an appropriate end mark for each sentence. Then label each sentence *declarative, imperative, interrogative,* or *exclamatory.*

  1. The human brain reaches its full weight by the seventh year of life
  2. Read the next chapter in your textbook for homework
  3. Where did you find that stationery
  4. What an exciting show that was
  5. A hot drink will make you feel cooler than an ice-cold one
  6. Will you hold all my telephone calls
  7. What is the distance between the wingtips of a Boeing 747
  8. Oh, the basement floor is covered with a foot of water
  9. I didn't understand what you said
 10. Because of the braking effect of the moon, the rotation of the earth slows down

Periods and Abbreviations

Using abbreviations is a good way to write faster when you are taking notes, but they should usually be avoided in formal writing, such as compositions and research papers.

Rule 27e Use a period after most abbreviations.

The following list contains some abbreviations that are acceptable in formal writing. Use the dictionary to check the spelling and punctuation of other abbreviations.

TITLES WITH NAMES   Mr.   Ms.   Mrs.   Rev.   Dr.   Sr.
TIMES WITH NUMBERS   A.M.   P.M.   B.C.   A.D.

Lt. Raymond L. Mason, Jr., received the Purple Heart.
At exactly 2:00 P.M., I will receive the award.

If a statement ends with an abbreviation, only one period is needed at the end of the sentence. If an interrogative or an exclamatory sentence ends with an abbreviation, both a period and a question mark, or a period and an exclamation point, are needed.

We should meet at 7:00 P.M.
Should we meet at 7:00 P.M.?

Note: A few special abbreviations are used without periods. Following are a few examples.

ABC	American Broadcasting Company	PA	Pennsylvania
mph	miles per hour	km	kilometer

EXERCISE 2 *Writing Abbreviations*

Number your paper 1 to 10. Then write the abbreviations that stand for the following items. Include periods where needed. If you are unsure of the spelling or the punctuation of a particular abbreviation, look it up in the dictionary.

1. Senior
2. New Jersey
3. Master of Arts
4. September
5. Captain
6. Avenue
7. et cetera
8. millimeter
9. pound
10. cash on delivery

Commas

Although there may seem to be many comma rules, commas have basically only two purposes: to separate items and to enclose items.

Commas That Separate

If commas did not separate certain items from each other, all writing would be subject to constant misunderstanding. There is a difference, for example, between *pineapple juice and cheese* and *pineapple, juice, and cheese.* Following are specific situations in which commas should be used to separate items.

Items in a Series A series is three or more similar items listed in consecutive order. Words, phrases, clauses, or short sentences that are written as a series are separated by commas.

Rule 27f	Use commas to separate items in a series.

WORDS January, February, and March are the best months for working on indoor hobbies. [nouns]
We swept, scrubbed, and polished the floor before our company arrived. [verbs]

PHRASES We searched for his keys throughout the house, along the driveway, and in the car.

CLAUSES We don't know who should march in first, where we should sit, or how the diplomas will be handed out.

SHORT SENTENCES The curtain fell, a brief silence followed, and then there was wild applause.

When a conjunction connects the last two items in a series, a comma is optional. It is always best, however, to include the comma before the conjunction in order to eliminate any possible confusion or misunderstanding.

CONFUSING I like pea, chicken, tomato and onion soup. [Do you like tomato soup or tomato and onion soup?]

CLEAR I like pea, chicken, tomato, and onion soup. [The last comma makes the meaning clear.]

If conjunctions connect all the items in a series, no commas are needed unless they make the sentence clearer.

Their new apartment is large **and** roomy **and** bright.

Note: Some expressions, such as *needle and thread,* are thought of as a single item. If one of these pairs of words appears in a series, it should be considered one item.

For breakfast we had our choice of yogurt, ham and eggs, or hot cereal.

Adjectives before a Noun A conjunction sometimes connects two adjectives before a noun. When the conjunction is omitted, a comma is sometimes used instead.

Driving across the long, narrow bridge was frightening.

Rule 27g Use a comma sometimes to separate two adjectives that directly precede a noun and that are not joined by a conjunction.

There is a test you can use to decide whether a comma should be placed between two such adjectives. Read the sentence with *and* between the adjectives. If the sentence sounds natural, a comma is needed.

COMMA NEEDED I enjoyed eating that fresh, crisp salad.
　　　　　　　　[*Fresh and crisp* sounds natural.]
COMMA I enjoyed eating that fresh tossed salad.
NOT NEEDED [*Fresh and tossed* does not sound natural.]

EXERCISE *Using Commas to Separate*

Number your paper 1 to 10. Then write each series or each pair of adjectives, adding a comma or commas where needed. If a sentence does not need any commas, write *C* after the number.

EXAMPLE We ate dinner did the dishes and went to a movie.
ANSWER ate dinner, did the dishes, and went to a movie

  1. Alaska Texas and California together make up more than a quarter of the total United States acreage.
  2. Put your shirt in the closet on your bed or in your top drawer.

3. An alligator has thick scaly skin.
4. The ocelot and the cheetah and the jaguar belong to the cat family.
5. Dr. Salk's discovery of a polio vaccine was a brilliant scientific achievement.
6. I don't know where they went what they are doing or when they'll be back.
7. The rabbit stopped at the clearing looked around and hopped across.
8. The tall dark-haired swimmer walked to the end of the diving board and dived in a graceful arc.
9. We visited several historic places in Philadelphia.
10. The three best sandwiches in this restaurant are tuna fish ham and cheese and roast beef.

Compound Sentences   The independent clauses in a compound sentence can be combined in several ways. One way is to join them with a comma and one of the coordinating conjunctions—*and, but, or, nor, for, so,* or *yet.* (A semicolon, or a semicolon and a transitional word, can also be used between independent clauses that are not separated by a conjunction. *See pages 294–297.*)

Rule 27h   Use a comma to separate the independent clauses of a compound sentence if the clauses are joined by a coordinating conjunction.

My sister has caught two fish, but I haven't caught any.
Friday night is prom night, and Sunday is graduation day.
She wants to leave the meeting, yet it seems too early.

No comma is needed in a very short compound sentence—unless the conjunction *yet* or *for* separates the independent clauses.

NO COMMA   We invited them and they came.
  COMMA   I lost, yet I still felt happy.

Note: Do not confuse a sentence that has one subject and a compound verb with a compound sentence that has two sets of subjects and verbs. A comma is *not* placed between the parts of a compound verb when there is only one subject.

COMPOUND SENTENCE   I worked last night, and John attended the meeting. [comma]
  COMPOUND VERB   I worked last night and couldn't attend the meeting. [no comma]

EXERCISE **4** *Using Commas with Compound Sentences*

Number your paper 1 to 10. Then write each sentence, adding a comma where needed. If a sentence does not need a comma, write *C* after the number.

1. Cod can lay up to five million eggs at one time but very few of the eggs hatch and mature.
2. You should hurry or we'll be late.
3. The giant panda is a relative of the raccoon but can weigh up to 300 pounds.
4. People have been very generous yet the hospital fund needs another three thousand dollars for new equipment.
5. At first glance the desert may seem to lack life but it actually is alive with many different plants and animals.
6. Dad will pack us a lunch or we'll eat in the cafeteria.
7. The spinal cord relays information between the brain and the rest of the body and controls the reflexes.
8. Sue and I can come tonight and can help you move the books into the library.
9. Not many people came yet I had a very good time.
10. Wild pigs will eat almost anything but they won't overeat.

Introductory Elements   A comma is needed to separate certain introductory words, phrases, and clauses from the rest of the sentence.

Rule 27i   Use a comma after certain introductory elements.

WORDS   **Yes,** those were my exact words. [*No, now, oh, well,* and *why* are other introductory words that are set off by commas—unless they contribute to the meaning of a sentence: Yes *was his answer.*]

PREPOSITIONAL PHRASE   **Throughout the entire baseball game,** Jessie pitched only one inning. [A comma comes after a prepositional phrase of four or more words. (Punctuation of shorter phrases varies. See the last set of examples that follows.) Never place a comma after a phrase or phrases followed by a verb: *Through the fog shone a dim light.*]

PARTICIPIAL PHRASE   **Hunting for my old jacket,** I found a long-lost pair of gloves.

M e c h a n i c s · **775**

INFINITIVE PHRASE USED AS AN ADVERB **To surprise Ellen,** we all hid in the kitchen. [A comma does not follow an infinitive phrase that is used as the subject of a sentence: *To forgive him was a wise decision.*]

ADVERB CLAUSE **Before they came in,** they removed their boots.

OTHER **In June 1986,** 320 seniors graduated.
Far above, a flock of geese flew by. [Commas are used in these sentences to avoid confusion.]

EXERCISE *Using Commas with Introductory Elements*

Number your paper 1 to 20. Then write the introductory elements that should be followed by a comma, adding a comma after each one. If a sentence does not need a comma, write *C* after the number.

1. In the fifteenth century Chinese scholars compiled a 22,937-volume encyclopedia.
2. If you start at 8:00 A.M. you'll reach the summit by noon.
3. Standing on a scaffold on the tenth floor two men were washing the windows of the large office building.
4. No we will not be attending the open house.
5. To give her family security Louisa May Alcott began writing.
6. After tomorrow I will be a high school graduate.
7. As the band tuned up the audience found their seats.
8. Walled by lava cliffs Crater Lake can be reached by footpaths.
9. According to a recent poll taken in our school 42 percent of the seniors have already been hired for summer jobs.
10. To find the best route to Atlanta Stephanie checked the map.
11. After Barry Paul will take his turn.
12. Knocking down every tackle in his path Seth plowed forward for a touchdown.
13. Well that was a surprise!
14. Of the six papers to be typed three have been completed.
15. To report on the game is my assignment.
16. Why are you dressed in that costume?
17. To the top of the tree scampered the squirrel.
18. When he was less than thirteen years old Alfred Tennyson wrote a 6,000-line epic poem.
19. After cooking Roger took a short nap.
20. To answer your question I will have to do some research.

Commonly Used Commas   Commas are probably used most often to separate the items in a date or an address.

Rule 27j   Use commas to separate the elements in dates and addresses.

Notice in the following examples that a comma is also used to separate the last item in a date or the last item in an address from the rest of the sentence.

> On Monday, October 3, 1980, my younger brother was born.
>
> Send your résumé to Ms. Faye Buscone, Hoffman Company, 520 Johnson Street, Madison, Wisconsin 53703, before June 30. [No comma is placed between the state and the ZIP code.]

If items in an address are joined by a preposition, no comma is needed to separate them.

> The company moved its headquarters to 45 Jackson Boulevard **in** Tacoma, Washington.

Note: No comma is needed when just the month and the year are given.

> Neil Armstrong walked on the moon in July 1969.

Rule 27k   Use a comma after the salutation of a friendly letter and after the closing of all letters.

SALUTATIONS	Dear David,	Dear Grandmother,
CLOSINGS	Sincerely yours,	Love,

EXERCISE *Using Commas Correctly*

Number your paper 1 to 10. Then write each sentence, adding a comma or commas where needed.

1. On March 30 1937 Franklin Roosevelt established the Okefenokee Swamp as a national wildlife refuge.
2. How long had you lived in Springfield Illinois before you moved to Portland?
3. If you are interested in applying for the job you should talk with the personnel director.
4. You can write to me at the University of Missouri Box 1254 Columbia Missouri 65201 after September 1.

5. Tacoma Washington lies between the Olympic Mountains and the Cascade Range.

6. Write to Writer's Supplies 843 Woodcove Avenue Pittsburgh Pennsylvania 15216 for free samples.

7. In the process of cleaning out the closet I found a long-lost sweater.

8. In 1988 77,900 patents for inventions were granted but only 25,546 were granted in 1901.

9. Students working as stagehands for the play should be at the meeting but those trying out for acting parts are not required to attend.

10. On June 19 1846 the first baseball game with organized rules was played at Elysian Fields in Hoboken New Jersey.

EXERCISE *Cumulative Review*

Number your paper 1 to 20. Then write each sentence, adding a comma or commas where needed. If a sentence is correct, write *C* after the number.

Inventors and Inventions

1. Among the inventions of Thomas Edison are the light switch an electric pen and the microphone.

2. The parking meter was invented in Oklahoma City and was the brainstorm of Carlton Magee.

3. To pay off a debt Walter Hunt invented the safety pin.

4. Margaret E. Knight patented an improved paper machine and invented a machine for cutting out shoes.

5. James Watt was not the inventor of the first steam engine but he did improve the steam engine in 1769.

6. After Humphrey O'Sullivan had walked all day on the hot hard pavements of Boston he invented the rubber heel.

7. Joseph Friedman invented the first flexible plastic straw.

8. Amanda Theodosia Jones invented the vacuum process of preserving food and tried to establish a factory that would use her process.

9. To improve methods of farming Englishman Thomas Coke invented a new method of crop rotation during the 1700's.

10. Leonardo da Vinci designed a flying machine and Benjamin Franklin invented bifocals.

11. On June 22 1882 the U.S. Patent Office granted a patent for a propeller-driven rocking chair.

12. Until the envelope was invented in 1839 people folded their letters and sealed them with wax.
13. According to the United States Patent Office records a man named Chester Greenwood held patents on earmuffs and many other items.
14. Fixing a tricycle John Dunlop accidentally invented an inflatable tire.
15. Patented by George B. Hansburg the Pogo stick became an American fad during the 1920's.
16. When Sybilla Masters succeeded in inventing a machine that reduced corn into meal food preparation methods were greatly improved.
17. King Camp Gillette started his Gillette Safety Razor Company in 1901 and patented the safety razor in 1904.
18. Before the birth of Christ the Chinese made beautiful porcelain.
19. Whitcomb L. Judson patented an early form of the zipper in 1893.
20. Lee De Forest invented a vacuum tube in 1907 and this device helped develop electronic equipment.

Commas That Enclose

Some sentences contain expressions that interrupt the flow of a sentence. These expressions usually supply additional information that is not necessary for understanding the main idea of a sentence. If one of these interrupting expressions comes in the middle of a sentence, use two commas to enclose the expression—to set it off from the rest of the sentence. If an interrupting expression comes at the beginning or at the end of a sentence, use only one comma.

Direct Address   Any name, title, or other word that is used to address someone directly is set off by commas. These interrupting expressions are called nouns of *direct address*.

Rule 271   Use commas to set off nouns of direct address.

> **Kenneth,** what did you do with the sports page?
> Hurry**,** **Matt,** or we'll be late.
> What time is it**,** **Maria?**

Parenthetical Expressions These expressions add meaning but are only incidental to the main idea of the sentence.

Rule 27m Use commas to set off parenthetical expressions.

Following is a list of common parenthetical expressions.

Common Parenthetical Expressions		
after all	however	nevertheless
at any rate	I believe (guess,	of course
by the way	hope, know,	on the contrary
consequently	think)	on the other hand
for example	in fact	therefore
for instance	in my opinion	to tell the truth
	moreover	

By the way, did you notice Tony's new haircut?

Your advice, **of course,** was helpful.

We will proceed as planned**, nevertheless.**

Note: Commas are used to set off the expressions in the preceding box *only* if the expressions interrupt the flow of a sentence.

COMMAS **On the other hand,** we enjoyed the dancing.

NO COMMAS Wear that glove **on the other hand.** [In this sentence *on the other hand* is necessary to the meaning of the sentence.]

Expressions other than those listed in the preceding box can also be parenthetical if they interrupt the flow of the sentence.

Irises**, like tulips,** grow from bulbs.

Contrasting expressions, which often begin with *not, but, but not,* or *though not,* are also considered parenthetical expressions.

Peggy, **not Angela,** will sing a solo at the concert.
The actor**, though not well-known,** will star in the play.

Occasionally an adverb clause will also interrupt a sentence.

The temperature**, if it hits 93,** will set a record today.

Appositives   An appositive with its modifiers renames, identifies, or explains a noun or a pronoun in the sentence.

Rule 27n   Use commas to set off most appositives and their modifiers.

Mr. James**, my English teacher,** attended Ohio State.

I would like the first entrée**, roast turkey with stuffing.**

An appositive is occasionally preceded by the word *or, particularly, notably,* or *especially.* Some appositives that are introduced by *such as* are also set off by commas.

Many insects**, especially honeybees,** cross-pollinate fruits.

Take warm clothing**, such as sweaters and wool socks.**

An appositive is not set off by commas if it identifies a person or a thing by telling which one or ones. Often these appositives are names and have no modifiers.

The verb *eat* is an irregular verb. [Which verb?]
My cousin **Lucy** is a dental assistant. [Which cousin?]

When adjectives, titles, and degrees are in the appositive position, they are also set off by commas.

ADJECTIVES   The lake water**, clear and cold,** felt refreshing.
TITLES   Franklin R. Moore**, Sr.,** is our chief of police.
DEGREES   Alicia Ray**, M.D.,** has an office on Broad Road.

EXERCISE 8   *Using Commas with Interrupters*

Write each sentence, adding a comma or commas where needed. If a sentence does not need any commas, write *C* after the number.

1. The sea otter's existence has been threatened by its two great enemies killer whales and humans.
2. Lydia have you met Mr. Robert Kahn Jr.?
3. The St. Lawrence Seaway I believe makes over 8,000 miles of coast accessible to large ocean vessels.
4. Did you know Eugene that there was a phone call for you?
5. The Greens not the Goldsteins are moving to Atlanta.
6. The hikers cold and hungry huddled around the campfire.
7. Babe Ruth's pitching skill if we are to believe the sports writers of his time was excellent.

8. The great playwright Lillian Hellman was born in 1905.
9. Several teachers especially Mr. Herman and Ms. Costa were particularly helpful.
10. A frog takes in water through its skin not its mouth.
11. Uriah Heep the villain in Charles Dickens's *David Copperfield* was the focus of my English composition.
12. Hannah like Lucia manages a vegetable stand.
13. William Carlos Williams M.D. was a noted poet.
14. The great soprano Beverly Sills became the director of the New York City Opera Company in 1979.
15. A tarantula's bite though not usually fatal is quite painful.

Nonessential Elements Like other interrupters you have just reviewed, some participial phrases and some clauses are not needed to make the meaning of a sentence clear or complete. When a phrase or a clause is not needed to complete the meaning of a sentence, commas are used to enclose it.

Rule 27o   Use commas to set off a nonessential participial phrase or a nonessential adjective clause.

A participial phrase or an adjective clause is nonessential (nonrestrictive) if it supplies extra, unnecessary information. To decide whether a phrase or a clause is nonessential, read the sentence without it. If the phrase or the clause could be removed without changing the basic meaning of the sentence, it is nonessential. A phrase or a clause that modifies a proper noun is almost always nonessential.

NONESSENTIAL PARTICIPIAL PHRASE   Cellophane**, made from wood pulp,** was invented in 1900. [Cellophane was invented in 1900.]

NONESSENTIAL ADJECTIVE CLAUSE   The ostrich**, which is the largest of all birds,** can outrun a horse. [An ostrich can outrun a horse.]

An essential (restrictive) phrase or clause identifies a person or a thing by answering the question *Which one?* Therefore, no commas are used. If an essential phrase or clause is removed from a sentence, the basic meaning of the sentence will be unclear or incomplete. (An adjective clause that begins with *that* is usually essential.)

ESSENTIAL
PARTICIPIAL
PHRASE

The lizard **called the gecko** can drop its tail and grow a new one. [*The lizard can drop its tail and grow a new one.* The phrase is needed to identify which lizard; otherwise, the sentence would mean that *all* lizards can drop their tails and grow new ones.]

ESSENTIAL
ADJECTIVE
CLAUSE

The book **that you wanted** was out of the library. [*The book was out of the library.* The clause is needed to identify which book was out of the library.]

EXERCISE   9   *Using Commas with Nonessential Elements*

Number your paper 1 to 10. Then write each sentence, adding a comma or commas where needed. If a sentence does not need any commas, write *C* after the number.

1. The exoskeleton of an insect is made of chitin which is lighter and far more flexible than bone.
2. The first public pay telephone installed in Connecticut in 1889 charged ten cents for a call.
3. Ralph Winters fishing in Beaver Brook caught a ten-inch trout.
4. Scientists who examine and classify insects are called entomologists.
5. We watched the geese flying south.
6. The senior playing right tackle is my cousin.
7. Did you speak to Ms. Velez who organized the county track meet?
8. Amelia Earhart who was the first woman to fly across the Atlantic alone won the Distinguished Flying Cross.
9. In the Bay of Fundy located between New Brunswick and Nova Scotia the tide sometimes rises ten feet in one hour.
10. The flag that inspired Francis Scott Key to write our national anthem had only 15 stars.

Application to Writing

A proverb is a wise saying that applies to many situations. Write a short essay about an incident in your life to which one of the following proverbs applies: *Don't cry over spilled milk* or *Half a loaf is better than none.* As you edit your essay, check for the correct use of end marks and commas.

EXERCISE *Cumulative Review*

Number your paper 1 to 20. Then write each sentence, adding a comma or commas where needed. If a sentence does not need any commas, write *C* after the number.

1. The smallest dinosaurs were about 2½ feet long and the largest were about 90 feet long.
2. Porpoises and dolphins and whales will drown if they stay underwater too long.
3. This basket was woven by Dudley Frasure whose work is the subject of a documentary film.
4. During a severe windstorm or high gale a skyscraper may sway up to six inches on either side.
5. If all cod eggs produced live fish there would be no room left in the oceans for water.
6. To photograph this event you must set the camera at a thousandth of a second.
7. The holiday is celebrated on the 8th not the 12th.
8. An air temperature of 134°F was recorded on July 10 1913 in Death Valley California.
9. Redwood trees produce bark that is up to 10 inches thick.
10. Coyotes highly adaptable animals are known to travel up to 35 miles per hour when pursuing prey.
11. Mozart wrote his last and many think his greatest symphony in fewer than 16 days.
12. The famous ocean scientist Jacques Cousteau appeared in the documentary series about marine exploration.
13. The song that became the official national anthem of the United States in 1931 was "The Star-Spangled Banner."
14. The Fourth of July or Independence Day has been celebrated as a national holiday ever since Revolutionary times.
15. In the average human body four to five quarts of blood are circulated every minute.
16. Virginia Dare born on August 18 1587 was the first child born of English parents in the New World.
17. Garter snakes though reptiles do not lay eggs.
18. We packed a picnic lunch and left for the beach at nine o'clock on Saturday morning.
19. The evening was cool breezy and delightful.
20. Geoffrey Chaucer the author of *The Canterbury Tales* was probably the most important writer in medieval England.

Mechanics: Editing for Correct Use of Commas

When you edit your written work, always check to see whether you have used any commas incorrectly. In addition, look to see whether you have mistakenly left commas out.

Checking Your Understanding   Write the following paragraphs, adding commas where needed. You will need to add 20 commas.

Elizabeth Blackwell was the first woman to earn a medical degree but she had to travel a long hard road to get that degree. Even though 29 medical schools had refused to admit her she persisted. After three years of private study Blackwell was finally accepted to the Medical Institute of Geneva New York. The director doubtful and concerned passed her application on to the students for their approval. Thinking it was a joke everyone agreed to admit her. When Blackwell arrived however she was greeted with shock and anger. She was ridiculed ignored refused lodging and barred from some classroom activities.

Graduating at the head of her class on January 23 1849 Blackwell continued her studies in London and Paris. She finally returned to New York City and there she opened a hospital in 1853. Called the New York Infirmary for Woman and Children it was staffed by women. With the help of Emily her younger sister Blackwell added a medical college for women in 1868. After a few more years she returned to England and helped found the London School of Medicine for Women.

Writing an Expository Essay   Do you like your name? Do you think it had any effect over the years on how your personality developed? If you could have a new name, what would you like it to be? Brainstorm answers to these questions. Then write an expository essay in which you explain the significance of your name. *Application:* As you edit your essay, check to see whether you have used commas and capital letters correctly.

27

Review

A **Understanding Sentence Structure**   Number your paper 1 to 10. Write an appropriate end mark for each sentence. Then label each one *declarative, imperative, interrogative,* or *exclamatory*.

  1. Tofu is a good source of protein
  2. Call Michael when you get home
  3. Did you see the exam schedule
  4. I didn't receive the test results
  5. The British word for *elevator* is *lift*
  6. How thrilled I was to hear from you
  7. Isn't she the captain of the volleyball team
  8. Congratulations You've passed your driver's test
  9. How invigorating an early-morning swim can be
 10. Will you close the screen door when you leave

B **Using Commas Correctly**   Number your paper 1 to 15. Then write each sentence, adding a comma or commas where needed. If a sentence does not need any commas, write *C* after the number.

  1. Between now and next week you should learn the music for the first two numbers.
  2. The terrain hilly and rocky made travel by car or truck virtually impossible.
  3. The little island was a great place for a rest for it was sparsely populated.
  4. Medical research though expensive often pays for itself in life-saving discoveries.
  5. A person who enjoys traveling on rough waters should take the ferry to Nova Scotia.
  6. Sally Tompkins a captain in the Confederate army ran a hospital at her own expense in Richmond Virginia.
  7. Winter sports such as sledding and skating are popular in the North.
  8. You need quarters not dimes for the washing machines at the laundromat.
  9. The pony express which has lived in legend for more than a century existed for less than two years.

10. Although approximately 70 percent of the surface of the earth is covered with water only 1 percent the experts agree is really drinkable.

11. On May 9 1936 the German airship *Hindenburg* landed at Lakehurst New Jersey after its first successful flight across the Atlantic Ocean.

12. A potato contrary to popular belief has about as many calories as an apple.

13. Lamb not pork was the main course.

14. Edgar Allan Poe wrote poetry edited literary magazines and created the modern detective story.

15. The bicyclists lining up to start this race have come from all over the United States.

Mastery Test

Number your paper 1 to 10. Write each sentence, adding a comma or commas where needed. Then add an appropriate end mark.

1. In a large pond goldfish can actually add more than a foot to their length

2. I bought a wrench but the store was out of the paint I needed for the kitchen

3. Numerous species of butterflies like birds fly south for the winter

4. Mary Goddard who was a United States postmaster was the printer of the Declaration of Independence

5. Before sky divers open their parachutes they travel through the air as fast as 200 miles an hour

6. That old creaky chair in the dining room broke when I sat on it yesterday

7. Have you returned the toaster oven to Mendrall Products 305 Forty-first Street Sidney New York 13838

8. Thomas Edison Charles Dickens and the Irish playwright Sean O'Casey never graduated from grade school.

9. Hearing the wild applause the actors waited a moment before they took their bows

10. In 1955 55 cities throughout the world had a million people or more

28 Other Punctuation

Diagnostic Test

Number your paper 1 to 10. Then write each sentence, adding apostrophes, semicolons, colons, hyphens, quotation marks, and other punctuation marks needed with direct quotations. Only a sentence with a speaker tag *(he said, she asked)* is considered a direct quotation.

EXAMPLE   Wendy asked Do you want to ride with us?
ANSWER   Wendy asked, "Do you want to ride with us?"

1. Which class do you have next Sheila asked.
2. The names of the seven continents are spelled with the same first and last letters Antarctica, Europe, Asia, Australia, Africa, and America (North and South).
3. Some seniors voted for an afternoon graduation however, most voted to hold it in the evening.
4. Watch out for that pothole Jeffrey called.
5. Hay fever is not caused by hay it is caused by pollen.
6. Everyone will need the following items a pencil, an eraser, and some scrap paper.
7. Thirty two students havent signed up Andrew stated.
8. You should try ice skating Kate suggested Its fun.
9. The party at the Smiths house will begin at 7 00 P.M.
10. Only 12 drawings have been submitted to the magazine-cover contest the rest are graphic designs.

Apostrophes

Although end marks and commas are the punctuation marks most commonly used, all marks of punctuation are important. This chapter will cover all the punctuation marks besides end marks and commas—such as apostrophes.

You probably use apostrophes with contractions every time you write, but an apostrophe has another important and very common use. It is used with nouns and some pronouns to show possession.

Apostrophes to Show Possession

By using an apostrophe, you can indicate that nouns and some pronouns are showing possession.

The Possessive Forms of Nouns The possessive of a singular noun is formed differently from the possessive of a plural noun.

Rule 28a Add 's to form the possessive of a singular noun.

To form the possessive of a singular noun, write the noun without adding or omitting any letters. Then add 's at the end.

> friend + 's = friend's   This is my friend's house.
> road + 's = road's   The road's surface needs repaving.
> quarter + 's = quarter's   I need a quarter's worth of nickels.

Singular compound nouns and the names of most businesses and organizations form their possessives in the way other singular nouns do.

> Her mother-in-law's birthday is tomorrow.
> I will order her flowers from Maher's Florist Shop.

To form the possessive of a plural noun, write the plural form of the word without making any changes. Then look at the ending of the plural noun. The ending will determine the way you will form the possessive.

Rule 28b Add only an apostrophe to form the possessive of a plural noun that ends in s.

If the plural noun ends in *s*, add only an apostrophe.

girls + ' = girls'   The girls' softball team has won!
Nelsons + ' = Nelsons'   The Nelsons' dog is a setter.
weeks + ' = weeks'   She lost two weeks' time.

If a plural noun does not end in *s*, add *'s* to form the possessive—just as you would to a singular noun that does not end in *s*.

men + 's = men's   Where is the men's locker room?
oxen + 's = oxen's   The oxen's barn was cleaned.

Note: Do not confuse a plural possessive with the simple plural form of a noun.

POSSESSIVE   Mrs. Grayson is the twins' teacher.
PLURAL   Mrs. Grayson teaches the twins.

EXERCISE ◀ 1 ▶ *Forming the Possessive of Nouns*

Number your paper 1 to 20. Then write the possessive form of each noun.

1. mother	**6.** day	**11.** Tuesday	**16.** city
2. cover	**7.** women	**12.** officers	**17.** penny
3. Karen	**8.** year	**13.** birch	**18.** David
4. Palmers	**9.** geese	**14.** men	**19.** doctor
5. Cheyenne	**10.** world	**15.** babies	**20.** bears

EXERCISE ◀ 2 ▶ *Using the Possessive of Nouns*

Number your paper 1 to 10. Then write each word that needs an apostrophe or an apostrophe and an *s*.

1. A tiger stripes often serve as camouflage.
2. Who has Sunday paper?
3. All the books jackets are in good condition.
4. How long will your sister-in-law visit last?
5. We enjoyed the children art exhibit.
6. Thompson Market on the Berlin Turnpike needs some part-time help.
7. Mr. Murphy is taking a year leave of absence.
8. Is that young woman Theresa sister?
9. Please buy a dollar worth of green beans at the store.
10. The Wongs business is flourishing.

The Possessive Forms of Personal Pronouns   Personal pronouns and the pronoun *who* show possession by changing form, not by adding an apostrophe.

> This is **his** coat, but **whose** coat is that?

None of the following possessive pronouns include apostrophes.

Possessive Pronouns			
my, mine	his	its	their, theirs
your, yours	her, hers	our, ours	

Note: Do not confuse a contraction with a possessive pronoun. A possessive pronoun does not include an apostrophe, but a contraction does. *Its, your, their,* and *theirs* are possessive pronouns. *It's, you're, they're,* and *there's* are contractions. *(See page 679 for more information about possessive pronouns.)*

The Possessive Forms of Indefinite Pronouns   An indefinite pronoun forms its possessive in the same way a singular noun does—by adding *'s. (See page 540 for a list of common indefinite pronouns.)*

> No one**'s** oral report will be given tomorrow.
> Did you ask for anyone**'s** advice?

EXERCISE *Using the Possessive of Pronouns*

Number your paper 1 to 10. Then rewrite any incorrectly written possessive form of a pronoun. If all of the pronouns in a sentence are written correctly, write *C* after the number.

1. You're research papers are due on Friday.
2. Everyones suggestions should be considered.
3. I think this cap is mine, but it could be his.
4. Who's telephone number is this?
5. Her's is the one with the purple stripes.
6. It's time to take the dog for it's distemper shot.
7. Someone's jacket was left in the bleachers.
8. Your's arrived first thing this morning.
9. There time cards should be put over there.
10. Neither ones photograph won a prize.

Other Uses of Apostrophes

An apostrophe is used to write contractions, to form certain plurals, and to show joint and separate ownership.

Apostrophes with Contractions An apostrophe is substituted for letters omitted in a contraction.

Rule 28c Use an apostrophe in a contraction to show where one or more letters have been omitted.

are nøt = aren't   that is = that's
we háve = we've   let us = let's
I wíll = I'll   of the clock = o'clock

The only contraction in which any letters are changed or added is th contraction for *will not,* which is *won't.*

EXERCISE ◆4▸ *Writing Contractions*

Write the contraction for each pair of words.

I. do not	**6.** who is	**II.** were not	**16.** there is
2. I have	**7.** they are	**12.** it is	**17.** does not
3. did not	**8.** will not	**13.** you are	**18.** are not
4. let us	**9.** I am	**14.** has not	**19.** we have
5. we will	**10.** is not	**15.** I would	**20.** have not

Apostrophes to Show Joint and Separate Ownership In written work apostrophes can signal either joint or separate ownership. One apostrophe is used to show joint ownership; two or more apostrophes are used to show separate ownership.

Rule 28d Add 's to only the last word to show joint ownership.
Add 's to each word to show separate ownership.

In the following example, the canoe belongs to Paul and Craig. Since both people own the canoe, an apostrophe is added to the second name only.

Paul and Craig's canoe has been returned.

If one of the words in a phrase showing joint ownership is a possessive pronoun, the noun must also show possession.

Paul's and **his** canoe has been returned.

In the following example, Paul and Craig own separate canoes; therefore, an apostrophe is added to each name.

Paul's and Craig's canoes have been returned.

Apostrophes to Form Certain Plurals The plural of certain items and words is formed by adding an apostrophe and an *s.*

Rule 28e Add 's to form the plural of numbers, letters, symbols, and words that are used to represent themselves.

Your *3*'s look like backward *E*'s.
Insert *$*'s where necessary in the financial statement.
You used too many *very*'s in your composition.

Note: Only the number *3*, the letter *E*, the dollar sign, and the word *very* are italicized in the examples above. Notice that the *'s* is not italicized. *(See page 800 for the use of italics or underlining, in such situations.)*

EXERCISE *Using Apostrophes in Special Situations*

Number your paper 1 to 10. Then write correctly each letter, symbol, or word that needs an apostrophe or an apostrophe and an *s.*

1. My typewriter types & but not +.
2. Their company uses Jones and Carey delivery service.
3. Does the word *referred* have two *r* or three?
4. Julie and César grades were the highest in our social studies class.
5. Lets get started no later than six oclock.
6. Points will be deducted if your *t* arent crossed and your *i* arent dotted.
7. Willie and her dog is only two months old.
8. Gary and Melinda photographs were exhibited at the fair.
9. Youve used 25 *however* in your report.
10. Theyll meet us at the town hall if they dont get delayed.

EXERCISE 6 *Cumulative Review*

Number your paper 1 to 10. Rewrite any incorrectly written letter or word. If a sentence is correct, write *C* after the number.

 1. Diego's article was well written, was'nt it?
 2. The Joneses and Taylors' apartments were just painted.
 3. The Queen of Englands picture seems to be everywhere in London.
 4. There's their neighbor, waiting at the bus stop.
 5. Teenager's interests certainly have changed over the past 50 years.
 6. Gorman' advertisement in this mornings' *Herald* features sneakers and sweatshirts.
 7. A student's life is very busy.
 8. The Raidens' son got two *A*'s on his report card, and their daughter got three on her's.
 9. Well need Dad's permission to go.
10. Aren't there two *c*s in *accumulate?*

Semicolons and Colons

By using the semicolon (;) and the colon (:), you can create sentence variety in your writing.

Semicolons

Two independent clauses not properly joined result in a run-on sentence. A run-on sentence can be corrected in any of several ways. One way to correct a run-on sentence is to join the clauses with a coordinating conjunction and a comma. *(See pages 634–635 for more information about correcting run-on sentences.)*

Monday is my birthday, **and** Tuesday is my mom's birthday.

The clauses in a compound sentence can be joined by a semicolon when there is no conjunction.

Rule 28f Use a semicolon between the clauses of a compound sentence when they are not joined by a conjunction.

Monday is my birthday; Tuesday is my mom's birthday.
The earthworm has no lungs; it breathes through its skin.

Note: Only closely related clauses should be joined by a semicolon. Ideas not closely related belong in separate sentences.

Semicolons with Transitional Words The clauses in a compound sentence can also be joined by a semicolon and a transitional word.

Rule 28g Use a semicolon between the clauses in a compound sentence when they are joined by certain transitional words.

The meeting was scheduled to begin at noon**; nevertheless,** it didn't start until one.

Following is a list of such common transitional words.

Common Transitional Words		
accordingly	furthermore	moreover
as a result	hence	nevertheless
besides	however	otherwise
consequently	indeed	that is
for example	in fact	therefore
for instance	instead	thus

Note: Some of the transitional words in the preceding box can also be used as parenthetical expressions within a single clause. *(See page 780 for more information about parenthetical expressions.)*

Notice in the following examples that the semicolon comes before the transitional word and that a comma follows the transitional word.

The loudspeaker wasn't working properly**; as a result,** people in the balcony couldn't hear the music very well.

Jamaica is covered with beautiful vegetation**; for example,** tropical fruits and flowers grow everywhere.

Semicolons to Avoid Confusion To make your meaning clear, you may have to substitute a semicolon for a comma.

Rule 28h Use a semicolon instead of a comma in certain situations to avoid possible confusion.

A semicolon is used instead of a comma between the clauses of a compound sentence if there are commas within a clause.

> Here is a jacket in yellow, blue, and green; but those are not Alexandra's favorite colors. [Normally a comma would come before a conjunction separating the clauses in a compound sentence.]

Semicolons are also used instead of commas between items in a series if the items themselves contain commas.

> The President's schedule includes stops in London, England; Paris, France; Florence, Italy; Geneva, Switzerland; and New Delhi, India. [Normally commas would separate the items in a series.]

Note: See Chapter 27 for comma rules.

EXERCISE ◄ 7 ► *Using Semicolons*

Number your paper 1 to 10. Write each word that should be followed by a semicolon and then add the semicolon.

1. Poison ivy is not ivy it is a member of the cashew family.

2. The vegetable stand was out of fresh corn therefore, I bought some peas.

3. I want to write my research paper on the poetry of Shelley, Keats, or Wordsworth but I can't decide which poet interests me the most.

4. The site of the 1898 Klondike gold rush wasn't Alaska in fact, it was the Yukon Territory of Canada.

5. The county fair will be held on Saturday, June 8 Sunday, June 9 and Monday, June 10.

6. Geoffrey Chaucer wrote during the Middle Ages William Shakespeare wrote during the Elizabethan Age.

7. I completed my weekend chores several hours early thus, I had more time for leisure activities.

8. Pocahontas's real name was said to be Matoaka Pocahontas was a family name.

9. I will put away the milk, the yogurt, and the cottage cheese or they will turn sour.

10. In the Northern Hemisphere, water goes down drains counter-clockwise in the Southern Hemisphere, it goes clockwise.

EXERCISE *Using Semicolons and Commas*

Number your paper 1 to 10. Then write the following sentences, adding semicolons and commas where needed.

1. The Sahara covers an area of about 3,500,000 square miles Europe covers about 4,100,000 square miles.
2. I have lived in Detroit Michigan Lincoln Nebraska and Ames Iowa.
3. Every seat in the auditorium was filled in fact some people had to be turned away.
4. The temperature today reached 102 it broke all records.
5. A queen bee never uses her stinger on workers drones or people but she will use it on another queen bee.
6. Our bake sale was a success we raised ninety dollars.
7. The test will cover Chapter 5 Sections 1 and 2 Chapter 6 Sections 5 and 6 and Chapter 7 Sections 3 and 4.
8. The traffic lights at Main and Belmont were not working during rush hour however not a single problem resulted.
9. Florida is not the southernmost state in the United States Hawaii is farther south.
10. You may have your senior picture taken at eight nine or ten but the earliest appointments are less crowded.

EXERCISE *Writing Sentences*

Write compound sentences that follow the directions below.

1. Join the clauses with a comma and a conjunction.
2. Join the clauses with a semicolon only.
3. Join the clauses with a semicolon and the word *moreover.*
4. Join the clauses with a semicolon and the word *however.*
5. In the first clause, include a series of words. Then join the clauses with a semicolon.

Colons

A colon is used most often to introduce a list of items that is about to follow in a sentence.

Rule 28i Use a colon before most lists of items, especially when a list comes after an expression such as *the following.*

When I applied for the job, the employer required the following: a résumé, two references, and a writing sample.

A colon, however, does not follow a verb or a preposition.

NO COLON   Required forms of identification include a driver's license, a passport, or a birth certificate.

COLON   You will need one of the following forms of identification: a driver's license, a passport, or a birth certificate.

NO COLON   Salt is used for making glass, building roads, and tanning leather.

COLON   Salt is used in the following processes: making glass, building roads, and tanning leather.

Remember that commas separate items in a series. *(See page 772.)*

A colon is also used to introduce a formal statement or a quotation that does not have a speaker tag.

The question before the budget committee was this: How can property taxes be reduced? [The formal statement begins with a capital letter.]

In Shelley's "Ode to the West Wind," we read this line: "If winter comes, can spring be far behind?"

Colons are also used in several conventional situations.

BETWEEN HOURS AND MINUTES	6:30 P.M.
BETWEEN BIBLICAL CHAPTERS AND VERSES	Psalms 46:10
BETWEEN PERIODICAL VOLUMES AND PAGES	*Futura* 16:3−8
AFTER SALUTATIONS IN BUSINESS LETTERS	Dear Sir or Madam:

Note: See page 357 for the use of a colon in introducing a long quotation.

EXERCISE *Using Colons*

Number your paper 1 to 10. Then write each word or number that should be followed by a colon and add the colon. If a sentence does not need a colon, write *C* after the number.

1. The following words are all twentieth-century creations *beautician, highbrow,* and *superhighway.*

2. The decision to be made is this Who will introduce the President at the convention?
3. That dealership sells cars, trucks, and vans.
4. Four women are represented in the U.S. Capitol's Statuary Hall Frances Willard, Maria Sanford, Florence Rena Sabin, and Esther Hobart Morris.
5. If we leave at 6 15, we should be at your house by 6 45.
6. Theodore Roosevelt is known for this saying "The only man who never makes a mistake is the man who never does anything."
7. To complete my coin collection, I need a 1963 penny, a 1940 dime, and a 1976 quarter.
8. The text for last Sunday's service was Joshua 1 9.
9. On our trip this summer, we plan to visit the following cities New Orleans, Montgomery, and Atlanta.
10. The question before the committee is this Should new members be installed twice a year?

EXERCISE *Cumulative Review*

Number your paper 1 to 10. Then write the following sentences, adding semicolons, colons, and commas where needed.

1. Benjamin Franklin played three instruments the harp the guitar and the violin.
2. I remembered the capitals of Georgia Texas and Utah but I had forgotten that Frankfort is the capital of Kentucky.
3. Some gorillas have learned sign language others have learned to read and write.
4. There are some places I have never visited in the city for example I have not yet been to the art museum.
5. Cities named after presidents include Jefferson City Missouri Jackson Mississippi Lincoln Nebraska and Madison Wisconsin.
6. Sir Winston Churchill once wrote this line "History unfolds itself by strange and unpredictable paths."
7. It didn't take as long as I'd planned to plant the bulbs Kate and I finished the work in two hours.
8. An insect has three parts head thorax and abdomen.
9. Katharine Lee Bates wrote "America the Beautiful" in 1893 she was inspired by the view from Pikes Peak in Colorado.
10. Most caterpillars change into butterflies inside a chrysalis however moths usually metamorphose inside a cocoon.

Underlining

When words are printed in italics, they slant to the right *like this*. When you write, you can use underlining as a substitute for italics. Letters, numbers, words, and titles should be underlined in certain situations.

Rule 28j Underline letters, numbers, and words when they are used to represent themselves. Also underline foreign words that are not generally used in English.

LETTERS, NUMBERS	When you write your compositions, your capital q's look like 2's.
WORDS, PHRASES	In Shakespeare's time the word <u>gentle</u> meant "noble."
FOREIGN WORDS	In Hebrew <u>shalom</u> means "peace."

Note: Only the *q* and the *2* in the first example are underlined—not the *'s*.

Rule 28k Underline the titles of long written or musical works that are published as a single unit. Also underline the titles of paintings and sculptures and the names of vehicles.

Long works include books, periodicals, newspapers, full-length plays, and very long poems. Long musical compositions include operas, symphonies, ballets, and albums. Vehicles include airplanes, ships, trains, and spacecraft. Titles of movies and radio and TV series should also be underlined.

George Eliot wrote <u>Silas Marner</u>.

Henrik Ibsen's plays <u>Hedda Gabler</u> and <u>A Doll's House</u> were written in the latter part of the nineteenth century.

Wolfgang Amadeus Mozart composed the opera <u>Don Giovanni</u> in Italian and the opera <u>The Magic Flute</u> in German.

The <u>Gudgeon</u> was the first submarine to circle the earth.

We're now getting the <u>Philadelpha Bulletin</u> delivered to our house. [*The* is generally not considered part of the title of a newspaper or a magazine.]

Note: See pages 761–763 for the capitalization of titles.

EXERCISE ◆12◆ *Using Underlining*

Number your paper 1 to 10. Then write and underline each letter, number, word, or group of words that should be italicized.

1. In our city Meet the Press airs on television every Sunday morning.
2. Charles Schulz, who created the character Charlie Brown, was once a cartoonist for a well-known magazine, the Saturday Evening Post.
3. Leonardo da Vinci's painting The Last Supper is considered one of the great art treasures of the world.
4. In many of the world's languages, the word mother begins with the letter m.
5. The expression bury the hatchet means "to make peace."
6. Of all Dickens's books that I have read, I enjoyed Oliver Twist the most.
7. The term First Lady was not widely used until a comedy about Dolley Madison, called The First Lady in the Land, opened in New York in 1911.
8. "Time flies" is the meaning of the common Latin expression tempus fugit.
9. Kaddara, an opera produced in 1921, is about Eskimos.
10. Gus Grissom made the second United States manned spaceflight in Liberty Bell 7.

Quotation Marks

Knowing how to use quotation marks correctly when you write fiction is important because conversations cannot be written without them. Authors often use conversation to reveal important information about the characters and to add realism to fiction.

Quotation marks are also essential in research papers. If you omit or incorrectly use quotation marks in a research paper, you may, unwittingly, be plagiarizing someone else's words. Quotation marks show that the words you are writing are not your own—that they belong to someone else.

One of the most important things to remember about quotation marks is that they come in pairs. They are placed at the beginning and at the end of uninterrupted quotations and certain titles.

Quotation Marks with Titles

The titles of long works of art and publications are underlined. These long works, however, are usually composed of smaller parts. A newspaper has articles, for example, and a book can include chapters, short stories, short plays, or poems. When the titles of these smaller parts are written, they should be enclosed in quotation marks.

Rule 281 Use quotation marks to enclose the titles of chapters, articles, stories, one-act plays, short poems, and songs.

Quotation marks are also placed around the titles of essays, compositions, episodes from TV series, and movements from long musical compositions.

"I Observe" is my favorite chapter in <u>David Copperfield</u> by Charles Dickens.

"Facing the Future" was an informative article in <u>Time</u>.

Yesterday we read Robert Browning's poem "My Last Duchess" in our anthology <u>English Literature</u>.

EXERCISE *Using Quotation Marks with Titles*

Number your paper 1 to 10. Then write each title, adding quotation marks and underlining where needed.

1. Automation on the Line was an illustrated article in the Detroit News.
2. The drama class presented the one-act play The Happy Journey to Trenton and Camden by Thornton Wilder.
3. The band played Yankee Doodle as we marched by.
4. You can find the short story The Bear in the book The Works of William Faulkner.
5. The Elizabethan Stage was the title of my essay for the writing contest.
6. Are we supposed to read Keats's poem To Autumn or Shelley's poem To a Skylark for class tomorrow?
7. As Time Goes By is the famous song in the movie Casablanca.
8. Cloudburst is the last movement from Grofé's Grand Canyon Suite.

9. Have you read the chapter The Turning Point in our textbook The History of the World?

10. The article Buying a Used Car in Consumer Reports was very helpful.

Quotation Marks with Direct Quotations

Quotation marks are placed around a *direct quotation*—the exact words of a person. They are not placed around an *indirect quotation*—a paraphrase of someone's words.

Rule 28m   Use quotation marks to enclose a person's exact words.

DIRECT QUOTATION   Bill said, "I'm almost ready."
INDIRECT QUOTATION   Bill said that he was almost ready. [The word
                     that often signals an indirect quotation.]

A one-sentence direct quotation can be placed before or after a speaker tag, and it can also be interrupted by a speaker tag. In all three cases, quotation marks enclose *only* the person's exact words. Notice in the third sentence in the following examples that two sets of quotation marks are needed because quotation marks enclose only a person's exact words—not the speaker tag.

BEFORE   "The game was very suspenseful," he said.
AFTER   He said, "The game was very suspenseful."
INTERRUPTED   "The game," he said, "was very suspenseful."

Only one set of quotation marks is needed to enclose any number of quoted sentences—unless they are interrupted by a speaker tag.

He said, "The game was very suspenseful. We were tied in the last inning. Then Willie hit a home run."

Capital Letters with Direct Quotations   A capital letter begins a quoted sentence—just as it begins a regular sentence.

Rule 28n   Begin each sentence of a direct quotation with a capital letter.

"**Always** be sure to think before you speak," Priscilla warned.

Priscilla warned, "**A**lways be sure to think before you speak."
[Two capital letters are needed: one for the first word of the
sentence and one for the first word of the quotation.]

"**A**lways be sure to think," Priscilla warned, "before you
speak." [*Before* does not begin with a capital letter because it is
in the middle of the quotation.]

"**A**lways be sure to think before you speak," Priscilla warned.
"**T**hat is the best advice I can give you." [*That* begins with a
capital letter because it starts a new sentence.]

EXERCISE *Using Quotation Marks and Capital*
Letters with Direct Quotations

Number your paper 1 to 10. Then write each sentence, adding quotation marks and capital letters where needed. In this exercise place
a comma or an end mark that follows a quotation *inside* the closing
quotation marks.

Happiness   **1.** happiness is not a state to arrive at, but a manner of traveling,
commented Margaret Runbeck.
2. Those who won our independence . . . believed liberty to be the
secret of happiness and courage to be the secret of liberty, declared
Justice Louis D. Brandeis.
3. when one is happy, there is no time to be fatigued. being happy
engrosses the whole attention, E. F. Benson said.
4. Don Marquis mused, happiness is the interval between periods
of unhappiness.
5. when a happy moment, complete and rounded as a pearl, falls
into the tossing ocean of life, Agnes Repplier said, it is never
wholly lost.
6. happiness is not being pained in body or troubled in mind, commented Thomas Jefferson.
7. C. P. Snow said, the pursuit of happiness is a most ridiculous
phrase. if you pursue it, you'll never find it.
8. if happiness truly consisted in physical ease and freedom from
care, then the happiest individual, I think, would be an American
cow, William Lyon Phelps mused.
9. the happy do not believe in miracles, Goethe stated.
10. happiness is not a matter of events. it depends upon the tides of
the mind, Alice Meynell once said.

Commas with Direct Quotations   A comma is used to separate a direct quotation from a speaker tag.

Rule 28o   Use a comma to separate a direct quotation from a speaker tag. Place the comma inside the closing quotation marks.

Notice in the following examples that when the speaker tag follows the quotation, the comma goes *inside* the closing quotation marks.

> "Today's mail is late," she said. [The comma goes *inside* the closing quotation marks.]
>
> She said, "Today's mail is late." [The comma follows the speaker tag.]
>
> "Today's mail," she said, "is late." [Two commas are needed to separate the speaker tag from the parts of an interrupted quotation. The first comma goes *inside* the closing quotation marks.]

End Marks with Direct Quotations   A period marks the end of a statement or an opinion, and it also marks the end of a quoted statement or opinion.

Rule 28p   Place a period inside the closing quotation marks when the end of the quotation comes at the end of the sentence.

> He said, "I think I'll order lasagna." [The period goes *inside* the closing quotation marks.]
>
> "I think I'll order lasagna," he said. [The period follows the speaker tag, and a comma separates the quotation from the speaker tag.]
>
> "I think," he said, "I'll order lasagna." [The period goes *inside* the closing quotation marks.]

If a quotation asks a question or shows strong feeling, the question mark or the exclamation point goes *inside* the closing quotation marks. Notice that the question mark goes *inside* the closing quotation marks in the three examples that follow.

> She asked, "Where did you pick the apples?"
> "Where did you pick the apples?" she asked.
> "Where," she asked, "did you pick the apples?"

The exclamation point also goes *inside* the closing quotation marks in the following three examples.

> He exclaimed, "I'm thrilled that I've been hired!"
> "I'm thrilled that I've been hired!" he exclaimed.
> "I'm thrilled," he exclaimed, "that I've been hired!"

A quotation of two or more sentences can include various end marks.

> "Did you see the movie at Cinema I?" Laura asked. "It was the funniest movie I've ever seen!"

Question marks and exclamation points are placed inside the closing quotation marks when they are part of the quotation. Occasionally a question or an exclamatory statement will include a direct quotation. In such cases the question mark or the exclamation point goes *outside* the closing quotation marks. Notice in the following examples that the end marks for the quotations themselves are omitted. Only one end mark is used at the end of a quotation.

> Did Nancy say, "The class rings have arrived"? [The whole sentence—not the quotation—is the question.]

> I was so relieved when my teacher said, "There will be no more reports today"! [The whole sentence—not the quotation—is exclamatory.]

Note: Semicolons and colons go *outside* closing quotation marks.

> Robert Browning wrote, "That's my last Duchess"; thus he began one of the most famous poems of all time.

> Mrs. Rooney said that the following are "mandatory reading for seniors": *Macbeth* and *Great Expectations*.

EXERCISE *Using Commas and End Marks with Direct Quotations*

Write each sentence, adding commas and end marks where needed.

   1. "Most baby seals must be taught how to swim by their mothers" Martha told us
   2. Cheryl asked "Why should a right-handed bowler step out on the right foot "

3. "I was so cold my teeth were chattering " Beth exclaimed

4. "The safest way to double your money" Frank Hubbard advised "is to fold it over once and put it in your pocket"

5. I was really surprised and proud when the public service announcer said "The marching band from Barry High School has won second prize in the competition"

6. "Did you get that summer job you applied for " Tara asked

7. Ramón called "We've run out of gas "

8. Norman Douglas observed "Life is full of untapped sources of pleasure Education should train us to discover them"

9. Did the principal say "The Senior Prom is on June 20 and graduation is on June 23"

10. "Those fresh tomatoes were delicious " Megan said "Did you grow them yourself"

EXERCISE *Cumulative Review*

Number your paper 1 to 10. Then write each sentence, adding capital letters, quotation marks, and other punctuation marks where needed.

Quotes from
Famous
Authors

1. the applause of a single human being is of great consequence Samuel Johnson said

2. the most beautiful adventures explained Robert Louis Stevenson are not those we go to seek

3. we need to restore the full meaning of the old word *duty* Pearl Buck remarked it is the other side of *rights*

4. Joseph Conrad stated an ideal is often but a flaming vision of reality

5. make up your mind to act decisively and take the consequences no good is ever done in this world by hesitation Thomas Huxley warned

6. Janet Erskine Stuart said to aim at the best and to remain essentially ourselves are one and the same thing

7. welcome everything that comes to you André Gide advised but do not long for anything else

8. can anything be sadder than work left unfinished Christina Rossetti asked yes, work never begun

9. did the poet W. B. Yeats say good conversation unrolls itself like the dawn

10. I do not like arguments I seek harmony if it is not there, I move away Anaïs Nin stated

Other Uses of Quotation Marks

In long quotations in a report and in conversations in a story, quotation marks require special applications.

Quoting Phrases If you are quoting a phrase or the definition of a word, put quotation marks around the borrowed words only. Capital letters and commas are usually not needed. Notice in the following examples that the period goes *inside* the closing quotation marks when the phrase or the definition comes at the end of the sentence.

> During his inaugural address, John F. Kennedy said that the day should be spent as "a celebration of freedom."
>
> The word *mutual* means "given and received in equal amount."

Note: The word being defined in the preceding example is italicized (underlined). *(See page 800.)*

Writing Dialogue When you write dialogue—conversation between two or more people—begin a new paragraph each time the speaker changes. A new paragraph clearly indicates who is speaking.

The following dialogue from *A Christmas Carol* takes place between Scrooge's nephew Fred and Fred's wife Belle. Each quotation follows the rules you have just studied, but each time the speaker changes, a new paragraph begins. Notice also that actions or descriptions of the two characters are sometimes included within the same paragraph in which each one speaks.

> "Belle," said the husband, turning to his wife with a smile. "I saw a friend of yours this afternoon."
>
> "Who was it?"
>
> "Guess!"
>
> "How can I? Tut, don't I know?" she added in the same breath, laughing as he laughed. "Mr. Scrooge."
>
> CHARLES DICKENS

Note: An *ellipsis* (three dots) means the omission of part of a quotation. If an ellipsis comes at the end of a complete sentence, it is preceded by a period—making four dots.

> "I saw a friend of yours. . . ."

Quoting Long Passages   Quotation marks are not necessary when you quote five or more lines in a research paper. Instead, skip two lines and indent ten spaces along the left margin. Skip another two lines between the last line of the quoted material and the next part of your text. *(See page 357 for an example.)*

Quotations within Quotations   If a title or a quotation is included within another quotation, a distinction must be made between the two sets of quotation marks. To avoid any confusion, use single quotation marks to enclose a quotation or certain titles within a quotation.

"Is the song '76 Trombones' from *The Music Man?*" Li asked.

Lou said, "I wonder what he meant when he said, 'You'll be seeing me soon.'"

A quotation within a quotation follows all the rules covered in this section. Notice, in the second example, that the closing single quotation mark and the closing double quotation marks come together.

EXERCISE   **17**   *Cumulative Review*

Correctly rewrite the following dialogue between Ebenezer Scrooge and Bob Cratchit. Add punctuation and indentation.

From *A Christmas Carol*

> Hallo growled Scrooge in his accustomed voice as near as he could feign it. What do you mean by coming here at this time of day? I am very sorry, sir said Bob. I am behind my time. . . . Yes. I think you are. Step this way, sir, if you please. It's only once a year, sir pleaded Bob, appearing from the tank. It shall not be repeated. I was making rather merry yesterday, sir. Now, I'll tell you what, my friend said Scrooge. I am not going to tolerate this sort of thing any longer. Therefore . . . I am about to raise your salary!
>
> CHARLES DICKENS

Application to Writing

Taking the role of President of the United States, write a brief conversation in which you speak with the head of state of a foreign country. Punctuate and indent the dialogue correctly.

Other Marks of Punctuation

Hyphens, dashes, parentheses, and brackets are covered in this section.

Hyphens

A hyphen has several uses besides its most common use, dividing a word at the end of a line.

Hyphen with Numbers and Words   Certain numbers and fractions are written with a hyphen.

Rule 28q   Use a hyphen when writing out the numbers *twenty-one* through *ninety-nine*. Also use a hyphen when writing out a fraction that is used as an adjective.

Eighty-four seniors from Delton will graduate in June.

A two-thirds vote of the House is needed.

A fraction used as a noun is *not* written with a hyphen.

Two thirds of the town voted for the referendum.

Hyphens with Compound Nouns and Adjectives   Compound nouns and compound adjectives can be written as two separate words, combined as one word, or written as two or more hyphenated words. Since compound nouns and compound adjectives can take these different forms, it is always best to check the dictionary for the correct spelling.

Rule 28r   Use a hyphen to separate the parts of some compound nouns and adjectives.

COMPOUND NOUNS   sister-in-law, flare-up, secretary-general
COMPOUND ADJECTIVES   skin-deep, long-term, run-of-the-mill

Note: Never use a hyphen between an adjective and an adverb ending in *ly.*

That **superbly talented** musician is my uncle. [no hyphen]

Hyphens with Certain Prefixes Several prefixes and one suffix are always separated from their root words by a hyphen.

Rule 28s Use a hyphen after the prefixes *ex-*, *self-*, and *all-* and before the suffix *-elect.*

ex-champion   self-control   all-around   governor-elect

A hyphen is used with all prefixes before most proper nouns or proper adjectives.

mid-Atlantic   pre-Columbian   pro-American

EXERCISE 18 *Using Hyphens*

Number your paper 1 to 10. Then correctly write each word that should be hyphenated. If no word in the sentence needs a hyphen, write *C* after the number.

1. Is Madeline Nenno the stand in for the female lead in our school play?
2. The ex mayor of South Morrisville teaches at the University of Nebraska.
3. I still must type one third of my term paper.
4. Fifty six bushels of corn were picked today.
5. Can you name two mid Victorian poets?
6. The metal used in the sculpture is one fourth copper.
7. This report includes up to date statistics.
8. The solidly constructed house has already stood for over 200 years.
9. Jamie is unusually self reliant for such a young person.
10. The principal commended the students for their all out effort in the fund raising drive.

Hyphens to Divide Words When you write a research paper or a composition, you should—whenever possible—avoid dividing words at the end of the line.

Rule 28t Use a hyphen to divide a word at the end of a line.

If you must divide a word, use the guidelines listed on the following page.

Guidelines for Dividing Words

1. Divide words only between syllables.

hu▪morous or humor▪ous

2. Never divide a one-syllable word.

laugh   brought   save   lead

3. Never separate a one-letter syllable from the rest of the word.

DO NOT BREAK   a▪dore   e▪mit   i▪ris

4. Hyphenate after two letters at the end of a line, but do not carry a two-letter word ending to the next line.

BREAK   be▪lieve   re▪call   in▪vite
DO NOT BREAK   tight▪en   shov▪el   over▪ly

5. Usually divide words containing double consonants between the double consonants.

shim▪mer   oc▪cur   ship▪ping   stag▪ger

6. Divide hyphenated words only after the hyphens.

spur▪of▪the▪moment   father▪in▪law   self▪confident

7. Do not divide a proper noun or a proper adjective.

Olivero   Yonkers   Himalayan   Polish

EXERCISE *Using Hyphens to Divide Words*

Write each word, using a hyphen or hyphens to show where the word can be divided. If a word should not be divided, write *no*.

1. educate	**5.** governor	**9.** puzzle	**13.** decent
2. squeeze	**6.** octave	**10.** immune	**14.** Reggie
3. follow	**7.** permit	**11.** dress	**15.** method
4. event	**8.** planet	**12.** teenage	

Dashes, Parentheses, and Brackets

Dashes, parentheses, and brackets are used to separate certain words or groups of words from the rest of a sentence. Do not overuse these marks of punctuation, however, or substitute them for other marks of punctuation, such as commas or colons.

Dashes   Like a comma a dash is used to separate words or expressions. A dash, however, indicates a greater separation than a comma does. Dashes should be used in the following situations.

Rule 28u   **Use dashes to set off an abrupt change in thought.**

Several students——there were three——applied for the scholarship.

I've misplaced the envelope——oh, I see you have it.

Rule 28v   **Use dashes to set off an appositive that is introduced by words such as** *that is, for example,* **or** *for instance.*

If your car gets stuck—— for example, in mud, snow, or soft sand——apply power slowly, keeping the front wheels in a straight position.

Mary Ann Evans's pseudonym——that is, her pen name——was George Eliot.

Rule 28w   **Use dashes to set off a parenthetical expression or an appositive that includes commas. Also use dashes to call special attention to a phrase.**

The names of four states——Alaska, Arizona, Arkansas, and Alabama——begin with the letter *A.*

You can call me Monday or Wednesday——or Friday, for that matter——right after school.

Rule 28x   **Use dashes to set off a phrase or a clause that summarizes or emphasizes what has preceded it.**

June 6, 7, and 8——these are the dates of the county fair.

A book and a T-shirt——I got these gifts for my birthday.

Parentheses   Parentheses separate from the rest of the sentence additional information that is added, but not needed. Definitions and dates, for example, are sometimes enclosed by parentheses.

Rule 28y   Use parentheses to enclose additional information that is not needed in a sentence.

> Dylan Thomas (1914–1953) read his own poetry brilliantly.
>
> Samuel Clemens did not invent the name Mark Twain (which means "a depth of 2 fathoms, or 12 feet").

Note: A period follows a closing parenthesis that comes at the end of a sentence.

Brackets   When you write a research paper that includes quoted passages, you may need to use brackets.

Rule 28z   Use brackets to enclose an explanation within quoted material that is not part of the quotation.

> Richard Ellman wrote, "He [W. B. Yeats] displayed and interpreted the direction in which poetry was to go."

EXERCISE **20**   *Using Dashes and Parentheses*

Number your paper 1 to 10. Then write each sentence, adding dashes and parentheses where needed.

1. The Impressionist painter Claude Monet 1840–1926 painted many pictures of the same lily pads.
2. Running, swimming, and riding all these are good forms of exercise.
3. A number of countries in the world for example, Bolivia, Switzerland, and Austria have no seacoast.
4. I feel you are too young how shall I say it to be alone in the city.
5. A provision in author Willa Cather's will she died in 1947 prohibited publication of her letters.
6. The dogwood grows well in many states for instance, New York, Maryland, and Virginia.
7. I cannot I repeat, cannot hear the people in the balcony.
8. In 1895, Lieutenant Peary later Admiral Peary found one of the world's largest iron meteorites in Greenland.
9. Los Angeles 464 square miles is more than one third the size of Rhode Island 1,214 square miles.
10. The dates for some of this year's events graduation, prom, and picnic have been set.

Mechanics: Editing for Correct Punctuation

When you finish writing, always take a few extra minutes to edit your work for correct punctuation. Consider that time an insurance policy for your efforts.

Checking Your Understanding   Write the following two paragraphs, adding any punctuation marks that are needed.

There arent any hard and fast statistics nevertheless the expression OK is probably the most widely used American expression in the world. For example, during World War II, there was a special international soccer match. One team was composed of members from the following four countries Poland, Czechoslovakia, Denmark, and Norway. The team had serious difficulties because of the language differences. Finally one of Polands players shouted OK! Feeling confident that everyone finally understood the same thing, the team members went on to win the game.

Despite its international acceptance, the expression OK is really an all American expression. It first appeared in print in 1839 in a Boston newspaper, the Morning Post. A year later President Martin Van Buren he was born in Kinderhook, New York ran for a second term of office. He was called Old Kinderhook by his backers. The initials of his nickname were then used during the campaign. Later OK came into wide use as a catchword meaning all is right.

Writing a Narrative   What would you like to be doing 20 years from now? Write freely, exploring all possible ideas that come to your mind. Choose one and create a scene that places you 20 years in the future. Limit your narrative to a single location and add only one or two other characters. Include realistic dialogue to help the characterization come alive.   *Application:* As you edit your narrative, check for the correct use of all punctuation.

28 Review

A Using Punctuation Correctly Write the following sentences, adding any needed punctuation. (There are no direct quotations.)

 1. The conservation department puts rainbow trout into the streams the lakes are stocked with pickerel and perch.
 2. The prop committee still hasnt found the following items a straw hat a wicker chair and a large desk.
 3. Everyones enthusiasm at the pep rally encouraged the players on Newtons all star team.
 4. In the code the 2s stood for es.
 5. The Eighteenth Amendment the prohibition amendment was not ratified by Connecticut and Rhode Island.
 6. Most insects have no eyelids thus their eyes are always open.
 7. Six forty and ten these are the three correct answers.
 8. Its time to apply for the dogs new license.
 9. We have our choice of pink aqua or lavender but we dont know which color would be best for the room.
10. A tree snake appears to fly through the air however it merely glides on air currents.
11. We couldnt possibly be at your house by 7 30.
12. Shiny metals for example tin and copper turn into black powders when finely ground aluminum is an exception.
13. Gregor Mendel 1822−1884 was the Austrian botanist who developed the basic laws of heredity.
14. Bobs and Teds scores were the best theyve ever had.
15. Only two copies of the works of the Greek sculptor Myron have survived one of those is the sculpture Discus Thrower.
16. Three people Nancy Alex and Claire will represent the school at the conference in Philadelphia.
17. There are no penguins at the North Pole in fact there are no penguins anywhere in the Northern Hemisphere.
18. The question before the finance committee is this Which of the two investments will yield the greater return?
19. You can see the famous painting Mona Lisa by Leonardo da Vinci in the book Great Masterpieces of the World.
20. We will donate two thirds of the clubs earnings to a fund for famine relief.

B **Punctuating Direct Quotations**   Number your paper 1 to 10. Then write the following quotations, adding capital letters, quotation marks, and other punctuation marks where needed.

1. were taking Rex with us to the store Chris announced
2. what an enthusiastic audience this is Beth remarked
3. why didnt someone answer the telephone she asked
4. the clerk said these shirts will be on sale next week youll save two dollars on each one if you wait
5. the show I told you about Jake announced is about to begin
6. Pablo asked does soccer practice start at three oclock
7. there is nothing better Katharine Butler Hathaway said than the encouragement of a good friend
8. what is the rhyme scheme in this poem by Byron Ms. Otero asked
9. did you read the article Space Station Speculation in todays issue of the Washington Post Leila asked
10. Bryan said the dictionary definition of the word glint is a tiny bright flash of light

Mastery Test

Number your paper 1 to 10. Then write each sentence, adding apostrophes, semicolons, colons, hyphens, quotation marks, and other punctuation marks needed with direct quotations. Only a sentence with a speaker tag should be considered a direct quotation.

1. Switzerland has four official languages French, German, Italian, and Romansch.
2. Seeds from plants are often dispersed by ingenious methods for example, the milkweed seed rides on a tiny parachute.
3. Anyones guess is as good as mine.
4. My research paper answered this question What is the main conflict in Shakespeares play Hamlet?
5. Andrea said His self assured manner impressed everyone.
6. At 5 30 A.M. Roy and I headed for Pier Ten.
7. True chameleons can change to green, yellow, or brown the American chameleon can turn only green and brown.
8. Have you an umbrella Rebecca asked It looks as if its raining.
9. Did Mozart ever write an opera Dwayne inquired.
10. You just scored the winning point he cheered.

Appendix

Using a Word Processor

Whether you are simply writing a letter or are composing a report, a word processor will help you in all stages of the writing process. With a word processor (or a computer, a keyboard, and a word-processing program), you can open and name documents, create and store files, and input drafts on the monitor. After drafting compositions, you can then revise, edit, and even publish them. If you take the time to learn and master word-processing skills, you will find a word processor to be a great writing tool. You will be able to accomplish writing assignments more easily and quickly than by writing in longhand or using a typewriter.

The conveniences of word processing are available through *word-processing programs,* of which there are several. Once you learn the program available to you, you can easily learn another.

Prewriting

In the prewriting stage, almost any activity that you complete with paper and pencil can be done on a word processor. For instance, you could use the computer to explore subjects for writing by brainstorming, freewriting, and inputting journal entries. You could even use the computer to record your responses to books, stories, poems, and other literature. A computer is also an effective way to share ideas if you need to explore subjects by conferencing with another student.

To organize your ideas on a computer, you can create files listing possible writing subjects and then add to those lists any time you have a new idea. You could even create separate subject files for each of the different writing purposes and list "Things I Could *Explain,*" "Things I Would Like to *Describe,*" "Things I Would Like to *Persuade* Others to Think or Do," "Thoughts and Feelings I Would Like to *Express,*" and "Ideas to *Create* Stories, Poems, and Plays." After you have named and stored your subject files, you can read them at any time at the touch of a key. The following list suggests ways of how you can effectively use a word processor when prewriting.

Prewriting on a Word Processor

1. Create a subject file by inputting your answers to questions for exploring your interests and knowledge. *(See pages 12–13.)*
2. Create a reader's response file, in which you record your responses to literature. *(See pages 15–16.)*
3. Store your Learning Log in the computer or on a disk and update it by logging in the interesting information you learn in other subject areas. *(See page 15.)*
4. Explore a subject by listing elements or aspects of it, possible focuses or main ideas for a composition about it, possible working thesis statements, and possible supporting details. *(See pages 17–18, 20–23, and 26–29.)*
5. Freewrite about your observations, experimenting with descriptive and sensory details. *(See page 20.)*
6. List questions for developing a subject through inquiring. *(See page 24.)*
7. Input audience profiles or freewrite letters to real or imaginary members of your audience to help to clarify your ideas. *(See pages 18–19.)*
8. Use computer conferencing to explore a subject through dialogue with a partner if your class is working on computers that are interconnected. For group brainstorming you and your classmates can keyboard questions and responses directly onto one another's monitors.

You will find a word processor particularly helpful when you need to gather and organize information for writing an expository essay or a report. If your computer is linked to an information network, for instance, you can use electronic bulletin boards to access databases—computerized reference materials. You may even be able to communicate by electronic mail with experts on your subject. Then, as you gather information, you can maintain a computer file listing all your sources. Some programs will automatically generate in the correct form footnotes or entries for a works cited page. *(See pages 356–363.)*

Regardless of what your writing purpose is, you should take advantage of any software available to you that lets you create clusters, diagrams, outlines, and charts for classifying or for comparing and contrasting. *(See pages 22–23 and 114–115.)* Even if you do not have access to special software, grouping and ordering ideas and information are easy on a word processor. Keyboard commands allow you to copy and move, or cut and paste, blocks of text.

Drafting

On a word processor, drafting is a simple procedure. You can type and enter commands without worrying about the ends of lines, the beginnings of new pages, or any mechanical errors. With the technique of scrolling, you can read your document on the monitor, quickly move from one part of the document to another, and work on any part of the document. Keyboard functions allow you to move back and forth between drafting and revising as you rearrange, delete, or insert words, sentences, or paragraphs. Because you can delete any unwanted writing at the touch of a key, you are free to include alternative ways of expressing an idea or alternative versions of an introduction or a conclusion. Below are listed a few tips for using a word processor effectively when drafting.

Drafting on a Word Processor
I. Start by setting the format so that all your writing will automatically be in standard manuscript form. *(See page 43.)* Double-space or triple-space for easy marking on hard, or printed, copies.
2. Input your outline on a word processor and expand it into a composition by developing each head.
3. Save your work often—about every 20 minutes—and print hard copies often to work on when you are not at the computer.

Revising

You will find that working on a word processor really saves time when you are ready to revise your composition. After you have completed your draft, you can use networking, or electronic conferencing, to help evaluate your work. For example, once your classmates or other readers have read your composition on their monitors, they can directly input their reactions, questions, and suggestions for improving your draft.

Another timesaving strategy is to store revision checklists in the computer or on a disk for easy reference. You can also use software that includes a dictionary and a thesaurus to help you check your spelling and improve your word choices. The following examples suggest ways to use a word processor when you revise.

Revising on a Word Processor
1. Use the INSERT command to add ideas, details, transitions between sentences and paragraphs, and parenthetical citations.
2. Use the MOVE or CUT and PASTE commands to rearrange the order of words, sentences, and paragraphs.
3. DELETE unneeded words and details and any sentences or paragraphs that detract from the unity of your composition.
4. Use the FIND or SEARCH and REPLACE features to substitute words and phrases.

Editing and Publishing

The same keyboarding functions that help in revising also help in editing. For example, you can use the SEARCH and REPLACE commands to correct automatically and simultaneously a particular kind of error in all the places where it occurs. In addition, most word processing programs have a SPELL feature that automatically checks your spelling.

Before you edit your revised draft on a word processor, mark final corrections on a hard copy, or printout, using proofreading marks. To guide you in marking your copy, you could store your Personalized Editing Checklist and other editing checklists in the computer or on a disk for quick reference.

When using a word processor, publishing your work can be a creative challenge. Various design features of the computer program can enhance the appearance of your composition before the final printout. Design features include different sizes, styles, and decorative treatments of type, called *fonts*. Most programs also let you use files of ready-made graphics or even let you create graphics of your own.

Printing out a manuscript that you have designed yourself can give you a feeling of great accomplishment. Remember, however, that you can publish your manuscript electronically too. In electronic publishing you share your writing with readers through electronic mail or on a network bulletin board.

Through all the stages of the writing process, word processing simplifies many writing procedures and saves time. It also gives you convenient new ways to keep records and to express your creativity. Although a word processor cannot automatically make you a good writer, it can help you in many ways improve your writing skills.

Useful Conventions of Writing

Dividing Words. Although you should avoid dividing words whenever possible, sometimes doing so is necessary to keep the right-hand margin of your paper fairly even. When dividing words, follow the rules on pages 810–812.

Writing Numbers. In general, spell out the numbers one through ten. Use numerals for numbers above ten.

> two   ten   11   57   289   1,554   6,328,730

To avoid writing six or more zeros, use a combination of numerals and words.

> five million   94 million   216 billion   3.5 billion

Always spell out a number at the beginning of a sentence or revise the sentence.

> Three hundred twenty-seven votes were cast for Myer in the
> school board election.
> The voters cast 327 votes for Myer in the school board
> election.

Use numerals for dates, street and room numbers, page numbers, percents, decimals, and times with A.M. or P.M.

> July 14, 1789   room 8   page 5   2 percent   5:40 P.M.
>   125 Spring Street   7.2

Using Abbreviations. Most abbreviations should be avoided in formal writing. In particular, do not abbreviate names of states, countries, days of the week, months, weights, or measurements. See page 771 for examples of abbreviations that are acceptable in formal writing.

Quoting Long Passages. When you write a research paper and want to quote a passage of five or more lines from a source, skip two lines and indent ten spaces from the left margin. Quotation marks are not necessary for a quotation of this length. A colon is usually used in the sentence that introduces the quotation. *(See pages 797–798.)* Remember to give credit to the author for the quoted material. *(See pages 356–357.)*

Glossary of Terms

A

Action verb An action verb tells what action a subject is performing. *(See page 542.)*

Active voice Active voice indicates that the subject is performing the action. *(See pages 78 and 662.)*

Adjective An adjective is a word that modifies a noun or a pronoun. *(See page 546.)*

Adjective clause An adjective clause is a subordinate clause that is used like an adjective to modify a noun or a pronoun. *(See page 616.)*

Adjective phrase An adjective phrase is a prepositional phrase that is used to modify a noun or a pronoun. *(See page 585.)*

Adverb An adverb is a word that modifies a verb, an adjective, or another adverb. *(See page 549.)*

Adverb clause An adverb clause is a subordinate clause that is used like an adverb to modify a verb, an adjective, or an adverb. *(See page 612.)*

Adverb phrase An adverb phrase is a prepositional phrase that is used like an adverb to modify a verb, adjective, or adverb. *(See page 586.)*

Alliteration Alliteration is the repetition of a consonant sound at the beginning of a series of words. *(See pages 61 and 400.)*

Allusion An allusion is a reference to persons or events in the past or in literature. *(See page 262.)*

Analogies Analogies show the logical relationships between pairs of words. *(See pages 465 and 506.)*

Antecedent An antecedent is the word or group of words that a pronoun replaces or refers to. *(See page 685.)*

Antonym An antonym is a word that means the opposite of another word. *(See page 464.)*

Appositive An appositive is a noun or a pronoun that identifies or explains another noun or pronoun in a sentence. *(See page 589.)*

Assonance Assonance is the repetition of a vowel sound within words. *(See page 400.)*

Audience Audience is the person or persons who will read your work or hear your speech. *(See page 19.)*

B

Brainstorming Brainstorming means writing down everything that comes to mind about a subject. *(See pages 21–22.)*

Business letter A business letter has six parts: the heading, inside address, salutation, body, closing, and signature. *(See pages 413–414.)*

C

Card catalog The card catalog is a cabinet of drawers containing author, title, and subject cards for materials in a library. *(See pages 484–486.)*

Case Case is the form of a noun or a pronoun that indicates its use in a sentence. In English there are three cases: the *nominative case,* the *objective case,* and the *possessive case. (See page 671.)*

Characterization Characterization is a variety of techniques used by writers to show the personality of a character. *(See pages 262, 263, and 384.)*

Character sketch A character sketch is a summary or a chart of the important physical and personality characteristics of a fictional character. *(See page 384.)*

Chronological order Chronological order arranges events in the order in which they happened. *(See pages 28 and 107.)*

Classification Classification involves grouping similar types of information into categories. *(See pages 27 and 114–116.)*

Clause A clause is a group of words that has a subject and a predicate. *(See page 611.)*

Clustering Clustering is a brainstorming technique in which the writer writes a subject at the center of a page, writes supporting details, and connects those details to the subject with lines. *(See page 22–23.)*

Coherence A paragraph or an essay has coherence if the ideas in it are presented in logical order with clear transitions. *(See pages 100–101 and 160.)*

Comparative degree The comparative degree of a modifier is used when two people, things, or actions are compared. *(See page 715.)*

Comparison and contrast Comparison and contrast is a method of development in which the writer examines similarities and differences between two subjects. *(See pages 28, 153–155, and 276.)*

Complement A complement is a word that completes the meaning of an action verb. *(See page 569.)*

Complete predicate A complete predicate includes all the words that tell what the subject is doing or that tell something about the subject. *(See page 561.)*

Complete subject A complete subject includes all the words used to identify the person, place, thing, or idea that the sentence is about. *(See page 561.)*

Complex sentence A complex sentence consists of one independent clause and one or more subordinate clauses. *(See page 622.)*

Compound-complex sentence A compound-complex sentence consists of two or more independent clauses and one or more subordinate clauses. *(See page 623.)*

Compound noun A compound noun is a common noun with more than one word. *(See page 538.)*

Compound sentence A compound sentence consists of two or more independent clauses. *(See page 622.)*

Compound subject A compound subject is two or more subjects in one sentence that have the same verb and are joined by a conjunction. *(See page 563.)*

Compound verb A compound verb is two or more verbs that have the same subject and are joined by a conjunction. *(See page 563.)*

Concluding sentence A concluding sentence adds a strong ending to a paragraph by summarizing, referring to the main idea, or adding an insight. *(See page 94.)*

Conclusion A conclusion completes an essay and reinforces its main idea. *(See page 139.)*

Conjugation of a verb A conjugation of a verb lists all the singular and plural forms of a verb in its six tenses. *(See pages 650–653.)*

Conjunction A conjunction connects words or groups of words. *(See page 553.)*

Connotation The connotation of a word is the feeling that a word creates. *(See page 56.)*

Consonance Consonance is the repetition of a consonant sound in words. *(See page 400.)*

Context clue A context clue is the clue to a word's meaning provided by the sentence or passage in which the word is used. *(See page 451.)*

Cooperative learning Cooperative learning occurs when a group works together to achieve a goal or accomplish a task. *(See page 444.)*

Coordinating conjunction A coordinating conjunction is a single connecting word used to connect compound subjects, compound verbs, and compound sentences. *(See page 553.)*

Correlative conjunction Correlative conjunctions are pairs of conjunctions used to connect compound subjects, compound verbs, and compound sentences. *(See page 553.)*

Critical essay A critical essay presents an interpretation of a work of literature and supports that interpretation with details and quotations from the work. *(See page 257.)*

D

Dangling modifier A dangling modifier is a phrase that has nothing to modify in a sentence. *(See page 601.)*

Declarative sentence A declarative sentence makes a statement or expresses an opinion and ends with a period. *(See page 769.)*

Deductive reasoning Deductive reasoning is the thinking process of beginning with a general statement and applying it to a particular case. *(See page 193.)*

Demonstrative pronoun A demonstrative pronoun points out a person or a thing. *(See page 541.)*

Denotation Denotation of a word is a dictionary definition of a word. *(See page 56.)*

Descriptive paragraph A descriptive paragraph creates in words a vivid picture of a person, an object, or a scene. *(See page 109.)*

Developmental order In developmental order, information is organized so that one idea grows out of the preceding idea. *(See page 28.)*

Dewey decimal system The Dewey decimal system is used by libraries to arrange nonfiction books on shelves in numerical order according to ten general subject categories. *(See pages 481–482.)*

Dialogue A dialogue is a conversation between people. In writing, a new paragraph begins each time the speaker changes. *(See page 262.)*

Direct object A direct object is a noun or a pronoun that receives the action of a verb. *(See page 569.)*

E

Editing Editing is the stage of the writing process that follows revising. In this stage, writers polish their work by correcting errors and making a neat copy. *(See page 38.)*

Elliptical clause An elliptical clause is a subordinate clause in which words are omitted but understood to be there. *(See pages 614 and 683.)*

Essay An essay is a composition that presents and develops one main idea in three or more paragraphs. *(See page 136.)*

Essential phrase or clause An essential phrase or clause is essential to the meaning of a sentence and is therefore not set off with commas. *(See page 782.)*

Etymology An etymology of a word is the history of a word from its earliest recorded use to the present. *(See page 448.)*

Exclamatory sentence An exclamatory sentence expresses strong feeling and ends with an exclamation point. *(See page 770.)*

Expository paragraph An expository paragraph explains or informs with facts and examples or gives directions. *(See page 114.)*

F

Fact A fact is a statement that can be proved. *(See pages 187 and 440.)*

825

Fiction Fiction refers to prose works of literature, such as short stories and novels, that are partly or totally imaginary. *(See page 263.)*

Figurative language Figurative language is the imaginative, nonliteral use of language. *(See pages 58, 262, and 402.)*

First draft Writing the first draft is the second stage of the writing process. Writers use their prewriting notes to get their ideas on paper as quickly as possible. *(See page 30.)*

Free verse Free verse is verse without meter but with the rhythm of spoken language. *(See page 405.)*

Freewriting Freewriting is a prewriting technique of nonstop writing that encourages the flow of ideas. *(See page 13.)*

G

Gerund A gerund is a verb form ending in *-ing* that is used as a noun. *(See page 595.)*

H

Helping verb A helping, or auxiliary, verb and the main verb make up a verb phrase. *(See page 545.)*

Hyperbole Hyperbole is the use of exaggeration or overstatement. *(See page 402.)*

I

Imagery Imagery is the use of concrete details to create a picture or appeal to senses other than sight. *(See pages 262 and 402.)*

Imperative sentence An imperative sentence makes a request or gives a command and ends with either a period or an exclamation point. *(See page 769.)*

Indefinite pronoun An indefinite pronoun refers to an unnamed person or thing. *(See page 540.)*

Independent clause An independent (or main) clause can stand alone as a sentence because it expresses a complete thought. *(See page 611.)*

Indirect object An indirect object is a noun or a pronoun that answers the question *to* or *for whom?* or *to* or *for what?* after an action verb. *(See page 570.)*

Inductive reasoning Inductive reasoning is the thinking process of forming general conclusions based on facts. *(See page 190.)*

Infinitive An infinitive is a verb form that usually begins with *to* and is used as a noun, an adjective, or an adverb. *(See page 597.)*

Inquiring Inquiring is a prewriting technique in which the writer asks questions such as *Who? What? Where? When?* and *Why? (See page 24.)*

Interjection An interjection is a word that expresses strong feeling. *(See page 553.)*

Interrogative pronoun An interrogative pronoun is used to ask a question. *(See page 541.)*

Interrogative sentence An interrogative sentence asks a question and ends with a question mark. *(See page 770.)*

Intransitive verb An intransitive verb is an action verb that does not have an object. *(See page 542.)*

Introduction An introduction to an essay introduces a subject, states or implies a purpose, and presents a main idea. *(See page 138.)*

Irony Irony occurs in a work of literature when the opposite of what is expected occurs. *(See page 262.)*

Irregular verb An irregular verb does not form its past and past participle by adding *-ed* or *-d* to the present. *(See page 642.)*

J

Jargon Jargon refers to the specialized, often wordy, language used in a certain field. *(See page 57.)*

Journal A journal is a daily notebook in which a writer records thoughts and feelings. *(See page 15.)*

L

Linking verb A linking verb links the subject with another word in the sentence. This other word either renames or describes the subject. *(See page 543.)*

M

Metaphor A metaphor implies a comparison by saying that one thing *is* another. *(See pages 59, 84, 262, and 402.)*

Meter Meter is the rhythm of stressed and unstressed syllables in each line of a poem. *(See pages 262 and 401.)*

Misplaced modifier A misplaced modifier is a phrase or a clause that is placed too far away from the word it modifies, thus creating an unclear sentence. *(See pages 601 and 619.)*

Mood (1) In literature, mood is the atmosphere or feeling created by a work of literature. *(See page 262.)* (2) In grammar, mood is the way in which a verb expresses an idea. *(See page 665.)*

N

Narrative paragraph A narrative paragraph tells a real or an imaginary story. *(See page 106.)*

Nominative case The nominative case of a pronoun is used for subjects and predicate nominatives. *(See page 672.)*

Nonessential phrase or clause A nonessential phrase or clause is not essential to the meaning of a sentence and is therefore set off with commas. *(See page 782.)*

Nonfiction Nonfiction is prose writing that contains facts about real people and events. *(See page 256.)*

Noun A noun is a word that names a person, a place, a thing, or an idea.

A common noun gives a general name. A proper noun names a specific person, place, or thing and always begins with a capital letter. *(See pages 537–538.)*

Noun clause A noun clause is a subordinate clause that is used like a noun. *(See page 620.)*

O

Objective case The objective case of a pronoun is used for direct objects, indirect objects, and objects of a preposition. *(See page 675.)*

Objective complement An objective complement is a noun or an adjective that renames or describes the direct object. *(See page 571.)*

Onomatopoeia Onomatopoeia is the use of words whose sounds suggest their meanings. *(See pages 61 and 400.)*

Opinion An opinion is a judgment that varies from person to person. *(See pages 187 and 440.)*

Order of importance, interest, size, or degree Order of importance, interest, size, or degree is a way of organizing by arranging details in the order of *least to most* or *most to least. (See pages 28 and 118.)*

Outline An outline organizes information about a subject into main topics and subtopics. *(See pages 148–151.)*

P

Paragraph A paragraph is a group of related sentences that present and develop one main idea. *(See page 92.)*

Paraphrase A paraphrase is a restatement of an original work in one's own words. *(See page 311.)*

Parenthetical citation A parenthetical citation is a brief reference in a research paper to the source of borrowed information. *(See pages 360–361.)*

Participial phrase A participial phrase is a participle with its modifiers and complements—all working together as an adjective. *(See page 592.)*

Participle A participle is a verb form that is used as an adjective. *(See page 591.)*

Passive voice Passive voice indicates that the action of a verb is being performed upon its subject. *(See pages 78 and 662.)*

Peer conference A peer conference is a meeting with one's peers to share information and ideas. The peer conference is commonly used as a prewriting and revising strategy. *(See pages 21, 22, and 37.)*

Personal pronoun A personal pronoun refers to a particular person, place, thing, or idea. *(See page 539.)*

Personification Personification is a comparison in which human qualities are given to an animal, object, or idea. *(See pages 61 and 402.)*

Persuasive paragraph A persuasive paragraph states an opinion and uses facts, examples, reasons, and the testimony of experts to convince readers. *(See page 120.)*

Phrase A phrase is a group of related words that function as a single part of speech and do not have a subject and verb. *(See page 585.)*

Play A play is a composition written for dramatic performance on the stage. *(See page 262.)*

Plot Plot consists of the events in a story or a play. *(See pages 262 and 388.)*

Poem A poem is a highly structured composition with condensed, vivid language, figures of speech, and often the use of meter and rhyme. *(See pages 262 and 398.)*

Point of view In first person point of view, the narrator takes part in the story. In third person point of view, the narrator tells what happens to others and is not a character in the story. *(See pages 48, 107, 262, and 385.)*

Possessive pronoun A possessive pronoun is used to show ownership or possession. *(See page 679.)*

Predicate adjective A predicate adjective is an adjective that follows a linking verb and modifies the subject. *(See page 573.)*

Predicate nominative A predicate nominative is a noun or a pronoun that follows a linking verb and identifies, renames, or explains the subject. *(See page 573.)*

Prefix A prefix is a word part that is added to the beginning of a word and changes its basic, or root, meaning. *(See page 454.)*

Preposition A preposition is a word that shows the relationship between a noun or a pronoun and another word in the sentence. *(See page 551.)*

Prepositional phrase A prepositional phrase is a group of words that begins with a preposition, ends with a noun or a pronoun, and is used as an adjective or an adverb. *(See page 585.)*

Prewriting Prewriting is the first stage of the writing process. It includes all the planning steps that come before writing the first draft. *(See page 12.)*

Principal parts of a verb The principal parts of a verb are the *present,* the *past,* and the *past participle.* The principal parts help form the tenses of verbs. *(See page 641.)*

Pronoun A pronoun is a word that takes the place of one or more nouns. *(See pages 538–539.)*

Proofreading symbols Proofreading symbols are a kind of shorthand that writers use to correct their mistakes while editing. *(See page 39.)*

Propaganda Propaganda is the effort to persuade by distorting information or by disguising opinions as facts. *(See page 439.)*

Protagonist A protagonist is the principal character in a story. *(See page 288.)*

Publishing Publishing is the final stage of the writing process. At this stage writers present their work to an audience in final form. *(See page 42.)*

Purpose In writing, purpose is the reason for writing. *(See pages 18–19.)* The purpose of a speech is the reason for speaking. *(See page 431.)*

R

Regular verb A regular verb forms its past and past participle by adding *-ed* or *-d* to the present. *(See page 641.)*

Relative pronoun A relative pronoun relates an adjective clause to the modified noun or pronoun. *(See page 616.)*

Repetition Repetition is the repeating of a word or phrase for poetic effect. *(See page 400.)*

Research paper A research paper is a composition based on research drawn from books, periodicals, and interviews with experts. *(See page 330.)*

Résumé A résumé is a summary of a person's work experience, education, and interests. *(See page 419.)*

Revising Revising is the third stage of the writing process. At this stage a writer changes a draft as often as needed to improve it. *(See page 33.)*

Rhyme scheme Rhyme scheme is a pattern of rhymed sounds at the end of lines in poems. *(See pages 262 and 403.)*

Root A root is the part of a word that carries the basic meaning. *(See page 454.)*

Run-on sentence A run-on sentence is two or more sentences that are written as one sentence. They are separated by a comma or have no mark of punctuation at all. *(See pages 634–635.)*

S

Satire Satire is writing that often uses exaggeration to ridicule a flaw in human behavior or society. *(See page 214.)*

Sentence A sentence is a group of words that expresses a complete thought. *(See page 561.)*

Sentence combining Sentence combining is the method of combining short sentences into longer, more fluent sentences by using phrases and clauses. *(See pages 67–70.)*

Sentence fragment A sentence fragment is a group of words that does not express a complete thought. *(See page 631.)*

Setting Setting is the location and time of a story. *(See pages 262 and 387.)*

Short story A short story is a well-developed account of fictional characters resolving a conflict or problem. *(See page 381.)*

Simile A simile states a comparison by using the word *like* or *as*. *(See pages 59, 262, and 402.)*

Simple predicate A simple predicate, or verb, is the main word or phrase in a complete predicate. *(See page 561.)*

Simple sentence A simple sentence consists of one independent clause. *(See page 622.)*

Simple subject A simple subject is the main word in the complete subject. *(See page 561.)*

Sound devices Sound devices are ways to use sounds in poetry to achieve certain effects. *(See page 400.)*

Spatial order Spatial order arranges details according to their location. *(See pages 28 and 109.)*

Speech A speech is an oral composition presented by a speaker to an audience. *(See page 430.)*

Style Style is the characteristic way in which a writer uses language. *(See pages 370 and 394.)*

829

Subjunctive mood The subjunctive mood is used to express (1) a condition contrary to fact that begins with words such as *if, as if,* or *as though* or (2) a wish. *(See page 665.)*

Subordinate clause A subordinate (or dependent) clause cannot stand alone because it does not express a complete thought. *(See page 611.)*

Subordinating conjunction A subordinating conjunction is used in a complex sentence to introduce an adverb clause. *(See page 613.)*

Suffix A suffix is a word part that is added to the end of a word and changes its basic, or root, meaning. *(See page 454.)*

Summary A summary is a concise condensation of a longer piece of writing, covering only the main points of the original. *(See page 299.)*

Superlative degree The superlative degree of a modifier is used when more than two people, things, or actions are compared. *(See page 715.)*

Supporting sentences Supporting sentences explain or prove a topic sentence with specific details, facts, examples, or reasons. *(See page 94.)*

Symbol A symbol is an object, an event, or a creature that stands for a universal idea or quality. *(See pages 126, 262, and 402.)*

Synonym A synonym is a word that has nearly the same meaning as another word. *(See page 464.)*

T

Tense Tense is the form a verb takes to show time. The six tenses are the *present, past, future, present perfect, past perfect,* and *future perfect. (See page 650.)*

Theme Theme is the underlying idea, message, or meaning of a work of literature. *(See page 262.)*

Thesis statement A thesis statement states the main idea and makes the purpose of an essay clear. *(See pages 138, 156, 200, and 348.)*

Timed writing Timed writing is an essay test that must be written in a prescribed amount of time. *(See page 531.)*

Tone Tone is the attitude of a writer toward the subject of a composition. *(See pages 138, 172, and 234.)*

Topic sentence A topic sentence states the main idea of a paragraph. *(See page 94.)*

Transitions Transitions are words and phrases that show how ideas are related. *(See pages 102 and 118.)*

Transitive verb A transitive verb is an action verb that has an object. *(See page 542.)*

U

Understood subject An understood subject of a sentence is a subject that is understood rather than stated. *(See page 566.)*

Unity A paragraph or an essay has unity if all the supporting sentences relate to the main idea in the topic sentence. *(See pages 99 and 166.)*

V

Verbal A verbal is a verb form used as some other part of speech. *(See page 591.)*

Verb phrase A verb phrase is a main verb plus one or more helping verbs. *(See page 545.)*

W

Working thesis A working thesis is a preliminary thesis statement that is refined in the process of writing. *(See pages 147 and 344.)*

Works cited page A works cited page comes at the end of a research paper and lists all the sources cited in the paper. *(See page 363.)*

Index

A

a, an, 731

abbreviation: in formal writing, 771; with or without period, 771; state, postal-service list, 771

abstract nouns, 537

accept, except, 731

Achebe, Chinua, 87–90

action verbs, 542

active voice, defined, 78, 662

adapt, adopt, 731

adjective clause: defined, 616; distinguished from noun clause, 620; as misplaced modifier, 619; punctuation with, 617; relative pronoun in, 616, 618, 709; in sentence combining, 70

adjective phrase: defined, 585; as misplaced modifier, 600–601

adjectives: articles (*a, an, the*), 547, 731; cases of, 396; comparison of, 715–717; compound, 547, 810; distinguished from nouns, 547; noun used as, 547; position of, 547; predicate, 573, 574, 722; pronominal, 548; pronoun used as, 547; proper, 547

adventure story, writing an, 406–407

adverb clause: defined, 314, 612; punctuation with, 315, 613; in sentence combining, 315; subordinating conjunction in, 613

adverb phrase: defined, 586; as misplaced modifier, 600–601; punctuation with, 587

adverbs: comparison of, 715–717; defined, 549–550; distinguished from *-ly* adjectives, 549; distinguished from prepositions, 552; uses of, 549

advertisement, writing an, 123, 125

advice, advise, 210, 731

affect, effect, 731

Agatha Christie: An Autobiography, from, 217–222

agreement of pronoun and antecedent, 539

agreement of subject and verb, 40, 695; collective nouns, 704; compound subject, 698–699; contractions, 707; helping verb, 696; indefinite pronoun, 701; interrupting words, 697; inverted order, 703; linking verbs, 707; singular noun with plural form, 695–696, 705–706; title as subject, 708; words expressing amount, 704

ain't, 732

alliteration, 61, 400

all ready, already, 732

all together, altogether, 732

allusion, illusion, 732

allusion in literature, 262, 318

a lot, 732

among, between, 210, 732

amount, number, 733

an, a, 731

analogies, developing, 146, 207; in literature, 86; word, 465–467, 469, 506–508

analyzing: advertisements, 442; by clustering, 337; ideas, subjects, 337; a paragraph, 93, 117. *See also* Critical Thinking.

antecedent: agreement of pronoun with, 538, 685–686; defined, 685; vague or missing, 690

antonyms, 464

any more, anymore, 733

anywhere, 733

apostrophe: contractions with, 792; forming plural with, 793; possessive noun or pronoun with, 789–791; to show joint or separate ownership, 789

appositive: defined, 589; phrases, 589; punctuation with, 589, 813

arguable proposition, 188

articles, (*a, an, the*), 547, 731

as, like, 743

as far as, 733

assonance, 400

audience, for speech, 431; for writing 18–19, 228

cultures, attitudes and traditions, 86–92, 329

D

dangling modifier, 600–601
dash, 812–813
"Dead Men's Path," 87–90
declarative sentence, 769
deductive reasoning. *See* reasoning.
degrees of comparison, 716–717
demonstrative pronouns, 541
denotation, 56
dependent clause. *See* subordinate clause.
descriptive mode, 29, 109–113, 136, 182, 236–237, 387–388
details, adding, 33; brainstorming for, 21; classifying, 27; ordering, 28, 149, 233; selecting, 147, 231; strategies for organizing, 26, 148; types of, 144
development, methods of: analogy, 146; analysis, 337; cause and effect, 119, 207; classification, 27, 115; comparison and contrast, 28, 153, 170–171; descriptive details, 109–113; facts and examples, 114, 182–184, 187; incident, 183; reasons, 120, 182; steps in a process, 119
developmental order, 28
Dewey decimal system, 481–483. *See* library.
diagram, sentence, 626–627; adjective and adverb, 578–579; adjective and adverb clause, 626–627; adjective and adverb phrase, 604; appositive and appositive phrase, 604–605; complement, 579–581; complex sentence, 626–627; compound-complex sentence, 627; compound object, 579–580; compound sentence, 626; compound subject, 578; compound verb, 578; direct and indirect object, 579–580; gerund phrase, 606; infinitive phrase, 606–607; inverted order, 578; noun clause, 627; objective complement, 580; participial phrase, 605; possessive pronoun, 579; prepositional phrase, 604; simple sentence, 578; subject and verb, 578; subject complement, 580–581; understood subject, 578; verb phrase, 578

dialect, 728
dialogue, writing a, 135
Dickens, Charles, 175–180
dictionary, 492–499; accent marks, 494; arrangement, 492; definitions, 495–496; derived words, 496; diacritical marks, 494; entry words, 492; etymologies, 497; inflected forms, 496; multiple meanings, 495–496; part of speech labels, 495; pronunciation guide, 493–494; schwa, 494; spelling, preferred and variant, 492–493; syllable division, 493; synonyms, 495; usage labels, 495
Didion, Joan, 235
different from, 736
Dillard, Annie, 231
direct address, 779
direct object, 569; pronoun as, 671
discover, invent, 737
dividing words, 493, 812
documentation. *See* sources, using and citing.
doesn't, don't, 707, 737
done, 737
double comparison, 718–719
double negative, 211, 721, 737
drafting, 30–32; critical essay, 278–282; descriptive paragraph, 109–111; expository essay, 156–165; expository paragraph, 114–120; narrative paragraph, 106–108, 124–125; personal essay, 234–238; persuasive essay, 205; persuasive paragraph, 120–123; research paper, 348–364; short story, 390–392; summary, 307–312; thesis statement, 156–157; title, 165
drama: analyzing, 265; elements of, 262

E

each, both, 735

editing, 38–45, 80–81, 112–113; checklist, 169, 397; critical essay, 284–285; expository essay, 168–169; grammatical errors, 637, 667, 690, 711, 725; personal essay, 240–241; personalized checklist, 38; persuasive essay, 210–211; proofreading symbols, 38–39; punctuation errors, 785, 815; research paper, 366–367; short story, 396–397; summary, 314

effect, affect, 731

elements of literature, 262–265

ellipsis, 808

elliptical clause, 614–615, 683–685

else, in comparisons, 719

emigrate, immigrate, 738

emphasis, 565

emphatic form of verb, 652

employment skills, 415–422

empty expressions, 63–65

end marks, 768–787

endnotes, 362

English language: dialects, 728; etymology, American words, 448–449; formal, 729; history of, 447; informal, 730; Middle English, 448; modern, 448; nonstandard, 210, 730; Old English, 447; standard, 210, 729

essay, 136–140; body, 137–139; in college application, 425–426, 429; conclusion, 139; critical essay, 246–289; expository essay, 136–173; introduction, 137–138; literary essay, 246–289; personal essay, 216–245; persuasive essay, 174–215; structure, 137–140; supporting paragraphs, 139; thesis statement, 147, 156–157. *See also* expository essay.

essays about literature. *See* critical essay.

essential clause, 617

essential elements, 782–783

etc., 738

etymology, 448–449, 497

evaluating: evidence, 202; sources, 338. *See also* Critical Thinking.

evaluation: of literary work, 265; of

oral presentation, 436–437; using criteria for, 313

evaluative mode, 136, 182, 190–198, 202, 265–266, 306, 338–339

everywhere, 733

except, accept, 731

exclamation point, 770

exclamatory sentence, 770

expository essay, 136–173; defined, 136; drafting, 156–165; editing, 168–169; prewriting, 141–155; publishing, 169, 171; revising, 166; revision checklist, 167. *See also* essay.

expository paragraph, 114–120; analyzing, 117; classifying details, information, 114–115; development, method of, 114. *See also* paragraphs, expository.

expressive purpose, 224, 398

Extending Your Vocabulary
9, 53, 91, 135, 181, 223, 255, 297, 329, 379

F

facts, 187

fallacies. *See* logical fallacies.

faulty sentences, 72–74

fewer, less, 739

fiction, analyzing, 263; elements of, 262; locating in library, 481

figurative language, 58–62, 402–403; hyperbole, 402; imagery, 402; metaphor, 59, 84, 402; oxymoron, 402; personification, 61, 402, 755; simile, 59, 402; symbol, 126, 402

figures of speech. *See* figurative language.

focusing, 26

"Follower," from, 404

footnotes, 362

formal English. *See* English language.

former, latter, 739

Forster, E. M., 291–296, 297, 298, 301, 312

fragments: clause 632–633; other, 633; sentence, 40, 561, 631

free verse, 401. *See also* meter; rhythm.

freewriting, 13–14

Writing Is Thinking

analyzing subject, *337;* comparing, *60;* criteria for evaluations, *306;* developing analogies, *146;* evaluating evidence, *202;* generalizing, *96;* implying, *389;* inferring, *267;* interpreting experience, *229*

Acknowledgments

The authors and editors have made every effort to trace the ownership of all copyrighted selections found in this book and to make full acknowledgment of their use. Grateful acknowledgment is made to the following authors, publishers, agents, and individuals for their permission to reprint copyrighted material.

Page 3: "The Singing Lesson," from *The Short Stories of Katherine Mansfield.* Copyright 1922 by Alfred A. Knopf, Inc., and renewed 1950 by John Middleton Murry. Reprinted by permission of Alfred A. Knopf, Inc. **87:** "Dead Men's Path," from *Girls at War and Other Stories,* by Chinua Achebe, copyright © 1972, 1973 by Chinua Achebe is reprinted by permission of Doubleday & Company, Inc., and David Bolt Associates. **131:** From *A Room of One's Own,* by Virginia Woolf, copyright 1929 by Harcourt Brace Jovanovich, Inc.; renewed 1957 by Leonard Woolf. Reprinted by permission of the publisher. **137:** From "But Did They Floss?" by John Noble Wilford, from *The New York Times,* March 7, 1989. **139:** "The Fosbury Flop," from *How Did They Do That?* by Caroline Sutton, copyright © 1984. Reprinted by permission of William Morrow and Company, Inc. **154:** "Grant and Lee: A Study in Contrasts," from *The American Story,* Earl Schneck Miers, editor. Reprinted by permission of the U.S. Capitol Historical Society. **172:** From *Opposites,* by Richard Wilbur, copyright © 1973 by Richard Wilbur, Harcourt Brace Jovanovich, Inc. **183:** "Controlling Alaska's Wolves," by Jim Reardon, and "Wolves as Scapegoats," by James L. Pitts. Copyright © 1977 by the National Wildlife Federation. Reprinted from the August-September issues of *National Wildlife Magazine.* **217:** From *An Autobiography,* by Agatha Christie, is reprinted by permission of Hughes Massie Limited, London. **247:** "Shaving," from *The Girl from Cardigan,* by Leslie Norris; Gibbs Smith, publisher; copyright © 1988. Reprinted by permission. **291:** "The Beauty of Life," from *Albergo Empedocle and Other Writings,* by E.M. Forster, edited by George H. Thomson. Copyright © 1972 by George Thomson. Reprinted by permission of Edward Arnold Ltd. **299:** From *Charles Babbage, Father of the Computer,* by Dan Halacy. Copyright © 1970 by Dan Halacy. Reprinted with permission of Macmillan Publishing Company. **303:** From *In the Dark,* by Richard Meran Barsam. Copyright © 1977 by Richard Meran Barsam. Reprinted by permission of Viking Penguin, Inc. **309:** From *National Parks,* by Paul Jensen, copyright © 1964 by Western Publishing Company, Inc. Reprinted by permission. **311:** From *Science in the World Around Us,* by William C. Vergara, copyright © 1973. Reprinted by permission of the author. **321:** From *Shooting an Elephant and Other Essays,* by George Orwell, copyright 1950 by Sonia Brownell Orwell; renewed 1978 by Sonia Pitt-Rivers. Reprinted by permission of Harcourt Brace Jovanovich, Inc. **340:** From *In the Blink of an Eye,* by Richard C. Morais, from *Forbes* magazine, March 23, 1987. **358:** "Catching the Drift," from the September issue of *Science 84.* Reprinted by permission of *Science* magazine, copyright © the American Association for the Advancement of Science. **373:** "Quality," by John Galsworthy. Copyright 1912 Charles Scribner's Sons; renewal copyright 1940. Reprinted with the permission of Charles Scribner's Sons, from *The Inn of Tranquility,* by John Galsworthy. **400:** "Pretty," from *Collected Poems,* by Stevie Smith. Copyright © 1972 by Stevie Smith. New Directions Publishing Corporation. By permission of the publisher. **400:** "Snake," from *The Complete Poems of D.H. Lawrence,* copyright © 1964, 1971 by Angelo Ravagli and C.M. Weekly, executors of the Estate of Frieda Lawrence Ravagli. Reprinted by permission of Viking Penguin, Inc., **400:** From "The Hollow Men" and "Preludes," from *Collected Poems 1909–1962,* by T.S. Eliot, copyright 1935, 1936 by Harcourt Brace Jovanovich, Inc.; copyright © 1964 by T.S. Eliot. Reprinted by permission of Harcourt Brace Jovanovich, Inc., and Faber and Faber Ltd. **402:** From "She Tells Her Love. . . ." from *Collected Poems,* by Robert Graves. Copyright © 1975 by Robert Graves. Reprinted by permission of Oxford University Press, Inc., and A.P. Watt Ltd., on behalf of the executors of the Estate of Robert Graves. **404:** From "Follower," from *Poems 1965–1975,* by Seamus Heaney. Copyright © 1966, 1969, 1972, 1975, 1980 by Seamus Heaney. Reprinted by permission of Farrar, Straus and Giroux, Inc. and Faber and Faber Ltd. **517–518:** "Introduction" from *Contemporary Heroes and Heroines,* Ray B. Browne, editor, copyright © 1990 by Gale Research Inc. Used by permission of Gale Research, Inc.

Cover Design: Studio Goodwin-Sturges. Illustration: Mahler Ryder. Calligraphy: Colleen

Unit Openers Design: Studio Goodwin-Sturges. Photography by Ken O'Donoghue © D.C. Heath. Calligraphy: Colleen

Interior Calligraphy Lisa Tarca

Illustrations 2–9: Michael McLaughlin. **14, 124, 266:** Amy L. Wasserman, Collage Artist. **32, 50–53, 195, 330:** Joan Hall. **76:** Susan Spellman. **86–91:** Tom Olivieri. **130–135:** Winslow Pinney Pells. **174–182, 282:** Fred Lynch. **212:** © D.C. Heath. **216–223:** Joan E. Paley, Assemblages. **242:** Jennifer D. Paley, Collage. **246–252, 255:** Debra Strick. **253–254:** Susan Doheny, Hand-Coloring. **268:** Larry Ross/The Image Bank. **290–297:** Lark Carrier. **320–329:** Connie Connally. **358:** Patrice Rossi.

Picture Research Connie Komack/Pictures and Words; Martha Friedman.

Photographs 10: *The Artist's Sister, Mme. Pontillon, Seated on the Grass,* Berthe Morisot (French 1841–1895), 1873. Oil on canvas, 17¾″ × 28½″. The Cleveland Museum of Art. Gift of the Hanna Fund, 50.89. **11:** Ralph Mercer, © D.C. Heath. **28:** Photofest. **37:** © Jim Whitmer. **46:** Myrleen Ferguson/PhotoEdit. **51:** *Reading Woman with a Parasol,* Henri Matisse, 1921. Oil on canvas. Tate Gallery, London/Art Resource. **54:** *Secret of the Sphinx (Homage to Elihu Vedder),* Mark Tansey, 1984. Oil on canvas, 60″ × 65″. Courtesy of Curt Marcus Gallery, New York. **55:** Gates/Frederic Lewis Stock Photos. **64:** *Arena,* Salomé, 1982. Artificial resin on canvas, 78.7″ × 94.5″ (200 cm × 240 cm). Galerie Raab, Berlin. From the artist's private collection. **66:** Center for American Archeology, Kampsville, Illinois. **82:** *l,* Ellis Herwig/The Picture Cube; *tm,* Mikki Ansin/The Picture Cube; *bm,* Janeart/The Image Bank; *r,* Jeff Dunn/The Picture Cube. **84:** Bill Longcore/Science Source, Photo Researchers, Inc. **89:** © Robert Caputo. **92:** *Rocky Mountains and Tired Indians,* 1965. Acrylic on canvas, 67″ × 99½″. © David Hockney. **99:** UPI/Bettmann. **107:** University of Louisville Photographic Archives. **110:** *Porch, Provincetown,* 1977; from *Cape Light,* Plate 3 (cat. 87). © Joel Meyerowitz. **122:** Obremski/ The Image Bank. **136:** Man Ray/Culver Pictures, Inc. **143:** Steve Weber/Stock Imagery. **149:** *Tetrahedral Planetoid,* M.C. Escher, 1954. Woodcut printed from two blocks. National Gallery of Art, Washington. Cornelius Van S. Roosevelt Collections. **153:** *l & r,* North Wind Picture Archives. **162, 164:** Museum of Modern Art/Film Stills Archive. **170:** *tl,* Photo-world/FPG International; *tr & b,* Culver Pictures, Inc. **172:** *Not to Be Reproduced,* René Magritte, 1937. Oil on canvas. 81.3 cm × 65 cm. Museum Boymans-van Beuningen, Rotterdam. **180:** The Illustrated London News Picture Library. **185:** © Jim Brandenburg. **189:** *La Tristesse du Roi (Sorrow of the King),* Henri Matisse, 1952. Paper cut-out. Musee National d'Art Moderne/Giraudon/Art Resource. **192:** *l,* David Young-Wolff/PhotoEdit; *r, Boston Common at Twilight,* Frederick Childe Hassam, 1885–86. Oil on canvas, 42″ × 60″. Gift of Miss Maud E. Appleton. Courtesy, Museum of Fine Arts, Boston. **201:** *Country Road with Bridge,* © Mitchell Funk. **220:** Raymond Mander and Joe Mitcherson Theatre Collection. **224:** UPI/Bettmann. **227:** *Impression, Sunrise,* Claude Monet, 1872. Oil on canvas. Musee Mamottan/Giraudon/Art Resource. **232:** Gary W. Griffin/Earth Scenes. **238:** *The South Ledges, Appledore,* Frederick Childe Hassam, 1913. Oil on canvas. National Museum of American Art, Washington, D.C./Art Resource. **253:** The Bettmann Archive. **254:** *l,* The Bettman Archive; *r,* Culver Pictures, Inc. **256:** *Razor,* Gerald Murphy, 1924. Oil on canvas, 32⅝″ × 36½″. Dallas Museum of Art, Foundations for the Arts Collection. Gift of the artist. **259:** *l,* Lee Boltin Picture Library; *ml & mr,* Laurie Platt Winfrey, Inc.; *r,* Lee Boltin Picture Library. **261:** Raymond Mander and Joe Mitcherson Theatre Collection. **264:** *La Lecture (The Reading),* Berthe Morisot, 1888. Oil on canvas, 29½″ × 36½″. Museum of Fine Arts, St. Petersburg, Florida. Gift of Friends of Art in Memory of Margaret Acheson Stuart, 1981. **272, 280:** Doug Mindell, © D.C. Heath. **286:** North Wind Picture Archives. **294:** *La Grenouillère,* Claude Monet, 1869. Oil on canvas, 29⅜″ × 39¼″. Metropolitan Museum of Art, New York. Bequest of Mrs. H.O. Havemeyer, 1929. The H.O. Havemeyer Collection (29.100.12). **295:** *La Grenouillère,* Pierre Auguste Renoir, 1869. Oil on canvas, 26″ × 31⅞″. National Museum, Stockholm. Photograph by Statens Konstmuseer. **298:** *l, Paris, A Rainy Day,* Gustave Caillebotte, 1876–77. Oil on canvas, 212.2 cm × 276.2 cm. Charles H. and Mary F.S. Worcester Collection, 1964.336, photograph © 1990, The Art Institute of Chicago. All Rights Reserved; *r,* Tabuteau/The Image Works. **301:** *0–9,* Jasper Johns, 1959. Encaustic and collage on canvas, 20⅛″ × 35″. Ludwig

845

Collection. **305:** Photofest. **309:** *Coast Scene, Mount Desert*, Frederick E. Church, 1863. Oil on canvas, 36⅛″ × 48″. Wadsworth Atheneum, Hartford. Bequest of Mrs. Clara Hinton Gould. **312:** *Desert Landscape with Camels*, © Mitchell Funk. **316:** *tl*, UPI/Bettmann; *tr*, Don Perdue/Gamma-Liaison; *bl*, Inge Morath/Magnum Photos, Inc.; *br*, © Mikki Ansin. **335:** Patrick Pagnano/Courtesy of CBS News. **341:** Ian Berry/Magnum Photos, Inc. **347:** *Three Flags*, Jasper Johns, 1958. Encaustic on canvas, 30⅞″ × 45½″ × 5″. Collection of Whitney Museum of American Art. 50th Anniversary Gift of the Gilman Foundation, Inc., The Lauder Foundation, A. Alfred Taubman, an anonymous donor, and Purchase 80.32. **356:** Hank Morgan/Science Source, Photo Researchers, Inc. **368:** *tl*, Library of Congress/American Heritage Picture Collection; *tr*, © Lawrence Migdale; *ml*, Camilla Smith/Rainbow; *bl*, © Lawrence Migdale; *bm*, Dan McCoy/Rainbow; *br*, © Lawrence Migdale. **380:** *Dickens' Dream*, R.W. Buss. Reproduced by courtesy of The Dickens House, London. **384:** *Feeding the Ducks*, Mary Cassatt, 1894, First State. Drypoint over aquatint etching, 8⅝″ × 6³⁄₁₆″. The Metropolitan Museum of Art, New York. Bequest of Mrs. H.O. Havemeyer, 1929. The H.O. Havemeyer Collection (29.107.99). **386:** Al Francekevich/Stock Market. **394:** *Feeding the Ducks*, Mary Cassatt, 1894, Fourth State. Drypoint over aquatint etching. © Daniel J. Terra Collection, Terra Museum of American Art, Chicago. **399:** Elliot Erwitt/Magnum Photos, Inc. **404:** *Cradling Wheat*, Thomas Hart Benton, 1938. Tempera and oil on board, 78.7 cm × 96.5 cm. The Saint Louis Art Museum; museum purchase. **406:** *all*, Shooting Star. **434, 444:** Culver Pictures, Inc. **471:** Richard Laird/FPG International. **476:** Robert Frerck / Tony Stone Worldwide, Chicago. **485, 486, 487, 489, 493, 495, 496, 497, 499:** Doug Mindell, © D.C. Heath, hand-colored by Margery Mintz.

Cartoons **59:** Elivia Savadier © 1990. **103:** The Far Side © 1985 Universal Press Syndicate. Reprinted with permission. **141:** Drawing by C. Barsotti; © 1977, The New Yorker Magazine, Inc. **447, 455, 458:** Elivia Savadier © 1990. **503:** The Far Side © 1986 Universal Press Syndicate. Reprinted with permission. **520:** Calvin & Hobbes © 1990 Universal Press Syndicate. Reprinted with permission. **524:** Chris Demarest.